Personnel management in government

PUBLIC ADMINISTRATION AND PUBLIC POLICY

A Comprehensive Publication Program

Executive Editor

JACK RABIN
Professor of Public Administration and Public Policy
Division of Public Affairs
The Capital College
The Pennsylvania State University--Harrisburg
Middletown, Pennsylvania

1. *Public Administration as a Developing Discipline (in two parts),* Robert T. Golembiewski
2. *Comparative National Policies on Health Care,* Milton I. Roemer, M.D.
3. *Exclusionary Injustice: The Problem of Illegally Obtained Evidence,* Steven R. Schlesinger
4. *Personnel Management in Government: Politics and Process,* Jay M. Shafritz, Walter L. Balk, Albert C. Hyde, and David H. Rosenbloom
5. *Organization Development in Public Administration (in two parts),* edited by Robert T. Golembiewski and William B. Eddy
6. *Public Administration: A Comparative Perspective, Second Edition, Revised and Expanded,* Ferrel Heady
7. *Approaches to Planned Change (in two parts),* Robert T. Golembiewski
8. *Program Evaluation at HEW (in three parts),* edited by James G. Abert
9. *The States and the Metropolis,* Patricia S. Florestano and Vincent L. Marando
10. *Personnel Management in Government: Politics and Process, Second Edition, Revised and Expanded,* Jay M. Shafritz, Albert C. Hyde, and David H. Rosenbloom
11. *Changing Bureaucracies: Understanding the Organization Before Selecting the Approach,* William A. Medina
12. *Handbook on Public Budgeting and Financial Management,* edited by Jack Rabin and Thomas D. Lynch
13. *Encyclopedia of Policy Studies,* edited by Stuart S. Nagel

14. *Public Administration and Law: Bench v. Bureau in the United States,* David H. Rosenbloom

15. *Handbook on Public Personnel Administration and Labor Relations,* edited by Jack Rabin, Thomas Vocino, W. Bartley Hildreth, and Gerald J. Miller

16. *Public Budgeting and Finance: Behavioral, Theoretical, and Technical Perspectives,* edited by Robert T. Golembiewski and Jack Rabin

17. *Organizational Behavior and Public Management,* Debra W. Stewart and G. David Garson

18. *The Politics of Terrorism: Second Edition, Revised and Expanded,* edited by Michael Stohl

19. *Handbook of Organization Management,* edited by William B. Eddy

20. *Organization Theory and Management,* edited by Thomas D. Lynch

21. *Labor Relations in the Public Sector,* Richard C. Kearney

22. *Politics and Administration: Woodrow Wilson and American Public Administration,* edited by Jack Rabin and James S. Bowman

23. *Making and Managing Policy: Formulation, Analysis, Evaluation,* edited by G. Ronald Gilbert

24. *Public Administration: A Comparative Perspective, Third Edition, Revised,* Ferrel Heady

25. *Decision Making in the Public Sector,* edited by Lloyd G. Nigro

26. *Managing Administration,* edited by Jack Rabin, Samuel Humes, and Brian S. Morgan

27. *Public Personnel Update,* edited by Michael Cohen and Robert T. Golembiewski

28. *State and Local Government Administration,* edited by Jack Rabin and Don Dodd

29. *Public Administration: A Bibliographic Guide to the Literature,* Howard E. McCurdy

30. *Personnel Management in Government: Politics and Process, Third Edition, Revised and Expanded,* Jay M. Shafritz, Albert C. Hyde, and David H. Rosenbloom

31. *Handbook of Information Resource Management,* edited by Jack Rabin and Edward M. Jackowski

32. *Public Administration in Developed Democracies: A Comparative Study,* edited by Donald C. Rowat

33. *The Politics of Terrorism: Third Edition, Revised and Expanded,* edited by Michael Stohl

34. *Handbook on Human Services Administration,* edited by Jack Rabin and Marcia B. Steinhauer

35. *Handbook of Public Administration,* edited by Jack Rabin, W. Bartley Hildreth, and Gerald J. Miller
36. *Ethics for Bureaucrats: An Essay on Law and Values, Second Edition, Revised and Expanded,* John A. Rohr
37. *The Guide to the Foundations of Public Administration,* Daniel W. Martin
38. *Handbook of Strategic Management,* edited by Jack Rabin, Gerald J. Miller, and W. Bartley Hildreth
39. *Terrorism and Emergency Management: Policy and Administration,* William L. Waugh, Jr.
40. *Organizational Behavior and Public Management: Second Edition, Revised and Expanded,* Michael L. Vasu, Debra W. Stewart, and G. David Garson
41. *Handbook of Comparative and Development Public Administration,* edited by Ali Farazmand
42. *Public Administration: A Comparative Perspective, Fourth Edition,* Ferrel Heady
43. *Government Financial Management Theory,* Gerald J. Miller
44. *Personnel Management in Government: Politics and Process, Fourth Edition, Revised and Expanded,* Jay M. Shafritz, Norma M. Riccucci, David H. Rosenbloom, and Albert C. Hyde
45. *Public Productivity Handbook,* edited by Marc Holzer

Additional Volumes in Preparation

Handbook of Public Budgeting, edited by Jack Rabin
Handbook of Organizational Consultation, edited by Robert T. Golembiewski

ANNALS OF PUBLIC ADMINISTRATION

1. *Public Administration: History and Theory in Contemporary Perspective,* edited by Joseph A. Uveges, Jr.
2. *Public Administration Education in Transition,* edited by Thomas Vocino and Richard Heimovics
3. *Centenary Issues of the Pendleton Act of 1883,* edited by David H. Rosenbloom with the assistance of Mark A. Emmert
4. *Intergovernmental Relations in the 1980s,* edited by Richard H. Leach
5. *Criminal Justice Administration: Linking Practice and Research,* edited by William A. Jones, Jr.

Personnel management in government

Politics and process

Fourth edition, revised and expanded

Jay M. Shafritz

Graduate School of Public and International Affairs
University of Pittsburgh
Pittsburgh, Pennsylvania

Norma M. Riccucci

Graduate School of Public Affairs
University at Albany, State University of New York
Albany, New York

David H. Rosenbloom

School of Public Affairs
The American University
Washington, D.C.

Albert C. Hyde

Graduate School of Public and International Affairs
University of Pittsburgh
Pittsburgh, Pennsylvania

Marcel Dekker, Inc.   **New York • Basel • Hong Kong**

Library of Congress Cataloging-in-Publication Data

Personnel management in government: politics and process/Jay M.
   Shafritz...[et al.]. -- -- 4th ed., rev. and expanded.
         p.   cm. -- -- (Public administration and public policy; 44)
      Rev. ed. of: Personnel management in government/Jay M. Shafritz,
   Albert C. Hyde, David H. Rosenbloom.
      Includes bibliographical references and index.
      ISBN 0-8247-8590-8 (alk. paper)
      1. Civil service-- --United States-- --Personnel management.
   I. Shafritz, Jay M. II. Shafritz, Jay M. Personnel management in
   government. III. Series.
   JK765.S44   1992
   353.001-- --dc20   91-36052
                                                          CIP

This book is printed on acid-free paper.

MARCEL DEKKER, INC.
270 Madison Avenue, New York, New York 10016

Current printing (last digit):
10 9 8 7 6 5 4 3 2

PRINTED IN THE UNITED STATES OF AMERICA

Preface

This fourth edition is a radical revision and expansion of the third. While history does not change much, almost everything else about personnel management in government does. So much revision was needed because of rapid developments in the field and in American society that we invited Norma Riccucci of the State University of New York at Albany to help us cope. So the three musketeers are now four. All for one and one for all, in that we all accept whatever blame or credit that this book warrants.

Few things are as satisfying to textbook authors as the opportunity to do subsequent editions. It gives the chance not only to correct one's mistakes, but to take full advantage of all the advice that came from so many strangers and friends who read the earlier editions. We hope we corrected all the mistakes and dealt with all of the shortcomings occasioned by youth rushing to publication. Besides, this *youth* business no longer applies to most of us. Indeed, it seems fair to say that most of us have grown old with this book; but not so old that we cannot keep up with revisions indefinitely. After all, none of us has yet reached fifty—but three of us are getting close.

As before, we encourage communications from the scholarly and professional community. Given sufficient encouragement we would be willing to continue revising this book until we get it right.

Jay M. Shafritz
Norma M. Riccucci
David H. Rosenbloom
Albert C. Hyde

Acknowledgments

No book is born without debts. Special research assistance was provided by Todd Jonathan Alexander, Noah Justin, Mark Wendell, Stephanie Leigh, Leah Naomi, Sarah Tamar, Joshua Isaac, and Lila Ziva. For this edition we are particularly indebted to: Carolyn Ban, Robert Mallinson, Betty Pletenik, and Frank J. Thompson of the State University of New York at Albany; Joel M. Douglas of the Baruch College of the City University of New York; Jacquelyn J. Hawkins and Lois Utley of the New York State Civil Service Department; Jocelyn Johnston of Syracuse University; Christine Altenberger, Anita Caivano, Hanna Freij, Olivia Hidalgo-Hardeman, and Sheila Kelly of the University of Pittsburgh; and J. Steven Ott of the University of Maine.

Professor Michael Graham of San Francisco State University made major contributions to the chapter on comparable worth, in what has been a major research project of his reviewing legal developments in this area. Several MPA graduate students at San Francisco State were helpful, including Nancy Edmonson, Mary Kittelson, Tony Travers, and Philip Vince, each of whom wrote major research studies that were incorporated into this chapter. Finally, in closing our West Coast connection, Professor Raymond Pomerleau deserves thanks for his steadfast encouragement of this text and his thoughtful reviews of the past two editions.

A unique set of contributions has been made by four individuals in Washington who have helped update our research on pivotal events in several personnel functional areas. Fifi Donahue of the Office of Personnel Management (OPM) Office of Systems Oversight and Innovation contributed her expertise on productivity gainsharing and Total Quality Management (TQM). Gail Redd of the same office helped shape our research on performance management and appraisal. Anna Briatico of OPM focused our assessment of examination and recruitment. Karla Adler Hester, formerly with OPM but now with the GSA, provided significant research assistance on pay reform and compensation developments. These four individuals made invaluable contributions to this fourth edition. It is worth noting in general that in the 1980s, OPM conducted numerous studies and evaluations of various demonstration projects in addition to special studies on personnel policy problems that provided valuable insights into many personnel problems.

OPM was not alone in helping guide personnel management research in the 1980s and 1990s. The U.S. General Accounting Office continued its well-established role in providing a strong evaluative arm with numerous detailed and well-researched studies. A new force in personnel research also emerged. The U.S. Merit Systems Protection Board's Office of Policy Evaluation (OPE) under the guidance of Evangeline Swift and John Palguta has conducted a series of insightful, well researched, and pivotal studies of federal personnel policy. OPE researchers Paul Van Rijn, Harry Redd, John Crum, Bruce Mayor, Jamie Carlyle, Charles Friedman, Katherine Naff, Ron Finnell, and Keith Bell prepared these valuable studies that are referenced so frequently in these chapters. In addition to their research contributions, we have had the benefit of numerous helpful conversations with them over the past two years in discussing the pros and cons of new directions in federal personnel management.

There are several other academic colleagues (past, present, and future) who merit a word of thanks for their ongoing collaboration and helpful support over the years. At the University of Colorado at Denver, Sam Overman, from the University of Houston, the late Phil Whitbeck and formerly Paul J. Flynn, Ron Gilbert of Florida International University, and Larry Luton of Eastern Washington University. Finally, thanks go to Susan Brannigan for her research on the Boston police strike of 1919. Many of these colleagues might be suprised to find their names in this same paragraph, especially in a book about personnel management; but their interest is less pivotal than their influence, which in its own way has been substantial and sustaining over the past decade.

Introduction:
Why This Book?

Public personnel management is a rapidly changing occupation. It has had to be. While the whirlpool of public policy moves ever onward, it is the personnel administrators who inherit the debris of the policy process. The polity decides that equal employment opportunity is a goal that should never have been denied, but it is the personnel managers of the nation who are charged with making that objective a reality. The U.S. Supreme Court decides that all employee selection devices must be empirically validated, but it is the psychometricians of the personnel department who must create examinations so valid that they can literally stand up in court. The political executives of a jurisdiction negotiate new contracts with a public employee union, but it is the departmental personnel officer who is responsible for harmonious labor relations on a daily basis. Until the early 1960s, none of these issues had a significant impact on public personnel management in the United States. The public debate on making equal rights for all citizens a reality was only just beginning, civil service examinations were seldom validated, and the public employee union movement was embryonic. Today, these issues are central. Other aspects of the public personnel purview such as human resources planning, productivity measurement, and the design of work are now just beginning to make themselves felt in a significant way. Tomorrow, they will be as central. The major intent of this text is to expose the reader to the basic elements of the public personnel practice with an emphasis on the most pressing concerns of today and the most probable concerns of tomorrow.

This is not a "how-to-do-it" book written for people who want to be personnel experts in ten easy lessons. It is a "what-is-it" book written for people who seek or are engaged in managerial careers in the public sector and are in need of a basic introduction to, or a review of, public personnel machinations. The "nuts and bolts" of personnel processes vary considerably from jurisdiction to jurisdiction. Because of differing laws and customs, it would be futile to present the "one right way" for any given procedure. Instead, the procedural chapters concentrate on the essential theory and future trends of their subjects. With this information, a diligent reader will have the kind of conceptual foundation that will allow him or her to rapidly digest and master the procedural nuts and bolts that differ with every jurisdiction. Our focus is descriptive rather than prescriptive. The aim is to prepare a reader to go out and work in and with the public personnel world, not to prepare him or her to be a narrowly based personnel functionary. However, if the latter is one's goal, then this is the place to begin.

The essential difference between personnel management in the private sector and personnel management in the public sector can probably be summed up in one word—politics. The public personnel process is a political process. Frankly, that is what makes it so interesting as an area of study. It is our underlying premise that the public personnel process cannot be properly understood without an appreciation of its political dynamics. All of the actors in the public personnel world must accept their political fate—they cannot pretend either to themselves or to the public that they operate as a public sector counterpart to industrial personnel operations. The political nature of public personnel management must be faced maturely. Just as the first step in arresting alcoholism is to have the alcoholic admit that he or she is an alcoholic and will always be an alcoholic even after he or she stops drinking, the first step toward putting public personnel operations on a more realistic footing is for public executives and union leaders alike to admit that public personnel operations are political processes even when traditional political considerations cease to dictate the minutiae of personnel policy. Because political phenomena cannot be understood or appreciated outside their historical context, much such context is provided. Although this text begins with a historical account of the development of public personnel institutions and practices, many of the later chapters also contain significant doses of history as well. The largest audience for this text will be individuals preparing for careers in public management that may last many decades. Accordingly, they need a long view of the development of public sector labor relations or equal employment opportunity, to cite two examples, so that they may be better prepared to deal with future developments in these areas.

The astute reader will quickly notice that there are no footnotes in this book. If a work is referred to in a chapter, the full citation will be found in that chapter's bibliography. Most long quotations are kept in boxes, separate from the main body and rhythm of the text. Although this book hardly constitutes "light" reading, we saw no need to demonstrate our scholarly erudition at the cost of readability.

Read on. You've gone this far!

Contents

Preface   *iii*
Acknowledgments   *v*
Introduction: Why This Book?   *vii*

**Part I   History and Politics of Public
Personnel Management**

1   Civil Service Reform   **3**

Prologue: President Garfield's Assassination   3
The Historical Perspective   5
The Spoils System   5
The Motivation for Reform   10
The Impetus for Reform   12
Grant's Civil Service Commission   13
The Civil Service Reform Associations   15
Reform at the Federal Level   16
Municipal Reform Efforts   16
The Civil Service Reform Act of 1978   19
Bibliography   23

**2   Institutional Achievements of
the Reform Movement**   **25**

*Prologue: The Scandal That Destroyed the U.S. Civil
    Service Commission*   25
The Centrality of the Civil Service   27
The Pendleton Act   29

The Central Personnel Agency   32
Phase I—Policing   33
Phase II—Scientific Management   35
Phase III—Centralization   36
Phase IV—The Decentralization of Federal Personnel Operations   37
Phase V—The Demise of the Civil Service Commission   39
Phase VI—Reform 1979   40
Phase VII—Post-Reform Era   45
State and Local Institutional Arrangements   56
The Decline of the Commission Format   61
Bibliography   62

3   Politics of Public Personnel   67

Prologue: "Spoiling" the Merit System   67
Fudging the System   68
The Netherworld of Public Personnel Management   71
A Missing Professionalism   73
The Cultural Milieu   78
The Legacy of the Reform Movement   82
The Volcker Commission   92
Bibliography   93

Part II   Position Management

4   Human Resources Planning   97

Prologue: Work Force 2000 and the "Endangered"
    Civil Servant   97
The Environment for Human Resources Planning   101
Human Resources Planning in "Hard Times"   104
A Historical Overview of Human Resources Planning   107
Work Force Planning   110
Forecasting Human Resources Supply   115
Forecasting Organizational Demands   119
Work Force Quality in the Public Sector: A Framework
    for Evaluating Human Resources Planning   124
Bibliography   128

5   Classification and Compensation   131

Prologue: Classification & Compensation's Next Generation:
    The China Lake and Pacer Share Demonstration Projects?   131
The Origins of Position Classification   134

The Politics of Classification   139
The Factor Evaluation System   143
Pay Reform and the "Quiet Crisis"   149
Federal Pay Reform: 1990   154
Work Redesign and Technology   156
Bibliography   162

6   Recruitment, Examination, and Selection   167

Prologue: A Tale of Two Courts: The Griggs and
    Wards Cove Decisions   167
The Development of the Uniform Guidelines   171
The Importance of Public Employment   177
Personal Rank Versus Position Rank   181
Legal Aspects of Selection Methodology   182
Examinations and Validation   185
The Old World of PACE   191
The New World of ACWA   196
Bibliography   197

Part III   The Legal Environment of Public
Personnel Management

7   Equal Employment Opportunity and Affirmative Action   203

Prologue: Affirmative Action and the Courts   203
Abuses of the Past   208
The Development of EEO   213
The Organization of EEO   222
EEO Policy   229
Affirmative Action Plans   232
EEO Complaint Systems   235
Additional EEO Concerns   236
Sexual Harassment   238
The Lessons of EEO   242
Looking Toward the Future   245
Bibliography   246

8   Comparable Worth   251

Prologue: "A Penny for Your Thoughts"   251
What Is Comparable Worth?   252
The Female-Male Pay Gap: Causes and Cures   254
Legal and Judicial Developments   257

Executive and Legislative Developments   262
Comparable Worth in the 1990s: New Directions   272
Bibliography   272

9 Constitutional Issues of Public
Personnel Management   277

Prologue: Elrod v. Burns (1976)   277
The Public Employment Relationship   283
The Individual Rights Model   287
The Public Service Model   289
Freedom of Expression: Nonpartisan Speech   290
Political Neutrality   293
Freedom of Association   296
Liberty   297
Equal Protection   300
The Right to a Hearing   304
Privacy   307
The Right to Disobey   314
Ramifications   315
Bibliography   316

Part IV   Public Sector Labor Relations

10 Labor Relations:
Development and Scope   319

Prologue: The Boston Police Strike   319
Overview   321
The Unionization of Public Employees   341
The Civil Service Reform Act of 1978   345
State and Local Arrangements   351
Conclusion   355
Bibliography   357

11 Labor Relations:
Process, Participants, Tactics, and Politics   359

Prologue: The Demise of PATCO   359
The Right to Join and Form Unions   361
Establishing the Collective Bargaining Relationship   367
Unit Determination   369
The Scope of Bargaining   371
Unfair Labor Practices and Good Faith   373

Contents

Impasse Resolution   376
The Trouble with Third Parties   382
Strikes   383
Grievances   388
The Union Leader   391
The Public Employer   395
Tactics   399
Politics   402
Conclusion   403
Bibliography   404

Part V   Productivity

12   Productivity Improvement   407

Prologue: The Meter Reader on Roller Skates:
  Productivity Innovation in One American City   407
Understanding the "Productivity Environment"   409
Privatization and Productivity   413
What Is Productivity?   415
Measuring Productivity   417
Models of Productivity Management   424
Gainsharing and Shared Savings Plans   427
Summary: Will It Work? Will It Last?   428
Bibliography   432

13   Improving Quality   437

Prologue: "Getting It Right the Second Time:" Quality
  Improvement at NASA's Johnson Space Center   437
The Emergence of Quality: A Public Sector Odyssey   439
Empowerment or Participative Management   442
Quality of Worklife Programs: A Personnel Management
  Perspective   449
Implications for Human Resources Management   451
Bibliography   453

Part VI   Human Resources Development

14   Training and Development   457

Prologue: Teaching Employees a "New Way to Think:"
  A Case Study on the Limits to Training and Development   457
Training and Development in "Hard Times"   459

Training and Personnel Relationships   463
Methods of Training   466
Career Development and the Employee   470
On Planning Training   475
On Evaluating Training   478
Training and Development in the 1990s   483
Bibliography   484

15   Performance Appraisal   **489**

Prologue: The Debate Over Merit Pay   489
The Problem of Performance Appraisal   492
The Traditional Approach to Performance Appraisal   496
Changing the System: The Behavioral Focus   500
Assessment Centers   505
Bibliography   508

**Part VII   Future Challenges to Public
Personnel Management**

16   Work, Family, and the Future   **517**

Prologue: Family Leave Policies and Benefits   517
Changing Demographics of the Workplace   518
The Pregnancy Paradox: Benefits or Bias?   519
The History of Family-Related Benefits   527
Policies and Programs Aimed at Accommodating
    Family Responsibilities   529
The Future   535
Bibliography   536

Index   **539**

Part I
HISTORY AND POLITICS OF
PUBLIC PERSONNEL MANAGEMENT

1
Civil Service Reform

Prologue: President Garfield's Assassination

Just as it was the assassination of President John F. Kennedy in 1963 that fostered the congressional climate essential for the passage of his previously thwarted domestic legislative goals, it was the 1881 assassination of President James A. Garfield—who was elected the year before on a platform that called for a complete and radical civil service reform—that created the climate necessary for the passage of the nation's first significant reform measure—the Pendleton Act of 1883. Hollywood could hardly have written a scenario that was more conducive to reform. Garfield was not shot by a mere political fanatic or run-of-the-mill deranged mind. His assassin, Charles Guiteau, was a disappointed office seeker.

Knowing that the vice-president, Chester A. Arthur, was such a thorough spoilsman that he was removed from his post as head of the New York Customhouse by President Hayes for notorious partisan abuses, Guiteau on July 2, 1881 approached Garfield at a Washington railroad station and shot him with a pistol. The first wound in the arm was minor; the second in the back proved fatal. Almost immediately captured, Guiteau explained his action by asserting, "I am a stalwart and Arthur is president now." Obviously, Guiteau felt that Arthur would be more receptive to his petitions for office than Garfield had been. Although Guiteau was plainly insane, many reasonable people thought that this insanity differed only in degree from that of many political leaders of the period.

Although popular sympathy for civil service reform was certainly in the air, it was an idea whose time had by no means come. But Guiteau's bitter act changed the political climate precipitously. The reformers, who took a moralistic tone to begin with, were suddenly able to equate the spoils system with murder. This the public took to heart. Garfield was a martyr to the spoils system. Sympathy for Garfield, who dramatically took more than two months to die as he lingered on in pain, was equated with support for reform. With Garfield's death on September 19, 1881, the press turned its attention to Guiteau's sensational trial, in which the defendant, a lawyer, sought to defend himself, and the prosecution introduced into evidence a portion of the deceased martyr's vertebra. Guiteau was found guilty and hanged on June 30, 1882.

On January 16, 1883, President Arthur signed the Pendleton Act into law, creating the U.S. Civil Service Commission. Civil service reform did not result quite so dramatically from Garfield's martyrdom as may appear, however. The Pendleton Act hardly provided the framework of a modern

An Assassin's Letter to a Future Victim

March 26,1881

Gen. Garfield:

I understand from Col. Hooker of the Nat'l committee that I am to have a consulship. I hope it is the consulship at Paris, as that is the only one I care to take. Wish you would send in my name for the consulship at Paris. Mr. Walker, the present consul, has no claim on you for the office, I think as the men that did the business last fall are the ones to be remembered.

Very respectfully,

Charles Guiteau

U.S. Office of Personnel Management, Washington, D.C.

merit system, and its passage, although aided by Garfield's death, was predominantly a reflection of the political trends of the time.

The Historical Perspective

Just as an individual's life cannot be properly appreciated without reviewing the time of childhood and youth, the modern import of a social movement, in this case civil service reform, cannot be appreciated without reviewing the hopes of its founders, the environment that molded it, and its evolution over time.

Although a civil service has long been a feature of government, a career civil service based upon merit has until just recently been a historical novelty. Such corps have popped in and out of history since the days of ancient China, but merit systems in the modern sense had to await the advent of industrialization and the modern nation-state. Prussia, one of the constituent states of what was to become modern Germany, was the first modern nation to institute a merit system. It was this German civil service that inspired Max Weber's famous "ideal-type" bureaucratic model that is the point of departure for many present-day discussions of bureaucratic theory. Weber, a scholar of prodigious output, is considered in consequence to be one of the principal founders of the academic discipline of public administration. Prussia began its merit system in the mid-eighteenth century. France followed the Prussian model shortly after the revolution of 1789. Great Britain, after developing a professionalized civil service for India in the 1830s, adopted the concept for the homeland in the 1850s. The United States was among the last of the major industrialized nations to inaugurate a civil service based on merit.

The Spoils System

In 1976, presidential candidate Jimmy Carter promised the American people that if elected he would reform the federal civil service system that had been suffering so publicly from a variety of scandals concerned with both the probity of the officials managing the system and the competence of the system in general. On October 13, 1978, President Jimmy Carter signed into law the Civil Service Reform Act of 1978, which provided for the dissolution of the U.S. Civil Service Commission as of January 1, 1979. But this act was only the most recent culmination of a long history and tradition of reform.

American civil service reform is generally dated from the post-Civil War period, but the political roots of the reform effort go back much earlier—to the beginning of the republic. John Adams tended to maintain

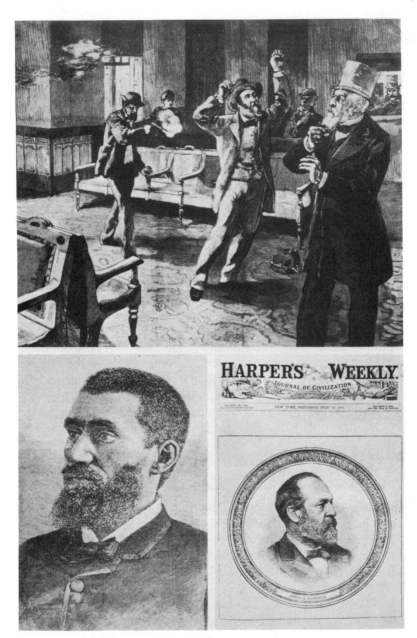

Drawings from *Harper's Weekly*, 1881. (Top) The firing of the second bullet, by W. A. Rogers. (Bottom left) Charles Guiteau by W. P. Snyder, and (bottom right) a cover featuring a fine engraving of President Garfield by George G. White. *Source: Harper's Weekly* (July 8, 1881 and July 23, 1881 issues).

the appointments of George Washington, but Thomas Jefferson was the first president who had to face the problem of a philosophically hostile bureaucracy. While sorely pressed by his supporters to remove Federalist officeholders and replace them with Republican partisans, Jefferson was determined not to remove officials for political reasons alone. Jefferson rather courageously maintained that only "malconduct is a just ground of removal: mere difference of political opinion is not." With occasional defections from this principle, even by Jefferson himself, this policy was the norm rather than the exception down through the administration of Andrew Jackson.

Andrew Jackson has been blamed for inventing the spoils system. High school students can tell you that upon becoming president he shouted "to the victor belong the spoils," and replaced every federal employee with one of his less competent friends. But the truth is much more subtle. Far from firing everybody, Jackson continued with the appointing practices established by his predecessors. The federal service prior to Jackson's administration was a stable, long-tenured corps of officials decidedly elitist in character and remarkably baren of corruption. Jackson for the most part continued with this tradition in practice. He turned out of office about as many appointees as had Jefferson. During his eight years in office (1829–1837) removals are generally estimated to have been less than 20 percent. As for that famous phrase "to the victor belong the spoils," it was neither uttered by Jackson nor recorded at all until the latter part of Jackson's first term as president. The famous phrase maker was Senator William L. Marcy of New York, who, in an 1832 debate with Senator Henry Clay of Kentucky, stated that the politicians of the United States "see nothing wrong in the rule, that to the victor belong the spoils of the enemy." Marcy was to get his comeuppance years later when as secretary of state under President Pierce he futilely sought to establish the rudiments of a career system for clerks in the State Department.

President Jackson's rhetoric on the nature of the public service was far more influential than his administrative example. While there was general agreement at the time that the civil service represented a high degree of competence and integrity, there was also widespread resentment that such appointments still tended to go to members of families of social standing at a time when universal white male suffrage had finally become a reality. To a large degree Jackson's contituency was made up of the previously disenfranchised and their sympathizers. In this context Jackson's rhetorical attack upon what had become an elitist and inbred civil service was well justified. In his most famous statement on the character of public office Jackson asserted that the duties of public office are "so plain and simple that men of intelligence may readily qualify themselves for their performance; and I cannot but believe that more is lost by the long continuance of men in office than is generally to be gained by their experience."

**President Jackson's Spoils Doctrine Was
Eloquently Stated in His Message to
Congress of December 8, 1829**

There are, perhaps, few men who can for any great length of time enjoy office and power without being more or less under the influence of feelings unfavorable to the faithful discharge of their public duties. Their integrity may be proof against improper considerations immediately addressed to themselves, but they are apt to acquire a habit of looking with indifference upon the public interests and of tolerating conduct from which an unpracticed man would revolt. Office is considered as a species of property, and government rather as a means of promoting individual interests than as an instrument created solely for the service of the people. Corruption in some and in others a perversion of correct feelings and principles divert government from its legitimate ends and make it an engine for the support of the few at the expense of the many. The duties of all public officers are, or at least admit of being made, so plain and simple that men of intelligence may readily qualify themselves for their performance; and I cannot but belive that more is lost by the long continuance of men in office than is generally to be gained by their experience....

In a country where offices are created solely for the benefit of the people, no one man has any more intrinsic right to official station than another. Offices were not established to give support to particular men at the public expense. No individual wrong is, therefore, done by removal, since either appointment to nor continuance in office is matter of right. The incumbent became an officer with a view to public benefits, and when these require his removal they are not to be sacrificed to private interests. It is the people, and they alone, who have a right to complain when a bad officer is substituted for a good one. He who is removed has the same means of obtaining a living that are enjoyed by the millions who never held office.

In claiming that all men, especially the newly enfranchised who did so much to elect him, should have an equal opportunity for public office, Jackson played to his plebian constituency and put the patrician civil service on notice that it had no natural monopoly on public office. Jackson's concept of rotation in office was basically conceived as a sincere measure of reform. As such it was enthusiastically supported by contemporary reformers. While Jackson's personal indulgence in spoils was more limited than commonly thought, he nevertheless established the intellectual and political rationale for the unmitigated spoils system that was to follow. Of course, Jackson's spoils doctrine would hardly have taken as it did were it not for the fact that the country was well prepared to accept it. Indeed, much of the venality of the spoils process was in full flower in state and local governments a full generation before it crept into federal office.

The spoils system flourished under Jackson's successors. The doctrine of rotation of office progressively prevailed over the earlier notion of stability in office. Presidents even began turning out of office appointees of previous presidents of the same party. President Millard Fillmore had dissident Whigs turned out in favor of "real" Whigs. When James Buchanan, a Democrat succeeded Franklin Pierce, also a Democrat, it was announced that no incumbents appointed by Pierce would be retained. This development led William Marcy to remark "they have it that I am the author of the office seeker's doctrine, that 'to the victor belong the spoils,' but I certainly should never recommend the policy of pillaging my own camp."

Abraham Lincoln as president followed the example of his predecessors and was an unabashed supporter and skillful user of the spoils system; his highly partisan exploitation of federal patronage was a great aid to the war effort. Paradoxically, while the spoils system reached its zenith under Lincoln, its decline may also be dated from his administration, for Lincoln refused to accede to the hitherto observed principle of quadrennial rotation after his reelection in 1864. This was the first significant setback that the principle of rotation had received since Jackson laid out its theoretical justifications. Yet through the height of the spoils period, there existed what some historians have called a "career service." Many clerks had continuous tenure all through this period, retaining their positions through competence, custom, and neutrality.

An Excerpt from the Henry Clay-William L. Marcy Senate Debates of 1832 During Which the Spoils Systems Was So Famously Defended

Mr. Clay: It is a detestable system, drawn from the worst periods of the Roman republic: and if it were to be perpetuated; if the offices, honors, and dignities of the people were to be put up to a scramble, to be decided by the result of every Presidential election, our Govenrment and institutions, becoming intolerable, would finally end in a depotism as inexorable as that at Constantinople....

Mr. Marcy: It may be, sir, that the politicians of the United States are not so fastidious as some gentlemen are, as to disclosing the principles on which they act. They boldly preach what they practice. When they are contending for victory, they avow their intention of enjoying the fruits of it. If they are defeated, they expect to retire from office. If they are successful, they claim, as a matter of right, the advantages of success. They see nothing wrong in the rule, that to the victor belong the spoils of the enemy....

I have good reasons, very good reasons, for believing that it is the gentleman's rule of conduct to take care of his friends when he is in power. It requires not the foresight of a prophet to predict that, if he shall come into power, he will take care of his friends, and, if he does, I can assure him I shall not complain; nor shall I be in the least surprised if he imitates the example which he now so emphatically denounces.

The Motivation for Reform

The chronology of civil service reform is easily delineated. A variety of specific events and documents have provided a convenient framework for analysis. However, the motivations of those who led the reform movement has remained a clouded issue, lending themselves to a considerable speculation. Historians tend to agree that the leaders of the reform movement represented a socioeconomic class that was both out of power and decidedly antagonistic to those elements of society who were in power. In simplistic terms it was the WASP (white Anglo-Saxon Protestant) patricians versus the ethnic plebians. The social upheavals that accompanied the Civil War left in its wake what Richard Hofstadter has described as a displaced class of old gentry, professional men, and the civic leaders of an earlier time. This displacement, this alienation, did much to establish the "ins" versus the "outs" pattern of the politics of reform. Because the reformers blamed the professional politicians for their own political impotence, they struck at the source of his strength—the spoils system. President Grant inadvertently accelerated the demand for reform when, upon obtaining office, he not only excluded from patronage appointments the old gentry, but denied office to the editors of

---

Career and Patronage Side by Side

During the first forty years of the Republic ... there was no legislation dealing with appointments, examinations, promotions, removals, or any other familiar aspects of a personnel system except that establishing pay rates for clerks and officers. There was nevertheless a genuine career system based strictly on custom and on the deference that one gentlemen owed to another. Men became clerks in their early years and remained clerks often in the same office, until they died.... The country started its history with a career system that stood intact and unchallenged for the first forty years. It was the model to which the country has been steadily returning, with modern improvements ever since 1883. Contrary to almost universal opinion, this system did not disappear with the inauguration of Andrew Jackson in 1829. Jackson advocated and introduced the idea of rotation, for reasons which in 1829 commanded respect. But he rotated during his first administration not more than 20 percent of the federal employees and probably less. In his second term he rotated none.

Without pursuing the record of succeeding administrations, it may be said that from 1829 to 1861 and later, the career system continued alongside the patronage system. Heads of departments found that it was absolutely necessary to have in the key positions of middle-management men who knew their business, were familiar with the laws and rgeulations, and could protect them against mistakes.

Leonard D. White, "Centennial Anniversary," *Public Personnel Review*, 14 (January 1953), p. 6. Reprinted by permission of the International Personnel Management Association, 1850 K Street, N.W., Suite 870, Washington, D.C. 20006.

influential newspapers and journals. This was in contrast to Lincoln's policy of courting the press by bestowing a lavish patronage upon them. As a result, the press of both parties started speaking out more strongly than ever before in favor of reform.

As the American economy expanded during the last half of the nineteenth century, the orientation of the business community became less and less focused on parochial interests bounded by the neighborhood and more and more oriented toward urban, regional, and international markets. Economic determinists could well argue that the death knell of the spoils system was sounded when the ineptness of government began to hamper the expansion of business. It is noteworthy in this respect that the federal government made some efforts to institute merit system concepts in both the New York Post Office and the New York Customhouse several years before the passage of the Pendleton Act. Such reform measures, limited as they were, were a direct result of pressure from a business community that had grown increasingly intolerant of ineptness in the postal service and extortion by the customs service.

Depending upon your point of view, the advent of modern merit systems is either an economic, political, or moral development. Economic historians would maintain that the demands of industrial expansion—a dependable postal service, a viable transportation network, and so on—necessitated a government service based upon merit. Political analysts could argue rather persuasively that it was the demands of an expanded suffrage and democratic rhetoric that sought to replace favoritism with merit. Both economic and political considerations are so intertwined that it is impossible to say which factor is the exact foundation of the merit system. The moral impetus behind reform is even more difficult to define. As moral impulses tend to hide economic and political motives, the weight of moral concern that is undiluted by other considerations is impossible to measure. Nevertheless, the cosmetic effect of moral overtones was of significant aid to the civil service reform movement in the United States because it accentuated the social legitimacy of the reform proposals.

With the ever-present impetus of achieving maximum public services for minimum tax dollars, the businessman was quite comfortable in supporting civil service reform. Support for reform was just one of a variety of strategies employed by the business interests to have power pass from the politicos to themselves. The political parties of the time were almost totally dependent for a financial base upon assessments made on the wages of their members in public office. The party faithful had long been expected to kick back a percentage of their salary in order to retain their positions. A good portion of the Pendleton Act is devoted to forbidding this and other related methods of extortion. With the decline of patronage the parties had to seek out new funding sources. The business interests were more than willing to assume this new financial burden and its concomitant influence.

The Impetus for Reform

It was congressional disenchantment with the policies of President Andrew Johnson that instigated the first comprehensive and highly publicized proposals for a merit system based upon competitive examinations. Congressman Thomas A. Jenckes, a Republican of Rhode Island, sponsored several bills to curb the patronage power of the president by foisting a merit system upon him. Jenckes's proporsals—which borrowed heavily from the British model—were worthy in and of themselves; but they were obviously inspired, at least initially, by antipathy to President Johnson. While Jenckes's 1865 proposals advocated a civil service commission appointed by the president, a growing hostility toward President Johnson certainly motivated the strikingly novel feature of his 1868 proposals—"to furnish employment for the Vice-President by making him the head of a new department—that of the civil service." This was a thinly disguised effort to take patronage out of the hands of a president whose appointments tended to antagonize the Congress. Once Johnson was out of office, Jenckes reverted to his original proposal for a presidentially appointed commission to adminsiter a civil service merit system. But the Jenckes proposals, having to compete for public attention with Andrew Johnson's impeachment trial and the forthcoming Republican national convention, made little impact. Johnson's impeachment was occasioned by his violation of the Tenure of Office Act of 1867. Many of the opinion leaders of the time, including the *Nation* and the *New York Times* praised the act as

The Patrician Reformer

To the patrician reformer, the ideal government tended to be one by men like himself. They, he was sure, would treat all problems with no urge for self-aggrandizement and would mete out to each group a disinterested justice.

In seeking his ideal government, the patrician reformer frequently gave special emphasis to the establishment of a civil-service system. The "chief evil" of the day, explained Charles Bonaparte, a Marylander who had inherited a lofty family name and more than a million dollars' worth of real estate, was "the alliance between industrialists and a political class which thinks like industrialists...." These politicians would be replaced by "gentlemen ... who need nothing and want nothing from government except the satisfaction of using their talents," or at least by "sober, industrious ... middle class persons who have taken over ... the proper standards of conduct." The argument of Bonaparte was common in the literature of patrician reform. The whole civil-service movement, as the patrician Theodore Roosevelt later remarked, was decidedly one "from above downwards."

Eric F. Goldman, *Rendezvous with Destiny: A History of Modern American Reform* (New York: Knopf, 1965), pp. 18–19.

a sincere measure of reform that would bring stability to the government service. As the whole impeachment controversy can be viewed from one perspective as a struggle between the executive branch and the legislative branch for the control of patronage, the Jenckes proposal to have the vice president serve as a buffer between the president and the Congress does not seem so outlandish considering the time frame.

While the various reform proposals that Jenckes put forth during the Johnson administration owed their origins to mixed motives on the congressman's part, they did, nevertheless, serve as an important rallying point for reform agitation. The movers and shakers of the budding reform movement as well as many of the important newspapers and journals of the day gave the Jenckes proposals considerable attention and concomitant publicity. The civil service reform movement that eventually led to the Pendleton Act did not exist in 1866. Jenckes's initial reform proposals of 1865 and 1866 were literally ignored by the press and other national opinion leaders. Yet within five years the reform movements had mobilized to the extent that the president of the United States, Ulysses S. Grant, recommended civil service legislation to the Congress in 1870 and obtained it, at least in the form of a short rider, in 1871. Jenckes deserves considerable credit for this mobilization of opinion and attention. However, possibly because he did not pay enough attention to his own patronage garden, Jenckes was defeated for reelection in 1870 and thereupon retired from public life.

Grant's Civil Service Commission

In 1859 Ulysses S. Grant, as a private and obscure citizen, sought an appointment as a county engineer in Missouri and was denied it because he lacked the requisite political sponsorship. This may have inspired Grant's support for civil service reform when he became president. It is one of the cruelties of one-dimensional popular history that the first adminstration to make a large-scale effort at civil service reform should be most noted for its spoils system excesses. Reform, fleeting as it was, was achieved not after the careful and lengthy deliberations of the legislature, but mainly through the parliamentary skill of its proponents. On the last day of the legislative session of the Forty-first Congress in 1871, Senator Lyman Trumbull of Illinois attached to an otherwise unrelated appropriations bill a rider that authorized the president to make rules and regulations for the civil service. Surprisingly, the total bill was approved by both houses. Although Grant supported the measure, historians tend to argue that the bill passed not so much because of Grant's influence but because of an awakening public opinion that had been coalescing for several years around the Jenckes proposals. Contributing to this arousal were the recent exposés of Boss Tweed's operations in New York City and other journalistic ferment. The rider itself was only one sentence long and did not formally require the president to do anything. It certainly would not have passed had it been thought to be anything more than a symbolic sop to the reformers. The rider essentially authorized the president "to prescribe such rules and regulations for the admission of persons into the civil service of the United States as will best promote the efficiency thereof, and ascertain the fitness of each candidate."

To the surprise of almost everyone, Grant proceeded to appoint a Civil Service Commission shortly thereafter. He authorized the commission to establish and implement appropriate rules and regulations. The commission required boards of examiners in each department who worked under the commission's general supervision. All things considered, a viable program existed during 1872 and 1873. Several thousand persons were examined, and several hundred were actually appointed. But once the Congress realized that Grant was serious about reform and intent upon cutting into its patronage

---

Corruption in Perspective

The typical historian has been too loose in applying the term "corruption." Specifically, he labels a politically partisan civil service corrupt rather than inefficient; he equates the spoils system with corruption when honest spoils-men far outnumber dishonest ones; he pronounces Gilded Age politicians guilty of corruption for associating with corruptionists even while attacking guilty by association in his own day.

One apparent reason why the historian has exaggerated the corruption of the Gilded Age is his desire to enliven lectures and writings. All the world loves a scandal, and the historian is loathe to abandon the pleasure of dispensing "vicarious sin." More basically, the historian dislikes the dominant forces in the Gilded Age. The historian is usualy liberal, more often than not a Democrat. He is, typically hostile to big business, an advocate of government regulation, of strong executive leadership, and of a civil service staffed by experts. The post-Civil War era stands for all the historian opposes. It was an era of Republicanism, of big business domination, of few and ineffectual attempts at government regulation, of weak executives, and of an essentially nonprofessional civil service. The historian naturally dwells upon the shortcomings of the period, particularly on the failures of Ulysses S. Grant, whose political career both personifies all the historian abhors and symbolizes Gilded Age politics.

Another reason the historian has exaggerated corruption in this period is the bias of his sources. The most articulate individuals in this age were its severest critics.

Ari Hoogenboom, "Spoilsmen and Reformers: Civil Service Reform and Public Morality," in *The Gilded Age: A Reappraisal*, ed. H. Wayne Morgan (Syracuse, N.Y.: Syracuse University Press, 1963), p. 71.

powers, the program was terminated. Congress simply refused to appropriate funds for the work of the commission. Although the president formally abolished his commission in 1875, the enabling legislation, the rider of 1871, remains law to this day.

Although the first federal Civil Service Commission was short-lived, the experiment served an an important object lesson for later reform measures and established presidential prerogatives that are now taken for granted. For the first time the president was given unchallengeable authority over federal government personnel. The reform measures implied by the rider went far beyond the control of personnel. By authorizing the president to, in effect, provide himself with staff assistance, the rider of 1871 marks the beginning of the presidency's rise to the actual leadership of the federal administrative apparatus. It was by the authority of this rider as well as the later Pendleton Act that the president issued executive orders and rules concerning the civil service.

The policies that this first Civil Service Commission promulgated still haunt merit systems to this day. The word *haunt* in this instance seems exceedingly appropriate, for it is the dead hand of the past that is frequently keeping the public service from achieving its full potential. An analysis of the terminology and concepts developed by Grant's commission shows that many of the provisions that are taken for granted today in merit systems at all jurisdictional levels were first developed in 1871. It was this commission that first instituted the "rule of three"; that adopted the policy of restricting lateral entry and making initial appointments only at the entrance level; and that mandated that promotion within the service should be decided by competitive examinations limited to those already in the agency. It is ironic that this last measure, in such widespread use today and almost universally used in large police and fire departments, was found by the commission upon trial to be an unsuitable method to determine promotions. All of the above-mentioned measures were appropriate innovations at the time, but they have not aged well. Although the federal service is not generally confined by these particular constaints upon management, many state and local jurisdictions must live with these and similarly antiquated practices. Not only are they locked into such practices by legal mandates, tradition, and inertia, but the newly militant public employee unions, finding that such procedures that give a decided advantage to seniority over merit are to the advantage of their members, are ever more insistent that such provisions remain.

The Civil Service Reform Associations

With the demise of the Grant commission, reform took only a few halting steps until the Arthur administration. Rutherford B. Hayes, who succeeded

Grant, was personally in favor of reform, but with a Congress hostile to it, he did not press the matter beyond issuing an executive order requiring competitive examinations for the notoriously corrupt New York Customhouse and for parts of the New York Post Office. However, it was during the time of the Hayes administration that the various civil service reform associations were established. The first of these was the New York Civil Service Reform Association formed in 1877. By 1880 a variety of other cities had also organized assocations. The National Civil Service Reform League was formed at that time "to facilitate the correspondence and the united action of the Civil-Service Reform Associations." These associations were to be a potent force in the fight for reform over the coming decades. It was the New York association that in 1880 drafted a reform program that was to be submitted to Congress for consideration. Meanwhile, Senator George H. Pendleton, a Democrat from Ohio, had independenlty and unbeknown to the association introduced a version of one of Jenckes's old proposals in the Senate. When the association learned of this, it convinced the senator to replace his own bill with the one written by the association. Thus the "second" Pendleton bill, written by the New York Civil Service Reform Association, was submitted to the Senate during 1881. Two years later it would become law.

Reform at the Federal Level

There is no doubt that civil service reform would have come about without the 1881 assassination of President James A. Garfield. There is also no doubt that the assassination helped. While Garfield's assassination was certainly instrumental in creating the appropriate climate for the passage of "An Act to regulate and improve the Civil Service of the United States," popularly known as the Pendleton Act after Senator Pendleton, historians maintain that the Republican reversals during the midterm elections of 1882 had the more immediate effect on enactment. Civil service reform had been the deciding issue in a number of congressional contests. The state that harbored the greatest excesses of the spoils system, New York, even elected as governor the reform-minded mayor of Buffalo, Grover Cleveland. Thus when President Arthur signed the Pendleton Act into law on January 16, 1883, and created the United States Civil Service Commission, it was essentially a gesture by reluctant politicians to assuage public opinion and the reform elements.

Municipal Reform Efforts

Whereas the reformers first achieved success on the national level, the class basis of the reform impetus was essentially an urban phenomenon that was strongly tainted with nativism. In essence, the WASP middle class, being dismayed at what the ethnic hordes were doing to "their" city, called for reform. The public service has often been used by the ascending groups in American society as a vehicle for social advancement. Inevitably accompanying such changes has been a large measure of friction, distrust, and hostility. The continuity of this process is unbroken to this day. In this regard there is no significant difference between the successors of Jackson deposing members of the aristocratically tinged civil service to replace them with loyalists of common origin and today's displacement of white ethnic municipal officials with African-American stalwarts.

Chester Alan Arthur. *Source*: Office of Personnel Management, Washington, D.C.

What is happening with African-American groups in a number of American cities today is the same process of assimilation and socialization previously undergone by the various white ethnic groups. The groups that were displaced were quite vocal in indicating that the insurgents were grossly corrupt and were using public office largely for their private gain and for the advantage of their peers. Although such utterances are typically attributed to such factors as racism and religious prejudice, the foundation upon which these remarks are made—the venality of public office—is essentially sound. There is no doubt that each succeeding power group used public office to their private advantage. As each social group took advantage of whatever the local political process could offer, they advanced themselves socially, sent their children to college, and moved to the suburbs, leaving the machine and its style of politics to the next cycle of immigrants. Now both physically and generationally removed from the political atmosphere from which they benefited, they feel comfortable in viewing the present inhabitants of the buildings in which they were born as socially and morally inferior. Safely middle class, they can now afford to be reformers—especially now that reform is at somebody else's expense. The cycle is complete—they now feel as strongly about "those" people in the city as an earlier group felt about their grandparents.

Why the Pendleton Act Passed!

The outlook for the Republican party in 1884 was not promising; members of that party were filled with apprehension and the Democrats with anticipation. The "outs" were nearly in and the "ins" were nearly out. Yet the lameduck session of the Forty-seventh Congress had been elected in 1882 and was very much Republican. The congressional "outs," or at least those who very shortly would be "outs," were in a majority and controlled the presidency. It would be advantageous for Republicans to make permanent the tenure of their office holding friends while supporting the reform their constituents so obviously desired. Accordingly, the Republican senators met in caucus to discuss the Pendleton bill. Pending amendments were considered, and those offered by Republicans were generally approved. No vote was taken and nothing was done to bind senators to a particular course, but it was understood that all Republican senators with one or two exceptions would vote for the Pendleton bill. Republicans supported the bill for two reasons: they could pose as reformers in 1884 and win back lost support, and they could "freeze" Republicans in office behind civil service rules if the Democrats would win the election.

Ari Hoogenboom, *Outlawing the Spoils: A History of the Civil Service Reforme Movement, 1865–1883* (Urbana: University of Illinois Press, 1961) pp. 236–237.

Even assuming sympathetic attitudes on the part of the middle class, the manifestations of these attitudes are frequently dysfunctional to the aims of the "new immigrants." The middle-class idea of doing "good" for the lower class frequently means abolishing the means by which they themselves escaped from it. Although the programs of President Johnson's "War on Poverty" may or may not have significantly reduced the incidence of poverty in the United States, they did provide a patronage boom for the African-American community. When many of these programs were found to have unaccounted-for expenditures, padded payrolls, and little effect, indignant liberals and outraged conservatives would point to African-American leadership and say, "You've run these programs no better than the old-style, corrupt machine politicians." The general reply of some of the more outspoken African-American leaders was quite simply, "Why not? It was our turn!" And so it was. In achieving the Jacksonian intent, many segments of American society have been able to better themselves through politics; and having done so, they move on to disdain it. To deny the current inhabitants of the central city the means by which the white ethnic groups advanced themselves is as ethically dubious as many of the patronage practices that one might wish to see abolished. To ask the lower class to play middle-class politics is to change the rules of the game just when it is their turn to play. The import of this discussion is not to speak out in favor of corruption, but merely to observe some of its beneficial manifestations. The moral issues involved remain unresolved.

The Civil Service Reform Act of 1978

It should come as no surprise to the reader that public personnel management is in a time of transition. It was ever so. When the first textbook, Mosher and Kingsley's *Public Personnel Administration*, was published on this subject in 1936, the authors were able to state with great justification that "thorough-going reform of personnel administration is long overdue." This statement is equally true today, but with a crucial difference. While the early reform efforts concentrated upon creating institutions, the thrust of present day efforts is centered upon reforming institutions. It is a vexing philosophical question as to which reform effort is the more difficult undertaking.

Ironically, at the same time that the federal government has been pressuring state and local governments to adopt and strengthen merit systems, the commission form of administering them has been on the wane. Independent, structurally and politically isolated, personnel agencies of a regulatory nature have had great difficulty in serving the needs of elected executives and public managers. They become viewed as obstacles to efficiency and effectiveness and are sometimes unduly influenced by pressure groups. Ever since the 1930s efforts have been made to bring public personnel administration into greater harmony with public management in general. At state and local levels this is often attempted through the appointment of a single personnel director as the head of a central personnel agency which is clearly located within the executive chain of command. In some cases, a citizens' "oversight" group without rule-making authority complements this approach. According to Jean J. Couturier, the former executive director of the National Civil Service League, about "half the large governments in the U.S have abandoned the commission form of government for personnel management." Such changes in institutional arrangements do not necessarily militate against the maintenance of merit systems. Indeed, many of their supporters believe that personnel divisions or departments rather than commissions serve to strengthen merit procedures. However, the Nixon administration scandal in federal personnel administration, discussed in greater detail in Chapter 3, lends credence to

The Curse of Civil Service Reform

The civil service law is the biggest fraud of the age. It is the curse of the nation. There can't be no real patriotism while it lasts. How are you goin' to interest our young men in the country if you have no offices to give them when they work for their party? Just look at things in this city today. There are ten thousand good offices, but we can't get at more than a few hundred of them. How are we going' to provide for the thousands of men who worked for the Tammany ticket? It can't be done. These men were full of patriotism a short time ago. They expected to be servin' their city, but when we tell them that we can't place them, do you think their patriotism is goin' to last? Not much. They say: "What's the use of workin' for your country anyhow? There's nothin' in the game." And what can they do? I don't know, but I'll tell you what I do know. I know more than one young man in past years who worked for the ticket and was just overflowin' with patriotism, but when he was knocked out by the civil service humbug he got to hate his country and became an Anarchist.

This ain't no exaggeration. I have good reason for sayin' most of the Anarchists in this city today are men who ran up against civil service examinations. Isn't it enough to make a man sour on his country when he wants to serve it and won't be allowed unless he answers a lot of fool questions about the number of cubic inches of water in the Atlantic and the quality of sand in the Sahara desert? There was once a bright young man in my district who tackled one of these examinations. The next I heard of him he had settled down in Herr Most's saloon smokin' and drinkin' beer and talkin' socialism all day. Before that time he had never drank anything but whisky. I knew what was comin' when a young Irishman drops whisky and takes to beer and long pipes in a German saloon. That young man is today one of the wildest Anarchists in town. And just to think! He might be a patriot but for that cussed civil service.

From William L. Riordon, *Plunkitt of Tammany Hall* (New York: Dutton, 1963), pp. 11–12. Reprinted by permission of E. P. Dutton & Co.

the arguments of those who believe that personnel agencies can all too easily fall under the political influence of elected executives.

One of the more significant influences on current thinking about civil service reform has been the National Civil Service League's Model Public Personnel Administration Law, which was first promulgated in 1970. The organization that wrote the actual text of the Pendleton Act in the 1880s, creating the U.S. Civil Service Commission, in the 1970s was recommending the abolition of commission formats for public personnel management. The league would replace civil service commissions with a tripartite structure consisting of (a) a personnel division headed by a director of "cabinet" rank whose task would be to serve the needs of effective management; (2) some form of ombudsperson to provide recourse for employees—a role which conceivably could be fulfilled by a labor relations board; and (3) a citizen's advisory board to represent the public interest. In 1895 Chicago was one of the first American cities to create a civil service commission. In 1976 it became the first major city to abolish its civil service commission in favor of reforms espoused by the model law of the National Civil Service League. At the time nobody suspected that the federal government would be next.

Directly upon inauguration, President Jimmy Carter took the first step toward fulfilling his oft-repeated campaign promise of reorganizing the federal bureaucracy. A variety of task forces made up the president's reorganization project. One of these groups, the Federal Personnel Management Project, was responsible for reviewing the federal personnel system. On March 2, 1978, President Carter, with the enthusiastic support of the new Civil Service Commission leadership, submitted to the Congress his reform proposals. On that same day before the National Press Club, he further called his proposals to the attention of Congress by charging that the present federal personnel system had become a "bureaucratic maze which neglects merit, tolerates poor performance, and permits abuse of legitimate employee rights, and mires every personnel action in red tape, delay, and confusion."

The reform bill faced considerable opposition from federal employee unions, who thought the bill was too management-oriented, and from veterans' groups, who were aghast at the bill's curtailment of veterans' preferences. The unions lost. The veterans won. The bill passed almost totally intact. The major exception was the deletion of strong veterans' preference curtailments. The Senate passed the bill by voice vote and the House endorsed it by the wide margin of 365 to 8. On October 13, 1978, only six months after he had submitted it to the Congress, President Carter signed the Civil Service Reform Act of 1978 into law.

The act is almost the mirror image of the National Civil Service League's model law. In January of 1979 the U.S. Civil Service Commission was divided into two agencies: an Office of Personnel Management (OPM) to serve as

The Essence of Reform

Six months after the Civil Service Reform Act of 1978 took effect I asked an old friend, a personnelist in the Washington headquarters of one of the best known federal departments, how he liked working with the new Office of Personnel Management. He responded in mock astonishment, "Are you kidding? It's the same old Civil Service Commission crowd. Do you think they got smarter because they changed their name?"

He had a good point. While he could have said it in a nicer way, he was essentially accurate in characterizing the Office of Personnel Management as the same old "crowd." A look at the cast of characters—the heads of major divisions—at the Commission just prior to its demise and OPM just after its installation shows substantially the same *dramatis personae*. So it was perhaps too much to expect that my friend, who took years to learn to be absolutely contemptuous of the Commission, would learn to respect the OPM when he saw it as nothing more than the Commission with a face lift.

Is the OPM nothing more than the Commission with a face lift? A case can be made that the whole Civil Service Reform Act was not much more than reorganization for cosmetic effct; that is, much has changed on the surface but almost everything has stayed the same underneath. While others criticize the Act as too little too late, I concede their misgivings and say "better a symbolic Act than no Act." The show must go on! For if the Act fails in substance (which I only partially concede), it is an overwhelming success as symbol.

In large measure because of the scandals that arose during the Nixon-Ford years, the U.S. Civil Service Commission grew to symbolize corruption and incompetence. Of course only a minority of individuals engaged in corrupt behavior or exhibited incompetent tendencies. But that was enough to ruin a reputation. The Commission's "good name" could not be salvaged. Only a new name could remove the stigma of past indiscretions. The stigma was so great that the reformers went so far as to formally assert that it was not the giant Office of Personnel Managment that would be the successor agency to the Commission, but the little Merit Systems Protection Board. OPM would be a totally new entity—an organization without a history starting with a clean slate. It's a nice thought. But quite untrue except as a symbolic purging of the evils of the past. Yet on this plane of symbolic action it has been a considerable success.

My friend in Washington was wrong. While it may be the same old "crowd," they have literally put on a new face, publicly purged themselves of the evils of the past and seek to oversee the federal personnel system with new techniques and a new sense of mission. To me, that's reform. Alan K. Campbell and company deserve a lot of credit. You can't help but admire a federal manager who, upon inheriting a troubled and demoralized agency, destroys it only to find himself and practically all of his previously troubled agency born again on the White House organization chart.

Jay M. Shafritz, "The Essence of Reform," *Midwest Review of Public Administration* (September 1979), pp. 175–176.

the personnel arm of the chief executive, and an independent Merit Systems Protection Board (MSPB) to provide recourse for aggrieved employees. In addition, the act creates a Federal Labor Relations Authority (FLRA) to oversee federal labor–management relations.

While the act includes provisions for new performance appraisal systems, mandates new adverse action and appeals procedures, and requires a trial period for new managers and supervisors, probably its greatest management innovation is the creation of the Senior Executive Service (SES). The SES has pooled the most senior-level managers (GS-16 and up) into an elite 8,000-member executive corps that OPM has wide latitude in rewarding and punishing. Unfortunately, this elite group is bound to be known, perhaps with some affection, as the SES pool.

Bibliography

Aron, Cindy Sondik. *Ladies and Gentlemen of the Civil Service*. New York: Oxford University Press, 1987.

Aronson, Sidney H. *Status and Kinship in the Higher Civil Service*. Cambridge: Harvard University Press, 1964.

Banfield, Edward C., and James Q. Wilson, *City Politics*. New York: Vintage, 1963.

Carpenter, William Seal. *The Unfinished Business of Civil Service Reform*. Princeton, N.J.: Princeton University Press, 1952.

Cook, Charles, *Biography of an Ideal: The Diamond Anniversary History of the Federal Civil Service*. Washington, D.C.: U.S. Government Printing Office, 1959.

Couturier, Jean J. "The Quiet Revolution in Public Personnel Laws," *Public Personnel Management* (May–June 1976).

Crenson, Matthew A. *The Federal Machine: Beginnings of Bureaucracy in Jacksonian America*. Baltimore: Johns Hopkins University Press, 1975.

Dalby, Michael T., and Michael S. Werthman, eds. *Bureaucracy in Historical Perspective*. Glenview, Ill.: Scott, Foresman, 1971.

Dresang, Dennis L. *Public Personnel Management and Public Policy*. White Plains, NY: Longman Press, 1991.

Eriksson, Erik M. "The Federal Civil Service under President Jackson," *Mississippi Valley Historical Review*, 13 (March 1927).

Fish, Carl Russell. *The Civil Service and the Patronage*. New York: Russell & Russell, 1904, 1963.

Hofstadter, Richard. *The Age of Reform*. New York: Vantage, 1955.

Hoogenboom, Ari. *Outlawing the Spoils: A History of the Civil Service Reform Movement, 1865–1883*. Urbana: University of Illinois Press, 1961.

Josephson, Matthew. *The Politicos, 1865–1896*. New York: Harcourt, Brace, 1938.

McBain, Howard Lee. *DeWitt Clinton and the Origin of the Spoils System in New York*. New York: AMS Press, 1967.

Meriam, Lewis. *Personnel Administration in the Federal Government*. Washington, D.C.: Brookings Institution, 1937.

_____. *Public Personnel Problems: From the Standpoint of the Operating Officer*. Washington, D.C.: Brookings Institution, 1938.

Mosher, William E., and J. Donald Kingsley. *Public Personnel Administration*. New York: Harper & Bros., 1936.

Murphy, Lionel V. "The First Federal Civil Service Commisison, 1871–1875," *Public Personnel Review*, 3 (October 1942).

Rosenbloom, David H. *Federal Service and the Constitution*. Ithaca, N.Y.: Cornell University Press, 1971.

Sayre, Wallace. "The Triumph of Techniques Over Purpose," *Public Administration Review*, 8 (Spring 1948).

Shafritz, Jay M. *Public Personnel Management: The Heritage of Civil Service Reform*. New York: Praeger, 1975.

Stewart, Frank Mann. *The National Civil Service Reform League: History, Activities, and Problems*. Austin: University of Texas, 1929.

Tolchin, Martin, and Susan Tolchin. *To the Victor: Political Patronage from the Clubhouse to the White House*. New York: Random House, 1971.

Van Riper, Paul P. *History of the United States Civil Service*. Evanston, Ill.: Row, Peterson, 1958.

White, Leonard D. *The Federalists*. New York: Macmillan, 1948.

_____. *The Jeffersonians*. New York: Macmillan, 1951.

_____. *The Jacksonians*. New York: Macmillan, 1954.

_____. *The Republican Era*. New York: Macmillan, 1958.

2

Institutional Achievements of the Reform Movement

Prologue: The Scandal That Destroyed the U.S. Civil Service Commission

What follows is part of the introduction to the U.S. Civil Service Commission's Merit Staffing Review Team report *A Self-Inquiry into Merit Staffing*. The report, popularly known as the Sharon Report after the team director Milton I. Sharon, was made public in May 1976.

In the summer of 1973, the Civil Service Commision began an inquiry into the personnel management practices at the General Services Administration in Washington, D.C., which revealed widespread and systematic abuses of the civil service appointment system. This inquiry, as well as subsequent investigations at the Department of Housing and Urban Development and the Small Business Administration, disclosed the existence of politically-oriented employment practices intended to bypass and evade merit system requirements. While attempts at subverting merit principles were not unprecedented in the history of the Federal service, the practices uncovered by these Commission investigations were distinguished by the degree to which they were organized and systematized—and by the extent to which they were successful in evading merit system requirements.

Moving to put an end to what it saw as a frontal assault on the civil service merit system, the Commission brought about the prompt dismantling of the so-called "special referral units" and ordered the prompt cessation of other personnel practices contrary to civil service requirements. The Commission ordered the termination of illegal appointments and corrective action to bring other personnel practices into conformance with merit procedures.

But the Commission did not stop with case and system correction alone. In January, March, and August, 1974, in a move unprecedented in the Civil Service Commission's more than ninety-year history, the Commission's Executive Director issued letters of charges to nineteen officials of the three agencies, stating his intention to recommend that the Civil Service Commission take disciplinary action against them for having violated merit system requirements. The proposed disciplinary action included removal from the Federal service in seven cases, and 30- to 90-day suspensions without pay in the other twelve.

The Commission had never established specific procedures for bringing action against agency officials held to be responsible for merit system violations. It was necessary, therefore, to develop procedures for the purpose. To satisfy due process requirements, the procedures which were adopted provided for a record to be developed and considered by an Administrative Law Judge under formal administrative procedures, prior to a final decision by the Civil Service Commissioners.

The Administrative Law Judge's decision in the first of the cases, however, issued on May 9, 1975, was to dismiss the charges on the grounds that the Civil Service Rule relied upon as the basis for imposing discipline did not apply to the official who had been charged with its violation. This decision was appealed by the Executive Director to the Appeals Review Board but without success. On October 10, 1975, the Appeals Review Board upheld the Administrative Law Judge's interpretation of the Rule.

The second case produced the same result. The Administrative Law Judge dismissed the charges. The Executive Director again appealed to the Appeals Review Board. Before the Appeals Review Board decision was reached, however, the appeal was withdrawn. Simultaneously, on November 6, 1975, in a move that came as a surprise to many, the Commission announced that it was withdrawing all charges in the remaining cases. The construction placed by the Administrative Law Judge and the Appeals Review Board on the Civil Service Rule relied upon by the Commission in bringing the charges had convinced the Commission that the charges could not successfully be pressed. Altogether, almost two years had elapsed between the filing of the first charges and the decision to withdraw them.

It was expected that the officials who had been charged with merit system violations, as well as their employing agencies, would put forth arguments in their own defense. What the Commission did not foresee, however, was the nature of some of these defenses. In addition to the predictable legal arguments, the Commission found itself faced with allegations by the charged individuals and agencies that Commission officials themselves had participated in, or had knowingly permitted, practices of the kind the Commission was now condemning.

It was alleged that the Civil Service Commissioners had themselves engaged in the practice of making personal referrals of applicants for employment to Federal agencies, and that such referrals had resulted in, or had sought for those referred, preferential treatment not in accord with merit principles.

It was alleged that the Civil Service Commission had operated within its own organization a special referral unit which performed essentially the same specialized placement functions the Commission had found objectionable in other agencies. The Commission could not, the respondents argued, hold agency officials culpable for activities or functions which were paralleled by the Commission's own organizational structure and internal procedures.

It was alleged that high-ranking officials of the Commission had had prior knowledge that politically oriented employment systems were in operation and had done nothing to stop them. By its inaction, the argument ran, the Commission had implicitly condoned such practices, and it would be hypocritical for the Commission to penalize others for conduct it had itself knowingly permitted.

The allegations proved to be true.

The Centrality of the Civil Service

Superficially, few subjects would appear to be as dull to the public manager or even to the public personnelist—not to mention the average citizen or political scientist—as a discussion of the institutional aspects of public personnel administration in the United States. Civil service commissions and legislative committees dealing with the selection, pay, retirement, and benefits of public employees are seldom in the limelight. Indeed, even the scandalous subversion of the merit system during the Nixon administration received comparatively slight coverage by the nation's leading newspapers. In contrast, however, when one member of Congress takes up with a congressional page, another takes her staff on a "fact-finding" tour of world capitals, or a White House functionary allegedly snorts cocaine, the public is both titillated and indignant; such episodes can hold the country's interest for weeks. They may even engender modest reforms. Yet as anyone who will pause momentarily to give the matter a serious thought can see, this situation is highly incongruous. Such antics cost the taxpayers very little. On the other hand, when public personnel managers fail to fill positions with qualified individuals, are unable to motivate public employees, and do not work toward the most efficient and effective public service, the costs are truly incalculable. Even a brief exploration of this contention will serve to demonstrate its validity as well as to elucidate the fundamental importance of public personnel administration in modern governments.

Public employees constitute the core of government in developed nations.

They carry on the day-to-day business of government with expertise that is generally unavailable elsewhere in the society. Although many public service tasks are technical and highly structured in nature, a substantial proportion of civil servants are inevitably engaged in making decisions that have a fundamental impact on the general direction and content of public policy. For example, the use of "affirmative action" has been an important political issue in the United States for over two decades; yet it is a policy that was created by administrative fiat and was not mandated fully by legislation until the enactment of the 1978 reform. The American political system enhances the policymaking role of the public service in several ways. Elected officials often prefer to avoid making decisions on hotly contested political issues. In consequence, these matters are often thrust upon the judicial and administrative arms of government. The Congress, recognizing both its own limitations and the expertise of career administrators, has in recent decades delegated authority in a vast array of policy areas to the bureaucracy.

Given the role of civil servants in the modern state, it is of undeniable importance that the public service be able to attract and hold highly qualified people. It is equally important that career civil servants be efficiently and effectively utilized and highly motivated. In recent years the salaries and benefits of federal servants have run around $65 billion, or about 11 percent of the entire federal budget. If overhead and other costs were added, this figure would be far greater. Whether this money is well spent is not just a function of the general policy directions mandated by presidents, legislators, public servants, and other political actors; it is just as importantly a consequence of the recruitment and utilization of public employees. This can be illustrated with a simple arithmetical exercise. Today, there are over 2.1 million civilian federal servants—exluding the U.S. Postal Service—employed 40 hours a week, 50 weeks a year, or 2,000 hours a work year. Now, suppose that each employee wastes but one-half hour *per work year*. This would amount to 1,050,000 hours per year, or the equivalent of 525 work years for one employee (or conversely, the employment of 525 workers for a full year). In a more reasonable vein, let's assume that each federal servant wastes an hour per workday. In this case, we have approximately the following: (2,100,000 hours/day) (250 workdays/year) ÷ 2,000 working hours per year, or a total of 262,500 work years lost. This would be more than enough to fill the ranks of all but the largest federal agencies, with ample to spare. If state and local employees, who far outnumber their federal counterparts (see Table 2.1), were entered into the equation, the figure would be many times larger. The fiscal stakes involved in public personnel management are very high. It stands to reason that every effort must be made to develop effective institutional arrangements for making public personnel policy and overseeing its implementation. Yet the task is complex and difficult; and a fully satisfactory

Table 2.1. Government Civilian Employment (in thousands)

Year	Federal employees	State & local govt. employees	Total govt. employment (all levels)	Federal employees as % of total govt. employment
1980	2,821	13,542	16,363	17.2
1981	2,806	13,274	16,080	17.5
1982	2,768	13,207	15,975	17.3
1983	2,819	13,220	16,039	17.6
1984	2,854	13,504	16,358	17.7
1985	2,964	13,827	16,791	17.7
1986	2,967	14,157	16,791	17.3
1987	3,030	14,412	17,124	17.4
1988	3,054	14,781	17,442	17.1

Source: Adapted from "The Shape of Governments," *Federal Times*, January 30, 1989.

institutional framework for contemporary public personnel management has remained elusive. It is convenient to begin an analysis of the institutional side of public personnel administration by focusing on the federal level; for it is here that contemporary patterns began and have been most advanced.

The Pendleton Act

The Pendleton Act of 1883 or "An Act to Regulate and Improve the Civil Service of the United States" has been a remarkably durable piece of legislation. Within it was the framework for personnel management that was at the heart of the federal civil service system until 1979. The act created a United States Civil Service Commission as the personnel management arm of the president. While it was termed a commission, the U.S. Civil Service Commission was by no means independent. It was an executive agency that for all practical purposes was subject to the administrative discretion of the president. Its three bipartisan commissioners served at the pleasure of the president. The act gave legislative legitimacy to many of the procedures developed by the earlier unsuccessful Civil Service Commission during the Grant administration. Written into the act were requirements for open competitive examinations, probationary periods, and protection from political pressures. While the personnel program was to remain decentralized and in the control

What Is the Meaning of *Mickey Mouse*?

... pejorative term for many aspects of personnel administration. When Walt Disney's famous mouse made it "big" in the 1930s, he appeared in a variety of cartoon shorts that had him building something that would later fall apart (such as a house or boat) or generally going to a great deal of trouble for little result. So Mickey Mouse gradually gave his name to anything requiring considerable effort for slight result, including many of the Mickey Mouse requirements of personnel. The term is also applied to policies or regulations felt to be needless, silly, or mildly offensive.

Jay M. Shafritz, *Dictionary of Personnel Management and Labor Relations*, 2nd ed. (New York: Facts on File Inc., 1985).

of the departments, the Commission was authorized to supervise the conduct of examinations and make investigations to determine the degree of departmental enforcement of its rules. Of tremendous significance was the authority given to the president to extend merit system coverage to federal employees by executive order. Historically, the authority to extend also carried with it the authority to retract. Both Presidents McKinley and Eisenhower had occasion to remove positions from merit coverage by executive order. However, the Supreme Court's decision in *Rutan* v. *Republican Party of Illinois* (1990) makes patronage an unconstitutional basis for personnel actions affecting most public employees (see also Chapter 9).

The Pendleton Act was hardly a total victory for the reformers. It only covered just over 10 percent of the federal service. Actually the reformers were not at all anxious for near-universal merit system coverage. They well recognized the problems of creating the appropriate administrative machinery and were concerned that the reform program would be overburdened and subject to failure if complete reform were attempted all at once. With the ensuing years federal employees would be more and more brought under the jurisdiction of the Civil Service Commission or of other federal merit systems, such as those of the Foreign Service and the Tennessee Valley Authority. When President Reagan took office in 1981, only about 7,000 of approximately 3 million federal positions were specifically designated as potential patronage opportunities. When President Bush took office, there were slightly fewer of such appointments (see Table 2.2).

American presidents during the reform period typically entered office taking full advantage of their patronage prerogatives and left office with extensions of the merit system to their credit. This was the case with every

Table 2.2. Political Appointments Available to the Bush Administration

Federal agency	Schedule C appointment[a]	Other[b]	Total
Agriculture	226	82	308
Commerce	107	83	190
Defense	119	129	248
Education	125	223	348
Energy	68	40	108
EPA	17	33	50
GSA	28	20	48
HHS	79	73	152
HUD	91	44	135
Interior	54	57	111
Justice	59	222	281
Labor	72	35	107
SBA	38	32	70
State	162	891	1,053
Transportation	73	63	136
Treasury	43	50	93
USIA	29	196	225
Other (e.g, Postal Service, Veterans Administration)	400	1,218	1,618
TOTALS	1,790	3,491	5,281

[a]Schedule C positions are those appointed by the cabinet secretaries and agency directors, with final approval from OPM.

[b]"Other" includes, for example, presidential appointments requiring Senate approval, foreign service personnel, and various medical and legal staff positions.

Source: Adapted from S. Kellam, "Scramble on for Choice Appointments," *Federal Times*, December 5, 1988.

president from Arthur to Wilson. Merit system coverage went from 10 percent in 1884 to over 70 percent by the end of World War I. Generally, lame duck presidents being succeeded by someone of a different party would blanket in large numbers of employees in order to reduce the amount of patronage available to the opposition party. One of the ironies of civil service reform brought about by such blanketing in is that such initial reforms have a tendency to benefit those who may be the least meritorious.

Presidents undoubtably had mixed motives concerning their last minute extensions of the merit system. While they sincerely wished to deny the patronage prerogatives that they enjoyed to their successors, many had become truly disillusioned by their experiences with spoils and possibly repentant of their excesses. The definitive statement on the disillusioning aspects of political patronage is credited to President William Howard Taft who was moved to conclude that whenever he made a patronage appointment, he created "nine enemies and one ingrate." Actually this quip is generally attributed to all sophisticated dispensers of patronage from Thomas Jefferson to Louis XIV. The American presidency has produced only two memorable patronage jokes besides many of the appointees themselves. In addition to President Taft's remark, which seems to have been often borrowed by many a latter-day, lesser politico, there is the story of Abraham Lincoln, who, while lying prostrate in the White House with an attack of smallpox, said to his attendants: "Tell all the office seekers to come in at once, for now I have something I can give to all of them."

The Central Personnel Agency

As with many questions in public administration, the issue of how the overall public personnel function should be organized has been plagued by an attempt to realize several incompatible values at once. Foremost among these values have been those of "merit" or neutral competence; executive leadership, political accountability, and managerial flexibility; and representativeness. The main problem of the structural organization and policy thrusts of central personnel agencies has been that maximizing some of these values requires arrangements ill suited for the achievement of others. Thus, achieving neutral competence requires the creation of a relatively independent agency to help insulate public employees from the partisan demands of political executives. Yet the same structural arrangement will tend to frustrate executive leadership and the ability of political executives to manage their agencies. To facilitate executive leadership, on the other hand, the central personnel agency should be an adjunct of the president, governor, or other chief executive. Similarly, maximizing the value of representativeness may require a serious reassessment of traditional merit concepts and examinations, and the placement of personnel functions having an impact on equal employment opportunity in an equal employment or human rights agency. So doing, however, will also complicate the possibilities of achieving a high degree of executive leadership and neutral competence, as traditionally conceived. Matters are further confused by the rise of public sectior collective bargaining, which emphasizes

Theodore Roosevelt As Civil Service Commissioner

Although he professed still to be enjoying his work as Civil Service Commissioner, and to "get on beautifully with the President," an increasing restlessness through the spring and summer of 1894 is palpable in his correspondence. It would be needlessly repetitive to describe the battles he fought for reform under Cleveland, for they were essentially the same as those he fought under Harrison. "As far as my work is concerned," he grumbled "the two Administrations are much of a muchness." There were the same "mean, sneaky little acts of petty spoilsmongering" in government; the same looting of Federal offices across the nation, which Roosevelt combated with his usual weapons of publicity and aggressive investigation; the same pleas for extra funds and extra staff ("we are now, in all, five thousand papers behind"); the same fiery reports and five-thousand-word letters bombarding members of Congress; the same obstinate lobbying at the White House for extensions of the classified service; the same compulsive attacks upon porcine opponents, such as Assistant Secretary of State Josiah P. Quincy, hunting for patronage "as a pig hunts truffles," and Secretary of the Interior Hoke Smith, "with his twinkling little green pig's eyes."

All this, of course, meant that Roosevelt was having fun.

Edmund Morris, *The Rise of Theodore Roosevelt* (New York: Coward, McCann & Geoghegan, 1979), p. 472. Footnotes omitted.

employee—employer codetermination of personnel policy and the creation of independent public sector labor relations authorities.

The desire to simultaneously maximize these incompatible values accounts for many of the problematic aspects of the organization of the central personnel function. Arrangements satisfying some values inevitably raise complaints that others are being inadequately achieved. As the emphasis shifts from one value to another in conjunction with changing political coalitions and different perceptions of what is required in the public sector, structural changes also take place. Yet since the process of public personnel reform is somewhat cyclical, no set of arrangements will be immutable. Figure 2.1 shows a typical organization for a central personnel office.

Phase I—Policing

In the years immediately following the creation of the U.S. Civil Service Commission, its main role was that of policing. While this was certainly not its sole purpose, the commission was overwhelmingly concerned with preventing patronage encroachments by spoilspersons and in depoliticizing the federal

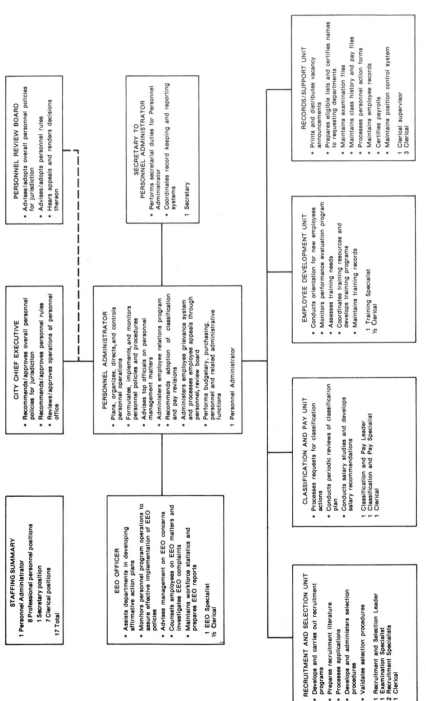

Figure 2.1. Organization of a central personnel office to serve a city of 4,000 employees. *Source:* U.S. Civil Service Commission, Bureau of Intergovernmental Programs, Organizing the Personnel Function: A Guide for Local Government Managers (Washington, D.C.: USCSC, April 1978), p. 15.

service. "Good" public personnel administration amounted to efficiently and effectively filling the ranks of the competitive service in a nonpartisan fashion. By the early 1900s this approach was viewed with less and less favor. The reformers had rationalized their wider political objectives in terms of efficiency, but depoliticization and selection through primitive open competitive exams failed to yield this result. In addition, the quest for greater efficiency became increasingly important as the government began taking on more complex tasks and as the regulatory policies it was pursuing began to penetrate the society and economy more deeply. Indeed, almost from the very moment that the reform movement achieved its fundamental success, clearer minds recognized its limitations in this regard. As early as 1887, in his famous essay "The Study of Administration," Woodrow Wilson wrote that "we must regard civil service reform in its present stages as but a prelude to a fuller administrative reform."

Phase II—Scientific Management

During the second and third decades of the twentieth century it was widely believed that a panacea for all administrative ills had been developed. A number of empirical observations, techniques, moral values, and premises concerning economics were loosely connected to form the "scientific management movement." At the center of its development was the thinking of Frederick Taylor who believed that management had a responsibility to determine "scientifically" how each and every task, both large and small, could be performed in the "one best way" by each worker. This would presumably yield far greater efficiency than the ad hoc techniques that had traditionally been developed and used by workers. Productivity would be further increased by adopting pay plans that were closely related to individual output. Were the whole world organized in this fashion, abundance and harmony would reign supreme. The thrust of these thoughts was to turn the individual employee into an appendage of an organizational machine, rather than to adapt organizational arrangements to individual talents and idiosyncracies.

In government, the concerns of "scientific management" were translated into an attempt at developing a more scientific personnel administration. The notions that there was "one best way" of doing a job and that one type of person could perform best in any given kind of position required the development of scientifically derived standards and the standardization of positions. Consequently, position classification moved to the core of public personnel administration. The content of the job or a group of similar jobs became the element upon which almost all else was based. Thus, more concern was devoted to ensuring that examinations were related to job requirements, rather than just to depoliticization as in the earlier period. The public service increasingly

Whose Merit? How Much?

The late Henry Aronson, who spent some 30 years developing and enforcing merit system standards for state agencies, used to tell this story: In the late '30s a certain Southern state paid little attention to the federal merit requirements newly established for grant-in-aid programs. Persuasion and threats accomplished nothing, and finally Uncle Sam began action to "cut off the water"—as politically unthinkable an action then as now. The governor of the state sent an assistant to see Aronson, who gave him the full sales business on merit system principles. When Henry paused, the emissary said, "Well, Mr. Aronson, the guv'nor—he b'lieves in the merit system—he just b'lieves that his friends have more merit than his enemies."

David T. Stanley, "Whose Merit? How Much?" *Public Administration Review*, 34 (September-October 1974), p. 425.

began to revolve around positions rather than people, and the rank was securely vested in the former rather than in the latter. The philosophic essence of this approach was written into law with the enactment of the Classification Act of 1923.

Phase III—Centralization

Until the 1930s the commission remained primarily an examining agency. Indeed, until that time position classification, efficiency ratings, and retirement programs were separately administered elsewhere. Other aspects of personnel administration, including training, promotion, transfer, health and safety, employee relations, and working conditions, were subject to almost no central direction or influence. The absence of coordination and responsibility inherent in this situation was increasingly deplored; and in 1931 the commission called for the integration "in one administrative body of all Federal agencies which have to do with personnel in the civil service." In the following three years, the commission was given authority for position classification, efficiency ratings, and retirement administration. This did much to make it more of a genuine central personnel agency, but its role was still far from complete in this regard. Moreover, most of its functions were cast in a negative vein. Having policed the spoilsperson in the past, the commission now found itself applying rather restrictive regulations to bureau chiefs and other federal employees, many of whom were themselves under the merit system. In addition, it performed its functions in a centralized fashion, which often presented difficulties in serving the managerial needs of various agencies. So negative was the commission's role and image that an analysis associated with the 1937

President's Committee on Administrative Management concluded that "many friends of the Commission...feel that the more constructive types of personnel activity cannot be carried effectively by an agency which necessarily must give so much attention to the enforcement of restrictive statutes." The commission's "policing" role was proving incompatible with the "friendly cooperation" required by the more positive aspects of centralized personnel administration. This realization heralded a new era in federal personnel administration.

Phase IV—The Decentralization of Federal Personnel Operations

Toward the close of FDR's first term it became increasingly clear that governmental administration was in a state of disarray. Agencies had overlapping and even contradictory functions, and controlling the "headless fourth branch" of government presented great difficulty. Roosevelt appointed the President's Committee on Administrative Management, chaired by Louis Brownlow, to study the administrative organization of the executive branch and to make recommendations for its improvement. The most important of these led to the creation of the Executive Office of the President, but the committee also had a profound effect on thinking about public personnel administration. Believing that "personnel administration lies at the very core of administrative management," and that "to set it apart or to organize it in a manner unsuited to serve the needs of the Chief Executive and the executive establishments is to render it impotent and ineffective," the committee sought the establishment of a whole new institutional framework for this function. Because the committee found the Civil Service Commission to be generally unresponsive to the needs of agency management, it recommended that the commission be replaced by a Civil Service Administration, headed by a single administrator appointed by and responsible to the president. A seven-member Civil Service Board would be appointed "to act as a watchdog of the merit system and to represent the public interest." Although these recommendations were not then enacted into law, they are similar to reforms implemented in 1979. In any event, decentralized personnel administration eventually became the order of the day. During 1938 President Roosevelt issued an executive order that required each agency to establish a division of personnel supervision and management.

The federal bureaucracy underwent a tremendous expansion during World War II. Recognizing that the growth of the federal service made centralized personnel administration largely a thing of the past, a 1947 executive order by President Truman accordingly stressed decentralization. The president declared that "personnel management is a primary responsibility of the head of each agency, and his officials who are responsible for the economical and

Decentralization

Another common reform theme is the decentralization of certain functions normally performed by a central personnel agency. Such actions are designed to place more decision-making authority in the hands of line managers, commensurate with their accountability to the public. The functions may include recruiting, examining, and position classification, with the central personnel agency usually retaining responsibility for the preparation of interagency class specifications and examination material, and post-auditing personnel actions relating to the decentralized functions.

The 1979 Merit System Standards specifically permit such decentralization as long as post audit procedures are maintained by a central personnel agency with effective enforcement authority to correct improper actions made by line agencies. In other words, a line agency with delegated authority to perform such personnel actions can assume responsibility for meeting the requirements of the Standards without the central personnel agency surrendering all of its accountability. For example, the central personnel agency may delegate to operating agencies responsibility for allocating individual positions to classes while retaining the specification writing function centrally and conducting post audits of the agency classification actions. Also, examinations could be decentralized in a similar fashion. Decentralization of position classification in the Federal Government has long been a necessary practice. It would be difficult to imagine position classifiers traveling from one central location, or even from ten regional locations, to classify jobs all over the country and even the world. However, the development and maintenance of classification standards, which is the basis for the allocation of positions in the agencies, is accomplished by the central office.

U.S. Office of Personnel Management, *Personnel Management Reform*, 1, no.1 (September 1979), pp. 2–3.

efficient conduct of the work." Under the order, agency heads and their designated subordinates were expected to plan, organize, coordinate, and control all personnel management programs in the agency. They were assigned the responsibility of ensuring that personnel management was effective and efficient. Moreover, the order required that "authority for the conduct of personnel matters within each agency should be delegated to the extent compatible with provisions of law and economical and efficient administration to those officials responsible for planning, directing and supervising the work of others." As a result of this approach, which was also written into the Classification Act of 1949, agencies are currently responsible for position classification, evaluation, promotion, a good deal of recruitment efforts, and a host of other personnel functions. All of the major studies of the federal bureaucracy, the Brownlow Committee, the First and Second Hoover Commissions, and others have strongly endorsed the decentralized approach to public personnel management. Yet decentralization has also had some costs, both in terms of weakening the merit system, as in the Nixon years, and in creating something of an identity and image "crisis" for the Civil Service Commission.

Phase V—The Demise of the Civil Service Commission

It is not surprising that the transition from the role of policing the federal personnel system to that of "serving" agency management placed considerable strains upon the Civil Service Commission (CSC). What becomes of a regulatory agency that acts as a servant for the group it was originally established to regulate? The transition turned what was once an image crisis into an identity crisis. Criticism came from many quarters. Some found the CSC too responsive to special interests. Marver Bernstein observed that the "Commission's role with respect to veteran's preference and similar provisions is not merely that of policeman [sic]; it is also an agency at the service of a clientele group." Its image was one of an agency engaged in "hemming in the line operator with restrictive rules governing job classification, appointment, promotion, transfer, salary change, and dismissal of employees." Others, such as Louis Gawthrop, were critical of the commission because it "consistently resisted major innovations in the federal career process." Supervisors at virtually all levels were troubled by its inspection (later called "evaluation") activities, which sometimes pointed out the shortcomings of agency personnel policy and agitated rank-and-file employees. Conversely, and somewhat ironically, still others, including Ralph Nader, criticized the commission for failing to use its authority. With regard to its activities in the area of equal employment opportunity, Nader had observed that there was no doubt whatsoever concerning the adequacy of the commission's authority to do its job. "It has ample authority, leverage, and disciplinary powers vis-á-vis other federal agencies, but it has been reluctant to use these tools."

In an effort to overcome its poor image and to find a new role after the decentralization of the 1940s, the commission tried to serve the needs of a diversity of groups, many of which have conflicting interests and some of which favor a substantial weakening of the merit system. Thus, it sought to serve the needs of Congress and the president, management and labor, as well as veterans, women, and other protected-class groups seeking recourse from discriminatory treatment. It tried to stress "merit," executive leadership, and representativeness all at once, to the possible detriment of each of these values. No wonder its chair asked, "What is the role of the Civil Service Commission in these fast-changing times?... Why do we exist? What is our identity? What is our purpose? Whom do we represent?"

On a formal level, these questions could be answered by enumerating the commission's functions as a central personnel agency:

1. To recommend legislation
2. To encourage departments and agencies to improve their personnel management
3. To promulgate governmentwide personnel policies and standards under law
4. To develop personnel programs
5. To centrally operate certain personnel services
6. To provide technical assistance to agencies
7. To evaluate the effectiveness of personnel management in the agencies
8. To adjudicate employee appeals
9. To secure compliance with civil service laws and merit principles.

Yet such a response is unsatisfactory because it fails to indicate in whose interest and to what ends these functions should be performed. Nor was the commission able to clarify these matters.

Ultimately, by 1978, the commission had been so racked by its conflicting roles, attempts to achieve mutually incompatible values, and its participation in the scandalous breaches of the merit system during the Watergate years that despite its long history it was reorganized out of existence by the Civil Service Reform Act of 1978.

Phase VI—Reform 1979

The 1978 Civil Service Reform Act constitutes the most sweeping attempt to change the nature of federal personnel administration since the passage of the Pendleton Act of 1883. The demands for widespread reforms had been growing since the 1930s. The Brownlow Committee in 1937 asserted that the Civil Service Commission seemed to have outlived its usefulness. The agency's general disarray during the early 1970s seemed to be additional evidence of its inadequacy. As bureaucratic power had grown during the post-New Deal era, the value of executive leadership took on added importance. By the 1970's it had become clear that the conventional strategies of strengthening the Executive Office of the President and providing the president with more power vis-á-vis the federal bureaucracy, such as reorganizational authority, still left the president and his political executives with insufficient managerial clout. Indeed, the expansion of the Executive Office of the President turned out to have distinct liabilities of its own. Yet from a political perspective, leaders of the Carter civil service reform effort continued to be concerned that "every new administration feels the negative aspects of the bureaucracy's pressure for continuity. New policy makers arrive with mandates for change and find that though they can change structures and appearances, it is very difficult to make dramatic changes in direction." In their view, the prevailing institutional arrangements for federal personnel administration stressed neutral competence in the form of rigidity and the protection of federal employees to such an extent that the concerns of executive leadership had been almost totally eclipsed.

Indeed, during the campaign to win support for the proposed reforms, the Carter administration constantly exposed the horrors of prevailing federal personnel administration. Among these were such issues as:

1. An award of about $5,000 in back pay to a postal worker who was fired for shooting a colleague in the stomach in a Manhattan post office
2. A 21-month paperwork maze to fire an $8,000-a-year Department of Commerce employee who consistently failed to show up for work without valid reasons
3. The existence of numerous $40,000- and $50,000-a-year employees who literally were "do-nothings"
4. The rating of 98 percent of all white-collar employees as "satisfactory" at a time when public confidence in the bureaucracy was very low and numerous major and minor scandals were being exposed
5. The firing of only 226 out of 2,800,000 civilian employees for inefficiency during 1977

In summing up the case against prevailing federal personnel administration, President Carter said, "There is not enough merit in the merit system. There is inadequate motivation because we have too few rewards for excellence and too few penalties for unsatisfactory work."

In addition, the Civil Service Commission had been under attack from civil rights groups and others interested in greater employment of African Americans, Latinos, and women in the federal service. At the beginning of the decade of the 1970s, efforts were made to divest the commission of the federal Equal Employment Opportunity program and place the program in the Equal Employment Opportunity Commission (EEOC). Thus, the commission had managed to lose the support of elements pursuing the values of executive leadership and representativeness. The commission and the federal personnel system were also criticized by some public employee labor unions who complained that scope of collective bargaining in the federal service was too limited and that the labor relations process was overwhelmingly dominated by management interests.

In combination, these forces generated enough support in the presidency and Congress to bring about the following major changes in federal personnel management:

1. The Civil Service Commission has been replaced by:
   a. An Office of Personnel Management (OPM) headed by a director

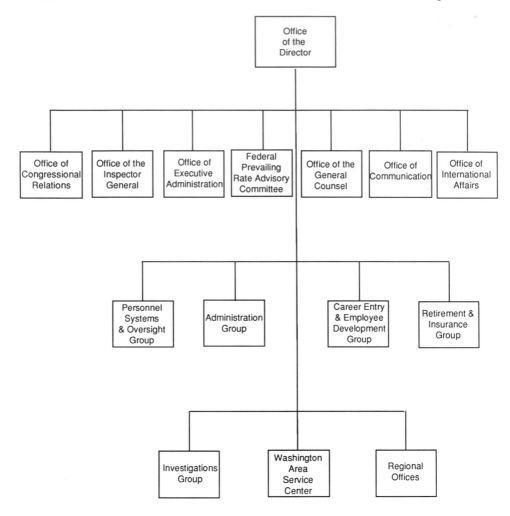

Figure 2.2. OPM organization chart, May 1990. *Source*: OPM.

appointed by the president with the advice and consent of the Senate for a four-year term, a deputy director, and up to five assistant directors (see Figure 2.2). The OPM has authority for the positive managerial functions that previously were vested in the commission. Among these are responsibilities for human resources management, evaluations, and enforcement of federal personnel laws and regulations. The OPM is an independent agency that is intended to work closely with the president and be the president's arm for managing the personnel aspects of the federal bureaucracy.

b. The Merit Systems Protection Board (MSPB), headed by a chair and two additional members holding seven-year nonrenewable terms, constitutes a "watchdog" of the federal merit system (see Figure 2.3). The bipartisan MSPB, whose members cannot be removed except for cause, received the commission's appeals functions. The MSPB also has general oversight functions and the authority to review OPM rules and regulations. In addition, when the reform act was first passed, the Office of Special Counsel (OSC) was created as a semi-independent body within the MSPB. The special counsel holds a five-year term of office and is removable only for cause.

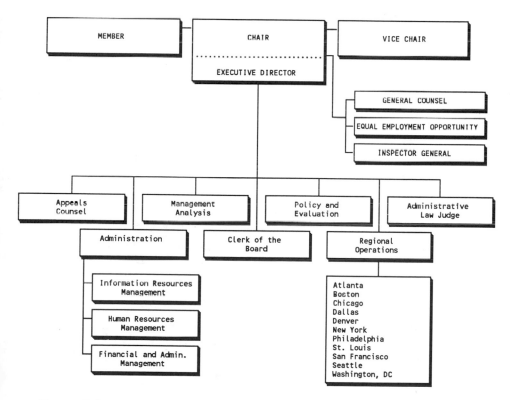

Figure 2.3.   U.S. Merit Systems Protection Board organization chart. *Source*: U.S. Merit Systems Protection Board, *Organization and Functions Manual* (Washington, D.C.: USMSPB, 1990).

What Are the Merit System Principles?

The Civil Service Reform Act of 1978 put into law the nine basic merit principles that should govern all personnel practices in the federal government and defined prohibited practices. The principles and prohibitions are:

Personnel Practices and Actions in the Federal Government Require:

- Recruitment from all segments of society, and selection and advancement on the basis of ability, knowledge, and skills, under fair and open competition.
- Fair and equitable treatment in all personnel management matters, without regard to politics, race, color, religion, national origin, sex, marital status, age, or handicapping condition, and with proper regard for individual privacy and constitutional rights
- Equal pay for work of equal value, considering both national and local rates paid by private employers, with incentives and recognition for excellent performance
- High standards of integrity, conduct, and concern for the public interest
- Efficient and effective use of the federal work force
- Retention of employees who perform well, correcting the performance of those whose work is inadequate, and separation of those who cannot or will not meet required standards
- Improved performance through effective education and training
- Protection of employees from arbitrary action, personal favoritism, or political coercion
- Protection of employees against reprisal for lawful disclosures of information

This official is responsible for investigating allegations of prohibited personnel practices, including such areas as political activity, "whistleblowing," discrimination, and arbitrary or capricious withholding of information sought under the Freedom of Information Act. The special counsel can bring charges against federal employees before the MSPB. (See the discussion, later in this chapter about the conversion of OSC to an independent agency within the Executive Branch, separate from the MSPB.)

2. The Federal Labor Relations Council was replaced by a more independent and less managerially based Federal Labor Relations Authority (FLRA). This agency, which is discussed at greater length in Chapter 10, has general oversight and regulatory authority for the conduct of labor relations in the federal service.

3. Although not part of the Civil Service Reform Act itself, the federal Equal Employment Opportunity (EEO) program was assigned to the

EEOC. The intent is to create independent enforcement of EEO regulations, as opposed to the previous practice of allowing the central personnel agency to sit in judgment of its own regulations in the face of allegations that they are discriminatory.

4. The top of the general schedule (GS) careeer structure, the "supergrades," was largely converted into a Senior Executive Service (SES). This change, which was prompted by the desire for managerial flexibility and executive leadership, facilitates the transfer of senior executive servants from position to position and from agency to agency. SES members can also be removed from the SES for unsatisfactory performance without meaningful appeal. At least 45 percent of all positions in the SES will be reserved for career officials and no more than 10 percent of all SES employees can be political appointees. In order to assure a measure of continuity and to protect career senior executive servants, they cannot be involuntarily reassigned within 120 days of the appointment of a new agency head or new noncareer supervisor.

5. A merit pay system was adopted for grades GS-13–15. Under this system managers may reward effective and efficient employees for their performance without having to promote them to a higher salary step or grade. Related to this was a bonus system authorized for SES members and a cash awards system created to reward any federal employee for superior accomplishment and cost savings.

6. A number of other reform elements include the modification of veterans preference, the creation of research and demonstration authority, and the sanctioning of whistleblowing that exposes violations of law or mismanagement, gross waste of funds, abuse of authority, or substantial and specific dangers to public health or safety. In addition, the creation and utilization of agency performance appraisal systems was mandated.

Phase VII—Post-Reform Era

The early years of the Civil Service Reform Act (CSRA) were marked by much turbulence. A primary reason for this can be attributed to the Carter administration's support for a long-term implementation process, whereby agencies were given several years to develop and implement the various new programs (e.g., merit pay and performance appraisal) called for by the act. This strategy proved to be detrimental to many of the act's components. As two notable critics of the CSRA have pointed out "such a long-term strategy is at odds with the nature of the American political system, which is notoriously unstable and oriented toward short-term results."

Although theoretically sensible, the long-term strategy was particularly inept in view of the politics of the CSRA. There was much support for many

**Officials and Employees Who Are Authorized to Take
Personnel Actions Are Prohibited from:**

- Discriminating against any employee or applicant.
- Soliciting or considering any recommendation on a person who requests or is being considered for a personnel action unless the material is an evaluation of the person's work performance, ability, aptitude, or general qualifications, or character, loyalty, and suitability.
- Using official authority to coerce political actions, to require political contributions, or to retaliate for refusal to do these things.
- Willfully deceiving or obstructing an individual as to his or her right to compete for Federal employment.
- Influencing anyone to withdraw from competition, whether to improve or worsen the prospects of any applicant.
- Granting any special preferential treatment or advantage not authorized by law to a job applicant or employee.
- Appointing, employing, promoting, or advancing relatives in their agencies.
- Taking or failing to take a personnel action as a reprisal against employees who exercise their appeal rights; refuse to engage in political activity; or lawfully disclose violations of law, rule, or regulation, or mismanagement, gross waste of funds, abuse of authority, or a substantial and specific danger to public health or safety.
- Taking or failing to take any other personnel action violating a law, rule, or regulation directly related to merit system principles.

U.S. Civil Service Commission, *Introducing the Civil Service Reform Act* (Washington, D.C.: U.S. Government Printing Office, November 1978), p. 2.

of the parts of the reform, but no comprehensive vision of public personnel policy was discernable. Thus, careerists could favor the MSPB; organized labor, the labor relations program; management and political executives, the merit pay and SES provisions; and protected-class persons and civil rights advocates, greater involvement of the EEOC in federal personnel policies.

Each of these interests sought to strengthen itself through the reform, but very few members of the reform coalition cared much about how the *whole package* would work. This was the politics of coalition building at its best and the prospects for successful implementation at their worst.

In addition, the act's emphasis on decentralization resulted in a number of managerial abuses as well as errors. Compounding these problems were the political realities associated with the election of Ronald Reagan, whose emphasis on political control of the federal bureaucracy rather than personnel management became a driving force behind the reform efforts.

How successful or effective have each of the major reforms been? As the following suggests, they have both succeeded and failed in reforming the federal system of personnel management.

1. Replacing the Civil Service Commission with:
   a. The OPM has produced mixed results. The OPM was initially successful in working toward its original goals of "improved federal management, stronger executive direction, and modernized personnel management." It emphasized, as was intended by the act, the value of *managing* human resources. Soon, however, rather than being a management tool for the president, the OPM had become an "instrument of political persuasion." In the words of Donald Devine, the OPM's second director, appointed by Reagan, "the skill and technical expertise of the career service must be utilized, but it must be utilized under the direct authority and personal supervision of the political leader who has the moral authority flowing from the people through an election." Under Devine, the OPM virtually lost its management orientation and has become a political instrument of the executive branch to assert and manage the values and partisan ideology of the president.

      Subsequent directors, Constance Horner and Constance Newman, worked hard to shift OPM back toward its intended managerial focus. Both Horner and Newman devoted great effort to such mechanics of federal personnel as reforming position classification and pay systems.
   b. The MSPB, while successful in establishing itself as an adjudicator of appeals brought by federal employees, continues to suffer from a perception that its decisions are biased toward management (see Table 2.3). This perception stems in large part from MSPB's decisions against appeals by air traffic controllers, who walked off their jobs in 1981 over a labor dispute with the federal government. In more recent years, the MSPB has undertaken and published a variety of important studies on the federal personnel system. It also issues reports evaluating aspects of OPM's performance.

      In addition, the OSC, at least in its first ten years of operation, was not very successful in fulfilling its role as protector of merit principles. This was due to a number of factors, including understaffing and skepticism on the part of federal employees and their unions as to the executive's actual commitment to a watchdog agency. Indeed, the powers of the special counsel were initially limited, especially in terms of its ability to protect whistleblowers from retaliation by federal employers.

Table 2.3. Analysis of Merit Systems Protection Board Decisions, through March 1986 (Selected Conduct Cases Where Agency Recommended Removal)

Category of action	Total cases	Agency removal	Recommendation: Other	MSPB decision: Removal	MSPB decision: Reinstate	MSPB decisions for agency/ managment (%)
Abusive language	21	15	6	12	3	80
Refusal to follow orders	63	47	16	30	17	64
Refusal to take fitness examination	9	7	2	6	1	86
Effect of acquittal	9	7	2	7	0	100
Conflict of interest	11	10	1	7	3	70
Sleeping on duty	8	7	1	5	2	71
Nepotism	2	1	1	1	0	100
Debts	5	4	1	1	3	25
Failure to pay taxes	7	6	1	3	3	50
Time and work records	26	21	5	16	5	76
Travel documents and expense accounts	11	8	3	5	3	63
Alcohol-related charges	28	24	4	18	6	75
Drug-related charges	40	37	3	26	11	70
Telephone & other equipment	3	1	2	0	1	0
Vehicles	25	9	16	5	4	56
Destruction of govt. property	9	4	5	3	1	75
Sex offenses	15	15	0	15	0	100
Sexual harassment	14	10	4	6	4	60
	306	233	73	166	67	71

Source: United States Merit Systems Protection Board Digest (St. Paul, Minn.: West Publishing Co., March 1986).

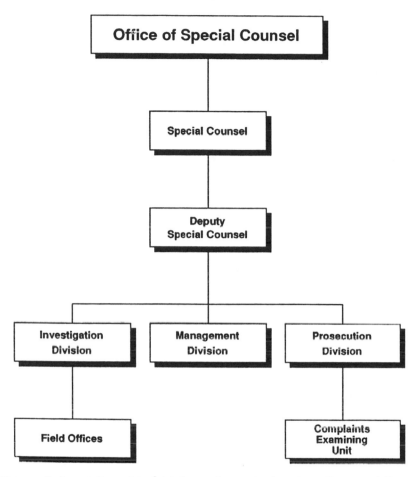

Figure 2.4. Office of Special Counsel organization chart. *Source: A Report to Congress from the Office of the Special Counsel* (Washington, D.C.: USOSC, 1989).

Some of these problems have been addressed by the passage of the Whistleblower Protection Act (WPA) of 1989, which converted the OSC into an independent agency within the executive branch (see Figure 2.4). Today, the OSC is completely separate and apart from the MSPB, and the powers of the special counsel have been enhanced, particularly in the area of protecting whistleblowers from punitive, retaliatory actions by federal agencies. Table 2.4 illustrates the number and types of complaints received by the OSC in one fiscal year.

Table 2.4. Allegations Contained in Complaints Received During FY 1989 by OSC

Nature of allegation	Number of complaints[a]
Alleged abuse of merit staffing requirements or procedures, primarily the alleged granting of unauthorized preference or advantage, or solicitation or consideration of unauthorized recommendations, deception, or obstruction of the right to compete, and attempts to secure withdrawal from competition [§§2302(b)(2), (4), (5), and (6)]	395
Alleged discrimination on the basis of race, color, sex, national origin, religion, age, or disabling conditions [§2302(b)(1)(A)-(D)]	333
Alleged reprisal for whistleblowing [§2302(b)(8)]	245
Alleged reprisal for exercise of a right of appeal [§2302(b)(9)]	190
Allegations which did not cite or suggest any prohibited personnel practice or prohibited activity[b]	185
Alleged violation of a law, rule, or regulation implementing or concerning a merit system principle [§2302(b)(11)]	126
Alleged violation of a law, rule, or regulation, or gross mismanagement, gross waste of funds, abuse of authority, or a danger to public health or safety [§1213(c) or §1213(g)][c]	112
Allegations of other activities allegedly prohibited by civil service law, rule, or regulation [§1216(a)(4)]	68
Alleged Hatch Act violation by a federal employee [§1216(a)(1)]	63
Alleged discrimination on the basis of non-job-related conduct [§2302(b)(10)]	58
Alleged Hatch Act violation by a state or local government employee [§1216(a)(2)]	39

(continued)

Table 2.4.   *(continued)*

Nature of allegation	Number of complaints[a]
Alleged arbitrary or capricious withholding of information requested under the Freedom of Information Act [§1216(a)(3)]	34
Alleged nepotism [§2302(b)(7)]	33
Alleged discrimination on the basis of marital status or political affiliation [§2302(b)(1)(E)]	9
Alleged coercion of political activity [§2302(b)(3)]	1
Total	1,891 [d]

[a]This category refers to the number of complaints that contained a particular allegation.

[b]Although these types of complaints may not, on their face, indicate the existence of any matter within the OSC's investigative jurisdiction, follow-up contact is made with the complainant to ascertain the exact nature of the complaint, and to determine whether there is any basis for further OSC action.

[c]These types of allegations are treated as whistleblower allegations that may be referred to the agency concerned under §1213(c) or §1218(g) for agency review. Nevertheless, if the allegation concerns an employment matter, the OSC carefully reviews it to determine whether the matter may be treated as an allegation of a prohibited personnel practice or other prohibited activity within its investigative jurisdiction. If so, the OSC investigates the matter.

[d]Each complaint may contain more than one allegation. Thus, this total exceeds the total number of complaints actually received by the OSC (1,239).

Source: A Report to Congress from the Office of the Special Counsel (Washington, D.C.: USOSC, 1989).

2. The FLRA has been relatively efficient and "evenhanded" in addressing and resolving labor-management problems and disputes. The FLRA, however, has been unsuccessful in gaining judicial deference. Its rulings and decisions have been overturned at a much higher rate by the courts than they have been upheld (see Chapter 11). Moreover, the courts, in several opinions, have issued harsh criticisms of the FLRA for its inconsistent and illogical decisions.

3. The civil service reform, as noted earlier, included a reorganization of EEO. It has helped EEO efforts insofar as oversight of the federal EEO program was transferred to the independent EEOC. In fact, as described in greater detail in Chapter 7, the EEOC was successful in abolishing a major obstacle to the achievement of EEO goals—the Professional and Administrative Careers Exam (PACE). The PACE was a so-called merit exam, of which the CSC was an ardent defender. Such exams tend to have an adverse effect on EEO efforts, and so the EEOC has been more opposed to their use than the CSC.

What is the Whistleblower Protection Act (WPA) of 1989?

The WPA is a federal statute that amended the Civil Service Reform Act (CSRA) to enhance protections against reprisal for employees disclosing wrongdoings in the federal government. The WPA made some of the following changes to the CSRA:

- The OSC is no longer a part of the MSPB; instead, the OSC is now an independent agency within the executive branch.

- A showing of reprisal no longer requires proof that a supervisor had a specific intent to retaliate against a whistleblower. It is enough that a personnel action was taken "because of" a protected whistleblower disclosure.

- Employees alleging that a personnel action was taken because of whistleblowing have a new "individual right of action" (IRA) before the MSPB, with appeal rights to federal court. Before employees may exercise this right, they must first seek assistance from the OSC. Attorney fees and other costs are available to employees who prevail before the MSPB or the courts.

- A threat to take or not take a personnel action because of whistleblowing or the exercise of a lawful appeal right is a prohibited personnel practice.

- Employees who file an IRA, or any appeal in which it is alleged that a personnel action was because of whistleblowing, can request a stay of a personnel action from the MSPB.

- Agency heads may grant a preference in transfers or reassignments when the MSPB finds that an employee has been a victim of a personnel action because of whistleblowing.

- The taking of an adverse personnel action because of a refusal by an employee to obey an order that would require the employee to violate a law is clearly defined as a prohibited personnel practice.

Source: *A Report to Congress from the Office of Special Counsel* (Washingotn, D.C.: USOSC, 1989), pp. 17–18.

Despite the relative success of this institutional reorganization, however, the federal government's EEO program, which goes well beyond the scope of the civil service reform efforts, has not been wholly satisfactory. The federal service is more socially diverse today, but it is white women more than any other persons or groups that have made the most progress. African Americans and Latinos continue to lag behind, particularly in terms of holding jobs at the upper levels of the federal government. Nevertheless, the CSRA does make it federal policy to eliminate the "underrepresentation" of EEO target groups.

4. Perhaps the most disappointing aspect of the CSRA has been the SES, which got off to a poor start. SESers charged that they were being subjected to illegitimate political pressures and many resigned or retired. In fact, by 1985, over half of the original SES cadre had left office (see Table 2.5). Moreover, relatively few SESers have moved from agency

Table 2.5.   Executive Agencies that Employ 50 or More Senior Executives (as of September 30, 1989)

Agency	Career SES	Noncareer SES	Total
Department of Health and Human Services	514	37	551
Department of the Treasury	479	21	510
NASA	499	4	503
Department of the Navy	441	4	445
Department of Energy	403	22	425
Department of Commerce	349	57	406
Department of Transportation	327	27	354
Department of Agriculture	291	38	329
Department of the Army	318	7	325
Office of the Secretary of Defense	273	31	304
Department of Veterans Affairs	287	6	293
Department of the Interior	226	32	258
Environmental Protection Agency	232	16	248
Department of Justice	207	35	242
Nuclear Regulatory Commission	213	2	215
Department of the Air Force	188	5	193
Department of Labor	150	15	165
General Services Administration	96	22	118
Department of State	88	18	106
Department of Housing and Urban Development	79	19	98
National Science Foundation	93	4	97
Office of Management and Budget	66	6	72
Department of Education	54	13	67
National Labor Relations Board	57	3	60
Office of Personnel Management	45	8	53
Securities and Exchange Commission	50	2	52

Source: Senior Executive Service Pay Setting and Reassignments (Washington, D.C.: Merit Systems Protection Board, 1990), p. 19.

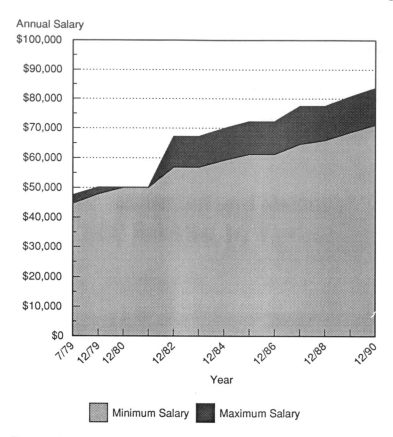

Annual Salary

Figure 2.5. Minimum and maximum SES salaries by year. Note: These figures do not reflect the higher pre-1982 salaries of those who had held Executive Level IV positions. Nor do they include those pre-1982 court-ordered retroactive revisions of 1984. *Source: Senior Executive Service Pay Setting and Reassignments* (Washington, D.C.: Merit Systems Protection Board, 1990), 4.

to agency, which has frustrated realization of the ideal of developing top-level federal managers who are familiar with a broad range of policy areas.

Pay has also lagged, causing further disaffection among SESers (see Figure 2.5). Overall, the SES leaves open to question whether a personnel system based on narrow position classifications and intense specialization in professional fields and policy areas can produce a flexible corps at the top that can bring a broad vision of the public interest to bear on the formulation and design of public policy.

5. The original merit pay system for grades GS-13–15 has proven to be "demoralizing and counterproductive." Its biggest failure has been its

inability to meet its primary goal: improving the performance of federal managers by establishing a link between pay and performance. To redress this problem, a new system was created in 1984—the Performance Management Recognition System (this is under revision at this writing). It, too, however, has not been very effective in linking reward structures to the performance of federal workers.

The federal government remains committed to the assumption that pay-for-performance will work, but the underlying politics of personnel simply have not supported this premise. Such a linkage may be possible only in an ideal sense where politics is "separate" from administration. Interestingly, the public personnel community is generally willing to challenge this flawed pay-for-performance principle behind closed doors, but no one is willing to admit publicly that the "emperor is wearing no clothes!" It is unlikely that such an admission will be made in the near future, given the overwhelming emphasis on improving the image of government, especially at the federal level.

6. Other reforms incorporated in the CSRA have also met with mixed results. Most notable is Title VI of the act, which called for the development of research and demonstration projects to explore new and improved approaches to federal personnel management. The demonstration provisions in particular would allow federal agencies to suspend civil service law under certain circumstances in order to improve the quality of such personnel functions as recruitment, hiring, performance appraisal, and classification and pay.

The research provisions of the reform act were quickly gutted when Donald Devine was appointed to head the OPM. Devine, aggressively pursuing and fostering Reagan's posture of economic austerity, drastically cut existing research efforts and also abolished the Research Management Division, which was created by OPM's first director, Alan Campbell, to oversee the research provisions mandated by the CSRA.

The demonstration provisions also ran into funding problems. However, the few demonstrations that were funded have proven to be relatively effective. For example, the Navy's China Lake demonstration, which is the largest and most ambitious to date, has provided line managers with the flexibility needed to hire and retain high quality employees. Other demonstration projects at such agencies as the Federal Aviation Administration and the National Institute of Standards and Technology (formerly the National Bureau of Standards) have been equally successful.

The next several years will continue to pose questions and challenges for the various reform components of the CSRA. Efforts to redress some of the problems are underway and various "reforms" to the reforms continue to be proposed by the federal government, federal employee unions, and other interested parties.

State and Local Institutional Arrangements

Influenced by the example of the 1883 Pendleton Act, state and local jurisdictions began to institute civil service commissions, but this was a very slow process. While New York State adopted a merit system that same year and Massachusetts did so during the following year, it would be more than 20 years before another state did so in 1905. By 1935 only 12 states had formally instituted merit systems. These early efforts weren't all successes. Connecticut had its first civil service law repealed while Kansas kept its statute as law, but refused to vote appropriations for it. Nor were these laws necessarily effective even when kept on the books. For example, New York State, which had the most stringent prohibitions against political assessments on the salaries of public employees since 1883, had widespread "voluntary" contributions to the party at least through the 1930s. Indeed, a special probe in Onondaga County (Syracuse) in the late 1970s alleged the widespread practice of political assessment.

Perhaps the most striking difference in public personnel management found among different jurisdictional levels in the United States is that the merit system and the commission form of administering it have been far less successful in state and local governments than at the federal level. The reasons for this have been largely political. Although national politicians once relied dearly upon patronage for securing and maintaining their positions, the federal government never fell under the control of a unified political machine. At most it was dominated by a coalition of state and local political "bosses." At the state and local levels, however, another picture was once common. While less important in recent decades, political machines once ruled supreme at these levels, and especially in local politics. Even where this was not the case, the "spoils" tradition was often strong. Consequently, with some exceptions, until the post-World War II period, the politics of patronage was largely able to forestall the adoption of effective merit-oriented reforms.

While some cities, including New York, Albany, Buffalo, Syracuse, Chicago, Evanston, and Seattle, introduced merit systems during the 1880s and 1890s, the vast number of local jurisdictions were left untouched by the first wave of civil service reform. During the progressive era of the early 1900s, when corruption and "bossism" were among the prime targets of muckrakers and reform politicians, progress was also made in many cities, including Los Angeles, San Francisco. Pittsburgh, Cincinnati, Cleveland, St. Louis, and Baltimore. Overall, only 65 cities had created civil service commissions by 1900. By 1930 that number had risen to 250. As of the mid-1980s, less than 12 percent of cities with populations exceeding 50,000 lacked merit systems, and only about 60 percent of all state employees were formally under merit systems.

The reader should be aware that all statistics concerning merit system coverage are inherently deceptive. While such figures may be numerically accurate, they merely indicate that merit systems are "on the books," not that they exist in practice. The surveys of merit system coverage that are annually undertaken by a variety of good-government groups are typically administered by mailed questionnaire. These statistics are by no means ascertained by empirical investigation. Consequently, while the arithmetic of these surveys may be impeccable, the resulting summaries frequently belie the true extent of merit system coverage. Remember, the city of Chicago has an excellent merit system on the books, yet it has managed to retain its well-earned reputation as the most famous large American city with patronage abuses. Even attempts to minimize the use of patronage have led to its manifestation in other forms. Court-imposed orders, for example, curtailed the late Mayor Washington's direct power over patronage hiring in the mid- to late-1980s in Chicago, but he was very skillful and effective in awarding city contracts on a patronage basis. In this sense, he retained indirect control over jobs in the city. Ultimately, even systematic legal efforts to eliminate patronage abuses have not ended the doling out of government largesse based on partisan politics.

Subnational jurisdictions followed the federal merit system example in many respects: bipartisan civil service commissions became common, examining methods and related administrative detail were frequently similar, and prohibitions concerning political assessments and other varieties of interference were legally binding many years before a general pattern of compliance appeared. In some areas, such as position classification programs and retirement provisions, a variety of local jurisdictions were many years ahead of the federal service. However, at the local level the pattern of reform that evolved contained a crucial difference—the civil service commission was made administratively and presumably politically independent of the jurisdiction's chief executive officer. The commission format was mandated by political, not administrative considerations. Then, as now, the illogic of divorcing the control of personnel from programmatic authority was recognized. Nevertheless, the more immediate goal of defeating the influences of spoils was paramount, and thus the rationale for the commission device was quite reasonable. Not only would it be independent from the party-controlled government, but its three- or five-part membership would be in a better position to resist political pressures than could any single administrator. Appellate functions, especially, are better undertaken by a tribunal than by a solitary judge. Not insignificantly, a commission provides a political safety valve by making room for special-interest representation, such as racial, religious, or employee groups.

It wasn't very long before the rationale for the independent commission was seriously challenged. As the city manager movement developed early in this century, managers—nonpartisan reform-type managers at that—found themselves burdened with the same kinds of restrictions upon their authority over personnel that had been designed to thwart the spoilsperson. These managers thus asserted that the original reason for establishing an independent personnel agency, namely, lack of confidence in the appointing authority, did not exist with regard to them. They felt, quite reasonably, that the personnel function should be integrated with the other administrative functions under the executive. While this line of reasoning made considerable headway where the city manager concept was firmly entrenched, it had little applicability for most of the larger cities where merit system provisions implemented only a few years earlier had degenerated into a sham. This was achieved by the dual process of appointing persons unsympathetic to merit system ideals as civil service commissioners and by restricting the work of the commission by denying adequate appropriations. In response to such "starve'em out" tactics, many jurisdictions later enacted ordinances providing that a fixed percentage of each year's budget would be for the administration of the merit system.

Despite these rather inauspicious beginnings, the merit system has now taken a firm hold in most sizable public jurisdictions. All cities with a population of over 250,000 have some provisions for a municipal civil service system. The smaller the number of employees in a jurisdiction, the less likely it is to have a merit system. Two basic factors have accounted for the continued growth of merit systems at the state and local levels. First, as the scope and nature of state and local employment changed it was almost inevitable that patronage appointees would have to give way to those with greater technical training and an interest in public service careers. It should be remembered in this context that even in the federal government at its worst, the spoils system never substantially abused positions requiring technical skills. To some extent, then, the complex functions of government, rather than the ideas of civil service reformers, have led to the relative demise of spoils practices.

At this same time, the federal government has thrown its weight in favor of the development of forceful merit systems at the state and local levels. Beginning in the 1930s, it has adopted a variety of measures to coerce or induce states to use merit procedures where federal funding is involved. Federal standards for this purpose were issued in 1939 and revised in 1948 and 1971. The most important step in this process has been the enactment of the Intergovernmental Personnel Act of 1970 (IPA). The act declared that "since numerous governmental activities administered by the State and local governments are related to national purpose and are financed in part by Federal funds, a national interest exists in a high caliber public service in State and local governments." First, the federal CSC and now OPM were charged with developing elaborate standards for merit systems and were given the authority

The Statutory Basis for Merit Systems

An effective merit personnel system starts with a clear mandate in law.

The statutory provisions can be fairly short and general or quite detailed. Too much detail in a law, especially of a procedural nature, can stand in the way of progress because laws are difficult to change when change is needed. On the other hand, too little detail, especially where rights and obligations are concerned, can cause problems of interpretation and also open the way to circumventing the purpose of a merit system.

It is desirable to keep the statutory language as general and flexible as possible leaving most details to be spelled out in administrative rules and regulations authorized by the statute.

a. State Constitutions or Local Charters

The basic authority for a merit system is often found in a State constitution or local charter adopted by the vote of the people. The constitutional or charter provision is usually in the form of a broad statement expressing the will of the people that their government be staffed by persons who are selected on the basis of merit.

Some State constitutions and local charters, however, go into more detail and contain provisions for the appointment and terms of office of the Civil Service Commissioners, the appointment of the Personnel Director, the powers and duties of these officials, and requirements for reporting on the activities of the merit system organization.

b. State Statutes or Local Ordinances and Resolutions

State statutes and local ordinances generally contain considerably more detail than is found in the constitutions or charters. They may either be based on a constitutional or charter provision or enacted independently of the legislative body.

The merit system organization and the major functions of the central administering body will usually be spelled out in the statute. Generally, the statute will direct a specified agency or person to issue the necessary rules and regulations which have the effect of law, and the necessary administrative procedures to carry out the provisions of the statute.

Other statutory provisions will cover such matters as pay, retirement, labor relations, conflicts of interest, and other essential components of a modern public personnel system.

If all the major components of the merit personnel system are not covered in one basic public personnel statute but, instead, are covered in several different statutes, it is desirable to codify all such provisions in one public personnel title of the State statutory code or comparable local instrument.

c. Civil Service or Personnel Rules and Regulations

Detailed provisions for operating a merit system are generally found in the rules and regulations issued by the central personnel agency or other designated agent of the jurisdiction, whether a civil service commission, a personnel board, or a personnel director. The rulemaking and regulatory authority is usually set out in the statute.

U.S. Civil Service Commission, *Guide to a More Effective Public Service ... The Legal Framework* (Washington, D.C.: Bureau of Intergovernmental Personnel Programs, August 1974), pp. 5–6.

to allocate grants for improving state and local personnel systems. In addition, the act made possible the temporary interchange of personnel between jurisdictions, allowed the use of federal training facilities for state and local government employees, and created a mechanism for the collection, coordination, and dissemination of information of public personnel administration. Few provisions of the IPA are in force today, however, since the act was virtually gutted under the Reagan administration's program of "new federalism."

What Is the Intergovernmental Personnel Act of 1970?

... federal statute designed to strengthen the personnel resources of state and local governments by making available to them a wide range of assistance. The act contains a declaration of policy that (1) the quality of public service at all levels can be improved through personnel systems that are consistent with merit principles, and (2) it is in the national interest for federal assistance to be directed toward strengthening state and local personnel systems in line with merit principles.

Specifically, IPA:

1. Authorizes the U.S. Civil Service Commission (now the Office of Personnel Management) to make grants to help meet the costs of strengthening personnel management capabilities of state and local governments in such areas as recruitment, selection, and pay administrations, and for research and demonstration projects;

2. authorizes grants to help states and localities develop and carry out training programs for employees, particularly in such core management areas as financial management, automatic data processing and personnel management (the grant programs of the IPA Act were eliminated in 1981);

3. authorizes awards for Government Service Fellowship grants to support graduate-level study by employees selected by state and local governments;

4. authorizes a wide range of technical assistance in personnel management to be made available to state and local governments on a reimbursable basis;

5. provides for the temporary assignment of personnel between federal agencies and state and local governments or institutions of higher education.

6. allows employees of state and local governments to benefit from training courses conducted for federal employees by federal agencies;

7. fosters cooperative recruitment and examining efforts; and

8. makes the Office of Personnel Management the sole federal agency responsible for prescribing and maintaining merit system standards required under federal grant programs.

Jay M. Shafritz, *Dictionary of Personnel Management and Labor Relations*, 2nd ed. (New York: Facts on File, Inc., 1985).

The Decline of the Commission Format

Ironically, at the same time that the federal government has been pressuring state and local governments to adopt and strengthen merit systems, the commission form of administering them has been on the wane for reasons similar

---

What Is the Meaning of *Mobility Assignment?*

. . . term generally used for the sharing of talent between the federal government and states, local governments, and institutions of higher education, as authorized by Title IV of the Intergovernmental Personnel Act of 1970, Public Law 91–648.

Title IV is designed to : (1) improve the delivery of government services at all levels of government by bringing the specialized knowledge and experience of skilled people to bear on problems that are of mutual concern to state or local jurisdictions and the federal government; (2) strengthen intergovernmental understanding, broaden perspective and increase capacity of personnel resources; and (3) help preserve the rights and benefits of employees so they will be better able to accept temporary assignments.

The ground rules for IPA Mobility Assignments are as follows:

1. Assignments can be made to or from federal agencies and states, local governments, and private and public colleges and universities for any period up to two years. They must be with the consent of the employee and for work of mutual benefit to the jurisdictions involved.

2. Employees can be assigned on a "detail" or leave without pay basis. If on detail, the employee is considered to continue on active duty with the organization from which detailed. If on leave, the employee goes on the rolls of the receiving organization.

3. No person-for-person exchange is required, although this can and does happen.

4. Federal employee salary, job rights, and benefits are protected, and travel and moving expenses are authorized.

5. For state, local and university employees, Title IV permits federal agencies to pay the employer's share of certain fringe benefits where this is appropriate, but job rights and continuation of benefit coverage remain the responsibility of the state or local employer.

6. Program officials of participating governments arrange assignments. Costs of the assignment, including salary, may be shared or borne entirely by either jurisdiction. This is subject to negotiation.

For further information contact the Intergovernmental Personnel Programs Division of the Office of Personnel Management.

Jay M. Shafritz, *Dictionary of Personnel Management and Labor Relations*, 2nd ed. (New York: Facts on File, Inc., 1985).

to the abolition of the commission format at the federal level. Put simply, independent, structurally and politically isolated personnel agencies of a regulatory nature have great difficulty in serving the needs of elected executives and public managers. They become viewed as obstacles to efficiency and effectiveness and are sometimes unduly influenced by pressure groups.

The development of satisfactory institutional arrangements for the formulation and implementation of public personnel policy presents several complexities and difficulties that cannot be readily resolved. At the heart of the overall problem is the diversity of roles played by central personnel agencies and the tension among several of them. Originally, the central personnel agency as we now know it in the United States was created to carry out the purposes of civil service reform. While some of these institutions have done admirably in this regard, the merit system in and of itself has been of limited efficiency in contributing to the development of highly effective and efficient public bureaucracies. While the merit system has gone far to recruit better people for public employment, it has seldom helped a chief executive to maximize the potential of his or her organization. The reasonable suggestion, incorporated in the federal Civil Service Reform Act of 1978, that the personnel system should be subordinated to the control of a chief executive, can result in undesirable politicization. It is important for public managers and students of public personnel administration to confront this matter. All too often they have echoed the view that efficiency is the number one axiom of administration without considering whether it is fully compatible with democracy, fairness, and apolitical public services. Improvements in the institutional arrangements involved in public personnel administration can certainly be made, but those searching for simplistic structural solutions to the overall problem are likely to be disappointed. Deep-seated and intractable social and political problems cannot be resolved with organizational cosmetics. The tension between the society's desire for depoliticized, merit-oriented public services and its interest in enabling its elected representatives to effectuate their policies is likely to make the nature of institutional arrangements for public personnel administration subject to constant reevaluation and modification for many decades to come.

Bibliography

Aronson, Albert H. "State and Local Personnel Administration." In *Biography of an Ideal*, edited by the U.S. Civil Service Commission. Washington, D.C.: U.S. Government Printing Office, 1974.

Ban, Carolyn, and Norma M. Riccucci, eds. *Public Personnel Management: Current Concerns, Future Challenges*. White Plains, N.Y.: Longman Press, 1991.(See, in particular, Ban's "The Navy Demonstration Project.")

Bellone, Carl J. "Structural vs. Behavioral Change: The Civil Service Reform Act of 1978," *Review of Public Personnel Administration* (Spring 1982).

Bernstein, Marver. *The Job of the Federal Executive*. Washington, D.C.: Brookings Institution, 1958.

Bussey, Ellen M., ed. *Federal Civil Service Law and Procedures*. Washington, D.C.: Bureau of National Affairs, Inc, 2nd edition, 1990.

Campbell, Alan K. "Civil Service Reform: A New Commitment,"*Public Administration Review*, 38 (March-April 1978).

Couturier, Jean J. "The Quiet Revolution in Public Personnel Laws," *Public Personnel Management*, 5 (May-June 1976).

Freedman, Anne. "Doing Battle with the Patronage Army: Politics, Courts, and Personnel Administration in Chicago," *Public Administration Review*, 48 (September/October 1988).

Gawthrop, Louis. *Bureaucratic Behavior in the Executive Branch*. New York: Free Press, 1969.

Golembiewski, Robert T., and Michael Cohen, eds. *People in Public Service: A Reader in Public Personnel Administration*, 2nd ed. Itasca, Ill.: F. E. Peacock Publishers, Inc., 1976.

Hall, Chester. "The United States Civil Service Commission," *Public Personnel Review*, 28 (October 1967).

Hampton, Robert. "The Basic Question," *Civil Service Journal*, 13(January March 1973).

Heclo, Hugh. *A Government of Strangers: Executive Politics in Washington*. Washington, D.C.: Brookings Institution, 1977.

Ingraham, Patricia W. and David H. Rosenbloom, "Symposium on the Civil Service Reform Act of 1978," *Policy Studies Journal*, 17 (Winter, 1988-89).

Ingraham, Patricia W. and Carolyn Ban, ed. *Legislating Bureaucratic Change: The Civil Service Reform Act of 1978*. Albany, N.Y.: State University of New York Press, 1984.

Kaufman, Herbert. "Emerging Conflicts in the Doctrines of Public Administration," *American Political Science Review*, 50 (December 1956).

Knudsen, Steven, Larry Jakus, and Maida Metz. "The Civil Service Reform Act of 1978," *Public Personnel Management*, 8 (May-June 1979). For an official OPM response to this article, see Alan K. Campbell, "Letter to the Editor," *Public Personnel Management*, 8 (September-October 1979).

Kramer, Kenneth W. "Seeds of Success and Failure: Policy Development and Implementation of the 1978 Civil Service Reform Act," *Review of Public Personnel Administration* (Spring 1982).

Lee, Robert D. Jr. *Public Personnel Systems*, 2d ed. Rockville, MD: Aspen Publishers, 1987.

Mosher, Frederick C. *Democracy and the Public Service*, 2d ed. New York: Oxford University Press, 1982.

Patten, Thomas H. Jr. *Classics of Personnel Management*. Oak Park, Ill.: Moore, 1979.

————. "Where Was the Commission?" *Good Government* (Spring 1975).

Pearce, Jone L. and James L. Perry, "Federal Merit Pay: A Longitudinal Analysis," *Public Administration Review*, 43 (July/August 1983).

Perry, James L., Beth Ann Petrakis, and Theodore K. Miller, "Federal Merit Pay, Round II: An Analysis of the Performance Management and Recognition System," *Public Administration Review*, 49 (January/February 1989).

Rosen, Bernard. *The Merit System in the United States Civil Service*. Monograph for the Committee on Post Office and Civil Service of the House of Representatives. Washington, D.C.: U.S. Government Printing Office, 94th Cong., 1st sess., December 23, 1975.

Rosenthal, Harvey. "In Defense of Central Control of Public Personnel Policy," *Public Personnel Review*, 28 (October 1967).

Rutan v. Republican Party of Illinois, 58 *Law Week* 4872 (1990).

Seidman, Harold and Robert Gilmour. *Politics, Position, and Power: The Dynamics of Federal Organization*, 4th ed. New York: Oxford University Press, 1986.

Shafritz, Jay M. *The Public Personnel World: Readings on the Professional Practice*. Chicago: International Personnel Management Association, 1977.

Sorauf, Frank J. "The Silent Revolution in Patronage," *Public Administration Review* (Winter 1960).

Stahl, O. Glenn. *Public Personnel Administration*, 7th ed. New York: Harper & Row, 1976.

U.S. President's Committee on Administrative Management. *Report of the Committee with Studies of the Administrative Management in the Federal Government*. Washington, D.C.: U.S. Government Printing Office, 1937.

Weber, Max. *From Max Weber: Essays in Sociology*, translated and edited by H. H. Gerth and C. W. Mills. New York: Oxford University Press, 1958.

Wilson, Woodrow. "The Study of Administration," *Political Science Quarterly*, 55 (December 1941). Originally published in 1887.

3
Politics of Public Personnel

Prologue: "Spoiling" the Merit System

When Fred Malek was the chief of the Nixon administration's White House personnel office he occasioned the drafting of the *Federal Political Personnel Manual*, popularly known as the Malek Manual. As Frank J. Thompson has suggested, "the Malek manual is to personnel administration what Machiavelli's *The Prince* is the broader field of political science." Malek's infamous manual did not specifically advocate the violation of any law; rather it encouraged the systematic and widespread abuse of the spirit of the federal merit system. In fairness, it must be added that the Nixon administration did nothing in this regard that was not done in earlier administrations. The Nixon Republicans were simply more comprehensive—more ambitious—in their abuse of the merit concept. They felt that their friends, their fellow Republicans, had more merit than strangers with like qualifications but differing affiliations. The nonpartisan processes of appointments based upon merit were merely an administrative inconvenience that could be overcome by mastering the minutiae of the civil service regulations. The politicos were out to beat the careerists at their own game. They nearly won!

The best way to appreciate the usefulness of the Malek Manual is to read an excerpt:

> Let us assume that you have a career opening in your Department's personnel office for a Staff Recruitment Officer. Sitting in front of you is your college roommate from Stanford University in California who was born and raised in San Francisco. He received his law degree from Boalt Hall at the University of California. While studying for the bar he worked at an advertising agency handling

newspaper accounts. He also worked as a reporter on the college newspaper. Your personnel experts judge that he could receive an eligibility rating for a GS-11.

The first thing you do is tear up the old job description that goes with that job. You then have a new one written, to be classified as GS-11, describing the duties of that specific Staff Recruitment Officer as directed toward the recruitment of recent law graduates for entry level attorney positions, entry level public information officers for the creative arts and college news liaison sections of your public information shop, and to be responsible for general recruiting for entry level candidates on the West Coast. You follow that by listing your selective criteria as follows: Education: BA and LLB, stating that the candidate should have extensive experience and knowledge by reason of employment or residence on the West Coast. Candidate should have attended or be familiar with law schools, and institutions of higher education, preferably on the West Coast. The candidate should also possess some knowledge by reasons of education or experience of the fields of college journalism, advertising, and law.

You then trot this candidate's Application for Federal Employment over to the Civil Service Commission, and shortly thereafter he receives an eligibility rating for a GS-11. Your personnel office then sends over the job descriptions (GS-11) along with the selective criteria which was based on the duties of the job description. When the moment arrives for the panel to "spin the register" you insure that your personnel office sends over two "friendly" bureaucrats. The register is then spun and your candidate will certainly be among the only three who even meet the selective criteria, much less be rated by your two "friendly" panel members as among the "highest qualified" that meet the selection criteria. In short, you write the job description and selective criteria around your candidate's Form 171.

There is no merit in the merit system!

Fudging the System

The perversion of most civil service merit systems for private, administrative, and especially partisan ends is one of the worst kept yet least written about secrets in government. While the general textbooks on state and local government frequently take cognizance of this situation, traditional texts on public personnel administration have tended to deal with this subject as if it were an abnormal malignancy instead of an inherent and frequently beneficial part of governmental personnel management. This is faulty perspective. Senator Daniel P. Moynihan (N.Y.) long ago noted that corruption must be recognized as "a normal condition of American local government." Similarly, it must be recognized that the perversion of merit system principles is a normal condition of the public personnel process. This latter situation is not necessarily as unhealthy and undesirable as the former. Frequently such "perversions"

Who Was Niccolo Machiavelli (1469–1527)?

. . . most famous management analyst of the Italian Renaissance, is often credited with having established the moral foundations of modern personnel management. In *Discorsi sopra la prima deca di Tito Livio* ("Discourses on the First Decade of Tito Livy") he offers his advice to all staff specialists:

> If you tender your advice with modesty, and the opposition prevents its adoption, and owing to someone else's advice being adopted, disaster follows, you will acquire very great glory. And, though you cannot rejoice in the glory that comes from disasters which befall your country or your prince, it at any rate counts for something.

Jay M. Shafritz, *Dictionary of Personnel Management and Labor Relations*, 2nd ed. (New York: Facts on File, Inc., 1985).

are essential if actual merit is to be rewarded within the "merit" system. Unfortunately, other considerations seem just as likely to apply.

Throughout the United States, public personnel merit systems tend to operate on two different planes within the same jurisdiction. The great majority of civil service employees within merit systems are able to enter and advance on the basis of their own talents and the design of the system. However, at the same time and within the same system, there are two groups of individuals that enter and advance according to criteria other than that provided for in merit system regulations.

The first group of employees consists of all those who were appointed for considerations other than personal fitness. Hidden here are the political appointees beyond those policy-making and confidential positions that are usually the executive's legal prerogative. The extent of such placements depends upon such factors as the strength and longevity of the merit system, the political culture of the community, and the integrity of the executive who, having taken an oath to uphold all the laws of his or her jurisdiction, can only make such appointments in violation of the spirit, if not the letter, of the oath.

While the merit system is frequently perverted for traditional political ends, it is similarly abused for more scrupulous purposes. The excessively rigid procedures for entering and advancing in most merit systems have long been recognized as being a decided hindrance to effective management practices. In order to compensate for the lack of managerial discretion occasioned by such rigidities, career civil servants as well as other highly qualified individuals have either been advanced or initially installed through a fudging of the civil service regulations—this is the same process by which politicos are foisted upon the merit system. The procedural morass designed to keep

A Few Examples of How Civil Service Systems are "Fudged"

Model	Process
• "Tailoring"	"Preferred" candidate is identified. Qualifications for position in vacancy announcement tailored to skills of preferred candidate. Preferred candidate hired or promoted. This practice is technically legal, but goes beyond the spirit of civil service law.
• "Bridging" a permanent appointment	Agency targets highly qualified (i.e., "preferred") candidate. To avoid a hiring delay, candidate is hired on a temporary line, which is later converted, or bridged to a permanent line. This practice is technically legal, but goes beyond the spirit of civil service law.
• Provisional appointment	Create a new job title or reclassify an existing one into "unique" title. Hire the "preferred" candidate as a provisional, pending development of a new test for the new title. Wait several years for the test to be developed if at all. This practice is technically legal but goes beyond the spirit of civil service law.
• "Soliciting" a declination	Convince persons ranked high on civil service list to turn job offer down. To do so, candidate must be convinced that the work is undesirable and unpleasant. Or, a bargain will be made whereby the candidate is promised a "helping hand" for some other current or future job vacancy. This practice is clearly illegal.

Note: This represents just a sample of techniques. The examples presented here have been employed at least at the federal level of government.

Source: Adapted from Ban, Carolyn. "The Realities of the Merit System," in *Public Personnel Management: Current Concerns, Future Challenges* (Carolyn Ban and Norma M. Riccucci, eds.) White Plains, NY: Longman Press, 1991).

out the bad is frequently as effective in keeping out the good. In consequence, what exists in fact, although it is nowhere de jure, is a first-class and second-class civil service. This classification is not a reflection on the quality of any given individual or of the productive value of each class, but merely a reference as to how they are treated by those who work the merit system. While the members of the civil service proletariat must be content with careers bounded by the full force of the frequently unreasonable and always constraining regulations, others—those fortunate enough to be recognized for their talents as well as those recognized in spite of their talents—benefit markedly by having

What Is the Meaning of *No-Show Jobs*?

. . . government positions for which the incumbent collects a salary but is not required to report to work. While no-show jobs are by their nature illegal, they are not uncommon. In 1975, when a New York State Assemblyman was tried in Albany County Court for authorizing no-show jobs on his legislative payroll, he claimed discriminatory prosecution and asked that his case be dismissed because the practice was so commonplace. The judge concurred and the case was dismissed. See *Albany* (N.Y.) *Times-Union*, September 23–28, 1975.

Jay M. Shafritz, *Dictionary of Personnel Management and Labor Relations*, 2nd ed. (New York: Facts on File, Inc., 1985).

these same regulations waived, fraudulently complied with, or simply ignored when it is to their advantage.

The Netherworld of Public Personnel Management

Appropriately, the entire fudging process operates in a netherworld; neither openly nor secretly, but in the shadows similar to a black market. In both instances, operations typically continue without serious interference despite the obviousness of their illegality or immorality and a surfeit of condemnatory rhetoric. Managers all too frequently find that it is impossible for them to fulfill their mandates by fully abiding by the structural constraints of the civil service system. However, since the public manager is in a position to command and/or influence an appropriate fudging of the system, the fudge is made by her personnel functionaries. Such netherworld products take forms suitable to the exigencies of the situation. Thus, in one context they could be an otherwise undeserving reallocation of a position to a higher grade level, or the exceptional lowering of the passpoint on a promotional exam in order to pick up a favored candidate, or the easing of the qualifications required for a particular position.

The netherworld products vary with the special requirements of any given jurisdiction. The public manager, being the customer of these specially made products, pays for them either (1) negatively—by not imposing sanctions of some kind upon the personnel office; or (2) positively—by providing individual rewards for the personnelists or granting additional resources for the other operations of the personnel office. A formal approach bound by the "system" would not allow the manager the flexibility that she demands. In sum, since she can command the resources to, in effect, "buy" the products that she needs for the accomplishment of her mission, a black market of sorts—a netherworld—grows up to serve her.

There is little incentive for elective and appointive public managers to strive to reform the administrative system that nurtures the netherworld. Since they tend to be short termers compared to the career officials in the civil service systems, there is little payoff for them to be concerned with the broad issues of personnel management. Therefore, while their substantive program accomplishments may be significant, their impact on or interest in the human-resources posture of their respective agencies tend to be inconsequential. When the flexibility that they deem essential for mission accomplishment is formally denied to line managers, it is almost invariably obtained informally via administrative finesse. Line managers, being the mission-oriented officers that they are, tend to exhibit a wanton disregard for the means—ethical and otherwise—by which their personnel resources are obtained. A personnel officer is judged by her ability to produce results—not by her lucid explanations of why the civil service regulations make it impossible to hire this person or to promote that one.

Reprinted by permission of the International Personnel Management Association, 1850 K Street, N.W., Suite 870, Washington, D.C. 20006.

The obvious danger of personnel managers as well as other managers using excessive zeal in seeking to achieve their agency's mission and thereby going beyond the proper range of their discretion is well recognized. This is an inherent and necessary risk in all managerial delegation. Unreasonable constraints only exacerbate the danger and increase the frustration. When legislative mandates that reflect neither administrative wisdom nor experience are viewed as barriers to managerial effectiveness, they tend to intensify the bureaucratic search for an appropriate circumvention. There is even significant evidence that organizational superiors support such tactics by discouraging subordinates from fully reporting just how they have accomplished their missions because of concerns for legal culpability. For example, a Brookings Institution study by Herbert Kaufman has found that executives in public agencies "may resort to the strategy of discouraging feedback about administrative behavior because they privately *approve* of the behavior they know they should, according to law and morality, prevent."

There is nothing systematically illegitimate about maintaining a public personnel netherworld. Indeed, there is considerable precedent for awarding public employment advantages to special groups such as veterans. What is so contemptible about the public personnel netherworld is not its operations, which are frequently benign, but its *hypocrisy*.

The netherworld of public personnel administration is more than just another informal organizational mechanism working to complement the formal structure by compensating for its shortcomings. It's an insidious cancer that quietly and relentlessly erodes the budding professionalism and spirit of the personnel establishment. In addition to whatever trauma it causes for the participants in its dramas, it serves to subvert the democratic processes of government by institutionalizing a system of governance that is neither known by the public nor formally sanctioned by their elected representatives. For example, by inviting applicants to apply for positions when a candidate has already been preselected, the netherworld perpetuates countless frauds upon the public, thus extending its infectious malaise of cynicism to the citizenry. While organizational and party politics will always be with us, there is no appropriate place for this kind of institutionalized hypocrisy in the public bureaucracies of the United States. Actually, the amount of hypocrisy in public personnel operations and other managerial functions compares favorably with the private sector; but with a crucial difference—public personnel hypocrisies are generally forbidden by law.

A Missing Professionalism

A political official determined to have her way with personnel matters can usually find career officials who are willing to be "realistic" about such things. But this assertion begs the significant question of why the career administrators, the personnel operatives, are so willing to be "realistic." Certainly the various merit systems could not be manipulated as facilely as they are if it were not for the technical expertise of the personnel establishment. The personnel process could hardly be abused as it is were it not for what Chester I. Barnard, in his 1938 classic *The Functions of the Executive*, has termed the "zone of indifference." Public officials are commonly in the dubious legal and moral position of conspiring with their personnel operatives to misrepresent facts and events to civil service commissions, the jurisdictions' employees, and the public. For example, a job vacancy may be announced as open to all when, in reality, a candidate has been preselected; or a promotion may be justified on merit when the only thing meritorious about the employee may be her political sponsorship. Personnel directors and their staffs tend to assist in these perversions of their established merit systems because such actions are acceptable to them. Such actions are within their "zone of indifference." This is not to say that personnelists will do absolutely anything that their superiors wish. Some things are just too gross. Clericals cannot generally be made into supergrades; but a law graduate with practically no professional experience can be if her other credentials—meaning political endorsements—are appropriate.

A personnelist's "zone of indifference" shrinks and expands according to her perceptions of the legitimacy of her orders. Career bureaucrats tend to give elected and appointed officials the benefits of any doubts that they may have over the extent of their authority. To do less would be to reject the fundamental democratic notion of political control. In this context, subordinate compliance is essential for democratic government. But is such compliance equally democratic when it requires the violation of legislative and judicial mandates? What may be obvious in a philosophy seminar is not so facile in practice. Considerable evidence exists that subordinates in American civilian and military bureaucracies will violate a variety of moral and legal

---

What Is the Meaning of *Nepotism*?

. . . any practice by which officeholders award positions to members of their immediate family. It is derived from the Latin *nepos*, meaning nephew or grandson. The rulers of the medieval church were often thought to give special preference to their nephews in distributing churchly offices. At that time, "nephew" became a euphemism for their illegitimate sons.

Jay M. Shafritz, *Dictionary of Personnel Management and Labor Relations*, 2nd ed. (New York: Facts on File, Inc., 1985).

provisions rather than disobey their superiors. Vietnam, Watergate, and the Iran-Contra Affair are ready examples.

It seems fair to suggest that a leading occupational hazard of public personnel operatives is an *enlarged* "zone of indifference." The main symptom of this problem is a chronic cynicism addressed mainly to personnel functions—frequently extending to the whole panoply of public administration. According to the report on a 1970 symposium of young personnel professionals held at the Federal Executive Institute, cynicism "has all too often been the common feeling among personnel people about their work." The symposium noted that the basic medium of communication and identification among personnelists "has been a sharing of horror stories, a 'can you top this' of frustrations and disappointments of the personnel administration 'game.' " The basic cause of this disabling cynicism is the disparity between what the personnelist desires to be in her organization and the role that is foisted upon her. This disparity, leading to a poor self-image, is compensated in part by the development of cynical attitudes toward her work.

Why is there so little resistance to the netherworld operations on the part of personnelists? Why do they seem to be such willing accomplices in activities that they know to be ethically dubious? The answer is to be found by examining the tangential consequences of their lacking professionalism. Personnel, while an ancient function, is a comparatively recent occupation. It was during the time frame between the two world wars that personnel emerged as a permanent occupational specialty in both industry and government. The various federal departments have only had formal divisions of personnel since 1938. Personnel has not yet been fleshed out as a profession.

Chester I. Barnard's "Zone of Indifference"

The phrase "zone of indifference" may be explained as follows: If all the orders for actions reasonably practicable be arranged in the order of their acceptability to the person affected, it may be conceived that there are a number which are clearly unacceptable, that is, which certainly will not be obeyed; there is another group somewhat more or less on the neutral line, that is, either barely acceptable or barely unacceptable; and a third group unquestionably acceptable. This last group lies within the "zone of indifference." The person affected will accept orders lying within this zone and is relatively indifferent as to what the order is so far as the question of authority is concerned. Such an order lies within the range that in a general way was anticipated at time of undertaking the connection with the organization.

Chester I. Barnard, *The Functions of the Executive* (Cambridge: Harvard University Press, 1938), pp. 168-169.

People are attracted to personnel work by expediency and not by a premeditated decision to undertake years of specialized training in preparation to a life's work. The great majority of personnel operatives enter the field, not because of any longstanding desire, but due to happenstance. Consequently, their orientation toward the employing organization differs markedly from that exhibited by professionals such as medical doctors and scientists.

Alvin W. Gouldner, the well-known sociologist, has identified two latent social soles that manifest themselves in organizational settings. The first role, that of a "cosmopolitan," tends to be adopted by true professionals. It assumes a small degree of loyalty to the employing organization, a high commitment to specialized skills, and an outer reference-group orientation. The second role, that of a "local," tends to be adopted by nonprofessionals. It assumes a high degree of loyalty to the employing organization, a low commitment to specialized skills, and an inner reference-group orientation. While these role models are extremes and represent the two ends of a continuum, they go far to explain why personnel operatives tend to be so compliant with netherworld operations. Because they are not true professionals, their loyalty lies not with professional and ethical obligations but with their immediate organization. There is little sense of commitment to specialized skills or to reference groups outside the immediate organization. Indeed, their immediate organization is their reference group; and it is from this group that the personnelist takes her behavioral cues. The pull that any sense of professionalism has on her is so slight that it can neither prevent her from conspiring to pervert the merit system nor comfort her if she resists.

Of course, this is changing. There is a variety of indications that many of the worst abuses of the netherworld will decline somewhat in the coming years even if no formal reforms are undertaken. The maturing of public administration and public personnel administration as professional fields of endeavor will tend to increase the cosmopolitan outlook of its practitioners. Indeed, such professional associations as the American Society for Public Administration and the International Personnel Management Association move personnelists in that direction. The tremendous growth of academic programs in public administration has generated a lively concern with administrative ethics. Various conspiracies within government, such as Watergate, have directed great attention to the problem of ethical behavior in the public service if only by serving as an object lesson on what happens if you get caught.

But more significant than all of the ethical considerations is the simple fact that the public personnel function is rapidly growing to include a variety of new skills in such areas as human resources planning, productivity measurement and bargaining, job design, and test validation, among others. In fact, many personnel departments, in accordance with their expanding scope, are

What Is the Meaning of *Ethics?*

. . . a set of moral principles or values. There are many ethical individuals working as personnel operatives. However, their ethical standards tend to reflect their personal background rather than some abstract standards of personnel management. While professional codes of conduct have been put forth by a variety of organizations— such as the American Society for Personnel Administration . . . and the International Personnel Management Association (see below)—their impact has been inconsequential.

Thomas H. Patten, Jr., in "Is Personnel Administration A Profession," *Personnel Administration* (March–April 1968), has succinctly summarized the dilemma of ethical codes for personnel managers:

> In a showdown disagreement with higher management, the personnel administrator who cited his professional ethical code as a basis for a course of action (assuming he had also complied with the law) could be regarded as either a naive, high-minded idealist or simply a fool. He would also be brave to so jeopardize his mealticket and future employment status. In any event, if he were to stand firm and threaten quitting as a sanction for his convictions, the letter or resignation would probably be eagerly awaited by a disgusted management (but one well pleased to be rid of a cloud-nine character).

Code of Ethics for the International Personnel Management Association

I pledge that, according to my ability and my judgment, I will pursue these goals and keep these commitments:

I will respect and protect the dignity of individuals, honoring their right to fair consideration in all aspects of employment and to the pursuit of a rewarding career without regard to race, sex, religion, age, or national origin.

I will foster and apply management practices and merit principles which motivate employees to develop their full capability as competent, productive members of their organization.

I will endeavor to insure that full and early consideration is given to the human aspects of management plans and decisions.

I will assist employees and management in understanding and fulfilling their mutual responsibilities and obligations.

I will give freely of my knowledge and my time in the counseling and development of those pursuing a career in personnel management and will contribute to the development and dissemination of professional knowledge for the improvement of the art.

I will treat as privileged, information accepted in trust.

I will not compromise, for personal gain or accommodation, my integrity or that of my employer, but will faithfully respect and apply this Code in the conduct of my professional duties and responsibilities.

Jay M. Shafritz, *Dictionary of Personnel Management and Labor Relations*, 2nd ed. (New York: Facts on File, Inc., 1985).

changing their name to human resources departments, and personnelists are often referred to as human resources managers.

Managers will tend not to abuse the sensibilities of employees they need. They can well afford to abuse the sensibilities of a bunch of clerks who have so little intrinsic skill that they would have tremendous difficulty finding a comparable-paying job in another organization. The sooner that personnelists obtain these new tools, the sooner management will realize that they are more than a bunch of clerks. This will all eventually come to pass; but it may be a long wait.

The Cultural Milieu

Public personnel management is constantly being judged in the wrong context. It is erroneously viewed as a public sector counterpart to industrial management systems. However, the private sector analogy holds true only for a portion of the total public personnel function, the size of that portion being directly related to the politicization of the jurisdiction. Thus public personnel operations cannot be properly understood or evaluated outside the political context of the host jurisdiction. The determinant of any given community's attitudes toward the quality and vigor of its public personnel program is the political culture of the geographic area concerned. It was Thomas Jefferson, a political observer of some skill, who noted that "some states require a different regimen from others." Indeed, the only way to find an explanation for the extreme variations of the quality or vigor of American civil service systems is to examine the cultural context of American governmental units.

The meritoriousness of a public personnel operation varies for a variety of reasons. Contributing significantly to the variations is the substantial disagreement as to just what constitutes a quality operation. While some zealots advocate the tightest possible merit system mechanisms, others with equal vigor and concern for the efficacy of operations cry out for greater discretion on the part of managers and an eventual dissolution of "strait jacket" civil service procedures. While honest critics may differ on what constitutes a quality personnel program, one quiet yet dominant fact remains: the quality or style of operations is determined only in the lesser part by well-meaning critics or even by the personnel administrators themselves; the crucial determinant is the political will of the community or jurisdiction as expressed by its political culture and manifested by the administrative style of public programs.

James Q. Wilson in his book *Varieties of Police Behavior* demonstrated that the style of police operations in eight communities reflected not some abstract standard of quality or professionalism but the expressed and/or

What Is the Ethics in Government Act of 1978?

. . . federal statute that seeks to deal with possible conflicts of interests by former federal executive branch employees of imposing postemployment prohibitions on their activities. The restrictions in the law are concerned with former government employees' representation or attempts to influence federal agencies, not with their employment by others. What is prohibited depends on how involved a former employee was with a matter while with the government and whether he or she was one of a specified group of senior employees.

implied desires of the community. For example, the police were either exceedingly lenient or exceedingly strict with minor legal violations depending upon the perceived degree of community concern one way or another. A similar condition exists with personnel operations. Merit systems arrayed along a continuun tend to be tight and legalistic or open to manipulation in reflection of community attitudes. Since public personnel agencies typically have a policing role to perform, it is useful to compare their operating premises to those of police departments in the same jurisdiction. Wilson considers a police department to have a "watchdog" style of performance if it is one in which order maintenance is perceived to be the prime function of the department. Such a police operation will tend to ignore law infringements, such as minor traffic violations, bookmaking, and illegal church bingo, that do not involve "serious" crimes. Correspondingly, a public personnel agency exhibiting this style might knowingly accept false information as the basis for a position reallocation, might encourage unsuspecting applicants to apply for a job vacancy for which a candidate has been preselected, or might allow the equal-rights provisions of recent legislation to be ignored or abused. Of course, all these activities or nonactivities are subject to occasional crackdowns. Just as the police periodically shut down illegal gambling operations in response to the political needs of the police chief or mayor, watchdog-style personnel operations periodically tighten up their classification procedures or pump new life into their upward mobility programs in response to the political needs of the appointed or elected executives. The thrust of the watchdog style in both instances is to maintain order, to ensure a smooth, nondisruptive running of the community or bureaucracy. Legal considerations and official operating mandates are paramount only when the "heat is on." Of course, the standard operating procedures of a police or personnel department will tend to be more legalistic in communities that are so disposed. But how do you account for or even determine such dispositions?

While a community's political culture is seldom articulated, it nevertheless serves as a source of definition. By determining the values to be applied to any given problem set, the political culture ensures that the decisional process is filtered through its value system prior to administrative action. Just as other aspects of culture create an individual's needs hierarchy by subconsciously ranking the importnce of such things as new clothes, big cars, and religion in one's life, the political culture is a significant influence in establishing an individual's hierarchy of role obligation whereby her legalistic responsibilities are placed above or below her obligations to political party, kinship group, coreligionists, and so on. It establishes the parameters of the systemically legitimate activities in which an individual may participate without incurring community sanctions. Even when corruption is rife, it is the cultural environment that sets the limits and direction of such corruption. Melvin M. Belli, the famous lawyer, relates a story illustrative of this. Years ago Belli traveled to Paris to represent his client, movie star Errol Flynn, who had a legal tangle with a French firm. When Belli arrived, the French lawyer on the case advised him that there was nothing to worry about—"we have given the judge 200,000 francs and the case is in the bag." When Belli wondered aloud what would happen if the other side were to give the judge 300,000 francs, his French associate became indignant and replied, "But Monsieur, he is a *French* judge—he only takes from one side!"

While passing mention of the importance of the cultural context of public management has long been made by organization theorists, a viable classification of the various American political cultures was not achieved until the mid-1960s with the work of Daniel J. Elazar of Temple and Bar Ilan Universities. Elazar classified the political subcultures of the United States by examining three sets of factors for each locality studied: the sources of political culture such as race, ethnicity, and religion; the manifestations of political culture such as political attitudes, behavior, and symbols; and the effects of political culture such as political actions and public policies. In this manner

---

Sir Thomas More on Public Service Ethics

Cardinal Wolsey: Now explain how you as a Councilor of England can obstruct those measures for the sake of your own, private, conscience.

Sir Thomas More: Well—I believe, when statesmen forsake their own private conscience for the sake of their public duties—they lead their country by a short route to chaos.

Robert Bolt, *A Man For All Seasons*, act I, scene 2.

he was able to identify the political subcultures for each of several hundred American communities.

Elazar finds that the overall American political culture consists of three major subcultures: the individualistic, the moralistic, and the traditionalistic (see Table 3.1).

The individualistic political culture "holds politics to be just another means by which individuals may improve themselves socially and economically."

In the moralistic political culture politics is conceived "as a public activity centered on some notion of the public good and properly devoted to the advancement of the public interest."

The traditionalistic political culture is reflective of "an older precommercial attitude that accepts a substantially hierarchical society as part of the ordered nature of things, authorizing and expecting those at the top of the social structure to take a special and dominant role in government."

As political culture is essentially a value system, it can best be understood in terms of the boundaries that it sets for political behavior. It sets limitations on political behavior and provides subliminal direction for political actions. Overall a political culture influences the operations of the larger political system by (1) molding the community's perceptions of the nature and purposes of politics; (2) influencing the recruitment of specific kinds of people to become active in government as holders of elective offices, members of the

Table 3.1.   Views of Elazar's Three Political Subcultures Toward Bureaucracy and Merit Systems

	Subculture		
	Individualistic	Moralistic	Traditionalistic
View of bureaucracy	Ambivalent (Undesirable because limits favors and patronage, but good because it enhances efficiency)	Positive (Brings desirable political neutrality)	Negative (Depersonalizes government)
Kind of merit system favored	Loosely implemented	Strong	None (Should be controlled by political elite)

Source: Adapted from Daniel J. Elazar, *American Federalism: A View from the States*, 2nd ed. (New York: Crowell, 1972), p. 100.

bureaucracy, and political workers; and (3) subtly directing politicians and public officials in the light of their perceptions.

The study of political culture would seem to offer great predictive potential for the efficacy of governmental operations. One would expect that the inhabitants of a political culture viewing public office as essentially a means of personal gain would be unlikely to support a strong merit system. Conversely, a culture with a high moral ethic would be unlikely to maintain a spoils system for public office. While Elazar's political subculture designations are far from definitive, they do provide a crude index of the cultural manifestations that can reasonably be anticipated. Thus Minnesota, with its overwhelmingly moralistic orientation, would be expected to have strong merit systems, while Chicago, with its individualistic orientation, would be expected to have an extensive patronage program. Similarly, parts of the South, are traditionalistic, being less likely to embrace the merit system.

If, as Elazar maintains, the political culture is the crucial determinant in merit system viability, then the particular mechanics of a merit system operation would seem to have little influence on its overall success or failure. In effect, jurisdictions with the exact same legislative mandates, operating regulations, and staffing patterns will function one way within a moralistic political culture and in quite a different manner within an individualistic political culture. By extrapolating from what is known about the political culture of the environment, it is therefore possible to make reasonable predictions about the manner in which any civil service system would function within that culture. While one subculture is usually dominant, it is a rare jurisdiction that does not have another subculture influencing the community to a lesser extent. Actually, much of the country has been forced into the formal requirements of the moralistic political culture because it is the most rhetorically acceptable. Civil service systems formally reflective of the individualistic and traditionalistic political subcultures could hardly be reconciled with the conflicting national values of equal access and fair play! Nevertheless, the analysis of political culture is invaluable in explaining why such strong merit systems are ineffectual in certain cultural environments.

The Legacy of the Reform Movement

The reform movement as a matter of strategy held that politics should be removed from the business of government. Woodrow Wilson maintained in his famous 1887 article, "The Study of Administration," that "administration lies outside the proper sphere of politics. Administrative questions are not political questions. Although politics sets the tasks of administration, it should not be suffered to manipulate its offices." While a variety of writers has expanded upon the themes established by Wilson, Herbert Kaufman has best articulated the desire of the reformers by labeling it the "quest for neutral competence." While this quest has had noble origins and commendable intent, it has brought in its wake the pollutant of mediocrity.

One of the lasting legacies of the reform movement, with its emphasis upon the creation of independent civil service commissions, was the divorcing of personnel administration from general management. How did this unfortunate situation develop? It was certainly not the intent of the reformers that the public service should become dominated by those seeking small jobs and great security. The impetus of the reform movement was of necessity essentially negative—destroy the spoils system—rather than positive. In the last century the scope of governmental operations was of such a dimension that the managerial implications of reform were hardly relevant. Besides, for the time, the abolition of spoils alone was a major managerial improvement in itself as it frequently implied that the incumbent would actually perform the duties of the position. By and large, the extent of concern for positive personnel management was evidenced by the impetus for position classification programs that offered the radical idea of equal pay for equal work. But classification programs did not come into fashion until the 1920s and 1930s. Personnel management during the early reform period was limited to the essentials: discovering who was on the payroll, providing equitable salaries, and recording attendance. The reform task was so immense that the emphasis had to be on the negative or policing aspects of personnel management—that in itself was positive.

The original intent of the reformers has tended to be forgotten or misinterpreted over time. A partial return to these original precepts of civil service reform would go far toward reconciling the artificial separation of personnel from management. The reformers tended to be of the opinion that if the front door or entrance to the civil service was protected from political influences, then the back door or the question of removals would take care of itself. Theoretically, there would be no incentive for a politically appointed or elected executive to remove a competent employee if he could not be replaced by a political cohort. Accordingly, the Pendleton Act of 1883 and subsequent state and local legislation made no provision for removals. Actually, the reform movement leaders were quite openly in support of management's absolute prerogative of removal for all but religious or political reasons. George William Curtis, one of the founders in 1881 and later the president of the National Civil Service Reform League, was quite supportive of management's unimpaired discretion. In commenting upon removal restrictions, he declared that "it is better to take the risk of occasional injustice from passion and prejudice . . . than to seal up incompetency, negligence, insubordination, insolence, and every other mischief . . . by requiring a virtual trial at law before an unfit or incapable clerk can be removed."

Viewed historically, it was the persistent abuse of management's prerogative of removal that led to its curtailment. The new federal civil service law had hardly been in effect when it developed that removals were commonly being made for partisan reasons and upon secret charges. However, it wasn't until 1897 that an executive order of President McKinley's provided that removals were not to be made in the competitive service except for just cause and upon written charges. The Lloyd-LaFollette Act of 1912, expanding upon an executive order of President Theodore Roosevelt, further required that removals were to be made only to promote the efficiency of the service. While employees were entitled to notice, charges, and an opportunity to reply, final authority remained with department heads and there was no appeal for a reversal to either the Civil Service Commission or the courts. It wasn't until the 1940s that this situation changed under the dual impetus of legislative provisions for civil rights and veteran's preference. The Ramspeck Act of 1940 prohibited discrimination in federal employment because of race, color, or creed, thus providing for the first time a binding appeal beyond the department levels. As this provision of the law was poorly enforced, it had little impact. However, the Veteran's Preference Act of 1944 established the right of veterans to appeal dismissals to the Civil Service Commission. Since more than half of the postwar federal service consisted of veterans, this changed the whole nature of removal proceedings. For the first time, department heads and their assistants had to approach dismissal actions with the thought that they would possibly have to justify such actions to a neutral third party or have their decisions reversed. Subsequent civil rights and related legislation

---

What Is the Meaning of *Meritocracy*?

... word coined by Michael Young, in his *The Rise of the Meritocracy, 1870–2033* (London: Thames & Hudson, 1958; Baltimore: Penguin Books, 1961). Referring to a governing class that was both intelligent and energetic, yet sowed the seeds of its own destruction because of its obsession with test scores and paper qualifications that eventually forced those deemed to have lesser IQs to revolt. A favorite slogan of the revolutionaries was "Beauty is achievable by all." Today meritocracy is often used to refer to any elitist system of government or education. The grisly connotation of the word's original use has been effectively forgotten.

Jay M. Shafritz, *Dictionary of Personnel Management and Labor Relations*, 2nd ed. (New York: Facts on File, Inc., 1985).

has given almost all federal employees possible grounds upon which they could appeal a dismissal action.

The removal procedures are now cumbersome and time-consuming enough for a manager that marginal employees may be tolerated where they once were not. It is frequently easier to seek additional staff than to remove those that are incompetent or nearly so. In this regard we have come full circle. A long-recognized fault of the spoils system was the creation of otherwise unnecessary positions to compensate for the inadequacies of political appointees. Public managers are still doing the same today, but now they are doing so to compensate for their merit system employees who are unproductive.

The growth of procedural inhibitions toward removals at the local level has been a similar story. Because employees who had been appointed following competitive examinations tended to be removed arbitrarily, presumably for political reasons, restrictions evolved upon the appointing officer's removal power. The first kind of restriction was typically a requirement that an employee facing removal be given a written statement of the reasons for his pending dismissal. While the employee had an opportunity to reply, she had no opportunity for appeal unless the removal was for political or religious reasons. Only then would a civil service commission have the right to review and possibly reverse the decision. As abuses of the new merit system became more common, greater restrictions came to be placed upon the appointing officer. In effect, the power to remove an employee was taken away from the appointing authority and given to the personnel agency—usually a civil service commission. The state of Illinois pioneered with this development in 1895 by requiring that employees be removed only "for cause" and providing for a formal hearing where an employee could oppose the dismissal with a defense. The policy of using the civil service commission as an appeals board for disciplinary actions was eventually incorporated into the model civil service laws of the National Civil Service League and the National Municipal League.

With this significant change the function of the civil service commission was radically altered. No longer did it serve simply to ensure that political considerations did not prevail in public employment, but it had gained the lawful right to review all of the personnel actions of management. The civil service commission with its new-found power of investigation and reinstatement had suddenly taken from management what had been its absolute prerogative—the right to fire an employee it deemed incompetent. Because of this development almost all present day disciplinary actions on the part of management are subject to a morass of administrative due process in a quasi-judicial setting. Such hearings are appropriately quasi-judicial because they are based upon a right of appeal mandated by legislation or provided for in a city or state constitution. Those hearing the appeal must take care that they conduct themselves with the detachment and deportment of the judiciary, for their decisions can be overturned by a higher court if the appellant's rights are not appropriately protected.

Reflective of the American legal tradition, government employees tend to be presumed innocent of incompetence until they are proven otherwise. Because the burden of proof is entirely upon management, disciplinary actions are seldom entered into unless documented evidence is overwhelming and only then with great trepidation, for the manager is really putting herself and all of her previous actions toward the employee in question on trial.

There is no more pressing problem in managing the public service than the increasing inability of the manager to control the work situation. According to John W. Macy, Jr., Chair of the U.S. Civil Service Commission during the administrations of President Kennedy and Johnson, "virtually every round-table discussion of problems facing public managers will quickly turn to the inability of the manager to discipline nonproductive or insubordinate employees or to dismiss those who have ceased to be productive or constitute chronic supervisory problems." It is certainly true that the legal framework exists that allows managers to dispose of incompetent and marginal employees. Nevertheless, it has long been recognized that a variety of significant factors tends to mitigate against any such action. It was observed by Mosher and Kingsley in their 1936 text that the manager "may have the ultimate power of discharge so far as the law goes, but as the record of removals shows, he is not accustomed to use it because of attendant circumstances." Listed below are eight such "attendant circumstances" of the present day.

1. It takes a tremendous amount of time to build up a case that will, in effect, stand up in court. While the organization may know that Jane Doe has, for years, been only half as productive as the other employees in her class, this has to be documented over a sustained period of time. The large amount of managerial time that has to go into building such a case is all too frequently an inhibitor of any action at all.

2. Even if this great investment of time and energy is undertaken, the eventual result is always a gamble. One never knows what mitigating circumstances the hearing officers may choose to recognize. Remember, civil service commissioners may conduct themselves as, and have the integrity of, judges; but equally like judges that are the product of a political process and subject in one fashion or another to its pressures.

3. Few things can kill an organization's morale as effectively as having within the work group an individual publicly proclaimed by management to be unworthy of her position yet lingering on for month after month after month—possibly even retaining her position after the due process battle is over. In this latter situation a management decision to initiate dismissal proceedings all over again is tantamount to persecution. The last thing that

organizations need is an incompetent martyr for other disgruntled employees to emulate. Organizational morale, like physical well-being, is always a most delicate balance. Appropriately, one does not introduce malaise unless there is relative certainty that the eventual outcome will be benign.

4. Managers, being individuals of a practical bent, frequently see the advantage of transferring, or of allowing a transfer of, a marginal employee to another segment of the organization. Experienced administrators rarely fire anybody—they merely arrange for a transfer to an outlying field office. This solves one manager's problem by pushing it upon another. Besides, a new work environment sometimes has a beneficial effect upon some employees. This process is certainly more economical from the manager's point of view than formal proceedings. Of course, if it is not possible to arrange a transfer, the next best thing is to make the employee ineffectual within your own organization yet comfortable enough so that she has no reason to complain. After all, from the manager's position, it is frequently easier to get an increased budget allocation for an additional employee than to seek to remove a wayward individual.

5. Most organizations possess a large degree of inertia, and this is especially true when it comes to the problem of removing people. Most social organisms have a decided tendency to protect their inept members. What better evidence is there of this than with performance reporting. Tough managers all too frequently turn into wimps in order to avoid the embarrassing personal situation of dealing with the poor performance of an employee. In consequence, efficiency ratings have tended to be a conspicuous failure. If and when a manager decides to take action against an employee, she is frequently faced with a number of years' worth of satisfactory ratings. In building her case against the employee she will undoubtedly have to explain why an employee who had been performing satisfactorily for so many years "suddenly" went bad.

6. One cannot ignore the unions. They exist mainly to protect the jobs and work-related prerogatives of their members. Any threat to their most basic needs—jobs for their members—will have them rattling their sabers as loudly or as discreetly as the situation warrants. Why should a manager sour her union relationships over one miscreant employee? Besides, the union has almost unlimited resources for lawyer's fees and so forth to pit against the manager's already overburdened staff and the decidedly limited talent available from the personnel office. Against such odds, why fight? Surely the salary of one less than fully productive employee is a cheap price to pay for harmonious union relations. But then what's to prevent that one from growing to be a significant portion of the total work force?

7. The dismissal of a marginal employee may do that individual excessive harm. It is one thing to fire a young man or woman who, after

The Mayor's Dilemma

Regardless of the job patronage they already control, mayors complain about civil service. Mayor White [of Boston] called for curtailing or circumventing civil service which he labeled "a detriment to effecting change quickly in an urban society." Civil servants, he explained, are unaccountable to political organizations, enabling them to remain free from the checks and balances which elected officials must cope with. Protected by law and by increasingly powerful municipal unions, they can resist changes in policy without suffering either the loss of their jobs or a cut in their salary. No corporation president could run his company, the mayors argue, with this empty shell of command over his employees: authority without power or control. Adding to their difficulties as mayor is the public belief that they do command, causing the shower of blame which inevitably rains on them when services fail to run optimally.

Martin Tolchin and Susan Tolchin, *To the Victor. . .: Political Patronage from the Clubhouse to the White House* (New York: Random House, 1971), pp. 72–73.

adjusting to the disturbance this causes in his or her life, will eventually find another position. It is another matter altogether to fire a person who has reached an age where she is neither entitled to adequate pension benefits nor even likely to gain another position of similar monetary reward. Consequently there is a great and understandable laxity toward taking action against a whole horde of middle-aged marginal performers. The organization, so it is felt, simply by retaining them for so many years incurs an obligation to them. This phenomenon could rather descriptively be termed compassionate corruption.

8. There is seldom adequate incentive for a line supervisor to be held accountable for her lack of punitive action toward deserving employees. Why should she risk creating a difficult interpersonal situation with all of her subordinates for some vague notion of the public interest? Unless there is some extraordinary pressure upon her for productivity, there is simply no incentive for her to take the hard action that is occasionally the duty of all managers. The public manager is not, after all, the proprietor of her own small business; the actions or inactions of her employees, unless they exhibit some gross misconduct, do not directly affect her own interests. Why should she be the one manager in her jurisdiction to take the waste of public funds seriously enough to take concrete action? Does it not take an individual of intense ideological conviction to act upon her beliefs when all around her indicate contrary attitudes? Before interfering with a system that tolerates marginally performing employees a reasonable person would have to be sure of the legitimacy of her actions. Precedence creates legitimacy. To upset what has evolved as the natural order of things may be socially and morally illegitimate while at the same time being legally appropriate.

All of the above factors tend to mitigate against managers undertaking disciplinary or removal actions. While state and local jurisdictions vary in their degree of protection for employees, it is reasonable to infer that whenever a strong merit system exists, procedural safeguards tend to undermine the authority of managers.

One cannot deal with the subject of procedural safeguards for public employees without delving into several value questions. Are all discipline-inhibiting safeguards really necessary? Why shouldn't managers have the absolute discretion to discharge employees for reasons other than religious or political as the original reformers envisioned? The essential question here is one common to American jurisprudence: is it more desirable to chance having one person treated unjustly or to provide for due process procedures that may allow many individuals to escape punitive sanctions? The whole thrust of the U.S. Supreme Court rulings on the procedural rights of criminal suspects has been to strengthen the procedural rights of individuals at the expense of the discretion of law enforcement agencies. Just as the job of the police officer has been made more difficult by the expansion of constitutional safeguards, the task of public managers has been made grossly more complicated by the expansion of the procedural rights of public employees. In each instance these expansions were the direct result of past abuses of discretion. Just as the theoretical foundations of the American legal system prefer to allow guilty persons to go free rather than chance the conviction of an innocent individual, American civil service merit systems at all levels of government prefer to retain their marginal and incompetent employees rather than risk doing an injustice to an individual. Yet even within this elaborate system of procedural safeguards abuses occur. But they are very minor compared to the vast amount of protection that procedural due process affords the public employee.

Those who have fought hardest for these safeguards over the years—the employees themselves, their union representatives, and the politicians who saw electoral support in the issue—tend to respond to the hamstringing of management's traditional prerogatives with the "there is no such thing as a bad apple" argument. If the organization suffers from inhibited productivity, the fault lies not in ourselves, but in our managers. Considering that most of the public management corps—the lower and middle levels—benefit from the same protective cocoon as do the rank and file, there is a thriving germ of truth in this allegation. Managers at all levels in all jurisdictions find themselves in an almost untenable position. They can neither urge their charges on to greater productive heights nor effectively impose sanctions of sufficient weight to frighten the workers into productive acts. With their backs collectively to the wall, public managers have no real choice as to action—they must learn to manage.

The evolution of public personnel practices can be organized into transition periods. The implementation of Jacksonian democracy and the advent of the reform movement are two of the more obvious phases of historical transition. Both of these previous transitions were essentially those of power—one political faction assuming office at the direct expense of another—although higher motives were invariably proclaimed. Today we are in the midst of a transition that is radically different in dimension. Because of the factors just enumerated, life tenure has been effectively achieved by the majority of civil service employees. Happily, not all employees take advantage of this, and the degree of turnover is roughly comparable to that in private industry. But generally speaking, only those comparatively few employees who have grossly violated the norms of conduct of their peer group are ever formally dismissed. This being the situation, where does it lead? Now that public managers are finding themselves increasingly "boxed in" with employees of decidedly mixed motivations and attitudes toward their work, they have no real choice but to work with what they have. With the managerial luxury of discharging a poor or marginal performer rapidly disappearing, there is

Would You Work for the Government?

Question: "In the next 20 years, where do you think a young person who _____ would do better—in business, government, in a profession such as law or medicine, or teaching?"

	Business	Govt.	Profession	Teaching	None/ Not Sure
Is a go-getter	56%	19%	13%	4%	8%
Wants to make money	47	14	31	2	6
Is well-organized and efficient	41	20	20	11	8
Gets along with people	31	20	15	25	9
Wants to lead a well-ordered life	27	14	28	20	11
Has a first-rate mind	25	20	32	13	10
Is highly creative	24	8	28	30	10
Likes to have a good time	23	18	20	13	26
Wants security	22	26	34	9	9
Has good leadership qualities	21	53	9	11	6
Is Idealistic	18	19	20	29	14
Dislikes pressures	10	16	19	21	34

Source: Reprinted from the Report of the National Commission on the Public Service (Washington D.C., 1989).

An Assessment of Government Performance

Federal Effectiveness at Different Functions

Question: How effective is the federal government at _____ ?

	Very Effective	Effective	Ineffective	Not Effective At All	Don't Know
Maintaining military defenses	19%	69%	8%	1%	2%
Cleaning up toxic and hazardous wastes	5	38	48	6	3
Regulating doctors' fees and hospital costs	3	21	56	15	4
Providing social security for retirement	10	65	20	4	2
Providing welfare for the poor	8	61	26	2	3
Providing retraining programs for workers in declining industrics	4	33	44	8	11
Providing special reading, math, and computer programs for young black children	5	27	41	6	22
Providing farm price supports to protect the income of farmers	11	41	33	6	9
Helping out American banks that have bad loans in Africa and Latin America	6	32	25	4	33
Supporting research and development in high-technology areas	12	59	15	2	11

Source: Reprinted from the *Report of the National Commission on the Public Service* (Washington, D.C., 1989).

a newfound impetus to have the managerial applications of the behavioral sciences fill this disciplinary void. Public managers feeling themselves left with nothing but bluster as a managerial tool must turn increasingly in this direction. The transition will be achieved when life tenure is no longer viewed so much as an obstacle to managerial effectiveness as an opportunity to develop each employee to his or her fullest potential.

The Volcker Commission

The chapters presented in this section have looked at some of the many abuses that can occur in civil service. They have also pointed to various efforts to combat these abuses. One of the most recent efforts has been the establishment in 1987 of the National Commission on the Public Service—better known as the Volcker Commission, named after its Chair, Paul A. Volcker. The primary charge of the commission was to address and respond to the "quiet crisis" in government, a crisis marked by government's poor image, government's inability to attract and retain high-quality employees, and the inability of government "to respond effectively to the needs and aspirations of the American people." In short, the task of the Volcker Commission has been to "rebuild the public service."

In order to meet this goal, the commission has proposed several recommendations or courses of action to be taken by the Congress, the president, educational institutions, and public servants (see box). Although it is too soon to determine how effective the commission's efforts have been, it is certainly being hailed as a "catalyst" for change in the federal civil service.

The Volcker Commission's Recommendations for "Rebuilding the Public Service"

First, Presidents, their chief lieutenants, and Congress must articulate early and often the necessary and honorable role that public servants play in the democratic process, at the same time making clear they will demand the highest standards of ethics and performance possible from those who hold the public trust.

Second, cabinet officers and agency heads should be given greater flexibility to administer their organizations, including greater freedom to hire and fire personnel, provided there are appropriate review procedures within the Administration and oversight from Congress.

Third, the President should highlight the important role of the Office of Personnel Management (OPM) by establishing and maintaining contact with its Director and

(continued)

The Volcker Commission's Recommendations *(continued)*

by ensuring participation by the Director in cabinet level discussions on human resource management issues.

Fourth, the growth in recent years in the number of presidential appointees, whether those subject to Senate confirmation, noncareer senior executives, or personal and confidential assistants, should be curtailed.

Fifth, the President and Congress must ensure that federal managers receive the added training they will need to perform effectively.

Sixth, the nation should recognize the importance of civic education as a part of social studies and history in the nation's primary and secondary school curricula.

Seventh, America should take advantage of the natural idealism of its youth by expanding and encouraging national volunteer service.

Eighth, the President and Congress should establish a Presidential Public Service Scholarship Program targeted to 1,000 college or college-bound students each year, with careful attention to the recruitment of minority students.

Ninth, the President should work with Congress to give high priority to restoring the depleted purchasing power of executive, judicial, and legislative salaries.

Tenth, if Congress is unable to act on its own salaries, the Commission recommends that the President make separate recommendations for judges and top level executives and that the Congress promptly act upon them.

Eleventh, the President and the Congress should give a higher budget priority to civil service pay in the General Schedule pay system.

Twelfth, the President and Congress should establish a permanent independent advisory council, composed of members from the public and private sector, both to monitor the ongoing state of the public service and to make such recommendations for improvements as they think desirable.

Source: Reprinted from the *Report of the National Commission on the Public Service* (Washington, D.C., 1989).

Bibliography

Ban, Carolyn and Norma M. Riccucci, eds. *Public Personnel Management: Current Concerns, Future Challenges*, White Plains, N.Y.: Longman Press, 1991.

Barnard, Chester I. *The Functions of the Executive*. Cambridge, Mass.: Harvard University Press, 1938.

Elazar, Daniel J. *American Federalism: A View from the States*, 2nd ed. New York: Crowell, 1972.

Fish, Carl Russell. *The Civil Service and the Patronage*. New York: Russell & Russell, 1904, 1963.

Gouldner, Alvin W. "Cosmopolitans and Locals: Towards an Analysis of Latent Social Roles, I," *Administrative Science Quarterly*, 2 (December 1957).

Grimes, Andrew J., and Philip K. Berger. "Cosmopolitan-Local: Evaluation of a Construct," *Administrative Science Quarterly*, 15 (December 1970).

Ingraham, Patricia W., and David H. Rosenbloom. *The State of Merit in the Federal Government*. Prepared for the National Commission on the Public Service, Washington, D.C., 1990.

Kaufman, Herbert. *Administrative Feedback in Monitoring Subordinates' Behavior*. Washington, D.C.: Brookings Institution, 1973.

————. "Emerging Conflicts in the Doctrines of Public Administration," *American Political Science Review*, 50 (December 1956).

Macy, John W. Jr. *Public Service: The Human Side of Government*. New York: Harper & Row, 1971.

Meriam, Lewis. *Personnel Administration in the Federal Government*. Washington, D.C.: Brookings Institution, 1937.

Mosher, Frederick C. *Democracy and the Public Service*, 2nd ed. New York: Oxford University Press, 1982.

Mosher, William E., and J. Donald Kingsley. *Public Personnel Administration*. New York: Harper & Bros., 1936.

Report of the National Commission on the Public Service (Volcker Commission). Washington, D.C., 1989.

Ritzer, George, and Harrison M. Trice. *An Occupation in Conflict: A Study of the Personnel Manager*. Ithaca, N.Y.: New York State School of Industrial and Labor Relations, Cornell University, 1969.

Rosenbloom, David H. *Public Administration: Understanding Management, Politics, and Law in the Public Sector*, 2nd ed. New York: Random House, 1989.

Savas, D. E., and Sigmund S. Ginsburg. "The Civil Service—a Meritless System?" *The Public Interest*, 32 (Summer 1973).

Shafritz, Jay M. "The Cancer Eroding Public Personnel Professionalism," *Public Personnel Management*, 3 (November-December 1974).

Shafritz, Jay M. "Political Culture: The Determinant of Merit System Viability," *Public Personnel Management*, 3 (November–December 1974).

————. *Public Personnel Management: The Heritage of Civil Service Reform*. New York: Praeger, 1975.

Sharkansky, Ira. "The Utility of Elazer's Political Culture: A Research Note," *Polity*, 2 (Fall 1969).

Thompson, Frank J. *Classics of Public Personnel Policy*, 2nd ed. Pacific Grove, CA: Brooks/Cole Publishing, 1990.

————. *Personnel Policy in the City: The Politics of Jobs in Oakland*. Berkeley: University of California Press, 1975.

Vaughn, Robert G. *The Spoiled System: A Call for Civil Service Reform*, New York: Charterhouse, 1975.

White House Personnel Office. "Malek Manual." In U.S. Senate, Select Committee on Presidential Campaign Activities, Executive Session Hearings, Watergate and Related Activities: Use of Incumbency—Responsiveness Program, Book 19, 93rd Cong., 2nd sess. Washington, D.C.: U.S. Government Printing Office, 1974.

Wilson, James Q. *Varieties of Police Behavior: The Management of Law and Order in Eight Communities*. Cambridge, Mass.: Harvard University Press, 1968.

Wilson, Woodrow. "The Study of Administration," *Political Science Quarterly*, 2 (June 1887).

Part II
POSITION MANAGEMENT

4
Human Resources Planning

Prologue: Work Force 2000 and the "Endangered" Civil Servant

When governments look back at the 1980s, they will remember a variety of new political factors and economic conditions that they had not faced before. From a personnel standpoint, up until 1980, federal, state, and local governments experienced some form of growth, sometimes rapid, sometimes slow, but growth nonetheless. The 1980s will surely be remembered as the decade that replaced the growth concept with privatization, productivity enhancement, expenditure and revenue limitation initiatives (a la Proposition 13), automatic deficit reduction, retrenchment, reductions in force (rifs), and furloughs and other modes of cutback management concepts.

But from a human resources planning perspective, the most significant event may well have been the publication in 1987 of a modest little volume from the Hudson Institute titled *Workforce 2000: Work and Workers for the 21st Century*. This research report dared to suggest that the ample labor markets that organizations and especially governments had relied upon for decades were coming to an end. It also predicted that unless American policy makers took active steps to address new challenges in technology, international competition, and social demography, America's premier position in the world's top economic rankings was in jeopardy. The bottom line was even more direct—without a major reform of the policies and institutions that govern the workplace, the work force needed for the future would not be there.

The report, *Workforce 2000*, is an illustration of the challenge facing public sector human resources planning. It addresses trends in both supply (the quantity and quality of the work force) and demand (the educational and technological skill requirements of jobs) in overall dimensions. Organizations—public, nonprofit, and private—must then extrapolate from these trends to determine how competitive they are at present and need to be in the future to capture their "fair share" of qualified workers. The consequences are immense.

To get a sense of what *Workforce 2000* projects, a short summary of the most critical demographic assumptions about workers and jobs is in order.

On workers, *Workforce 2000* states:

1. The population and the work force will grow more slowly than at any time since the 1930's.
2. The average age of the population and the work force will rise, and the pool of young workers entering the labor market will shrink.
3. More women will enter the work force.
4. Minorities will be a larger share of new entrants into the work force.
5. Immigrants will represent the largest share of the increase in the population and the work force since the first World War.

On jobs, *Workforce 2000* states:

1. The fastest-growing jobs will be in professional, technical, and sales fields requiring the highest education and skill levels.
2. Of the fastest-growing job categories, all but one (service occupations) require more than the median level of education for all jobs.
3. New jobs in service industries will demand much higher skill levels than the jobs today.

What does this mean for the basic federal, state, or local government agency? It means that they will be increasingly hard pressed to compete in future a labor markets (see Tables 4.1 and 4.2). Consider the plight of one organization recently highlighted in a major newspaper. Long regarded as a model employer, this organization has had to make major concessions to fill its shift and weekend work requirements. Not only did it have to offer more flexible work scheduling plans with premium pay for overtime shifts, it had to launch major training programs in both technical job skills and language skills to bring its work force up to speed. To stay competitive in a very tight national labor market, many of its branches also offered educational tuition assistance programs and child care arrangements. (Chapter 16 provides more information on the importance of child care benefits to the future work force.) This is not the Social Security Administration, the military, the Department of Motor Vehicles, or your local public hospital. The organization is MacDonalds. If this corporation has problems, imagine the plight of public sector organizations.

Table 4.1. The Projected Growth of Professional and Management-Related Positions in the Federal Government

Occupational category	Share of federal employment (%)	
	1986	2000
Management related	14.1	15.2
Engineers, architects, surveyors	5.2	6.0
Natural and computer scientists	5.2	5.4
Social scientists	0.8	0.8
Lawyers and judges	0.9	1.0
Teachers, librarians, counselors	1.1	1.1
Health care	4.1	4.2
Technicians	8.9	10.0
Marketing and sales	0.5	0.5
Administrative support	25.1	21.4
Service	6.2	6.3
Construction trades	2.2	2.3
Mechanics, installers, repairers	6.2	6.6
Precision production	2.0	2.0
Plant and system	0.4	0.5
Helpers and laborers	3.1	2.9

Source: Adapted from *Civil Service 2000* (Washington, D.C.: U.S. Office of Personnel Management, 1988).

Public sector organizations face even larger problems because of their rigid compensation systems and lagging pay rates which are, in many parts of the country, simply noncompetitive. Today's public sector human resources planning issues obviously overlap into compensation, recruitment, and training areas, and as such, will be touched on in later chapters. But make no mistake about the message of *Workforce 2000*. The civil servant of the past is very likely to be an endangered species if current work force policies are not altered and true attention given to work force planning issues. The Office of Personnel Management (OPM) commissioned its own version of "Work Force 2000," aptly titled *Civil Service 2000*. A quote from this report nicely sums up why human resources planning is so critical to public personnel management:

> The Federal government faces a slowly emerging crisis of competence. For years, many Federal agencies have been able to hire and retain highly-educated, highly-skilled workforces, even though their wages, incentives, and working conditions

Table 4.2. The Math and Language Skills Require for Federal Jobs by the Year 2000

Occupation	Mean math skill rating[a]	Mean language skill rating[b]	Employed (1986)	New jobs (1986–2000)	Rate of growth
Engineers, architects, and surveyors	5.1	5.0	110,253	19,489	17.68
Natural and computer scientists	5.7	5.6	109,440	6,920	6.32
Social scientists	4.5	5.1	17,022	521	3.06
Teachers, librarians, and counselors	3.3	4.5	23,063	71	0.31
Health care	4.4	5.1	86,187	4,746	5.51
Technicians	3.9	4.0	187,412	17,608	9.40
Marketing and sales	3.3	3.6	10,960	624	5.69
Administrative support	2.7	2.9	530,032	(68,200)	−12.87
Service	2.2	2.6	131,057	5,649	4.31
Construction trades	2.8	2.9	45,889	2,552	5.56
Mechanics, installers, and repairers	2.5	2.6	130,743	11,851	9.06
Precision production	2.2	2.3	43,012	178	0.41
Plant and system	2.7	2.7	9,224	405	4.39
Helpers and laborers	1.1	1.2	64,838	(2,750)	−4.24

[a]Jobs with a math skill rating of 4 or above require the use of algebra, statistics, or trigonometry. A job rated 1 or below requires only the ability to add or subtract two-digit numbers.

[b]Jobs with a language skill rating of 5 or above require employees to read literature, scientific/technical journals, financial reports, or legal documents. Jobs rated below 1 require employees to read simple messages, follow oral instructions, and fill out requisitions or work orders.

Source: Adapted from *Civil Service 2000* (Washington, D.C.: U.S. Office of Personnel Management, 1988).

have not been fully competitive with those offered by private employers. But as labor markets become tighter during the early 1990's, hiring qualified workers will become much more difficult. Unless steps are taken now to address the problems, the average qualifications and competence of many segments of the Federal workforce will deteriorate, perhaps so much as to impair the ability of some agencies to function.

The Environment for Human Resources Planning

All organizations face considerable problems regarding the use of their human resources. In public organizations, which are service- and information-oriented, employees tend to be the most significant resource. Personnel-related costs generally constitute between 50 and 70 percent or more of an operating budget, and so the need for planning in this area is particularly acute. The primary incentive for such planning is directly related to two factors: the amount of change or turnover in personnel and the levels of expense that personnel involve as a majority resource item. Consider the statistics in Table 4.3 for the federal government, which illustrate the numbers of accessions (i.e., new or renewed hirings of employees) and separations (i.e., the numbers of resigned, discharged, retired, or laid-off employees).

Obviously, 1980 was an anomaly—an election year marking a transition from one administration to another of a different party, which accounts for the extremely large jump in separation rates. Overall, the numbers seem pretty stable. In fact, the size of the federal government throughout the 1980s was very stable. The separation data presented in Table 4.3 are also somewhat deceiving in that sizable parts of the separations each year come from the expirations of temporary appointments and temporary employment resignations. Add in the fact that nearly 40 percent of the separations are in the postal service, and a rather different picture of the current federal work force

Table 4.3. Number of Accessions and Separations in the Federal Government, Excluding Postal Service, 1970–1987 (in thousands)

Year	Total civilian employees	Total accessions	Total separations (%)	Total resignations (%)
1970	2645.0	727.0	796.7 (30.1)	334.4 (12.6)
1975	2741.0	564.2	588.9 (21.5)	212.9 (7.8)
1980	2772.0	995.2	1004.0 (36.2)	227.7 (8.2)
1985	2902.0	692.1	585.6 (20.2)	238.6 (8.2)
1986	2895.0	598.7	557.5 (19.3)	208.7 (7.2)
1987	2972.0	637.6	637.6 (21.5)	206.1 (6.9)

Source: U.S. Statistical Abstracts, Washington, D.C.: U.S. Department of Commerce, 1989.

begins to emerge, one with a resignation rate of less than 10 percent. But what really counts is to recognize that change in the composition and character of a work force emerges gradually. This means that good human resources planning should be able to spot and track trends involving supply and demand in advance.

But unfortunately, it also means that there are limits to the solutions. Consider the plight of many state universities across the country. For several years now, personnel offices in universities have been warning administrators about the looming retirement of a significant proportion of college teachers, especially in the social sciences. Estimates are that over 40 percent of current teaching faculty will be retiring before 1995. The current supply of Ph.D.'s is not going to be able to provide replacements; there simply aren't that many potential graduates in the pipeline. This is a good example of the dilemma of good human resources planning—it can identify the problem, but changing policy and institutional actions is another matter.

Organizations normally view their personnel resources as a unique category of investment that requires considerable effort, time, and cost to recruit, select, evaluate, train, and staff effectively. Generally, more highly trained and experienced employees will achieve greater levels of productivity; so the development of (meaning the investment of resources in) employees seems a rational long-range decision. But the actual investment in terms of imparted skills and maturity of judgment remains inside the individual, who may or may not stay within the organization. The individual employee's attitude about the organization's investment or lack of investment in his or her development will naturally affect present levels of both productivity and commitment to the organization. As expensive as personnel is, the cost of turnover, replacement, and redevelopment adds on even more.

What does it cost to replace an employee? Of course, the answer varies with the organization, but Wayne Cascio in his book *Costing Human Resources* has developed a format complete with formulas to calculate the costs of turnover. Cascio calculates that about 12 to 15 percent of the compensation levels being recruited against. Since there's little reason to doubt that the higher the salary level being recruited for, the higher the proportionate cost of filling the vacacy would be, this cost formula is a rather disturbing validation of what personnel managers have known intuitively for years. It is expensive to replace personnel—and the expense is even greater if the wrong choice is made.

Although the need for human resources planning seems obvious, translating that need into a specific planning program is a more difficult matter. The same questions that plague planning in general must be addressed here. Who should do the planning for the organization—top management or

Measuring the Costs of Personnel Replacement

Separation costs	Replacement costs	Training costs
1 Exit interview costs	5 Advertising and recruiting communication costs	11 Informational and orientation literature
2 Administrative costs to separate employee	6 Preemployment and administrative costs	12 Formal training and orientation costs
3 Separation pay	7 Entrance interview costs	13 On-the-job instruction (breaking in)
4 Unemployment taxes (if applicable)	8 Staff and organizational meetings and reviews	14 Other job training programs (technology, other job skills)
	9 Medical examinations, security clearances, references file checks	
	10 Administrative costs and functions to place individual into employee status—payroll, fringe, and all insurance coverages	

Source: Adapted in part from Wayne F. Cascio, *Costing Human Resources* (Boston: Kent, 1982).

lower operating levels? Should planning be long-range or short-range, formal or informal, proactive or reactive, "blue sky" or realistic? How often should plans be updated? What planning techniques should be used? How and by whom will the planning be evaluated?

Different answers to these questions do not mean that any one planning approach will be better than another. This depends upon the size, complexity, and needs of the organization and the amount of uncertainty involved. However, there is a difference in techniques between what might be termed strategic planning (or planning that *integrates* management strategies based on some anticipation of needs) and adaptive learning (the formation of management strategies based on an *incremental* approach of observing and evaluating dissatisfaction with current performance). While both strategic planning and adaptive learning can lead to change, only a strategic planning approach can be categorized as a *planned change approach*. Effective human resources planning as a strategic planning approach must involve a systematic process of analyzing external conditions and organizational needs *and* delineating management strategies and tactics to make responsive changes.

This is not an easy assignment. The arrival of a new decade affords personnel managers a unique perspective to reflect on the increasing difficulty for human resources planning. And unlike the assumption of the 1980s that all the challenges were on the demand side (new technology, new organizational arrangements), the 1990s will present major challenges on the supply side. In one sense, the ample labor markets of the 1970s and 1980s negated the seriousness of human resources planning. In the tight labor markets of the 1990s, in which public sector jurisdictions will be increasingly hardpressed to compete, public sector organizations will have to take human resources planning very seriously indeed.

Human Resources Planning in "Hard Times"

Governments at all levels have faced budget constraints and fiscal shortages that have seemed at times to be quite unpredictable. Personnel offices have added new scenarios (and vocabulary) to their human resources planning efforts, such as "planning for retrenchment," "downsizing the organization through attrition," and "cutback management" using "furloughs, rifs, and other personnel budget reduction techniques." What does all this mean? It means simply that if the budget gets cut or if there's an unexpected decline in revenues, governments begin to scramble to find ways to cut expenditures to balance their budgets. And since personnel costs are such a large portion of the budget, they are by necessity part of that process.

The late Charles Levine, who is generally credited with coining the term *cutback management*, addressed the importance of human resources planning for public sector organizations facing budget declines. In his view, long-term personnel forecasting was a vital first management strategy that could have major impacts on reducing the effects of budget decline and the costs of uncertainty. This was especially important since budgetary uncertainty has a major negative effect on employee morale and negative attitudes toward the organization. Unfortunately, the methods he prescribed are little more than information-gathering tactics, useful in the short run to outline options for stressed decision makers, but far less effective in evaluating the impacts on the organization's work force quality and productivity.

More useful to human resources planning is a typology of cutback management strategies and their resulting impacts on the work force Levine developed with George Wolohojian. The typology (see Figure 4.1) looks at human resources impacts in terms of both the degree of uncertainty (in this case, how likely the situation is to be restored to normal during the next budget cycle) and the extent of the decline (how severely the budget is going to be cut).

In strategy I, as Figure 4.1 shows, the agency assumes a modest budget cut and a quick return to normal. It practices a *stretching*, keeping all its personnel, deferring optional personnel expenditures such as travel and training, and possibly instituting a hiring freeze, which then uses nonreplacement and attrition to lower personnel costs. The work force remains hopeful. In strategy II, the severity of the budget cut is much higher but hopes for some return to normal remain. A *prioritizing* strategy is taken up, protecting certain programs and staffing levels tied to those programs, but scaling down others. The organization may try to use the scaling down efforts as a budgetary ploy to raise public outcries (e.g., eliminating summer recreation programs or closing libraries on weekends). But if it honestly prioritizes its programs and the budget cuts are not lessened, some employees will ultimately respond by attempting to switch to protected programs, leaving at the first possible opportunity, or protesting and lobbying for change through the union or other professional organizations. The latter strategy is partially intended as an additional strategy to bring public pressure to restore the budget cuts.

The third and fourth strategies assume that some type of change is inevitable. In these cases, political uncertainty is low and the agency has to

EXTENT OF BUDGET CUTBACK

U N C E R T A I N T Y	I. Stretching/searching	II. Prioritizing/protecting
	III. Muddling/selective withdrawal	IV. Slashing/retrenchment

Figure 4.1. A typology for cutback management strategies. *Source* Charles H. Levine and George Wolohojian. "Retrenchment and Human Resources Management: Combatting the Discount Effects of Uncertainty," in Hays and Kearney, eds., *Public Personnel Administration: Problems and Prospects* (Englewood Cliffs, N.J.: Prentice-Hall, 1983).

face the music that whatever changes are made are unlikely to be restored. In strategy III, *selective withdrawal*, the agency faces a mild cutback. It cautiously chooses low-priority programs and abandons them. It also places a high priority on productivity measures emphasizing efficiency. Programs facing this approach often place more emphasis on increasing outputs by cutting back on quality levels, using more technology and or less costly personnel resources (paraprofessionals or volunteers). Work force impacts are several. Some individuals in withdrawn programs are transferred. Many not wishing to change over either leave or concentrate their efforts on finding other jobs. One is reminded of the story of a regional office of a major federal agency that was "reorganizing" in response to some gradual but permanent cuts in its budget. The office instituted a forty-hour, four-day work week schedule, which was a tremendous boost for morale. In the words of the director, "now the employees had a free day to look for other jobs."

Finally, there is the worst case scenario—strategy IV, *retrenchment*. The budget cuts are severe and they seem permanent. In some examples, agencies actually fear for their continued existence. The cutback management approach is to reorganize and streamline the priority programs, eliminate the programs with the least political support, and make major cuts in the personnel budget via rifs or furloughs. Ironically, when an agency goes under this type of siege mentality, personnel often cling to the organization as tightly as possible. In part this is because organizations rarely get into a strategy IV immediately. In most cases, agencies will go through various aspects of stretching, prioritizing, and even withdrawal well before they come to total retrenchment. This usually means that the most mobile employees will have already left. Those that are left are the most committed or the most incapable of leaving for whatever reason. While morale and anxiety levels may not be great, those that see an organization through this strategy are likely to be there until the very end.

The typology presented in Figure 4.1 is useful in explaining why human resources planning has difficulty in responding to resource scarcity and organizational decline. The most obvious service it can perform would be to forecast the effects of various program cutbacks on staffing levels and potential attrition rates. It is central to evaluating what the separation and retirement rates will be in given years and how they will affect personnel budgets. But the true lesson for human resources planning is the political uncertainty variable. As long as political uncertainty is high, agency heads will be optimistic and think incrementally. Everything will be righted next year, and there's no reason to make any gloomy forecasts for an unwanted future. But human resources planning can be instrumental in planning for both the long-range future and the short-range consequences of cutback management. It is important that personnel management accept the importance of human resources planning and understand what it can do to help prepare for "Work Force 2000" or next year's budget dilemma.

A Historical Overview of Human Resources Planning

A longstanding problem with the term *human resources planning* or *work force planning*, is definitional. Simply put, it means different things to different people. There is no universally accepted definition of what work force planning is or consensus on what activities should be associated with it. Organizations claiming that they do "work force planning" appear to use a wide variety of methods to approach their own unique problems.

Although work force planning seems to emulate a formalized strategy for response to current and anticipated problems, many of its definitions bear little resemblance to each other, either in terms of substance or methodology. James Walker defines human resources planning as "the process of analyzing an organization's human resources needs under changing conditions and developing the activities necessary to satisfy these needs." Such a definition sees human resources planning as more than a simple personnel function but one that involves the entire management process. This is vastly different from the older concepts of labor force or work force planning. It is important, however, that one realize that the confusion over what earlier versions of work force planning were and what human resources planning is hides a very significant development—in fact, a true evolution in substance and methodology.

Historically, work force planning was, and of course still remains, an integral part of numerous public and private programs whose objective is to affect the labor market in order to improve the employment status and welfare of individuals (see Table 4.4). These goals of the Full Employment Act of 1946 are reflected in training and development programs for African Americans, the aging, the disabled, and other disadvantaged groups. The programs are primarily designed to further the use, development, and retention of individuals as members of the labor force. As such, the programs have a macro focus in that they deal with the aggregate labor force of the nation or region.

Labor force planning efforts undertaken by organizations also reflect the concern for balancing supply and demand; that is, at the organizational level, planning involves managing the organization's assets. However, at the "economy" level, planning involves managing the nation's assets. The distinction is apt—planning in both cases involves projecting and managing the supply and demand of human resources, only at different levels.

But what do these planning levels specifically involve? Both are concerned with future demand aspects; that is, what the requirements for the future

Table 4.4. The Evolution of Human Resources Planning

Periods and emphasis	Conditions and events	Techniques introduced or emphasized
1900–1940 Work engineering Hourly personnel	Search for efficiency in production Labor-intensive, unskilled Modern work organization, division of labor, professional management Union movement	Task measurement/ simplification Testing for employee selection Skills training Payroll budgeting and control Labor relations Welfare programs
1940–1960 Productivity and continuity Hourly/managerial	Talent shortage due to war Emphasis on productivity for wartime and postwar demand Increased mechanization, automation Job satisfaction/productivity studies	Organization charting Management backup charting for replacements University executive development programs Work group effectiveness and leadership style changes Attitude surveys, human relations programs
1960s Balancing supply and demand Managerial, professional, and technical employees	Sputnik-stimulated demand for high-talent personnel Age 30–40 gap; shortage of scientists and engineers Rapid organizational expansion and diversification Multinational expansion Rapid technological change, risking obsolescence Civil Rights Act Student/youth activism Vietnam War	Intense college recruitment Fast-track programs; career ladders Skills inventories Matrix organizations Assessment centers Disadvantaged/hardcore programs Formalized forecasting activity Experiments with mathematical models Job enrichment projects Performance goal setting
1970s Affirmative action	Court- and government-imposed goals and timetables New legislation (OSHA, age discrimination, ERISA, privacy, etc.)	Models used in setting AA goals Computer-based information systems Human resource planning functions established

(continued)

Table 4.4. *(continued)*

Periods and emphasis	Conditions and events	Techniques introduced or emphasized
Salaried employees, particularly the protected classes	Concern for retention, utilization of present staff; cost control "Women's liberation" movement "Discovery" of midlife crisis Energy crisis	Human resource analysis related to business planning and budgeting Assessment of human resource costs and benefits Early retirement and outplacement Quality of worklife and productivity programs "Zero-base" budgeting Broadening of managerial development (multifunctional)
1980s Work and career management All employees	Consolidation of federal law governing personnel practices and administration Aging of the work force Competition among young managers for responsibility Accelerated unionization of professionals and managers Expansion of adult education	Job-related criteria for personnel decisions (hires, promotions, pay, terminations, etc.) Individual career planning Work analysis a tool for designing jobs, forecasting needs, organization, etc. Flexible work schedules Direct use of computer systems; development of flexible models
1990s and beyond 2000 Individual autonomy within large-scale work organizations All employees	Energy, food, other resource shortages Limited work available; increased leisure time Stress on family, privacy, personal independence Extended life expectancy, improved health Legislation governing pensions, health insurance, and lifetime income security	Reshaping of work environments and customs Work sharing; reduced work week Extended vacations, sabbaticals Job matching/career guidance by government and employers New careers in emerging fields of communications, health, energy sciences, etc.

Source: Adapted from James W. Walker, *Human Resources Planning* (New York: McGraw-Hill, 1980), p. 6–7.

work force will be. At the macro level this means projecting what skills will be in demand to service the economy. At the micro level, this entails projecting specific requirements for the work force of the organization, or what quantities and qualities of personnel will be needed to carry out organizational objectives.

Both levels are concerned also with future supply aspects. At the macro level this means that projections must be made on what the national labor force will consist of in terms of future skills, both surpluses and deficits. For the micro level, the organization must forecast what its future work force will consist of as well as evaluate its competitive position in order to decide what quantities and qualities of personnel it can encourage to enter the organization as replacements.

Although there is a certain symmetry in terms of the supply-and-demand aspects for labor force planning at both levels, the methodologies involved in the processes are quite dissimilar. The objectives involved are also different in that an organization's work force policy may be efficient when viewed from its own perspective, but quite dysfunctional to the national economy. For example, an organization may fire X number of employees (whose skills is in surplus nationally) and hire X number of new employees (whose skill is in deficit nationally). A macro-oriented work force decision might have called for retraining some of the old employees about to be displaced. However, from the organization's vantage point, the training cost and the delay involved may have rendered that option inefficient.

Work Force Planning

The late 1960s and early 1970s saw numerous advancements in human resources planning at the organizational level. The planning tools available to management multiplied considerably. Major technical advancements in computers, information systems theory, and modeling and simulation methodologies were applied in such a way to the problems of supply and demand that a new second generation of work force planning was created (see Figure 4.2). These relate to either of two planning elements:

Organizational requirements planning—The projection and analysis by organizational management of the categories and quantities of job skills needed to implement organizational programs.

Work force planning—The projection and analysis of the quantities of each category of current workers' skills that will be available to the organization in future periods.

Each element has, of course, numerous components and processes. Work force skills planning, probably the more advanced element in terms of the

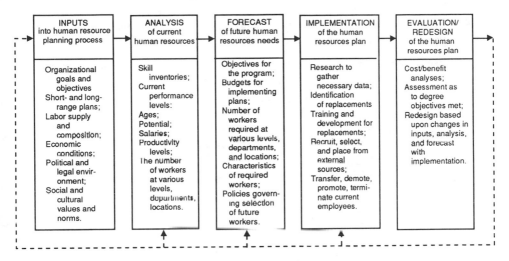

Figure 4.2. The human resources planning process. *Source*: Adapted from Richard W. Beatty and Craig Schneier, *Personnel Administration*, Reading, Mass Addison-Wesley Publishing Company, 1982.

present state of the art, involves techniques that focus on three separate exercises:

1. *Attrition projections*—Forecasting the impact of changes in the quantity of specific categories within the work force because of separations
2. *Adjustment projections*—Forecasting the impact of changes in the current work force involving those employees who change some aspect of their status (functional skills, preference, employment categories, grade levels, and so on)
3. *Current recruitment projections*—Forecasting the impact of current recruitment efforts and special policy programs (such as African-American and Latino recruitment, and lateral entries)

The logic of work force skills planning requires that the above components reflect all of the possibilities of the status changes that an employee can undergo in the organization. In essence, there are four such possibilities of situational change:

1. Employees can enter the organization (new hires).
2. Employees may leave the organization (separation).
3. Employees can change their grade level (be advanced or demoted).

4. Employees can change their skill characteristics (change job skills, change positions, change employment status, and so on).

The use of some type of model combining the forecasts for both requirements and skills planning would provide the basic components for constructing an organizational plan for recruitment purposes.

Methodologies for determining attrition, adjustments, and recruitment projections are integral parts of the overall planning effort involved in producing some type of work force plan that indicates what the future work force will look like given current assumptions. Work force planning also recognized that the time dimension would vary the focus of various forecasting efforts. Forecasts were expected to vary between short-range periods (usually less than two years) and intermediate and long-range periods (from two to five years and beyond).

Organizational requirements planning is a far more abstract process in that the needs of future programs are obviously more difficult to predict and are more subjective. Despite the advent of some fairly sophisticated modeling and forecasting techniques, the available methodologies for this are not universally accepted or employed. In the private sector, forecasts for organizational needs are usually based on sales and market forecasts by various unit managers. Since control is generally more internalized, decentralized, and less dependent upon outside review channels, these forecasts have a better chance of being realistic. Of course, the growth assumptions that dominated the thinking on work force planning have also changed in the last decade. In the new era of "downsizing," private sector organizations have had to readjust many of their forecasts. Organizations in the public sector have even less control over their future plans, and the likelihood of their being able to specify the equivalent of a market forecast and have it accepted for three to five years into the future is slim.

Forecasting continuous work force demand or future program requirements is an especially difficult process in the public sector milieu. A common approach seeks to link such forecasting to the budgeting cycle; but the inherent instability of public sector budgets usually prevents this approach from being effective. The adoption of Delphi techniques and decision analysis forecasting represent processes that attempt to overcome this problem. In essence, these processes purport to "quality" and weigh the various forecasts being made in order to increase the probability that the most accurate projections are given appropriate emphasis by the organization. These techniques are characteristic of the second generation of work force planning. Justifications for this genre generally focus on its supply-and-demand balancing aspect, the purpose being to ensure that the organization has the right types of people in the right positions at the right times.

Second-generational work force planning techniques have been widely employed in the public sector, albeit with varying success. Back in the 1970s, Lee and Lucianouic conducted a research survey of 775 state and local governments, federal agencies, and private corporations in order to identify the progress made to date in establishing such planning systems. The survey sought information on three types of work force planning efforts:

1. Computerized information systems to provide summary data by occupation on employment, labor turnover, job vacancies, and wage category
2. Methodologies to make short- and long-range projections of employment levels, additional work force requirements, training needs, and separations
3. Action programs that offer management alternative procedures to relieve some work force problems and help others from occurring

Survey results indicated that even in this early period of human resources planning evolution, over one-third of the respondents had developed or were using one of the three specified work force planning system components, and nearly half were in the process of developing or planning to develop additional tools. This trend does not, however, belie the fact that less than 5 percent of the respondents indicated that they had developed a reasonably sophisticated work force planning system. Of those work force planning systems developed or developed in part, 80 percent made use of computers and 60 percent were using or developing projection methodologies. Such projections were primarily concerned with future levels of total employment, retirements, additional work force requirements (replacements plus growth), employment in selected occupations, and training needs. Techniques employed ranged from the relatively simple (based on past trends and "best judgment"), used by two-thirds of those making forecasts, to sophisticated simulation models employing Delphi techniques, Markov chain models, and regression analysis.

With the exception of the Department of Defense, most of the systems described were relatively new, the average system's age being two and a half years. In the 1980s, the expected technological "life span" of most computerized systems was well under five years, while in the 1990s, system life spans of under two to three years will be more the norm. This means that forecasting systems can be upgraded or even totally replaced to reflect new technological developments. Although this gives public sector organizations more access to work force forecasting systems, it does not mean that such systems will be universally adopted. The larger an organization is (by employment size), the more likely it will have some kind of work force planning system. Clearly this is changing, as *Workforce 2000* has demonstrated. A better rule would be that the more dependent the budget is on personnel and highly qualified workskills, the more imperative a proactive human resources planning process is for any organization.

The final problem with second generation work force planning has been the arrival of this new "era of resource scarcity," discussed earlier in this chapter. In retrospect, the 1970s will come to be viewed as the good old days for governmental organizations in terms of sustained growth and stability. The 1980s ushered in contracting out, privatization, and budgetary retrenchment, with jurisdictions cutting back programs and laying off employees. Even the Defense Department, the big winner in the 1980s in terms of growth, faces a spectacular reduction in its own new era of *glasnost*, democratization of Eastern Europe, and global disarmament. If the so-called peace dividend is realized, the Defense Department is projecting a massive cut in military personnel, both domestic and abroad.

Obviously, when political and economic circumstances change as dramatically as international events have in the last two or three years, the entire forecasting emphasis must change. Basic planning assumptions have changed significantly. Most public sector organizations expect little real growth in overall employee population. Many, in fact, foresee long-range multiyear shifts and in some cases reductions in the number of personnel working in government. There will be fewer blue-collar jobs, but increases in service workloads. *Civil Service 2000* predicts 157,000 new white-collar jobs and 107,000 fewer blue-collar federal jobs.

As a result, the work force planning focus is shifting to internal change and reprogramming. It is focusing on occupational shifts, such as predicting the impacts on technology and automation on the work force. Automation is a good example of how work force planning is adjusting. Most public sector organizations have gone to computers and automation to be more productive and to hold the line on having to hire new workers. The biggest effects are expected in administrative, clerical, and office services. Using the federal government as an example, the effects thus far have been quite modest. In fact, there has been a 4 percent increase since 1970 in these occupational categories. But clerical levels have declined by just over 10 percent in the last ten years. Of course, computer specialists have doubled over the same time frame.

Work force planning systems can be an important information source to personnel managers. As a system, it requires a variety of ongoing judgments at various managerial levels as to what anticipated needs (either pluses or minuses) will be (organizational requirements planning). In addition, the system contains components that provide for current accountability and projection of changes to the current work force. This is a system that can answer the following questions, which are particularly important as we move into the 21st century:

1. What is the current status of the organizational work force (e.g., how many persons, and with what type of skills will leave or transfer)?

2. Where will current plans take the organization X years hence—what will this mean in terms of work force requirements (e.g., what are the impacts of technology and changes in occupational needs caused by changing workloads)?
3. Where will the current work force be in terms of skills X years hence given current policies (e.g., is the aging of the work force being considered)?
4. What changes must be made now to bring the future work force into balance with anticipated needs (e.g., what will the recruitment and training priorities be)?
5. What will be the impact of interim or short-range personnel policies (such as rifs, furloughs, and vacancy and wage freeze policies) on long-range supply and retention of personnel?

At this point, it is necessary to focus with more detail on the supply-and-demand aspects of human resources planning.

Forecasting Human Resources Supply

A variety of techniques have been employed in attempting to forecast what a current organizational work force will resemble X years hence. The key to such exercises has been to predict the turnover rate for the organization; that is, the numbers and kinds of employees who will leave the organization for various reasons, whether voluntary retirement, medical or disability retirement, death, leave without pay, or resignation. The initial techniques used reflected the fact that for the most part the turnover that was available to organizations was not very comprehensive. Typically, various modes of trend analysis would be utilized to calculate three-to-five year averages in the number of separations by category. This average could then be recalculated each year and would form the projection for the coming year. (In forecasting methodology, this updating of the mean is known as establishing a "moving average.") Still, this method is much like calculating tomorrow's weather based solely on the weather of the previous week. Unless the organization is a very stable one, the method is not very satisfactory.

Methods of statistical analysis offer numerous ways to go beyond the limited applicability of the historical approach. For example, simple five-year means can be replaced with a weighted mean based on the different sizes of the work force categories; a trend line analysis might be used when the more recent years are especially significant in calculating expected attrition.

Considerable research and analysis has also been expended in pursuit of other methods to forecast turnover. If the variables that influenced turnover could be identified, it has been argued, then forecasting might be relatively simple to predict. For example, one type of analysis would attempt to focus on motivational factors and the organizational environment and project the impact of these influences—whether positive or negative—on the number of resignations, retirements, and so forth that could be expected. Historical ranges would be constructed for past years for each turnover category, and depending upon the organization's analysis of its expected environmental factors, a forecast could be made of how many employees would probably leave.

The most common method of identifying the causal factors of turnover has been some type of exit interview. Such interviews attempt to discover the reasons for quitting or leaving at that particular time. But several problems can be encountered, thus rendering this approach for forecasting turnover fruitless. First, employees do not often relate their real reasons for leaving, particularly if they are concerned about future references. There is no incentive for them to be frank or honest since they are terminating their association with the organization. Second and more important, however, is that the number of possible factors for leaving can be so numerous and involved that meaningful analysis is virtually hopeless. For example, a simplistic psychological test for workers' preferences developed by Tomkins and Horn identified 655 basic factors and combinations of factors that were potential influences on the decision to leave a job.

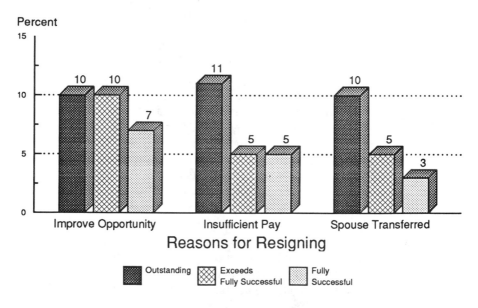

Figure 4.3.   Most important reasons for resigning, according to performance rating. *Note*: Reasons shown are ones with more noteworthy comparisons. *Source*: *Why Are Employees Leaving the Federal Government?* (MSPB, 1990), p. 15.

Of course, there are exceptions where the use of exit interviews or in this case exit surveys can provide important information, especially for public personnel policy. Recently, the U.S. Merit Systems Protection Board (MSPB) developed an exit survey that was sent to over 2,800 federal employees who had separated from government in 1989. This broad-based survey attempted to identify what factors most influenced the decision to leave (see Figures 4.3 and 4.4). The MSPB listed forty-six different factors and asked the survey respondents to rank those that were most critical in making their decision. Not surprisingly, given all the press about the adverse effects of the federal pay gap (it purportedly now lags private sector compensation rates by over 25 percent), compensation and advancement reasons were top ranked (28 percent of surveys). But most survey respondents cited multiple reasons for leaving and the MSPB's report concluded that different groups of federal employees (varying by age, grade, sex, location, and performance rating) had different rankings of reasons, the policy implication thus being that corrective strategies to reduce turnover must focus specifically on each category of employee to be most effective.

For distinct organizations, the recognition that turnover or attrition rates should be based on the characteristics of the work force itself represented

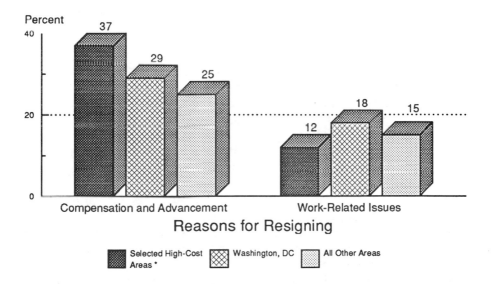

Figure 4.4. Most important reasons for resigning, according to location of work. *Note*: Reasons shown are ones with the more noteworthy comparisons. *Source*: Why Are Employees Leaving the Federal Government? (MSPB, 1990), p. 15.
*New York, Boston, Los Angeles, San Francisco.

Table 4.5. A Transitional Matrix for Estimating Internal Movement of Human Resources

Time Period 1 (by job category)		A	B	C	D	E	F	G	H	I	J	Out	Total (%)
						Time Period 2 (5 years later)							
						Job category							
Vice president	A											1.00	1.00
Department head	B	1.00											1.00
Division head	C		.11	.83								.06	1.00
District head	D			.03	.97								1.00
Unit head	E				.10	.87	.03						1.00
Technician II	F					.05	.90					.05	1.00
Technician I	G						.35	.65					1.00
Secretary	H								.85			.15	1.00
Clerk II	I								.10	.65	.05	.20	1.00
Clerk I	J									.10	.50	.40	1.00
% of total organizational recruitment								.18	.62		.20		1.00

Note: In percentages. A five-year time interval is employed.
Source: Adapted from Richard W. Beatty and Craig Schneier, *Personnel Administration* (Reading, Mass.: Addison-Wesley Publishing Company, 1982).

a major step in the development of work force planning skills. This concept means that depending on such characteristics as sex, age, and length of service, the choices made by individuals will exhibit probabilistic frequency patterns. The logic of this approach is based in part on the fact that retirements and resignations constitute the primary withdrawal categories from the work force. In addition, most resignations will occur early (with short time of service) and retirements will be blocked out over a very specific time span (the years of retirement eligibility).

The forecast process involves the use of matrices for various work categories correlating age by length of time or service. Employees in the retirement zone and the resignation zones can be aggregated in their various age categories. The total matrix can then be used to calculate projections for deaths and disability retirements. The accuracy of these matrices in predicting turnover is based on transitional probability factors. A transitional probability factor is a linear programming concept that essentially illustrates movement from one time period to another (see Table 4.5). In this case, it is the probability of a change going from a past period to a new period. In order to project the turnover for any given cell of the matrix, the number of employees in that cell is multiplied by the transitional probability factor. For example, if the organization has 100 people reaching their first year of eligibility (and historically one-fourth of the employees retire as soon as they are eligible), then multiply the number of new eligibles (100) by the transitional probability factor (.25) in order to obtain the retirement projections for that cell of the matrix—in this case, 25. To work effectively, this type of projection analysis requires that transitional probability factors be calculated for the various categories of attrition based on the past experience of the organization. Of course, some sort of data base on separation actions must be maintained on a cumulative basis to ensure accurate forecasts. For a more detailed analysis, one should examine the OPM's classic work by Clark and Thurston on this subject—*Planning Your Staffing Needs*.

Forecasting Organizational Demands

A very different set of problems is encountered in predicting organizational requirements over time. The problem with demand forecasting is that the emphasis is usually on the incremental portion of change. Forecasting consists of making predictions based upon the observed regularities of the past. The supply models just discussed certainly use this premise as their base, but forecasting must also allow for certain changes, whether technological, organizational, or policy-oriented, which disrupt the progression of the observable regularity of the past. Such disruptions are the primary concern of demand forecasting. If demand forecasting is to be accurate, qualitative information must somehow be obtained from those closest to the decision. Supply forecasting, on the other hand, has gained, with the advent of computerized personnel information systems, a much more accessible and quantifiable data base.

One approach to forecasting organizational demand for human resources is to incorporate the human resources concept into organizational planning. Essentially, as the organization's long-range planning and budgetary processes occur, they must include specific references to future personnel requirements. It remains to be determined how an organization can integrate information from management at the top policy, operational, and personnel levels (if, indeed, all levels are involved) into one coherent human resources plan. Delphi techniques are the most impressive methodologies developed to date in terms of piecing together various opinions to arrive at a future consensus. Delphi techniques involve asking various individuals or groups for their opinions and weighting their responses with some factor that considers their relative importance or influence on the situation, their expertise, their past forecasting accuracy, and so on. When all the opinions are weighted and aggregated, a calculation can be obtained as to the likely probability of a future situation.

The Delphi Technique: A Hypothetical Example

The figure below presents a hypothetical decision tree designed to predict the probability of an increase in staffing for an agency that is considering a new training office. The question of the new staff seems to hinge on whether or not the organization's budget is to be cut. In the example, the group of organizational influentials consists of 20 individuals who "vote" on one of four outcomes. But the final outcome shows that 16 of 20 voters believe the training office will be established anyway. This Delphi exercise concludes that the probability of new training being established is .8—and the organization would do well to begin plans for staffing this new office.

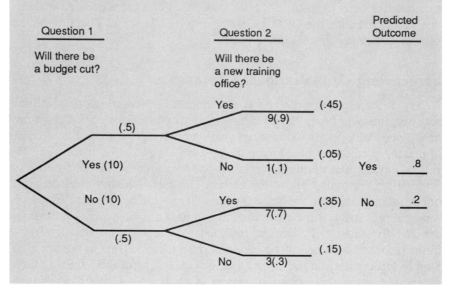

The Delphi technique can also reroute results through the same individuals or groups as a further check, this time weighting responses with their intensity of belief.

The OPM's decision analysis forecasting technique is an excellent application of the Delphi concept. Developed in the 1970s specifically for human resources planning at the executive level, it utilizes decision analysis network theory to set up planning considerations in the form of decision trees. The technique develops staffing requirements by:

1. "Decomposing" each human resources planning problem into relevant factors
2. Quantifying subjective preferences and probability judgments for each problem factor

3. Combining the available data plus these quantified judgments into a table
    of predictions

The Delphi technique's great strength is that it outlines future outcomes. This
is in itself a major development in forecasting organizational demand for human
resources. The organization is thus able to recognize alternatives and plan
out each option in terms of human resources requirements. This technique
recognizes the real difficulty in charting out the future in times of great uncertainty. Given current environments, this is by no means a revelation. The
best that can be hoped for is that possible paths can be charted out in advance
as an aid to rational decision making, thus increasing the possibility that our
future choices will be informed ones.

New conceptual advances in work force planning will mean that while
current planning techniques involved in predicting future work force requirements and skill levels are important, present practice simply does not
go far enough. The present concept can be expaned by bringing planning
methodology to the various strategies that an organization must employ if
it is to manage the interaction of its future needs and resources. The term
human resources planning, as discussed earlier, has been advanced as the
title for this concept—a third generation of planning, following labor force
and work force planning (see Figure 4.5). Human resources planning
recognizes one further aspect of interaction—the attitudes and aspirations of
the individuals occupying the positions being analyzed.

This means that if an organization has a current problem or anticipates
a future problem in meeting its requirements, it should consider a variety
of options to meet those needs. For example, if an agency had identified via
its organizational work force planning exercise that five energy-science
specialists would be required to deal with problems relating to new energy
sources over the next two years, the alternative routes to consider in filling
these needs can be costed out using human resources planning: X number
of such skilled individuals could be reassigned from less important work being performed elsewhere if indeed the skills were present; X number could
be trained via special academic training programs or cross-functional professional work programs, if time permitted; or X number of specialists could
be hired from the outside as new employees.

The organization could choose one or a combination of any of one above
strategies. The point is that human resources planning recognizes the in-
terdependence of each of these options and should project an actual cost and
the political feasibility of each. Any feasibility measure must include consideration of the impact on the individuals associated with any option. Since
any given option would naturally impact on other aspects of the organization's work force, each involves and requires for effective implementation

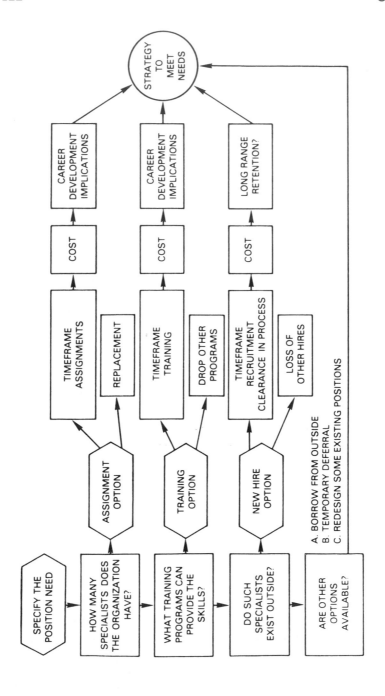

Figure 4.5. The human resources planning approach.

the realization of human resources management. In effect, a comprehensive human resources plan maps out the options available to the organization to meet the needs for energy specialists. Likewise, in dire economic straits, it can map out the options and impacts of retrenchment or reprogramming alternatives.

Human resources planning also prefigures a further development in personnel management. As the various programs and processes of personnel become increasingly interactive and complex, human resources planning may emerge as the only integrated systems approach capable of effecting rational decision making. Even now, personnel processes can be viewed as so interactive that in terms of an impact flow chart, they resemble a maze. The advent of more participative management styles and greater concern for the rights of individuals in the organization may make this development an imperative.

Logic suggests that human resources planning will become an even more significant decision-making process in the future. However, unless work force planning as a discipline continues to grow, it may fall into the same disrepute as economic forecasting did in the early 1970s and political forecasting is being revisited by today. To avoid this fate, work force planning will have to develop in two directions: establishing new planning methodologies and beginning new types of planning efforts. Given the current environment of scarce resources, advancement in methodologies does not seem as promising as expanding the scope of work force planning activities.

The major advances in work force planning in the future will more than likely be in new directions. Applications of human resources planning techniques are imminent in several areas: linking interactive functions of personnel management, considering individual reactions and preferences, charting new forms of organizations, and developing new types of information.

For some time, the complexity and interrelatedness of personnel decisions has been recognized. Placements, training, intake selections, promotions, and separations all impact on each other and present alternative routes for organizations to meet human resources needs. Human resources planning approaches in the future will be increasingly concerned with mapping and costing out these various components within the personnel management process.

Perhaps the most sensitive area of concern for human resources planning will be in considering the individual. That organizations can no longer get by without recognizing an individual's needs and desires is becoming obvious. Human resources planning will need to consider the preferences of individual employees and to examine the impact of personnel management decisions on employees. James W. Walker in *Human Resources Planning* considers this area so critical that career development is incorporated as a major dimension in his model of human resources planning.

Human resources planning techniques must also be concerned with rapidly changing organizational structures. As computer technology and increased communications capabilities make possible more decentralized working environments and as project teams become more commonplace, human resources planning may be applied in whole new areas. For starters, there may be major shifts in the content of work and the skills required. For example, there have been some interesting projections on how computerized knowledge systems will change both professional work and even the nature of professional judgment. Over time professionals will spend far less time memorizing, gathering information, analyzing, and reasoning and far more time in the areas of intuition and perception. It promises to be a fascinating future, one that goes far beyond the placement emphasis in human resources planning, which considers planned assignment of individuals in terms of the specific needs of various projects to ensure effective use of employees and effective project operations.

Finally, human resources planning will confront new types of information needs. Organzations are going to want to plan for and assess such employee characteristics as personality type, interpersonal skill, and other aptitudes. (Obviously, organizations will need to be vigilant of the possibility of discrimination when characteristics such as "personality type" are employed.) Data formats for such information are not yet available, but the need is there. Organizations are no longer going to be content with simply filling vacancies with available candidates; rather, they may want a personality type X, skills orientation type Y, and supervisory-aptitude type Z manager to "match" a specific position environment.

Work Force Quality in the Public Sector: A Framework for Evaluating Human Resources Planning

These new directions might change the entire character of human resources planning, perhaps evolving into a fourth generation, but the rationale behind human resources planning is obvious. Public sector organizations in particular must be increasingly concerned about the capabilities of their human resources. This is part of the message of *Workforce 2000*, but it goes beyond even this. Behind the human resources planning process is a new and very dramatic expression of these concerns—the movement toward *work force quality assessment* (see Figure 4.6).

Perhaps the best way to comprehend this movement thrust is to examine a quote from a 1989 joint MSPB-OPM conference on work force quality. The preface to the report asks:

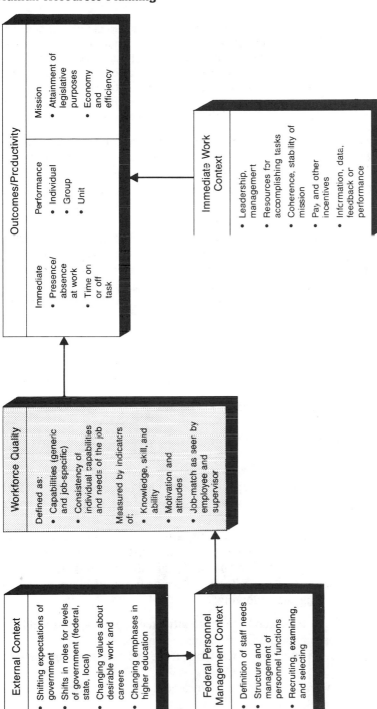

Figure 4.6. Work force quality and its larger context. *Source:* U.S. General Accounting Office, *Federal Workforce: A Framework for Studying Its Quality Overtime* (Washington, D.C.: USGAO, 1988), p. 17.

How do the qualifications of Federal employees compare to their counterparts in the state and local governments or in the private sector? Has the quality of the Federal workforce remained stable over the last 10 to 20 years or has it increased or decreased? Do we have well qualified employees in some occupations and geographic areas and poorly qualified employees in others? How has workforce quality affected the services Government provides? Should we be concerned about the current quality of the Federal workforce?

The resounding answer to these questions was largely a "we don't know." Work force quality represents the evaluation counterpoint to human resources planning, but with much more of a qualitative focus. How should or could a personnel manager respond to an agency director, city manager, or legislative committee if asked, "Do you know and how do you know whether our current work force quality is better or worse?"

That question, more or less, is asked by MSPB in its periodic survey of merit principles; about 10,000 federal employees are surveyed. Managers in the 1986 and 1989 surveys responded as follows to whether they felt the quality of applicants for professional and administrative jobs at entry, middle, and senior levels had changed as follows (the percentages vary across levels in the question):

	Became Worse (%)	Stayed the same (%)	Improved (%)
1986	35–36	33–40	24–31
1989	41–52	34–42	14–23

While the data are certainly not conclusive, the trend is hardly positive. More managers across more categories see a decline offsetting an improvement in quality during the 1980s.

The U.S. General Accounting Office issued a 1988 report noting that no suitable definitions or research methodologies exist to measure work force quality. They have proposed their own study design that would sample various occupational groups within the federal government and develop indicators capable of determining the following:

Entering work force—How good are those attracted to federal jobs and how do they compare with others hired elsewhere?

Current work force—How good is the work force and how has that changed over time?

Separations from work force—Is the government losing its best employees?

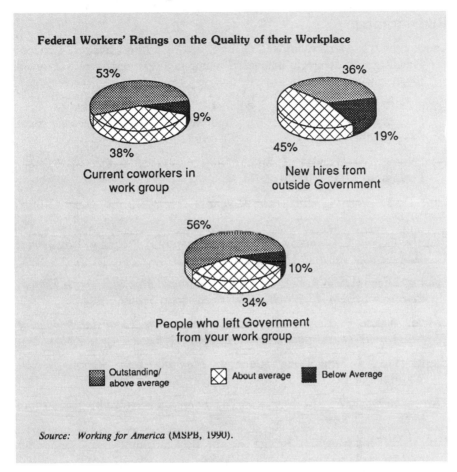

Federal Workers' Ratings on the Quality of their Workplace

53%
9%
38%
Current coworkers in
work group

36%
19%
45%
New hires from
outside Government

56%
10%
34%
People who left Government
from your work group

Outstanding/
above average   About average   Below Average

Source: Working for America (MSPB, 1990).

Incidentally, MSPB and OPM have jointly started a federal task force on work force quality designed to recommend policy actions and research methodologies to evaluate work force quality. What the work force quality debate in the 1990s will represent is the last part of the message of *Workforce 2000*. In previous eras, economic and political quality aspects were taken for granted. Quantity was the major focus of work force planning efforts focusing on supply and demand calculations. In the coming era of tight labor supplies, smaller work forces, and dynamic workplace and technology factors, quality will redefine quantity, and this will be the new framework that will most appropriately be used to assess human resources planning.

Bibliography

Baird, Lloyd, I. Meshoulam, and G. DeGive. "Meshing Human Resources Planning with Strategic Business Planning," *Personnel*, vol. 60, no. 5 (September–October 1983).

Davey, Bruce W. and Larry S. Jacobson. *Computerizing Human Resource Management*. Alexandria, Va.: International Personnel Management Association, 1987.

Bartholomew, D. J. and A. R. Smith. *Manpower and Management Science*. Lexington, Mass.: Heath, 1971.

Bell, D. J. *Planning Corporate Manpower*. London: Longman Group, 1974.

Blakely, Robert T. "Markov Models and Manpower Planning," *Industrial Management Review*, 11, no. 2 (Winter 1970).

Burack, Elmer H. and Robert D. Smith. *Personnel Management: A Human Resource System Approach*. New York: John Wiley, 1982.

Cascio, Wayne F. *Costing Human Resources: The Financial Impact of Behavior in Organizations*. Boston: Kent, 1982.

Clark, Harry L. and Dona Thurston. *Planning Your Staffing Needs*. Washington, D.C.: U.S. Government Printing Office, 1977.

Clowes, Kenneth W. *The Impact of Computers on Managers*. Ann Arbor, Mich.: UMI Research Press, 1982.

Coil, Ann. "Job Matching Brings Out the Best in Employees," *Personnel Journal*, vol. 63, no. 1 (January 1984).

DeSanto, John F. "Workforce Planning and Corporate Strategy," *Personnel Administrator*, vol. 28, no. 10 (October 1983).

Gillespie, Jackson E., Wayne E. Leininger, and Harvey Kahalas. "A Human Resource Planning and Valuation Model," *Academy of Management Journal*, 19, no. 4 (December 1976).

Greer, Charles R. and Daniel L. Armstrong. "Human Resource Forecasting and Planning: A State of the Art Investigation," Faculty working paper, Oklahoma State University, Stillwater, 1979.

Heneman, Herbert G. III and Marcus Sandver. "Markov Analysis in Human Resource Administration: Applications and Limitations," *Academy of Management Review*, 2, no. 4 (October 1977).

Hyde, Albert C. and Jay M. Shafritz. "HRIS: Introduction to Tomorrow's System for Managing Human Resources," *Public Personnel Management* (March–April 1977).

Hyde, Albert C. and Torrey S. Whitman. "Workforce Planning: The State of the Art," in *The Public Personnel World*, edited by Jay M. Shafritz. Chicago: IPMA, 1977.

Johnston, William B. *Workforce 2000: Work and Workers for the 21st Century*. Indianapolis: the Hudson Institute, 1987.

Lee, Robert and William M. Lucianouic. "Personnel Management Information Systems for State and Local Government," *Public Personnel Management* (March/April 1975).

Leigh, David R. "Business Planning is People Planning," *Personnel Journal*, vol. 63, no. 5 (May 1984).

Levine, Charles H. and George Wolohojian. "Retrenchment and Human Resources Management: Combatting the Discount Effects of Uncertainty," in *Public Personnel Administration: Problems and Prospects*, Stephen Hays and Richard Kearney, eds. Englewood Cliffs, N.J.: Prentice-Hall, 1983.

Miller, James R. "Revitalization: The Most Difficult of All Strategies," *Human Resource Management*, vol. 23, no. 3 (Fall 1984).

Mills, D. Quinn. "Human Resources in the 1980's," *Harvard Business Review*, 51, no. 4 (July–August 1970).

Morrison, Malcolm H. "Retirement and Human Resource Planning for the Aging Work Force," *Personnel Administrator*, vol. 29, no. 6 (June 1984).

Naff, Katherine and Paul Vin Rijn, "The Next Generation: Why They Are Leaving," *The Bureaucrat* (Summer 1990).

Niehaus, Richard J. *Computer-assisted Human Resources Planning*. New York: Wiley-Interscience, 1979.

Nkomo, Stella M. "The Theory and Practice of HR Planning: The Gap Still Remains," *Personnel Administrator* (August 1986).

Odiorne, George S. "Human Resources Strategies for the Nineties," *Personnel*, vol. 61, no. 6 (November–December 1984).

Perry, Lee T. "Key Human Resource Strategies in an Organizational Downturn," *Human Resource Management*, vol. 23, no. 1 (Spring 1984).

Rich, Wilbur C. "Career Paths for Public Managers: Upward but Narrow," *Personnel*, vol. 61, no. 4 (July–August 1984).

Rowland, Kenndrith M. and Scott L. Summers. "Human Resources Planning: A Second Look," *Personnel Administrator*, vol. 26, no. 12 (December 1981).

Schein, Edgar H. "Increasing Organizational Effectiveness through Better Human Resources Planning and Development," *Sloan Management Review* (Fall 1977).

Ulschack, Francis. *Human Resource Development: The Theory and Practice of Need Assessment*. Reston, Va.: Reston, 1983.

Uyar, Kivilcim M. "Markov Chain Forecasts of Employee Replacement Needs," *Industrial Relations*, 11, no. 1, (February 1972).

U.S. Congress, Congressional Budget Office. *Employee Turnover in the Federal Government*, 1986.

U.S. Congress, Office of Technology Assessment. *Technology and the American Economic Transition*, 1988.

U.S. Congress, Office of Technology Assessment. *Technology and the American Economic Transition*, 1988.

U.S. General Accounting Office, *Federal Workforce: A Framework for Studying Its Quality Over Time*, 1988.

U.S. Merit Systems Protection Board & U.S. Office of Personnel Management. *A Report on the Conference on Workforce Quality Assessment*, 1989.

U.S. Merit Systems Protection Board. *Why Are Employees Leaving the Federal Government?* 1990.

U.S. Merit Systems Protection Board. *Who is Leaving the Federal Government?* 1989.

U.S. Office of Personnel Management. *Civil Service 2000*, 1988.

Walker, Alfred. *HRIS Development*. New York: Van Nostrand, 1982.

Walker, James W. "Evaluating the Practical Effectiveness of Human Resource Planning Applications," *Human Resource Management*, 13, no. 1 (Spring 1974).

Walker, James W. *Human Resources Planning*. New York: McGraw-Hill, 1980.

5

Classification and Compensation

Prologue: Classification and Compensation's Next Generation—the China Lake and Pacer Share Demonstration Projects?

Perhaps no aspect of public personnel administration has been more criticized than classification and compensation policies and procedures. Developed from principles originating from scientific management at the turn of the century, classification was designed to bring structure and regulation into organizations that had few management control systems and little understanding of division of work and job responsibilities. Times have changed, but managers lament that for the most part public sector classification and compensation systems have not. In a new era requiring flexibility, responsiveness, teamwork, and innovative personnel policies, managers have too often felt that classification and compensation systems are more a part of the problem than of the solution.

When the 1978 Civil Service Reform Act was put together, the reformers envisioned a series of special projects to develop classification and compensation innovations. Title VI authorized demonstration projects in which existing civil service rules would be waived and new systems developed and evaluated. In 1980 one of the most ambitious demonstration projects ever undertaken was begun at the Naval Weapons Center in China Lake, California, and the Naval Ocean Systems Center in San Diego. In the mid-1980s, a parallel effort was initiated at the Air Force's McClellan Air Force Base in a union environment.

What makes these particular demonstration projects so different is their reliance on a unique and more flexible classification system that aggregated separate grade levels into broader categories called pay bands. Both demonstration projects then used a totally different compensation scheme. In the case of China Lake, a performance appraisal system tied compensation to performance levels. At McClellan (called Pacer Share) individual performance appraisals were to be replaced completely with a productivity gainsharing system.

Why were these demonstrations so radical? The answer is in what they were both rejecting—the federal job classification system. To understand how the current classification system works one has to see the total complexity that the system is trying to manage. On one side, there is the General Schedule (GS) system which defines nearly 450 different white-collar occupations into eighteen grades or compensation levels. On the other side stands the federal wage system (FWS) which divides blue-collar work into nearly 350 occupations with fifteen grade levels. Organizational managers have to use the "system" to place people into their work roles; they write job descriptions for new hires that are reviewed and classified in terms of grade level before an authorization to fill the position can be given.

The same system is confronted when work roles and duties change over time. The position must be classified if the supervisor wants to change the work roles, assignment, or the compensation levels for individuals in the organization. Obviously, managers are going to complain if there is extensive paperwork (there is), if there are delays (usually), and if they feel that classifiers are trying to tell them how to run or structure their organization (whether this is true or not, this impression is inevitable). In an era of centralization, stability, and prescribed work arrangements, the classification system was viable. In current organizational climates characterized by decentralization, rapid change, and discretionary work arrangements, managers are going to view classification systems as excessively rigid, narrow, overspecialized, inefficient, and too time-consuming.

The advantage of pay banding comes from combining grade levels and simplifying occupational categories. In fact, pay banding is not an original idea developed just for the demonstration projects. In a 1969 report, *Job Evaluation and Ranking in the Federal Government*, the idea of grade reduction was proposed as a solution to problems of rigidity and arbitrariness. It was felt that fewer overall grades with broader within-grade levels would provide more flexibility and authority for managers. Using the China Lake project as an example, the following steps were taken:

1. Five career paths were created covering separate major occupational groups, assuring that employees in comparable jobs would get comparable pay evaluations.

2. Each career path was divided into pay bands that combined at least two or more GS grades, giving each pay band a salary range of at least 50 percent (by comparison, the maximum range within a single GS grade is less than 30 percent).
3. Finally, individuals are paid at least the minimum pay rate in their pay band with increases tied to either performance levels or some other type of incentive plan.

Does pay banding work? Is this the next generation of classification and compensation? Every demonstration project authorized under Title VI requires a systematic evaluation. The Office of Personnel Management (OPM) itself has its own evaluation unit, the Office of Systems Innovation and Simplification (OSIS), which has prepared major studies of both China Lake and McClellan. In the more recent case of McClellan, numerous difficulties, including budget shortfalls and unexpected employee and union configurations have delayed major assessments on this important project, but early results are very promising. However, ample evaluations have been conducted on China Lake that reflect on the promise and pitfalls of pay banding and the development of performance-based pay systems. The General Accounting Office (GAO) has even conducted a major study of the Navy demonstration projects.

In the case of China Lake, the evaluations conclude that revised personnel practices that rely on pay banding for classification, appraisal, and pay are workable. However, both OPM and GAO advised caution in drawing general conclusions because of other mitigating factors and external events. Initially OPM noted that overall salary costs increased 6 percent more for the demonstration sites than for the control sites. Not surprisingly, attitudinal surveys showed higher pay satisfaction among most employees at the demonstration sites and a greater sense of "connectedness between pay and performance." A later OPM study has shown that pay banding at China Lake does not have a dissimilar effect on salary costs as pay levels at the control sites have caught up to demonstration project levels.

This question about increased salary costs is important. Obviously, any experiment would have to be viewed more favorably by participants if overall salary levels simply increased. The intent behind the demonstration projects is to prove it is budget-neutral and that it can either work without increasing costs or produce benefits that outweigh the costs. Probably most of the federal personnel community believes that pay banding will increase overall salary costs over time. As the U.S. Merit Systems Protection Board (MSPB) noted in its 1989 review of *OPM's Classification and Qualification Systems*:

> Over a longer time span, the Board is still inclined to believe that pay banding will increase overall salary costs, all other things being equal. Of course, even

if pay banding does increase costs, it may still be a valuable enhancement to the classification system.

For all the promise, pay banding and a new generation of classification and compensation simplification is far from being a reality. In addition to determining the cost and budget impacts, there are other problems relating to pay comparability and performance appraisal. Critics are concerned that the drive to simplification will hinder comparisons between specific jobs, making salary surveys more complex and blurring distinctions about job values within organizations. Others are worried about the increased pressure on performance appraisal practices. Pay banding shifts the classification focus from specific positions to more emphasis on an individual's performance within a broader pay band as determined by the manager. Given the less than distinguished history of performance appraisal practices in government, some wonder as MSPB questioned whether ". . . Government's appraisal tools and processes are up to the demands of a system using broad pay bands"? Of course, the counterargument is that the above freedom, flexibility, and increased managerial discretion is precisely the goal of this potential innovation that links classification and compensation systems.

The Origins of Position Classification

In the beginning, salaries of public employees had been individually determined by legislative statute or by departmental administrators. Consequently, the first modern position classification plans were intended to remedy conditions of excessive political and personal favoritism in determining the duties and pay of public employees. It wasn't until 1902 that the federal government began to give serious consideration to the establishment of a classification program. In its annual report, the U.S. Civil Service Commission began to urge that positions be classified "on the basis of duties performed and to make compensation uniform for work of the same kind." Although Presidents Theodore Roosevelt and Taft were openly sympathetic to the installation of such a program, the Congress was not so inclined until 1912, when it authorized the Civil Service Commission to establish a division (later bureau) of efficiency to develop a system of efficiency ratings on the premise that standard salaries should be adopted for similar kinds of work.

Although the federal government had ambiguous feelings toward position classification during this time period, there was considerable reform activity at the state and local levels. In 1912 Chicago became the first jurisdiction to implement a position classification program. Later in the same year, Illinois was the first state to do so. Within the next two decades position classification plans were implemented by many of the largest state and local jurisdictions and certainly by all the progressive ones.

The Language of Position Classification

Job Evaluation. A broad term meaning any approach, method, or process that distinguishes among jobs for the purpose of establishing rates of pay.

Job Analysis. The process of gathering and assessing facts about jobs in order to determine their proper classification. Any of several techniques may be used for job analysis so long as the technique is objective and accurately identifies and measures all significant aspects of jobs. The results of a thorough job analysis provide input into recruitment, selection, and training programs in addition to the classification process.

Factors. These are aspects of a job such as nature of supervision received or exercised, guidelines available, complexity of the work, impact of decisions, relationships with others, mental demands and working conditions. These dimensions of a job are used for purposes of evaluation.

Factors are used in both "whole job" and factor point approaches to position classification. The "whole job" approach, however, does not define each factor and degree in advance nor does it use numerical points to weight each factor. In contrast, factor point systems evaluate each factor separately and give each one a numerical value according to how strongly the factor is represented in the job. The points for all of the factors are added to arrive at the total amount for the job, which determines its classification.

Position. Any combination of duties and responsibilities, assigned by competent authority, to be performed by one person. A position may be full or part-time, temporary or permanent, filled or vacant; it is distinguished from an employee who may at any time be assigned to it.

Positions are fundamental units of classification just as they are the smallest elements within the organization structure. The emphasis on the position as the unit of evaluation is a significant concept. It focuses attention on what is done rather than on who performs it and thus avoids the subjective judgments that are inevitably associated with evaluating people. The concept also underscores another fundamental of position classification—that management ultimately controls the classification of positions by approving the assignment of specific duties and responsibilities to be performed.

Job. Any combination of duties and responsibilities to be performed by one or more employees that is identical in all significant respects so that a single descriptive word or title can be used to identify the work and employees can be readily transferred from one position to another without noticeable interruption of performance. Examples include the jobs of trash collectors, hoseman, voucher clerk, urban planner, etc., all of which may be performed by one or more employees.

Class. A "class" is a grouping of positions for which the duties, responsibilities and qualification requirements and conditions of employment are sufficiently alike to justify the same treatment with respect to pay, selection, and other personnel processes. At times, the terms "jobs" and "class" may be used interchangeably through "class" is a broader concept, normally encompassing more than one job.

(continued)

Classes generally are defined as broadly as is feasible so long as the test of similarity in treatment is met. This contributes to efficient and cost effective management by reducing the number of categories for which it is necessary to separately recruit, examine, certify, train and establish pay levels. Nevertheless, there are always cases where a narrowly defined class must be established for a few or even a single position because different personnel procedures must be used.

Class Series. Class series can be likened to occupational career ladders. They usually begin with an entry level which contains positions to be filled by persons with the basic preparation necessary to enter the occupation. Beyond the entry level, class series ordinarily progress through commonly identified levels in the field of work in this fashion:

> Experienced level—jobs that are typically performed by persons who have acquired a good knowledge of the field and are able to perform a wide range of tasks typical of the occupation; frequently termed the "journeyman" level.

> Advanced level—positions usually performed only by persons with considerable experience who are able to handle the most difficult and complex work in the field; frequently termed the "expert" level.

> Supervisory and administrative levels as necessary.

Class series indicate the normal lines of promotion within a field of work. By dividing the field into commonly identified levels they permit the recruitment and induction into the service of persons at commonly identified stages in their career development from outside the service. Hence, the formation of class series requires a good knowledge of the common patterns of career development that characterize occupations.

Occupational Group. This represents the largest grouping of occupations (classes) that can be feasibly related for purposes of recruitment, selection, transfer, promotion and training. It also provides a fundamental category for the application of compensation policies.

The position, class, class series, and occupational group are the basic categories of a system of position classification. Together, they comprise a classification plan which is an orderly grouping of all positions in the organization according to kind of work and level of difficulty and responsibility.

U.S. Office of Personnel Management, *Position Classification: A Guide for City and County Managers* (Washington, D.C.: U.S. Government Printing Office, November 1979), pp. 3–5.

In 1919, the Congress created the Congressional Joint Commission on Reclassification of Salaries. The commission's report, issued in 1920, announced that "equal pay for equal work as a standard for employment does not prevail in the U.S. Civil Service." (See Chapter 8 on comparable worth for a discussion of this concept in a different context.) The commission maintained that it was the lack of a comprehensive position classification plan that caused so many gross inequities in pay and concomitant problems of organizational structure, morale, excessive turnover, and inefficiency. Because the commission was mandated to propose remedies for the problems it encountered, the commission's staff developed a comprehensive classification system that evaluated positions according to duties, qualifications, and responsibilities. The basic principles were codified in the Classification Act of 1923, which set up the method for job standardization, drew up grade levels and salary levels for each grade, created five series to group occupational categories, and established the Personnel Classification Board (abolished in 1932 and transferred to the Civil Service Commission) as the central classifying authority. The 1923 act was a major precedent or foundation for practically all position classification systems at the state, local and national levels. The principle that were promulgated were very much reflective of the scientific management movement, which was so influential at that time; so it is hardly surprising that their implied view of the individual worker is that of a human interchangeable machine part.

The principles established in 1920 were as follows:

1. That *positions* and *not individuals* should be classified.
2. That the duties and responsibilities pertaining to a position constitute the outstanding characteristics that distinguish it from, or mark its similarity to, other positions.
3. That qualifications in respect to the education, experience, knowledge, and skill necessary for the performance of certain duties are determined by the nature of those duties. Therefore, the qualifications for a position are important factors in the determination of the classification of the position.
4. That the individual characteristics of an employee occupying a position should have no bearing on the classification of the position.
5. That persons holding positions in the same class should be considered equally qualified for any other position in that class.

By the Second World War, there were substantial new pressures on the federal classification system. The sheer increase in numbers of positions and resulting deluge of classification actions that were needed as government grew made the idea of one central classifying authority impossible. Increasing numbers of white-collar jobs were presenting problems in classifying for a system that was predominantly based on blue-collar jobs. The result was a major revision of the system in the Classification Act of 1949. The 1949 act created the GS pay plan with eighteen grade categories to cover white-collar workers. Blue-collar workers were grouped into a Craft, Protective, and Custodial (CPC) pay plan. Amendments in 1954 would change the CPC pay schedule to a wage grade system in which blue-collar workers were linked to local prevailing rates. Finally, the Classification Act of 1949 specified classification standards (i.e., detailed statements of job duties and qualifications for each grade level). The result was, as the MSPB recently noted, "These grade level criteria have come to be viewed as if they were cast in stone since they have only had one minor modification in the last 40 years" (see Figure 5.1 and Table 5.1).

These changes lessened some of the administrative difficulties but did not abate managerial pressures. The most constant complaint about classification procedures, the one gripe that is heard above all of the rest, is that the system places primary emphasis on the position rather than on the qualifications and abilities of an individual incumbent. This situation generates dysfunctional activities in order to compensate for the inflexibility of the classification system. As long as organizational structures try to maintain the principle established by the 1920 *Report of the Congressional Joint Commission on Reclassification of Salaries*—namely, that "the individual characteristics of an employee occupying a position" shall have no bearing on the classification of the position—administrators, recognizing the futility of maintaining such a principle, will compensate via administrative finesse; that is, by fudging the system.

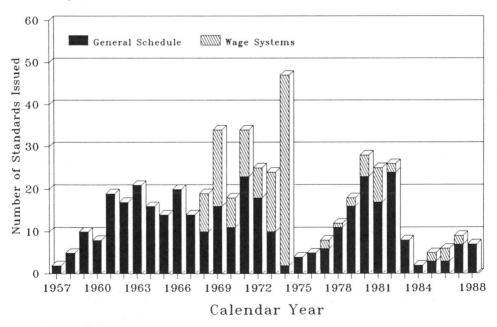

Figure 5.1. Numbers of OPM classification standards which are still in use, by year published (1957 to 1988). *Source*: *OPM's Classification and Qualification Systems* (U.S. MSPB, 1989).

Table 5.1.   Number and Percent of OPM White-Collar (GS)
Classification Standards Still in Use, by Time Period Issued
(1951–88)

Time period	Number of standards issued	Percentage of total
1951–58	8	2
1959–63	75	20
1964–68	74	20
1969–73	78	21
1974–78	28	7
1979–83	88	24
1984–88	22	6
	373	100

Source: OPM'S Classification and Qualification Systems. (U.S. MSPB, 1989.)

The Politics of Classification

Public personnel programs have perennial problems with the uses and abuses of position classifications—formal job descriptions that organize all jobs in a given organization into classes on the basis of duties and responsibilities for the purpose of delineating authority, establishing chains of command, and providing equitable salary scales. Although position classifications are almost universally recognized as essential for the administration of a public personnel program, they are frequently denounced, sometimes justifiably, as unreasonable constraints on top management, sappers of employee morale, sources of pay discrimination (see Chapter 8 on comparable worth), and for being little more than polite fictions in substance. As with other aspects of traditional public personnel administration, they often represent what Wallace Sayre has called the "triumph of techniques over purpose."

In seeking to thwart the excesses of spoils politics, the reform movement instituted many civil service procedures that have inadvertently had the effect of thwarting effective management practices as well. Thus, the negative role of the public personnel agency in guarding the merit system has commonly been more influential than the positive role of aiding management in the maintenance of a viable personnel system. This contradictory duality of function in public personnel operations is nowhere more evident than with position classification procedures.

All public personnel agencies have a dual role to play within their organizations. They are both the enforcer of the myriad civil service laws, rules,

The Position Classifier's Dilemma

Position classifiers may fall into two extreme profiles. One resembles the zealous police officer who tickets anyone, whether garbage collector or mayor. The other profile resembles a philanthropist, a person who approves all requests for grade and salary increases automatically. The first profile requires a combative personality. The zealot must constantly be prepared to fight to ensure that the official standards, and her interpretation of them, prevail. The zealot proclaims a high ethical and moral purpose. She feels personally responsible for the taxpayer's money, and treats the official standards as Holy Writ. The zealot is a fundamentalist.

The second profile possesses a personality that is resigned to bureaucratic "reality." He curries favor with superiors and employees alike. To disappoint no one is his motto. As the fundamentalist seeks her reward in another world, the philanthropist obtains his pleasure in this world. The philanthropist's generosity makes him an object of love and attention. His vested interest is in serving others, creating good will, and earning a special place in the hearts and minds of his benefactors.

While some position classifiers may actually fall neatly into these two profiles, most probably do not. People do, however, tend to develop habit patterns, and these patterns may enable any individual classifier to gravitate predominantly toward either the zealot or the philanthropist profile. Most position classifiers are sensitive to the prevailing winds in their respective agencies. They learn to sense what is expected of them by their superiors, and they adapt.

Adapted from Michael L. Monroe, "The Position Classifier's Dilemma," *The Bureaucrat*, 4 (July 1975, pp. 205–206. (Changes have been made in gender terminology.)

and regulations and a servitor to the jurisdiction's executive. There is frequently considerable conflict over what role the personnel agency should take in its activities. Is it a policing agency or a service department? Of course, it must be both at the same time. If the personnel agency makes a severe shift to one side or the other, it loses its effectiveness to either the executive or the public. And it must serve both—if not equally, at least fairly.

To a program manager, budget office administrator, or civil service commission, positions are neat packages that represent specific salaries. Ultimately, the management of positions is a budgetary process. If position classification is thought of as essentially an accounting procedure, the whole system becomes more rational. Because all personnel actions are equated to money, all changes, no matter how insignificant and/or beneficial, must be properly justified through appropriate procedures. Obviously, this is inefficient.

Peter Drucker, perhaps the most renowned and influential of American business management theorists, offers an explanation for this "seeming" irrationality. Drucker maintains that government is an inherently poor manager because it is of necessity obsessed by procedure in order to establish account-ability. But, the merit system apparatus of position classifications, examina-tions, and certification procedures grew up in direct response to previous abuses (something *business* management theorists usually overlook, since they tend to have little understanding of how government systems and operations—including personnel—work). Chiefly due to partisan or spoils politics, as ad-dressed in earlier chapters, individuals were unable to effectively and equitably manage personnel operations. As such, discretion over these matters was taken out of their hands and given to "unemotional," "impartial," and, in some circumstances, "irrational" procedural safeguards. The honest administra-tion of the public's business was too important a matter to leave to an in-dividual's discretion. It is precisely because governmental and especially public personnel procedures attempt to assign accountability for everything that public management operations grow to be outrageously expensive when compared to similar functions in private industry. According to Drucker, government has no choice but to tolerate this extra expense. Although the high costs of accountability cannot be eliminated, they can be mitigated, but such mitiga-tion frequently has the personnel agency transferring some of its discretionary powers to the line managers.

The principles and procedures of position classification that are gener-ally used in the public service are throwbacks to the heyday of the scientific management movement. They were conceived at a time—the 1920s and 1930s—when this school of management thought held sway, and they have never really adapted to the modern currents of management thought that began in the 1930s. After all, a classification plan is essentially a "time-and-motion" study for a governmental function. The duties of the larger organization are divided into positions in order to prevent duplication and enhance efficiency. A position is not a person but a set of duties and responsibilities fully equivalent to an interchangeable machine part because that is exactly what it represents—a human interchangeable part. Because the political reformers of this period were fervently seeking a rationale for separating politics from administra-tion, it proved an effective strategy to maintain that administration was a science and thus had to be operated according to the dictates of "the" experts.

The reformers operated from the premises articulated by Woodrow Wilson and Frank Goodnow—that politics and administration should be separate. Their success in any given instance can be measured by the number of personnel control mechanisms that prevent elected officials and appointed program managers from implementing their electoral mandate. What was once a ge-nuine triumph for the public good is rapidly turning into a Pyrrhic victory. Because the most basic doctrines of position classification were established prior to World War II, current practices effectively ignore many of the ad-vances in management science and theory that have occurred since then.

Technical worker in the state of New York. *Source*: New York State Civil Service, Albany, New York.

While management practices in the private sector changed with the human relations and behavioral movements, public personnel administrators held firm to the outdated methods of position classification because of its pseudoscientific pretentiousness that lent so much credence to the "equal pay for equal work" motto of the civil service reformers. Current position classification practices are best thought of as being of mixed parentage, being derived more or less equally from two contemporary early twentieth-century movements—scientific management and civil service reform.

As control devices, position classifications are doubly unsuccessful. First, they prevent program managers from having the discretion essential for the optimum success of their mission. Second, they generate an astounding amount of dysfunctional activity whose sole purpose is to get around the control devices. Although the controls are frequently and successfully circumvented, the costs of such activity take away resources from the organization's prime goals.

Position classifications easily lend themselves to what Chris Argyris terms organization pseudoeffectiveness, "a state in which no discomfort is reported but in which, upon diagnosis, ineffectiveness is found." Because the underlying ineffectiveness is not immediately evident, the costs of maintaining the existing position classification structure does not seem disproportionate. The true costs are hidden by the informal compensatory mechanisms, and will influence the organization negatively.

A common example of this situation concerns the problem of grade escalation—an increase in grade (and pay) that may or may not be justifiable in terms of increased responsibilities and qualifications. The pressures upon supervisors for grade escalations or position reallocations are understandably powerful. Such pressures can be internal as well as external because supervisors can frequently have their own status improved when those working under them are upgraded. Grade escalations are pseudoeffective if their primary motivation is bureaucratic empire building. The classification process conveniently lends itself to the ends of bureaucratic empire building because it is a relatively inexpensive and conveneient way to puff up the formal organizational structure without disturbing current operations. Thus a substantial and impressive paper reorganization with its incumbent new flowcharts, and revised chains of command can be had for the price of a position reallocation. This cannot be done, of course, without the expenditure of a great deal of imagination and time that should more properly contribute to the agency's mission.

The Factor Evaluation System

In 1967 the House Committee on Post Office and Civil Service decided that "a comprehensive review should be made of all classification and ranking systems in the federal service." Thereupon a comprehensive survey of federal classification practices was undertaken by the Subcommittee on Position Classification. The subcommittee's report was a detailed indictment of current practices. It found that:

1. Although job evaluation and ranking should provide the basis for good personnel management, many believed it was not doing so.
2. Classification and ranking systems had not been adapted to, maintained, or administered to meet the rapidly changing needs of the federal government.

3. Classification was not generally used as a management tool. Many officials commented that the only function of classification in their organization was a basis for fixing pay.

These findings were so serious that they led directly to the passing of the Job Evaluation Policy Act of 1970. This act asserted that it was the sense of the Congress that there be a coordinated classification system for all civilian positions and that the U.S. Civil Service Commission should exercise general supervision and control over it. The Civil Service Commission was authorized to establish a planning unit that would submit its final report within two years and then cease to exist. This unit became known as the Job Evaluation and Pay Review Task Force. The final report of the task force, released in January 1972, is popularly known as the Oliver report after the task force director, Philip M. Oliver. The Oliver report declared the federal government's classification and ranking systems obsolete. The task force recommended a new job evaluation system. The new system was field-tested and revised. Finally, in December 1975, the Civil Service Commission approved the implementation, over a five-year period, of the *factor evaluation* system for nonsupervisory positions.

The factor evaluation or factor comparison system is designed to be accurate and flexible, yet simple and relatively inexpensive. But even more

Job Evaluation and Class and Comp Systems

Job evaluation has been defined in a number of different ways. Today, it is mainly seen as the overall process by which organizations develop "job worth" hierarchies, and it is through job evaluation that formal classification and compensation (class and comp) systems in both public and private sectors are set. The antiquated job evaluation techniques that continue to underlie most class and comp systems result in, among other things, pay disparities between women and men; and between whites and people of color.

A number of states, particularly in the 1980s, became more and more concerned with these pay disparities. As such, many began to reevaluate their class and comp systems in order to, as the New York State Center for Women in Government has stated, "determine whether assumptions about the value of jobs and the assignment of job titles to salary grades have been distorted by the sex or race of the typical job incumbent." Studies have shown that such "distortions" are widespread, thus giving way to job evaluation systems that are more equitable in orientation and outcome.

New York State Center for Women in Government. *Comparable Worth Study* (Albany, N.Y.: October 1985).

important, it hoped to secure the active involvement of operating management, thus helping to reduce the "them or us" mentality that has come to be associated with traditional control-oriented classification methods. The federal government's use of this factor evaluation system is seen by some as a return to the classification practices of the 1920s. Indeed, the first factor comparison system was installed by Eugene J. Benge at the Philadelphia Transit Company in 1926. The factor comparison system is naturally a hybrid of traditional position classification systems; but the differences are significant. In the case of traditional classifications, different combinations of factors were used for different positions; the factor evaluation system uses the same factors for all positions. In the case of traditional classifications, grade levels were ascertained by the weight and eloquence of narrative descriptions; the factor evaluation system determines grade levels by comparing positions directly to one another. In short, the factor evaluation system seeks to take traditional classification concepts a step further into rationality (see Table 5.2).

The main ingredient of a factor evaluation system is, obviously, the factor—any of the various key elements individually examined in the evaluation process. Although there is an infinite number of specific factors that pertain to differing jobs, the factors themselves can usually be categorized within the following groupings:

1. *Job requirements*—The knowledge, skills, and abilities needed to perform the duties of a specific job
2. *Difficulty of work*—The complexity or intricacy of the work and the associated mental demands of the job
3. *Responsibility*—the freedom of action required by a job and the impact of the work performed upon the organizational mission
4. *Personal relationships*—The importance of interpersonal relationships to the success of mission accomplishment
5. *Other factors*—Specific job-oriented elements that should be considered in the evaluation process, e.g., physical demands, working conditions, accountability, number of workers directed

Once the factors of a position have been identified, it can be ranked; that is, the factors of one position are compared to another. Such a factor comparison can have only three outcomes. Any given factor must be higher than, lower than, or equal to the factor of another position. When positions are ranked by factors, all of the factors of each position are compared and an overall ranking is achieved.

The crucial focus of a factor comparison system is the benchmark—a specific job at a specific point within an array of evaluations. Each series of choices based on ranking one position as compared to another results in a composite or total of the choices. These, when assigned numerical values,

Table 5.2.   Comparisons Between Nonquantitative and Quantitative Approaches to Position Classification

Nonquantitative (position classification)	Quantitative (factor point)
1. Installation and maintenance	
Requires the least time to install and can be accomplished by staff with less in-depth technical background.	Take more time to develop and requires more specialized staff. Expensive to install.
Classification decisions depend on skills and judgment of classifier. Takes many years for average classifier to acquire skills needed to make valid judgments.	Standard factor definitions and point scales facilitate classifying new positions and restructuring or reclassifying existing ones. Can be applied by trained staff with less extensive classification experience and takes less time to train classifiers.
Needs extensive salary surveys for initial installation and ongoing maintenance. Adjustment of pay scales depends more on external salary comparisons.	Needs less extensive salary survey but requires conversion of data into wage curve to derive actual pay raise.
2. Acceptance	
System is widely known, which makes it easy to gain acceptance. In actual operation, disagreements may arise because decisions are mostly judgmental.	Fear of the unknown and high costs of installation may generate resistance. Once understood, acceptance tends to be high, especially among lower-paid employees.
Does not always provide easily justifiable or convincing rationale for classification decisions.	Facilitates resolution of classification appeals and grievances.
3. Technical adequacy	
Decisions are judgmental and could lead to varying results when made by different classifiers.	Points assigned to job factors provide objective and consistent measure of job value.
Does not define internal relationships by job factors.	Permits internal comparisons of positions, factor by factor.
Responds easily to changing labor market conditions by adjusting salary levels of entire occupational groups	Requires modification of factor definitions or point scales to reflect external labor market conditions.

Source: U.S. Office of Personnel Management, *Position Classification: A Guide for City and County Managers* (Washington, D.C.: U.S. Government Printing Office, November 1979), pp. 6–7.

yield a score that assigns position X and position Y to specific points within an array of evaluations. Each time such determinations are made, they add to the array, thereby increasing the number of benchmarks. Each addition to the number of benchmarks facilitates arriving at the ranking choices for other jobs not yet evaluated. Finally, when all of the jobs within an organization have been evaluated, they all become benchmarks. Once this has been achieved, all the positions within an organization would have, in effect, been compared to each other; each would have found its place in the classification and pay plans because it was found to rank higher than, lower than, or equal to its neighboring positions.

The factor evaluation system that the federal government assembled for its use was based on the following nine factors:

1. *Knowledge required by the position*—This factor measures the nature and extent of information or facts that the worker must understand to do acceptable work (e.g., steps, procedures, practices, rules, policies, theory, principles, and concepts) and the nature and extent of skills/abilities necessary to apply this knowledge.

2. *Supervisory controls*—This factor covers the nature and extent of direct or indirect controls exercised by the supervisor, the employee's responsibility, and the review of completed work. Controls are exercised by the supervisor in the way assignments are made, instructions are given to the employee, priorities and deadlines are set, and objectives and boundaries are defined. Responsibility of the employee depends upon the extent to which the employee is expected to develop the sequence and timing of various aspects of the work, to modify or recommend modification of instructions, and to participate in establishing priorities and defining objectives. The degree of review of completed work depends upon the nature and extent of the review, e.g., close and detailed review of each phase of the assignment; detailed review of the finished assignment; spot check of finished work for accuracy; or review only for adherence to policy.

3. *Guidelines*—This factor covers the nature of guidelines and the judgment needed to apply them. Jobs vary in the specificity, applicability, and availability of guidelines for performance of assignments. Consequently, the constraints and judgmental demands placed upon employees also vary. For example, the existence of specific instructions, procedures, and policies may limit the opportunity of the employee to make or recommend decisions or actions; however, in the absence of procedures or under broadly stated objectives, the employee may use considerable judgment in researching literature and developing new methods.

4. *Complexity*—This factor covers the nature and variety of tasks, steps, processes, methods, or activities in the work performed, and the degree to which the employee must vary the work, discern interrelationships and

deviations, or develop new techniques, criteria, or information. At the low end of the scale, the work involves few clear-cut and directly related tasks or functions.

5. *Scope and effect*—This factor covers the purpose of the assignment and the effect of work products both within and outside the organization. At the lower end of the scale, the purpose is to perform specific routine operations that have little impact beyond the immediate organizational unit. At the high end of the scale, the purpose is to plan, develop, and carry out vital administrative or scientific programs that are essential to the missions of the agency or affect large numbers of people on a long-term or continuing basis.

6. *Personal contacts*—This factor includes face-to-face contacts and telephone and radio dialogue with persons not in the supervisory chain. The nature of contacts ranges from those with other employees in the immediate work unit to contacts with high-ranking officials outside the agency. In between are many variations.

7. *Purpose of contacts*—The contacts covered by this factor range from the factual exchanges of information to situations involving significant or controversial issues and differing viewpoints, goals, or objectives.

8. *Physical demands*—This factor covers the requirements and physical demands placed on the employee by work assignments. This includes physical characteristics and abilities (e.g., specific agility and dexterity requirements) and the physical exertion involved in the work (e.g., climbing, lifting, pushing, balancing, stooping, kneeling, crouching, crawling, or reaching). To some extent the frequency or intensity of physical exertion must also be considered; for example, a job requiring prolonged standing involves more physical exertion than a job requiring intermittent standing.

9. *Work environment*—This factor considers the risks, discomforts, or unpleasantness that may be imposed upon employees by various physical surroundings or job situations.

But the factor evaluation system provided only a Band-Aid for the wounds of the federal classification system and the need for pay reform. It offered better and more efficient methods but it could not address the deterioration of the entire classification system. By the early 1980s this was all too apparent, as the trend to reallocate positions upward (frequently referred to as "grade escalation" or "grade creep") continued unabated.

In August of 1983, OPM issued a moratorium on the issuance of classification standards. This was a remarkable admission on the part of OPM as they in effect refused to put more resources into creating and updating standards when the system clearly need total revision. The moratorium lasted until 1986, when OPM announced new initiatives to move toward more flexible and simplified standards. A major thrust of this movement is to experiment with "multi-occupation classification guides" that are designed to be more general and compare similar work across different occupational categories to avoid being overly specialized or narrow. Finally, the new initiatives promise more delegation of authority to agencies and more flexibility for managers.

But the above may be too late. As one federal personnel manager, Lyn Meridew Holley (chief of position classification at the Customs Service), noted in a 1990 article:

> The job classification system has been in a state of progressive deterioration for more than a decade, culminating in 1983 when OPM ceased altogether to develop or update job classification standards. The system for developing job classification standards (and training those who use them) has not been fundamentally improved since the 1950's, even while resources available to develop and update standards have shrunk, and the rate of change in occupations has increased. The job classification system should be redesigned, retooled, and recalibrated. The problem of inaccurate position classification cannot be solved unless the pay problem is addressed.

Pay Reform and the "Quiet Crisis"

The problem of pay reform, while complex, is primarily one of political will. At the federal level, the system was basically created by the Federal Salary Reform Act of 1962 and the Federal Pay Comparability Act of 1970. As mentioned, the idea of paying blue-collar workers wages that were based on prevailing wage rates of local private sector counterparts has long been established. For white-collar workers, private sector comparability came in the above statutes. Up to the 1950s the problems were numerous, in part because of congressional reluctance to approve pay increases for higher grade levels and the difficulty in relating pay adjustments across different pay systems.

It was the Salary Reform Act of 1962 that first required the president to submit an annual report to Congress evaluating federal wage rates against the private sector's. This report established basic salary surveys by agencies and required a recommendation by the president for an annual salary adjustment. Of course, congressional action was required to approve the request. Further complicating the political requirements of getting Congress to legislate, there was an eighteen-month lag built into the process from the first survey actions to implementation. These problems led to minor corrections in the Federal Salary Act of 1967 and a major revision in the 1970 Federal Pay Comparability Act.

The Pay Comparability Act of 1970 codified the principle that federal pay rates would be comparable to private sector wage rates for similar work. More important, it created separate mechanisms to make pay adjustments. A primary organ with responsibility for wages called the pay agent was created, consisting of the directors of the Office of Management and Budget (OMB),

The Classification Game

Consider, for example, a woman who works as a secretary stenographer for a high administrator in a police department. Because her boss is buried under paperwork and generally prefers to write drafts of her letters in longhand, she spends her time typing and filing papers rather than taking dictation. If this situation persisted, civil service rules require that the position be downgraded (e.g., to a class called typist). Such a downgrading is, however, very unlikely because those who play the classification game lack either the resources or will to do much about the situations. For one thing, those with information about the misclassified position lack the incentive to report it to those in authority. The woman occupaying the position obviously has little reason to unveil her activities since a downgrading could cost her money, status, and self-esteem. Nor does her boss wish to act. Reclassification would create personal unpleasantness with her subordinate and could eat up hours she wished to spend on other matters. Besides, few supervisors wish to develop reputations as penny pinchers when it comes to their employees' salaries. In addition, the administrator may believe that any high-level official of significance has a secretary stenographer. Her prestige therefore depends on keeping the position from being downgraded.

Frank J. Thompson, "Classification as Politics," in *People in Public Service*, 2nd ed., ed. Robert T. Golembiewski and Michael Cohen (Itasca, Ill.: Peacock Publishers, 1976), pp. 525–526. (Changes have been made in the gender terminology.)

OPM, and the Labor Department (the secretary of labor actually being added by amendment in 1977). The Advisory Committee on Federal Pay was also established to get recommendations from the public. Finally, the Federal Employees Pay Council, representing labor unions and employees organizations, was created.

However, section 5305(c)(1) of the act adds a subtle but major change. It stipulates:

> If, because of national emergency or economic conditions affecting the general welfare, the President should, in any year, consider it inappropriate to make the pay adjustment required. . . . he shall prepare and transmit to the Congress before September of that year such alternative plan with respect to a pay adjustment as he considers appropriate.

Finally, the act provided for a legislative veto provision stating that if either house of Congress vetoed the president's alternative pay plan, then the pay recommendation provided for in the pay agent's and advisory committee's annual report would be approved instead. Thus, despite the best intentions, the Pay Comparability Act paved the way for the current 30 percent pay gap that now exists between federal and private sector wages. Since the Carter administration, the annual adjustment has been basically the president's alternate pay plan because of one excuse or another given that decries economic necessity to ward off further inflation, counteract the deficit, or whatever the current economic fad term is for American economic problems. Over two decades, the Congress has seldom overridden the president's alternative pay plan.

But all of this discussion of classification and compensation reform has taken on special meaning in the 1990s because of the increasing significance of the public sector pay gap. In 1989, the National Commission on the Public Service under the direction of Paul A. Volcker, issued its report, *Leadership for America*, calling for desperately needed public service revitalization and urging a significant salary increase for the federal civil service. This was not a sudden development. The OPM had previously concluded in its report *Civil Service 2000*, that "federal compensation is increasingly noncompetitive . . . public esteem for civil servants has been declining and the prestige of government jobs has been falling . . . [and] low pay and low prestige have been exacerbated by outdated management practices and needless aggravations." The GAO has recently surveyed many federal agencies and reports major recruitment and retention problems, especially in geographic areas with higher costs of living.

Of course the above problems are not limited just to federal civil service. State and local governments and nonprofit organizations are now facing increasing competition in current low unemployment conditions and from other legal and budgetary constraints. It has been difficult to gauge accurately how well state and local governments have fared in the 1980s in their compensation practices. For one thing, most face unions that are not restrained from bargaining over wages as are their federal counterparts. Second, the linkage between political elected executives and legislators and civil servants is more pronounced (and more visible, in part because professionals generally get paid more than politicians). For example, the governor of New York was in a 1988 survey the highest paid state official at $130,000 but the superintendents of schools in New York City ($150,000) and Dade County, Florida ($135,000) get more, as did the police chief in Los Angeles ($136,000). Most surveys of state and local governments show such incredible degrees of variance that it's hard to make comparisons, not only in terms of who gets what but why.

Perhaps more significantly, the fiscal situation of many states and cities has changed dramatically from a feast to famine cycle. Sporadically difficult times in the early 1980s were followed by surpluses in many states and cities in the mid-1980s, but the end of the decade brought a major crunch that had states and cities running in the red, raising taxes, and cutting personnel costs either through layoffs or hiring freezes. State and local governments are in a bind. As *Governing* magazine termed it, in a recent article by Elder Witt on the state and local compensation gap, "[t]he core issue is quality. As the needs of government grow more complex, the public sector is drawn into competition with private industry for skilled people: engineers, nurses, computer specialists and able managers." There is a superb example of one innovative approach that aptly summarizes this dilemma. The city of San Diego reorganized its data processing division as a nonprofit organization, in large part to be able to set competitive salaries to attract and hold the computer and information systems talent it needed for the city, but not to the point of distorting the total wage system for the rest of city employees.

Problems surrounding pay seem most pronounced at the federal level. Here, the term "quiet crisis" refers not only to recruitment and retention implications of compensation and performance. Morale and political perspectives are major aspects of the crisis as well. One of the most forceful evaluations has been the recent survey results of the *Government Executive*, as reported by Clark and Wachtel, which conducted a first-time poll of nearly 4,000 federal managers. Poll results strongly confirm continued dedication and concern for public sector work but immense alienation toward the personnel system they operate under. Regarding compensation—70 percent felt that their pay was unfair, and 74 percent felt that current merit pay and bonus systems were unfair. Still, over 90 percent favored the concept of pay for performance, and many noted support for pay innovations as a part of civil service simplification and ongoing reform. The innovations most often mentioned are China Lake and the McClellan Pacer Share project, which are demonstration projects sponsored under Title VI of the Civil Service Reform Act, already discussed in the prologue.

What then are the main threads of the "quiet crisis" that will impact on the new environment? The pay gap is usually the first topic mentioned. The Volcker Commission has already gone on record indicating that by the end of the 1980s the gap between federal and private sector wages had reached canyon proportions of over 25 percent. In fact, the pay gap in 1990 was now estimated at 30 percent by the report of the Advisory Committee on Federal Pay (see Figure 5.2). But other salary surveys contend that the gap may be smaller. Others reiterate the timeworn argument that other factors must be considered. Although the same white-collar occupations tend to pay more money in the private sector, salary surveys can't take into account the enhanced job security that most federal workers enjoy (and many other employees do not).

But perhaps the most telling statistic tied to the pay gap issue is the question of pace. In 1988, an election year, federal employees received a 4.1% increase, the largest increase of the decade. But the decade trend is more onerous. In fact, both OPM and the Federal Advisory Committee on Pay have noted that federal white-collar salary increases have not kept pace with

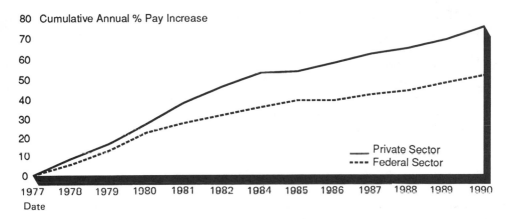

Figure 5.2. Federal/private sector pay gap (1977 to 1990). Federal pay adjustments were made in October for years 1977 through 1982. Adjustments were shifted to January for 1984 through 1990; therefore, 1983 does not appear on the horizontal axis. *Source: Recruitment and Retention: Inadequate Federal Pay Cited as Primary Problem by Agency Officials* (U.S. General Accounting Office, September 1990), p. 13.

inflation. Current estimates are that over the past twenty years, federal employees have lost on the average nearly 20 percent of their purchasing power. While the debate over the size of the pay gap and how it can be remedied given current budget deficit levels continues, federal salaries lag further behind.

The pay gap is further exacerbated by cost of living differentials in different parts of the country. With a few exceptions, federal government salaries are the same no matter what part of the country you work and reside in, so in New York City or San Francisco (where living costs are high), salaries are extremely noncompetitive while in Atlanta or Pittsburgh (where living costs are lower), salaries are competitive. The current federal initiative "locality pay" is designed to offset these differences by paying higher wages based on regional cost of living differences.

Pay reform in the 1990s is on everyone's agenda (both the Bush administration's and the Congress's) but so is the federal budget deficit. The result is an environmental constraint called "budget neutrality." This means that salaries can be increased, but total dollars paid for federal department programs and operations must stay constant. Governments face tough choices under budget conditions that must be budget neutral. Salaries can be increased but must be offset by either productivity gains or other cost reductions. Of course, these cost reduction strategies could include decreasing the total number of positions, lowering grade levels, or making other personnel cost reductions.

The second question is quality of the work force. Do pay and performance evaluation policies negatively impact who stays and who leaves the federal work force (see Table 5.3)? This incredibly complex and difficult question has been addressed by a number of significant studies. The Congressional Budget Office (CBO) dealt with this issue directly in a 1986 study. The study concluded that quit rates were not extensive when compared to other organizations and that the greatest turnover was with clerical workers. The CBO explored briefly the problem of who is leaving the public service. Their conclusion was that a "healthy pattern" existed in that there was no "disproportionate turnover" among higher rated managers.

In July 1988, the MSPB further examined the quality retention issue. Their study showed more support for the "desirable pattern," which they calculated for the 1984–1985 year. Their findings, as shown in Table 5.4, contrasted 26 percent of unsatisfactorily rated employees leaving government compared to only 6 percent of those employees given an outstanding rating who had left.

This pattern, it is argued, indicates that the crisis is not as serious as claimed. However, there simply isn't enough evidence to draw any real conclusions. More data are required, as well as a more comprehensive definition of quality in a work force. Much of the interest in attrition was to use it as a key index factor for setting compensation and recruitment strategy first articulated in 1984 in OPM's somewhat controversial report *Reforming Federal Pay: An Examination of More Realistic Alternatives*.

Federal Pay Reform: 1990

There is little doubt that the various reports and studies surrounding the quiet crisis motif have served a useful purpose in creating the best opportunity for pay reform in the last twenty years for the federal government. Pay reform legislation was hammered out in congressional conference in the fall of 1990, producing the Federal Pay Reform Act of 1990.

The act focuses its greatest impacts on new linkages to local private sector wage rates, or what is termed *locality pay*. This emphasis is perhaps the most important feature of pay reform at this time because it is the only way to stave off pressure for splintering the GS system. If agencies can't get relief to pay their personnel wages that are competitive in high cost areas, their only course of action is to push for their own separate special pay system. Some federal agencies, such as the Defense Department, Justice, and NASA have advocated having their own systems for some time. Locality pay, it is argued, would enable agencies to recruit and retain qualified personnel at prevailing local wage rates.

Table 5.3. Respondents Said Pay and Job Availability Were Primary Reasons to Leave and to Decline Federal Employment

Retention factors and percentage who said "reason to leave"	Recruitment factors and percentage who said "reason to decline"
Pay (78.3)	Pay (72.5)
Job availability (71.3)	Job availability (63.6)
Staffing (51.6)	Length of recruitment/hiring process (39.0)
Career opportunities (45.7)	Benefits (33.1)
Benefits (37.0)	Physical environment (31.2)
Physical environment (35.4)	Staffing (29.7)

Source: Recruitment and Retention: Inadequate Federal Pay Cited as Primary Problem by Agency Officials. (U.S. Government Accounting Office, 1990).

To close the pay gap, the current legislation calls for 5 percent raises across the board for 1992, 1993, and 1994. In 1994, surveys of high-cost areas will show the remaining gap and extra salary raises will be paid to workers in those areas that close the gap by 20 percent. These extra increases would be paid until the year 2003 at a rate of 10 percent of the remaining gap. To handle critical local situations, the president is authorized to extend immediate salary increases of 8 percent. Special provisions for federal law enforcement officials amounting to 4 to 16 percent salary increases for high-cost areas

Table 5.4. Results of MSPB's Survey on the Retention of "Quality" Employee

	Performance Rating				
	Unacceptable	Minimally successful	Fully successful	Exceeds fully successful	Outstanding
Total employees rated	4,203	4,440	475,981	435,394	247,854
(Percent)	<.5%	<.5%	41%	37%	21%
Total employees leaving government	1,138	853	37,459	23,670	15,609
(Percent)	27%	19%	8%	5%	6%

Source: "Who is Leaving the Federal Government? An Analysis of Employee Turnover," (MSPB, 1989).

in 1992 are also included. There are also provisions to alter substantially the pay system for administrative law judges.

How the cost will be paid for in this era of budget neutrality is not quite as clear. About $3.6 billion has been budgeted by the Bush administration over the next five years (that's roughly 3 percent of the total annual federal payroll costs), but that is only half of what is needed to make the necessary salary increases. Departments and agencies are supposed to provide the other half by reducing turnover and managing other payroll costs. Finally, the sums targeted for this pay reform package only extend for five years, leaving future congressional and administration leaders to determine where the funding will come from after 1995.

Will it work? Initially, any reform that closes the pay gap will have a chance, and certainly no one in the personnel community wants to face the alternative. OPM director Constance Newman, put it very bluntly in a speech, reported by Gerson in 1990:

> There will be some pay reform that will go through this session. . . . All recognize that otherwise we will lose control over the federal pay system, because DOD, DOE, the FBI and others are able to cut their own deals—and there is belief that that will not be good for the system, because the agencies getting their own pay systems will be those with strong ties to budget dollars. The funds will not necessarily go out based on the needs of the nation, to agencies like Education, Labor, HHS—because those agencies will not carry the same weight.

Work Redesign and Technology

Perhaps the greatest area of emphasis that classification has neglected is the dynamic nature of work itself. By definition, classification has concerned itself with harnessing people to organizational structures, mainly because control and accountability were inherent in structure and hierarchy. The world of work in the 1980s was no longer so designed, and the 1990s promises to be even less so.

In part, it is the attitude of workers and the importance of their motivation. In the public sector, this is extraordinarily critical (in contrast to earlier times when commitment, loyalty, and motivation were assumed as constants). It is not just a case of unions, work strikes and stoppages, or other job actions, nor is it a shift in political values and the desire to become more politically involved in order to represent specific interests. It goes far beyond this— major problems of individual attitude about work are present in almost every attitudinal survey taken of government employees.

Questions about the nature of work strike to the very core of what classification and compensation seek to address. Three factors must be addressed:

1. Is work performed the same way (*work methods*) in this new era less than affectionately called "the automated technology era?" Are workers getting the training needed to keep up with job changes and the introduction of new technology?
2. Have the *relationships* of workers toward their work roles and toward their supervisor/subordinates changed?
3. Have the *attitudes and preferences* of workers changed toward work, performance, and the organization?

One need only consider the computer and its impact to see that work methods have changed. Recent evaluations of the URBIS project at the University of California at Irvine (a 25-year panel study of the management and effect of computerization in local governments) show extensive applications of computer technology. In 1985 cities averaged over eighty different computer applications and 84 percent of all managers and staff indicated that their work involved extensive interaction with computers. A prediction made in the mid-1980s that there would be a ratio of one computer for every white-collar worker in government is rapidly becoming a reality. On the flip side, the recent MSPB study of federal workers shows only 42 percent of employees responding positively as to whether or not they are being trained in new technology as it is introduced.

Relationships and attitudes are more difficult to evaluate. Cummings and Strivastva make a convincing case, as Table 5.5 illustrates, that there is no longer any one type of work arrangement that determines relationships and levels of authority. The world of work is moving increasingly toward the "emergent work environment," where neither the organization nor the individual is in control; an arena that is highly dynamic and characterized by its "uncontrolled nature." This is almost a description of a world of work beyond classification, or at least beyond the type of classification developed to date.

To some extent, many public sector personnelists have positions that have characteristics of "emergent work." However, this does not mean that classification is hopeless. In fact, what most organizational managers seek is increased flexibility to respond more quickly to dynamic environments and still retain some measure of integration of organizational efforts. In broad personnel management terms, this objective centers on work redesign as a management strategy (see Table 5.6). Work redesign has been around since the mid-1960s in both the private and public sectors and is considered by some theorists as only another stage in work planning that begins with work simplification of the scientific management era.

A number of techniques are variously associated with work redesign, which has developed an extensive literature describing its theory and

Table 5.5.   A Typology of Work Agreements

Category of work agreement	Source of work determination	Level of worker discretion	Source of authority review
Prescribed	Not determined by self, determined by organization	Fixed; judgment exercised within prespecified bounds	Authority in supervisors
Contractual	Jointly determined by self and others in organization	Flexible; discretion determined by bargaining and dual commitment to results	Authority in work contracts
Discretionary	Determined by self but not by others	Individual has almost total task discretion	Authority in organizational sanctions
Emergent	Work determined by environment, neither individual nor others have control	Variable and un-controlled; in-dividual most cope with each situation on a separate basis	Authority in envi-ronment—indiv-iduals must res-pond to situa-tions and general societal/en-vironmental laws

Source: Adapted from T. G. Cummings and S. Srivastva, *Management of Work* (Kent, Ohio: Kent State University Press, 1977), pp. 27–28.

implementation. Work simplification, job enlargement, job enrichment, semiautonomous team building—all are parts of the work redesign environment. The first modern experiment with work redesign occurred in the 1940s as a job enlargement program undertaken by Thomas Watson at IBM. This program was started by giving assembly line workers a larger number of different tasks in order combat boredom and monotony. In one sense, this early experiment set the tone for much of the direction of work redesign—moving away from defining jobs and positions in terms of the simplest, most mechanical, and most efficient divisions of labor—to any strategy or arrangement that changed specific jobs or groups of interrelated jobs with the objective of improving the quality of the individual's work experience, motivation and interest, and hence long-range on-the-job productivity.

In short, work redesign seeks to motivate the worker through the work itself—by making it more rewarding, more satisfying, more challenging,

Table 5.6. The Evolution of Work Redesign: Periods, Emphasis, Concepts, and Techniques

Periods and emphasis (some significant theorists)	Concepts and techniques
1. Job simplification 1800–1940s (Taylor, Scientific Management)	1. Rationalization of tasks and work: to replicate scientifically one most efficient way of producing output.
2. Job enlargement 1955–1960s (Walker and Guest; Davis and Canter)	2. Horizontal task loading: changing positions by increasing number, control, and variety of tasks performed so that worker can identify better with work process
3A. Job enrichment 1960s–1970s (Herzberg; Ford and Gillette)	3A. Vertical task loading: work redesign as the key to employees' psychological growth, emphasis on improving individuals responsibility, recognition, and achievement
3B. Integrated work/organizational redesign (Hackman and Oldham; Janson and Purdy; Lawler)	3B. Changing core job dimensions: (skill variety, task identity and significance, autonomy); job redesign but as a motivational strategy and a design for employee development
4. Self-maintaining organizations (Emery and Trist; Davis)	4. Development of autonomous work teams: (emphasis on self-regulation through use of team building, new forms of organizations, new management roles)

and enhancing the level of involvement of the worker in the work. Initially two major approaches were used: job enlargement and job enrichment. Job enlargement involved changing the range of work responsibilities by giving each worker a greater variety of work tasks in order to reduce boredom and excessive repetition. Job enrichment, developed later, employed a more qualitative focus, since it enabled workers to take more responsibility for the schedule, pace, control, and preliminary management of the work being performed. Perhaps the best distinction, albeit a technical one, that can be drawn between these two approaches is that although they both involve work redesign, one focuses on "horizontal task" change, the other on "vertical task" change. Horizontal tasks are work activities performed at similar levels involving division of various specialized labors, while vertical tasks involved more hierarchical relationships in work, crossing worker levels, schedules, and other organizational planning and management functions.

Both job enlargement and job enrichment assume certain constancies about work methods, uses of employees' skills levels, participation, and organizational structures. It is the later stages of work redesign that jettison these assumptions and focus on a path that reintegrates organizational and individual roles. Davis and Taylor, and Hackman and Oldham are but a few work redesign theorists who emphasize that work redesign works best when it goes beyond merely changing job content and changes indivdiual work roles, organizational structures, and management relationships.

What will be changed are work variety, task identity, task significance and definition, worker autonomy, and levels and sources of feedback/communications. Expected results will be higher levels of experienced meaningfulness in work, greater experienced responsibility and commitment to work outcomes, and more knowledge of actual work results and performance outcomes. This is an extraordinary agenda that strikes to the heart of many jobs that are viewed as soulless and incapable of producing real motivation, job satisfaction, work quality, and productivity.

How will this ultimately affect classification? It should have an incredible impact. Thus far, work redesign efforts in the public sector have only received cursory attention, because initial attempts to redesign jobs have been viewed as experiments or demonstration projects. No commitment has been made and thus classification has been able to ignore it. But this is changing just as classification practices are responding to pay banding and other civil service simplification initiatives. Work redesign is more than a series of temporary adjustments that are designed to improve motivation but that leave no real marks on organizations or personnel management practices.

Perhaps the best indication of the totality of change incorporated into work redesign is found in its next stage—the movement toward autonomous work teams. American work organizations—public, private, and nonprofit— have been struck by many aspects of the international economic challenge, but two organizational aspects stand out: fewer levels or layers of hierarchy and the proclivity toward work teams that are largely self motivated and internally managed. Japanese organizations are famous for their teamwork and quality circles, which experts point out are obtained by a mixture of leadership, training, and strong values that drive individual performance and group accomplishment. The societal model itself reinforces the educational role of superiors and loyalty from subordinates.

While there are major social and cultural differences between American organizations and Japanese or European, the movement toward autonomous work teams is growing in the United States. Driven in part by economic incentives and new technological advances in communication, the concept of work groups supervising themselves, planning their own development, and functioning as work teams will have radical impacts on organizational structures and personnel systems. The impacts on classification alone will be major. Autonomous work teams assume:

1. Cross-training of all individuals to perform in each other's work roles, and constant work rotation of team members
2. Joint determination and redefinition of the work process, technology, and team work roles adjustment
3. Participative management with either no supervisory roles or rotated supervisory roles
4. Compensation methods would tie significant portions of pay to gainsharing and group incentives in which all members of the work team benefit equally for their cooperation

Under this arrangement, classification and compensation would have to focus on group inputs and outputs and move to some form of knowledge-based compensation. There is some private sector experience with "knowledge-based pay," as this concept is known, especially in production environments. Pay rates for individuals are keyed to acquisition of additional skills, and as they are rotated through and master new skills, the pay rate advances. The top rate of compensation is obtained when all the skills have been mastered. One can see how this type of compensation concept would fit the autonomous work team readily, and as the individuals are rotated and cross-trained into the organization. Adding some form of group incentive or gainsharing system would complete the arrangement.

Gainsharing and group-based incentive plans present a final set of headaches for classification and compensation systems. The logic fits a number of current management needs—how to link a portion of each person's pay to some measure of productivity and performance or the gains accrued to the organization due to more efficient work efforts. Historically, gainsharing dates back to 1896, when Henry Towne incorporated such payments into his factory's wage system. Some key distinctions must be made first. Gainsharing or "shared savings plans," as they are sometimes called, are cooperative efforts and differ from individual incentive plans.

On an individual level, incentives or pay for performance concepts have been used extensively in the public sector. (They will be discussed in the performance appraisal chapter.) By definition, they are competitive in that the individual's bonus is based on his or her performance measured against the group average or group standard. Such a concept doesn't fit well into the autonomous work team concept. Competitive pay arrangements don't foster cooperation, nor do they create incentives for one person to assist or train another, since such activities take away from time that could be spent earning your own bonus.

Gainsharing assumes equal payouts to all team members. Equal benefits are created by improving the performance levels of the lowest skilled team member or facilitating the highest skilled. It is a work group decision and the team members see how each work decision affects work outcomes and share equally in the results. Much of the current impetus to try gainsharing systems is taken from the compensation policies of some Japanese firms that pay out over 25 percent of worker's wages in two annual bonuses determined by the firm's economic performance. There will be more discussion of current gainsharing and shared savings plans in Chapter 12 in the context of productivity management.

Bibliography

Argyris, Chris. *Integrating the Individual and the Organization*. New York: John Wiley and Sons, 1964.

Balkan, David B. and Luis R. Gomez-Mejia. "Toward a Contingency Theory of Compensation Strategy," *Strategic Management Journal* (March–April 1987).

Ban, Carolyn. "The Navy Demonstration Project: An Experiment in Experimentation," in Carolyn Ban and Norma M. Riccucci, eds., *Public Personnel Management: Current Concerns, Future Challenges*. White Plains, N.Y.: Longman Press, 1991.

Beatty, Richard W. and James R. Beatty. "Some Problems with Contemporary Job Evaluation Systems," In Helen Remick, ed., *Comparable Worth and Wage Discrimination*. Philadelphia: Temple University Press, 1984.

Blank, Rebecca M. "An Analysis of Worker's Choice Between Employment in the Public and Private Sectors," *Industrial and Labor Relations Review* (January 1985).

Boston Federal Executive Board. *Competing for the Future: A Report on the Effects of Federal Pay Policy on Public Service*. Boston, March 1989.

Bowey, Angela and Richard Thorpe. *Payment Systems and Productivity*. London: Macmillan, 1986.

Clark, Timothy B. and Marjorie Wachtel. "The Quiet Crisis Goes Public," *The Government Executive* (June 1988).

Classifiers Column. Newsletter of the Classification and Compensation Society, Washington D.C., vols. 20 and 21.

Cummings, Thomas G. and S. Srivastva. *Management of Work*. Kent, Ohio: Kent State University Press, 1977.

Davis, Louis E. and James C. Taylor. *Design of Jobs*. Santa Monica, Calif.: Goodyear, 1979.

DeSanto, John F. "Higher Pay for Good Performance: The Average Grade Approach," *Public Personnel Management*, vol. 9, no. 4 (1980).

Doherty, Mary H. and Ann Harriman. "Comparable Worth: The Equal Employment Issue of the 1980's," *Review of Public Personnel Administration*, vol. 1, no. 3 (Summer 1981).

Drucker, Peter. "The Sickness of Government," *The Public Interest* (Winter 1969).

Duggan, Martin L. "The Bottom Line on Federal Pay," *Labor Law Review* (January 1985).

Forrer, J. *A Federal Position Classification System for the 1980's*. Washington, D.C.: U.S. Government Printing Office, 1981.

Fredlund, Robert F. "Criteria for Selecting a Wage System," *Public Personnel Management*, 4 (September–October 1976).

Ganschinietz, Bill and Stephen McConomy. "Trends in Job Evaluation Practices of State Personnel Systems," *Public Personnel Management*, vol. 12, no. 1 (Spring 1983).

Gerson, S. R. "Newman's Views," *Classifer's Column* (June/July 1990).

Chropade, Jai and Thomas J. Atchison. "The Concept of Job Analysis: A Review and Some Suggestions," *Public Personnel Management*, vol. 9, no. 3 (1980).

Gilbert, G. Ronald and Ardel Nelson. "The Pacer Share Demonstration Project: Implications for Organizational Management and Performance Evaluation," *Public Personnel Management* (Summer 1989).

Government Employee Relations Report. *Reforming the Federal Pay System: Special Report* (December 1989).

Greenough, William C. and Francis P. King. *Pension Plans and Public Policy*. New York: Columbia University Press, 1976.

Hackman, Richard and Greg R. Oldham. *Work Redesign*. Reading, Mass.: Addison-Wesley, 1980.

Halachmi, Arie. "Information Technology, Human Resources Management, and Prductivity," in Carolyn Ban and Norma M. Riccucci, eds., *Public Personnel Management: Current Concerns, Future Challenges*. White Plains, N.Y.: Longman Press, 1991.

Holley, Lyn Meridew. "Pay Reform and Job Classification," *The Bureaucrat* (Spring 1990).

Hyde, Albert C. "The New Environment for Compensation and Performance Evaluation in the Public Sector," *Public Personnel Management* (Winter 1988).

Hyde, Albert C. and Jay M. Shafritz. "Position Classification and Staffing," in *Public Personnel Administration*, edited by Stephen W. Hays and Richard C. Kearney. Englewood Cliffs, N.J.: Prentice-Hall, 1983.

Ippolito, Richard A. "Why Federal Workers Don't Quit," *The Journal of Human Resources* (Spring 1987).

Jensen, Ollie A. "An Analysis of Confusions and Misconceptions Surrounding Job Analysis, Job Evaluation, Position Classification, Employee Selection, and Content Validity," *Public Personnel Management*, 7 (July–August 1978).

Lust, John and Charles Fay. "The Impact of Compensation and Benefits on Employee Quit Rates," *Compensation and Benefits Management* (Summer 1989).

Maccoby Michael. *Why Work?* New York: Simon & Schuster, 1988.

McCarthy, Eugene M. *The Congress and the Civil Service: A History of Federal Compensation and Classification*. Background paper for National Commission on the Public Service, 1989.

Milkovich, George and Jerry M. Newman. *Compensation*. Homewood, IL: Business Publications, Inc., 1987.

Naff, Katherine C. and Raymond Pomerleau. "Productivity Gainsharing: A Federal Sector Case Study," *Public Personnel Management* (Winter 1988).

National Academy of Public Administration. *The Quiet Crises of the Civil Service: The Federal Personnel System at the Crossroads*, December 1986.

National (Volcker) Commission for the Public Service. (Leadership for America.) Washington, D.C., 1989.

Oliver, Philip M. "Modernizing a State Job Evaluation and Pay Plan," *Public Personnel Management*, 5 (May–June 1976).

Penner, Maurice. "How Job-Based Classification Systems Promote Organizational Effectiveness," *Public Personnel Management*, vol. 12, no. 3 (Fall
1983).

Perlman, Kenneth. "Job Families: A Review and Discussion of Their Implications for Personnel Selection," *Psychological Bulletin*, vol. 80, no.
1 (January 1980).

Remsay, Arch S. "The New Factor Evaluation System of Position Classification," *Civil Service Journal*, 16 (January–March 1976).

Report on Job Evaluation and Ranking in the Federal Government. Committee on Post Office and Civil Service, Subcommittee on Position Classification, 91st Cong., 1st Session, House Report no. 91-28. Washington, D.C.,
February 27, 1969.

Sayre, Wallace S. "The Triumph of Techniques Over Purpose," *Public Administration Review* (Spring 1948).

Shafritz, Jay M. *Position Classification: A Behavioral Analysis for the Public
Service*. New York: Praeger, 1973.

Siegel, Gilbert B. "Compensation, Benefits and Work Schedules," *Public
Personnel Management* (Summer 1989).

Smith, Russ. "Job Redesign in the Public Sector," *Review of Public Personnel Administration*, vol. 2, no. 1 (Fall 1981).

Suskin, Harold (ed). *Job Evaluation and Pay Administration in the
Public Sector*. Chicago: International Personnel Management Association, 1977.

Thompson, Frank J. "Classification as Politics," in *People in the Public Service*, edited by R. T. Golembiewski and M. Cohen. Itasca, Ill.: Peacock,
1976.

U.S. Civil Service Commission. *A Report on Study of Position Classification Accuracy in Executive Branch Occupations under the General
Schedule*. Washington, D.C.: 1978.

U.S. Congressional Budget Office (CBO). *Employee Turnover in the Federal
Government: A Special Study*. February 1986.

U.S. General Accounting Office (GAO). *Federal Workforce: Pay, Recruitment, and Retention of Federal Employees*. February 1987.

———. *Federal Workforce: Pay, Recruitment, and Retention of Federal
Employees*. September 1990.

U.S. General Accounting Office (GAO). *Locality Pay for Federal Employees*. June 1989.

————. *Federal Pay: Comparisons with the Private Sector by Job and Locality*. May 1990.

————. *Federal White-Collar Employee Salary Reform*. March 1990.

U.S. Merit Systems Protection Board (MSPB). *OPM's Classifiction and Qualification Systems: A Renewed Emphasis, A Changing Perspective*. November 1989.

U.S. Office of Personnel Management (OPM). *Integrated Salary and Benefits: Programs for State and Local Government*. Washington, D.C.: U.S. Government Printing Office, November 1979.

————. *Position Classification: A Guide for City and County Managers*. Washington, D.C.: U.S. Government Printing Office, November 1979.

————. *Federal White-Collar Pay System: Report on a Market-Sensitive Study*. Washington, D.C.: August 1989.

White, Robert D. "Position Analysis and Characterization," *Review of Public Personnel Administration*, vol. 4, no. 2 (Spring 1984).

Winn, Russ. "A Comparison of Internal and External Factors Affecting Voluntary Turnover," *Review of Public Personnel Management* (Fall 1984).

Witt, Elder. "Are Our Governments Paying What It Takes to Keep the Best and the Brightest?" *Governing* (December 1988).

6

Recruitment, Examination, and Selection

Prologue: A Tale of Two Courts—The *Griggs* and *Wards Cove* Decisions

Few things seemed as certain in the human resources management world as the direction set by the federal court system in the early 1970s to eliminate employment discrimination. This movement, stemming out of the unanimous U.S. Supreme Court decision in *Griggs* v. *Duke Power Company* (1971), and affirmed through various statutory laws and presidential executive orders, made discriminatory hiring practices a major target for elimination. But things change; even courts! In the 1980s, President Ronald Reagan's appointment of several conservative judges began to result in a very different set of outcomes and decisions, even in seemingly fundamental areas as the barring of employment discrimination. Through several decisions in 1989, a badly divided Supreme Court ruled that while the goal of barring employment discrimination was still valid, the means to reach the goal was subject to dispute. This prologue highlights the two Court cases in question, which are, in reality, the product of two different Supreme Court environments. In short, it is a tale of two very different Courts.

   Griggs v. *Duke Power* involved the personnel practices of the Duke Power Company's power-generating facility at Draper, North Carolina, known as the Dan River steam station. In 1964, the Dan River station employed ninety-five workers and was organized into five departments. The station's lowest paying jobs were in its labor department, where the highest paying job paid less than the lowest paying job in the other four departments. Promotions within each department were generally based on seniority. The station employed fourteen African Americans by 1964, all of whom worked in the labor department.

In 1955, the company began to require a high school education for initial placement in all departments except labor. This policy effectively prohibited African Americans from working in any department but labor. Then, on July 2, 1965, which just so happened to be the effective date of the Civil Rights Act of 1964, the company added an additional requirement for new employees. In order to qualify for placement in any department but labor, it was necessary to pass two aptitude tests. Later that year, the company eased up on its policy of requiring high school diplomas for transfers from the labor department to any of the other departments; it was now willing to allow incumbent employees to qualify for transfer by simply taking the two aptitude tests.

The tests used by the Dan River steam station were the Wonderlic personnel test, designed to measure general intelligence, and the Bennett mechanical comprehension test. These tests did not and were not intended to measure the ability to perform successfully in any particular type of job. Not surprisingly, the tests were actually more restrictive than the previous requirement for a high school diploma because the requisite scores used by the company approximated the national median for high school graduates. On a national basis only about half of all high school graduates would have been able to gain the requisite scores.

In early 1966, the "racial barrier" at the Dan River station was broken. An African-American employee, a high school graduate who had worked for Duke Power since 1953 in the labor department, was promoted. His promotion came five months after charges had been filed with the Equal Employment Opportunity Commission (EEOC) against the company. The next year, thirteen of the African-American employees at Dan River steam station, all of whom had been denied promotion because they scored low on the aptitude tests, filed a class-action suit against their employer, the Duke Power Company.

Who Was Socrates (470–399 BC)?

. . . ancient Greek philosopher who established the intellectual foundations of modern employment testing when he asserted that "The unexamined life is not worth living."

Jay M. Shafritz, *Dictionary of Personnel Management and Labor Relations*, 2nd ed. (New York: Facts on File, Inc., 1985).

They charged that the company's requirements of a high school education and passing scores on intelligence tests for selection or promotion within the company were discriminatory and violated Title VII of the Civil Rights Act of 1964. While Title VII forbids discriminatory employment practices, it does allow the use of professionally developed ability and aptitude tests for employment practices, provided there is no intent to discriminate. The *Griggs* case finally made its way to the U.S. Supreme Court only after a district court and a Court of Appeals rejected the contentions of the African-American employees at Dan River.

A unanimous Supreme Court in 1971 reversed the lower court decisions and ruled in favor of the African-American employees. The Court ruled that Title VII of the Civil Rights Act of 1964 "proscribes not only overt discrimination but also practices that are fair in form, but discriminatory in operation." Thus, if employment practices that are operating to exclude African Americans or other protected-class persons "cannot be shown to be related to job performance, the practice is prohibited." The Court dealt a blow to restrictive credentialism when it stated that, while diplomas and tests are useful, "Congress has mandated the common-sense proposition that they are not to become masters of reality." In essence, the Court found that the law requires that tests used for employment purposes "must measure the person for the job and not the person in the abstract."

The *Griggs* decision originally applied only to the private sector, but since passage of the Equal Employment Opportunity Act in 1972, which extended the provisions of Title VII of the Civil Rights Act to cover public employees, the *Griggs* decision opened the doors to a new era in public employee testing and selection. What was at stake, as most organizations were to find, was not the actual practice, selection policy, or testing device in use, but the applied *results*, or the ways in which policies or practices brought about discriminatory *impact* on various special groups (gender, age, ethnicity, and race being the most important categories for which adverse impact must be avoided). So, as the *Griggs* Court said,

> good intent or absence of discriminatory intent does not redeem employment procedures or testing mechanisms that operate as "built-in headwinds" for minority groups and are unrelated to measuring job capability. . . . Congress directed the thrust of the [Civil Rights] Act to the *consequences* of employment practices, not simply the motivation.

It was to a quite different Supreme Court that the *Wards Cove* v. *Atonio* case found itself before in 1989. Wards Cove Packing Company operated several salmon canneries in Alaska; it essentially used two types of employees. There were unskilled jobs on the cannery lines that were held predominantly by nonwhites, while the noncannery jobs (skilled positions such as boat

In Search of the "Best Qualified" Job Candidate

The U.S. Supreme Court, in its 1987 *Johnson* v. *Transportation Agency* (107 S.Ct. 1442, 1987 at p. 1457) ruling said that there may *never* be a best qualified job applicant. Quoting from a brief submitted by the American Society for Personnel Administration, the Court said that "[i]t is a standard tenet of personnel administration that there is rarely a single, 'best qualified' person for a job . . . final determinations as to which candidate is 'best qualified' are at best subjective."

operators, accountants, and medical personnel) were held predominantly by whites. Almost all the cannery jobs paid wages below the noncannery jobs. Furthermore, there was almost complete separation between the two groups of employees in that nonwhite and whites lived in separate dormitories and ate in separate dining facilities. Justices Stevens and Blackmun, in their dissenting opinions in this case, went as far as to remark that "the salmon industry, as described by this record takes us back to a kind of overt and institutionalized discrimination we have not dealt with in years: a total residential and work environment, organized on principles of racial stratification and segregation, which . . . resembles a plantation economy."

Justice White delivered the majority opinion for this 5-4 decision by refuting the interpretation provided in *Griggs* that forbade employment practices that result in "disparate impact" (i.e., that produce discriminatory results, even if the practices themselves are neutral). The majority ruling rejected the standard of comparison established by *Griggs* in which a prima facie disparate-impact case could be established by comparing simply the percentage of minorities in each job category. In its place was a new standard, which compared the "qualified job force" in the labor market to the racial makeup of the jobs in question. The Court majority said:

> If the absence of minorities holding such skilled positions is due to a dearth of qualified nonwhite applicants (for reasons that are not petitioners' fault), petitioners' selection methods or employment practices cannot be said to have had a "disparate impact" on nonwhites.

The Court went the extra step to make clear its new position on where the burden of proof was regarding disparate impact. It stated that "any employer having a racially unbalanced segment of its work force could be hauled into court, and made to undertake the expensive and time-consuming task of defending the business necessity of its selection methods." *Wards Cove* effectively overturned the landmark *Griggs* ruling by shifting the burden of proof to the plaintiffs, requiring them to demonstrate that specific employment practices of the company have *caused* the statistical disparity between work force groups and jobs. As Linda Greenhouse, reporting for the *New York Times* said, this places "insurmountable obstacles in the path of workers seeking to bring a common type of employment discrimination lawsuit under the Civil Rights Act of 1964." Moreover, it "could prove so onerous to plaintiffs that employers might feel free to abandon affirmative action plans."

Of course, there was vigorous dissent, bordering on disbelief on the part of the four dissenting justices. They stated that the majority ruling in *Wards Cove* reargues the intentions of *Griggs*, the Title VII precedents, and even the acceptance within society of the *Griggs* decision as a fundamental ruling. The dissenting justices ended with a cynical note: "One wonders whether the majority still believes that race discrimination—or more accurately, race discrimination against nonwhites—is a problem in our society, or even remembers that it ever was."

An ending to this tale of two Courts must be delayed. *Wards Cove* and several other related conservative Court actions generated a backlash and spurred legislative reaction in the form of a new 1990 Civil Rights Act, which, if it had not been vetoed by President Bush, would have counteracted regressive Supreme Court rulings such as *Wards Cove* (see also Chapter 7). Because the Senate failed to override the veto by one vote, *Wards Cove* holds for now. In the interim, the Supreme Court has added a new, and by all accounts moderate-conservative justice, Mr. Souter, who replaces Justice Brennan, one of the Court's most liberal justices. Congressional leaders, as of this writing, have already signaled their intentions to pass an even stronger Civil Rights Bill for 1991. This tale is definitely "to be continued. . . ."

The Development of the Uniform Guidelines

Although *Wards Cove* and several other Court rulings have limited grounds for litigation and changed the burden of proof in job discrimination cases, there remains a considerable bulwark of legal framework that regulates selection and hiring practices. Following the *Griggs* decision, the courts provided more specific guidance on testing practices. In 1973, in *U.S.* v. *Georgia Power Company*, the Fifth Circuit Court of Appeals reaffirmed job-relatedness as the critical requirement. In this case, the Georgia Power Company had used a separate validation process for its testing instruments that did not correspond with how the tests were being used for making employment and promotions decisions. The court ruled that job-relatedness in this case can only be construed as part of the selection decision-making process. The Supreme Court in 1975 provided more definitive instructions on what job-relatedness entailed. In *Albemarle Paper Company* v. *Moody*, the Court struck down a rather late constructed job-testing and validation procedure because it failed to demonstrate job relevance. The company in this case had conducted a job analysis based on only a few select jobs and concentrated on the job requirements for employees at the highest levels in those jobs. Basically, tests were developed that were keyed to higher level, job-experienced whites, but were used to make hiring decisions for inexperienced minorities for lower-level jobs. In rejecting this practice, the Court ruled that it was essential for valid testing that a job analysis study relate entry-level applicants to higher positions and that criteria measurement be established to determine job-specific abilities to the positions in question. The message to all employers using examinations was rather clear: a well-planned and rigorously constructed validation study would be required to "ensure" any examination from legal challenges.

These early 1970s legal decisions about testing and selection helped lead to the development of the *Uniform Guidelines on Employee Selection Procedures* issued jointly by the EEOC, the former U.S. Civil Service Commission, and the Departments of Labor and Justice. They were the result of nearly fifteen years of arguments among federal agencies and scores of individually issued procedures that often created more chaos than clarity. Finally, in 1978, the guidelines were formally issued, completing a process that established a uniform government employment policy.

The *Uniform Guidelines* are the central set of rules for selection procedures that apply to both the public and private sectors. Of course, most federal government agenices are covered, as are any state and local government agencies that employ more than fifteen people or receive federal revenue assistance. The same concept applies to private sector employers: if they have fifteen or more employees hired for twenty weeks in the year, or receive any form of government contract or subcontract, they must also abide by the *Uniform Guidelines*.

What the *Uniform Guidelines* cover is equally pervasive. Simply put, all procedures used in making "employment decisions" are covered. This would include, for example, application forms, minimum application requirements, any performance test, reviews of past training and experience, all written tests, all oral interviews or tests, and even performance reviews of someone hired on a trial or probationary basis. It is also important to add, as the courts have made abundantly clear, that "employment decisions" include more than the recruiting and hiring process. An employment decision includes retention, promotion, separation or firing, performance review, and training decisions. In effect, whenever one employee is chosen over another, this constitutes a "selection decision."

The *Uniform Guidelines* detail minimum standards for validation, explain different forms of validity, and document evidential requirements for demonstrating validity. Figure 6.1 is provided to give an indication of the scope of the *Guidelines*. The serious student of public or private personnel management must have a working familiarity of the *Guidelines*.

Figure 6.1. Uniform guidelines (table of contents) on employee selection procedures.

COMPREHENSIVE TABLE OF CONTENTS

GENERAL PRINCIPLES

1607.1. Statement of Purpose
A. Need for Uniformity — Issuing Agencies
B. Purpose of Guidelines
C. Relation to Prior Guidelines
1607.2. Scope
A. Application of Guidelines
B. Employment Decisions
C. Selection Procedures
D. Limitations
E. Indian Preference Not Affected
1607.3. Discrimination Defined: Relationship Between Use of Selection Procedures and Discrimination
A. Procedure Having Adverse Impact Constitutes Discrimination Unless Justified
B. Consideration of Suitable Alternative Selection Procedures
1607.4. Information on Impact
A. Records Concerning Impact
B. Applicable Race, Sex and Ethnic Groups For Record Keeping
C. Evaluation of Selection Rates. The "Bottom Line"
D. Adverse Impact And The "Four-Fifths Rule"
E. Consideration of User's Equal Employment Opportunity Posture
1607.5. General Standards for Validity Studies
A. Acceptable types of Validity Studies
B. Criterion-Related, Content, and Construct Validity
C. Guidelines Are Consistent with Professional Standards
D. Need For Documentation of Validity
E. Accuracy and Standardization
F. Caution Against Selection on Basis of Knowledges, Skills or Abilities Learned in Brief Orientation Period
G. Method of Use of Selection Procedures

H. Cutoff Scores
I. Use of Selection Procedures for Higher Level Jobs
J. Interim Use of Selection Procedures
K. Review of Validity Studies for Currency
1607.6. Use of Selection Procedures Which Have Not Been Validated
A. Use of Alternate Selection Procedures to Eliminate Adverse Impact
B. Where Validity Studies Cannot or Need Not Be Performed
(1) Where Informal or Unscored Procedures Are Used
(2) Where Formal And Scored Procedures Are Used
1607.7. Use of Other Validity Studies
A. Validity Studies not Conducted by the User
B. Use of Criterion-Related Validity Evidence from Other Sources
(1) Validity Evidence
(2) Job Similarity
(3) Fairness Evidence
C. Validity Evidence from Multi-Unit Study
D. Other Significant Variables
1607.8. Cooperative Studies
A. Encouragment of Cooperative Studies
B. Standards for Use of Cooperative Studies
1607.9 No Assumption of Validity
A. Unacceptable Substitutes for Evidence of Validity
B. Encouragement of Professional Supervision
1607.10. Employment Agencies and Employment Services
A. Where Selection Procedures Are Devised by Agency
B. Where Selection Procedures Are Devised Elsewhere
1607.11. Disparate Treatment
1607.12. Retesting of Applicants

(continued)

1607.13. Affirmative Action
A. Affirmative Action Obligations
B. Encouragement of Voluntary Affirmative Action Programs

TECHNICAL STANDARDS

1607.14. Technical Standards for Validity Studies
A. Validity Studies Should be Based on Review of Information about the Job
B. Technical Standards for Criterion-Related Validity Studies
  (1) Technical Feasibility
  (2) Analysis of the Job
  (3) Criterion Measures
  (4) Representativeness of the Sample
  (5) Statistical Relationships
  (6) Operational use of Selection Procedures
  (7) Over-Statement of Validity Findings
  (8) Fairness
    (a) Unfairness Defined
    (b) Investigation of Fairness
    (c) General Considerations in Fairness Investigations
    (d) When Unfairness Is Shown
    (e) Technical Feasibility of Fairness Studies
    (f) Continued Use of Selection Procedures When Fairness Studies not Feasible
C. Technical Standards for Content Validity Studies
  (1) Appropriateness of Content Validity Studies
  (2) Job Analysis for Content Validity
  (3) Development of Selection Procedure
  (4) Standards For Demonstrating Content Validity
  (5) Reliability
  (6) Prior Training or Experience
  (7) Training Success
  (8) Operational use

  (9) Ranking Based on Content Validity Studies
D. Technical Standards For Construct Validity Studies
  (1) Appropriateness of Construct Validity Studies
  (2) Job Analysis For Construct Validity Studies
  (3) Relationship to the Job
  (4) Use of Construct Validity Study Without New Criterion-Related Evidence
    (a) Standards for Use
    (b) Determination of Common Work Behaviors

DOCUMENTATION OF IMPACT AND VALIDITY EVIDENCE

1607.15. Documentation of Impact and Validity Evidence
A. Required Information
  (1) Simplified Recordkeeping for Users With Less Than 100 Employees
  (2) Information on Impact
    (a) Collection of Information on Impact
    (b) When Adverse Impact Has Been Eliminated in The Total Selection Process
    (c) When Data Insufficient to Determine Impact
  (3) Documentation of Validity Evidence
    (a) Type of Evidence
    (b) Form of Report
    (c) Completeness
B. Criterion-Related Validity Studies
  (1) User(s), Location(s), and Date(s) of Study
  (2) Problem and Setting
  (3) Job Analysis or Review of Job Information
  (4) Job Titles and Codes
  (5) Criterion Measures
  (6) Sample Description
  (7) Description of Selection Procedure
  (8) Techniques and Results
  (9) Alternative Procedures

Figure 6.1.   *(continued)*

Investigated
(10) Uses and Applications
(11) Source Data
(12) Contact Person
(13) Accuracy and
Completeness
C. Content Validity Studies
(1) User(s), Location(s), and
Date(s) of Study
(2) Problem and Setting
(3) Job Analysis — Content of
the Job
(4) Selection Procedure and its
Content
(5) Relationship Between
Selection Procedure and
the Job
(6) Alternative Procedures
Investigated
(7) Uses and Applications
(8) Contact Person
(9) Accuracy and Completeness
D. Construct Validity Studies
(1) User(s), Location(s), and
Date(s) of Study
(2) Problem and Setting
(3) Construct Definition
(4) Job Analysis
(5) Job Titles and Codes
(6) Selection Procedure
(7) Relationship to Job
Performance
(8) Alternative Procedures
Investigated

(9) Uses and Applications
(10) Accuracy and Completeness
(11) Source Data
(12) Contact Person
E. Evidence of Validity from
Other Studies
(1) Evidence from Criterion-
Related Validity Studies
(a) Job Information
(b) Relevance of Criteria
(c) Other Variables
(d) Use of the Selection
Procedure
(e) Bibliography
(2) Evidence from Content
Validity Studies
(3) Evidence from Construct
Validity Studies
F. Evidence of Validity from
Cooperative Studies
G. Selection for Higher Level Jobs
H. Interim Use of Selection
Procedures

DEFINITIONS

1607.16. Definitions

APPENDIX

1607.17. Policy Statement on Affirmative
Action (see Section 13B)
1607.18. Citations

Source: Federal Register, vol. 43, no. 166 (Friday, August 25, 1978).

Figure 6.1. *(continued)*

At the heart of the *Guidelines* is the concept of "adverse impact." (This is the disparate impact controversy embodied in *Griggs* and *Wards Cove*, as discussed in the prologue to this chapter.) This concept refers to the establishment of an "80 percent" or "4/5ths" rule, which is used to determine minimum evidence of "discrimination." The 80 percent rule stipulates that if the selection rate for any group is less than 80 percent of that for other groups, this constitutes evidence of adverse impact in the selection device. This does not mean that the selection device cannot be used, but it must be carefully *validated* if the 80 percent rule is violated. Essentially a "burden of proof" change is incorporated into the legal process surrounding selections. Under the "old rulings" (i.e., beginning with *Griggs*), if there is adverse impact, the burden of proof shifted to the organization to defend and show that there are valid reasons for the result and that no intent to discriminate is involved. Under the new ruling (i.e., *Wards Cove*), adverse impact is not enough to reverse the burden or proof. The individual or "unselected one" must demonstrate either the *intent* to discriminate or some causality between each employment practice and statistical job disparities.

It is important to point out that prior to *Wards Cove*, it was only in cases arising under the Constitution that intent rather than results determined the existence of discrimination. This was made clear in the Court's landmark 1976 *Washington* v. *Davis* decision. In this case, an entry-level police officer exam administered by the District of Columbia's police department disproportionately screened out African American applicants (four times as many African Americans failed the exam as whites). The African Americans filed suit, arguing that the police department's written exam was racially discriminatory and violated the Due Process Clause of the Fifth Amendment to the Constitution. Because the case was filed under the Fifth Amendment as opposed to Title VII, the adverse impact standard was not applied. The *Washington* Court said that this standard "is not the constitutional rule." The Court said: "Disproportionate impact is not irrelevant, but it is not the sole touchstone of an invidious racial discrimination foridden by the

---

What Exactly Is Adverse Impact?

The *Uniform Guidelines* state that evidence of adverse impact exists when "a selection rate for any race, sex or ethnic group . . . is less than four-fifths (4/5ths) or eighty percent (80%) of the selection rate for the group with the highest selection rate."

The *Guidelines* provide the following example:

Applicants	Hires	Selection rate/ percentage hired
80 Whites	48	48/80 or 60%
40 Black	12	12/40 or 30%

"A comparison of the black selection rate (30%) with the white selection rate (60%) shows that the black rate is 30/60, or one-half (50%) of the white rate. Since the one-half (50%) is less than 4/5ths (80%) adverse impact is usually indicated."

"Questions and Answers to Clarify and Provide a Common Interpretation of the Uniform Guidelines on Employee Selection Procedures," *Federal Register*, vol. 44, no. 43 (March 2, 1979), p. 11998.

Constitution. Standing alone, it does not trigger the rule. . . ." The Court instead relied on whether the police department *intended* to discriminate against the African-American job candidates. The Court found no intent to discriminate, therefore ruling in favor of the police department (for a further discussion, see Chapter 9). Based on *Wards Cove*, it may be that Title VII cases will move in the same direction.

In 1978, the U.S. Supreme Court decided another precedent-setting case in *U.S.* v. *South Carolina*. In this case, a lower court ruling was upheld concerning the use of a test designed by a national testing corporation for selection decisions involving school teachers. Even though there was adverse impact, the Court ruled that there was no intention to discriminate and that proper validation procedures had been followed. (This case was brought under the Fourteenth Amendment, Title VII, and the Civil Rights Acts of 1866 and 1871). While the legal verdict is still out in the selection and employment area, the technical vocabulary and methodological expertise required to understand the key issues involved is a permanent fixture, and more guidance is on the way. At the urging of the General Accounting Office, as well as such professional associations as the International Personnel Management Association, the EEOC has begun a comprehensive review of the *Uniform Guidelines*. Unfortunately, the review began in 1984 and, as of this writing, a projected end date is not yet in sight!

The Importance of Public Employment

Perhaps the biggest reason that employment practices—recruitment, selection, and placement—have emerged as such a highly controversial area of personnel management is that the stakes are so high. Public sector employment, like government, was at one time relatively small. But by the late 1980s, over 17 million persons (3 million federal, 4 million state government, and over 10 million local government) worked for government, accounting for almost 15 percent of the total work force. When workers in not-for-profit organizations are added, one expert, Eli Ginzberg, estimates that total "public employment" is over one-third of all American workers. Government is not only the largest single work "industry," but has been one of the most important sources of employment for women, African Americans, Latinos, and other protected-class persons (see Chapter 7). When one then considers the tremendous implications that government employment holds for the economic health of American communities and the aspirations of various interest groups, it is understandable that the processes controlling entry to these jobs are subject to both intense scrutiny and widespread concern.

What was once a matter of the spoils system versus the merit system has given way to disputes about equity and representativeness. Historically,

government has been conceived of in terms of its efficiency, whether the decisions and actions of its functionaries were good or bad for the public weal.
This concern bypassed two increasingly significant aspects of bureaucracy—its
utility as a source of jobs and economic betterment for the citizenry and its
social composition as an indicator of political power and representation in
a democracy. The latter concept of equity implies that the distribution of
government jobs should be approximately proportional to, or representative
of, the population at large. The importance of equity can not be underestimated.
Samuel Krislov, in his classic work *Representative Bureaucracy*, argues that
only if government is representative will it have the credibility to accomplish
its agenda in any orderly and effective fashion. Equity also entails that the
percentage that a particular reference group occupies in the recruiting population should correspond to the percentage of positions it occupies at all levels
of the bureaucracy.

The process of employment has three basic components: recruitment,
selection, and placement. Once an organization has ascertained a specific staffing need and a corresponding funding source for a new human resource,

---

**Early Recruiting Effort of the
U.S. Civil Service Commission**

THE EDITOR   May 22, 1891
  American Architect
    Boston, Massachusetts

SIR:

The Commission tenders the inclosed notice of examination for draftsman for publication, but has no means of paying for its publication, and neither such tender nor
this letter must be regarded as in any sense creating a liability on the part of any
one to pay for inserting the notice. It is simply hoped that you will regard it as an
act of justice to those who wish to be examined for the public service to give them,
as far as practicable, the information needed for that purpose, and that you will think
the notice of so much interest for your readers and the public generally that you
will be willing to publish it as information.

Thanking you for past favors,

                              Very respectfully,

                                        THEODORE ROOSEVELT
                                        Acting President

Letters of Theodore Roosevelt, Civil Service Commissioner, 1889–1895 (Washington, D.C.:
U.S. Civil Service Commission, 1958), p. 16.

it will initiate an employment process. The first step is some form of recruitment—the process of advertising staffing needs and encouraging candidates to apply, from both inside and outside the organization. *Recruitment* is designed to provide the organization with an adequate number of viable candidates from which to make its selection decision. *Selection* is the process of reviewing the job candidates and deciding who will be offered the position. *Examinations* in their many varieties are the dominant selection tool. Selection will tend to automatically order the last step in the process, *placement*—the assignment of the new employee to the position so that work can begin.

With the increasing size, importance, and professionalization of public sector employment, some of the more traditional problems regarding recruitment have, for the most part, dissipated. These problems primarily focused on the difficulty of attracting people to apply for work in the public sector. Compared to the private sector, pay was generally inferior and the prestige or status of government work was low. But this changed in the 1970s. Because of the union movement and legislation mandating pay comparability, government employees, at least in the larger jurisdictions, generally began to enjoy fairly competitive fringe benefit and salary packages. This movement slackened in the 1980s, but has now been renewed by recent pay reform legislation passed by the federal government (see Chapter 5 for a further discussion). Still, one indicator of the economic health of an area is the number of applicants for public employment. In hard economic times government agencies are flooded with applications.

The main objective of recruitment can be said to be the generating of an adequate number of qualified applicants from which a good selection decision can be made. An applicant is any individual who submits a completed application form for consideration. Indeed, it is often said that the first phase of the examining process consists of filling out the application blank. If applicants do not provide the necessary information documenting their minimum qualifications, they are not given any further consideration; that is, they are not permitted to take the formal examination. However, it is not uncommon for applicants who qualify in every respect for a position to be refused consideration. Many positions above the entry level are open only to individuals already employed with the jurisdiction. Outsiders, no matter how qualifed, may not be admitted to such promotional examinations. Sometimes, union agreements make the recruiting base even more restrictive. When promotional examinations are held on a departmental basis, a department may have no choice but to accept all of the low scorers in its own department before it may consider higher scoring individuals from other departments.

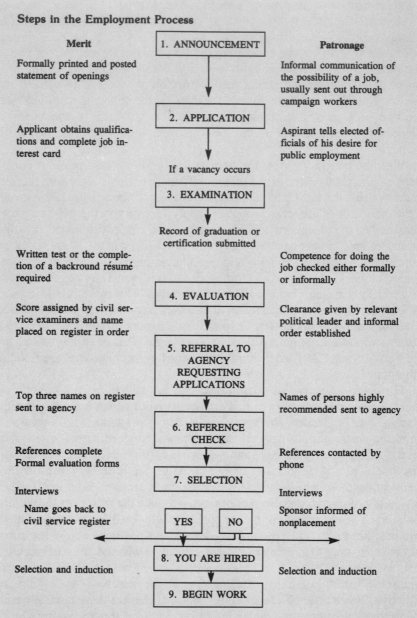

Steps in the Employment Process

Merit	1. ANNOUNCEMENT	Patronage
Formally printed and posted statement of openings		Informal communication of the possibility of a job, usually sent out through campaign workers
	2. APPLICATION	
Applicant obtains qualifications and complete job interest card		Aspirant tells elected officials of his desire for public employment
	If a vacancy occurs	
	3. EXAMINATION	
	Record of graduation or certification submitted	
Written test or the completion of a backround résumé required		Competence for doing the job checked either formally or informally
	4. EVALUATION	
Score assigned by civil service examiners and name placed on register in order		Clearance given by relevant political leader and informal order established
	5. REFERRAL TO AGENCY REQUESTING APPLICATIONS	
Top three names on register sent to agency		Names of persons highly recommended sent to agency
	6. REFERENCE CHECK	
References complete Formal evaluation forms		References contacted by phone
	7. SELECTION	
Interviews		Interviews
Name goes back to civil service register	YES NO	Sponsor informed of nonplacement
Selection and induction	8. YOU ARE HIRED	Selection and induction
	9. BEGIN WORK	

Reprinted from Jerome B. McKinney and Lawrence C. Howard, *Public Administration: Balancing Power and Accountability* (Oak Park Ill.: Moore Publishing, 1979), p. 287. Copyright © 1979 Moore Publishing Company Inc.

Personal Rank Versus Position Rank

There are essentially two kinds of jobs for which governments recruit: those that offer personal rank and those that only offer position rank. Rank-in-person systems, such as the Foreign Service and the military, are oriented toward bottom-entry career ladder patterns, whereby individuals normally progress from the lowest to higher ranks. These systems usually have an "up or out" feature whereby a member who is not promotable to the next higher grade after a set period of time is either dismissed or forced to retire. Therefore, employment decisions are related to overall career potential and the capability to perform a wide range of responsibilities. Rank-in-position systems, based primarily on the classification and level of the position held by the employee, are far more common. Here it is the set of work responsibilities ascribed to the position that carries authority. Individuals, by virtue of having qualified for the position, being selected for the position, and holding the position, take its authority as their own only during tenure in that particular position.

These two systems, rank-in-person and rank-in-position, have employment processes that differ markedly:

Concerning recruitment—The rank-in-person system seeks relatively inexperienced high-potential young people to start a career at the entry level, while the rank-in-position system seeks individuals who can perform a specific position's duties.

Concerning selection—The rank-in-person system selects individuals on the basis of their long-range potential and aptitude to perform at various levels through the course of a career, while the rank-in-position system selects individuals on the basis of their ability to perform a specific set of duties for one position or for positions in a certain job family.

Concerning placement—The rank-in-person system has flexible assignments that periodically change. Training is often included as part of an assignment change in order to provide newly needed skills. Individuals must keep themselves available for any geographic or functional assignment. In contrast, with the rank-in-position system new assignments are tied to promotions and to the meeting of specific standards. Individuals must usually initiate and consent to placement changes.

While these two systems are nearly separate as analytical constructs, in reality both systems tend to pay attention to both aspects—the person and the position. The intermingling of these systems, their standing side by side in many organizations with some means of access into each other (what is termed conversion) has further ensured this common perspective. Yet, the orientations of rank-in-person and rank-in-position systems are quite different

Position Classification and Personal Ranking

The two chief methods used by government to establish hierarchical structures within the civil service are position classification and personal ranking. Position classification is essentially job-oriented and focuses attention on the organization and its immediate functions. The personal ranking system concentrates on the individual and his personal status.

The core of position classification is the concept of the "position" as an abstract entity apart from the employee. The position is viewed as a group of duties and responsibilities requiring the services of one employee. From an organizational viewpoint, a position is the smallest administrative unit of an organization. In a position classification system an individual employee is considered to "fill a position" and he achieves promotion by progression from one "position" to a higher-level "position" within the organization's structure.

The personal ranking system, also called the "career system" or "rank classification," is oriented to the personnel of an organization rather than directly to the organizational structure. It is distinguished from position classification by establishment of a rank hierarchy which exists apart from the administrative structure of the organization, whereas position classification adheres rigidly to organizational lines.

The position classification method is used extensively in the United States in the federal civil service and by many state and local public jurisdictions. It is used sparingly outside of the United States by Canada, Brazil, and, to some extent Russia. The much older personal ranking system has its roots in the class society of Western Europe and is used in the British and French civil service as well as in most other European countries. Personal ranking is not unknown in the United States with familiar applications in the academic world, military service and the foreign service.

Daniel F. Halloran, "Why Position Classification?" *Public Personnel Review*, 28 (April 1967), p. 89. Reprinted by permission of the International Personnel Management Association, 1850 K Street, N.W., Suite 870, Washington, D.C. 20006.

in terms of who is to be employed and for how long. As such, employment practices will be appropriately oriented.

Legal Aspects of Selection Methodology

In the United States, important public issues most often become legal problems, and this is certainly the case with the central question of public employment examinations—test validity. While the validity of such exams could be theoretically determined by psychologists and other social scientists, they could only offer their professional opinions, whereas the opinion of a federal judge provides binding social legitimacy. When the historians of personnel operations look back at the past few decades, they no doubt will write that the courts markedly accelerated the sophistication of employment examinations (but, as we have seen in the prologue to this chapter, the change from *Griggs* to *Wards Cove* has resulted in a whole new area of concern about testing instruments).

The heart of the selection process is the examination. While there are a variety of examination formats, their common objective is to determine whether or not an individual has a specified skill or ability. The idea of using tests to select individuals for "positions in the public trust" is a very old one dating back to ancient China, which initiated the use of examinations for employee selection. The Pendleton Act of 1883, which put the federal government on the road to widespread merit system coverage, foreshadowed the character of the examinations process when it mandated "open competitive examinations" that "shall be practical in their character, and so far as may be possible shall relate to those matters which will fairly test the relative capacity and fitness of the persons examined." As the British Civil Service was the greatest single example and infuence upon the American reform movement, there was considerable concern that a merit system based upon the British system of a competitive academic examinations would be automatically biased

---

Perceptions of Abuse in Federal Government Hiring

A sample of personnel specialists* in the federal government observed the following prohibited personnel practices:

Practice	Percentage
Selection based on friendship	43
Selection based on family relationship	23
Denial of job because of race, national origin, color, religion, or gender	21
Denial of job because of age	17
Denial of job because of disability	9
Influence to quit job competition to help another	8
Competitive selection based on political affiliation	7
Denial of job for political affiliation	2

*Survey conducted in 1988; sample consisted of 3,500 personnel specialists.

Adapted from U.S. Merit Systems Protection Board, *Federal Personnel Management Since Civil Service Reform: A Survey of Federal Personnel Officials* (Washington, D.C.: USMSPB, November 1989), p. 5.

in favor of college graduates. As higher education was essentially an upper-class prerogative in the America of the last century, this was reminiscent of the aristocratic civil service that the Jacksonian movement found so objectionable only fifty years earlier. Mandating that all examinations be "practical in their character" presumably neutralized any advantage that a college graduate might have. (The first entrance examination designed specifically for liberal arts graduates would not be offered by the U.S. Civil Service Commission until 1934.)

Over the years, the primacy of examination practicality was often breached. But that primacy was loudly reaffirmed by the U.S. Supreme Court's 1971 *Griggs* v. *Duke Power Company* decision. The intent of the original civil service reform of the 1880s, that the more privileged elements of society not have an elitist advantage over the less privileged in seeking public employment, was in essence supported by the U.S. Supreme Court in 1971, albeit in the context of a private sector case. And, although the Court's ruling in *Wards Cove* rejected the disparate impact theory, it did not alter the doctrine of job relatedness. Job relatedness remains the paramount consideration in choosing a selection device. The legality of any test now hinges on its ability to predict success on the job, casting everything else under intense scrutiny. Even jobs in police and fire departments, which for years maintained certain physical requirements, have had to be reviewed in the light of real job relatedness. Many women and disabled individuals were formerly excluded from jobs requiring high levels of physical capabilities. Police and fire departments have to conduct detailed job analyses to determine what the "real" requirements are in terms of strength, height, weight, or physical endurance.

Job relatedness, validity, prediction, criterion measurement—what do these mean? More important, what requirements do they establish for personnel managers who wish to develop and use examinations? One must begin with the purpose of an examination. Exams are devices or instruments designed to measure individual differences. In some cases, the measurement problem can appear to be quite simple. Take for example, a written examination to obtain a driver's license. The measurement accomplished through the exam is that those who achieve a prespecified minimum score (usually 70 percent) receive licenses; those who fail get to take the test again. But the more basic question involves what's being measured, or what the criteria are. In this case, questions about state traffic laws, driving safety practices, and traffic signs are used as the criteria for measurement. The assumption behind the driver's test is that a passing score represents an adequate measurement of who will be a relatively safe driver. The criteria are thus, as Wayne Cascio defines them, "operational statements of goals or desired outcomes." While there are many problems with driver licensing from an examination-selection perspective that could be discussed, it must be recognized that the problems

Validating the New York City Civil Service Exam for Firefighter

A 1982 court-imposed effort to hire women into the New York City Fire Department involved the validation of a physical agility exam. In *Berkman* v. *City of New York*, the exam was found by a federal district court judge to have an adverse impact on women. To validate the test, the city established standards based on the performance of incumbent male firefighters (i.e., the city used a concurrent validity strategy). Although a number of women passed the exam, many failed, particularly the second time it was administered. . . . The test was once again challenged under Title VII because of its adverse impact on women, but it was upheld on appeal in 1987 on the grounds that it was valid. . . . In effect, the "valid" test did not facilitate a determination of necessary physical strength or predict qualifications for the job. Rather, it simply showed that some women can perform equally as well as incumbent men.

Norma M. Riccucci, "Merit, Equity and Test Validity: A New Look at an Old Problem," *Administration and Society* (May 1991).

of individual measurement for personnel selection decisions are of much greater magnitude and infinitely more complex.

The use of examinations in employment selection faces two critical problems of measurement: reliability and validity. Reliability concerns stability and consistency: Does the test measure accurately over time? Validity speaks to *relevance* and inherent accuracy: Does the test measure what it is designed to measure? Organizations have not been very concerned with reliability, in part because exams are changed so frequently and in part because of the primacy of validity and job relevance. The key dimension to validity, as previously mentioned, has been job relatedness. Job relatedness means essentially that the criteria being measured in the test are relevant and significant factors in the jobs for which selection decisions are to be made. With these terms introduced, it is now appropriate to look at how they are put into practice.

Examinations and Validation

There are two kinds of examinations: assembled and unassembled. The latter are typically used for professional and managerial positions; they mainly consist of an extensive review and evaluation of a candidate's background. Many professional job candidates have already demonstrated their proficiency. Physicians need a state license to practice medicine; lawyers cannot practice law until they pass a state bar examination. It is obviously wasteful for a jurisdiction to seek to duplicate professional examinations. Sometimes they

Winston Churchill on Examinations

I had scarcely passed by twelfth birthday when I entered the inhospitable regions of examinations, through which for the next seven years I was destined to journey. These examinations were a great trial to me. The subjects which were dearest to the examiners were almost invariably those I fancied least. I would have liked to have been examined in history, poetry and writing essays. The examiners, on the other hands, were partial to Latin and mathematics. And their will prevailed. Moreover, the questions which they asked on both these subjects were almost invariable those to which I was unable to suggest a satisfactory answer. I should have liked to be asked to say what I knew. They always tried to ask what I did not know. When I would have willingly displayed my knowledge, they sought to expose my ignorance. This sort of treatment had only one result: I did not do well in examinations.

This was especially true of my Entrance Examination to Harrow. The Headmaster, Dr. Welldon, however, took a broad-minded view of my Latin prose: he showed discernment in judging my general ability. This was the more remarkable, because I was found unable to answer a single question in the Latin paper. I wrote my name at the top of the page. I wrote down the number of question 'I'. After much reflection I put a bracket around it thus '(I)'. But thereafter I could not think of anything connected with it that was either relevant or true. Incidentally there arrived from nowhere in particular a blot and several smudges. I gazed for two whole hours at this sad spectacle: and then merciful ushers collected my piece of foolscap with all the others and carried it up to the Headmaster's table. It was from these slender indications of scholarship that Dr. Welldon drew the conclusion that I was worthy to pass into Harrow. It is very much to his credit. It showed that he was a man capable of looking beneath the surface of things: a man not dependent upon paper manifestations. I have always had the greatest regard for him.

Winston S. Churchill, *A Roving Commission: My Early Life* (New York: Scribner's, 1931), pp. 15–16.

are even forbidden to do so. For example, Congress has mandated that the OPM not offer written examinations for legal positions.

Assembled examinations are far more common, being any means by which individuals are tested to see if they have the ability to perform the prescribed responsibilities of a particular work assignment or position. There are three basic varieties of assembled examinations: written, oral, and performance. Written examinations, which are the least expensive to administer to large candidate populations, are the most common. Performance examinations are essential when specific skills must be demonstrated (e.g., typing, pipefitting, or truck driving). Oral examinations are appropriate when interpersonal skills are needed for a position and/or when the position is at such a level of sophistication that it is not cost effective to create a special written examination for it. Sometimes examinations are given in two parts (oral or performance sections may only be given to candidates who have previously passed a written portion). In such cases, the scoring process is weighted, for example, 70 percent of the total examination may be for the written portion and 30 percent for the oral. Since examinations are expensive to develop and monitor, only very large or very "rich" jurisdictions such as the federal government and the more highly populous cities and states can afford the staffs of psychologists, the consulting expenses, and other sources of testing expertise that are necessary to develop and maintain a comprehensive testing system. Consequently, many jurisdictions find it economical to grant contracts to private testing firms to develop their examinations, analyze the results, and evaluate the testing system's effectiveness.

Examining tools can now be challenged as discriminatory. Job success is a complex matter and not generally attributable to any single factor. To ensure job relatedness, organizations must identify the appropriate criteria that "contribute" to job success, and then ensure that whatever testing devices are used accurately measure those criteria. Those responsible for examination preparation have no choice but to develop their testing techniques on the assumption that they will have to be defended in a legal challenge.

The utility, economy, and equity of selecting individuals for public service by using objective examinations is obvious, yet the examining process itself poses many problems. Critics contend that written examinations are, at best, imperfect predictors of job performance. The complexity of successful job performance involves a great many variables—quality of supervision, adequacy of training and orientation, motivation, working conditions, peer relationships, and interpersonal environments, among others, any of which may surpass in importance the cognitive skills that are evaluated on written tests.

It has long been conceded that written examinations are imperfect selection devices. As long as it could be maintained that everybody was being treated equally unfairly by the testing process, the problem of cultural bias did not emerge. But that fiction was sunk by the concern for equal employment opportunity. Now, it is asserted that while written examinations may be somewhat unfair to all, they are more unfair to some. There are three categories of bias in testing that may adversely affect such protected-class persons as African Americans and Latinos: the test content, the testing atmosphere, and test use.

Test content has been the subject of intense scrutiny over the past few years. For example, efforts to counter cultural bias have led to the inclusion, in reading tests, of passages by minority authors or about various racial groups. But most subsequent work by psychologists has led to the conclusion that test content (except in cases in which specialized historical and cultural background knowledge is being examined) does not make a sizable difference.

Culturally Fair Tests

During the first few years of the controversy concerning test bias against minority-group members, many individuals felt that an answer to this problem was to develop a test or set of tests that were "culture fair," thus limiting the effects of disadvantaged backgrounds. A basic assumption behind this approach was that differences between minority- and majority-group members on traditional pencil-and-paper verbal tests were due to factors associated with the tests themselves.

One factor often suggested is that test items are culturally "loaded" or familiar only to those individuals who share white middle-class experiences. For example, the content of many intelligence tests may not be familiar to the culturally deprived. An item that has the word "umbrella" in one of the questions might be "unfair" because some people in our society may not know what it is. A 100-item test developed by Williams (1975) provides a dramatic example of this "effect" operating in reverse. The test is called the Black Intelligence Test of Cultural Homogeneity (BITCH) and is intended to be a "cultural-specific" test that taps the cultural experiences of blacks in this country. (Another such test is the Scales Inner City Intelligence Test [Scales, 1973]). When the BITCH is administered to both white and black subjects, there is virtually no overlap between the two distributions—the blacks score considerably higher. However, just because race correlates highly with test scores does not necessarily mean race has anything to do with performance on this test. That is, a middle-class black person raised in suburbia may perform just as poorly on the BITCH as a middle-class white person.

Richard D. Arvey and Robert H. Faley, *Fairness in Selecting Employees*, 2nd ed. (Reading, Mass.: Addison-Wesley Publishing Co., 1988), p. 192.

The potential problem with the testing atmosphere is greater. Although research in this area has been slight, initial indications are that factors such as the race of the examiner, the distance to be traveled to the examination place, and the reception at the test center may have an adverse impact on protected-class persons. There are so many unresearched potential variables that may interact in various ways. As such, little progress has been made in untangling the multiple interactions of such factors as personality, motivation, perception of peer group comparisons, perception of the likelihood of success, or relation to the examiner or examining place.

As mentioned, test usage has been the primary source of bias. Since the U.S. Supreme Court's decision in *Griggs*, job relatedness has become the mandated dictum of test usage. The process of assuring the unbiased application of test results is validation.

Just as there are different kinds of tests, there are different methods of assessing how well a test measures what it purports to measure. The process of compiling data to evaluate tests is referred to as validation. The more common kinds of test validity are *content, criterion*, and *construct*. Additionally, the term *face validity* must be distinguished and examined for its own separate importance. At the outset, it is important to note that the concepts of validity mentioned above are related to each other, although they can be examined as separate factors. In fact, educational psychologists generally insist that a complete review of any examination must necessarily examine all three types of validity.

Content validity means that the questions on the examination are directly related to the duties and responsibilities (i.e., the content) of the position. But how does a test become content valid? Before the examination is assembled, the personnel or test technician must discover the abilities required for the job title for which the test is being developed. There are different ways to get this information: (1) from the knowledge, skills, and abilities section of the job description or class specification; (2) by interviewing managers who supervise individuals who are presently in the positions for which the test is being written; or (3) via a job analysis. A job analysis is akin to a position classification field audit in that the technician goes into the organization in order to talk with and observe individuals presently in the job. From this data the technician can identify the *elements* of a position for which test questions must be written. In short, a testing device has content validity if it is developed to measure the specific requirements for a job (i.e., several related positions). It is generally conceded that if the area of knowledge to be examined is well defined with considerable consensus about field boundaries and emphasis, content validity is an important aspect of validation. As might be expected, however, agreement about the application of content validation parallels that of commonly accepted well-defined fields of knowledge and well-defined jobs. Let us suppose as an example, that a social case worker position required language fluency in Spanish. A content-valid examination for Spanish proficiency would be one that tested for specific vocabulary, speaking, and writing skills needed in that position.

Criterion-related validity involves another set of questions. Essentially we attempt to compare the test with certain external variables that are assumed to be characteristic of the behavior in question. This sounds more complicated but it really entails making an indirect prediction about future success. Suppose, using our case worker example, we wanted to select case workers who could learn Spanish over a two- to three-year period. We might use a language aptitude test that measured an individual's ability to learn languages. In actuality, this type of exam makes a prediction about the individual's likely success in foreign language acquisition by measuring memorization, speaking facility, and mental organization skills that are predictors of success in learning languages.

There are two strategies for demonstrating criterion-related validity—concurrent validity and predictive validity. Concurrent validity may involve giving a prospective examination to individuals already performing successfully on the job. Each of the incumbents could be independently rated by their supervisors on their actual job performance. Then the test scores and the ratings are correlated. If the better workers also obtain the better test scores, then the examination can be said to have concurrent validity.

Predictive validity could seek a similar correlation but would involve a time interval. An examination might be given to all applicants, and at a later date their test scores could be correlated with performance to see how accurate the original scores were in predicting success.

Both of these approaches to criterion validity have drawbacks. Concurrent validity has two particular problems. First, if previous employment decisions reflected discriminatory practices, validation results might be distorted by examining a group of "wrong employees." The difficulty relates to the time factor of experience. It may be that the variable being tested will be validated in experienced employees. However, some capabilities can only be acquired via experience. Therefore, such experience-based capabilities should not be a critical factor for entry. Concurrent validity is more an aid in the diagnosis of existing conditions than a predictor of future performance.

Predictive validity, in contrast, may provide accurate distinctions about future performance, but unfortunately, most organizations cannot afford it—either in terms of organizational disruption or expense. It may be unrealistic to expect many jurisdictions to establish an examinations program, hire a full range of scorers, place them, and wait a year or more to evaluate how well the test scores predicted success, and yet some jurisdictions are doing just that in response to or in anticipation of court pressures.

Leo Rosten's Maxim

When you get farther along, remember Leo Rosten's maxim: "First-rate people hire first-rate people; second-rate people hire third-rate people." Hire the best you can. Whenever I hired anybody, I'd ask myself: "How would I like to work for him—or her—someday?" The nod will go to the one I'd rather work for. This question is a real sleeper. It gets to such issues as: Are you protecting yourself against potential threats, or are you trying to get the best people you can? It also gets to the root of leadership. Once you've hired those assistants, if you're a true leader, you *will* be working for them—to help them become the best they can be.

Robert Townsend, *Up the Organization* (Greenwich, Conn.: Fawcett, 1970), pp. 213–214.

Construct validity involves examining the personal traits being measured by a test, such as honesty, enthusiasm or reliability. This is an important step in compiling a valid examination process, but it necessitates a lengthy and rather theoretical evaluation. While it is important to understand what the test is measuring, the emphasis to date has been on content and criterion validity, which are more direct measurements of how test results are being used.

A fourth type of validity—*face validity*—is not a true measurement of validity at all. It is simply an indication that the test, on the face of it, is relevant; that is, it seems to measure what it purports to measure to the perception of the test taker. Face validity is really a measure of the appropriateness, overall acceptance, or legitimacy of the test. Perhaps the most important thing about face validity is its power. Although not a true statistical measure of an examination, it can make an invalid test appear valid or, conversely, cause test takers to have considerable anxiety and disbelief about a valid test.

These approaches to validation speak to the heart of the selection process. Psychological and statistical measurement problems abound, but jurisdictions have reduced their questions to one: Will it hold up in court? While examinations were once simply a technical and administrative problem of the personnel department, they are now, as was made clear at the beginning of this chapter, of equal concern to a jurisdiction's legal office.

The Old World of PACE

Throughout the 1960s and 1970s, examinations were the real mainstay of the public service employment process. Of the nearly two million persons who applied for federal employment annually, between 50 and 60 percent of them took written examinations, and although about 60 percent of all candidates taking written examinations passed them, the likelihood of obtaining a job was considerably less. The case of the federal government's former PACE exam (Professional and Administrative Career Examination) nicely illustrates the problem here. Between 200,000 to 300,000 applicants competed annually for fewer than 15,000 PACE jobs. About 40 percent of those applicants were in the Washington, D.C. metropolitan area, where some 2,000 PACE jobs were available. To be considered for a PACE job in Washington meant scoring among the top 3 percent of all test takers.

Sometimes the odds seem almost impossible. Consider the probabilities of taking the Foreign Service officers exam. This annual exam offered for years by the Department of State became almost a "ritual" for many college graduates who were interested in working overseas as Foreign Service officers. The number of exam takers generally ranged from 20,000 to 25,000 for at most 200 positions. The State Department uses the written exam to

Profile of the "Typical" Federal Civilian Non-Postal
Employee as of March 31, 1987

The "typical federal civilian employee" is a topic of frequent interest for the news
media, businesses, private citizens, and organizations as well as the Congress, White
House, and other federal agencies. This factsheet lists the summary statistics often
requested for speeches, letters, and reports. (Data are for total on-board employment unless otherwise indicated [i.e., all work schedules] and may differ from other
releases due to coverage [e.g., agency, work schedule, tenure] and as-of dates.)

Demographic Characteristics

Age	41.9 years average for full-time permanent employees
Length of service	13.1 years average for full-time permanent employees
Retirement eligibility	10% of full-time permanents covered under Civil Service retirement (excluding hires since January 1984)
Education level	31% have bachelor's or higher degree
Gender	58% men and 42% women
Race and national origin	26.7% minority group members: 16.8% African American, 5.1% Latino, 3.1% Asian/Pacific Islander, 1.7% Native American
Disability Status	7% have disabilities
Veterans' preference	34% have veterans' preference (17% are Vietnam era veterans)
Retired military	5.0% of total: 0.5% officers and 4.5% enlisted personnel

Job characteristics

Annual base salary	$27,749 average for full-time permanent employees
	4% paid higher rates for retention in shortage occupations
Grade	8.3 average General Schedule grade
Pay system	72% General Schedule, 19% wage systems, and 9% others
Work schedule	93% full-time, 4% part-time, and 3% intermittent
Tenure	89% permanent appointments
	87% full-time permanent appointments
Occupation and PATCO	81% white collar (19% professional, 23% administrative, 17% technical, 20% clerical, 2% others)
	19% Blue Collar
Supervisory status	10% Supervisors, 2% managers, and 0.4% executives

(continued)

Job Characteristics (continued)

Union representation	76% eligible and 56% represented
Service (position occupied)	82% Competitive and 18% excepted
Agency	48% Department of Defense and 12% Veterans Administration
Geographic location	96% USA and 14% Washington, D.C. metropolitan area
Retirement plan	70% under Civil Service retirement (including 2% in special plan for law enforcement and firefighter personnel),
	6% under Civil Service retirement *and* Social Security,
	13% under federal employees retirement system *and* Social Security,
	9% under Social Security only,
	1% under foreign service retirement, and 1% none

Adapted from Christine E. Steele, U.S. Office of Personnel Management's Central Data File. Washington, D.C.; USOPM, 1987.

screen out approximately 1,000 candidates who are interviewed and tested further.

But from an organizational perspective, one can see the attractiveness of offering a nationwide, written, highly competitive (but open to all) examination to hire entry-level applicants, especially when the entry jobs in question represent a broad range of professional and administrative careers. The federal government has used such a testing concept since 1948 beginning with the junior management assistant exam and then moving to the FSEE, or the Federal Service Entrance Examination, in 1955. Such exams were geared primarily for college graduates or college seniors looking for work in the government. Of course, as long as the exam was testing applicants at a 20-to-1 ratio of applicants for jobs, it stood a reasonable chance of selecting top candidates. In 1974, the FSEE was replaced with PACE. PACE covered 118 occupations and brought entrants into the civil service at grades GS-5 or GS-7. Obviously, there were exceptions and college graduates with distinguished academic records could obtain exemptions from taking the PACE for certain occupational series, but the exam was the centerpiece for federal entry-level hiring.

Ironically, the death blow to the PACE examination came in 1980 as a result of a consent decree signed by the OPM in an out-of-court settlement

I ALWAYS WONDERED
HOW THESE PROMOTION
BOARDS WORK.

Reprinted by permission of the International Personnel Management Association, 1850 K Street, N.W.,
Suite 870, Washington, D.C. 20006.

over a suit alleging discrimination. The suit, *Luevano* v. *Campbell* (later
Luevano v. *Devine*), claimed that PACE had not been validated correctly and
that it resulted in adverse impact against African Americans and Latinos. The
U.S. Merit Systems Protection Board (MSPB) explained the circumstances
in their 1987 report, *In Search of Merit*:

> In Jaunary 1979, a group of minority candidates who failed to achieve passing
> scores on the PACE filed suit in Federal Court. Their suit charged that the PACE
> discriminated unfairly against minorities. Citing differences in the pass rates for
> whites (approximately 42%), Blacks (approximately 5%) and the Hispanics (ap-
> proximately 13%), these challengers contended that the differences were caused
> by test bias. . . . *Luevano* v. *Devine* never came to trial. Instead a consent decree
> was negotiated by the plaintiffs and the Department of Justice on January 9, 1981.
> . . . Abolishment of the PACE was a key requirement of the decree.

While the OPM denied the allegations stated above, they agreed to phase
out PACE over a four-year period in favor of a more specific occupational
testing procedure. In fact, in 1982, OPM changed its mind and abolished

the PACE examination immediately. To handle entry-level hiring, it established a highly decentralized "Schedule B" appointment authority for use until a new exam could be developed (see Table 6.1). Schedule B appointment authority has had a long history (since 1910), but had been primarily used by agencies to make "co-op" appointments in which students from universities or other schools were brought in under noncompetitive status; later, (after successful completion of their degree program and institutional training program), they would be converted to career conditional status. Agencies now became the focal point of the entry-level hiring practices. By 1985, OPM had developed several new examinations to cover more than half of the old PACE positions.

Ban and Ingraham have completed a comprehensive assessment of the

Table 6.1. Number of Individuals Appointed Through the Schedule B Professional and Administrative Career (PAC) Authority Each Calendar Year Since 1983 by Major Agencies

Department or Independent Agency	1983	1984	1985	First six months, 1986
Treasury	1,183	1,206	436	71
Army	307	1,067	747	151
Air Force	290	627	668	155
Navy	211	436	175	49
Department of Defense (not uniformed)	2	595	829	a
Health and Human Services	459	178	421	178
Education	0	52	33	0
General Services Administration	20	45	14	29
Environmental Protection Agency	0	38	36	25
Labor	3	8	146	0
Agriculture	0	6	16	3
Interior	0	2	8	2
Justice	2	1	13	0
Transportation	2	1	1	1
Small Business Administration	0	1	1	3
Energy	0	0	17	17
National Aeronautics and Space Administration	0	0	0	3
TOTALS	2,479	4,263	3,561	687

[a]Agency reported the data were not available at the time the responses to the MSPB inquiries were prepared.

Source: U.S. Merit Systems Protection Board, In Search of Merit: Hiring Entry-Level Federal Employees (Washington, D.C.: USMSPB, September 1987), p. 8.

Schedule B system in their 1988 *Public Administration Review* article, "Retaining Quality Federal Employees: Life After PACE." The good news, they report, is that agencies are "satisfied" with the Schedule B and new examinations processes, and that minority hiring has increased (about double the rate under PACE). The bad news is that the effect on the quality of the public service is difficult to determine and that the very few studies that have been done seem to indicate that internal hires are not as good as general exam hires. Ban and Ingraham, however, question a more serious concern: the compatibility of a decentralized, more narrowly specific job-focused hiring process with the longer range, more career-oriented needs of a quality work force premised on an effective merit system. Addressing just such needs, the OPM announced the opening on May 1, 1990 of a replacement examination process, called Administrative Careers with America, or ACWA.

The New World of ACWA

OPM's new examination system is premised on what it calls a "whole person approach." To measure the whole person, the process has both job-specific skills tests, using traditionally recognized verbal and quantitative testing elements, and an individual achievement record (or IAR), which analyzes the prospective employee's experiences and accomplishments in academic and other work experiences. The IAR, in effect, supplements the skills tests through a multiple choice questionnaire that examines other job-relevant performance factors.

To create ACWA, ninety-six different occupational series were grouped into six categories according to specific job-related knowledge, skills, and abilities (referred to as KSAs). A seventh category with job-specific requirements that has no testing component was also created. Overall, this establishes the following:

- Group 1: health, safety, and environmental occupations
- Group 2: writing and public information occupations
- Group 3: business, finance, and management occupations
- Group 4: personnel, administrative, and computer occupations
- Group 5: benefits, tax, and legal occupations
- Group 6: law enforcement and investigative occupations
- Group 7: positions with positive education requirements (e.g., a specific degree to qualify, such as economics or psychology)

The actual examination process of the six groups requiring exams involves a written test keyed to occupational context (in other words typical questions and materials that one might encounter in a specific job situation). Logic-based testing is also a critical dimension of the testing process. In this case, the verbal-based reasoning tests use the principles of logic, whereby the correct response to a question posed is a logical conclusion to a series of statements that are connected or related to each other. The use of logic-based testing is designed to avoid ambiguity and other forms of cultural wording bias. The total examination process weighs the test and the IAR equally in calculating a rating for each occupational group. As with past practices, an academically high achievement exemption is provided for college graduates with a 3.5 average or those graduating in the top 10 percent of their class.

The OPM is very optimistic that ACWA will erase the somewhat painful memories of the federal government's experience with career entry-level testing. First, ACWA signals a return to a single examination process that will both make recruitment efforts easier and open the federal examination process to more potential college applicants. The new designs in the selection procedure should, it is hoped, maintain job relatedness and avoid future legal problems, while at the same time improving affirmative action efforts. Initial studies project ACWA pass rates for minorities at more than seven times the old 4 percent pass rate of the PACE examination. The OPM is also counting on speeding up the hiring process with a variety of automated options, including computer-based delivery of examinations that might allow immediate testing at actual agencies.

But the new world of ACWA still faces formidable challenges. There has been a considerable education and awareness process in getting the word out to universities and colleges about the new exam. For the first offering in May of 1990, the number of test takers was considerably below (less than 20%) the average number of test takers for the PACE in its heyday. Some might contend that this is attributable in part to the lower prestige of federal public service; but, more likely, the largest factor is simply informing prospective applicants about the exam and the new process. A more telling problem was reported in an article in the December 17, 1990 edition of the *Federal Times* entitled "Budget Crises Snarls Recruitment." It reported that of the 55,000 applicants who passed the May exam, only 127 had been placed in federal jobs as of that month. The best testing process in the world isn't going to work if agencies can't hire those who pass the exams. Clearly, as these difficulties attest, the new world of ACWA is not without its own share of problems.

Bibliography

Albemarle Paper Co. v. *Moody* 422 U.S. 405 (1975).

American Psychological Association. *Standards for Education & Psychological Tests*. Washington, D.C.: APA, 1966.

Arvey, Richard, D. *Fairness in Selecting Employees*. Reading, Mass.: Addison-Wesley, 1979.

Ash, Ronald A. "Job Elements for Task Clusters: Arguments for Using Multi-Methodological Approaches to Job Analysis and a Demonstration of their Utility," *Public Personnel Management*, vol. 11, no. (Spring 1982).

Ban, Carolyn and Patricia W. Ingraham. "Retaining Quality Federal Employees: Life After PACE," *Public Administration Review* (May–June 1988).

Berwitz, Clement Jr. *The Job Analysis Approach to Affirmative Action*. New York: Wiley, 1975.

Blumrosen, Alfred W. "Strangers in Paradise: Griggs v. Duke Power Co., and the Concept of Employment Discrimination," *Michigan Law Review*, 71 (November 1972).

Byham, W. C. and M. D. Spitzer. *The Law and Personnel Testing*. New York: American Management Association, 1971.

Campbell, Joel T. "Tests Are Valid for Minority Groups Too," *Public Personnel Management*, 2 (January–February 1973).

Campion, Michael A. "Personnel Selection for Physically Demanding Jobs: Review and Recommendations," *Personnel Psychology*, vol. 36, no. 3 (Autumn 1983).

Cascio, Wayne. *Applied Psychology in Personnel Management*, 3rd ed. Englewood Cliffs, NJ: Prentice-Hall, 1987.

Cathcart, David A. and R. Lawrence Ashe, Jr. *Five-Year Cumulative Supplement to Schlei & Grossman's Employment Discrimination Law*. Washington, D.C.: Bureau of National Affairs, 1989.

Cronback, Lee J. *Essentials of Psychological Testing*. New York: Harper & Row, 1970.

Donovan, J. J., ed. *Recruitment and Selection in the Public Service*. Chicago: International Personnel Management Association, 1968.

Elliot, Robert H. "Selection of Personnel," in *Handbook on Public Personnel Administration and Labor Relations*, edited by Jack Rabin et al. New York: Marcel Dekker, 1983.

Gandy, Jay A. et al. "Development and Initial Validation of the Individual Achievement Record (IAR) Study." Washington, D.C.: U.S. Office of Personnel Management (November 1989).

Ghiselli, Edwin E. "The Validity of Aptitude Tests in Personnel Selection," *Personnel Psychology*, 1973.

_____. *The Validity of Occupational Aptitude Tests*. New York: Wiley, 1966.

Greenhouse, Linda. "The Court's Shift to Right." *New York Times*, (June 7, 1989), pp. A1/A22.

Griggs v. *Duke Power Co.*, 401 U.S. 424 (1971).

Holmen, Milton G. and Richard F. Docter. *Educational and Psychological Testing*. New York: Russel Sage Foundation, 1972.

Howell, William C. and Robert L. Dipboye. *Essentials of Industrial and Organizational Psychology*, revised edition. Homewood, Ill.: Dorsey Press, 1982.

Hunter, J. E. and R. F. Hunter. "Validity and Utility of Alternate Predictors of Job Performance," *Psychological Bulletin*, vol. 96 (1984) pp. 72–98.

Isaac, Stephen with William B. Michael. *Handbook in Research and Evaluation*. San Diego: Robert R. Knapp, 1981.

Krislov, Samuel. *Representative Bureacracy*. Englewood Cliffs, N.J.: Prentice-Hall, Inc., 1974.

Krislov, Samuel and David H. Rosenbloom. *Representative Bureaucracy and the American Political System*. New York: Praeger Publishers, 1981.

Lawsche, C. H. "A Quantitative Approach to Content Validity," *Personnel Psychology*, 28 (1975).

Ledvinka, James and Vida G. Scarpello. *Federal Regulation of Personnel and Human Resources Management*. Boston: PWS-Kent Publishing, 1991.

Matarazzo, J. D. and A. M. Wiens. "Black Intelligence Test of Cultural Homogeneity and Wechsler Adult Intelligence Scale Scores of Black and White Police Applicants," *Journal of Applied Psychology*, 62 pp. 57–63.

McClung, Glenn. " 'Qualified' vs. 'Most Qualified': A Review of Competitive Merit Selection," *Public Personnel Management*, 2 (September–October 1973).

Pearlman, Kenneth. "Job Families: A Review and Discussion of Their Implications for Personnel Selection," *Psychological Bulletin*, vol. 80, no. 1 (January 1980).

Primof, Eanest S. *How to Prepare and Conduct Job-Element Examinations*. Washington, D.C.: U.S. Government Printing Office, 1973.

Riccucci, Norma M. "Merit, Equity and Test Validity: A New Look at an Old Problem." *Administration and Society* (May 1991).

Robertson, David E. "Update on Testing and Equal Opportunity," *Personnel Journal* (March 1977).

Rosenbloom, David H. and C. Obuchowski. "Public Personnel Examinations and the Constitution: Emergent Trends," *Public Administration Review*, 37 (January–February 1977).

Rouleau, Eugene and Burton F. Krain. "Using Job Analysis to Design Selection Procedures," *Public Personnel Management*, 4 (September–October 1975).

Scales, R. Jr. *Scales Inner City Intelligence Test*. Wilmington, N.C.: Scales, 1973.

Schein, Edgar H. *Career Dynamics*. Reading, Mass.: Addison-Wesley, 1978.

Schlei, Barbara and Paul Grossman. *Employment Discrimination Law*, 2nd ed. Washington, D.C.: Bureau of National Affairs, 1983.

Sylvia, Ronald D. *Critical Issues in Public Personnel Policy*. Pacific Grove, CA: Brooks-Cole Publishing, 1989.

Taylor, Vernon T. *Test Validity in Public Personnel Selection*. Chicago: International Personnel Management Association, 1971.

Tenopyr, Mary L. "Content-Construct Confusion," *Personnel Psychology*, vol. 30 (1977).

Thomas, John C. and W. Donald Heisal. "The Modernization of Recruitment and Selection in Local Governments," in *Public Personnel Administration: Problems and Prospects*, edited by Steven Hays and Richard Kearney. Englewood Cliffs, N.J.: Prentice-Hall, 1983.

Thompson, Duane E. and Toni A. Thompson. "Court Standards for Job Analysis in Test Validation," *Personnel Psychology*, vol. 35, no. 4, (Winter 1982).

Trattner, M. H. *The Validity of Aptitude and Ability Tests Used to Select Professional Personnel*. Report for U.S. Office of Personnel Management, 1988.

U.S. General Accounting Office. *Federal Recruitment and Hiring*. Washington, D.C.: August 1990.

U.S. Merit Systems Protection Board. *In Search of Merit: Hiring Entry-Level Federal Employees*. Washington, D.C.: September 1987.

U.S. v. *South Carolina*, 434 U.S. 1026 (1978), *sub nom. National Educ. Ass'n* v. *South Carolina.*

Van Maanen, John. "Breaking In: A Consideration of Organizational Socialization," in *Handbook of Work, Organization, and Society*, edited by R. Dubin. Chicago: Rand-McNally, 1975.

Wards Cove Packing Co. v. *Atonio*, 57 *Law Week* 4583 (June 6, 1989).

Washington v. *Davis*, 426 U.S. 229 (1976).

Whitman, Torry S. and Albert C. Hyde. "Matching the Right Person to the Right Position," *Defense Management Journal* (March 1978).

Williams, R. L. *Black Intelligence Test of Cultural Homogeneity*, 1975. (Available from Robert L. Williams, Williams & Associates, Inc., 6374 Delmar Boulevard, St. Louis, Missouri 63130).

Zeidner, Rita L. "Budget Crises Snarls Recruitment," *Federal Times* (December 17, 1990).

Part III
THE LEGAL ENVIRONMENT OF PUBLIC PERSONNEL MANAGEMENT

Equal Employment Opportunity and Affirmative Action

Prologue: Affirmative Action and the Courts

In December 1979, the Transportation Agency of Santa Clara County, California, announced that it would be promoting one of its employees to the position of road dispatcher. Twelve county employees applied for the position, which involves record keeping and assigning crews, equipment, and materials to road maintenance jobs. Applicants were required to have a minimum of four years of dispatch or road maintenance experience with the county.

Among the applicants were Diane Joyce and Paul Johnson. Joyce had worked for the county for nine years, and had been in road maintenance since 1975. Johnson had been with the county for twelve years, as a road yard clerk and road maintenance worker, among other jobs. Both had occasionally worked out of class as road dispatchers.

Joyce and Johnson were among nine applicants deemed qualified for the job. Each was interviewed by a two-person board. Seven, including Joyce and Johnson scored above 70, thereby becoming eligible for the road dispatcher position. Johnson tied for the second highest score, a 75; Joyce was next with a 73. The top score was 80. A second set of interviews was held with three agency supervisors, who recommended that Johnson be given the promotion.

This rather common personnel story could well have reached its mundane conclusion with Johnson doing the road dispatching. Instead, it resulted in a landmark ruling by the U.S. Supreme Court, *Johnson* v. *Transportation Agency of Santa Clara County* (1987). Here's the rest of the story and why it is so important.

When Diane Joyce thought she might not be treated fairly in her competition with Paul Johnson, she contacted the county's Affirmative Action Office. Since 1978, the Transportation Agency was under an affirmative action plan that sought "an equitable representation of minorities, women and handicapped persons" in its work force. The plan specifically authorized the Transportation Agency "to consider as one factor the sex of a qualified applicant" when "making promotions to positions with a traditionally segregated job classification in which women have been significantly underrepresented." Based on this plan, an affirmative action coordinator recommended that the agency director promote Joyce and thereby make her the first female road dispatcher in the agency's history.

Faced with the choice between Joyce and Johnson, the director selected Joyce. He explained, "I tried to look at the whole picture, the combination of her qualifications and Mr. Johnson's qualifications, their test scores, their expertise, their background, affirmative action matters, things like that...I believe it was a combination of all those." No matter which person the director chose, the other was likely to file an equal employment opportunity (EEO) complaint, and possibly a law suit, as well.

After receiving a "right to sue" letter from the U.S. Equal Employment Opportunity Commission, Johnson took his case to federal district court. He prevailed there, convincing the court that he was more qualified than Joyce and that her sex was the "determining factor in her selection." His victory was ephemeral, however, as the district court was reversed on appeal by the federal court of appeals for the ninth circuit. The appeals court thought that the affirmative action plan was legal because it "neither unnecessarily trammeled the rights of other employees, nor created an absolute bar to their advancement." Johnson continued his effort to become a road dispatcher by asking the Supreme Court to take his case on a writ of certiorari, which it did.

At first thought, one might wonder how, as late as 1987, the legal issues posed by the Joyce-Johnson contest could be so unresolved that they divided federal judges and merited attention by the nation's highest court. After all, the basic legal framework for equal employment opportunity and affirmative action was established by Title VII of the Civil Rights Act of 1964 as amended by the Equal Employment Opportunity Act of 1972. Yet the language of these statutes, and amendments to them, allows for divergent interpretations. Indeed, even Supreme Court justices vociferously disagreed as to what these laws permitted.

Justices Brennan, Marshall, Blackmun, Powell, and Stevens, who constituted a majority, agreed that the Transportation Agency's procedure was legal. However, Stevens also filed a separate concurring opinion. Justice O'Connor concurred in the Court's judgment, but not in Brennan's majority opinion. Justice Scalia dissented. He was joined by Chief Justice Rehnquist.

Justice White joined in some parts of Scalia's dissent, but not in others. However, by the time the High Court finished dissecting the letter of the law, public personnelists had finally been given a fine, if not bright, line to walk in their pursuit of equal employment opportunities.

The basic legal problem raised by affirmative action plans like Santa Clara's is that Title VII of the Civil Rights Act (as amended) prohibits both public and private employers from "discriminating against any individual with respect to his compensation, terms, conditions, or privileges of employment, because of such individual's race, color, religion, sex, or national origin; or to limit, segregate, or classify his employees or applicants for employment in any way which would deprive or tend to deprive any individual of employment opportunities or otherwise adversely affect his status as an employee, because of such individual's race, color, religion, sex, or national origin." This language is clear enough, but it is not all the act has to say.

The statute also reads that nothing in Title VII "shall be interpreted to require any employer...to grant preferential treatment...to any group because" of an imbalance in the social composition of its work force. In *Steelworkers* v. *Weber* (1979), a majority on the Supreme Court held the latter clause to mean that although no employer would be *required* to grant preferences, employers were *permitted* to do so. While such reasoning may sound odd to the layperson, just why would a statute say that something is not required if it is clearly prohibited anyway? (This would be the equivalent of a law saying no one is required to commit murder!) Logically, then, preferences are permitted, but only insofar as they do not discriminate against or adversely affect individuals based on their race, color, religion, sex, or national origin.

At this point, one might ask, as did Justice Scalia in dissent, didn't the promotion of Ms. Joyce pursuant to Santa Clara's affirmative action plan discriminate against and adversely affect Mr. Johnson because of his sex? Here, the majority had a twofold response. First, Johnson was not actually harmed because he "had no absolute entitlement to the road dispatcher position. Seven of the applicants were classified as qualified and eligible, and the Agency Director was authorized to promote any of the seven. Thus, the denial of the promotion unsettled no legitimate firmly rooted expectation on the part of [Johnson]. Furthermore, while [he] was denied a promotion, he retained his employment with the Agency, at the same salary and with the same seniority, and remained eligible for other promotions." Second, and of greater importance, Santa Clara's plan had a number of qualities that made it legally acceptable under Title VII.

Affirmative action plans and procedures may be legal if they maintain a balance between the requirement of avoiding discrimination and the freedom to grant preferences to social groups. Establishing an acceptable balance requires that a plan have certain aspects, sometimes referred to as the quality of being "narrowly tailored." A narrowly tailored plan will:

1. Be voluntarily developed to eliminate or reduce a "manifest imbalance" of members of different social groups, such as males and females or blacks and whites, in a job classification
2. Avoid personnel actions, such as hiring and promotions, on the basis of race, sex, and so forth alone
3. Avoid unnecessarily trammeling the rights of employees who are not in the groups given preference or create "an absolute bar to their advancement"
4. Have a limited duration, such as attaining a balance in the work force as opposed to maintaining one indefinitely.

At least for the time being, the *Johnson* decision put to rest an issue that had been plaguing affirmative action since the U.S. Supreme Court issued its *Regents* v. *Bakke* and *Steelworkers* v. *Weber* decisions in 1978 and 1979, respectively. In *Bakke*, the Court was so divided that its resolution of the case was at once termed both a victory and a defeat for affirmative action. A majority of the justices would not support a "quota" system for admission to a state school, but a majority also seemed willing to accept the constitutionality of a flexible system whereby race, under certain circumstances, could serve as a criterion for admissions. A year later in *Weber*, however, the Court upheld the Kaiser Corporation's voluntarily developed affirmative action program, thereby striking an important victory in favor of private sector affirmation action. At the same time, though, the Court left uncertain whether affirmative action would be acceptable in the public sector.

Six justices of the Supreme Court in *Johnson* finally responded that affirmative action plans and procedures in the public sector could be legal. The Court's majority opinion even took great pains to explain to public personnelists the conditions that such plans must meet. Just as the shifting demographics of the nation's work force are beginning to bring much higher proportions of women, immigrants, African Americans, Latinos, and other protected-class groups into the labor market, the Supreme Court cleared the way for personnelists to use affirmative action to assure that members of these groups can have equal opportunities to compete for all the jobs for which they are qualified.

Yet the controversy over affirmative action is hardly over. First, because of the way the *Johnson* case was argued, the Court did not consider whether or not Santa Clara's affirmative action plan, although within the letter of the pertinent civil rights law, was actually in violation of the Constitution's Fourteenth Amendment, which guarantees individuals "equal protection of the laws." Although it's hard to imagine a practice being legal but unconstitutional, stranger judicial decisions can be found. Second, public personnelists are permitted to use narrowly tailored affirmative action, but will they? Finally, even if they do, will it be successful in reducing manifest social imbalances in the work force and in promoting equal opportunity? These are among the major personnel questions that will be answered during the 1990s.

Rulings in Brief: U.S. Supreme Court Decisions on Affirmative Action and EEO in 1989 and 1990

Case	*Decision*
Metro Broadcasting v. *F.C.C.* (1990)	The Court upheld, under the equal protection component of the Fifth Amendment, the constitutionality of *federal* programs aimed at increasing "minority" ownership of broadcast licenses.
Richmond v. *Croson* (1989)	The Court declared unconstitutional, under the Fourteenth Amendment's Equal Protection Clause, a *local* ordinance that called for setting aside 30% of public works contracts for "minority" or protected-class contractors.
Wards Cove v. *Atonio* (1989)	Plaintiffs, not employers, in Title VII disparate-impact cases have the burden of showing that the employment practices they are challenging are not a "business necessity." (For a further discussion, see Chapter 6.)
Price Waterhouse v. *Hopkins* (1989)	In some cases alleging *intentional* discrimination under Title VII, employers have the burden of showing that their refusal to hire or promote someone is *not* based on discrimination but legitimate reasons.
Martin v. *Wilks* (1989)	Under Title VII, white employees can challenge, *without* time limitations, affirmative action consent decrees settling employment discrimination dispute, even if they were not original parties to the consent decree.
Lorance v. *AT&T* (1989)	Women challenging the legality of a collectively bargained seniority system under Title VII must file suit within the first 300 days of the system's adoption.
Patterson v. *McLean Credit Union* (1989)	A claim of racial harassment cannot be brought under Section 1981 of the Civil Rights Act of 1866, thereby narrowing the scope of this provision.

President Bush Vetoes the Civil Rights Act of 1990

The Civil Rights Act of 1990, which sought to "neutralize" the regressive rulings issued by the U.S. Supreme Court in the 1989–90 term, was vetoed by President Bush. Mr. Bush argued that the anti-discrimination bill "employs a maze of highly legalistic language to introduce the destructive force of quotas into our national employment system." Obviously, argued proponents of the measure, President Bush does not truly understand what quotas are, and hence has totally missed the point on the bill. Senator Kennedy, who was one of the bill's sponsors said that the "President's veto of the Civil Rights Act of 1990 and his repeated efforts to pin the false label of quotas on this legislation are part of a disreputable tactic to appeal to public resentment and prejudice."

Congress was unable to override the President's veto.

Steven A. Holmes, "President Vetoes Bill on Job Rights," *New York Times* (October 23, 1990), pp. A1/B7.

Abuses of the Past

In the past three decades equal employment opportunity has become a major concern of public personnel administration in the United States. There are now a myriad of statutes, executive orders, judicial decisions, and administrative regulations intended to further EEO at all levels of government. However, as the prologue suggests, EEO means different things to different people and how it should be defined and implemented touches directly upon one of the most persistent political questions facing America today. Here can be seen the full politicality and widespread ramifications of personnel practices in the public sector. It is impossible to understand recent developments in the EEO realm, especially reliance on affirmative action, without at least a cursory understanding of the discriminatory practices of the past. Although other groups have been subjected to unequal treatment, discrimination against African Americans and women has been illustrative and perhaps most prevalent.

Even as the American revolutionaries were fighting the British for the right to establish a new political order, it was reasonably clear that whatever improvements the struggle for independence might bring to whites in the new world, African Americans were not very likely to receive a substantial share of the prospective benefits. Symbolically, this was demonstrated at the outset by General Washington, who, although in need of increased human resources power, was unwilling to use African-American troops. The issue of slavery aside, the first formal application of such an outlook toward free African

Americans came in 1810 when Congress enacted a law providing that "no other than a free white person shall be employed in conveying the mail." At least some of its proponents, including Postmaster General Gideon Granger, wanted to prevent African Americans from doing anything that "tends to increase their knowledge of natural rights, of men and things, or that affords them an opportunity of associating, acquiring and communicating sentiments, and of establishing a chain or line of intelligence." The law was subsequently modified, but remained on the books until it was repealed in 1865.

Although this provision applied only to postal employees, it is believed that there were no African Americans in the federal bureaucracy until 1867. After that date, African Americans made slow, but generally steady, numerical inroads. It appears that by 1928 they had achieved a proportion in the federal service roughly equal to their proportion in the nation as a whole. These gains came about both through politics and through the merit system. Politically, after the end of the Reconstruction period, the Republicans began to make a number of African American civil service appointments as a form of compensation to the group as a whole. Eventually a tradition was established of appointing African Americans to some minor posts in the District of Columbia and to diplomatic posts in black nations such as Liberia and Haiti. However, once white Southerners were able to disenfranchise African Americans through terror, poll taxes, and other devices, the Republicans began to lose interest in their lot and became reluctant to make additional African-American appointments.

During the latter part of the nineteenth century, as African-American gains under Reconstruction were wiped out, it appeared that the merit system might offer a lasting means of facilitating their appointment to the federal service. In 1883, when the merit system was enacted into law, there were 620 African Americans in the bureaucracy in Washington. By 1892 this number had increased to 2,393. In its *Eighth Annual Report*, the Civil Service Commission wrote: "Another excellent feature of the examinations in the Southern States has been the elimination not only of the questions of politics and religion but of the question of race." It maintained that "it is impossible to overestimate the boon to these colored [sic] men and women of being given the chance to enter the Government service on their own merits in fair competition with white and colored [sic] alike." But maintaining entry is sometimes more difficult than gaining entry. The civil service laws did little to prevent discrimination in dismissals and other aspects of personnel administration. Thus, in 1894, the Civil Service Commissioner Theodore Roosevelt observed that over the three or four preceding years, the War Department dismissed about two-thirds of the African Americans placed through examination. Such practices were exacerbated by the Taft and Wilson administrations. Taft believed that African Americans should not hold federal posts where whites complained of their

Landmarks for Women in the Federal Service

1775—Mary Katharine Goddard, the first woman to be employed by the national government, was appointed postmaster of the Baltimore Post Office.

1864—The first statutory recognition of federal employment for women established a maximum salary of $600 a year for women clerk-copyists. At that time, male clerks were being paid $1,200 to $1,800 a year.

1870—Congress passed a law which allowed agency heads to appoint women to higher-level clerkships "at their discretion." Based on interpretation of this law, agencies tended to appoint men only to higher-level jobs and women only to many lower-level jobs for the next 92 years.

1883—The Civil Service Act permitted women to compete in civil service examinations. A woman received the highest score on the first test—but she was the second person to be appointed from the register.

1893—After 10 years under the Civil Service Act, the federal departments in Washington were staffed by 8,377 men and by 3,770 women (31 percent of the Washington work force). Over the years, the number of female civil servants would fluctuate in response to depressions (decreases) and to wars (increases).

1920—The Women's Bureau was created and placed within the Department of Labor to formulate standards and policies aimed at advancing the employment opportunities of women.

1923—The Classification Act made mandatory the principle of equal pay for equal work.

1961—President Kennedy established the Commission on the Status of Women.

1962—The attorney general declared the 1870 law invalid. (Congress would repeal the law 3 years later.)

1963—The Federal Women's Program was established in response to recommendation from the President's Commission on the Status of Women.

1964—The Civil Rights Act prohibits discrimination based on gender in the federal service.

1967—Executive Order 11375 prohibited gender discrimination in the federal government.

1969—Executive Order 11478 integrated the Federal Women's Program into the overall Equal Employment Opportunity Program.

1971—The restriction on women bearing firearms as federal employees was removed, thereby opening many law enforcement jobs to women.

1973—Height restrictions were prohibited for most federal jobs, making many more jobs open to women.

1974—Leave provisions were changed to allow advancing up to 30 days of sick leave for maternity leave, similar to other leave situations.

1976—Veterans preference for peacetime service was eliminated for all persons who entered the military after October.

(continued)

1977—Congress repealed apportionment, which required the Civil Service Commission to take into account an applicant's voting residence when ranking applicants for consideration for federal employment.
1977—All federal jobs opened to women.
1981—Sandra Day O'Connor becomes the first female U.S. Supreme Court justice.
1988—Women constitute 48.2 percent of all white-collar federal employees. They hold a majority of the positions in each of the following fields: general administration, medical, library, personnel, legal, accounting, supply, and business.

See the Federal Women's Program, *Putting Women In Their Place* (Washington, D.C.: U.S. Government Printing Office, January 1979), pp. 16–19. (Updated by the authors.)

presence. Moreover, he began segregationist practices in the federal service by segregating census takers in Washington, restricting whites to whites and African Americans to African Americans.

The Wilson administration had an even greater impact on inequality. Although often considered one of the more "liberal" and "enlightened" presidents, Wilson, put simply, engaged in racist personnel policies. After openly appealing to the African American vote, which was largely Republican at the time, and winning more of it than had any other Democratic candidate for the presidency, he created widespread segregation within federal agencies and sanctioned the dismissal of large numbers of African Americans. In the following years, segregationist practices were continued and gained the sanction of the Civil Service Commission. In the words of one of its officials, the commission was in the practice of "not certifying Negroes [sic] to bureaus where they would be turned down or made unhappy." It wasn't until the New Deal that the treatment of African Americans in the federal service began to undergo significant change.

While the employment of women in the government service in America actually predates the formation of the union, women have generally not been treated as equals in the federal service. The relevant history of women and federal personnel administration began in 1861, when the Treasury Department first began the then "scandalous" practice of hiring female clerks. Similar to the experience of African Americans, discrimination against women was once formally sanctioned both by law and by official directive. The most important formal basis of inequality on the grounds of gender was derived from an 1870 statute, which ironically had been intended to give women greater equality: "Women may, in the discretion of the head of any department, be appointed to any of the clerkships therein authorized by law, upon the same requisites and conditions, and with the same compensations as are prescribed for men." The law was interpreted to allow appointing officers to exclude women for reasons unrelated to their capacity or the efficiency of the service, and until 1919 women were excluded from about 60 percent of the positions covered by examinations. Until the ratification of the Nineteenth Amendment in 1920 (guaranteeing women the right to vote), many women also found it difficult to compete for patronage positions. Unequal compensation had originally been provided for by law, and despite the 1870 statute it continued in some agencies until 1923, when the Classification Act established the requirement of equal pay for equal work, regardless of gender. However, it wasn't until 1937 that marital status became an illegal basis for discriminatory treatment.

Legal barriers and prejudice aside, women faced a number of substantial problems in gaining and retaining federal employment. First, as Cindy Sondik Aron points out in her book, *Ladies and Gentlemen of the Civil Service*, social norms frowned so much on middle-class women working outside the home that those "...who chose to become federal employees might well have felt they were jeopardizing not only their class status, but their gender identity as well." Second, female federal employees faced sexual harassment. As early as 1864, a congressional committee began to investigate charges that supervisors were seeking sex from their female subordinates. Popular writers belabored the theme that a federal clerkship would often be won at the cost of a woman's virtue. The Treasury, in particular, gained notoriety for sexual improprieties, although it is impossible to say how widespread they were. Finally, as Aron notes, "...government offices were clearly men's turf," for they spit, smoked, cursed, and sometimes showed up drunk—all of which the women workers were likely to find offensive at that time.

No doubt most of the women who joined the federal service in the latter half of the nineteenth century were "reluctant pioneers," as Aron puts it. Yet, the number of female employees in the executive departments in Washington, D.C. increased from none in 1859 to 6,882 by 1903. By 1930, about half of all federal clerical workers were women. Eventually, that proportion would rise to over 80 percent, creating new problems such as sex-segregated jobs and concerns over pay equity for women.

Despite the unique problems facing women, historically their experience in the federal service paralleled that of African Americans in many respects. For instance, until recent decades, both were confined almost entirely to the lower grades. Both groups also found it somewhat easier to obtain positions in factory-type operations, such as in mint and printing operations. As was the case for African Americans, the Civil Service Commission formally supported equality for women while at the same time accepting and even

Women are *slowly* entering into state trooper positions. *Source*: New York State Civil Service, Albany, New York.

abeting discrimination against them. As will be seen shortly, it was not until the 1960s that genuine change in this area began to occur.

The Development of EEO

Although there were a few earlier provisions affecting equal opportunity in federal personnel procedures, it was in 1941 that a serious EEO effort was begun. In order to forestall a threatened mass protest march by African Americans on Washington, President Franklin Roosevelt issued Executive Order 8802, which called for the elimination of discrimination based upon race, color, religion, or national origin within defense production industries and the federal service. A newly created Fair Employment Practice Committee was charged with the implementation of the program. By almost all accounts, however, the committee was weak and even somewhat uninterested in combatting discrimination in the federal service. In 1946, it met its demise through an amendment to an appropriations bill.

In 1948, President Truman created a Fair Employment Practices Board within the Civil Service Commission through an executive order. The board advanced EEO concepts considerably. Its "corrective action program" enabled individuals who believed that they had been subjected to illegitimate discrimination to launch a complaint. Such actions had to be initiated in the agency involved, so the board only heard cases on appeal, which limited its effectiveness. The board's other responsibilities were both ill-defined and ineffective. It held conferences with fair employment officers and outside organizations, conducted periodic surveys and appraisals, and sought the adoption of new recruitment techniques and better efforts at integrating the federal work force. In a way, the board's activities were a precursor of contemporary practices, although it believed that its direct action options were strictly limited by the need for "color blindness" and "merit." In judging the board, it should be remembered that it existed during the McCarthy era, when being sympathetic to racial equality was sometimes taken as evidence of communist leanings under the loyalty-security programs in existence at the time.

In 1955, the board was replaced by the President's Committee on Government Employment Policy. The new program reaffirmed the government's interest in nondiscrimination, but it went further in declaring that "it is the policy of the United States Government that equal opportunity be afforded all qualified persons, consistent with law, for employment in the Federal Government." This was interpreted to mean that the government was obligated to take whatever action it deemed reasonable to overcome societal inequities and to equalize opportunity itself, not just equalize the treatment of individuals. Under the new policy it was necessary to channel special efforts in recruitment, training, and other areas of personnel administration toward minority or protected-class groups that were thought to be proportionally underrepresented in the federal service as a result of societal inequalities. Accordingly, the program moved further in the direction of affirmative action and compensatory treatment. At the same time it maintained an interest in individual complaints and strengthened the system for their consideration.

By the time President Kennedy took office, the basic EEO concepts of today had been developed, if not carried to their logical ends or effectively implemented. However, it was not until the Kennedy administration that EEO became a central and major aspect of federal personnel administration. Between 1961 and 1965, the civil rights movement reached the pinnacle of its political importance and racial equality became a dominant national issue. Indeed, it was a sign of the times when Kennedy declared, "I have dedicated my administration to the cause of equal opportunity in employment by the Government."Accordingly, he issued yet another executive order, this time creating the President's Committee on Equal Employment Opportunity. The new committee gained prestige and some measure of political clout by including the vice president as its chair. It stressed affirmative action in the sense of making efforts to bring more African Americans, Latinos, and other protected-class groups into the federal service. These included recruitment drives at high schools and colleges heavily attended by these persons. Agencies were encouraged to provide better training opportunities for them as well. The committee also began the practice of taking an annual census of the employment of African Americans, Latinos, and other protected-class groups in government. Although it deemphasized the importance of complaints, believing that they were of only remedial importance, it nevertheless took steps to strengthen the complaint system. Finally, and most important, the commitee developed a new sense of realism in recognizing that "full equality of employment opportunity requires that we face up to the whole problem of equality itself." Accordingly, it began thinking along compensatory lines.

The Kennedy program was carried forward by President Johnson until 1965, when another reorganization occurred and a longer-lived program was initiated. The change was a result of many factors. The Civil Rights Act of 1964 declared that "it shall be the policy of the United States to ensure equal employment opportunities for Federal employees." It also created the Equal Employment Opportunity Commission to combat discrimination in the private sector and, consequently, the coordination of all federal civil rights activities became increasingly complex and difficult. Funding for the President's Committee on EEO ran into difficulty in Congress and it was decided to shift its responsibilities to the Civil Service Commission, where the program remained until 1979.

The Civil Rights Act also required EEO for women by prohibiting discrimination on the basis of gender. Prior to its enactment, Kennedy had created a Commission on the Status of Women and subsequently issued a memorandum requiring that appointments and promotions be made without regard to gender except under circumstances whereby the Civil Service Commission found differentiated treatment justifiable. In 1969 the Women's Program was fully incorporated into the overall EEO program for the first time.

The next major development in the evolution of the EEO program came in 1969, when President Nixon issued an executive order requiring agency heads to "establish and maintain an affirmative program of equal employment opportunity." The following year, Nixon changed the nature of EEO activities still further by creating a Spanish-Speaking Program within the overall EEO program. Designed to bring more members of the Spanish-speaking population into the federal service, it was subsequently renamed Hispanic

Why Gender was Added to the Language of Title VII of the Civil Rights Act of 1964

Gender discrimination in employment was by no means a significant concern of the civil rights advocates of the early 1960s. Its prohibition only became part of the Civil Rights Act of 1964 because of Congressperson Howard "Judge" Smith. As the leader of the South's fight against civil rights, he added one small word— *sex*—to prohibitions against discrimination based on race, color, religion, and national origin. He felt confident this amendment would make the proposed law ridiculous and cause its defeat. Smith was an "old style" bigot: in his mind one thing more ridiculous than equal rights for blacks was equal rights for women.

The "sex discrimination" amendment was opposed by the Women's Bureau of the Department of Labor, by the American Association of University Women, and by most of the Congress' leading liberals. They saw it as nothing but a ploy to discourage passage of the new civil rights law. The major support for adopting the amendment came from the reactionary southern establishment of the day. Because President Lyndon Johnson insisted that the Senate make practically no changes in the law as passed by the House, there was no discussion of gender discrimination by the Senate. The momentum for a new civil rights law was so great that Smith's addition not only failed to scuttle the bill, but went largely unnoticed.

Adapted from David H. Rosenbloom and Jay M. Shafritz, *Essentials of Labor Relations* (Reston, VA. Reston Publishing Co., 1985), pp. 63–64.

Employment Program and became an integral part of the government's EEO efforts. It has been effective in turning attention to the special circumstances of the Hispanic or Latino segment of the population.

The Equal Employment Opportunity Act of 1972 solidified the Civil Service Commission's authority in this area and placed the program on a solid statutory basis for the first time. It reaffirmed the traditional policy of nondiscrimination and empowered the commission to enforce its provisions "through appropriate remedies, including reinstatement or hiring of employees with or without back pay...[and issuing] such rules, regulations, orders and instructions as it deems necessary and appropriate." It also made the commission responsible for the annual review and approval of agency EEO plans and for evaluating agency EEO activities. The act also brought state and local governments under the federal EEO umbrella for the first time. The Equal Employment Opportunity Commission, heretofore primarily concerned with the private sector, was given similar authority over the nonfederal public sector.

Dothard v. *Rawlinson*
433 U.S. 321 (1977)

Facts—Plaintiff, a woman, applied for a position as a prison guard with the Alabama Board of Correction. When her application was rejected because she failed to meet the 120 lbs. weight requirement and the 5′2″ height requirement, she brought a class action suit under Title VII and the Equal Protection Clause of the Fourteenth Amendment. While the suit was pending, the defendant adopted a regulation establishing gender criteria for assigning prison guards to maximum security institutions for positions requiring continuing close proximity to inmates. Plaintiff amended her complaint to challenge this regulation.

A three judge Federal District Court found in favor of plaintiff.

Issue—Did the defendant's height and weight requirements constitute sex discrimination under Title VII?

Discussion—The Supreme Court stated that in a suit challenging facially neutral standards a plaintiff need only show a significantly discriminatory pattern in order to establish a *prima facie* case of discrimination and thus, shift the burden to the defendant of demonstrating job relatedness. The Court noted that women comprised almost 53% of the work force in the nation but only approximately 13% of the prison guards in Alabama. The District Court had found that the height requirement operated to exclude one third of the women in the U.S. but only 1.3% of the men. The weight restriction served to exclude approximately 22.3% of women but only 2.4% of men. The Supreme Court rejected defendant's argument that the use of generalized national statistics would not suffice to establish a *prima facie* case and that statistics concerning applications would be inadequate in that they would not meet them and would therefore, have a chilling effect on the number of women applicants. Noting that the defendant did not attempt to adduce countervailing statistical evidence, the Court upheld the District Court's finding of a statistical *prima facie* case of discrimination.

Regarding defendant's attempt to rebut the *prima facie* case by arguing that the height and weight requirements were related to strength and thus, were job related, the Court found that defendant had produced no evidence correlating height and weight with relative strength nor had a properly validated test (or for that matter any test) been employed. Accordingly, the Court affirmed the District Court's finding that the height and weight requirements violated Title VII.

Regarding the regulation prohibiting the assignment of female guards in all male maximum security correctional facilities, the defendant justified this overt sex discrimination citing Section 703(e) of Title VII which permits such discrimination where sex is a "bona fide occupational qualification" reasonably necessary to the overall operation of the enterprise.

The Court found that the bona fide occupational qualification exception was meant to be an extremely narrow exception to the prohibition of sex discrimination.

(continued)

Nevertheless, the Court concluded (in a split vote) that the regulation in question fell within the ambit of the 703(e) exception. The Court reasoned that while ordinarily, the argument that a job is too dangerous for a woman may be rebutted by noting that it is the purpose of Title VII to allow the individual to exercise free choice, the ability to maintain order in a male maximum security penitentiary "could be directly reduced by her [the guard's] womanhood." The Court found that under the conditions extant in the prison system under scrutiny (inmate access to guards, understaffed institutions, a substantial portion of the inmate population comprised of sex offenders), there are few deterrents to inmate assaults on women prison guards. The Court concluded on this basis that the District Court erred in ruling that being male is not a bona fide occupational qualification for the prison guard position and accordingly reversed this portion of the District Court's judgment.

U.S. Office of Personnel Management, *Equal Employment Opportunity Court Cases* (Washington, D.C.: U.S. Government Printing Office, September 1979), pp. 24–25.

In 1979, as a part of the overall federal civil service reforms then taking place, the enforcement aspects of the federal EEO program were transferred to the Equal Employment Opportunity Commission (EEOC). But while the EEOC gained responsibility for reviewing affirmative action plans and processing complaints of discrimination, the newly created Office of Personnel Management (OPM) contained an Office of Affirmative Employment Programs, which had responsibility for the Federal Women's Program, the Hispanic Employment Program, and programs for veterans, the disabled, and the "upward mobility" of members of these groups and protected-class groups in general. This change was opposed by some high-ranking OPM officials and several members of Congress on the grounds that it undesirably fragments authority for federal personnel management. The EEOC was also criticized for its huge backlog of cases and its history of ineffectiveness. These views notwithstanding, the transfer was part of the political price of building a consensus in favor of President Carter's reform package and it was generally supported by African Americans and other groups especially interested in federal EEO. Obviously, the Civil Service Commission's failure to develop much support for its implementation of EEO proved costly to the development of unified and coherent public personnel management. Once again, then, public personnelists were clearly reminded of the politicality of their jobs.

The transfer of major EEO responsibilities to the EEOC quickly turned out to be of major consequence for federal personnel administration. The EEOC was instrumental in forcing the OPM to discontinue the Professional and

Administrative Career Examination (PACE). The exam had an adverse impact on the employment of African Americans (as well as Latinos). Only 5 percent of the African Americans taking the exam passed it, and only 0.7 percent received a score high enough to even win consideration for hiring. By contrast, as of 1979, the passing rate of whites was 51 percent and 9 percent of them scored a 90 or higher, thereby making appointment likely. The exam was discarded in 1982, after the OPM failed to demonstrate satisfactorily that it was valid in the sense of one's score being predictive of the quality of job performance later on. PACE was the single major examination for entrance into the main career track in the General Schedule. Its demise gave individual agencies far greater responsibility for developing their own approaches to selection. Many federal agencies began to place greater reliance on unassembled examinations. Much more use was also made of Schedule B, which allows hiring based on noncompetitive examination (i.e., the applicant must pass an examination but is not ranked competitively with other applicants by score). A variety of other techniques were also used. These included relying on college grade point averages, recommendations, interviews, and highly specialized exams for specific positions.

Constance Horner, former director of OPM, claimed that personnelists faced a "nightmarish" situation in trying to screen some 300,000 to 500,000 yearly applicants for roughly 10,000 positions in the General Schedule's main administrative career track. But getting rid of the PACE also enhanced EEO. By 1990, OPM was set to try to maximize both efficient personnel administration and equal opportunity. It had spent about $100,000 to develop each of six broad examinations that, if all goes right, will not have an adverse impact on African Americans, Latinos and other protected-class groups, and will be highly predictive of on-the-job performance.

The civil service reform of 1978 not only gave the EEOC a major role in federal personnel practices, it also changed EEO policy substantially. The reform makes it federal policy to seek a "work force reflective of the Nation's diversity" by establishing that "recruitment should be from qualified individuals from appropriate sources in an endeavor to achieve a work force from all segments of society." Further, it requires that each executive agency's recruitment should be "designed to eliminate underrepresentation of minorities in the various categories of civil service employment within the Federal service." "Underrepresentation" in turn is defined as a situation in which members of a designated minority or protected-class group "within a category of civil service employment constitutes a lower percentage of the total number of employees within the employment category than the percentage that the minority constituted within the labor force of the United States." Any such underrepresentation is to be eliminated within the framework of merit, and programs to do so would presumably have to be narrowly tailored to avoid violating the legal rights of nonminorities. However, the statute leaves no doubt that federal personnel policy now views obtaining a socially representative work force as a major objective. In the early days of EEO programs, there was often a contest of merit *versus* representation; today, the goal is clearly merit *and* representation.

There are several lessons of contemporary relevance to be learned from the past. Foremost among these is the simple fact that the government had engaged in widespread discriminatory practices. African Americans, women, and members of other groups were not excluded on the basis of their qualifications but rather on the basis of their social characteristics. The merit system once created did not fully apply to them. In addition, the development of the federal EEO program indicated that while organizational change came frequently, substantive change has been elusive. Although the first-stage problem of equalizing the opportunity of protected-class persons to gain entrance to the federal service has been more or less resolved, these government employees still remain disproportionately concentrated in the lower grades of the bureaucracy. Whether equal opportunity has been created remains debatable. However, it is abundantly clear that more than five decades of federal EEO have not resulted in anything approaching substantive equality.

Racial Harassment: Alive and "Well" and Living in Your Workplace

The federal district court for the Eastern District of New York in *Snell* v. *Suffolk County* (1985) found illegal a number of abuses against African-American and Latino correctional officers by white correctional officers. The court noted, for example, that they "have repeatedly been mimicked in derogatory ways...In [one instance,] White correction officers dressed a[n] Hispanic inmate in a straw hat, sheet, and a sign that read 'Spic.' The White officers referred to the inmate as 'Ramos' son.' Officer Ramos complained...[but was] accused...of trying to 'make waves.'"

The court also directed attention to racist materials posted on official bulletin boards at the jail. The court pointed to, for example, "a cartoon depicting a Ku Klux Klan member who after shooting a Black person remarks to a ranger 'Whatcha mean, Out of Season?' Other racially-demeaning materials included a highly offensive depiction of a large-breasted Black woman in some form of native garb...a national geographic magazine-type photograph of a naked Black woman with the words 'Yo Mama' and a bone added about her head...a questionnaire that begins 'photo not necessary since you all look alike' and asks such questions as '[how many] years [spent] in local prisons?' and '[give] approximate estimate of income [from] theft, welfare...false insurance claims....'"

Figures 7.1 and 7.2 and table 7.1 capture the current federal EEO situation well. Great progress has been made in assuring that members of protected-class groups will have equal opportunity in the federal personnel system. There is no pronounced underrepresentation of them in the federal work force as a whole. However, members of these groups are still disproportionately concentrated in the lower levels of the federal service and they are seriously underrepresented in the upper grades. Consequently, today the EEO emphasis is less on eliminating barriers to the employment of protected-class persons than on developing greater upward mobility for them within the federal service. Affirmative action plans also stress recruitment to the higher levels to do away with marked imbalances in the social composition of the work force. Overall, public employment at the state and local governmental levels reflects similar patterns and concerns. However, just as there is considerable variation among individual federal agencies and regions in their employment patterns, there is great variation among the states, counties, municipalities, towns, authorities, and school and other districts that form all but one of the nation's 83,000 governmental jurisdictions.

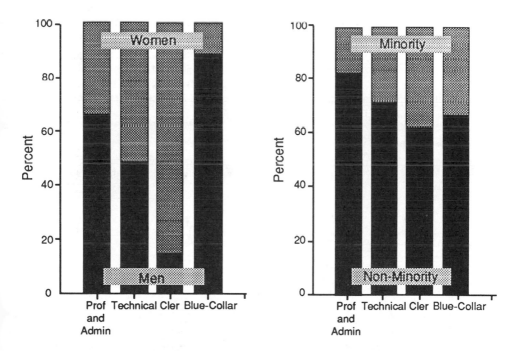

Figure 7.1. A varied federal work force by gender and race (1987). *Source*: U.S. Office of Personnel Management, *The Federal Work Force* (Washington, D.C.: OPM, 1989).

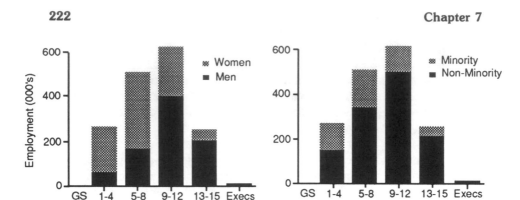

Figure 7.2. Women and protected-class persons in the federal work force by GS grade (1987). *Source*: U.S. Office of Personnel Management, *The Federal Work Force* (Washington, D.C. OPM, 1989).

The Organization of EEO

Although public sector EEO programs can be organized in a variety of ways, several pertinent organizational lessons have been learned from past experience. First, an agency administering EEO must have a credible record in its own dealings with protected-class persons. EEO agencies must practice what they preach. In this regard, the old Civil Service Commission (CSC) was particularly defective. In the 1970s, it was harshly criticized by the U.S. Commission on Civil Rights for adopting a role that "was characterized more by passivity than by 'leadership'; more by neutrality than by 'guidance'." Undoubtedly,

Table 7.1. Protected-Class Persons in the Federal Executive Branch (1987)

	Women	Men	Percentage of total	Civilian Labor Force (%)
African Americans	207,461	147,313	16.6	10.5
Latinos	41,478	67,425	5.1	8.0
Asian American/ Pacific Islander	26,064	41,721	3.2	2.2
Native American	17,995	18,614	1.7	0.7
TOTAL	292,998	275,073	26.5	21.4

Source: U.S. Office of Personnel Management, *The Federal Work Force* (Washington, D.C.: OPM, 1989).

the CSC's inadequate performance contributed strongly to support for the transfer of much of the EEO program to the EEOC.

Second, efforts to decentralize EEO and to integrate into all facets of public personnel management have not worked well at the federal level. The CSC's organizational scheme dispersed authority and responsibility among bureaus and officials that were often more sympathetic to traditional personnel practices than to EEO. Consequently, change was difficult and the discriminatory status quo was maintained to a substantial extent. Agencies had considerable responsibility for the development of their own EEO programs, including the authority to establish and implement affirmative action plans and to deal with many aspects of complaints of discrimination within broad guidelines set forth by the CSC. Authority and responsibility were also divided among headquarters and regional offices in such a fashion that the CSC's Office of Federal EEO, the main policy-making and oversight bureau, had little direct information concerning federal employment outside the Washington, D.C. metropolitan area. In essence, this meant that the affirmative action plans and agency activities covering over 90 percent of the federal work force were outside its purview. Moreover, the EEO offices in the headquarters of other agencies sometimes suffered from a similar problem and knew little about what was going on within their own field installations.

However, if decentralization of EEO activities in an effort to integrate equal opportunity with public personnel management generally have not worked well, efforts to implement EEO through a centralized enforcement agency also present difficulties. Historically, in the federal service at least, this approach has not worked well. EEO agencies outside the mainstream of personnel have been frustrated by the commitment of personnelists to "merit" even in the face of clear evidence that aspects of the merit system can be discriminatory. Moreover, public personnel is rather complicated and difficult for outsiders to comprehend—especially in its netherworld aspects. Even today the EEOC and the OPM are sometimes seriously at odds concerning policies that are relevant to EEO. Nevertheless, there is now some evidence from local governmental experience that EEO efforts will be more effective if responsibility for them is placed under the chief executive rather than in a personnel department or a civil service commission.

Another positive lesson was learned regarding the organization of efforts to further the employment of members of different groups covered by EEO. In 1970, a special Spanish-Speaking Program (subsequently renamed the Hispanic Employment Program) was initiated within the overall framework of federal EEO. It included Hispanic Employment Program coordinators who were to address the special needs of Latinos and to facilitate the application of EEO to them. Similarly, Federal Women's Program coordinators were to advise agency officials on the "special concerns" of women and were

The Language of EEO

Adverse effect. Differential rate of selection (for hire, promotion, etc.) that works to the disadvantage of an applicant subgroup, particularly subgroups classified by race, gender, and other characteristics on the basis of which discrimination is prohibited by law.

Adverse-inference rule. An analytical tool used by the Equal Employment Opportunity Commission (EEOC) in its investigations. The EEOC holds that when relevant evidence is withheld by an organization when the EEOC feels that there is no valid reason for such a withholding, the EEOC may presume that the evidence in question is adverse to the organization being investigated. The EEOC Compliance Manual permits use of the adverse-inference rule only if "the requested evidence is relevant," the evidence was requested "with ample time to produce it and with notice that failure to produce it would result in an adverse inference," and the "respondent produced neither the evidence nor an acceptable explanation."

Adverse impact. When a selection process for a particular job or group of jobs results in the selection of members of any racial, ethnic, or gender group at a lower rate than members of others groups, that process is said to have adverse impact. Federal EEO enforcement agencies generally regard a selection rate for any group that is less than four-fifths or 80 percent of the rate for other groups as constituting evidence of adverse impact.

Affected class. According to the U.S. Department of Labor's Office of Federal Contract Compliance:

> persons who continue to suffer the present effects of past discrimination. An employee or group of employees may be members of an affected class when, because of discrimination based on race, religion, sex, [sic] or national origin, such employees, for example, were assigned initially to less desirable or lower paying jobs, were denied equal opportunity to advance to better paying or more desirable jobs, or were subject to layoff or displacement from their jobs.

Employees may continue to be members of an "affected class" even though they may have been transferred or advanced into more desirable positions if the effects of past discrimination have not been remedied. For example, if an employee who was hired into a lower paying job because of past discriminatory practices has been subsequently promoted, further relief may be required if the employee has not found his or her "rightful place."

Affirmative action. When the term first gained currency in the 1960s, it meant the removal of "artificial barriers" to the employment of women and "minority" group members. Toward the end of that decade, however, the term got lost in a fog of semantics and came out meaning the provision of compensatory opportunities for hitherto disadvantaged groups. In a formal, *legal* sense, affirmative action now refers to specific efforts to recruit, hire, train, retain, and/or promote disadvantaged groups for the purpose of eliminating the present effects of past discrimination.

(continued)

Bona fide occupational qualification (BFOQ or BOQ). *Bona fide* is a Latin term meaning "in good faith," honest, or genuine. A BFOQ, therefore, is a *necessary* occupational qualification. Title VII of the Civil Rights Act of 1964 allows employers to discriminate against applicants on the basis of religion, gender, or national origin, when being considered for certain jobs if they lack a BFOQ. However, what constitutes a BFOQ has been interpreted very narrowly by the EEOC and the federal courts. Legitimate uses for BFOQs include, for example, female sex for a position as an actress or male sex for professional baseball player. There are no legally recognized BFOQs with respect to race or color. Overall, a BFOQ is a job requirement that would be discriminatory and illegal were it not for its necessity for the performance of a particular job.

Bottom-line concept. In the context of equal employment opportunity, the bottom-line concept suggests that an employer whose total selection process has no adverse impact can be assured that EEO enforcement agencies will not examine the individual components of that process for evidence of adverse impact. However, not all EEO enforcement agencies subscribe to the concept.

Business necessity. The major legal defense for using an employment practice that effectively excludes protected-class persons. The leading court case, *Robinson* v. *Lorrilard Corp.*, 444 F.2d 791 (4th Cir. 1971); *cert. denied*, 404 U.S. 1006 (1971), holds that the test of the business necessity defense

> is whether there exists an overriding legitimate business purpose such that the practice is necessary to the safe and efficient operation of the business. Thus, the business purpose must be sufficiently compelling to override any racial impact; the challenged practice must effectively carry out the business purpose it is alleged to serve; and there must be available no acceptable alternative policies or practices which would better accomplish the business purpose advanced, or accomplish it equally well with a lesser differential racial impact.

Chilling effect. Employment practices, government regulations, court decisions, or legislation (or the threat of these) may create an inhibiting atmosphere or chilling effect that prevents the free exercise of individual employment rights. A "chilling" effect tends to keep protected-class persons from seeking employment and advancement in an organization even in the absence of formal bars. Other chilling effects may be positive or negative, depending upon the "chillee's" perspective. For example, even discussion of proposed regulations can "chill" employers or unions into compliance.

Consent decree. Approach to enforcing equal employment opportunity involving a negotiated settlement that allows an employer to not admit to any acts of discrimination yet agree to greater EEO efforts in the future. Consent decrees are usually negotiated with the Equal Employment Opportunity Commission or a federal court.

Discrimination. In the context of employment, the failure to treat equals equally. Whether deliberate or unintentional, any action that has the effect of limiting

(continued)

employment and advancement opportunities because of an individual's gender, race, color, age, national origin, religion, physical disability is discrimination. Because of the EEO and civil rights legislation of recent years, individuals aggrieved by unlawful discrimination now have a variety of administrative and judicial remedies open to them.

Disparate effect.   Tendency of an employment screening device or criteria to limit the appointment opportunities of protected-class persons at a greater rate than for white males.

Employment practice.   In the context of equal employment opportunity, an employment practice is any screening device operating at any point in the employment cycle. If a discriminatory employment practice is not related to job performance, it will not be able to withstand a court challenge.

Equal Employment Opportunity (EEO).   Concept fraught with political, cultural, and emotional overtones. Generally, it applies to a set of employment procedures and practices that effectively prevent any individual from being adversely excluded from employment opportunities on the basis of race, color, gender, religion, age, national origin, or other facts that cannot lawfully be used in employment efforts. While the ideal of EEO is an employment system that is devoid of both intentional and unintentional discrimination, achieving this ideal may be a political impossibility because of the problem of definition. One person's equal opportunity may be seen by another as tainted with institutional racism or sexism. Because of this problem of definition, only the courts have been able to say if, when, and where EEO exists.

Equal employment opportunity counselor.   Specifically designated individual within an organization who provides an open and systematic channel through which employees may raise questions, discuss real and imagined grievances, and obtain information on their procedural rights. Counseling is the first stage in the discrimination complaint process. The counselor through interviews and inquiries attempts to informally resolve problems related to equal employment opportunity.

Equal employment opportunity officer.   Official within an organization who is designated responsibility for monitoring EEO programs and assuring that both organizational and national EEO policies are being implemented.

Fair Employment Practice Commission (FEPC).   Generic term for any state or local government agency responsible for administering/enforcing laws prohibiting employment discrimination because of race, color, gender, religion, national origin, or other factors.

Fair employment practice laws.   All government requirements designed to prohibit discrimination in the various aspects of employment.

Gender differential, also RACE DIFFERENTIAL. Lower than "regular" wage rate paid by an employer to female and/or African American and Latino employees. Such

(continued)

differentials were paid before the advent of current equal employment opportunity laws and are now illegal.

Gender discrimination. Any disparate or unfavorable treatment of an individual in an employment situation because of his or her gender. The Civil Rights Act of 1964 makes gender discrimination illegal except where a bona fide occupational qualification is involved.

Make whole. Legal remedy that provides for an injured party to be placed as near as may be possible, in the situation he or she would have occupied if the wrong had not been committed. The concept was first put forth by the U.S. Supreme Court in the 1867 case of *Wicker* v. *Hoppock*. In 1975, the Court held, in the case of *Albermarle Paper Company* v. *Moody* (422 U.S. 405), that Title VII of the Civil Rights Act of 1964 (as amended) intended a "make whole" remedy for unlawful discrimination.

Protected class. Any person covered by antidiscrimination legislation, including women, African Americans, Latinos, Asian/Pacific Islanders, Native Americans, persons over forty years of age, disabled persons, and Vietnam-era veterans.

Reading assistant. Reader for a visually impaired employee. Public Law 87-614 of 1962 authorized the employment of readers for visually impaired federal employees. These reading assistants serve without compensation from the government, but they can be paid by the visually impaired employees, nonprofit organizations, or state offices of vocational rehabilitation. They may also serve on a volunteer basis.

Reasonable accommodation. Once a disabled employee is hired, an employer is required to take reasonable steps to accommodate the individual's disability unless such steps would cause the employer undue hardship. Examples of "reasonable accommodations" include providing a reader for a visually impaired employee, an interpreter for a hearing-impaired person requiring telephone contacts, or adequate workspace for an employee confined to a wheelchair.

Religious discrimination. Any act that manifests unfavorable or inequitable treatment toward employees or prospective employees because of their religious convictions. Because of section 703(a)(1) of the Civil Rights Act of 1964, an individual's religious beliefs or practices cannot be given any consideration in making employment decisions. The argument that a religious practice may place an undue hardship upon an employer—for example, where such practices require special religious holidays and hence absence from work—has been upheld by the courts. However, because of the sensitive nature of discharging or refusing to hire an individual on religious grounds, the burden of proof to show that such a hardship exists is placed upon the employer.

Restrictive credentialism. General terms for any selection policy adversely affecting disadvantaged groups because they lack the formal qualifications for positions that, in the opinion of those adversely affected, do not truly need such formal qualifications.

(continued)

Representative bureaucracy. Concept originated by J. Donald Kingsley, in *Representative Bureaucracy* (Yellow Springs, Ohio: Antioch Press, 1944), which asserts that all social groups have a right to participation in their governing institutions. In recent years, the concept has developed a normative overlay—that all social groups should occupy bureaucratic positions in direct proportion to their numbers in the general population.

Retroactive seniority. Seniority status that is retroactively awarded back to the date that a woman or other protected-class group member was proven to have been discriminatorily refused employment. The U.S. Supreme Court has interpreted the "make whole" provision of Title VII of the Civil Rights Act of 1964 to include the award of retroactive seniority to proven discriminatees; however, retroactive seniority cannot be awarded further back than 1964—the date of the act.

Rightful place. Judicial doctrine that an individual who has been discriminated against should be restored to the job—to his or her "rightful place"—as if there had been no discrimination and given appropriate seniority, merit increases, and promotions.

706 Agency. State and local fair employment practices agency named for Section 706(c) of Title VII of the Civil Rights of 1964, which requires aggrieved individuals to submit claims to state or local fair employment practices agencies before they are eligible to present their cases to the federal government's Equal Employment Opportunity Commission. State and local agencies that have the ability to provide the same protections provided by Title VII as would the EEOC are termed 706 agencies. The EEOC maintains a list of the 706 agencies that it formally recognizes.

Systemic discrimination. Use of employment practices (recruiting methods, selection tests, promotion policies, etc.) that have the unintended effect of excluding or limiting the employment prospects of protected-class persons. Because of court interpretations of Title VII of the Civil Rights Act of 1964, all such systemic discrimination, despite its "innocence," must be eliminated where it cannot be shown that such action would place an unreasonable burden on the employer or that such practices cannot be replaced by other practices which would not have such an adverse effect.

Adapted from Jay M. Shafritz, *Dictionary of Personnel Management and Labor Relations*, 2nd ed. (New York: Facts on File, Inc., 1985).

"required" to "have empathy with and understanding of the special problems and concerns of women in the employment situation." Organization along these lines is important because the employment patterns of African Americans, women and other protected-class persons are sufficiently dissimilar to indicate that these persons should be treated separately rather than as a bloc.

EEO Policy

EEO policy development since the early 1970s has been largely a function of a larger struggle between those who believe in the inviolability of the merit system and those who think that "compensatory" or "benevolent" treatment should be applied in order to redress the practices of the past and/or create a public bureaucracy that is "representative" of the population at large. The "compensatory treatment" approach starts from the premise that past discrimination against protected-class persons makes nondiscrimination in the sense of color blindness insufficient to remove all the barriers to equality of opportunity. This position is often explained by drawing an analogy to a foot race. Imagine, ask proponents of compensatory treatment, a race between an African American and a white in which whoever reaches certain points along the course first receives rewards that help this runner to continue running, while the opponent receives nothing or is actually encumbered by arriving at these positions last. Imagine further that the white receives a headstart while the African American is forced to run the race with weights around his neck and limbs. For those who favor compensatory approaches, simply declaring an intent not to discriminate in the future is the equivalent of halting the race, removing the weights from the African American, and then allowing the contest to continue. "Doesn't equality of opportunity require more?" they ask. At the very least, many argue, the relative starting positions of African Americans and whites have to be equalized. Others believe that, because past discrimination against African Americans and other protected-class persons was so entrenched, "affirmative" steps must be taken to neutralize the past advantages obtained by white males. For many, therefore, "compensatory" treatment is not only a way of creating genuine equality of opportunity, it also serves as a remedy for past abuses.

A second line of argument in favor of compensatory treatment is more politically oriented. It stresses the political importance of positions in public bureaucracies and argues that the social composition of the public service is of great consequence. Thus, Samuel Krislov maintains that who gets to be a high-ranking civil servant is as important as who gets to be president, cabinet member, or members of Congress. In general, this approach can be subsumed under the concept of representative bureaucracy. This notion dates back to the presidencies of Thomas Jefferson and Andrew Jackson. It came into the literature of the social sciences in the 1940s and has gained increasing attention in recent years. It consists of several overlapping and intertwined meanings. Among these are the ideas that (1) all groups ought to have a right to influence and political participation; (2) the representation of social groups in a public bureaucracy binds members of those groups in general to the regime and the policies it seeks to implement; (3) a representative bureaucracy will therefore be in tune with the general ethos of the larger political community and consequently its effectiveness and efficiency will be enhanced; (4) the social representatives of various groups will seek to establish policies that are beneficial to the groups from which they come; and (5) as a result, a representative bureaucracy can compensate for the unrepresentative characteristics of legislatures, courts, and other aspects of a government. It is evident that to a very large extent the utility of a representative bureaucracy depends upon whether or not bureaucrats actually seek to represent the special needs of the groups from which they come and under what circumstances. Traditional theories about bureaucracy would argue that such behavior would be uncommon because bureaucrats operate in an impersonal manner and according to written and rigid rules. Empirical studies of this matter have come to different conclusions.

However, there is accumulating evidence that public administrators drawn from individual groups, such as African Americans or Latinos, are likely to have perspectives on issues of high salience to their group's status and interests that differ from that of white administrators. Similarly, a number of issues, including comparable worth (see Chapter 8) and pregnancy and maternity leaves (see Chapter 16), are particularly important to women, who put them on the personnel policy agenda as their numbers in the public sector work force grew dramatically during the 1970s and 1980s. At the very least, the wide range of concerns generally voiced in a highly pluralistic nation is more likely to be heard in a representative public service than in one drawn very disproportionately from a single social group.

Supporters of compensatory treatment also point to the role that the public sector has historically played in the upward mobility and assimilation of immigrant groups from Europe. There is much evidence that Irish, Italian, and Jewish immigrants and their progeny benefited from public employment. Not only do public sector jobs provide income, but they also convey the appearance that social groups have been accepted by the government as valued members of the political community. Furthermore, they enable members of these groups to pass on middle-class skills and attitudes to their offspring. Civil service jobs can also be used to establish networks of contacts that facilitate the entrance of other members of a social group into the public service.

At this point it might be asked, why not merit and representation at once? Need they be mutually exclusive? Doesn't contemporary public personnel policy combine merit and representation? In *theory*, there is no incompatibility between the two objectives. More practically, however, there is some tension, especially in a society such as the United States. Most bureaucratic jobs, and especially those in the higher ranks, are middle class in nature requiring middle-class literacy and educational credentials. Representation under merit is only likely to be obtained in a society in which all groups are distributed in equal proportions along the social class ladder. This, of course, is decidedly not the case in the United States, where African Americans, Native Americans, and the Latino population are still disproportionately economically disadvantaged. For example, in 1950, the median income of white families was 1.8 times that of African American families; in 1970, the equivalent figure was 1.6; in 1978, it was 1.7; and in 1987, the ratio stood very close to the 1950 figure, at 1.78. Relatedly, the African-American unemployment rate has remained substantially higher than that of whites: in 1973, it was 2.19 times the white rate, in 1983, 2.32 times, and in 1987, the rate was 13 percent for African Americans compared to 5.3 percent for whites, or 2.45 times greater for African Americans. In 1987, approximately one in every three African Americans lived in poverty whereas the same was true of about 1 in every 10.5 whites. In 1986, the average life expectancy of whites stood at 75.4 years, a full six years longer than for African Americans. Moreover, the growing "feminization" of poverty presents a new barrier to obtaining equal opportunity under conventional merit systems. Of course, in some cases the pursuit of EEO has clearly enhanced the objectives of the merit system by increasing the pool of qualified applicants for competitive positions. This has been especially evident in the removal of artificial barriers to competitive employment, such as unnecessary weight and height requirements.

Perhaps the biggest problem with the argument that there is tension between merit and representation stems from society's unequivocal acceptance of merit. For example, if a white woman or an African American scores lower than a white male on a "merit" exam, but is nonetheless hired, the argument is made that "merit has been sacrificed." But, has it really? Can we come to this conclusion without a thorough assessment of how merit is conceptualized and measured? And, why isn't this argument made when the "buddy" system is used to fill job vacancies? Is it even possible to identify "qualified" or "best qualified" job candidates through use of merit exams?

Well, the U.S. Supreme Court in *Johnson*, discussed earlier, may have answered some of these questions when it quoted a brief submitted by the American Society for Personnel Administration:

> It is a standard tenet of personnel administration that there is rarely a single, 'best qualified' person for a job...final determinations as to which candidate is 'best qualified' are at best subjective.

Even just "qualified" candidates may not be identified by merit exams because of the underlying biases in the exams themselves (e.g., cultural biases) as well as in the validation techniques used to make them "job-related."

As a matter of policy, the federal government, many state governments, and more than 90 percent of U.S. cities have moved from a strictly "color-blind," noncompensatory approach to one which creates "compensatory" treatment in the form of affirmative action. The Supreme Court's decision in the *Johnson* case (discussed in the chapter prologue) cleared the legal path for further reliance on this approach as long as it meets the requirements of "narrow tailoring."

Affirmative Action Plans

Traditionally, affirmative action meant the removal of "artificial barriers" to the employment of protected-class persons. However, the term has now come to include "compensatory treatment" as well. An affirmative action plan maps out an agency's strategy for furthering EEO during the period it covers. Typically, affirmative action plans cover such elements as:

1. Agency organization and resources for administering the EEO Program
2. Recruitment activities designed to reach and attract job candidates from all sources
3. Plans for fully utilizing the present skills of employees
4. Training for employees and fostering their upward mobility
5. EEO training for supervisors
6. Employment goals and timetables to achieve a representative work force

Many agencies and jurisdictions seek broad managerial and employee participation in the formulation of affirmative action plans. This approach counteracts a tendency for the plan to be unrealistic or unresponsive to the conditions in an agency. It also makes it less likely that the plan will be little more than a "paper" program.

The most controversial and important aspect of agency affirmative action plans has been the setting of employment goals and timetables to foster the hiring and promotion of women and members of minority or protected-class groups. A *goal* has been defined as a "realistic objective which an agency endeavors to achieve on a timely basis within the context of the merit system of employment." Goals are supposed to be formulated in areas in which "minority employment is not what should reasonably be expected" in terms of the "skills composition" of minorities in the recruiting area.

For the most part, this approach is realistic because it is geared to the actual conditions in any given department, agency, or bureau. However, it can lead to a great deal of decentralization in the setting of goals and timetables. This makes it difficult to generalize about the content of affirmative action plans or to evaluate their impact on employment patterns. Nevertheless, available policy analyses indicate that the social composition of American public services is changing in a way that comports with the objectives of EEO and affirmative action programs—albeit far too slowly for some critics.

During the 1970s, one of the pitfalls of affirmative action became evident. Women and African Americans disproportionately lost their public

Procedures for Processing Individual Complaints of Discrimination Based on Race, Color, Religion, Gender, National Origin, or Physical or Mental Disability

1. Employee contacts EEO COUNSELOR within 30 calendar days of alleged discriminatory action. COUNSELOR has 21 calendar days to attempt informal resolution.

   If final counseling interview is not completed in 21 days, COUNSELOR must on 21st day give written notice of right to file an individual complaint any time up to 15 calendar days after final interview.

2. If informal resolution fails, EMPLOYEE may file an individual formal complaint with DIRECTOR OF EEO, AGENCY HEAD, INSTALLATION HEAD, EEO OFFICER, or FEDERAL WOMEN'S PROGRAM MANAGER within 15 calendar days of final interview with COUNSELOR.

3. EEO OFFICER advises DIRECTOR OF EEO, who assigns INVESTIGATOR from jurisdiction or agency other than that in which the complaint arose.

4. Investigation conducted; COMPLAINANT given copy of investigative file. EEO OFFICER provides opportunity for informal adjustment.

5. If adjustment not made, EEO OFFICER notifies COMPLAINANT in writing (1) of proposed disposition, (2) of right to hearing and decision by AGENCY HEAD, and (3) of right to decision by AGENCY HEAD without a hearing.

6. If COMPLAINANT does not reply within 15 calendar days, EEO OFFICER may adopt proposed disposition as decision of the agency, providing he or she has been delegated this authority. Otherwise, complaint is forwarded to AGENCY HEAD (or his or her designee) for agency decision. Upon receipt of decision or any final decision, the EMPLOYEE may file a notice of appeal within 20 days to EEOC or may file a civil action in an appropriate U.S. District Court within 30 days.

7. If COMPLAINANT asks for hearing, agency requests EEOC to assign COMPLAINTS EXAMINER.

8. COMPLAINTS EXAMINER reviews file; remands complaint to agency if further investigation necessary; schedules and conducts hearing.

9. Hearings recorded and transcribed verbatim. COMPLAINTS EXAMINER makes findings, analysis, and recommends decision; forwards these and the complaint file to the AGENCY HEAD (or designee).

10. HEAD OF AGENCY (or designee) makes agency decision, based on file, giving COMPLAINANT a copy of COMPLAINTS EXAMINER'S report. Must give specific reasons for rejection or modification of COMPLAINTS EXAMINER'S recommended decision in detail.

11. COMPLAINANT has right to file a notice of appeal to EEOC'S OFFICE OF REVIEW AND APPEALS within 20 calendar days of receipt of agency's notice of final decision.

(continued)

Note:

1. COMPLAINANT has right to file civil action in an appropriate U.S. District Court:
   (a) Within 30 calendar days of his or her receipt of notice of final agency action on his or her complaint
   (b) After 180 calendar days from date of filing an individual complaint with agency if there has been no decision.
   (c) Within 30 calendar days of his or her receipt of notice of final action taken by EEOC on the complaint, or
   (d) After 180 calendar days from date of filing an appeal with EEOC if no EEOC decision.

   Filing of a civil action does not end the processing of an individual complaint by the agency or EEOC.

2. The agency shall furnish EEOC monthly reports on all individual complaints pending within the agency. If an agency has not issued a decision or requested EEOC to supply a complaints examiner within 75 calendar days of the date a complaint was filed, EEOC may require special action or assume responsibility for the complaint.

Supervisory and Communications Training Center, U.S. Office of Personnel Management, *Workshops on Sexual Harassment, Trainer's Manual* (Washington, D.C., u.d.), pp. 74–75.

sector jobs as many jurisdictions engaged in widespread cutbacks of their civil services. To some extent, this was a function of personnel policies operating on a "last in, first out" (LIFO) system. Where women and members of other protected-class groups have been "last in" due to discriminatory practices of the past, they are nonetheless likely to be "first out" when cutbacks occur. Seniority retention preferences can be based on several different factors, including time in the public sector work force, time in an agency, time in a collective bargaining unit, and time in a position. Depending upon precisely how a LIFO system operates, cutbacks can lead to "bumps" and "retreats" that are disproportionately harmful to the retention and level of employment of women and members of minority groups. It is important to note that bona fide seniority systems are both legal and constitutional, even though they may have this effect. Indeed, in *Memphis* v. *Stotts* (1984), the Supreme Court held that a bona fide seniority system could be used even if it led to the layoff of minority firefighters who had been hired specifically as part of a program to remedy the effects of past discrimination. Eventually the seniority versus

EEO problem may work itself out. However, at present, this is an area in which the objectives of some labor unions in negotiating seniority retention preferences are often at odds with the goals of EEO.

EEO Complaint Systems

Discrimination complaint systems are another central feature of EEO programs. Although these are largely remedial in their impact on the public service, they are important in several respects. First, complaint systems provide employees with an enforcement mechanism that enables them to protect their right of equal opportunity whenever they feel it is being violated. At the same time, complaint systems provide supervisory personnel and agencies with protection against false accusations that they are racist, sexist, or otherwise illegally discriminatory. Third, complaint systems tend to serve as indicators of public employers' commitment of EEO. Where discrimination is rarely found, administrative credibility in the EEO realm generally suffers.

Yet complaint systems have been very troublesome; they must process large numbers of sensitive complaints with efficiency, equity, and consistency. But doing so in large jurisdictions can be almost impossible. The federal government is illustrative of the problem. The system is so complex that it's less a wonder that it creaks on than that it works at all. Although discrimination cases are supposed to be closed within 180 days, the governmentwide average is about 1.5 years. In some agencies, it takes more than two years, on average, to close cases. Even in NASA, which seems to resolve complaints with space age efficiency compared to other agencies, the average is 218 days per case. In one traditional "green eye-shade agency," the General Services Administration, it once took six years to decide one aspect of an EEO complaint—the issue of "timeliness"! Worse yet, perhaps, in practice complainants face a heavy burden of persuasion. Out of 17,014 federal EEO complaints filed in 1987, only 91 resulted in clear findings of discrimination. Many more were probably settled to the claimant's satisfaction, but the road to justice is clearly long and arduous. It's also expensive—the cost to the government of processing a complaint is estimated at about $8,000.

Dealing with a "mixed case"—that is, an adverse action case involving a charge of illegal discrimination—is particularly cumbersome. It presents what former EEOC and OPM officials have termed as "disaster" and an "administrative nightmare." Such cases are acted upon by both the EEOC and the Merit Systems Protection Board (MSPB). When these two agencies cannot agree, an official from the White House may be drawn into the fray. It would be surprising if such cases were routinely resolved in less than a full year.

Effective complaint systems should provide the following:

1. Opportunities for fair, informal resolution of the matter
2. Timely hearings, decisions, and appeals
3. Impartial hearings divorced from the control of agency management
4. Sufficient remedies, including back pay, promotion, desired training, and so forth
5. Willingness to punish discriminatory supervisory personnel
6. Mechanisms by which general complaints challenging fundamental aspects of the personnel program, such as merit examinations, can be heard and resolved fairly

The importance of complaint systems was enhanced by the Supreme Court's decision in *Connecticut* v. *Teal* (1982). The EEOC had issued a somewhat complicated rule that enabled an employer to mount a "bottom line" defense against charges of discrimination if the selection rate among eligible minorities or women was at least 80 percent of the selection rate for white males. The Court held, however, that a racially balanced work force does not "immunize" the employer from liability for specific acts of discrimination.

Additional EEO Concerns

Equal opportunity essentially requires that artificial barriers not be placed in the way of qualified individuals seeking public or private employment and that once on the job all employees be treated in a nondiscriminatory fashion. In 1967, Congress enacted the Age Discrimination in Employment Act (ADEA)

Who Is Covered by the Age Discrimination in Employment Act?

In 1967, the Congress passed the Age Discrimination in Employment Act (ADEA), which made it illegal for private businesses to refuse to hire, to discharge, or to otherwise discriminate against an individual in compensation or privileges of employment, between the ages of 40 and 65. The act was amended in 1974 to apply to state and local governments. Age discrimination in federal employment was prohibited by executive order. The act was amended again in 1978 to raise to 70 the minimum mandatory retirement age for employees in private companies and state and local government. This 1978 amendment also banned forced retirement for federal employees at any age. The ADEA was once again amended in 1986 to remove age 70 as the upper limit for all employees (private and state and local government) *except* for (1) firefighters, (2) law enforcement officers, and (save the best for last!) (3) tenured university professors. These exceptions are repealed December 31, 1993, pending a determination of their feasibility.

**Faulty Complaint Process Holds
Equal Opportunity Hostage**

The equal employment opportunity (EEO) complaint process for federal employees, as many have pointed out, is extremely deficient. Thousands of discrimination complaints are filed with the Equal Employment Opportunity Commission (EEOC) each year, but time delays, conflicts of interest and lack of sanctions against federal employers have rendered the EEO complaint machinery ineffective, indeed biased! The EEOC and Congress are seeking to remedy this problem, and Eleanor Holmes Norton, former chair of the EEOC, was called upon to testify before the congressional panel charged with the investigation. The following represents excerpts from her testimony.

We can no longer afford a mechanism in which the federal agencies continue to investigate and take final action on complaints by the workers they employ. There are practical and financial reasons why the system was established in this manner, and political turf and concerns contribute to the continuation of the present system. However, these are not acceptable reasons for maintenance of an approach that has floundered and deprived federal workers of their rights for decades.

Think for a moment of the public outrage if the government permitted IBM or General Motors, for example, to investigate and take final action on complaints that violated Title VII of the Civil Rights Act of 1964. If these circumstances are unacceptable for private industry, by what tortured reasoning do we allow them to continue in the federal government?

Among other recommendations to improve the system, Norton proposed that we "remove" [federal] agencies from the investigative and hearing process entirely and centralize all discrimination functions within the EEOC."

Source: Adapted from *Federal Times* (August 27, 1990), p. 9.

to assure that age would not be treated as such a barrier by private employers. Subsequently, the act was applied to state and local employers. Enforcement authority was originally vested in the Department of Labor but was transferred to the EEOC as part of the federal service reform of 1978. Greater efforts have also been taken to assure that disabled persons are not summarily excluded from positions for which they are qualified. There has been movement from "categorical medical standards" to case-by-case medical/ accommodational analyses. Recent approaches regarding disabled persons emphasize the need to avoid rigid procedures in seeking to make adequate accommodations.

Veterans preference is another function that is sometimes subsumed within the framework of affirmative recruitment programs. It has been in conflict with the employment interests of women and, to a lesser extent, minorities. However, many public jurisdictions, including the federal government, have reasoned that such preferences enhance the opportunities of those who have been out of the civilian labor market for some time, and especially of those who have been disabled while serving the nation's military interests. Most states and the federal service provide a five-point advantage to veteran preference eligibles on entry ranking devices and ten-point preference to disabled veterans. In some places an absolute preference is used. In this case, available veteran preference eligibles must be hired or promoted before positions can be filled by other applicants or employees. Veteran preferences are also given for promotions and reductions in force in some jurisdictions. Some place a time limit on the period for which one can be eligible for veterans preference.

Finally, it should be remembered that equal opportunity is a concept that must be infused throughout public personnel administration. It pertains not only to the hiring and promotion of individuals, but to equal pay, comparable worth, and the treatment of employees on a day-to-day basis. No greater mistake could be made than equating EEO simply with the formal requirements of an affirmative action plan.

Sexual Harassment

Sexual harassment is a serious EEO concern and a form of prohibited discrimination. It is considered discrimination because it bases job actions or work arrangements on sex, which is prohibited by the Civil Rights Act of 1964 as amended. There is no single, standard definition of sexual harassment. However, it is usually thought of as "unwanted sexual attention." This definition is broad enough to encompass everything from coercion to touching to leering to offhand comments with sexual overtones.

Although its scope is inherently unknowable, there is considerable evidence that sexual harrassment is very widespread. Several surveys have indicated that a large number of women believe they have been subject to sexual harrassment in the workplace at one time or another. Indeed, the study *Sexual Harassment in the Federal Government*, released by the MSPB in June 1988, contained several shocking findings. First, sexual harassment is very widespread: "In 1987, 42 percent of all women and 14 percent of all men reported they experienced some form of uninvited and unwanted sexual attention." Second, "Many victims tried more than one response to unwanted sexual attention. Although later judged ineffective by most of them, almost half of all victims tried to ignore the behavior and did nothing in response. In 1987, only 5 percent of...victims said they took some type of formal action." Third, "During the 2-year period from May 1985 through May, 1987, sexual harassment cost the Federal Government an estimated $267 million. This cost is in addition to the personal cost and anguish many of the victims had to bear." Fourth, "Coworkers are much more likely than supervisors to be the source of sexual harassment. In 1987, 69 percent of female victims

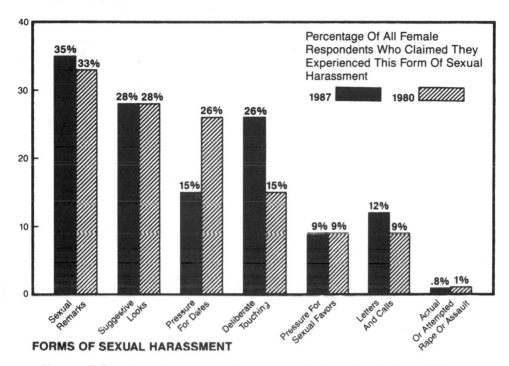

Figure 7.3.   Sexual harassment of women in the federal work force (1980 and 1987). *Source* U.S. Merit Systems Protection Board, *Sexual Harassment in the Federal Government* (Washington, D.C.: MSPB, 1988), p. 16.

and 77 percent of male victims said they were harassed by a coworker or another employee without supervisory authority over them." Finally, as Figure 7.3 indicates, some forms of sexual harassment seem to be increasing.

Perhaps the best way of thinking about the effort to eliminate sexual harassment is to realize that it is part of a larger historical attempt to eliminate sources of social or political friction from the civil service. Friction, being the antithesis of smooth-running efficiency, has long been deemed undesirable in the federal service. Politically, presidents from John Adams (1797–1801) through the Civil Service Reform of 1883 sought to eliminate partisan frictions in the federal work force. After reform, when it was no longer possible to appoint only Republicans or only Democrats, political neutrality was introduced to assure that partisanship would not become an intrusive force in work relationships. Socially, African Americans were first prohibited from holding federal service jobs, and subsequently segregated in the federal service as a means of eliminating racial frictions. Woodrow Wilson introduced widespread racial segregation in the federal service with the statement that

What is Sexual Harassment?

Sexual harassment* is any unwanted verbal or physical sexual advance or sexually explicit derogatory statements made by someone in the classroom or workplace, which are offensive or which cause the recipient discomfort or humiliation or which interfere with the recipient's education or job performance. It can include:

> Leering at a person's body
>
> Verbal harassment or abuse of a sexual nature
>
> Unnecessary touching, patting, pinching, or constant brushing against a person's body
>
> Subtle pressure for sexual favors
>
> Demanding sexual favors accompanied by implied or overt threats concerning one's grades, recommendations, job, performance evaluation, promotion, etc.
>
> Physical assault

Note: Although the majority of incidents involve a male supervisor, co-worker or instructor harassing a woman, the law also covers women harassing men, women harassing women, and men harassing men.

*Definition from N.O.W. and the Working Women's Institute, as it appears in a pamphlet prepared by the Affirmative Action Office, the University at Albany, State University of New York.

it would reduce such frictions. Eventually, society realized that the way to deal with the problem, to the extent that one exists, was not to prohibit African Americans and whites from working together but rather to require equal employment opportunity and nondiscrimination. These programs and principles are intended to assure that race, color, national origin, religion, and gender do not affect the treatment of individuals in the public service. In the past, women, like African Americans, have been banned from many jobs in the public service. Sometimes the rationale was that women presented "moral dangers," as when they would work in close quarters with men or travel with them. As in the other cases of friction, this approach is now thoroughly discredited. If moral dangers exist, they are to be eliminated not by excluding women from the public service but rather by taking all "sexuality" out of it—including sexual harassment. From a managerial perspective this is really the equivalent of taking partisanship or racial prejudice out of public personnel matters. A strong program to eliminate unwanted sexual attention should accomplish this.

What Responsibilities Does the Supervisor Have Regarding Sexual Harassment of Federal Employees?

Q: What is expected of supervisors in the area of personnel management?

A: As stated in section 250-5 of the Federal Personnel Manual you must: Make objective evaluations of the quality of individual performance, based on valid performance measurements and sound judgment;

Develop and motivate employees to reach their fullest potential;

Deal with all employees in a fair and equitable manner and in accordance with established policy, including the terms of negotiated agreements.

Any of the behaviors described in OPM's definition of sexual harassment would be contrary to these requirements. Therefore, it is expected that the supervisor will make it plain to all employees that sexually harassing behavior will not be tolerated in the organization, and they will circulate written statements of organization policy to all members of the organization, discussing implications as needed.

Q: What should a supervisor do if an employee complains of sexual harassment by another employee, subordinate, coworker, or other supervisory person?

A: The supervisor should listen to the employee and try to determine what action the employee would like to see in the situation. For example, the employee may desire only to inform the supervisor about the problem, to obtain some information from the supervisor about employee rights, choose to handle the situation without help, or want the supervisor to intercede.

Q: If the employee wants the supervisor's help in resolving the problem, what can the supervisor offer to do?

A: Speak to the offender privately about the organization's code of ethics and behavior, if appropriate, or about the discomfort and loss of productivity the offending behavior is causing; or call a meeting between harasser and the person who feels harassed to discuss and resolve the issue; or suggest the employee contact an EEO counselor, the personnel office or other person for procedural advice; or arrange for communication skills training for the harassed employee and others who would profit from such training with the intent of equipping those persons to deal more successfully with sexually harassing behavior.

Q: What should a supervisor do if he or she observes possibly sexual harassing behavior on the job?

A: The supervisor should inquire of the harassed employee whether the latter considers behavior to be harassing. The employee may need to be told that he or she does not have to tolerate sexually harassing behavior.

Supervisory and Communications Training Center, U.S. Office of Personnel Management, *Workshop on Sexual Harassment, Trainer's Manual* (Washington, D.C., n.d.), p. 68.

Eliminating sexual harrassment, or unwanted sexual attention, is also part of a larger political cultural issue of protecting rights and basic standards of decency in the public sector. Obviously, sexual coercion and other forms of harassment are demeaning and intended to assert illegitimate authority or power over other individuals. Even comments about another's sexuality can have this effect. Referring to a woman as "sweetie" or "honey" is essentially the same thing as referring to adult African Americans as "boys" and "girls." Such language and what it stands for politically and socially has no place in the public service.

Currently, sexual harassment is illegal under a number of statutes. Most important for noncriminal sexual harassment is the Civil Rights Act of 1964 as amended by the Equal Employment Opportunity Act of 1972. Under these statutes, the EEOC has authority to hear and resolve complaints of sexual harassment. In the federal service, the MSPB, which has authority over many breaches of personnel law, can also help protect those who are its victims or take action against federal personnel who engage in such behavior.

In 1986, the U.S. Supreme Court issued a landmark ruling in the area of sexual harassment. In *Meritor Savings Bank* v. *Vinson*, the Court ruled that "a violation of Title VII may be predicated on either of two types of sexual harassment: harassment that involves the conditioning of concrete employment benefits on sexual favors, and harassment that, while not affecting economic benefits, creates a *hostile* or offensive working environment." (Emphasis added.) The hostile environment standard is an important one because it suggests that a violation of Title VII on a sexual harassment claim is not dependent upon the victim's loss of promotion or employment. Ultimately, the Court's ruling here will encourage employers to develop policies and complaint procedures that will protect women from unwanted, unwelcomed sexual advances.

The Lessons of EEO

Public personnel administration has now witnessed five decades of EEO. A few crucial lessons can be drawn from this experience. First, there has been a tendency for EEO programs and administering agencies to be weak and ineffective. Placing EEO under the authority of agencies outside the personnel policy area engenders hostility from personnelists. It also limits the expertise of those seeking to implement EEO and makes it difficult to build equal opportunity into all facets of the personnel program. On the other hand, where personnel agencies, such as the U.S. CSC, have overall responsibility for EEO, there has been a pronounced tendency for them to treat the merit system as sacrosanct and to fail to investigate or deal with its relationship to inequality of opportunity. This is a dilemma that appears likely to be with us for some years to come.

A second lesson is that remedial techniques have had a steady but slow impact on the racial, ethnic, and gender composition of the public service. Although entrance barriers have been successfully overcome, minority and female employees remain disproportionately in the lower grades. Some ranks are so overwhelmingly staffed by these persons that they are virtually segregated. Given the racial tensions prevalent in the United States, this does not bode well for effective management or an effective public service. Today's EEO problem is primarily one of moving protected-class persons up the grade ladder. Unfortunately, many of the central EEO program elements are not well suited to this task, especially with regard to positions in the top third of the career bureaucracy. Even if discrimination were rife at these levels, many employees would be reluctant to launch formal complaints. To do so would be to expose the defects of the top management of one's agency, and while such "whistleblowing" would serve the public interest, it also takes an unusual degree of courage and is hardly likely to redound to the employee's benefit. Since a college education is a virtual prerequisite for employment in the highest ranks, government-provided training will not often serve as

---

The Principal Provisions of Title V of the
Rehabilitation Act of 1973, as Amended

Section	Provision
501	Requires affirmative action in federal employment
502	Requires that federal buildings be accessible
503	Requires federal contractors to develop affirmative action plans
504	Prohibits discrimination by federal agencies as well as institutions receiving financial assistance
505(b)	Requires that attorneys' fees be provided for the prevailing party in a Title V action

Adapted from Barbara Schlei and Paul Grossman, *Employment Discrimination Law*, 2d ed (Washington, D.C.: Bureau of National Affairs, 1983), p. 246.

a road of access. Nor will special recruitment efforts, especially whenever these are in competition with the private sphere. In short, the nature of social inequality in the United States limits the utility of many of the traditional incremental approaches for achieving EEO, and this is especially the case with reference to the upper level of public services.

Although the society's experience with compensatory techniques such as the use of goals and timetables is far from complete, it appears that these do not present the easy solution for which many had hoped. There is a tension between EEO and affirmative action that requires the latter to be narrowly tailored (and therefore limited).

Another lesson has been that it is desirable to address the needs of different EEO target groups separately, since their interests are not identical to one another. For example, the needs and interests of disabled persons may be very different from other protected-class groups. Indeed, this is evident in one of the most current issues in public personnel administration today—persons with AIDS, who are considered to be disabled either explicitly under certain state statutes (e.g., in Florida, Maine, Massachusetts, New York and New Jersey), or implicitly under the federal Rehabilitation Act of 1973 and the Americans with Disabilities Act (ADA) of 1990.

Finally, the Rehabilitation Act itself illustrates the lesson that, ever since the 1940s, EEO has been in a state of flux as public personnel responds to newly emerging issues and concerns. The act defines a disabled person as one who "(i) has a physical or mental impairment which substantially limits

---

Title I of the Americans with Disabilities Act of 1990.

The Americans with Disabilities Act (ADA) covers employers, employment agencies, labor unions and joint labor-management committees with twenty-five or more employees. (By 1994, it will cover employers, etc. with fifteen or more employees.) Excluded from coverage are the United States, any corporation wholly owned by the U.S. government or a bona fide private membership club (other than labor organizations).

According to the ADA, "[n]o covered entity shall discriminate against a qualified individual with a disability because of the disability of such individual in regard to job application procedures, the hiring, advancement, or discharge of employees, employee compensation, job training, and other terms, conditions, and privileges of employment."

Among those protected by the act are individuals who are in or have successfully completed rehabilitation for drug abuse or alcoholism. Congress, however, has to draw the line somewhere. The act states that "homosexuality and bisexuality are not impairments and as such are not disabilities under this Act"!

one or more...major life activities, (ii) has a record of such impairment, or (iii) is regarded as having such an impairment." (This definition is also incorporated in the ADA.) The act prohibits discrimination against "otherwise qualified handicapped individuals" (i.e., those who, "with reasonable accommodation," could perform the essential functions of a given job).

The U.S. Supreme Court has not explicitly found AIDS to be a covered disability under the Rehabilitation Act, but it has opened the doors for such an interpretation by the lower courts with its decision in *School Board of Nassau County* v. *Arline* (1987). In this case, the Supreme Court ruled that a public school teacher afflicted with the contagious disease of tuberculosis is a "handicapped individual" within the meaning of the Rehabilitation Act and, therefore, is afforded protection against employment discrimination by reason of the disability.

On the basis of this ruling, some lower courts have said that the Rehabilitation Act protects persons with AIDS from employment discrimination. For example, in *Chalk* v. *U.S. District Court, Central District of California and Orange County Superintendent of Schools* (1988), the U.S. Court of Appeals for the Ninth Circuit, relying on the Supreme Court's *Arline* decision, said that Section 504 of the Rehabilitation Act "allows the exclusion of an employee only if there is a *significant* risk of communicating an infectious disease to others." Based on myriad evidence presented by the medical community, the court found that there was no risk of Chalk, a teacher of hearing-impaired students, transmitting the virus to others. The court ordered Chalk to be reinstated to his teaching post.

Although not explicit, it appears that AIDS is also protected under the ADA, which was passed in 1990. (See Chapter 9 for a discussion of the constitutionality of testing for AIDS.) As of this writing, however, there are no court decisions interpreting this aspect of the law. In any event, EEO programs at all levels of government will be particularly vigilant of this issue in the coming years.

Looking Toward the Future

Federal EEO efforts began about half a century ago. Both policy development and progress have been incremental. As we move toward the year 2000, however, the skills required for public sector jobs will rise, and public employers will face a very different labor market. The OPM's *Civil Service 2000* (1988) predicts substantial increases in the number of positions requiring medium to very high language or math skills and a decline in positions requiring lesser skills. At the same time, it is predicted that:

Almost two-thirds of the new entrants into the work force between now and the year 2000 will be women. Demands for day care and for more time off from work for pregnancy and child-rearing will certainly increase, as will interest in part-time, flexible, and stay-at-home jobs. (For a further discussion, see Chapter 16.)

African Americans will make up 17 percent of the growth of the labor force between now and the year 2000, compared to their current 11 percent share of all workers.

Latinos will constitute an even greater fraction of the growth, with some 6 million new Latino workers added to the work force, 29 percent of the total increase. Not only are many African Americans and Latinos unprepared educationally for the higher skilled jobs being created, they are concentrated in declining central cities and slow-growing occupations that will limit their new employment opportunities. Although the federal government has traditionally been a large employer of African Americans, the increasing skill requirements of federal jobs could cap the growth of African American federal employment unless African American educational preparation, including rates of college graduation, rises.

Immigrants will represent the largest share of the increase in the population and work force since the first World War: approximately 600,000 legal and illegal immigrants are projected to enter the United States annually throughout the balance of the century. Because federal law and executive order sharply restricts the hiring of such workers (in the federal service) until they become U.S. citizens, federal employers in labor markets dominated by immigrants may find that they are in fierce competition for the native workers, unless these laws and orders are changed.

These predicted developments not only pose challenges to public sector EEO policy, they may require some fundamental rethinking of central aspects of personnel policy generally. For example, it is evident that job design will be a key to achieving and maintaining a socially representative public sector work force in the future. So will training, which will have to become more elaborate and innovative to meet the public sector's requirements as we approach 2000. If the employment outlook for African Americans and Latinos does not change otherwise, far more extensive public sector outreach programs may become highly desirable. But these are just a few of the changes that may be coming. From the perspectives of EEO and affirmative action, the public personnel agenda remains very dynamic.

Bibliography

Aaron, Henry J. and Cameran M. Lougy *The Comparable Worth Controversy*. Washington, D.C.: the Brookings Institution, 1986.

Aron, Cindy Sondik. *Ladies and Gentlemen of the Civil Service*. New York: Oxford University Press, 1987.

Asher, Janet and Jules Asher. "How to Accommodate Workers in Wheelchairs," *Job Safety and Health* (October 1976).

Bittker, Boris. *The Case of Black Reparations*. New York: Random House, 1973.

Bureau of National Affairs. *The Equal Employment Opportunity Act of 1972*. Washington, D.C., 1973.

Dresang, Dennis L. and Paul J. Stuiber. "Sexual Harassment: Challenges for the Future," in Carolyn Ban and Norma M. Riccucci, eds., *Public Personnel Management: Current Concerns, Future Challenges*. White Plains, N.Y.: Longman Press, 1991.

Eisinger, Peter K. *Black Employment in City Government, 1973-1980*. Washington, D.C.: Joint Center for Political Studies, 1983.

Elliot, Robert H. and T. Wilson, "AIDS in the Workplace," *Public Personnel Management*, 16 (Fall 1987).

Equal Employment Opportunity Commission. *Title 29—Labor, Chapter XIV—Part 1604—Guidelines on Discrimination Because of Sex Under Title VII of the Civil Rights Act of 1964, as Amended Adoption of Interim Interpretive Guidelines*. Washington, D.C., April 1980.

Goldberg, Alan. Sexual Harrassment and Title VII: The Foundation for the Elimination of Sexual Cooperation as an Employment Condition," *Michigan Law Review*, 76 (May 1978).

Greenhouse, Linda. "Court 5-4 Affirms a Right to Reopen Bias Settlements," *The New York Times* (June 13, 1989). p. A1.

_____. "The Year the Court Turned to the Right," *The New York Times* (July 7, 1989), p. A1.

Hall, Francine S. and Maryann H. Albrecht. *The Management of Affirmative Action*. Santa Monica, Calif.: Goodyear, 1979.

Hawkins, Jacquelyn J. "Considerations for Developing Model Sexual Harassment Policies and Complaint Procedures." *Equal Employment Opportunity Compliance Manual*. Prentice Hall, 1989.

Horn, Patrice D. and Jack C. Horn. *Sex in the Office: Power and Passion in the Workplace*. Reading, Mass.: Addison-Wesley, 1982.

Jackson, Diane P. "Affirmative Action for the Handicapped and Veterans: Interpretative and Operational Guidelines," *Labor Law Journal* (February 1978).

Johansen, Elaine. "Managing the Revolution: The Case for Comparable Worth," *Review of Public Personnel Administration* (Spring 1984).

Kelly, Rita Mae and Jane Bayes (eds.). *Comparable Worth, Pay Equity, and Public Policy*. Westport, Conn.: Greenwood Press, 1988.

Kranz, Harry. *The Participatory Bureaucracy: Women and Minorities in a More Representative Public Service*. Lexington, Mass.: Lexington Books, 1976.

Krislov, Samuel. *The Negro in Federal Employment*. Minneapolis: University of Minnesota Press, 1967.

_____ , and David H. Rosenbloom. *Representative Bureaucracy and the American Political System*. New York: Praeger, 1981.

Lewis, William G. "Toward Representative Bureaucracy: Blacks in City Policy Organizations, 1975–1985," *Public Administration Review*, 49 (May-June 1989).

Lovrich, Nicholas P., Brent S. Steel and David Hood "Equity Versus Productivity: Affirmative Action and Municipal Police Services," *Public Productivity Review*, 39 (Fall 1986).

Mackinnon, Catharine A. *Sexual Harassment of Working Women*. New Haven: Yale University Press, 1979.

Martin, Andrew Ayers. "Title VII Discrimination in Biochemical Testing for AIDS and Marijuana," *Duke Law Journal*, 129 (February 1988).

Neuberger, Thomas Stephen. "Sex as a Bona Fide Occupational Qualification under Title VII," *Labor Law Journal* (July 1978).

Neugarten, Dail Ann and Jay M. Shafritz. *Sexuality in Organizations: Romantic and Coercive Behaviors at Work*. Oak Park, Ill.: Moore, 1980.

Pati, Gopal C. "Countdown on Hiring the Handicapped," *Personnel Journal*, 57 (March 1978).

Quinn, Robert E. "Coping with Cupid: The Formation, Impact, and Management of Romantic Relationships in Organizations," *Administrative Science Quarterly*, 22 (March 1977).

_____ , and Patricia L. Lees. "Attraction and Harassment: Dynamics of Sexual Politics in the Workplace," *Organizational Dynamics* (Autumn 1984).

Rabin, Jack (ed.). "The Future of Affirmative Action and Equal Employment Opportunity: A Symposium," *Review of Public Personnel Administration*, 4 (Summer 1984).

Reichenberg, Neil E. *Employment Discrimination in the Workplace: The Impact of the 1988–89 Supreme Court Term*. Alexandria, VA: International Personnel Management Association, 1989.

Remick, Helen, (ed.). *Comparable Worth and Wage Discrimination: Technical Possibilities and Political Realities*. Philadelphia: Temple University Press, 1984.

Riccucci, Norma M. "Merit, Equity and Test Validity: A New Look at an Old Problem," *Administration and Society*, May 1991.

Rosenbloom, David H. *Federal Equal Employment Opportunity*. New York: Praeger, 1977.

Spann, Jeri. "Dealing Effectively with Sexual Harassment," *Public Personnel Management*, 19 (Spring 1990).

Thomas, Clarence. "Pay Equity and Comparable Worth," *Labor Law Journal* (January 1983).

U.S. Office of Personnel Management. *Civil Service 2000*. Washington, D.C.: Office of Personnel Management, 1988.

U.S. Merit Systems Protection Board. *Sexual Harassment in the Federal Government*. Washington, D.C.: Merit Systems Protection Board, 1988.

Vaughn, Robert G. *The Spoiled System*. New York: Charterhouse, 1975.

Wisniewski, Stanley C. "Achieving Equal Pay for Comparable Worth Through Arbitration," *Employee Relation Law Journal* (Autumn, 1982).

Cases

AFSCME v. *Washington State*, 770 F. 2d 1401 (9th Cir. 1985).

Chalk v. *U.S. District Court, Central District of California and Orange County Superintendent of Schools*, 840 F.2d. 701 (9th Cir.1988).

Connecticut v. *Teal*, 457 U.S. 440 (1982).

Fullilove v. *Klutznick*, 448 U.S. 448 (1980).

Griggs v. *Duke Power Company*, 401 U.S. 424 (1971).

Johnson v. *Transportation Agency of Santa Clara County*, 480 U.S 624 (1987).

Leckelt v. *Board of Commissioners*, 909 F.2d 820 (5th Cir. 1990).

Lorance v. *AT&T*, 490 U.S. 900 (1989).

Martin v. *Wilks*, 490 U.S. 755 (1989).

Memphis v. *Stotts*, 104 S.Ct. 582 (1984).

Meritor Savings Bank v. *Vinson*, 477 U.S. 57 (1986).

Metro Broadcasting v. *F.C.C.*, 111 L.Ed. 2d 445 (June 27, 1990).

Patterson v. *McLean Credit Union*, 491 U.S. 164 (1989).

Price Waterhouse v. *Hopkins*, 490 U.S. 228 (1989).

Raytheon Co. v. *Fair Employment & Housing*, 261 Cal. Rptr. 197 (Cal. App. 2 Dist. 1989).

Regents v. *Bakke*, 438 U.S. 265 (1978).

Richmond v. *Croson*, 488 U.S. 469 (1989).

School Board of Nassau County v. *Arline*, 480 U.S. 273 (1987).

Steelworkers v. *Weber*, 443 U.S. 193 (1979).

United States v. *Paradise*, 480 U.S. 150 (1987).

Wards Cove Packing Co. v. *Atonio*, 490 U.S. 642 (1989).

Washington v. *Davis* 426 U.S. 229 (1976).

8

Comparable Worth*

Prologue: "A Penny for Your Thoughts"

"FEMALE-MALE EARNINGS GAP NARROWS: GAINS IN 80'S FINAL-
LY PUT WOMEN'S PAY AHEAD OF BIBLICAL CALCULATION"; or
so ran a headline in a *Washington Post* column in August 1990. The column
referred to the Book of Leviticus in the Bible which contains the following
reference: "Your valuation of a male...shall be 50 shekels of silver....If the
person is female, your valuation shall be 30 shekels."

This ancient assessment of different values for males and females has
stood the test of time remarkably well in the American experience. Up until
1940, female median earnings stood at 58 percent of male earnings. By 1980,
it was just over 60 percent. Only in the 1980s has the 60 percent wage gap
narrowed. A recent study reported by the Bureau of Labor Statistics showed
the female-male earnings gap "narrowing significantly" to 65 percent by 1988.
(In the public sector, at the federal level, women earn about 62 percent of
men's salaries and in state and local governments, they earn about 71 percent of men's wages.) More important, the modest improvement was attributable to earnings per hour, not an increase in total hours worked. But
this news must be tempered by the bottom-line calculation—over the last
decade, the male-female earnings gap has shrunk about one cent a year. Total
male-female pay equity, at a rate of progress of one penny per year will require another thirty years or perhaps longer (see Tables 8.1 and 8.2)!

*The authors wish to acknowledge the contributions of Michael Graham of San Francisco State
University.

251

Table 8.1. Federal Government Employees' Annual Salaries for Select Occupations by Gender (1919)

Position	Female salary	Male salary
Cleaning	$300–399	$600–699
Personal	$300–399	$300–399[a]
Custodial	$720	$700–799
Subclerical (office messenger)	$500–599	$400–499
Telephone and telegraph	$900–999	$1,400–1,499
Typist	$1,000–1,099	$1,100–1,199
Stenography	$1,200–1,299	$1,200–1,299
Supervisor of clerks	$1,200–1,299	$2,000–2,099
Scientific lab aid	$900	$1,200
Statistician	$1,200	$2,300
Accountant	$1,400	$1,800
Publicity	$2,300	$2,700–3,099
Biological sciences	$1,800–2,400	$3,000–3,099

Note: Salary or range of salary upon entrance to federal government.
[a]Plus subsistence

Source: Norma M. Riccucci, *Women, Minorities, and Unions in the Public Sector* (Westport, Conn. Greenwood Press, 1990).

What Is Comparable Worth?

Comparable worth differs considerably from "equal pay for equal work." The latter, which is explicitly mandated by the Equal Pay Act of 1963 for public and private employers, is aimed more at pay *equality* between women and men peforming similar or equal work. A female maintenance worker, for example, must be paid the same wages as a male maintenance worker, assuming the content of the jobs is equal. Equal pay may be required even if the jobs are not identical, provided that they are similar in functions and required skills (*Schultz* v. *Wheaton Glass Co.*, 1970).

Comparable worth, on the other hand, is aimed at pay *equity*, seeking to pay women and men equal wages for different or dissimilar jobs of comparable value to an employer. It is much more abstract as well as political in nature than pay equality, given its emphasis on measuring the intrinsic worth of jobs. Pay equity measures have been more popular in the public sector than in the private sector, perhaps because public sector jobs are not specifically linked to the "free labor market" ideology that has been a major deterrent to the implementation of pay equity in the private sector. It is also

Table 8.2. Federal Government Employees' Average Annual Salaries for Select Occupations by Gender (1987)

Position	Female salary	Male salary
General administrative, clerical, and office services	$19,575	$32,982
Accounting and budget	$21,402	$32,397
Biological sciences	$22,946	$29,592
Transportation	$23,090	$36,444
Medical, hospital, dental, and public health	$23,584	$32,404
Business and industry	$23,891	$33,747
Personnel management and industrial relations	$24,191	$34,537
Legal and kindred	$24,555	$40,889
Education	$24,580	$30,571
Investigation	$24,974	$34,212
Engineering and architecture	$28,425	$37,879
Mathematics and statistics	$28,760	$42,191
Physical sciences	$29,008	$39,058
Social science, psychology, and welfare	$29,504	$37,627
Copyright, patent, and trademark	$34,189	$48,428
Total, full-time white collar	$22,071	$33,818

Source: Adapted from Lisa Young, "Average Annual Salaries of White Collar Employees," *Federal Times*, (June 19, 1989), p. 12.

important to note that comparable worth is not explicitly mandated by any federal legislation.

Comparable worth proponents argue, quite correctly, that jobs traditionally associated with women have been systematically undervalued in the marketplace. The net result is a disparity in pay for women when compared with that for jobs largely held by males. This compensatory bias against women, it is argued, can be demonstrated and subsequently eliminated by assessing the economic value of disparate occupations through the use of objective standards of evaluation. For example, although secretarial and janitorial jobs are dissimilar in function, it is argued that pay equity can be achieved by assessing such factors as working conditions and the amount of training, responsibility, and effort required for each job—in effect, using the classification function to determine the true value of the work being performed.

Critics of comparable worth vigorously counter those arguments. They state that the wage differential between men and women is more the result of career choice and market forces than sex discrimination. They point out that any pay gap that develops is produced over time. For example, male and female college graduates start out at comparable salaries once out of school. Moreover, opponents contend that employers, by definition, will pay higher wages for some occupations than others in order to remain competitive and to attract the best qualified personnel. Their responsibility is to be sensitive to the forces of supply and demand. Finally, critics of comparable worth maintain that job evaluation systems are inherently subjective. Therefore, any comparison of dissimilar jobs is at best arbitrary.

The issues inherent in comparable worth are complex and reflect a great deal about American social, political, and economic forces. By the late 1980s, there were approximately 60 million women working in the American labor force compared to 65 million males. This tremendous increase in female participation itself represents one of the most dramatic changes in labor economics over the last twenty-five years. Women are also remaining in the labor force. Traditionally, women would quit the labor force in high percentages for marriage and family responsibilities. Under this situation, it was argued that the marketplace would reward males for remaining. Of course, the counterargument runs that the lack of advancement opportunities and the wage gap provided negative incentives for women to stay.

But this is no longer the case (see, e.g., Chapter 16 on work and family). Why then, if female participation (in terms of entering and leaving) is comparable to male rates, should there be a wage gap? This question stands at the heart of comparable worth.

The Female-Male Pay Gap: Causes and Cures

A number of explanations for the wage gap between women and men as well as whites and people of color have been advanced in recent years. One explanation relates to occupational segregation. Women entering the labor force tend to go into certain occupations that society deems "appropriate" for them (See Tables 8.3 and 8.4); that is, they are socialized into thinking about jobs and professions as being either "female" or "male." The argument (which is specious at best!) then runs that as women begin to "crowd" certain job categories, the salary rate for such jobs becomes low because there is an abundant supply of workers. Moreover, the conclusion is then reached by opponents

Table 8.3.   Female Representation in
Select Occupations (1987)

Occupation	Percent
Engineer	12.6
Doctor	19.5
Lawyer	19.7
Professor	31.7
Teachers	73.6
Librarian	81.8
Nurse	95.1
Child care	96.1
Secretary	99.1

Source: Adapted from *U.S. Statistical Abstracts,*
1989.

comparable worth that women desire or choose these low-paying jobs, and
therefore the government should not interfere with women exercising their
choice. A great deal of the female-male wage differential is attributed to patterns of occupational segregation. In effect, women and men are in different
jobs to begin with and female-dominated jobs are the lesser-paying occupations.

Further compounding patterns of occupational segregation is the higher
percentage of females in part-time jobs compared to full-time (see Table 8.5).
The part-time/full time dimension has interesting side effects that show how
difficult it is to untangle the long-standing patterns of occupational segregation. Hospital nursing, for example, with its extensive shift work requirements,

Table 8.4.   Female Representation in Uniformed Services, in 1975, 1980,
and 1985

	1975	1980	1985
Police	3.7	6.1	9.2
Fire	.1	.4	.9
Corrections	10.2	13.4	15.4
Sanitation	.5	1.7	2.4
Percent in working-age population	40.0	42.5	44.2

Note: Figures represent women in uniformed, nonclerical jobs (e.g., police patrol officers, firefighters,
correctional officers, and sanitation workers), at local and, for police and corrections, state levels.

Source: Norma M. Riccucci, *Women, Minorities and Unions in the Public Sector* (Westport, Conn.: Greenwood Press, 1990).

Table 8.5. The Jobs and Earnings of Women in Full-Time Jobs (1987)

	Women		Men	
	All jobs	Full-time	All jobs	Full-time
Jobs	59,088,000	29,809,000	64,419,000	47,080,000
Median earnings	$10,618	$16,909	$19,878	$26,008

Source: Adapted from *U.S. Statistical Abstracts*, 1989.

has major staffing demands. One solution would be to raise salaries dramatically to attract more people (including men) into the profession. Other solutions involve creating weekend shift packages or other innovative flexible part-time arrangements that attract female nurses. Hospitals that employ flexible time plans solve their staffing problems in the short term, but their wage and compensation structures are preserved, thereby perpetuating patterns of occupational segregation. Nursing remains a 95% female-dominated job.

Others have argued that the female-male earnings gap is due to "market forces." They argue that organizations should pay only what the prevailing wage rate is for librarians, secretaries, nurses, and so forth. If there is an ample supply of qualified applicants for the organization's needs, the salary rate should reflect this. Conversely, if the organization needs truck drivers, computer programmers, or sanitation workers, they must pay the market rate which, in these as well as other cases, reflects, as the organization will argue, a scarcer supply of labor. One result is organizations paying truck drivers higher salaries than librarians or nurses, even though the educational qualifications and professional responsibilities of the latter may far exceed the former. Another by-product, which raises legal concerns, is the organization's creation of a major disparity in relative wages between female and male jobs, or what is called "gender-based wage discrimination."

But what happens when the organization has a comprehensive classification and compensation system? Modern "class and comp" systems, as discussed in Chapter 5, use job evaluation techniques to relate each job in the organization to each other. In public sector organizations, this affords a unique perspective. Nurses can be compared to truck drivers, librarians to sanitation workers, and so on. In short, since the job evaluation methods focus on the position requirements, they ignore the marketplace arguments of supply and demand. What does an organization do when it compares the position value of each of its occupations with the market-created realities of prevailing wages? When it follows the marketplace, it then builds in discrimination in wages that the marketplace has created.

Welcome then to comparable worth. It is a world of many dilemmas for public sector organizations. The public sector has always led the battle against discrimination, but its leadership in comparable worth has been a true test. Public sector organizations are particularly vulnerable to the conflicting political and economic currents within comparable worth. For example, if governments pay higher salaries for women, what will the budgetary effects be? Will higher salaries mean a reduction in the number of new jobs in various occupational groups? Will higher salaries for female jobs create incentives or disincentives to break down occupational segregation? Is the breakup of "male jobs" and "female jobs" a public policy objective arising out of comparable worth? And incidentally, shouldn't any compensation correction policy entail some kind of reduction in male wages presently or over time? The solutions to these many problems are tied tightly to the political processes and strategies of implementation. The potential impacts are simply enormous.

But the lessons of the marketplace are clear. A decade's progress has added one cent a year toward closing the gap. A penny for your thoughts!

Legal and Judicial Developments

During the 1980s, the concept of comparable worth became closely identified with "women's rights" and gender discrimination. At the start of the decade, it was called the "equal employment opportunity issue" of the decade. Now it is referred to as a "debate" or major "public policy issue." The prologue of this chapter attempted to set the stage by highlighting some of the issues, but comprehension of the issues must rest on a detailed examination of legislative, judicial, and executive actions that were taken in the 1980s.

The chief legal devices employed by advocates of comparable worth to achieve pay equity have included the Equal Pay Act of 1963 and Title VII of the Civil Rights Act of 1964, as amended. The two acts are closely linked. As noted earlier, the Equal Pay Act generally prohibits gender-based pay inequality for "equal work," but it also provides for four "affirmative defenses," or exceptions. In other words, lower pay for one sex can be justified when such payments are based on:

1. A nondiscriminatory system
2. A merit system
3. A system that measures earnings by quantity or quality of production
4. A wage differential based on any additional factor other than gender

The other statute, Title VII, specifically prohibits all employers from discriminating in their business practices on the basis of gender. In an attempt to avoid a conflict between the two acts, Congress added the so-called Bennett Amendment to Title VII in 1964. This amendment provides that an employer may "differentiate" the amount of employee's wages if such payments are based on the affirmative defenses of the Equal Pay Act.

Initial judicial interpretations of the Equal Pay Act tended to be extremely narrow. More specifically, because of its "equal work" provision, the act was held not to apply to instances of gender-based wage discrimination in which jobs were merely comparable rather than the same. Thus, the act was held to apply only to persons who performed "substantially equal" jobs, but not to dissimilar forms of employment requiring the same degree of skill, responsibility, and effort. Early interpretations of the Bennett Amendment also appeared to indicate that no lawsuits alleging discrimination in compensation could be brought under the provisions of Title VII unless the "equal work" standard of the Equal Pay Act was involved.

However, everything changed with the landmark U.S. Supreme Court decision in *County of Washington, Oregon* v. *Gunther* (1981). In *Gunther*, four female guards who worked in the women's section of a county jail were found to have been paid only 70 percent of what the county paid its male guards. The four female guards were discharged when the county eliminated the women's section of the jail. Following this action, the former guards filed suit to recover back pay, charging the county with intentional gender discrimination in violation of both Title VII and the Equal Pay Act.

In an opinion delivered by Justice Brennan, the Court held that even when jobs are not substantially equal under the Equal Pay Act, a claim of intentional wage discrimination under Title VII is not precluded. To achieve this result, the Court ruled that the Bennett Amendment incorporates only the four "affirmative defenses" of the Equal Pay Act, not its equal work provision. Justice Brennan pointed out that inclusion of the equal work standard would mean that a female victim of wage discrimination would be unable to gain relief under Title VII unless her employer also employed a man in an equal job at a higher rate of pay. This situation, he concluded, would have the unintended effect of sanctioning discrimination against women in a statute that Congress had specifically designed to overcome it.

But the Court wasn't done yet. It went on to emphasize that *Gunther* was not a comparable worth case. Both men and women performed the same job. Nor was the Court required to make its own "subjective assessment of the value of male and female guard jobs, or attempt by statistical technique or other method to quantify the effect of sex discrimination on the wage rates." Instead, the Court maintained that it reached its decision solely on the objective facts of the case as they related to the prohibition on discrimination contained in Title VII. Nevertheless, because it refused to incorporate the equal work provision, the Court expanded the scope of Title VII beyond the Equal Pay Act, and thus opened up the possibility that comparable worth claims could be brought in subsequent cases.

The *Gunther* case legitimized comparable worth. Yet, although the Supreme Court removed the major legislative obstacle to comparable worth suits, it provided no guidelines for the lower federal courts to follow. Consequently, in the two years following the *Gunther* decision, the lower courts proceeded cautiously and were hesitant to act. Indeed, one report characterized the lower court response as expressing a "great hostility to the comparable worth concept." As one lower court judge remarked a year later, "the Supreme Court's recognition of intentional discrimination may well signal the outer limit of legal theories cognizable under Title VII." Thus, the lower courts tended to impose liability against employers only in cases of intentional discrimination against women whose salaries were set lower than males performing equal or functionally related jobs. And, in the few cases where comparable worth claims were considered, they were rejected for failure to prove intent to discriminate.

However, a highly publicized (but short-lived, as will be seen shortly) exception to this pattern of judicial restraint was found in the case of *American Federation of State, County and Municipal Employees (AFSCME)* v. *State of Washington* (1983). In this case, Federal District Court Judge Jack Tanner awarded $400 million in back pay to approximately 15,000 predominantly female state civil service employees. The facts of the case are somewhat complex. In the early 1970s the governor of Washington ordered an investigation in response to complaints that the state's Department of Personnel and Higher Educational Personnel Board had perpetuated discriminatory salary practices against female employees. An outside consulting firm was hired to conduct a study of the problem. The study included sixty-two predominantly female job classifications and fifty-nine predominantly male job classifications, with the term *predominantly* defined as 70 percent dominance by one sex or the other. The study concluded that women tended to be paid 20 percent less than men for jobs of comparable worth, and that the disparity in pay increased with the importance of the job.

Subsequent studies updated these findings and produced a comparable worth formula to determine the value of each job. The formula was based on knowledge and skills, mental demands, accountability, and working conditions; points were then assigned to these criteria in order to compute the rates of compensation. However, because of budget constraints, the state refrained from enacting the comparable worth plan into law.

In response, AFSCME filed a class action suit alleging state discrimination on the basis of sex in violation of Title VII. To support this claim, AFSCME did the following:

1. Cited the state's own comparable worth studies
2. Produced statements of various state officials acknowledging the pay disparity problem, as well as their desire to correct it
3. Cited the state's failure to take prompt action to correct the noted discriminatory practices

4. Provided evidence that the state had historically segregated jobs on the basis of gender

In its defense, the state argued that the studies were only informational and therefore there was no intent to discriminate. In addition, the state defended its market-based compensation system by maintaining that it was cost effective, provided a good method to recruit and retain employees, based salaries on a fair and uniform system, and minimized disruption of the work force.

Judge Tanner found the state of Washington liable for the pay disparities, noting that no compelling reason was provided by the state to outweigh the nation's interest in eliminating wage discrimination against "employees in predominately female job classifications." Judge Tanner also found an intent to discriminate on a number of grounds. These included:

1. The "deliberate" perpetuation of the 20 percent pay disparity between female and male job classifications with the same number of job classification points
2. Statements made by past and present state officials that the state's method of market-based compensation was discriminatory
3. The state's failure to pay those affected by discriminatory practices their evaluated worth as established by the state's own studies

On the basis of these findings, Judge Tanner ordered the back pay award noted above and issued an order for injunctive relief. The injunctive order required the state to cease all practices that maintained or perpetuated discrimination in the state's system of compensation and to base wages on the comparable worth plan (belatedly) adopted by the state after the filing of the lawsuit.

The *AFSCME* decision was the first to hold an employer liable for violations of Title VII due to wage disparities in functionally unrelated jobs. However, in September 1985, a unanimous three-judge panel of the U.S. Court of Appeals for the Ninth Circuit reversed Judge Tanner's decision. In an opinion written by Judge Anthony Kennedy (now on the U.S. Supreme Court), the panel held that neither the disparate impact theory nor the disparate treatment theory had been properly applied by the trial court to establish liability under the provisions of Title VII. The court agreed that proof of intent to discriminate is not necessary under disparate impact theory. However, it did maintain that "disparate impact analysis is confined to cases that challenge a specific, clearly delineated employment practice at a single point in the job selection process." The court further noted that the complexities of a compensation system are incompatible with this approach. For example, the state of Washington based its compensation system on a variety of factors that included budget proposals, market surveys, administrative recommendations, and legislative enactments, all of which are difficult to isolate and assess. Thus, the court concluded that the state's decision to base its system of compensation on these factors and others, did not establish liability under disparate impact theory.

In establishing a charge of intent to discriminate, AFSCME argued that the state's reliance on and perpetuation of market rates for setting salaries inferred a purpose to discriminate. To support this argument, AFSCME cited statistical evidence contained in the state's comparable worth studies, and derived from it a historical pattern of lower wages to predominantly female employees. While the district court judge was willing to accept this evidence, the appellate court was not, stating that the evidence was insufficient to establish intention to discriminate. The higher court held that it had not been shown that the state was motivated by impermissible gender-based considerations in setting salaries because the state did not create the market disparity, and "neither law nor logic deems the free market system a suspect enterprise." The court also found nothing in either the language or legislative history of Title VII to indicate that Congress had intended "to abrogate fundamental economic principles such as the laws of supply and demand or to prevent employers from competing in the labor market."

Although the appellate court did concede that under certain circumstances intent to discriminate may be derived from statistical evidence, it cautioned that such evidence, standing alone, is insufficient under disparate treatment analysis. Rather, the weight accorded statistical evidence is determined by specific and independent testimony, or other corroborative evidence of discrimination. Since none of the plaintiffs in the case had testified with regard to specific instances of discrimination, the statistical evidence failed to establish intent. Finally, the appeals court rejected AFSCME's contention that because it commissioned the studies, the state of Washington was obligated to implement a system of compensation based on comparable worth. Such a holding, according to the court, would penalize rather than commend an employer for undertaking such an effort, not to mention discourage other employers from undertaking such studies.

Following the Ninth Circuit decision in *AFSCME*, a petition for rehearing was filed, but later withdrawn because of a settlement between AFSCME and the state of Washington. The settlement provided $41.5 million for pay increases to all classified state employees due comparable worth "raises," with the objective of achieving full pay equity by 1992. A projected expenditure of over $475 million has been set to "rectify the wage gap." The settlement also clarified concerns about the wage adjustments; specifically, increases would be given to raise salaries that were below the comparable worth line but salary decreases for those occupations above the line were prohibited.

The settlement, however, ended the case, thereby precluding an appeal to the U.S. Supreme Court. In effect, the Ninth Circuit's ruling remains intact, and the question of the ability of state or federal courts to require comparable worth consistent with or in enforcement of Title VII of the Civil Rights Act of 1964 is unresolved.

In the *Gunther* case, the Supreme Court opened up the possibility for comparable worth suits to be brought under Title VII. However, because of the narrowness of the ruling, it was left to the lower courts to develop standards of proof. As the previous discussion shows, whatever legal impetus was created with *Gunther* has been severely impaired by recent judicial developments. The most recent defeat, at this writing, came in 1989 with dismissal by a federal district judge of the largest pay equity lawsuit filed in the nation (a 1984 California State Employee's Association suit on behalf of 60,000 female workers). In throwing out the union's claim, the federal judge ruled that "the state's pay scale reflected market rates not deliberate sex discrimination." In discussing the ruling, a *New York Times* column in October 1989 opened up with an accurate description of the current and future outlook of comparable worth. It stated: "The campaign for pay equity for women, considered innovative legal theory 10 years ago, is sputtering in the court but flourishing at the bargaining table." Indeed, it flourishes in a number of arenas outside the courts.

Executive and Legislative Developments

As the courts have wrestled with comparable worth issues, the impetus for change has shifted gears into the "political arena." More recently, it is the actions of federal, state, and local administrative agencies bargaining with unions and legislatures that have become pivotal in bringing about comparable worth solutions. Collective bargaining agreements currently represent the most pivotal dimension to understanding the resolution of pay equity problems.

Addressing and resolving pay equity problems at the bargaining table may seem a somewhat undesirable political solution, but this has been necessitated by the lack of legislative action. Indeed, the process might be simpler and cleaner if there were significant congressional action at the national level or even state statutes mandating comparable worth. Such is not the case. Several states have appropriated funds to "implement" comparable worth, based on pay equity studies or other methods, but comprehensive legislation has not been the preferred model of action.

Only one state, Minnesota, has passed a statewide pay equity statute, despite the fact that over half of the states introduced such bills in the 1980s. However, a number of states have taken significant steps to implement comparable worth (see Table 8.6). At last count (according to the National Committee on Pay Equity, a Washington D.C.-based nonprofit organization

Table 8.6.   State Comparable Worth Activity (1989)

	No action	Research/data collection	Pay equity study	Pay equity adjustment/ implementation
Alabama		X		
Alaska	X			
Arizona		X		
Arkansas	X			
California				X
Colorado		X		
Connecticut				X
Delaware	X			
Florida				X
Georgia	X			
Hawaii				X
Idaho	X			
Illinois				X
Indiana		X		
Iowa				X
Kansas		X		
Kentucky		X		
Louisiana		X		
Maine				X
Maryland			X	
Massachusetts				X
Michigan				X
Minnesota				X
Missouri		X		
Mississippi		X		
Montana			X	
Nebraska		X		
Nevada		X		
New Hampshire		X		
New Jersey				X
New Mexico				X
New York				X
North Carolina		X		
North Dakota			X	
Ohio			X	
Oklahoma			X	
Oregon				X
Pennsylvania				X
Rhode Island				X

(continued)

Table 8.6. *Continued*

	No action	Research/data collection	Pay equity study	Pay equity adjustment/ implementation
South Carolina		X		
South Dakota				X
Tennessee		X		
Texas		X		
Utah		X		
Vermont				X
Virginia		X		
Washington				X
West Virginia			X	
Wisconsin				X
Wyoming			X	

Source: Adapted from *Pay Equity Activity in the Public Sector* (Washington, D.C.: National Committee on Pay Equity, 1989), pp. 10–11. These actions have been taken by the state legislature, the governor, or a state agency.

that monitors developments in this area), by the end of the 1980s, a dozen states and over 1,500 local governments (to include cities, towns, counties, school districts, and so on) had changed their salary and job classification practices to reflect some type of comparable worth solution. Compared to a universe of fifty states and 83,000 governments of all types, this may seem minute, but the precedent set by their example and the ensuing change promises greater impact in the 1990s.

Federal Developments

The federal experience provides a superb example of the difficulty of legislating comparable worth. In 1983, Senator Cranston of California introduced the first comprehensive comparable worth legislation—the Pay Equity Act of 1983. This act would have encouraged public and private employers to use job evaluation systems that were not sex-based, required extensive reporting from the Equal Employment Opportunity Commission (EEOC), and reinterpreted Civil Service Act language stating that equal pay should be provided to federal employees doing work of "equal value." Among other premises, the bill clearly announced legislative intent to remedy the fact that the average earnings of female workers are below those of similar male workers and to prohibit "discriminatory wage differentials."

The following year, Representative Mary Oakar of Ohio introduced "House Resolution 5092," with language very similar to the Senate bill

Unions in Support of Comparable Worth?

Unions have a considerable stake in the comparable worth issue because comparable worth seeks to restructure one of the most important considerations for unions—wage systems. The news media suggest that unions are extremely supportive of comparable worth and have taken measures to attain equal pay for comparable worth.

But, some unions—both public and private—have either intentionally discriminated against women or have failed to rectify past or historical discriminations against them. Unions have frustrated women's efforts to gain access to certain jobs and have made little progress in advancing them to leadership positions within unions themselves. What then, encourages unions to engage in the bitter and costly battle to end discrimination against women in compensation and classification systems?

There are several possible answers. One factor may be that women will press their unions for protection from pay discrimination. With more women in more places in the work force, they are a force to be reckoned with by any union that expects to survive. On the more positive side of the ledger, in an era of overall dwindling union membership, unions will campaign for pay equity in hopes of attracting women. Then, some unions will support comparable worth and others will oppose it. Perhaps a good illustration of where unions stand on the issue can be seen in a review of the case law, since lawsuits represent an accurate legal account of unions' position on pay equity. Consider the following:

Case	Employment Sector		Union Type		Union Position	
	Public	Private	Craft	Industrial	For	Against
St. Louis Newspaper Guild v. Pulitzer Pub. Co. 618 F.Supp. 1468 (1985)		X		X	X	
AFSCME v. County of Nassau 609 F.Supp. 695 (1985)	X			X	X	
AFSCME v. City of New York 599 F.Supp. 916 (1984)	X			X	X	
Hawaii Government Employees Association, AFSCME v. State of Hawaii 38 FEP Cases 1126 (1985)	X			X	X	

(continued)

Case	Employment Sector		Union Type		Union Position	
	Public	Private	Craft	Industrial	For	Against
AFSCME v. State of Washington 770 F.2d. 1401 (9th Cir. 1985)	X			X	X	
Connecticut State Employees Association v. State of Connecticut 31 FEP Cases 191 (1983)	X			X	X	
EEOC v. Affiliated Foods and Teamsters Union 34 FEP Cases 943 (1984)		X		X		X
Briggs v. City of Madison 536 F. Supp. 435 (1982)	X			X		X
Power v. Barry County, Mich. Fraternal Order of Police 539 F. Supp. 721 (1982)	X		X			X
Taylor v. Charley Brothers 25 FEP Cases 602 (1981)		X		X		X
Penn, Human Relations Comm. v. Hempfield Township and Teamsters 16 FEP Cases 1348 (1976)	X			X		X
American Nurses Assoc. v. State of Illinois 783 F.2d 716 (7th Cir. 1986)	X			X	X	

Certainly, the above figures do not provide the total picture of union involvement in comparable worth. But, the important point to be made is that not all unions and affiliated locals, whether operating in the public or private sector, support comparable worth.

Source: Adapted from Norma M. Riccucci, Women, Minorities, and Unions in the Public Sector (Westport, Conn.: Greenwood Press, 1990).

introduced by Cranston. The House bill focused both on public and private employers, attempted to eliminate discriminatory job classifications, and required extensive involvement on the part of the EEOC to insure compliance. Representative Oakar introduced subsequent bills with much narrower scope; for example, the Federal Employees Pay Equity Act, which passed the House by a vote of 415 to 6 in June of 1984, sought to achieve pay equity within the federal government. Another bill, which passed only by a 259 to 162 vote in October of 1985, focused on the need for a special study of discriminatory wage practices and the impacts on women, African Americans, Latinos, and other protected-class persons.

While positive support in the Democratic-controlled House of Representatives was obtained, the then Republican-controlled Senate showed little interest and support for pay equity legislation, no matter how proposed. Even after the Democrats regained control of the Senate, pay equity legislation was not a priority. In the last half of the 1980s, Congress was sideswiped by federal budget and deficit issues, not to mention concern with an ever-widening pay gap between federal and private sector wages, last reported at 28 percent. The pay equity crisis was overtaken by the "quiet crisis," the term used to describe the increasing dissatisfaction with all pay levels in the public sector (see Chapter 5 for a further discussion). This is not surprising, since any issue concerning white women and people of color usually becomes a low priority when issues involving the "general" work force are at stake.

The executive branch, under Republican leadership in the 1980s, was at first genuinely anti-comparable worth, and then uninterested in pursuing it. The most prominent and progressive developments from the executive branch came during the Carter administration, during which the EEOC, then headed by Eleanor Holmes Norton, had been active (albeit cautiously) in developing and promoting comparable worth law. The commission filed a "brief" in support of the plaintiff in the *Gunther* Case, held hearings, and commissioned the widely used National Academy of Sciences study, *Women, Work, and Wages: Equal Pay for Jobs of Equal Value*.

But, the executive branch's position on comparable worth changed dramatically under the Reagan administration. In June of 1984, the EEOC, headed by Clarence Thomas, held what it called "consultations" on the issue of comparable worth. Hearings were designed to accept testimony from chosen witnesses to assist the commission in assessing the merits of comparable worth as a remedy for gender discrimination in employment. When the final report came out in September, as expected, the position was one of support for equal pay for equal *work*; but the concept of comparable worth was rejected as inappropriate for solving problems of wage discrimination. The EEOC stated flatly that methods existed to resolve such problems and that they are best handled through these channels. Finally, in June of 1985, the EEOC ended months of speculation about what it would do with the 266 backlogged comparable worth claims. In a landmark action—it rejected comparable worth claims as proof of discrimination, ruling that comparable worth was not recognized under Title VII.

The EEOC's position during this time paralleled that of the U.S. Commission on Civil Rights, the independent body established in 1957 to, among other things, "study and collect information concerning legal developments constituting discrimination or a denial of equal protection of the laws because of race, color, religion, sex, age, handicap, or national origin." A majority of members on this commission voted to reject the doctrine of comparable worth. (The two dissenting votes came from Commissioners Mary Frances Berry and Blandina Cardenas Ramirez, who supported the doctrine.) The commission's position, as stated in a 232-page study, was that "comparable worth, as a theory of discrimination, is profoundly and irretrievably flawed." Indeed, Clarence Pendleton, then chair of the commission, denounced the concept as the "looniest idea since Looney Tunes came on the screen."

Of course, there are other federal bodies or agencies that are able to influence comparable worth. The U.S. General Accounting Office (GAO), while not holding an official position, has been extremely active in completing several major substantive studies on pay equity, including an extensive options study that details legal and methodological aspects of comparable worth. GAO has even surveyed the states regarding their pay equity actions, to include job evaluation methodologies and establishment of a comparable worth policy. While GAO has acknowledged the existence of a wage gap between females and males, it has consistently indicated that the causes are undetermined and cannot be positively linked to discrimination. What GAO has contributed is a steady stream of information regarding the issues and methodologies for conducting a federal pay equity survey within the federal work force.

GAO's counter, on the other side, has been the Office of Personnel Management (OPM). In September 1987, OPM released its own major report on comparable worth, entitled "Comparable Worth for Federal Jobs: A Wrong Turn Off the Road Toward Pay Equity and Women's Career Advancement." The title itself left little doubt where OPM stood on the pay equity issue. OPM's conclusions were that "no concrete evidence to substantiate the comparable worth argument" could be found and that federal female employees were making major strides in taking professional positions, breaking down occupational barriers, and closing the wage gap. It was obvious at this point that a federal administrative solution to the pay equity problem was virtually impossible. The resulting gridlock in the federal congressional-executive arena has shifted attention to strategies and approaches taken by state and local governments.

State Governmental Developments

The absence of a strong federal mandate has left state governments to their own devices. During the 1980s, the GAO estimated that the great majority of states had in place some form of statute or study upon which to premise some form of comparable worth action. But this has led to some rather contradictory developments. The Council of State Governments in its annual surveys of the state governments noted a number of states that appropriated funding for implementing comparable worth in accordance with, for example, collective bargaining arrangements.

The case of Washington State has already been detailed under legal events, but it is worth adding that as early as 1983, Washington had appropriated $1.5 million pay equity raises and then set aside over $40 million for pay raises after 1987. The settlement reached by AFSCME and the state—which ended the litigation—moved the full implementation of comparable worth up by one year earlier than what the state legislature had set for its objective. Iowa and Wisconsin also appropriated funding for comparable worth raises via collective bargaining arrangement. Ohio, Oregon, Massachusetts, Connecticut, New Jersey, and New York also made appropriations to achieve pay equity based on recommendations from pay equity or job evaluation studies. And there have been other states which totally reversed directions on pay equity; for example, the New Mexico legislature reneged on its second year appropriation for pay equity raises and North Carolina closed down its pay equity study in midstream.

What is of interest in the local experience is the sense of a new development away from legislated initiatives toward local political implementation. Most critical are neither new statutes nor studies, but rather how localities (and states) proceed with their own variations of strategies for implementing comparable worth at the local level of government. Many of these approaches are ad hoc, with one-time adjustments and very unpredictable results. Once implemented, the willingness to restudy and readjust may lessen dramatically. Indeed, the road to implementation may be more disruptive than expected, as the New Mexico experience illustrates.

California provides some excellent case experiences with pay equity. California has both a comparable worth statute and a pay equity study. It also has, at this writing, a strongly divided state government (a Republican governor opposed to comparable worth; a Democratically controlled state legislature in favor of it; a strong group of employee unions also in favor of comparable worth; a state population generally in favor of tight fiscal constraints on state and local budgets, and various local governments opposed to judicial and legislated mandates on comparable worth). The state experience has been for the governor to veto any legislated comparable worth settlements and push all such adjustments to the bargaining table, where settlements are then rejected because of fiscal pressures.

California's experience is exceptionally diverse. While the state clearly has the "tools" on hand to mandate comparable worth, it has shown considerable reluctance in implementing comparable worth, for whatever reasons. The lesson to be learned in California will revolve around the impacts of collective bargaining, budgets, and voter referendums. It may be less a case of "why or why not" as opposed to "how much." The experience to date of some of California's largest cities is as follows:

- In Los Angeles, the union and the city successfully bargained over pay equity raises that would not require a pay equity study. Their approach was a pure "negotiated" comparable worth agreement impacting some 4,000 city employees.
- In San Jose, extensive union negotiations provided a piecemeal settlement in what is usually regarded as the first comparable worth city following a nine-day strike in 1981. Indeed, San Jose's personnel director described the experiences of this first major city to implement comparable worth as akin to "opening Pandora's box." The city was beset with major financial problems and although it made its initial commitments for 7 to 8 percent wage adjustments for pay equity, concerns about its abilities to pay for the future have played a major role in leaving San Jose's situation unsettled.
- In San Francisco, negotiated union settlements for pay equity adjustments were put on the ballot in 1985 and subsequently defeated by voters. In 1986, a modified proposal was accepted by the voters that provided for annual pay equity surveys and board of supervisors' reviews. Then the city was beset by major financial problems that ultimately put the unions in the position of trading pay equity wage increases for regular salary increases. Even for a city like San Francisco, famous for its turbulent political environment, the path of comparable worth in the 1980s was legendary.

What each of these major California city's experiences indicates is that comparable worth solutions via the bargaining process include a vastly different set of variables than simply legal principles and administrative processes. And, it seems clear that the "action" in most states and localities will be at collective bargaining tables or on the desks of personnel and compensation managers. Two variables will be critical in determining "how much" comparable worth will be "negotiated": political strength of the interested parties and budgetary constraints. In this negotiating process, the true essence of the new "politicization" of comparable worth will be determined.

There is, of course, one major exception—Minnesota, where comparable worth was mandated by the state legislature. Beginning with a 1979 Hay Associates study of Minnesota's 30,000 plus state employees, the state

Comparable Worth in Minnesota

The implementation of comparable worth for local and state employees has proceeded farther in Minnesota than in any other state in the nation. In 1982, Minnesota passed the State Employees Pay Equity Act, which established equitable compensation relationships as "*the* primary" wage-setting consideration for employees of the state of Minnesota. The total cost of the complete, four-year (1983–87) implementation in new salary money added to permanent salary costs was $22 million, or 3.7% of the 1983 baseline salary. This sum provided the necessary wage increases for underpaid female-dominated classes, making Minnesota the first state to pass and fully implement a comparable worth policy for state employees. The Local Government Pay Equity Act, passed in 1984, broke new ground by requiring all local jurisdictions to make comparable worth "*a* primary" consideration in compensation and prescribed a process by which jurisdictions could determine if pay inequities exist.... By August 1987, 90% of local governments had...embarked on an implementation plan.

Sara M. Evans and Barbara J. Nelson, *Wage Justice: Comparable Worth and the Paradox of Technocratic Reform* (Chicago: University of Chicago Press, 1989), p. 3.

responded with a $21.7 million settlement (spread over two years) to correct identified wage discrimination deficiencies. Legislation was then passed that mandated comparable worth in all state government agencies. The law provided for an ongoing review by requiring the Commissioner of Employee Relations to submit detailed reports on existing wage inequities to the legislature annually. The two-year period to enact comparable worth statewide then passed to a second phase involving all local governments. Local units of government were required to develop job evaluation systems and implement comparable worth by October 1985. Significantly, the Minnesota laws recognize that pay equity adjustments are subject to collective bargaining and as such are part of the collective bargaining process.

Minnesota became the first case of comprehensive-legislated comparable worth among state governments. The costs were not insignificant, with state implementation reaching 3.7 percent of total annual payroll (or 1 percent per year), and local government implementation reaching 2.6 percent of the total annual payroll. The adjustments for the over 8,000 employees affected averaged over $1,600 for the first year. Rothchild and Watkins have provided one of the first evaluations of Minnesota's state experience with a more guarded review of the local government phase. In their words, there were no wage freezes, layoffs, strikes, or lawsuits. Women working for the state increased by 6 percent over the implementation period and the numbers of women working in nontraditional jobs went up by 19 percent. Morale remained high, due in part to the 80 percent prevailing support of comparable worth concept among the work force. While local government results have lagged somewhat, they still conclude that overall results are positive.

Comparable Worth in the 1990s: New Directions

Where comparable worth will go in the 1990s is to a great extent a product of the comparable worth experience in the United States for the 1980s. What began as a major legal development in *Gunther* at the start of the decade has ended up at the negotiating table in various cities and state governments across the nation. Although private sector firms and compensation experts have expressed reservations and perhaps some concern about comparable worth, for the most part private sector action has been quite limited. It is in the public sector that comparable worth has become politicized, moving mostly in a fragmented ad hoc process.

Yet, despite the efforts of some public sector employers to achieve pay equity, job segregation—which, as noted earlier, greatly contributes to pay disparities—continues to exist. Sociological studies continue to find up to 60 percent of occupational categories being segregated into female or male jobs. Barbara Bergmann notes that "substantial equality" is decades away and that females still face serious discrimination in the job market, primarily via job segregation wherein the mean wage is adversely affected by any dominant ratio of females in job categories. This form of discrimination may well filter up through the organization, as Ellen Auster and Robert Drazin's 1988 study of wage differences between women and men in a large private sector financial services organization demonstrates. There were increasingly significant wage differences at the higher levels of the organization despite the fact that females scored slightly higher on performance ratings than their male counterparts.

As with many other major policy issues in the United States, the proof is in the implementation. In the case of comparable worth in the 1980s, that proof has not been realized. Time will tell in the 1990s.

Bibliography

Aron, Cindy Sondik. *Ladies and Gentlemen of the Civil Service*. New York: Oxford University Press, 1987.

Auster, Ellen and Robert Drazin. "Sex Inequality at Higher Levels in the Hierarchy." *Sociological Inquiry*, Spring 1988.

Bergmann, Barbara R. *The Economic Emergence of Women*. New York: Basic Books, 1986.

The Bureaucrat. In "Point-Counterpoint," Patricia Shroeder, "OPM Missed the Point," p. 8 and Constance Horner "Argument Undermined" p. 9. (Winter 1987–1988).

The Bureau of National Affairs (BNA). *Pay Equity and Comparable Worth: A BNA Report* (1985).

Chi, Keon S. "Comparable Worth in State Governments," in *Book of the States*. The Council of State Governments 1986, pp. 291–294.

Cook, Alice H. "Pay Equity: Theory and Implementation" in Carolyn Ban and Norma M. Riccucci (eds.), *Public Personnel Management: Current Concerns, Future Challenges*. White Plains, N.Y.: Longman Press, 1991.

Evans, Sara M. and Barbara J. Nelson. *Wage Justice: Comparable Worth and the Paradox of Technocratic Reform*: Chicago: University of Chicago Press, 1989.

Horrigan, Michael W. and James P. Markey. "Recent Gains in Women's Earnings: Better Pay or Longer Hours," *Monthly Labor Review* (July 1990).

Johansen, Elaine. *Comparable Worth: The Myth and the Movement*. Boulder, Colo.: Westview Press, 1984.

Kelly, Rita Mae and Jane Bayes (eds.). *Comparable Worth, Pay Equity, and Public Policy*. Westport, Conn.: Greenwood Press, 1988.

Edward Lazear, (ed.). *The Journal of Economic Perspectives*, 1989.

Luton, Larry S. and Suzanne Thompson. "Progress in Comparable Worth: Moving Toward Non-Judicial Determination," *Review of Public Personnel Management* (Spring 1989).

Nelson, Barbara J. "Comparable Worth: A Brief Review of History, Practice and Theory," *Minnesota Law Review* (May 1985).

Remick, Helen (ed.) *Comparable Worth and Wage Discrimination* Philadelphia: Temple University Press, 1984.

Riccucci, Norma M. *Women, Minorities and Unions in the Public Sector*. Westport, Conn: Greenwood Press, 1990.

——————. "Union Liability for Wage Disparities Between Women and Men," *University of Detroit Law Review*, vol. 65 (Spring 1988).

Scheibal, William, "AFSCME v. Washington: The Continued Viability of Title VII in Comparable Worth Actions," *Public Personnel Management*, vol. 17, no. 3, (Fall 1988), pp. 315–322.

Sorenson, Elaine. "The Wage Effects of Occupational Sex Composition: A Review and New Findings," in Anne Hill and Mark R. Killingsworth (eds), *Comparable Worth: Analyses and Evidence*. Ithaca, N.Y.: Cornell University Press, 1989.

Treiman, D. J. and H. J. Hartman (eds.). *Women, Work, and Wages: Equal Pay for Equal Value*. Washington, D.C.: National Academy Press, 1981.

U. S. Commission of Civil Rights. *Comparable Worth: Issue for the 80's, A Consultation of the U.S. Commission on Civil Rights*, vol. 1, *Papers*; vol. 2, *Proceedings*, (June 6–7, 1984).

U. S. General Accounting Office. *Description of Selected Systems for Classifying Federal Civilian Positions and Personnel*, GAO/GGD-84-90 (July 13, 1985).

U. S. General Accounting Office. *Distribution of Male and Female Employees in Four Federal Classification Systems*, GAO/GGD-85-20 (November 27, 1985).

U. S. General Accounting Office. *Options for Conducting a Pay Equity Study of Federal Pay and Classification Systems*, GAO/GGD-85037 (March 1, 1985).

U. S. General Accounting Office. *Pay Equity: Status of State Activities*, GAO/GGD-86-141BR (September 1986).

U. S. Office of Personnel Management. *Comparable Worth for Federal Jobs: A Wrong Turn Off the Road Toward Pay Equity and Women's Career Advancement* (September 1987).

Cases

Angelo v. *Bacharach Instrument Co.*, 555 F2d 1164 (3d Cir. 1977).

Bond v. *Madison County Mutual Insurance Co.*, 653 F.2d 1173 (7th Cir. 1981), *cert. denied*, 454 U.S. 1146 (1982).

Brennan v. *Prince William Hospital Corp.*, 503 F2d 282 (4th Cir. 1974), *cert. denied*, 420 U.S. 972 (1975).

Briggs v. *City of Madison*, 536 F.Supp. 435 (W.D. Wisc. 1982).

California State Employees Association v. *State of California*, 724 F. Supp. 717 (N.D. Cal. 1989).

Connecticut State Employees Assoc. v. *State of Connecticut*, 31 Fair Empl. Prac. Cas. (BNA) 191 (D. Conn. 1983).

Christensen v. *Iowa*, 563 F2d 353 (8th Cir. 1977).

County of Washington v. *Gunther* 452 U.S. 161 (1981).

Davis v. *California*, 613 F2d 957 (D.C. Cir. 1979) at 962.

Francoeur v. *Corroon & Black Corp.*, 552 F. Supp. 403 (W. D. Wisc. 1982).

Lemons v. *Denver*, 620 F2d 228 (10th Cir. 1980).

Power v. *Barry County*, 539 F. Supp. 721 (W.D. Mich. 1982).

Spaulding v. *University of Washington*, 704 F2d 686 (9th Cir. 1984) at 703.

State of Washington v. *AFSCME*, 770 F2d 1401 (1985).

Texas Department of Community Affairs v. *Burdine*, 450 U.S. 48 (1981).

Wilkins v. *University of Houston*, 654 F2d 388 (5th Cir. 1981) at 395.

Wirtz v. *Wheaton Glass Co.*, 421 F.2d 259 (3rd Cir.) *cert. denied*, 398 U.S. 905 (1970).

9

Constitutional Issues of
Public Personnel Management

Prologue: *Elrod* v. *Burns* (1976)

The use of public jobs for political patronage in America is a practice almost as old as the American political experience itself. In colonial days, the British used patronage widely and often abusively; the creation of sinecures and the sale of public office were a central aspect of colonial public administration. Indeed, so incensed were the Americans with these practices that in the Declaration of Independence they included the complaint that King George III had "erected a multitude of new offices, and sent hither swarms of officers to harass our people, and eat out their substance." But by the time the spoils system rolled into full swing in the 1840s, patronage could be considered as American as apple pie. As President Jackson pointed out, rotation in office is a democratic principle, and one that makes the public service accountable to the electorate. Nor can it be doubted that among the lasting benefits of patronage has been the creation of a strong two-party political system. The use of political patronage for democratic ends was a major aspect of American political development. It is not surprising, therefore, that despite the efforts of civil service reformers to eradicate patronage practices at all levels of government, some jurisdictions managed to hold on to hallowed traditions. But what the reformers missed, the Supreme Court took care of in *Elrod* v. *Burns* —a case that well illustrates the extent of judicial involvement in contemporary public personnel administration.

The facts of the case were rather straightforward and reminiscent of events that have taken place throughout the history of the nation. In December 1970, the sheriff of Cook County (Chicago), Illinois, a Republican, was replaced by Richard Elrod, a Democrat. Elrod, along with "boss" Richard J. Daley, the Democratic organization of Cook County, and the Democratic Central Committee of Cook County, adhered to the time-honored practice—employed by his Republican predecessor as well—of replacing all noncivil service employees of his office who were unable to win the approval of the Democratic Party with new appointees. John Burns and other "deposed" Republican employees brought suit on the grounds that their First and Fourteenth Amendment rights had been abridged by their dismissals. This complaint was somewhat remarkable because they had received their jobs in the same general way as the Democrats who replaced them.

The Supreme Court held the dismissals to to be unconstitutional, but its members could not fully agree on precisely what the problem with them was. Justice Brennan announced the judgment of the court in an opinion joined by Justices White and Marshall. While recognizing that "patronage practice is not new to American politics," Brennan also maintained that "the cost of the practice of patronage is the restraint it places on freedoms of belief and association." In order to justify these costs, in his view, the government had to demonstrate some compelling logic for the use of patronage: "In short, if conditioning the retention of public employment on the employee's support of the in-party is to survive constitutional challenge, it must further some vital government end by a means that is least restrictive of freedom of belief and association in achieving that end, and the benefit gained must outweigh the loss of constitutionally protected rights."

What possible justifications might exist? First, patronage might help to ensure effective government and the efficiency of public employees. Those workers holding the same political views as the head of a governmental agency might work harder toward implementing official policy. To this argument, Brennan's terse reply was, "We are not persuaded." Clearly, the history of patronage indicates that it breeds inefficiency, corruption, and ineffective administration.

Second, patronage might yield greater political accountability. Brennan was quick to point out, however, that this objective could be accomplished by limiting patronage to policy-making positions, which was not the situation back in Cook County.

Third, patronage might be necessary for the maintenance of strong political parties and thus for the democratic process as well. Although this line of thought has substantial force—political parties, weakened by civil service reform and voter participation, began dropping at the same time that patronage was being limited—Brennan did not believe that the elimination of the practice being challenged specifically would "bring about the demise of party politics."

In Brennan's view, therefore, although the ends associated with arguments in favor of patronage were laudable, the means itself were unsatisfactory

THE BILL OF RIGHTS

Amendment I

Congress shall make no law respecting an establishment of religion, or prohibiting the free exercise thereof; or abridging the freedom of speech, or of the press, or the right of the people peaceably to assemble, and to petition the Government for a redress of grievances.

Amendment II

A well regulated Militia, being necessary to the security of a free State, the right of the people to keep and bear Arms, shall not be infringed.

Amendment III

No Soldier shall, in time of peace be quartered in any house, without the consent of the Owner, nor in time of war, but in a manner to be prescribed by law.

Amendment IV

The right of the people to be secure in their persons, houses, papers, and effects, against unreasonable searches and seizures, shall not be violated, and no Warrants shall issue, but upon probable cause, supported by Oath or affirmation, and particularly describing the place to be searched, and the persons or things to be seized.

Amendment V

No person shall be held to answer for a capital, or otherwise infamous crime, unless on a presentment or indictment of a Grand Jury, except in cases arising in the land or naval forces, or in the Militia, when in actual service in time of War or public danger; nor shall any person be subject for the same offence to be twice put in jeopardy of life or limb, nor shall be compelled in any criminal case to be a witness against himself, nor be deprived of life, liberty, or property, without due process of law; nor shall private property be taken for public use without just compensation.

Amendment VI

In all criminal prosecutions, the accused shall enjoy the right to a speedy and public trial, by an impartial jury of the State and district wherein the crime shall have been committed; which district shall have been previously ascertained by law, and to be informed of the nature and cause of the accusation; to be confronted with the witnesses against him; to have compulsory process for obtaining witnesses in his favor, and to have the assistance of counsel for his defence.

Amendment VII

In Suits at common law, where the value in controversy shall exceed twenty dollars, the right of trial by jury shall be preserved, and no fact tried by a jury shall be otherwise re-examined in any Court of the United States, than according to the rules of the common law.

Amendment VIII

Excessive bail shall not be required, nor excessive fines imposed, nor cruel and unusual punishments inflicted.

Amendment IX

The enumeration in the Constitution of certain rights shall not be construed to deny or disparage others retained by the people.

Amendment X

The powers not delegated to the United States by the Constitution, nor prohibited by it to the States, are reserved to the States respectively, or to the people.

Note: The first ten Amendments (Bill of Rights) were ratified effective December 15, 1791.

because they abridged public employee's rights too severely. Consequently, Brennan thought that patronage dismissals violated the First and the Fourteenth Amendments.

Justices Stewart and Blackmun concurred in a much narrower opinion: "The single substantive question involved in this case is whether a nonpolicy making, nonconfidential government employee can be discharged from a job that he is satisfactorily performing upon the sole ground of his political beliefs. I agree with the Court that he cannot."

Chief Justice Burger dissented. He argued that a state's right to use a patronage system was protected by the Tenth Amendment. This would be especially true where the state, as in the case of Illinois, "pointedly decided that roughly half of the Sheriff's staff shall be made up of tenured career personnel and the balance left exclusively to the choice of the elected head of the department."

The Chief Justice, along with Justice Rehnquist, also joined in a wide-ranging dissent by Justice Powell.* According to Powell's judgment: "History

---

*Justice Stevens, who was involved with the case at an earlier time, did not participate. However, his previous involvement left no doubt that he would have provided a sixth vote against patronage.

U.S. Supreme Court Courtroom *Source*: Collection of the Supreme Court of the United States.

and long prevailing practice across the country support the view that patronage hiring practices make a sufficiently substantial contribution to the practical functioning of our democratic system to support their relatively modest intrusion on First Amendment interests. The judgment today unnecessarily constitutionalizes another element of American life—an element certainly not without its faults but one which generations have accepted on balance as having merit."

The Supreme Court holding in *Elrod* was strengthened by its action in *Branti* v. *Finkel* (1980). The case involved the patronage dismissals of assistant public defenders in Rockland County, New York. In finding the removals to be unconstitutional, a majority of the Supreme Court expanded the *Elrod* ruling by holding that "the ultimate inquiry is not whether the label 'policymaker' or 'confidential' fits a particular position; rather, the question is whether the hiring authority can demonstrate that party affiliation is an appropriate requirement for effective performance of the public office involved."

  Elrod and *Branti* went a long way toward making patronage *dismissals* unconstitutional. But what about making other personnel actions, such as hiring, promotion, transfer, or "dead-ending," based on partisanship? In 1990, a full decade after the *Branti* decision, a slim majority of the Supreme Court ruled in *Rutan* v. *Republican Party of Illinois* that "unless... patronage practices are narrowly tailored to further vital government interests, we must conclude that they impermissibly encroach on First Amendment freedoms..." Practically speaking, then, partisan intrusion into public personnel administration should become a thing of the past and the merit orientation of most contemporary public personnel should be strengthened considerably.

  There are at least two lessons public personnelists should draw from these cases. First, and most specifically, the use of patronage will be constitutional only if it can be demonstrated that partisan affiliation is strongly related to effective job performance. Second, and more generally, the role of the judiciary in contemporary public personnel management cannot be overlooked. Here "a practice as old as the Republic," as Justice Powell put it, was found to be unconstitutional as the result of evolving judicial concepts and perspectives. If something as traditional as patronage can now be found to violate the Constitution, certainly other aspects of public personnel administration are also vulnerable. Constitutional law is ever changing; public personnel managers must remain abreast of it lest they find themselves on the losing side.

  The Supreme Court's action in *Elrod* v. *Burns* points to the continuing relevance of the Constitution as part of the framework for American public personnel management. Its ruling that a practice as old as the republic itself is now unconstitutional is indicative of the constantly changing nature of constitutional doctrines affecting public employment and of the potential scope of judicial intervention in public personnel management. Whereas in the past a chapter such as this would have been unnecessary, today the public personnel manager can ignore the Constitution only at the risk of having fundamental aspects of the personnel program, including examinations, disciplinary systems, aspects of collective bargaining, and affirmative action, overturned in court. In addition, it is important for public personnel managers to understand judicial concepts and values because so much of contemporary public personnel administration has been conditioned by the judiciary. In this chapter, we will explore the contemporary constitutional status of public employees, its rationale, and its ramifications for public personnel management.

The Public Employment Relationship

Employment creates a relationship between the employer and the employee that encompasses a variety of rights, obligations, and mutual expectations. This employment relationship can be regulated by statutory law, common law, contract law, collective bargaining agreements, and custom and practice in the workplace. It can also be regulated by constitutions. In the United States, it is very largely the federal and state constitutions that distinguish the *public* employment relationship from arrangements in the private sector. With the exception of the Thirteenth Amendment's proscription of slavery and involuntary servitude, the U.S. Constitution does not directly affect the private employment relationship. However, under current judicial interpretations, the Constitution does convey to public employees broad substantive, procedural, and equal protection rights. As a result, the judiciary has become an active partner in public personnel administration. But it wasn't always this way. Historically, the public employment relationship has had three phases.

The first phase was the longest, lasting from the adoption of the Constitution in 1789 to the 1950s. It treated the public employment relationship as very similar to the private employment relationship, that is, largely unregulated by the Constitution. Employment in both sectors was considered to be at the "will" of the employer, who, insofar as the Constitution was concerned, could hire and fire employees for virtually any reason whatsoever, or no reason at all. This approach made the spoils system possible and ironically also set forth the first constitutional justifications for prohibiting public employees from taking an active part in partisan politics. For the sake of convenience, this appproach can be called the "private sector model."

In terms of constitutional interpretation, the private sector model was sustained by what became known as the doctrine of privilege. Under this approach it was generally accepted that since there was no constitutional right to public employment, it was a privilege to hold a government job. Moreover, because such employment was voluntary rather than compulsory, public employees had few rights that could not be legitimately abridged by the government in its role as employer. The logic behind this position is still best conveyed by Justice Holmes's often quoted statement that "the petitioner may have a constitutional right to talk politics, but he has no constitutional right to be a policeman." Under this approach, public personnel administration was free to place virtually any conditions it saw fit upon public employment, and the judiciary played almost no role in this policy area.

The doctrine of privilege and the private sector model contained a certain logic, but they also had substantial defects. Most important, as the size of public employment increased to the point where about 16 percent of the work force held public jobs, it became evident that the rights of a substantial

Personnel Managers Beware!

The material in this chapter is hardly academic. A local governmental public personnel manager who violates the federal constitutional or statutory rights of employees or applicants may be held personally liable for monetary damages awarded as a result of a civil suit against him or her. Several U.S. Supreme Court decisions have eroded the traditional immunity of public administrators from such liability. In general, the local personnel administrator would not be immune from suit if his or her conduct violated "clearly established statutory or constitutional rights of which a reasonable person would have known." Monetary damages assessed against such a personnelist may be intended to compensate the individual illegally or unconstitutionally treated, and in some cases they may be punitive as well. In the latter instance damages would go beyond making the wronged individual "whole"; they would be intended to punish the personnelist and serve as a deterrent against breaches of individual rights in the future. Municipalities can also be sued if their personnel policies violate federally protected statutory or constitutional rights. They are liable if such violations actually occurred regardless of what the city should "know" about the status of such rights. Punitive damages cannot be awarded against municipalities in cases of this type. When dealing with current employees, federal personnelists appear to be exempt from such liabilities because Congress provided an alternative remedy by creating an elaborate adverse action appeals system. State personnelists also appear to be exempt under current interpretations of federal law, though they may face liabilities under state law. Public personnelists at all levels of government who exercise adjudicatory roles are absolutely immune from such suits. A sticky issue for state and local personnelists is figuring out what they *reasonably* should know about individuals' rights, with the federal courts determining what's reasonable. A good place to start is by considering the constitutional values inherent in the cases and approaches discussed in this chapter.

For further information, see David H. Rosenbloom, *Public Administration and Law* (New York: Marcel Dekker, Inc., 1983), and David H. Rosenbloom and James D. Carroll, *Toward Constitutional Competence* (Englewood Cliffs, N.J.: Prentice-Hall, 1990).

proportion of the population could be abridged by governments in their roles as employers. And abridge these rights they did! During the late 1940s and early 1950s, governments at all levels developed "loyalty-security" regulations to protect themselves against subversive employees. But one's definition of *subversive* tended to vary with one's politics and geographic location. Consequently, some federal employees were charged with such dangerous activities as favoring peace and freedom, being critical of the American Legion and public power projects, being related to someone who might have had procommunist leanings, having "communist literature" and "communist art" in their houses, living with unmarried members of the opposite sex, learning

Russian, and favoring racial integration. Some employees were even asked whether they regularly read the *New York Times,* attended church, or had intelligent, clever friends and associates.

The habit of abusing the constitutional rights of public employees lasted longer than the "red scare" of the early post-World War II period. Since the much feared worldwide communist revolution failed to occur, personnelists turned their attention to the domestic sexual revolution of the 1960s. In the National Security Agency, employees were routinely asked such questions as

1. When was the first time you had sexual relations?
2. How many times have you had sexual intercourse?
3. Have you ever engaged in homosexual activities? In sexual activities with an animal?
4. When was the first time you had intercourse with your spouse?
5. Did you have intercourse with your spouse before you were married? How many times?

Some federal employees were also asked to respond, in true/false format on personality tests, to such statements as, "My sex life is satisfactory," and

CHAPMAN

WE HAVEN'T FIGURED OUT A WAY TO FIRE YOU YET, SMEDLEY, BUT WE'RE WORKING ON IT.

S-28

Reprinted by permission of the International Personnel Management Association, 1850 K Street, N.W., Suite 870, Washington, D.C. 20006.

The Use of Polygraph Tests for Preemployment Screening

The U.S. District court for the Southern District of Texas in *Woodland* v. *City of Houston* (1990) found unconstitutional a polygraph test that inquired about:

a. The applicant's religion, religious practices, or lack of them;
b. The applicant's consensual sexual activity, except to the extent that the act was unlawful in the jurisdiction where it took place and involved a minor and occurred within three years of the screening;
c. Extramarital sex;
d. Crimes committed as a child, except to the extent they involved a felony or a physical injury or a sexual assault in the jurisdiction within which they occurred, or the applicant was tried and convicted for them as an adult;
e. The use of marijuana, except to the extent that it was used unlawfully by the applicant in the jurisdiction where it was used within the six months preceding the screening process; illegal use of marijuana cannot be used to disqualify an applicant unless similar level offenses are similarly used as disqualifications, like traffic, drinking or hunting violations;
f. Adult criminal behavior, except to the extent that the applicant committed a felony, a sexual assault, theft, a Class A misdemeanor, or caused serious injury;
g. Theft, unless it involved at least $25 and occured within the twelve months before the screening process or there have been four thefts within the three years preceding the screening process;
h. Membership in organizations, except to the extent that the applicant is currently or, within the previous five years, has been an active member of an organization which advocates violent, unlawful acts;
i. Drug use, unless the questions are about the applicant's illegal use of uppers, downers, steroids, or cocaine in the last twelve months; or hallucinogens within five years; or heroin within twelve months and more than one use in five years.

"There is little love and companionship in my family as compared to other homes."

Questions of this nature placed severe strains upon the federal employee's First Amendment and privacy rights. However, the abuses did not stop there; federal servants were also subject to coercion that infringed upon their right of liberty under the Fifth Amendment. Not only were they required to attend lectures and films on such topics as racial integration and the cold war, but in 1966 Senator Ervin observed that there was "outright coercion and intimidation of employees to buy everything from savings bonds to electric light bulbs for playgrounds."

At a time when public employment was rapidly growing, many feared that such governmental power over this segment of the population could pose a threat to democracy. Not only were the rights of a substantial number of citizens abridged, but concerted coercion could also turn them into a significant political force. Perceptive observers recognized that governments could also limit the rights of other citizens receiving other privileges, and in the modern administrative state this could have included everyone who receives welfare benefits, social security, government contracts, passports, and even driver's licenses. Clearly, the doctrine of privilege was ill suited to modern political conditions in democratic regimes, and its demise was not limited to the realm of public employment.

The Individual Rights Model

Beginning in the 1950s, the federal judiciary became more sensitive to the threats to individual rights posed by the private sector model and the doctrine of privilege in its broad application. Several Supreme Court justices urged that the public employment relationship be controlled by the Constitution's guarantees and that an individual not be required to sacrifice his or her constitutional rights as a condition of becoming a public employee. Public employees, like other citizens, had constitutional rights that were inviolable—even in the context of the employment relationship.

At first these views were voiced mostly in dissent. But by the early 1970s, the doctrine of privilege had been completely discarded by the judiciary. For example, in *Board of Regents* v. *Roth* (1972), the Supreme Court averred that it had "fully and finally rejected the wooden distinction between 'rights' and 'privileges' that once seemed to govern the applicability of procedural due process rights." A year later, in *Sugarman* v. *Dougall*, it again "rejected the concept that constitutional rights turn upon whether a governmental benefit is characterized as a 'right' or as a 'privilege.'" But replacing the doctrine of privilege with one that is more balanced does not promote undue judicial intervention in public personnel management, and enabling public managers and employees to understand their respective rights and obligations has been difficult for the judiciary. Just as the doctrine of privilege was doomed by its simplicity in an age of complex public administration, a general judicial inclination to treat the constitutional rights of public employees as essentially the same as those of other citizens proved inadequate.

Initially, the doctrine of privilege was replaced by the doctrine of substantial interest. It held that whenever there was a "substantial interest," such as the individual's reputation, the employee, facing possible dismissal, had a right to a procedure to determine whether legitimate grounds for the removal really existed. This procedure would generally consist of a hearing of some sort, perhaps including the rights of confrontation and cross-examination.

In addition, the new doctrine started from the premise that the government could not condition the granting of public employment on the individual's sacrifice of some constitutional right. This had the impact of shifting the burden of proof to the government when cases came before the judiciary.

The doctrine of substantial interest gave public employees considerable constitutional rights, but it did not serve the needs of either the judiciary or public personnel managers very well. Indeed, it led to an ever-increasing number of cases involving the public employee's constitutional position and to great perplexity over what actually constituted a substantial interest. From the perspectives of public personnel management it meant that constitutional issues were often raised and that personnel managers had to be able to anticipate judicial rulings. Given the wave of protest that swept government employees in the late 1960s, the doctrine of substantial interest seemed to make government itself ungovernable.

As the Supreme Court wrestled with the perplexities involved in the constitutional aspects of the public employment relationship and as its membership changed during the Nixon and Ford administrations, another approach developed. This involved the assessment of each and every case on its own merits and the avoidance of the development of a broad constitutional doctrine specifying the general outlines of the constitutional rights of public employees. Good examples occurred in the area of mandatory maternity leaves, where the the Supreme Court held that these could not commence without an individualized determination of a woman's physical capability to continue at her public sector job (except very late in the normal term of a pregnancy), and in the area of barriers to the public employment of aliens, where the Court held that they could be banned from some jobs but not others.

The "individualized" approach multiplied the practical deficiencies of the doctrine of substantial interest and is best attributed to the Supreme Court's inability to develop a dominant coalition among its members on public employment issues. Thus, the approach encouraged further litigation and made public personnel management more difficult by requiring the individual treatment of individual employees. For instance, how can a personnel manager plan on recruiting for a replacement for a woman going on maternity leave when no one is sure when that leave will commence? Similarly, how can it be determined in advance of a judicial ruling which positions can legitimately be reserved for citizens? One lower court even held that race might sometimes, but not always, be constitutionally used as a factor in job assignments. Yet it provided little guidance on the matter. In sum, the individual rights model of the public employment relationship seemed inadequate to the needs of modern, coherent public personnel management. The doctrine of privilege afforded public employees virtually no constitutional protection, but at least it was clear. The individual rights model afforded them expansive constitutional rights, but it lacked clarity. Beginning in the mid-1970s, the Supreme Court formulated a model of the public employment relationship more suited to the contemporary public service state.

The Public Service Model

Unlike earlier models of the public employment relationship, the public service approach seeks to strike a functional balance among the sometimes competing concerns of the government as employer, the interests of public employees in exercising constitutional rights, and the public's interest in the way its affairs are run by public administrators. Especially important in the latter category are the efficiency, honesty, and political responsiveness of the public service. Rather than being defined solely from the perspectives of personnel management or employee rights, the public employment relationship is currently being developed with a vision toward its impact on matters of broad public concern, including the electoral process (as in the patronage cases). Since modern public personnel managers can hardly be effective if they are oblivious to any of these interests, following the constitutional law has become an important part of the personnelist job.

Before proceeding with an examination of the content of leading constitutional decisions pertaining to public personnel management, it is an affordable luxury to pause to consider what that content should ideally be. The public service model of the public employment relationship helps us to identify several central concerns. First, the nonpartisan political speech of public employees must be protected. This enables them to engage in whistleblowing and debates over public policy. Public employees often know more about their agencies and various aspects of policy than any other group. Moreover, unlike politicians, they do not have to worry about getting elected. Consequently, as Herbert Storing pointed out, the civil service can "bring to bear on public policy its distinctive view of the common good or its way of looking at questions about the common good." It is essential to the development of an informed electorate that they be able to communicate their ideas to the citizenry.

Second, in a society that values liberty, restrictions on the private lives of public employees must be held to a minimum. One's social and intellectual proclivities off the job should not be a concern of public personnel administration unless they have some direct and harmful bearing on one's performance at work. While the same might be said for the economic affairs of public employees, concern with conflict of interest might legitimately outweigh the individual's right to privacy. Illegal substance abuse might also be of legitimate interest to the governmental employer, even if no manifestations of it are evident on the job. The private use of illegal drugs has had such a major impact on violent crime and social decay in the United States that it cannot be considered "victimless." Some illegal drugs also cause health problems, which could be of legitimate interest to an employer, as might be alcohol abuse or smoking.

Third, in placing restrictions upon the constitutional rights of public employees, it must always be remembered that these may have a detrimental impact on recruitment. Although there may be candidates for jobs despite such impositions, there is evidence suggesting that in the past, especially during the loyalty-security era, the federal government was unable to attract the kind of talent it sought. In part this was because such people were unwilling to work in an atmosphere of coerced conformity and suspicion.

Finally, a balance must be struck between the need to protect employees from arbitrary and capricious adverse actions and the requirement of allowing public managers enough flexibility to deal effectively with inefficient and incompetent employees. Even the civil service reformers of the 1870s and 1880s, who sought to reduce patronage dismissals, were opposed to dismissals by lawsuit. Of course, striking the precise balance is no small feat. Perhaps the central lesson to remember is that in a day and age when such a large segment of the population is publicly employed, political democracy requires democratic public personnel management. We turn now to a review of the contemporary constitutional case law concerning public personnel management.

Freedom of Expression: Nonpartisan Speech

The late 1960s witnessed growing militancy and political activism on the part of public employees. To some extent this was related to the demise of the doctrine of privilege, which provided them with more freedom. For instance, some federal employees engaged in demonstrations against the war in Southeast Asia, signed antiwar and pro-civil rights petitions, and wrote open letters to government officials advocating political positions. In addition, some formed groups in order to advance political causes and even to press for the creation of what might be called "participatory bureaucracy." The objectives of the latter were to reduce hierarchy to a minimum, increase the participation of middle-level employees in public policy making and in the structuring of the bureaucracy, and establish the principle that an employee has a right to refuse to perform work that is contrary to his or her conscience. Hence, the public personnel manager may now be confronted with a host of new situations that were unthinkable only a few years ago. The central constitutional question here is, "How far may employees go in publicly opposing their agencies' leadership and policies without being legitimately disciplined?"

The judiciary has been developing the public service model in this area. The most recent significant case in which the Supreme Court explained the constitutional law regarding public employees' freedom to engage in non-partisan speech is *Rankin* v. *McPherson* (1987). The case involved the dismissal of a deputy county constable who, after hearing of an assassination attempt on President Reagan, said to a fellow employee in the constable's office, "Shoot, if they go for him again, I hope they get him." Another employee overheard the remark and reported it to Constable Rankin. Rankin discussed the matter with Ms. McPherson and then fired her. In turn, she sued for reinstatement, back pay, costs, fees, and other equitable relief.

In a somewhat surprising 5–4 decision, a majority of the Supreme Court held that McPherson's dismissal was unconstitutional in violation of her rights to freedom of speech. In so doing, the majority set forth the general constitutional framework for determining whether public employees' non-partisan remarks are constitutionally protected. The Court built upon an earlier case, *Pickering* v. *Board of Education* (1968), in noting that the key consideration is to strike a balance between the interests of the governmental employer in promoting efficiency and those of the employee as a citizen commenting on matters of public concern. Consequently, the threshold question is whether an employee's remarks can be considered to address a matter of public concern. This is an important element in the public service model because it is assumed that public employees often have information about public policies and the operation of the government that can help to inform the electorate.

If an employee's speech is on a matter of public concern, then "in performing the balancing, the statement will not be considered in a vacuum; the manner, time, and place of the employee's expression are relevant, as is the context in which the dispute arose." Among the factors of special pertinence are "whether the statement impairs discipline by superiors or harmony among coworkers, has a detrimental impact on close working relationships for which personal loyalty and confidence are necessary, or impedes the performance of the speaker's duties or interferes with the regular operation of the enterprise."

In applying this framework specifically to McPherson's comment, the Court found that her remark was of public concern because it was part of a larger conversation regarding Reagan's policies. It was also constitutionally protected since "[t]he burden of caution employees bear with respect to the words they speak will vary with the extent of authority and public accountability the employee's role entails. Where, as here, an employee serves no confidential, policymaking, or public contact role, the danger to the agency's successful function from that employee's private speech is minimal." Consequently, "at some point," for an employee such as McPherson, such statements "are so removed from the effective function of the public employer" that they cannot constitutionally be the basis for dismissal.

The Rankin approach affords considerable protection to public employees' right to freedom of nonpartisan expression. However, as with many aspects of constitutional law, it can require public personnelists and employees to exercise subtle judgment. First, how can one always be sure whether a remark such as McPherson's is on a matter of public concern? The dissenting justices offered little encouragement here because, unlike the majority, they concluded that the remark did *not* meet the threshold test of being on a matter of public concern. Second, if one concludes that a remark does meet the threshold test, it is still necessary to strike the correct balance. Here again, the dissenting four justices disagreed with the majority five. Clearly, the most tenable approach for public personnelists is to employ the Court's general framework and follow the constitutional law closely in this area. As the federal district courts apply the Supreme Court's approach to differing situations, the extent of public employees' rights to freedom on nonpartisan expression will be delineated further.

In the meantime, it can be reported that a public employee's remarks on a matter of public concern made in a private conversation with a supervisor are subject to the kind of balancing considerations articulated in the *Rankin* case, but that according to the *Rankin* majority, "a purely private statement on a matter of public concern will rarely, if ever, justify discharge of a public employee." Further, a federal employee appears to have a firm constitutional right to inform federal officials of violations of federal law. Additionally, public employees' constitutional rights to freedom of expression on matters of public concern have been held to encompass private communication with a supervisor, the filing of lawsuits, and "symbolic speech"—specifically, police officers removing the American flag from their uniforms to protest racial discrimination in the police force. These protections apply not only to personnel actions involving dismissal, but also to refusals to hire, demotions, transfers, refusals to promote, letters of reprimand, and reprisals in the form of reductions in force (rifs). They apply to probationary as well as to permanent employees. Despite the breadth of these protections, prepublication clearance agreements in the area of national security are currently considered valid and can create an obstacle to informing the electorate about the performance of agencies such as the CIA. An even more important exception to the public employee's right to speak out on matters of public concern are regulations prohibiting their participation in partisan political campaigns.

Political Neutrality

Political activity by public employees has presented a persistent problem in the United States. In an earlier day, when public bureaucracies were less obviously engaged in the making of public policy and when administration was considered distinct from politics, the political neutrality of civil servants was thought to be a necessity for efficient, democratic government. The notion of political neutrality was first introduced by President Jefferson when he issued a circular declaring that the federal employee was expected not to attempt to influence the votes of others or to take part in electioneering, "that being deemed inconsistent with the spirit of the Constitution and his duties to it." But it was not until the introduction of civil service reform in the 1880s that restrictions on the political activities of public employees became common and effective. The undesirable aspects of a partisan and politically active public service were made evident by the spoils system. Public employees, either through their own volition or as a result of coercion, were deeply engaged in partisan politics. Sometimes, although drawing their salaries from the public treasury, they performed no public functions at all, only partisan ones. Administration became partisan, employees were forced to vote for the party in office, their salaries were "taxed" (assessed) by the parties, and the corruption and personnel turnover associated with partisanship became a serious problem.

Depoliticization of the public service was crucial to the objectives of civil service reform and the spoils system gave the reformers plenty of arguments in favor of it. In the words of George William Curtis, a leading reformer, "the tap root of the evils and abuses which reform would destroy is the partisan prostitution of the civil service." Regulations intended to assure the partisan neutrality of the federal service were issued shortly after the enactment of the Pendleton or Civil Service Act of 1883. However, it was not until 1907 that political neutrality became an important feature of the federal service. In that year President Roosevelt changed the civil service rules to forbid employees in the competitive service from taking active part in political management or in political campaigns. At the same time the rule explicitly allowed such employees to express privately their opinions on all political subjects. The Civil Service Commission (CSC) was charged with enforcing this provision. But by the commission's own admission, it was impossible to provide a complete list of the activities in which an employee could not engage. Consequently, decisions have been largely made on a case-by-case basis, and by 1940 a kind of case law had developed in over 3,000 rulings.

In 1939 matters were complicated by the passage of the first Hatch Act. It extended the coverage of political activity restrictions to almost all federal employees, whether in the competitive service or not. The impetus for this legislation came primarily from a decrease in the proportion of federal employees who were in the competitive service. This was a direct result of the creation of several New Deal agencies that were placed outside the merit system. Senator Hatch, a Democrat from New Mexico, had worked for several years to have legislation enacted that would prevent federal employees from being active in political conventions. He feared that their involvement and direction by politicians could lead to the development of a giant national political machine.

From the perspective of public personnel management, the Hatch Act created some confusion. It allowed federal employees to express their views freely on all political subjects rather than only to express them privately. However, it also proclaimed that the act was intended to prohibit the same activities that the CSC considered illegitimate under the 1907 regulations, which allowed only private expression. The second Hatch Act (1940) extended these regulations to positions in state employment having federal financing and allowed public employees to express their opinions on "candidates" as well as political subjects, but not as part of a political campaign. Penalties for violation of the first Hatch Act have been softened considerably over time. Originally removal was mandatory, but by 1962 the minimum punishment was suspension for 30 days.

It has never been possible to define completely the activities political neutrality regulations prohibit. However, the following are among the major limitations:

1. Serving as a delegate or alternate to a political party convention
2. Soliciting or handling political contributions
3. Being an officer or organizer of a political club
4. Engaging in electioneering
5. With some exceptions, being a candidate for elective political office
6. Leading or speaking to partisan political meetings or rallies

The constitutionality of these regulations was first upheld by the Supreme Court in *United Public Workers* v. *Mitchell* (1947). The court was divided 4 to 3. The majority adopted the private sector model of the employment relationship. It held that the ordinary constitutional rights of federal employees could be abridged by Congress in the interest of increasing or maintaining the efficiency of the federal service. The minority, on the other hand, could find nothing special about public employees that justified placing such limitations upon them. In the years following this decision, as the doctrine of privilege began to erode and ultimately met its demise, several courts cast increasing doubt on the constitutionality of regulations of this nature. In fact, in *National Association of Letter Carriers (NALC)* v. *CSC* (1972), the Court of Appeals for the District of Columbia Circuit declared the Hatch Act to be unconstitutional because its vague and "overbroad" language made it impossible to determine what it prohibited. In a somewhat surprising

Hatch Act Coverage of State and Local Employees

In General

Federal law prohibits partisan political activity by an officer or employee of a State or local agency if his or her principal employment is in connection with an activity which is financed in whole or in part by loans or grants made by the United States or a Federal agency. The law is enforced by the United States Merit Systems Protection Board. (If you have any question as to whether this law applies to you, ask the Board to resolve it. Don't rely solely on the advice of your friends, fellow workers or others who do not have special knowledge of this law—you may receive erroneous advice, as others have.)

Federal Financing

In many State, County, and Municipal governments the following programs receive financial assistance from the Federal Government:

1. Public Health
2. Public Welfare
3. Housing, Urban Renewal, and Area Redevelopment
4. Employment Security
5. Labor and Industry
6. Highways and Public Works
7. Conservation
8. Agriculture
9. Civil Defense
10. Aeronautics and Transportation
11. Anti-poverty
12. Law Enforcement

Principal Employment

In most cases employment with the State or local agency is the principal employment of the officer or employee concerned. If she or he has another job or jobs, factors such as the amount of time spent on each job, proportionate income received, etc., are considered in determining which constitutes her or his principal employment.

U.S. Civil Service Commission, *State and Local Employees Political Participation* (Washington, D.C.: U.S. Government Printing Office, pamphlet No. GC-39); Civil Service Reform Act of 1978, P.L. 95-454 (Oct. 13, 1978).

decision, however, the Supreme Court reaffirmed its decision in *Mitchell* when the *NALC* case reached it on appeal. The Court reasoned that despite some ambiguities, an ordinary person using ordinary common sense could ascertain and comply with the regulations involved. It also argued that its decision did nothing more than to confirm the judgment of history that political neutrality was a desirable or even essential feature of public employment in the United States.

The Supreme Court's decision, of course, does nothing to prevent Congress from modifying or abandoning the restrictions on political activity. After losing in court, public employee unions and other opponents of political neutrality turned their attention increasingly in the legislative direction. By March 1976 they were successful in gaining congressional approval of a bill repealing the Hatch Act, but this was vetoed by President Ford and never became law.

In 1990, the Hatch Act was once again at the center of political controversy. After an intensive drive by unions representing federal employees, Congress voted by overwhelming margins (334 to 87 in the House; 67 to 30 in the Senate), to allow federal employees to hold office in national, state, and local political organizations and to engage in widespread campaigning activity while off duty, and not in uniform or in government offices or vehicles. However, President Bush vetoed the effort to "un-Hatch" federal employees and Congress failed to override his veto. Bush claimed the revision would politicize the federal service.

The 1990 act would have strictly outlawed any activity seeking to coerce federal employees or intimidate them into performing partisan activities. Most political observers seemed to agree that freeing up federal employees to actively support partisan candidates would have benefited the Democrats more than the Republicans. Of course, unionized federal employees would have benefited the most from un-Hatching, since there is often more to gain through politics than is available within the crimped scope of bargaining that predominates in labor relations with most nonpostal federal workers (see Chapters 10 and 11).

There seems little doubt that public sector labor organizations will also seek modification of restrictions on the political activities of state and local public employees as well. How important to public administration the repeal of such restrictions may be remains to be seen. It is somewhat alarmist to assume that repeal will lead to the demise of merit and the reinstitution of spoils practices. One of the primary objectives of the Hatch Acts and similar regulations was to prevent public employees from being coerced into the performance of partisan services, and it is at least plausible that the growth of unionism, protections against arbitrary adverse actions, and the Supreme Court's rulings in *Elrod* v. *Burns* and *Branti* v. *Finkel* have made coercion increasingly unlikely. Moreover, there is no reason to assume that political selectin will replace merit as a result of a liberalization of restrictions on the political activities of public employees.

Freedom of Association

The public employee's freedom of association was broadly guaranteed for the first time by the Supreme Court in *Shelton* v. *Tucker* (1960). Subsequent cases have upheld the public employee's right to join a labor union and even to have membership in subversive organizations or organizations with illegal ends as long as they do not personally support or participate in such activities. In the 1970s, however, the thorny problem of public employee's right *not* to join organizations came to the fore.

As we saw in the prologue, in *Elrod* v. *Burns*, five Supreme Court justices agreed that rank-and-file public employees could not be compelled to join or support political parties on pain of dismissal. In *Abood* v. *Detroit Board of Education* (1977), the Court was confronted with an "agency shop" arrangement "whereby every employee represented by a union—even though not a union member—must pay to the union, as a condition of employment, a service fee equal in amount to union dues." The Court reasoned that such arrangements are common in private employment and can be considered a fundamental aspect of collective bargaining. Although when applied in the public sector it interferes with the civil servant's freedom of association, "such interference as exists is constitutionally justified by the legislative assessment of the important contribution of the union shop to the system of labor relations."

Agency shop arrangements are coercive but they are a price often paid in the hope of establishing stable labor relations. While the Court was willing to accept this, it opposed the practice of forcing employees to pay for the union's spending of funds "for the expression of political views, on behalf of political candidates, or towards the advancement of other ideological causes not germane to its duties as collective bargaining representative." In other words, public employees can be compelled to pay for a union's collective bargaining activities, but not its general political and social endeavors. This right was strengthened substantially by the Supreme Court's holding in *Chicago Teachers Union* v. *Hudson* (1986), that "... the constitutional requirements for the Union's collection of agency fees include an adequate explanation of the basis for the fee, a reasonably prompt opportunity to challenge the amount of the fee before an impartial decisionmaker, and an escrow for the amounts reasonably in dispute while such challenges are pending." Both the *Abood* and *Chicago Teachers Union* decisions fit the public service model in that they seek to assure that public employees will not be coerced to join and unreasonably support unions, but rather will remain free to identify primarily with their governmental employer, if they so choose.

Liberty

As discussed earlier, over the years there has been a tendency for governments to place a variety of restrictions upon the personal liberty of their employees. During the 1970s, the Supreme Court handed down several important decisions in this area.

In *Cleveland Board of Education* v. *LaFleur* and *Cohen* v. *Chesterfield County School Board*, argued and decided together in 1974, the Court addressed the issue of mandatory pregnancy leaves. The policies being challenged were particularly arbitrary and harsh by requiring leaves to commence early in the term of a pregnancy while at the same time serving no rational purpose. Indeed, Justice Powell expressed the opinion that the policies were aimed at preventing schoolchildren from gazing upon pregnant teachers. Teachers were also banned from returning to their jobs until three months after the birth of their children. The Court found such policies to be unconstitutional. It did so, however, not on the basis of a violation of equal protection of the laws, but rather on the grounds that "by acting to penalize the pregnant teacher for deciding to bear a child, overly restrictive maternity leave regulations can constitute a heavy burden on the exercise of ... protected freedoms." The Court held that with the exception of a regulation forcing the employee to go on leave a few weeks prior to the expected date of the birth of her child, regulations based on elapsed time rather than on the individual's capability to continue at her job were constitutionally unacceptable. (See Chapter 16 for a further discussion of pregnancy leave policies.)

The constitutionality of grooming regulations for male police officers was at issue in *Kelley* v. *Johnson* (1976). The regulations included such requirements as "sideburns will not extend below the lowest part of the exterior ear opening, will be of even width (not flared), and will end with a clean-shaven horizontal line." Although a lower court reasoned that "choice of personal appearance is an ingredient of an individual's personal liberty," the Supreme Court found no constitutional infirmity in the regulations. In fact, it placed the burden of proof on the employees, challenging them to "demonstrate that there is no rational connection between the regulation ... and the promotion of safety of persons and property." The Court went on to reason that since such regulations make police more identifiable and may contribute to an *ésprit de corps,* they cannot be considered irrational. Such logic, of course, is peculiar to say the least. It's difficult to imagine how sideburns and the like could possibly obscure the uniforms and badges police wear to facilitate identification; and since it was the president of the local Patrolmen's Benevolent Association who, in his official capacity, was challenging the regulation, it is difficult to imagine how it could have enhanced morale. What explains the Court's decision, then, is primarily its desire to avoid public personnel management issues of limited importance that can be dealt with in other forums, including lobbying and collective bargaining.

In a more or less related fashion, in *McCarthy* v. *Philadelphia Civil Service Commission* (1976), the Supreme Court upheld the constitutionality of residency requirements for municipal employees in the face of a challenge to them on the grounds that they unconstitutionally abridge the individual's

Cleveland Board of Education v. *LaFleur* 414 U.S. 632 (1974)

Facts—Pregnant public school teachers in Ohio and Virginia challenged the constitutionality of the mandatory leave regulations of their school boards. The Ohio rule required plaintiff to take unpaid pregnancy leave five months before her expected childbirth, and to make application at least two weeks before her departure. She was not eligible to return to work until the next regular semester after her child reached three months of age. The Virginia rule required one of the plaintiffs to give at least six months notice, and to leave work at least four months, before the expected birth. Re-employment was guaranteed no later than the first day of the school year after she was declared re-eligible. Both rules required a physician's certificate attesting to the teacher's physical fitness before her return. The Court of Appeals for the Sixth Circuit held the Ohio local school board's rule unconstitutional whereas the Court of Appeals for the Fourth Circuit held the Virginia local school Board's rule constitutional.

Issue—Do mandatory pregnancy leave regulations that set arbitrary dates for the commencement of leave violate the 14th Amendment?

Discussion—Freedom of personal choice in matters of marriage and family life is one of the liberties protected by the Due Process Clause of the 14th Amendment. Neither the necessity for continuity of instruction or the State interest in keeping physically unfit teachers out of the classroom can justify the sweeping mandatory leave rules. They violate the Due Process Clause because they create irrebuttable presumptions that unduly penalize a female teacher for deciding to bear a child. The arbitrary cutoff dates, which come at different times of the school year for different teachers, have no valid relationship to the State's interest in preserving continuity of instruction so long as the teacher is required to give substantial advance notice of pregnancy. The rules conclusively presume that every teacher is physically incapable of teaching when she is four or five months pregnant, when such ability is, in fact, an individual matter and administrative convenience alone cannot validate arbitrary rules. Cleveland's arbitrary and irrational three-month return provision also violated due process in that it creates an irrebuttable presumption that the mother is not fit to resume work. The time limit serves no legitimate State interest and unnecessarily penalizes the female teacher for asserting her right to bear children. This, too, is not germane to maintaining continuity of instruction.

U.S. Office of Personnel Management, *Equal Employment Opportunity Court Cases* (Washington, D.C.: U.S. Government Printing Office, September 1979), p. 7.

liberty. In the Court's view, the case, which involved a firefighter, established a "bona fide continuing residence requirement" of constitutional acceptability. It did not, however, provide a comprehensive explanation of this position. Consequently, it is unclear as to whether all such regulations are constitutional or whether there are limits on a public employer's right to require that its employees live within its jurisdictional boundaries. In considering residency requirements, local jurisdictions should remember that while there are economic benefits to be gained, one of the liabilities is political—public employees may emerge as a major voting bloc in favor of benefits that the local government can ill afford.

Massachusetts Board of Retirement v. *Murgia* (1976) is another case that fits the public service vision. There, the Supreme Court accepted the constitutionality of a mandatory retirement age of 50 for state police officers. In contrast to the maternity leave cases, it did not think that individualized determinations of fitness were constitutionally required since the regulation applied at "a stage that each of us will reach if we live out our normal span."

As noted earlier, a difficult constitutional question concerns the impact of public employees' exercise of protected rights and liberties off the job on their suitability for governmental employment. Different courts have come to different conclusions regarding the strength of the nexus between private conduct and public employment that the government must show in dismissing or disciplining its employees, and in refusing to hire applicants. However, after reviewing myriad judicial decisions, Robert Roberts and Marion Doss concluded that in recent years: "With respect to the dismissal of state and local employees for off-duty conduct...state and federal courts consistently have found that public employers need only demonstrate a very general relationship between the off-duty conduct of their employees and job performance to withstand constitutional challenges...." For example, in *Fraternal Order of Police, Lodge No. 5* v. *City of Philadelphia* (1987) the federal Court of Appeals for the Third Circuit sustained a police department requirement that applicants for a special investigative unit submit detailed information regarding their physical and mental health, alcohol consumption, gambling activity, membership in associations, and financial status. The court accepted the government's position that such matters were strongly related to the applicants' suitability. On the other hand, in *Thorne* v. *City of El Segundo* (1983), the Court of Appeals for the Ninth Circuit could find *no* rational nexus between the sexual conduct of an applicant and her suitability for a civilian clerical position in a police department. The main lesson for personnelists in such cases is that they must be prepared to show some connection between the employee's or applicant's conduct and the interests of the public service. Gratuitous prying or allegations of immorality can easily violate the Constitution.

Equal Protection

During the 1970s and 1980s, the equal protection rights of public employees became highly complex. As the disparate impact of some personnel devices (e.g., merit examinations) became better understood and as efforts were undertaken to remedy past discrimination against African Americans, women, and members of other groups, new constitutional questions were posed. The Supreme Court responded with a host of decisions that were sometimes evasive and confusing. However, by the late 1980s, the main framework for assessing public employees' constitutional rights to equal protection of the laws became relatively clear.

A large part of the issue of the constitutionality of disparate impact was resolved in *Washington* v. *Davis* (1976). The case presented a very serious constitutional challenge to contemporary public personnel administration because it involved a common problem. The written qualifying examination used to screen applicants for a police training program in the Washington, D.C. metropolitan area had a disproportionately harsh impact on African Americans. Indeed, it disqualified four times as many of them as whites. Several lower court cases involving similar issues had resulted in decisions banning the use of such examinations and sometimes in the judicial imposition of "quotas" as a remedy for previous discrimination through merit exams. Ordinarily in such circumstances, the burden of proof shifted to the government to demonstrate the validity of the examinations. Since proving the validity of exams is so difficult, shifting the burden of proof was often tantamount to deciding the case against the government. Ironically, if *Elrod* v. *Burns* had the effect of constitutionalizing the merit system, equal opportunity decisions tended toward the conclusion that the merit system was generally in unconstitutional violation of equal protection. The Supreme Court sought to deconstitutionalize this area of the public employment relationship. It reasoned that there is a wide variety of public policies that affect African Americans differently from whites, and consequently not result but *intent* was the key to constitutionality. It upheld the constitutionality of the exam on the grounds that an invidious discriminatory purpose had not been shown. Thus, public personnel policies and activities that have differential impacts on various social groups are nevertheless constitutional unless they are *intended* to harm one of these groups. Even then they may be constitutional if the harm is not invidious, or if the harm serves some compelling governmental interest, and if the policies are "narrowly tailored" (see the prologue to Chapter 7 and the discussion below).

At the time it was decided, it appeared that *Washington* v. *Davis* was of limited importance in public personnel management because prevailing statutory law, unlike the Constitution, looked at results rather than intentions. Thus, while an examination or other practice might be constitutional, it might also be illegal if it had a harsh racial or gender impact. But the significance of *Washington* v. *Davis* became evident in *Personnel Administrator* v. *Feeny* (1979). The case involved a challenge to the constitutionality of that state's veterans preference law on the grounds that it violated the equal protection rights of women. The case could not be brought under the Equal Employment Opportunity Act of 1972 because it specifically omits veteran preference regulations from its purview. The Supreme Court noted that the impact of the Massachusetts law on the "public employment opportunities of women has...been severe." Nevertheless, it upheld the law's constitutionality on the grounds that the resulting discriminatory effect on women was not intentional. The Court observed that women veterans were likewise entitled to preference.

The main result of the *Washington* v. *Davis* and *Personnel Administrator* v. *Feeny* decisions is to provide legislators and public personnel managers with more leeway in dealing with public employees and public employment. While purposeful invidious discrimination is likely to be found unconstitutional, practices that harm women, African Americans, Latinos, and other protected class persons as a by-product of their intended impacts can withstand constitutional scrutiny.

Perhaps of even greater significance, in *United States* v. *Paradise* (1987), the Supreme Court upheld the constitutionality of remedial affirmative action. Although the Court failed to formulate a majority opinion, the views of the justices voting in favor of affirmative action are very likely to frame future decisions in this area. The case involved a particularly egregious record of discrimination against African Americans by the Alabama Department of Public Safety. In 1972, a federal district court found that Alabama had acted unconstitutionally in excluding African Americans from its force of state troopers for almost four decades. It issued an order requiring the department to cease discriminating and to use a "quota" system to remedy the impact of past discrimination on the racial composition of the force. The court's order had some impact, but by 1979 there were still no African Americans in the department's upper ranks. The department then agreed to promote African Americans, but after two years elapsed, none had been advanced. After more legal wrangling, the court ordered that "for a period of time," at least 50 percent of those promoted to the rank of corporal be African American, if qualified African American candidates were available. It also imposed a 50 percent promotional requirement in the other upper ranks, but only on the conditions that (1) there were qualified African-American candidates, (2) in the ranks covered, less than 25 percent of the department's work force was African American, and (3) the department failed to establish a promotion plan for the rank involved that did not have an adverse impact on African Americans. After the department proceeded to promote eight African Americans and eight whites under the district court's order, the United States (in the incarnation of the solicitor general), appealed the district court's order on the grounds that it violated equal protection. The court of appeals upheld the district court, as did the Supreme Court on further appeal.

Justice Brennan announced the judgment of the High Court in an opinion joined by Justices Marshall, Blackmun, and Powell. Brennan reasoned that although "it is now well established that government bodies, including courts, may constitutionally employ racial classifications essential to remedy unlawful treatment of racial or ethnic groups subject to discrimination," two issues remained. First, was the district court's plan sufficiently "narrowly tailored" to pass constitutional muster? Brennan responded affirmatively because the plan was "temporary and flexible" and applied "only if qualified blacks are available, only if the Department has an objective need to make promotions, and only if the Department fails to implement a promotion procedure that does not have an adverse impact on blacks."

Second, was the district court's order realistically related to the percentage of African Americans in the relevant work force? Again Brennan responded affirmatively, thereby concluding that the plan met the test of narrow tailoring.

Justice Stevens concurred in the Court's judgment in an opinion that was even more strongly in favor of affirmative action. He thought that the record of discrimination was so overwhelming that the district court clearly had the authority to impose the remedy it chose and that it was unnecessary to be so concerned with narrow tailoring.

In a separate concurring opinion, providing very useful guidance to public personnelists, Justice Powell restated the main facets of narrow tailoring:

1. The efficacy of alternative remedies
2. The planned duration of the remedy
3. The relationship between the percentage of minority group members in the relevant population or work force
4. The availability of waiver provisions [for instance, is the plan waived if there are no qualified minority applicants?]
5. The effect of the remedy upon "innocent" third parties

The last aspect is especially important in affirmative action. Justice Powell wrote that "the effect of the order on innocent white troopers is likely to be relatively diffuse. Unlike layoff requirements, the promotion requirement at issue in this case does not 'impose the entire burden of achieving racial equality on particular individuals.'...Although some white troopers will have their promotions delayed, it is uncertain whether any individual trooper, white or black, would have achieved a different rank, or would have achieved it at a different time, but for the promotion requirement."

On the other hand, in *Wygant* v. *Jackson Board of Education* (1986), the U.S. Supreme Court found an affirmative action plan intended to maintain racial balance in the work force during periods of layoffs unconstitutional. Justice Powell, writing for the Court majority, said that the affirmative action plan imposed too great a burden on "innocent" individuals, "resulting in serious disruption of their lives."

Who Are the "Innocent" Individuals in Race and Gender Discrimination Cases?

Justice Stevens, writing the dissenting opinion in *Martin* v. *Wilks* (1989), said that the "white respondents in this case are not responsible for [the] history of discrimination [in this country], but they are nevertheless beneficiaries of the discriminatory practices that the litigation was designed to correct. Any remedy that seeks to create employment conditions that would have [been] obtained if there had been no violations of law will necessarily have an adverse impact on whites, who must now share their job and promotion opportunities with blacks. Just as white employees in the past were innocent beneficiaries of illegal discriminatory practices, so is it inevitable that some of the same white employees will be innocent victims who must share some of the burdens resulting from the redress of the past wrongs."

Four members of the Supreme Court dissented in *Paradise*, on a variety of grounds, including their belief that the plurality's view of narrow tailoring was "standardless." Based on all the opinions expressed in the case, it is likely that, at least in the near future, discussions of the constitutionality of affirmative action measures will be cast in terms of narrow tailoring. Presumably, in the process, the requirements of narrow tailoring will be more finely honed.

In passing, it should be noted that equal protection issues sometimes arise in the context of collective bargaining. For instance, an exclusively recognized bargaining agent (union) may be granted privileges, such as the use of a public agency's internal mailing system, that are withheld from other groups. Similarly, the public employer may agree to "checkoff" dues; that is, withhold money from employees' paychecks, for an exclusively recognized union but refuse to provide the same service for other groups. Although such practices create different statuses and privileges for groups, for the most part the courts have not found them in violation of the constitutional requirement of equal protection. Rather, the judiciary has tended to reason that there is a rational basis for matters associated with "exclusive recognition" because that status is fundamental to contemporary collective bargaining (see Chapters 10 and 11).

The Right to a Hearing

The Constitution protects citizens against governmental denial of "life, liberty, or property, without due process of law." A technical definition of *due process* is problematic, but generally it is taken to mean "fundamental fairness." In public personnel management the issues raised by the due process clause are (1) under what conditions does the Constitution require that adverse actions be accompanied by hearings? and (2) what protections must be afforded to public employees at such hearings?

Foley v. *Connelie* 435 U.S. 291 (1978)

Facts—The plaintiffs, in a class action, charged that a State statute which limited the appointment of state troopers to applicants who are U.S. citizens violated the Equal Protection Clause of the 14th amendment. A three judge District Court held that the statute was constitutional.

Issue—Can a State constitutionally limit its State Troopers to citizens?

Discussion—The Supreme Court held that citizenship may be a relevant qualification for fulfilling important nonelective positions held by officials who participate directly in the formulation, execution, or review of broad public policy. The Court held that a State need only show some rational relationship between the interest sought to be protected and the limiting classification. Inasmuch as police officers are clothed with authority to exercise an almost infinite variety of discretionary powers which can seriously affect individuals, citizenship bears a rational relationship to the demands of the particular position, and States may limit the performance of such responsibility to citizens.

U.S. Office of Personnel Management, *Equal Employment Opportunity Court Cases* (Washington, D.C.: U.S. Government Printing Office, September 1979), p. 37.

In *Board of Regents* v. *Roth* (1972), the Supreme Court established the principle that although there is no general constitutional right to a hearing, one might be constitutionally required in individual instances. This would be true under any one of four conditions:

1. Where the removal or nonrenewal was in retaliation for the exercise of constitutional rights such as freedom of speech or association
2. Where the adverse action impaired the individual's reputation
3. Perhaps not fully distinguishable from the above, where a dismissal or nonrenewal placed stigma or other disability upon the employee that foreclosed his or her freedom to take advantage of other employment opportunities
4. Where one had a property right or interest in the position, as in the case of tenured or contracted public employees

It is evident that this decision left about as many questions unanswered as resolved. While this may make for interesting law review articles, it leaves the public personnel manager in a difficult position. For instance, how is one to know what constitutes a charge that might seriously and adversely affect one's reputation or chances of earning a livelihood in a chosen occupational area? Such a question is inherently unanswerable under current constitutional ruling because it is only after a specific set of facts has been litigated that the practitioner can receive sufficient guidance to deal constitutionally with many situations. However, by then it may be too late, as the number of cases reaching the courts in this area tends to confirm. Thus far, for instance, it has been held that removals or nonrenewals for fraud, racism, lack of veracity, and, at least in connection with high-level urban employment, absenteeism and gross insubordination can violate the constitutional requirement of procedural due process in the absence of a hearing. It has also been strongly suggested that removal at an advanced age, except as part of a general retirement system, tends to preclude subsequent employment and therefore requires the application of due process. On the other hand, a charge of being "antiestablishment" has been found not to create a sufficient impairment of reputation so as to afford constitutional protection. For the public personnel manager, the point is not to ask whether these holdings are consistent or reasonable, but rather to be fully aware that an employee's right to procedural due process protections in adverse actions, where the reasons for the actions are supplied, must be evaluated on a multidimensional basis, including such factors as the nature of the charge, the type and level of the position, the age of the individual, and the employee's prospects for employment elsewhere. Under these circumstances, it is evident that each case is largely a separate one. The best rule for public personnel management would be either to (1) avoid giving reasons for adverse actions, insofar as possible, despite the obvious costs of such an approach in terms of employee morale and the possibilities for arbitrary decisions; (2) communicate the reason to the employee in strict privacy; or (3) hold a hearing in each and every case, whether required by statute and regardless of the expense involved.

The first two options were legitimized by the Supreme Court's decision in *Bishop* v. *Wood* (1976). It held that at least in the case of an employee *without* legal job protection, "in the absence of any claim that the public employer was motivated by a desire to curtail or penalize the exercise of an employee's constitutionally protected rights, we must presume that official action was regular and, if erroneous, can best be corrected in other ways. The Due Process Clause...is not a guarantee against incorrect or ill-advised personnel decisions." Furthermore, in *Codd* v. *Velger* (1977), the Supreme Court held that hearings need not be held in any event if the employee is not challenging "the substantial truth of the material" upon which a dismissal or other adverse action is based. Whatever the merits of this as constitutional law, its desirability as public personnel policy is questionable and consequently public personnel managers may opt to hold hearings even where they are not constitutionally required.

In *Cleveland Board of Education* v. *Loudermill* (1985), the Supreme Court *required* the third approach, that of holding a hearing, whenever the public employee had a property interest in his or her job. The property interest can be conferred by a statute or regulation prohibiting dismissal except for "cause." In the Court's words, "The essential requirements of due process...are notice and an opportunity to respond. The opportunity to present reasons, either in person or in writing, why proposed action should not be taken is a fundamental due process requirement.... The tenured public employee is entitled to oral or written notice of the charges against him, an explanation of the employer's evidence, and an opportunity to present his side of the story." In addition, such an employee will generally be entitled to a more elaborate posttermination hearing.

Sometimes a public employee will be dismissed or disciplined for a number of reasons, only some of which are constitutionally impermissible. For instance, an employee whose performance is poor enough to warrant dismissal may make some derogatory public comments about the agency for which he or she works. The comments may prompt dismissal proceedings, but they may also be constitutionally protected. Under the prevailing case, *Mt. Healthy City School District Board of Education* v. *Doyle* (1977), in such circumstances the governmental employer would have to show "by a preponderance of the evidence that it would have reached the same decision...even in the absence of the protected conduct." This rule fits the public service model well; on the one hand, public employees cannot immunize themselves from legitimate adverse actions by exercising constitutionally protected rights; while on the other, agencies must meet a heavy burden of persuasion when they take action against employees that might be in retaliation for the exercise of such rights.

Privacy

The constitutional privacy rights of public employees currently constitute an area of considerable interest. The Fourth and Fourteenth Amendments protect individuals against *unreasonable* governmental searches and seizures. In the course of a normal day's work, a supervisor might enter an employee's workspace to retrieve a file, manual, or similar item. The supervisor might take the item off the top of the employee's desk, perhaps from a desk drawer, or even from an open briefcase. But a supervisor might also look through an employee's desk, filing cabinet, or briefcase in search of evidence of poor performance, illegal activity, or controlled substances. How should the constitutional right to privacy be framed in the context of public employment? Here, too, the public service model provides for a balancing among the interests of the employee, the employer, and the public.

A divided Supreme Court wrestled with establishing such a balance in *O'Connor* v. *Ortega* (1987). The case involved the search of a doctor's office at a state hospital and the seizure of its contents, which included such personal items as a Valentine's card, a photograph, and a book of poetry sent to him by a former resident physician. Although all the members of the High Court agreed that public employees such as Dr. Ortega have rights under the Fourth Amendment that can restrain administrative searches in the workplace, they disagreed on the scope of these rights. The plurality opinion was written by Justice O'Connor and joined by Justices White and Powell, and Chief Justice Rehnquist. She reasoned that "individuals do not lose Fourth Amendment rights merely because they work for the government instead of a private employer." But the legitimacy of administrative searches depended on two factors. First is the threshold issue of whether or not the employee has a reasonable expectation of privacy in the circumstances involved. The issue of such an expectation, in turn, breaks down into two elements: (1) did the employee actually have an expectation of privacy, and (2) was it one that society was prepared to accept as reasonable? In O'Connor's view, "given the great variety of work environments in the public sector, the question of whether an employee has a reasonable expectation of privacy must be addressed on a case-by-case basis." Again, until the case law develops further, many personnelists will face a judgment call when trying to determine whether or not an employee has such an expectation.

Second, according to the plurality even if the employee did have such an expectation, an administrative search would be constitutionally permissible if the government could show that "both the inception and the scope of the intrusion ... [were] reasonable." Justice O'Connor argued that a reasonableness test was more appropriate than a requirement that the government have a warrant or probable cause.

Justice Blackmun dissented in an opinion joined by Justices Brennan, Marshall, and Stevens. They agreed that the further "development of a jurisprudence in this area might well require a case-by-case approach." However, the dissenters argued that the plurality was far too quick to substitute a reasonableness standard for that of warrants or probable cause.

Justice Scalia, by contrast, concurred, but agonized little over what standard should be employed: "searches to retrieve work-related materials or to investigate violations of workplace rules—searches of the sort that are regarded as reasonable and normal in the private-employer context—do not violate the Fourth Amendment."

Although the *O'Connor* case places a framework on thinking about public employees' constitutional rights to privacy in the workplace, it is neither definitive nor comprehensive. The courts have more recently been laboring over perhaps the major privacy issues in the public sector today—mandatory testing of public employees for drug use and AIDS.

To date, the leading Supreme Court decision on drug testing is *National Treasury Employees Union* v. *Von Raab* (1989). There, the Court upheld drug

Executive Order 12564 of September 15, 1986: Drug-free Federal Workplace

I, RONALD REAGAN, President of the United States of America, find that:

Drug use is having serious adverse effects upon a significant proportion of the national work force and results in billions of dollars of lost productivity each year;

The Federal government, as an employer, is concerned with the well-being of its employees, the successful accomplishment of agency missions, and the need to maintain employee productivity;

The Federal government, as the largest employer in the Nation, can and should show the way towards achieving drug-free workplaces through a program designed to offer drug users a helping hand and, at the same time, demonstrating to drug users and potential drug users that drugs will not be tolerated in the Federal workplace;

The profits from illegal drugs provide the single greatest source of income for organized crime, fuel violent street crime, and otherwise contribute to the breakdown of our society;

The use of illegal drugs, on or off duty, by Federal employees is inconsistent not only with the law-abiding behavior expected of all citizens, but also with the special trust placed in such employees as servants of the public;

Federal employees who use illegal drugs, on or off duty, tend to be less productive, less reliable, and prone to greater absenteeism than their fellow employees who do not use illegal drugs;

The use of illegal drugs, on or off duty, by Federal employees impairs the efficiency of Federal departments and agencies, undermines public confidence in them, and makes it more difficult for other employees who do not use illegal drugs to perform their jobs effectively. The use of illegal drugs, on or off duty, by Federal employees also can pose a serious health and safety threat to members of the public and to other Federal employees;

The use of illegal drugs, on or off duty, by Federal employees in certain positions evidences less than the complete reliability, stability, and good judgment that is consistent with access to sensitive information and creates the possibility of coercion, influence, and irresponsible action under pressure that may pose a serious risk to national security, the public safety, and the effective enforcement of the law; and

Federal employees who use illegal drugs must themselves be primarily responsible for changing their behavior and, if necessary, begin the process of rehabilitating themselves.

Federal Register, vol. 51, no. 180 (September 17, 1986).

testing in the Customs Service for those employees who both engage in drug interdiction and drug law enforcement and carry firearms. The majority noted that the process of drug testing infringed on the employee's privacy interests. (The employee was taken to a toilet in which the water had been dyed to prevent adulteration and required to provide a urine sample while a monitor

Cheating on Your Drug Test??

Byrd Laboratories of Austin, Texas is offering "100 percent pure urine samples" for $49.95 a bag. The firm also publishes a brochure entitled "Success in Urine Testing," which promises "passing" scores on corporate or government urine testing. The firm's most popular item today is "instant urine," since it has a longer shelf life than actual urine samples. Also coming soon, according to a company spokesperson, is freeze-dried urine.

Another option, of course, is Diet Mountain Dew soda, which has the exact same pH and density of urine!

Anne Laurent, "Texas Firm Offering 'Clean' Urine by the Bag," *Federal Times* (January 5, 1987), p. 11, and *Newsweek* (July 31, 1989), p. 5.

listened.) But the Court reasoned that due to the sensitive nature of their jobs, the employees had a diminished expectation of privacy, and that the tests were constitutionally permissible insofar as they were reasonable. A key point in the decision was that the tests were reasonable even though there was no suspicion that any individual employee had been using illegal drugs. In *Skinner* v. *Railway Labor Executives* (1989), the Court used similar logic in upholding drug testing for certain categories of railway workers.

The framework established in *Von Raab* relies heavily on the public service model's concern that the public be well served by the terms of the public employment relationship. There is a clear and strong public interest in assuring that customs agents charged with drug enforcement are not themselves users of illegal drugs. As *Skinner* suggests, workers upon whose performance the public's safety depends are another category of public employees who might constitutionally be subject to drug testing. But there are also millions of public employees whose functions are such that their performance poses no serious risk to public safety. As it stands today, the Fourth and Fourteenth Amendments protect such employees from drug tests. However, if there is a strong individualized suspicion that a particular employee is using illegal substances, the governmental employer may be able to require a drug test, regardless of the employee's position. And what makes this even more interesting is the low "hit rate" for federal employees tested for drug use (see Tables 9.1 and 9.2).

Perhaps the leading decision on the constitutionality of testing for the AIDS virus is *Glover* v. *Eastern Nebraska Community Office of Retardation* (1989). In this case, a state agency providing services to mentally retarded persons required any employee who has direct contact with agency clients

Table 9.1. Selected Hit Rates for Federal Civilian Drug Testing

		Period	Tests	Positives	Hit rates
1.	Department of Transportation	July 1988– Sept 1989	20,414	115	0.6%
2.	Drug Enforcement Administration	July 1988– Sept 1989	1,222	5	0.4%
3.	Depot System Command, Department of the Army	May 1986– Sept. 1989	13,861	110	0.8%
4.	Army Chemical and Nuclear Weapons Security Program	1988	7,680	44	0.6%
5.	U. S. Postal Service	Sept. 1987– May 1988	5,465	515	9.4%
6.	Department of Interior		2,800	13	0.5%
7.	Department of the Army	July 1988– Sept. 1988	3,938	28	0.7%
8.	Department of Housing and Urban Development	January– June 1990	134	0	0%
9.	National Aeronautics and Space Admin.	1990	120	2	1.7%
10.	Department of Commerce	1990	223	2	.8%
11	Department of Energy	1989–1990	602	1	.1%
12.	GSA	1989–1990	263	8	.3%
13.	HHS	1990	17	0	0%

Source: Adapted from Frank J. Thompson, Norma M. Riccucci, and Carolyn Ban, "Drug Testing in the Federal Workplace: Leadership by Example?" Conference paper, American Political Science Association, 1990. (Also see, Thompson, Riccucci and Ban, 1991.)

to undergo testing for AIDS and hepatitis B viruses. The agency justified such testing on the grounds that it sought to protect the safety of the developmentally disabled persons it served as well as all employees of the agency.

The U.S. Court of Appeals for the Eighth Circuit ruled that mandatory testing for AIDS and hepatitis B violated the employees' Fourth Amendment rights against unreasonable searches and seizures, because the agency's interest in protecting the safety of its clients did not outweigh the privacy

Table 9.2. Disposition of Employees Testing Positive for Drugs in Selected Agencies

Action	Department of Transportation July 1988 Sept. 1989 (N = 115)	Depot System Command, Army May 1986 Sept. 1989 (N = 110)	Drug Enforcement Administration July 1988– Sept. 1989 (N = 5)	Agencies combined (N = 230)
Exit				
Fired	18%	20%	100%	21%
Resigned or	(7)	(6)	(20)	(7)
Retired	(11)	(14)	(80)	(14)
In rehabilitation	11	8		10
Completed rehabilitation	70	41		55
Permanently reassigned or demoted to non-testing designated position	0	31		15

Source: U.S. General Accounting Office (GAO), *Action By Certain Agencies When Employees Test Positive for Illegal Drugs* (Washington: GAO/GGD-90-565S, 1990). This table adapted from Frank J. Thompson, Norma M. Riccucci, and Carolyn Ban, "Drug Testing in the Federal Workplace: Leadership by Example?" Conference paper, American Political Science Association, 1990.

Who Should Be Tested for Drug Use?

Former Attorney General Edwin Meese sought to justify testing virtually all employees in the U.S. Department of Justice. The followint positions were designated for testing:

- " 'Space Management Specialist' because 'unwise space usage determination' could result in the rental of excess office space;

- 'Administrative Assistant' because of the threat of 'improper inventory control';

- 'Secretary' in the procurement office because of the possibility of 'inappropriate contract awards';

- 'Mail Clerk' in the legislative affairs office because of the potential to 'jeopardize important legislative priorities';

- 'Secretary/Stenographer' in the Anti-trust Division because the ultimate result of drug use would be higher prices, lower quality of goods and services, and decreased competitiveness for American business in world markets."

Here are other positions designated for testing by a number of federal agencies:

- "In the Department of Health and Human Services, 'Economist,' 'Management Analyst,' 'Accountant,' and 'Actuary' positions...because there *might* be 'inaccurate analysis of complex technical information,' and employees in these positions could give bad 'advice to policymakers';

- the Department of Interior designated 'Secretary/Typist' positions for drug testing in instances where the employee is responsible for *typing* the personal disclosure forms of agency administrators because 'serious financial hardships for a top-level Department official could result from an improper decision of divestiture';

- the 'Public Affairs Specialist' [in the Interior Department] is also to be tested because employees 'are in a position to substantially influence national news stories and could advance ideas in contradiction of the Administration's positions!' "

Committee on Post Office and Civil Service, U.S. House of Representatives, *Oversight Hearing on Administration Plans to Drug Test Federal Work Force* (June 16, 1988), pp. 99–101.

rights of its employees. The court said that the agency's "articulated interest in requiring testing does not constitutionally justify requiring employees to submit to a test for the purpose of protecting the clients from an infected employee."

Also important to the court in *Glover* was the potential for disease transmission. Here, the court said that "the risk of transmission of the AIDS virus from staff to client, assuming a staff member is infected with [the AIDS virus] ... is extremely low, approaching zero. The medical evidence is undisputed that the disease is not contracted by casual contact. The risk of transmission of the disease to clients as a result of a client biting or scratching a staff member, and potentially drawing blood, is extraordinarily low, also approaching zero."

The U.S. Supreme Court declined to review *Glover* and so the decision of the appeals court will remain intact for the time being (see Chapter 7 for a discussion of employment discrimination under statutory law due to AIDS).

Finally, the courts may be more lenient with preemployment drug and AIDS testing, as well as other routine medical screening, providing that the procedures involved in the collection of urine or blood samples are not overly obtrusive. In *Fowler* v. *New York City Department of Sanitation* (1989), the federal district court reasoned that preemployment physical examinations, including urinalysis are "simply too familiar a feature of the job market on all levels to permit anyone to claim an objectively based expectation of privacy in what such analysis might disclose." It is important to remember, though, that these cases address administrative searches and concerns, not law enforcement efforts to apprehend those engaged in criminal conduct. In the latter situation, warrants or probable cause, rather than reasonableness, are required.

The Right to Disobey

Among the constitutional rights now held by public employees is a right to refuse to engage in an unconstitutional act. This nascent right grows out of the liability that public servants may face if they violate the constitutional rights of individuals upon whom they act in their official capacities, including their subordinates. In *Harley* v. *Schuylkill County* (1979), a federal district court confronted the situation of a prison guard who was dismissed because he refused to take an action that would have violated an inmate's Eighth Amendment rights, which prohibit cruel and unusual punishment. After noting that the guard "would have been liable for a deprivation of [the inmate's] constitutional rights if he had proceeded to obey the order given to him," the judge reasoned that "the *duty* to refrain from acting in a manner which would deprive another of constitutional rights is a duty created and imposed by the constitution itself. It is logical to believe that the concurrent right [to refuse to act unconstitutionally] is also one which is created and secured by the constitution. Therefore, we hold that the right to refuse to perform an unconstitutional act is a right 'secured by the Constitution...'"

It is unlikely that many public administrators will face situations in which asserting a constitutional right to disobey will be appropriate. However, successfully refusing to disobey may require that the employee (1) sincerely believe that the order is unconstitutional, and (2) be correct in claiming that the proposed action is, in fact, unconstitutional.

Ramifications

As a result of shifting judicial approaches, the public employment relationship now has a substantial component that is determined by constitutional law. Having moved from the private sector model through the individual rights model, the judiciary is currently guided by the public service model of how the Constitution should be applied in the context of public employment. Today, the courts seek to balance the interests of the employee, the governmental employer, and the public in reaching their decisions. It is this approach that enables the Supreme Court to allow the restriction of public employees' First Amendment rights in the context of regulations for partisan political neutrality, while also protecting these same rights in connection with patronage dismissals. In the Court's view, evidently, political neutrality contributes to the proper functioning of the public service, whereas patronage dismissals detract from it. In the same vein, the Court has broadly protected public employees' speech on matters of public concern, in large part because their remarks can help to inform the public about the operation of the government.

The public service model has important ramifications for public personnel management. First, it requires that public personnelists and supervisors understand the constitutional rights of public employees. This can be difficult because the extent of their rights often depends on an elaborate balancing of several factors, as illustrated by the *Rankin* v. *McPherson* case. The public personnelist or other administrator who lacks reasonable knowledge of employees' constitutional rights runs the risk of being held personally liable for violations of those rights.

Second, public personnel administration has been deeply affected by the expansion of public employees' constitutional rights. For instance, some degree of due process is now routinely incorporated into adverse action procedures. No personnelist can rationally contemplate instituting a drug testing program without consulting the constitutional law. The same is true in assessing whether or not the private conduct of an employee or applicant can be made the basis for a discharge, denial of employment, or other adverse action. Third, public personnel administration has become judicialized to an extent. Hearings are now routine in the dismissal of employees having a property interest in their jobs. They are also required by the *Chicago Teachers Union* case in resolving disputes over agency shop or fair share fees. Fourth, in some areas, public personnel concepts have been essentially disregarded by the judiciary. For example, in the *Elrod* case, the distinction between employees being under the merit system or outside it carried no weight. Finally, and fully evident, public personnel administration has become much more complicated as it has been infused with constitutional concerns.

One of the perplexing aspects of the constitutional component of the public employment relationship is how frequently courts and judges are divided over the outcome of cases. In some cases reviewed in this chapter, the Supreme Court was divided 5 to 4; in others, it could reach a judgment, but not a majority opinion. Such narrow margins suggest that changes are likely and that personnelists should be on the lookout for them. Regardless of the overall trends during the 1990s, however, personnelists will have to respond to the opportunities and challenges presented by developments in the constitutional component of the public employment relationship.

Bibliography

Goldman, Deborah D. "Due Process and Public Personnel Management," *Review of Public Personnel Administration*, 2 (Fall 1981).

Harvard Law Review. "Developments in the Law—Public Employment," vol 97 (May 1984), pp.1611–1800. (Authors not identified.)

Riccucci, Norma M. "Drug Testing in the Public Sector: A Legal Analysis," *The American Review of Public Administration*, (June 1990).

Roberts, Robert N. and Marion T. Doss, "The Constitutional Privacy Rights of Public Employees," *International Journal of Public Administration*, 14 (May 1991).

Rosenbloom, David H. *Federal Service and the Constitution*. Ithaca, N.Y.: Cornell University Press, 1971.

_____. "Constitutional Law and Public Personnel in the 1980s," *Review of Public Personnel Administration*, 8 (Spring 1988).

_____ and James D. Carroll, *Toward Constitutional Competence: A Casebook for Public Administrators*. Englewood Cliffs, N.J.: Prentice Hall, 1990.

Thompson, Frank J., Norma M. Riccucci, and Carolyn Ban, "Biological Testing and Personnel Policy: Drugs and the Federal Workplace," in Carolyn Ban and Norma M. Riccucci (eds.), *Public Personnel Management: Current Concerns, Future Challenges*. White Plains, N.Y.: Longman Press, 1991.

_____. "Drug Testing in the Federal Workplace: An Instrumental and Symbolic Assessment," *Public Administration Review*, 51 (November/December 1991).

Vaughn, Robert G. "Public Employees and the Right to Disobey," *Hastings Law Journal*, 29 (November 1977).

Cases

Abood v. *Detroit Board of Education*, 430 U.S. 209 (1977).

AFSCME v. *Woodward*, 406 F.2d. 137 (1969).

Bishop v. *Wood*, 426 U.S. 341 (1976).

Board of Regents v. *Roth*, 408 U.S. 564 (1972).

Branti v. *Finkel*, 445 U.S. 506 (1980).

Broadrick v. *Oklahoma*, 413 U.S. 601 (1973).

Chicago Teachers Union v. *Hudson*, 475 U.S. 292 (1986).

Civil Service Commission v. *NALC*, 413 U.S. 548 (1973).

Cleveland Board of Education v. *La Fleur*, 414 U.S. 632 (1974).

Cleveland Board of Education v. *Loudermill*, 470 U.S. 532 (1985).

Codd v. *Velger*, 429 U.S. 624 (1977).

Cohen v. *Chesterfield County School Board*, 414 U.S. 632 (1974).

Elrod v. *Burns*, 427 U.S. 347 (1976).

Fowler v. *New York City Department of Sanitation*, 704 F. Supp. 1264 (1989).

Fraternal Order of Police v. *City of Philadelphia*, 812 F.2d. 105 (1987).

Glover v. *Eastern Nebraska Community Office of Retardation*, 867 F. 2d. 461 (8th Cir. 1989), *cert. denied*, 110 S.Ct. 321 (1989).

Harley v. *Schuylkill County*, 476 F. Supp. 191 (1979).

Kelley v. *Johnson*, 425 U.S. 238 (1976).

Martin v. *Wilks*, 490 U.S. 755 (1989).

McAuliffe v. *New Bedford*, 155 Mass. 216 (1982).

McCarthy v. *Philadelphia CSC*, 424 U.S. 645 (1976).

Mt. Healthy City School District Bd. of Education v. *Doyle*, 429 U.S. 274 (1977).

NALC v. *CSC*, 346 F. Supp. 578 (1972).

National Treasury Employees Union v. *Von Raab*, 489 U.S. 656 (1989).

O'Connor v. *Ortega*, 480 U.S. 709 (1987).

Personnel Administrator v. *Feeney*, 422 U.S. 256 (1979).

Pickering v. *Board of Education*, 391 U.S. 563 (1968).

Rankin v. *McPherson*, 483 U.S. 378(1987).

Rutan v. *Republican Party of Illinois*, 497 U.S. ____; 110 S.Ct.2729 (1990).

Shelton v. *Tucker*, 364 U.S. 479 (1960).

Skinner v. *Railway Labor Executives Association*, 489 U.S. 602 (1989).

Snepp v. *U.S.*, 444 U.S. 507 (1980).

Sugarman v. *Dougall*, 413 U.S. 634 (1973).

Thorne v. *City of El Segundo*, 726 F. 2d. 459 (1983).

United Public Workers v. *Mitchell*, 330 U.S. 75 (1947).

United States v. *Paradise*, 480 U.S. 149 (1987).

Washington v. *Davis*, 426 U.S. 229 (1976).

Wygant v. *Jackson Bd. of Education*, 476 U.S. 267 (1986).

Part **IV**
PUBLIC SECTOR
LABOR RELATIONS

10
Labor Relations: Development and Scope

Prologue: The Boston Police Strike

On the afternoon of September 9, 1919, most of Boston's patrol officers turned in their badges and went on strike. Although there were many grievances, the major issue immediately involved was the right of the police to form a union and to affiliate with the American Federation of Labor (AFL). Should the police be allowed to form a union, engage in collective bargaining, strike? Would such activity be in the public interest? Would it pose a threat to the public order and democracy? Although the ensuing three-day strike did little to answer these questions, it shocked the nation's conscience and transformed a laconic, almost invisible state governor into a national hero.

The drive for unionization and collective bargaining had been spurred by the reprehensible conditions under which the patrol officers had to work. Their starting salary was $1,000, of which some $200 went for equipment and uniforms. Annual increases were $100 to a maximum salary of $1,600. In May 1919 the city had authorized the first pay raise in six years, $200 for all patrol officers. This increase was far outweighed by the skyrocketing cost of living, which had gone up 86 percent during the period. The patrol officers averaged an 87-hour work week and had to put up with outrageous working conditions. The patrol officers' wives constantly complained of the cockroaches which accompanied their husbands home and shared their clothing. Vermin-eaten helmets were also a source of displeasure. Although there was a civil service system, the police commissioner, a gubernatorial appointee, was not required to promote on the basis of promotion lists. Thus, a patrol officer could rank at the top of the eligible list and remain there, despite

319

openings, until retirement. Personal acceptability to the commissioner was the key to success.

Once the strike began, politics came to the fore. Boston's mayor, a "good-government" Democrat, sought to work out a compromise despite his opposition to the union. The police commissioner, a gubernatorial appointee, was adamant in his desire to break the union. The Republican governor of Massachusetts, Calvin Coolidge, preferring inaction, did little until the strike's final day. The evidence suggests that all three sought some political advantage from the situation, and one, of course, won the whole show.

Despite the efforts of some police officers and volunteers to maintain order, Boston reverted to a Hobbesian state of nature. Criminals of all persuasions flocked to the city and joined Boston's home-grown hoodlums in sacking it. Van after van was filled with stolen bounty. When lawlessness and mob rule gained the upper hand, the mayor exercised authority, on the basis of two old state statutes, to wrest control of the police from the commissioner and to call upon men from the State Guard. He further requested not less than "three regiments of infantry fully equipped for field service" from the governor. Coolidge responded by sending the entire State Guard and by putting himself in control of these troops as well as the police department. By September 11, some 7,000 guards were patrolling Boston's streets, the strikers were summarily discharged, and order was more or less restored.

It was at this moment that Coolidge, whose luck was legendary, received the political break of his life. Samual Gompers, head of the AFL, unwittingly provided the opening that ultimately made Coolidge the thirtieth president of the United States. Gompers protested the police commissioner's refusal to allow the union to affiliate. As the nation watched, Coolidge responded with his famous assertion that "there is no right to strike against the public safety by anybody, anywhere, anytime." With those words, Coolidge, an unimpressive cold, and "sourish" man, captured the public's imagination. Amid civic disintegration and chaos appeared a commonsensical Yankee who knew what was right and what was wrong and was willing to take a forceful stand against elements that seemed threatening to the nation. The tidal wave of support for Coolidge among the press and public swept him into the vice-presidential slot on the 1920 Republican ticket. When Harding died in 1923, he became president.

The Boston police strike in 1919 was the nation's first genuine taste of a municipal labor problem. Although many years elapsed between the strike and the emergence of the present period of permanent crisis in public sector labor relations, the basic problems involved are essentially the same and remain without substantial resolution. In the past two and a half decades, governments have sought to come to grips with the public sector labor relations problem by creating a legal basis for collectively bargaining with public employees.

Overview

During the past quarter century, collective bargaining has emerged as a fundamental feature of public personnel administration. A process that was once considered antithetical to the constitutional principles of the United States and likely to lead to chaos and anarchy has become part and parcel of day-to-day personnel management in the public sector. Matters that were once left to managers' discretion and considered appropriate for scientific study, such as position classification and pay, are now regularly negotiated through collective bargaining in many jurisdictions. The exercise of authority in the workplace, once thought to be a managerial prerogative, is now commonly constrained by labor contracts and negotiated procedures for resolving workers' complaints or grievances. It is fair to say that collective bargaining has revolutionized many aspects of public personnel management. But as in the case of many developments of this magnitude, its impact has varied from place to place. Moreover, the specifics of collective bargaining processes vary widely among different jurisdictions in the United States. There is not even a singular collective bargaining format at the federal level. These facts make it difficult to gain a solid understanding of public sector collective bargaining. Case studies of individual bargaining instances abound, as do more systematic analyses of the general processes and broad impacts of collective bargaining procedures. Yet, overall, relatively little attention has been devoted to developing a theoretical overview of public sector collective bargaining that will facilitate understanding its evolution and problematic aspects in a more comprehensive, systematic, and complete fashion. We will attempt to present such an overview in the next few pages in the hope that it will aid students and public personnelists in organizing their thoughts on the vast array of activity that goes under the label of public sector labor relations. Specifically, the theoretical overview developed here rests on the observations that (1) society has sought to use the prevailing private sector collective bargaining model in the public sector; (2) it is widely believed that the private sector model does not fit perfectly in the public sector; (3) consequently, adjustments have been made to make the model comport better with conditions in the public sector; (4) these adjustments tend to reduce the coherence and systematic character of the collective bargaining model; (5) as a result, the practice of collective bargaining in the public sector is still characterized by a number of dysfunctions that frequently place labor relations in a state of crisis.

The Private Sector Model

In the United States, the origins of collective bargaining in the private sector can be traced back at least as far as the 1790s. Throughout the nineteenth century, labor organizations experimented with a number of approaches, including local unions, national unions, and craft unions. These were the forerunners of modern industrial unions, welfare unionism (i.e., concern for workers' economic *and* social welfare), business unionism (i.e., concern for workers' compensation and working conditions only), and the development of labor-oriented political parties and social movements. Society, too, experimented with a number of responses to these developments, including (1) outlawing all combinations of workers as illegal conspiracies; (2) using injunctions to break unions, prohibit their concerted activities, and imprison their leadership; and (3) eventually abandoning both these approaches in favor of a federally-mandated general model of collective bargaining in private employment affecting interstate commerce.

The latter model was codified in a number of statutes. These provided an explicit legal framework for the private sector collective bargaining model that had evolved through long experiences and countless negotiations and confrontations. Their main contribution to public policy was specifically to delineate the boundaries of the model that had evolved, specifying the rights of labor and management, indicating the practices that would be considered unfair and/or illegal, and creating an administrative agency (the National Labor Relations Board) to oversee the operation of the model, adjudicate disputes pertaining to it, and make rules to clarify its content. Insofar as these statutes changed the model that had developed, they did so by outlawing certain common practices, such as the closed shop and some types of picketing and boycotting, and by seeking to assure that labor unions were democratically organized and free of corruption. The model ratified and clarified by these statutes is exceedingly complex in some of its attributes, and its rules often have no parallel in the public sector. For instance, the rights of those engaging in concerted activity often depend upon whether their motivation is recognitional, economic, to insure safety, or to protest unfair practices. Handbilling is treated differently from picketing, and the latter's legality may depend on the extent to which an advocated boycott is of a product that is one of many being offered for sale or is merged with other products in a fashion that makes their sale impossible without it.

Despite its complexity, however, the private sector model contains only a few fundamental assumptions that are critical to its operation, but are either absent from the public sector or must be seriously modified when applied to government employment. These are as follows:

1. The parties to collective bargaining are legally coequal. Their respective rights are delineated by collective bargaining statutes. Neither party can unilaterally alter the content of these statutes or abrogate the legal rights of the other.
2. In bargaining, the parties are likely to be constrained by market forces. Labor will not demand an economic package that will make the employer

The Language of Labor Relations

Agency Shop—A provision of a collective agreement stating that nonmembers of an organization employed in the bargaining unit must pay the employee organization a sum for its representational services as a condition of continuing employment. The agency shop was designed as a compromise between the employee organization's desire to eliminate the "free rider" by means of compulsory membership, and management's desire to make employee organization membership voluntary.

American Federation of Labor-Congress of Industrial Organizations (AFL-CIO)—A federation of craft and industrial unions, as well as unions of a mixed structure. Created in 1955 by the merger of the AFL and the CIO, the AFL-CIO is not in itself a bargaining agent. Its primary functions are education, lobbying, and providing aid to unions in the organizing process.

Arbitrator—An impartial third party to whom disputing parties submit their differences for decision (award). An ad hoc arbitrator is one selected to act in a specific case or a limited group of cases. A permanent arbitrator is one selected to serve for the life of an agreement or a stipulated term, hearing all disputes that arise during this period.

Authorization card—A statement signed by an employee authorizing an organization to act as her representative in dealings with the employer, or authorizing the employer to deduct organization dues from her pay (checkoff).

Award—In labor-management arbitration, the final decision of an arbitrator, sometimes binding on both parties to the dispute.

Bargaining agent—An employee organization that is the exclusive representative of all workers, both members and nonmembers of the organizations within a bargaining unit.

Bargaining unit—A group, class, or category of employees that has been determined by the employer as appropriate to be represented by an employee organization for purposes of collective bargaining.

Certification—Determination by the National Labor Relations Board (NLRB), Public Employment Relations Board (PERB), or an independent impartial agency that a particular employee organization is the majority choice, and hence the exclusive bargaining agent, of all employees in a particular unit.

Checkoff—A deduction of union or other employee organization dues, assessments, and initiation fees from the pay of all members by the employer (for which the employee must give written permission).

Contract bar—A denial of a request for a representation election, based on the existence of a collective agreement.

Decertification—Withdrawal by an appropriate agency of an organization's official recognition as exclusive negotiating representative.

(continued)

The Language of Labor Relations *(continued)*

Escalator clause—A collectively bargained contract clause that ties wage rates to the cost of living during the period of an agreement so that wages fluctuate with the cost of living. Escalator clauses are designed to keep real wages reasonably stable during the term of the contract.

Exclusive negotiating rights—The right and obligation of an employee organization designated as majority representative to negotiate collectively for all employees, including nonmembers, in the negotiating unit.

Fact-finding—Investigation of a labor-management dispute by an individual, a board or a panel, usually appointed by a PERB. Fact finders sometimes issue reports that describe the issues in the dispute and frequently make recommendations for their solution.

Featherbedding—Practices, usually by employee organizations, such as demanding payment for work not performed, refusing to allow adoption of laborsaving equipment, and creating nonessential jobs.

Free rider—A union term describing a person who is working in a bargaining unit and is eligible for union membership, but does not join the employee organization.

Grievance—A statement of dissatisfaction, usually by an individual, but sometimes by the employee organization or management, concerning interpretation of a collective bargaining agreement or traditional work practices. The grievance machinery (i.e., the method of dealing with individual grievances) is nearly always spelled out in the employee organization contract.

Injunction—A court order restraining individuals or groups from committing acts that the court determines will do irreparable harm. There are two types of injunctions: temporary restraining orders, issued for a limited time and prior to a complete hearing; and permanent injunctions, issued after a full hearing, in force until such time as the conditions that gave rise to their issuance have been changed.

Joint bargaining—Process in which two or more unions join forces in negotiating an agreement with a single employer.

Lockout—A suspension of work initiated by the employer as the result of a labor dispute. The antithesis of a strike, which is initiated by the workers. Used primarily to avert a threatened strike.

Management prerogatives—Rights that management feel are exclusively theirs and hence not subject to collective negotiations. These rights are often expressly reserved to management in the collective negotiations agreement.

Mediating—Usually used interchangeably with conciliation to mean an attempt by a third party to bring together the parties to a dispute. The mediator has no power to force a settlement, but sometimes suggests compromise solutions. Not to be confused with arbitration.

(continued)

The Language of Labor Relations *(continued)*

Multiemployer bargaining—Collective bargaining covering more than one company in a given industry, or more than one employer in a given area. For example, "metropolitanwide" collective bargaining for police, firefighters, and other municipal workers might be more efficient than collective bargaining for each group of workers by jurisdiction.

No-strike and no-lockout clause—Provision in a collective agreement in which the employee organization agrees not to strike and the employer agrees not to lock out for the duration of the contract.

Open shop—Those establishments in which there is no employee organization. Also sometimes applied to places of work in which there is an employee organization, but where employee organization membership is not a condition of employment or of continuing employment.

Picketing—Publicizing, by demonstrating near the location of the dispute, the existence of a labor dispute. Also an attempt to persuade workers to join a work stoppage, or to discourage customers from patronizing a business establishment, or both.

Ratification—Formal approval of a newly negotiated agreement by vote of the organization members affected.

Scab—A union term for a worker who refuses to go out on strike with his or her co-workers. Also a worker who is hired to replace a striking worker.

Scope of bargaining—The actual issues negotiated by labor and management at the bargaining table. *Mandatory* issues are those that must be bargained over by law. *Nonmandatory* or permissive issues are those which are bargained over on a voluntary basis, if management agrees (these are "management prerogatives"). *Prohibited* issues are those which may not be bargained over by law.

Shop steward (union steward, building representative)—Employee organization representative of a group of workers who carries out organization duties at the employment site (e.g., handles grievances, collects dues, recruits new members). Elected by organization members in the plant, office, or schools, or appointed by higher organization officials. The shop steward usually continues to work at her regular job, and handles employee organization duties only on a part-time basis.

Slowdown—A deliberate reduction of output on the part of the workers in an attempt to win concessions from the employer.

Strike—A work stoppage in a plant, government, or industry for the purpose of gaining concessions from the employer. There are several types: a general strike, a strike by all or most organized workers in a given community; wildcat strike, a spontaneously organized strike, triggered by an "incident" on the job and usually of short duration; a sympathy strike, a strike by workers not directly involved in a labor dispute in an attempt to show labor solidarity and bring pressure on an employer in a labor dispute.

(continued)

The Language of Labor Relations *(continued)*

Unfair labor practice—A practice on the part of either union or management that violates provisions of national or state labor relations acts.

Union shop—Provision in a collective agreement that requires all employees to become members of the union within a specified time after hiring (typically 30 days) or after a new provision is negotiated, and to remain members of the union as condition of continued employment.

Vesting rights (vesting, vested rights)—Applicable to many pensions or retirement plans; refers to the pension rights that permit employees to terminate employment before attaining retirement age, but without forfeiting accrued pension rights financed through employer contributions.

Whipsawing—The tactics of negotiating with one employer at a time, using each negotiated gain as a lever against the next employer.

Work stoppage—A temporary halt to work initiated by workers or employer, in the form of a strike or lockout. This term was adopted by the Bureau of Labor Statistics to replace "strikes and lockouts." The terminology arose largely from the inability of the Bureau of Labor Statistics (and, often, the parties) to distinguish between strikes and lockouts since the initiating party is not always evident.

Work to rule—A type of slowdown in which workers perform only those activities or duties specified in their job descriptions. Employees will also follow procedures "to the letter," further contributing to the slowdown. By adhering to formal job descriptions and complying with organizational rules and regulations, employees cannot be disciplined.

Zipper clause—A clause incorporated in a negotiations document to ensure that negotiations will not be reopened for a specific period of time, such as a one- or two-year period.

Adapted from *A Glossary of Terms: Collective Negotiations in Education*. (The University at Albany, State University of New York and the New York State Education Department, Albany, NY: 1968).

uncompetitive with other firms, at least in the short run. Management faces a labor market that prevents it from paying wages that are uncompetitive with other employers in the same market.

3. Economic issues are "distributive," i.e., in view of market forces, a gain for one side—labor or management—necessarily means less for the other. Management and labor are both paid out of a firm's earnings from the sale of a service, product, or natural resource; the economic contest between them is partly over the distribution of those earnings after other costs have been paid.

4. Economic contests can appropriately be settled by strikes and/or lockouts.

Although this model clearly does not fit the public sector perfectly, it has been relied upon primarily because it is a form of labor relations with which the society, labor leaders, lawyers, industrial relations experts, judges, and politicians are very familiar. When public employees demanded the opportunity to engage in collective bargaining and governments began to grant it to them, it was natural for both to think in terms of the private sector model. However, several modifications of its assumptions were generally adopted.

Modifications for the Public Sector

For most of the period during which the private sector model was evolving, there was nearly universal agreement that collective bargaining was inappropriate for the public sector. For the most part, until the 1960s and 1970s, governments and their component units simply refused to engage in collective bargaining with their employees. Those that did recognize unions or employee associations sometimes sought to engage in a "meet and confer"approach that allows employees to voice requests but does not provide a format for actual collective bargaining. Yet, labor's drive for full collective bargaining rights in the public sector rendered the earlier approaches politically and organizationally untenable. Public employees were a rapidly growing segment of the economy. They had the constitutional right to organize; once they did so, they wanted to assert their power through collective bargaining—and they were able to lobby and employ concerted action, such as picketing and strikes, in order to achieve this objective. The traditional opposition to public sector collective bargaining was overwhelmed by events. Nevertheless, doubts about the appropriateness of collective bargaining in the public sector were expressed in a number of ways that violated the premises of the private sector model:

1. Public sector collective bargaining regulations do not treat the parties as coequal. The government, that is, one of the parties, *establishes the process*, the rights of the other party, and the scope of bargaining (i.e., what can and cannot be legally bargained over). Management rights, that is, the government's own rights, are often put forth in expansive terms. The designation of matters that are "fit for negotiation" and the definition of what can be submitted to arbitration, if anything, are often exceedingly narrow. For instance, for most of the federal government service, items on which bargaining is prohibited include wages, hours, agencies' missions, budgets, organization; their right to hire, assign, direct, lay off, retain, suspend, remove, demote, or discipline employees; agencies' right to assign work, contract out, and fill positions; and their right to take action in emergencies. Although it is an old-fashioned term, in essence the relatively narrow scope of bargaining

found in many public sector jurisdictions is an outgrowth of the concept of governmental "sovereignty." Sovereignty, in turn, is a reflection of the fundamental legal inequality of the parties. (The concept of sovereignty will be further addressed later in this chapter.) The government is hardly a neutral third party to its own negotiating process.

2.   The market is a more remote constraint on public sector collective bargaining. Government revenues are raised primarily through taxation and the provision of monopoly services for user fees. The demand for their services may not fluctuate much. A government whose taxes are too high and services too sparse or poorly performed may become uncompetitive with neighboring jurisdictions. Some of its residents and potential new residents may move to these jurisdictions. Nevertheless, unlike the private sector firm, the uncompetitive government is not likely to disappear. Some of its services may be stopped, others may be curtailed, but its essential functions are likely to be maintained on at least a minimal level. Nor can the "uncompetitive" government move to another region or country in search of lower labor costs. Labor's demands for compensation are consequently muted most when a government is on the verge of bankruptcy—but this is a very high price to pay for effective labor relations. Governments may respond to this situation through residency requirements that impede labor mobility and tie the welfare of public employees to the jurisdictions for which they work.

3.   Economic issues are not truly distributive, at least among the parties to the collective bargaining negotiations. If rank-and-file workers are paid more, it does not mean that public managers and political officials will necessarily be paid relatively less. Indeed, they may be paid *more* in order to maintain the status imputed by traditional pay ratios. Since those signing labor agreements on behalf of the public employer are dealing with "other people's money" (the taxpayer's), the economic relationship of the parties to the bargaining does not have the same direct adversary quality as is typically found in the private sector.

4.   The nature of government services and the sources of its revenues are such that the society finds it desirable to prohibit strikes and lockouts as a means of resolving impasses. The majority of states prohibit strikes altogether; several allow the strike, but only under certain conditions, and generally not when a governmental body determines that it threatens the public health, safety, or welfare (see Chapter 11). The strike, of course, is an integral and essential aspect of the private sector model. Its absence makes it difficult for public employees to levy severe sanctions on management. Consequently, public managers may fail to take labor's demands seriously and unionized public employees may work for extended periods without a current contract—a situation that is extremely rare in the private sector.

Department of Treasury, IRS v. Federal Labor Relations Authority,
110 S. Ct. 1623 (1990)

Facts—During a round of contract negotiations with the Internal Revenue Service
(IRS), the National Treasury Employees Union (NTEU) proposed that if employees
wished to raise objections to the contracting out of work by the IRS, they could do
so through the grievance and arbitration provisions of the negotiated contract. The
IRS refused to bargain over the proposal on the grounds that it was not negotiable
under Title VII of the Civil Service Reform Act of 1978. The NTEU challenged
the IRS before the Federal Labor Relations Authority (FLRA), which ruled that the
IRS was required to negotiate over the proposal.

Issue—Are federal agencies required to bargain over proposals that could directly
or indirectly affect their ability to contract government work out to the private sector (a practice often referred to as privatization)?

Decision—The U.S. Supreme Court ruled against the FLRA (and, hence, the union).
Referring to section 7016 of the Civil Service Reform Act of 1978 (which defines
"management rights"), the Court said that "nothing in the entire Act ... shall affect
the authority of agency officials to make contracting out determinations."

Adjusting the Model

The modification of the fundamental assumptions of the private sector model
upon its transfer to the public sector promotes certain changes. Many of these,
including procedures for unit determination, recognition, certification, contract and election bars, the union shop, and administrative oversight of the
collective bargaining process are important (and will be discussed at a later
point); but they are not critical to the operation of the collective bargaining
model. Three, however, have a very fundamental impact on how public sector collective bargaining operates differently from private sector practices.
One is the fragmented character of the public employer. It is often characterized
by a separation of powers that requires labor to present its demands to different
units of government. Compensation may require legislative approval; the
judiciary is involved in the definition of public employees' rights and
obligations and in the determination of which issues are arbitral; the executive
is responsible for day-to-day personnel matters, including job design, position classification, assignment, promotion, and adverse actions. Even where
bargaining is with a unified employer, such as a special district or school
board, the public, as taxpayers, as consumers of a service, and as the electorate, is often deeply involved. Although it may be extending the concept
of fragmented or "multilateral" employer too far, the electorate is clearly

perceived by elective political authorities as a direct participant in government. Private firms also pay attention to their customers, of course, but their executives cannot be appointed or recalled by them.

Second, the absence of the right to strike or its highly regulated character requires that the public sector develop substitute procedures for resolving intractable disagreements (i.e., "impasses"). To date, a host of mechanisms have been tried, including mediation; fact-finding, with or without recommendation; interest arbitration, be it voluntary, compulsory, binding, or nonbinding; final offer of the whole package or issue-by-issue varieties or with the option of making the award on the basis of the fact finder's report; mediation-arbitration; and superconciliation. These approaches are discussed in the next chapter, but the main point here is that several of them have no parallel in the private sector.

Third, the relatively limited scope of bargaining found in the federal government and in some state and local jurisdictions forces unionized employees to seek elsewhere what cannot be discussed at the negotiating table. Hence, public sector unions often concentrate a good deal of their efforts on lobbying and electoral politics. Unions representing private employees also engage in these political activities. However, in many municipalities, public sector unions are such a major force that it becomes difficult to disentangle collective bargaining from political action.

A Loss of Coherence

These deviations seriously violate the systematic and coherent quality of the private sector model. The fragmented character of the employer and the limited scope of bargaining require that a great deal of labor relations take place away from the collective bargaining table and outside the realm of grievance procedures as well. Unions necessarily have to seek their demands in forums where the collective bargaining model is *irrelevant*. Lobbying is appropriate for the legislative forum. Electioneering and contributing to campaigns is useful where elective officials hold the key to what labor wants. The judiciary is the forum for asserting legal and constitutional rights. The latter go well beyond noneconomic matters, as the adjudication of "comparable worth" at the initiation of organized public sector labor illustrates (see Chapter 8). The multilateral character of public employers also makes coordination of labor relations difficult for governments and detracts from the development of comprehensive, well-thought-out responses to labor's demands. It further complicates the problem of developing proactive approaches to effective labor-management relations.

The impasse procedures used in the public sector have some virtues, but they are characterized by two serious flaws. First, they are not a true substitute for the exercise of economic power that is associated with the strike in the private sector. This is precisely why the private sector has almost no equivalent to the reliance placed on the arbitration of economic matters in the public sector. Even where standards for arbitration include "acceptability" or "ability to pay," such impasse resolution procedures fall far short of approximating the use of economic force. (Indeed, the core problem is that even the *strike* in the public sector may not do this as it may leave governments better off financially by virtue of taxes collected but not expended on the wages of strikers or the provision of struck services.) Second, many have observed that these impasse procedures tend to suppress the vigor of negotiations by creating "ritual," "chilling," and "narcotic" effects, which will be discussed in the next chapter. But in the private sector, vigorous bilateral negotiations are considered the heart of the process—and seriously reducing their vitality is viewed as a violation of the collective bargaining model itself.

As a result of these differences, the public sector model is less systematic and coherent than the private. It is open-ended in terms of participants, much activity takes place away from the bargaining table, and it does not have a mechanism, such as a strike or lockout, to force the parties to take each other's position seriously and to bring the contest to a logical closure.

Dysfunction

In the past, there has been a tendency to argue that the failures of public sector collective bargaining were due to its relative immaturity. Among its common dysfunctional aspects have been illegal strikes, unfair refusal to grant unions recognition, incomprehensible parity agreements, governmental inability to pay for agreements, employees working for extended periods without a current contract, arbitrators' awards that are set aside through litigation, and a wide range of unfair practices on both sides. However, nowadays some practitioners and students of public sector labor relations are questioning whether there are not serious problems with the public sector collective bargaining model itself. Primary among these are the narrow scope of bargaining and fragmented character of the public employer, which have the following consequences:

1.   They encourage employees to organize, but leave their expectations frustrated because there is not enough to talk about at the bargaining table. Unions therefore turn to *lobbying* and to *prohibited* concerted activity, such as strikes, in an effort to compel government to respond to their demands. Alternatively, unions are seeking to place more and more in labor-management committees, which address, in a cooperative fashion, issues of mutual concern to labor and management. (Issues such as wages, however, are never addressed by labor-management committees.)

2.   Impasse resolution not only suffers from the effects noted previously, it also "judicializes" the collective bargaining process and takes decision

What Is Labor-Management Cooperation?

Mutual concerns by labor and management over such issues as productivity, poor morale, unsafe working conditions, and cutback management have led to the formation of labor-management committees (LMCs). Such cooperative endeavors allow labor and management to address a common need to tackle a mutual problem that cannot be addressed in an adversarial way at the bargaining table.

One of the earliest and best-known cooperative efforts in the public sector was undertaken during the early days of the Tennessee Valley Authority (TVA), the government corporation formed in the 1930s for controlling flooding and for generating electric power. The TVA and the Tennessee Valley Trades and Labor Council formed a cooperative committee to address such issues as productivity, improving the quality of work and services, and increasing morale.

Today, joint labor-management cooperation is virtually a staple of public sector labor relations. It exists at every level of government and for a variety of purposes.

Adapted from Norma M. Riccucci, *Women, Minorities and Unions in the Public Sector* (Westport, Conn.: Greenwood Press, 1990).

making out of the hands of the parties. This frequently gives private individuals de facto authority over aspects of governmental budgets and matters of public policy. As such, important qualities of representative government can be compromised—which is precisely why some governments prefer a narrow scope of bargaining and to avoid binding arbitration of economic matters.

3. The collective bargaining model turns labor into the adversary of management and into the adversary of the taxpaying or service fee-paying public. Public employees, once commonly called "public servants" and once thought to exercise a "public trust," are still charged with carrying out the public interest. So are public managers. Neither is paid out of profits; neither should claim to have monopoly on defining the public interest. So where is the conflict between them? Perhaps it is over the authority imputed by hierarchical relationships—but then the problem is likely to be more inherent in the character of traditional public management than in the absence of effective means for collective bargaining. Similarly, any institutionalized process that routinely forces public employees to present themselves as adversaries of the community for which they work is inherently polarizing and often an obstacle to achieving the benefits of "community."

One could probably point to other dysfunctions that arise from the kind of public sector collective bargaining model that has emerged. However, at this point the more appropriate question may be, "Where do we go from here?"

One answer is "nowhere," for perhaps the current model is more or less the best we can do with a very complicated problem that demands an elaborate and ever-shifting balance among several competing concerns. Or it may be that we can tinker around with the public sector model in ways that will eventually improve it substantially. Alternatively, it may be possible to reduce some of the difficulties presently associated with public sector collective bargaining by allowing greater democracy in the workplace. During the past decade or so, many private firms and public agencies have experimented with ways of enabling rank-and-file workers to participate more in the designing and assigning of work and to share in what once was considered the exercise of managerial prerogative and authority.

In sum, when we think about labor relations in the public sector, it is useful to bear in mind that the basic model we have adapted is derived from long experience in the private sector and that its fit in the public sector is imperfect. It is with these "imperfections" that public personnelists are often most concerned. Having presented a broad framework for understanding the development of collective bargaining in the public sector, we will now turn our attention to the main events and specific formats that have formed public sector labor relations.

Origins

For most of the period after the civil service reform of the 1880s, public employees were viewed as a stabilizing force in government. In the public's view, at least as judged by traditional stereotypes, public employees were threatening only in a passive way. At worst, they were inefficient, lazy, committed to pointless routines, and lacking in individual initiative. Yet their reputed docile, complacent, and conservative natures provided a measure of comfort. While they might be unduly costly to the taxpayer, they presented little challenge to the citizenry's freedom, liberty, and ultimate sovereignty. In the words of the president of the U.S. Chamber of Commerce in 1928, "The best public servant is the worst one. A really efficient public servant is corrosive. He eats holes in our liberties." Yet labor problems have always been just below this placid surface and have erupted from time to time. Perhaps the first major labor dispute affecting the operations of the federal government occurred in 1839 when workers in a Philadelphia naval shipyard went out on strike. However, the organization of public sector labor prior to the demise of the spoils system was obviously premature, and it was not until the 1880s that important developments began to occur.

As has generally been the case in federal labor relations, postal employees provided the major impetus for change. In the late 1880s, post office workers began to organize in affiliation with the Knights of Labor. Their first national organization, the National Association of Letter Carriers, was established in

What Is the Postal Alliance?

In 1913, the National Alliance of Postal Employees was formed, because of the Railway Mail Association's policy of barring African-American clerks. The Postal Alliance was composed mainly of African-American railway mail clerks, but other postal employees were also welcomed. In fact, a faction of the National Association of Letter Carriers (NALC) sought for years to require African-American letter carriers to join the Postal Alliance in order to rid the NALC of African-American carriers. A resolution at the NALC's 1927 convention stated:

> Whereas the conditions in the south, as well as the entire Association of the United States, in respect to the colored members of the National Association of Letter Carriers, in that in many of the Branches the colored members have come to majority, and, therefore, places them in authority, causing a disruption in the ranks of the membership....
>
> Whereas their strength in voting has proved without question in these Branches that white letter carriers have been compelled to either withdraw their membership or take the embarrassment of being defeated to positions of local officers and representation in our National Conventions, and
>
> Whereas the higher-minded and considerate colored carriers have recognized these conditions, and desiring to avoid any future trouble have instituted an organization for the colored civil service employees, which is known as the Postal Alliance, its purposes are for the protection of the colored employees and improvement of the service; therefore be it
>
> Resolved, That this convention goes on record as endorsing this organization, and appeals to all colored carriers to avail themselves in its membership in order that peace may be preserved in the service.... (*The Postal Record*, 1927:408).

The postal alliance still exists today as the National Alliance of Postal and Federal Employees. The alliance no longer has collective bargaining rights with the Postal Service, but it does with other federal agencies.

Adapted from Norma M. Riccucci, *Women, Minorities and Unions in the Public Sector* (Westport, Connecticut: Greenwood Press, 1990).

1890. The National Federation of Postal Clerks followed shortly thereafter and received its charter from the AFL in 1906. These developments had important consequences for federal labor relations policy.

In the early 1900s the government became increasingly wary of the lobbying pressure exerted by postal organizations. Given their geographic dispersion, they have always been in a strategic position to play upon vulnerabilities of members of Congress. In 1902 an effort was made to counteract this strength. A so-called gag order was issued which forbade employees and their associations from petitioning Congress for wage increases and other improvements in working conditions, except through proper departmental channels. This approach immediately gave rise to efforts by the postal organizations to secure the right to organize and to lobby. By 1912 they were successful; the Lloyd-LaFollette Act of that year guaranteed federal employees the right both to join unions that did not authorize the use of strikes and to petition Congress either individually or through their organization. The act remained the only statutory basis for the organization of federal employees until the passage of the Civil Service Reform Act of 1978 (see Table 10.1).

The Long Gestation

Despite these relatively early developments public employee unions did not move to the forefront of labor relations until the 1960s. There are several reasons for this, the heart of them being the peculiar nature of government. First, as discussed in the overview section, it has long been thought that collective bargaining is an improper model for the public sector because of the nature of sovereignty. Although many political philosophers have dealt exhaustively with this concept, here it is only necessary to state its basic meaning: that the ultimate power to decide questions of public policy for the entire political community must lie in some individual or body. In the United States the citizenry as a whole is seen as the sovereign, with the government resting on its consent and exercising its will. The government itself is divided into different branches with separate and overlapping powers as a means of ensuring that neither it nor any of its units becomes the ultimate sovereign. In terms of public labor relations, a formal application of the concept of sovereignty would seem to preclude collective bargaining. Only the citizenry, speaking through the government, its representative, would have the authority to establish conditions under which public servants would work. From this perspective, employee-employer codetermination of working conditions, or even bargaining among the participants over these conditions, constitutes a breach of sovereignty because the political community would have to yield some of its authority to a nongovernmental, nonrepresentative group.

These issues become even more difficult when the question of "Who shall bargain for the state?" is posed. Two of the stickier problems in public sector labor relations are finding a meaningful line between management and labor and determining how, if at all, management shall be represented in *its* demands concerning working conditions (see Chapter 11). When employee organizations engage in collective bargaining vis-à-vis other nonelected, nonpolitically appointed public employees who are also protected by a merit system, the extent to which the political community has ceded its sovereignty becomes abundantly clear. The issue is hardly academic. Even though bargaining over matters such as wages and hours is often not possible with

Table 10.1.   Major Labor Relations Policies Covering Federal Workers

Law	Major Provisions	Employees covered
Lloyd-LaFollette Act (1912)	Gave federal employees the right to join unions that did not authorize strikes; guaranteed federal employees the right to petition Congress for redress of their grievances.	Technically postal workers, but interpreted to cover all federal workers.
Taft-Hartley Act (1947)	Section 305 prohibits federal employees from striking.	Federal, including postal.
Executive order 10988 (1962)	Gave federal employees the right to form and join unions and to engage in collective bargaining over noneconomic issues. Wages and fringe benefits would continue to be determined by Congress. Allowed for use of advisory arbitration over grievances.	Federal employees except for those in the FBI and CIA, and certain managerial and supervisory employees.
Executive order 11491 (1969)[a]	Expanded scope of bargaining, provided for secret ballot elections, restricted certain internal affairs (e.g., financial) of unions, created the Federal Labor Relations Commission to administer 11491, created the Federal Mediation and	Same as those covered under executive order 10988.

(continued)

Table 10.1. *Continued*

Law	Major Provisions	Employees covered
Executive order 11491 *(continued)*	Conciliation Service (FMCS) and Federal Service Impasses Panel (FSIP) to settle labor disputes and resolve impasses.	
Postal Reorganization Act (1970)	Incorporates most of the provisions of the National Labor Relations Act (NLRA) of 1935, which covers private sector employees. But, striking is prohibited, as is any form of union security other than voluntary checkoff of union dues. Empowers the National Labor Relations Board (NLRB), which oversees the NLRA, to oversee labor relations in the postal service.	Postal workers.
Civil Service Reform Act, Title VII (1978)	Labor rights of covered federal workers now guaranteed by federal law. Solidified provisions incorporated in previous executive orders. FLRC replaced by the Federal Labor Relations Authority (FLRA), the FSIP now a separate entity within the FLRA. Scope of bargaining clarified. Provides for binding arbitration over grievances.	All federal workers except for supervisory personnel, members of the armed services, and employees in the postal service, foreign service, FBI, CIA, GAO, NSA, and TVA.

[a]Executive orders 11616 (1971) and 11838 (1975) further modified and strengthened the labor relations program in the federal government.

career managers, virtually all collective bargaining agreements will have some budgetary ramifications and many have very important policy consequences. Yet it may be the case that neither party involved is directly responsible or accountable to the electorate, and sometimes not even under the immediate control of politically-elected or appointed authorities. In essence, collective bargaining demands that the sovereign sacrifice some of its authority. While in recent years events have overridden the traditional concern with sovereignty, the matter nevertheless retains its theoretical importance. Indeed, as late as 1968, the attorney general of Nevada ruled that sovereignty prevented public employees from joining organizations whose goal was collective bargaining. The federal courts have since reversed this approach and have held that restrictions on the right to organize unions are unconstitutional. Nevertheless, public employees still lack a constitutional right to bargain collectively, and as unions become more and more involved in matters of public policy, it is likely that some of these traditional concerns with sovereignty will reappear in new types of legislation.

A second factor limiting the development of collective bargaining in the public sector has been the nature of governmental services. To a large extent governments have a monopoly over their functions and/or operate in areas where there is little possibility of attaining a profit. Thus, governments provide a set of highly diverse services which are not or cannot be provided by the private sector. Among these are defense of the political community, law enforcement, regulation of the economy, and foreign and domestic policy-making in general, to name a few. Even where government provides services that can be furnished privately, such as education and transportation, it often does so with the view that service to the political community rather than profitability is of paramount importance. To take a subterranean example, a city may deem it desirable or even necessary to provide subway service. However, the economics of such transportation may be such that it is impossible to make the user pay the entire cost. To do so might, for example, drive up the cost of such services to the extent that potential riders search for other means of getting around. From an economic standpoint, such a falling demand might require a curtailment of service, precisely what the city wanted to avoid in the first place. In such a case, one solution is obviously to make the general population rather than just the specific users of such services bear some of the costs of its operation. There may be no injustice in this as even nonusers stand to benefit from the operation of subway lines within their city. Similar arguments can be made with reference to education and a host of other functions. When governments provide public goods, the whole community is the intended beneficiary.

Thus, much of what government does is characterized by its essential quality, by low or zero profitability, and/or by commitment to the political community. Police and fire protection, public health, transportation, and education are examples. In such cases, the applicability of traditional collective bargaining sometimes presents difficulties. This is evident in the case of job actions by essential government workers. For example, it is often said—based more on hysteria than fact or experience—that police, firefighters and other public employees in essential and safety services often hold the public welfare as a hostage to their demands. Although collective bargaining has taken place in such settings *and* without the dreaded apocalypse that many warn of, most government employers continue to restrict the rights of public sector employees and their unions in essential services.

This is true even in the case of nonessential services. In the private sector there is generally at least one ultimate check on collective bargaining. Workers and their leadership realize that it is possible to drive a company out of business by demanding or receiving too much. Where labor agreements bankrupt private firms, these businesses and the jobs they provide may disappear—something that neither side of the collective bargaining table wants to see. Although this situation is often complicated by monopoly or oligopoly, tariffs to regulate competition from abroad, and other elements, it is nevertheless an important constraint on collective bargaining agreements in the private sector. However, there is no equivalent moderating influence in the public sector. One of the dominant characteristics of government is that its outputs (products) are seldom subject to evaluation in external markets. Revenues are raised largely through taxation and borrowing rather than through the sale of goods and services. Moreover, while many cities face severe fiscal woes and even bankruptcy, they nonetheless cannot close their doors and move away. Many services must be maintained even by a government which cannot pay for them. Consequently, while collective bargaining may raise expenditures and result in some loss of jobs for public employees, not all face the possibility of losing their livelihood. Indeed, those most likely to retain their jobs may also be the leading power bloc in a union. Although governments are wont to plead that they cannot afford increased benefits for their employees, and although this may often be the case, public employees, conditioned by society's tendency to try to make them the first victims of an economic downswing and by the public's low esteem for them in general, are likely to believe that there is more funding available than meets the eye and to view the possibility of schools, police and fire services, and other functions being forced to shut down with an air of unreality. Hence, the normal constraints of the free market are much weaker on collective bargaining in the public sector. Another way of looking at this is that while labor markets prevent governments from paying their workers too little, markets on the output side do not prevent them from paying too much.

A third factor inhibiting the organization of government employees has

Table 10.2. Union Membership in Public and Private Sectors (1986–1989)

	Percentages			
Employment sector	1986	1987	1988	1989
Public	36.0	36.0	36.7	36.7
Private	17.5	17.0	16.8	16.4

Note: Expressed as percentage of employed workers.
Source: Calculated from various January issues of *Employment and Earnings* (Washington, D.C.: U.S. Bureau of Labor Statistics).

been the varied nature of government occupations and the traditional composition of the public work force. Occupation has traditionally provided the major basis for employee organization. Yet occupation cannot provide the sole basis of organization in large governments because it would create such a plethora of representational units that the government would be continually mired in negotiations. Thus New York City once bargained with 400 separate units. Today federal employees are engaged in thousands of occupational classifications. The representation of each would be entirely impossible if the government were to do anything other than negotiate collective bargaining agreements. Dealing with the 4,000 or so bargaining units now extant is a serious strain. Yet if occupation is not to be the basis of organization, what can take its place? Government service in general or even employment in a specific agency may not provide a sufficient commonality of interest among employees to make collective bargaining feasible. As a result of this situation, bargaining unit determination has become a major problem in public sector labor relations.

When we turn our attention from the nature of government occupations to the composition of the public sector work force, it can be seen that there are other barriers to the organization of public employees. These are most pronounced on the federal level, where employees are widely dispersed in a geographic sense. Although politicians and newspaper editors may be given to tirades about "those bureaucrats in Washington," only about 10 percent of all federal employees are actually located in the nation's capital. Organizing even among employees with a commonality of interest under such circumstances presents very considerable difficulties. In addition, the public sector work force contains relatively large proportions of protected-class persons, such as women, African Americans, and Latinos, who historically have been somewhat reluctant to organize, due in part to the discriminatory treatment against them by unions. Moreover, government consists largely of white-collar employees who traditionally have not provided fertile ground for organization.

A final reason why unionization was relatively late in becoming a major characteristic of the public sector has been the widespread use of the merit system. Merit systems and civil service protections have presented many difficulties from the perspectives of collective bargaining. The protection they afford against arbitrary adverse actions has been a significant deterrent to unionization. They made less important the traditional union goal of providing job security. Given that it is only since the 1960s that unions have bargained effectively over wages and hours, many civil service employees have simply found it unnecessary to organize and pay union dues.

The Unionization of Public Employees

At times the barriers to unionization of public employees and the institution of collective bargaining in the public sector have seemed insuperable, yet today public employees are more unionized than workers in the private sector. In the 1960s and 1970s, unionization of the public services grew at an unprecedented pace. For example, between 1962 and 1968, public employee organizational membership increased some 136 percent as compared to a 5 percent increase over the same period in the private sector. Since 1968, about 50 percent of all eligible nonpostal federal employees have been union members. Unionization of postal workers has reached about 90 percent, which is truly a phenomenal figure. By 1980, about 54 percent of all full-time municipal employees were union members, as were about 40 percent of state employees and 35 percent of county employes. School district employees showed an even higher propensity to join unions, with almost 60 percent of them being members. The figure for special governmental districts was about 36 percent.

These figures pertain to actual union membership. However, they underestimate the impact of unionization because unions represent all workers in recognized bargining units whether these workers are union members or not. Consequently, the number of employees represented by unions and covered by collective bargaining agreements tends to be considerably larger than the number of union members per se. In fact, in some cases, as many as three or four workers may be covered by an agreement for each union member in a bargaining unit. All told, today a very large proportion of public employees are therefore represented by labor unions.

What accounts for the tremendous growth of unionization and collective bargaining in the face of so many obstacles? Several factors have been identified.

1. At the federal level membership in labor organizations has been permissible since the late 1800s and early 1900s and collective bargaining of some kind took place in some agencies, such as the Government Printing Office,

the Tennessee Valley Authority, and the Department of the Interior prior to the 1960s. However, the greatest impetus was supplied by President Kennedy in 1962, when he issued executive order 10988. It has been referred to as the "Magna Carta" of labor relations in federal employment. It outlined a process of collective bargaining in most civilian agencies. Moreover, the Kennedy order asserted that "the participation of employees in the formulation and implementation of personnel policies affecting them contributes to the effective conduct of the public business." Virtually in one fell swoop, the order legitimized collective bargaining in the federal service and defused opposition to it there and elsewhere.

2. Although the Kennedy order applied only to federal employment, it made it difficult to argue that collective bargaining was inappropriate in the public sector. No longer could state and local officials assert with impunity that collective bargaining was antithetical to constitutional principles and representational government. After all, the President of the United States strongly supported it.

3. A growing awareness by the labor movement that unionization and union strength in the private sector was diminishing. These organizations sought to unionize unorganized sectors of the economy, including public employment, which at the time was growing very rapidly. Many unions representing public employees are "mixed unions" because they also represent private sector workers. The Service Employees International Union (SEIU) and the Teamsters Union are examples.

4. The financial resources and skill that national unions could bring to bear on their efforts to organize public employees.

5. The stifling impact of position classification and pay systems on the upward mobility of employees in large public bureaucracies.

6. A general sense among clerical employees that their earning power could be enhanced and their rights protected through collective bargaining.

7. A growing sense among professional employees, such as teachers, that professionalism and unionization could go hand in hand. In other words, collective bargaining could be used to achieve professional goals.

8. The spillover effect of union organizational drives on more placid employee associations. In order to protect their appeal and organizational base, many of the latter became more aggressive in demanding a right to bargain collectively.

9. The radicalizing effect of what has been described by Carl Stenberg as " 'the head-in-the-sand' attitude of many public employers, rooted in the traditional concept of the prerogatives of the sovereign authority and distrust of the economic, political, and social objectives of unions—an attitude which has made questions of whether employee organizations will be recognized for the purpose of discussing grievances and conditions of work with management the second most frequent cause of strikes."

The Decline in Private Sector Unionism

More and more private sector unions are targeting public employees for unionization. This is due in large part to the decline in private sector union membership. Here are some of the factors contributing to this decline:

- Changing values of American workers—Young workers are not knowledgeable about the history of unionism, in particular the oppression of workers, which led to unionization. Young workers are also more interested in upward mobility, aspiring to be part of "management," than solidarity and collective action for the good of all workers.
- Economic conditions—The U.S. has experienced declining business activities and relatively little economic growth in the past several years.
- Foreign competition—The importation of foreign goods and services has led to the loss of jobs for Americans and a decline in union membership.
- Wage/benefit spillover—Economic spillovers from union to nonunion establishments keep the interests of nonunion workers satisfied.
- Union avoidance/busting—Various strategies and tactics (e.g., locating a business in nonunion geographic regions) employed by management to keep unions out.
- Promanagement inclination in government—The current and immediate past federal administrations have been hostile to labor interests.
- Effectiveness of strikes declining—The use of the strike has been weakened by several factors, including (1) economics; that is, where workers cannot afford to be on strike, thereby making them more willing to cross picket lines; (2) public apathy, which in turn permits (3) tougher business attitudes toward striking workers; that is, the "social norm" pressuring organizations not to hire "scabs" or replace striking workers is virtually gone—now, organizations will permanently replace striking workers, and this is perfectly legal; and, (4) automation, which makes strikers replaceable.

These factors were extremely important in the growth of public sector unionization during the 1960s and 1970s. Moreover, once unions were able to organize public employees and negotiate contracts, they had the opportunity to demonstrate their desirability to those workers who remained unorganized. To some extent this enabled public sector unions to enroll members of groups that had traditionally been skeptical of unionization, such as African Americans and women (see Table 10.3). Nevertheless, unionization has hardly been uniform. We have already noted that public employee unionization varies with occupation or function. It has also varied with geographic region. For the most part, the southeastern and sunbelt states have been more resistant to public employee and private sector unionization than other states, especially those in the northeast and Great Lakes regions.

Having discussed some general considerations about public sector unionization and collective bargaining, we now turn our attention to an outline of federal and state legal provisions.

Table 10.3. Percentages of Female and Minority Union Membership (Public and Private Sectors)

Employment sector	Total unionized	White male	Minority male	White female	Minority female
Public (all levels)					
1977	32.1	37.6	43.3	17.5	31.5
1980	33.8	39.2	42.9	21.2	32.3
1985[a]	34.9	35.8	37.5	34.4	31.3
Private					
1977	23.3	28.3	34.5	14.4	23.0
1980	22.3	27.0	33.0	14.3	23.3
1985[a]	14.4	19.0	21.6	7.2	14.0

Note: Data could not be broken down by individual "minority" group members.
[a]1985 data are tabulated from the Current Population Survey (CPS), U.S.Bureau of the Census.
Source: Adapted from Norma M. Riccucci, *Women, Minorities and Unions in the Public Sector* (Westport, Conn.: Greenwood Press, 1990).

The Federal Collective Bargaining Program

Despite some limited earlier developments, it was not until 1949 that organized civil servants began a strong campaign to reverse the opposition to collective bargaining in the federal government and to ensure more uniform procedures. Their specific objective was to secure more formalized legal recognition and a greater role in determining working conditions in the federal bureaucracy. By 1956, they had succeeded in obtaining the Democratic party's commitment to the "recognition by law of the right of employee organizations to represent their members and participate in the formulation and improvement of personnel policies and practices." During the presidential election campaign of 1960, Democratic nominee John F. Kennedy reaffirmed his party's earlier position, and, after his election, he made good on his campaign promise by issuing Executive Order 10988 (January 17, 1962). Intended to promote "employee-management cooperation in the federal service," it was premised upon assumptions that encompassed traditional public personnel administration thinking.

In some ways, the Kennedy program, though innovative, was nevertheless "too little, too late." It reflected many of the traditional concerns with public sector collective bargaining and consequently did not create an effective or lasting format for federal labor relations. The program contained a very strong management rights clause, a limited scope of bargaining, and prohibitions against strikes. No special means for resolving impasses were developed. Union recognition provisions were complex and provided for both collective bargaining and meeting and conferring. In retrospect, the program was a very important half-step toward a comprehensive system of labor relations in the federal government. It set in motion two forces that eventually played a major role in the creation of contemporary public sector collective bargaining systems: (1) the legitimization of such collective bargaining, and (2) a substantial incentive for unions to seek to organize federal employees.

The Kennedy program was radically revised by Executive Order 11491, issued by President Nixon in 1969. But Nixon's comprehensive effort to set federal labor relations on a sound and contemporary basis was also short-lived. It was replaced by the two statutes that frame most federal collective bargaining today—the Postal Reorganization Act of 1970 and the Civil Service Reform Act of 1978.

The Postal Reorganization Act

The Postal Reorganization Act followed on the heels of the chaotic and disastrous postal strike of 1970, in which some 200,000 workers joined. It models collective bargaining in the Postal Service, which has some 700,000 employees, along private sector lines to a substantial, although not complete, extent. It empowers the National Labor Relations Board to resolve questions of representation and charges of unfair labor practices. It extends the scope of negotiations by allowing postal unions with exclusive recognition to bargain over wages, hours, and other conditions and terms of employment. Moreover, unlike the Kennedy and Nixon executive orders, the act does not contain a management rights clause, which implies that the scope of negotiations should be very similar to that found in private sector labor relations. The major departure from private sector practice is that the act prohibits strikes and requires fact-finding or, when necessary, binding arbitration to overcome impasses. In the view of some, the act tended to make the rest of the federal labor relations program somewhat obsolete because there is little logic in treating the postal service as a unique case. However, the Civil Service Reform Act of 1978, the next significant development in federal labor relations, did not follow its lead.

The Civil Service Reform Act of 1978

The enactment of Title VII of the Civil Service Reform Act of 1978, sometimes called the Federal Service Labor-Management Relations Statute, represented the achievement of a goal sought by organized labor since the 1940s. At long last federal labor relations were made to rest upon a comprehensive statute rather than a series of executive orders. The AFL-CIO was especially supportive of the change, which can be interpreted as creating a relatively permanent framework for federal collective bargaining. Future changes will have to be brought about through legislation rather than by more easily proclaimed executive orders. And labor's strength in Congress can be formidable.

Although the act solidified the gains won by labor over the years, it did not fundamentally change the federal labor relations process. It does not apply to supervisors, members of the armed forces or foreign service, and employees of the General Accounting Office (GAO), the Federal Bureau of Investigation, the Central Intelligence Agency, the National Security Agency, the Tennessee Valley Authority, or the post office. Among its most important features are:

1. The establishment of the Federal Labor Relations Authority (FLRA). The new agency is substantially divorced from federal personnel management and is intended to act as a neutral entity. It is headed by a chair and two additional members selected on a bipartisan basis and holding their terms for five years. They are removable only for cause. A general counsel to the FLRA is also appointed for a five-year term. The FLRA is authorized to make determinations concerning appropriate bargaining units, supervise elections

The Postal Strike

On March 17, 1970, members of the Manhattan-Bronx Branch 36 of the National Association of Letter Carriers (NALC) voted to strike the U.S. Postal Service. For the first time in the agency's 195-year history, it was neither "rain, sleet, nor gloom of night," but rather picket lines that stopped the U.S. mail.

At issue was the low wage scale for postal carriers. Starting pay was $6,100 per annum, "rising" to $8,442 over a twenty-one-year period. In New York City alone, this left 7 percent of the carriers on welfare of one sort or another. The local union was seeking a new scale that would range from $8,500 to $11,700 and would provide cost-of-living increases. The union also wanted the maximum to be attainable after five years instead of twenty-one and sought a twenty-year half-pay retirement option among other fringe benefits.

But the strike was not called simply for economic reasons; politics was involved as well. Specifically, a kind of three-cornered game of "chicken" had been developing, and the strike was used to break a deadlock. The Nixon administration, unhappy with the operating effectiveness and "organizational philosophy" of the post office, had sought to transform it from an ordinary department into a government corporation. Nixon made future pay raises dependent upon congressional and postal union support of his plan. A week prior to the outbreak of the strike, the House Post Office Committee, which is ordinarily heavily influenced by organized postal workers, approved a bill providing for a 5.4 percent pay increase for lower-grade employees. However, it failed to include the cost-of-living increases that were demanded by the postal unions. Feeling that no other recourse was available, the Manhattan-Bronx branch of the NALC opted to flex its muscle.

(continued)

The Postal Strike *(continued)*

The strike was scheduled for 12:01 A.M. of March 18. By 1:00 A.M. police reported that picket lines had sprung up outside Manhattan's central postal facility. As the day progressed, the head of the Manhatten-Bronx Postal Union said he expected the 25,000 clerks, mail handlers, and other employees he represented to honor the picket lines. Then the strike spread across the East River to Brooklyn and Queens. Once the post office was shut down in New York, it was inevitable that tons of mail would begin to pile up not only there but in other post offices across the country.

Of course, there are laws against this sort of thing. Indeed, federal statutes provide for criminal sanctions against striking federal employees. However, despite these and court injunctions prohibiting the strike, the workers did not return to their jobs. Herman Sandbank, executive vice-president of the NALC, in the style of many union leaders, told the government where to put its injunctions and what to do with its laws: "The men will defy any injunction. They'll stay out until hell freezes over."

Next, the strike spread across the Hudson River to New Jersey and northward to Connecticut. Eventually it went westward and southward, and soon postal facilities in many major cities throughout the nation were paralyzed. Union leaders seemed to lose control of the situation, and the strike took on a wildcat flavor. Ultimately, some 200,000 postal workers joined in.

Within a week, Nixon declared a national emergency and sent 27,500 National Guards to sort and deliver mail in New York City. However, to sweeten this coercive pill, the government for the first time in history agreed to allow wages, which hitherto had always been set through the legislative process, to be negotiated between union and government representatives. That ended the strike. Subsequently, the Postal Reorganization Act was passed, establishing the corporate framework sought by Nixon and providing for collective bargaining with postal employees in the future.

and certify exclusive bargaining agents, decide appeals from agency determinations that issues are nonnegotiable, and hold hearings and resolve complaints concerning unfair labor practices (ULPs). In addition, the general counsel has independent investigatory authority. The Federal Service Impasses Panel (FSIP), a separate entity within the FLRA, continues to resolve impasses when appropriate.

2. The act clarifies some aspects of the scope of bargaining. The following working conditions are *nonnegotiable:* (1) matters established by law, such as position classifications, Hatch Act enforcement, and pay; (2) governmentwide rules and regulations; (3) rules and regulations of an agency or primary national subdivision, unless the FLRA has determined that there is no compelling need to prohibit negotiations or a union represents a majority of the affected employees (who comprise a single bargaining unit);(4) management rights, including interpretation of the agency's mission, determination

of its budget, organization, number of employees, and internal security, and the right to take personnel actions involving the assignment of work, contracting out, promotions, and emergency actions. However, management may elect to negotiate over the following, which are deemed *permissive* subjects of bargaining: (1) the numbers, types, and grades of employees or positions assigned to an organizational subdivision, work project, or tour of duty; and (2) technology, the means, or the methods of performing work. *Mandatory* bargaining subjects include: (1) conditions of employment that do not fall into either of the above categories; (2) procedures for implementing actions within management's preserved rights; (3) appropriate arrangements for employees adversely affected by management's exercise of its reserved rights; and (4) a grievance procedure, which must allow for conclusion by binding arbitration.

The FLRA has confronted the tension between the substantive non-negotiability of management's rights and the mandatory negotiability of procedures for implementing exercises of these rights by adopting the doctrine that if a union proposal regarding procedures would prevent the agency from "acting at all," then the proposal is nonnegotiable. The theoretical underpinnings of the acting at all doctrine have been sharply criticized and it is uncertain whether it will continue to be sustained in the future. However, it allows for more vigorous bargaining, within an already crimped framework, than the management-favored alternative of prohibiting bargaining if the proposal would create an "unreasonable delay" in the exercise of reserved rights.

There is also a tension between the nonnegotiability of management rights and the mandatory negotiability of arrangements for employees adversely affected by the exercise of such rights. Here, by contrast, the FLRA adopted a standard that was found too narrow by the courts. It sought to prohibit the negotiation of proposals that "directly interfered" with management's rights. However, the judiciary overturned this standard in favor of one requiring bargaining unless the proposal impinged on management's rights to an "excessive degree."

3. Contract enforcement is to be largely through grievance procedures. Negotiated grievance procedures must be fair and simple, provide for expeditious processing, allow the union or an aggrieved employee to present and process cases, and, as noted earlier, provide for binding arbitration. Grievances cannot pertain to disputes involving prohibited political activities, retirement, health or life insurance, suspensions and removals for national security reasons, examinations, certifications, appointments, and classifications that do not result in an employee's reduction in grade or pay. The grievance procedure may cover or exclude "appealable actions," such as breaches of equal employment opportunity regulations or adverse actions that fall within the jurisdiction of the Equal Employment Opportunity Commission (EEOC)

and/or the Merit Systems Protection Board (MSPB). Literally tens of thousands of grievances have gone to binding arbitration. These are summarized in the Office of Personnel Management's Labor Agreement Information Retrieval System (LAIRS). Awards can include back pay and other make-whole remedies. Exceptions to interest arbitration or grievance awards (not involving adverse actions) may be filed with the FLRA. The agency will overturn awards when it finds them contrary to federal laws, rules, or regulations or if they are considered defective on some ground that the federal courts have used to reject similar arbitration awards under regulations pertaining to the private sector.

    4.   Impasses can be brought to the FSIP upon the request of either party. When the FSIP agrees, arbitration can be used to resolve impasses.

    5.   Exclusive recognition continues as the major basis of collective bargaining. The act continues a policy first established by President Ford in 1975 that encourages the use of larger bargaining units by allowing units to consolidate without elections providing the unions and agencies involved agree and the FLRA grants approval. As a result of this policy, the average size of bargaining units has risen. In 1980, there were more than 2,600 bargaining relationships. Throughout the postreform period, roughly 60 percent of the work force covered by the statute has been organized in bargaining units represented by an exclusive agent.

    6.   The act includes a number of miscellaneous provisions that are important to collective bargaining. It allows federal workers to engage in informational picketing. Unions are granted that right to have represented employees' dues withheld from their paychecks (dues checkoff) at no cost, but each employee is free to either authorize or refuse to authorize such withholding. Official time is authorized for employees in labor negotiations to the same extent that management time is authorized. Thus, labor negotiators are now paid for the time they spend in negotiations. Agencies such as the Office of Personnel Management (OPM), the General Services Administration, and the State Department (excluding the Foreign Service), which issue personnel regulations having applicability to their work forces governmentwide, must consult with unions representing their employees prior to making substantive changes.

    The Civil Service Reform Act led to several incremental improvements. Especially important has been the negotiation of grievance procedures, which has reduced the need to rely on adverse action appeals systems. The latter are expensive for the government, which bears the entire cost. According to the OPM, currently over 90 percent of negotiated grievance procedures provide that the costs of arbitration, if necessary, will be split between the union and the agency.

    It is evident that to a considerable extent the quality of the federal labor relations program depends on the FLRA. The Labor-Management Relations Statute is complex and requires fine tuning through FLRA rulemaking and adjudication. It also requires that the FLRA decide cases in a timely fashion and be evenhanded with regard to labor and management. Analysis of the FLRA's record from 1979 to 1987 suggests that the agency has succeeded in some respects, but failed in others. On the plus side, tens of thousands of ULP cases have been resolved under its purview. In 1986, the median number of days to resolve a ULP without an appeal was 63; the median number of days with an appeal was another 51. Earlier, in 1980, the respective figures were 81 and 104 days. The FLRA also appears to be fair in that its decisions do not seem to favor either management or labor in any consistent fashion. However, on the negative side, the FLRA has not utilized its rulemaking authority to improve the system of labor relations in the federal government. Moreover, its adjudicatory competence has been questioned because its decisions are so frequently overruled by the federal circuit courts on review. In fact, in reported decisions by the circuit courts, the FLRA's interpretation of the statute was rejected in 53 percent of the cases and upheld in 47 percent. The agency tended to be affirmed more frequently in scope of bargaining cases than in ULPs. In a few instances, the reviewing courts were exceptionally harsh on the FLRA. For instance, in *Professional Airways Systems Specialists, MEBA, AFL-CIO* v. *FLRA* (1987), the circuit court noted that "the confusion and inconsistency within the Authority is abundantly evident." Moreover, the FLRA's record on review showed no substantial improvement over time. Among other factors, some FLRA officials cite the complexity of the statute and the difficulty of the cases in explaining why the agency has not fared better in court. Whatever one concludes concerning the agency's competence, however, it does seem clear that the FLRA has not yet eliminated ambiguity in interpreting the Labor-Management Relations Statute.

Many criticisms of the federal labor relations program remain. The limited scope of bargaining continues to lead to frustration on the part of unions and employees. Bargaining over grievance procedures is mandatory, but that is an issue of authority in the workplace rather than one of economic interest. Wages and hours remain outside the scope of bargaining, for most federal employees, as do many aspects of personnel administration that are critical to the quality of work life. In the eyes of some, the federal labor relations program will remain vastly underdeveloped unless the statute is rewritten. It has also been alleged that neither management nor labor takes negotiations seriously enough. Labor recognized that what it can win at the bargaining table is very limited, so it continues to devote major efforts to lobbying in Congress for better pay and working conditions for federal employees. Management realizes that the scope of bargaining is so narrow that it really does not have to bargain over much. Moreover, since federal employees are forbidden to strike, the amount of damage union activity can do to an agency seems limited. Sometimes labor will vent its frustrations by bringing a host of grievances. But while inconvenient for management, such abuse of grievance procedures is often expensive and self-defeating for labor. Partly for these reasons, labor has also tended to allege a large number of unfair labor practices, which must be resolved by the FLRA, and generally cost the unions little or nothing. Finally, it appears that many managerial personnel would benefit from better training for labor relations.

State and Local Arrangements

The development of the federal labor relations program indicates the general direction that has been taken in the whole area of public sector collective bargaining. The major emphasis has been on the creation of a right to organize and to gain recognition and a process for negotiating and resolving impasses. Once the programs got underway, earlier fears for sovereignty and public order were somewhat alleviated. As unions representing federal employees gained strength in terms of numbers, experience, resources, and legitimacy, they began demanding a more comprehensive role in the determination of personnel matters affecting federal employees. One major result of the federal experience so far has been a movement toward making federal labor relations practices closer to those found in the private sphere. This is especially evident with regard to postal employees. At the state and local level there have been similar developments. However, there is a good deal more variation and some state programs are far more developed than others.

State and local employees have come up against certain constraints that never affected the federal government, since federal employees were granted the right to organize as early as 1912. Prior to 1968 it was generally believed that the First Amendment did not protect the right of public employees to organize labor unions; therefore, states were free to prohibit them. However, this position was reversed during that year when a U.S. Court of Appeals in *McLaughlin* v. *Tilendis* held that regulations prohibiting public employees from organizing were unconstitutional. Although laws which forbade unionization, such as those in North Carolina and Alabama, were not specifically involved in the case, the decision cast grave doubt on their constitutionality. The decision did not require that governments engage in collective bargaining, and so a host of options remained open to state lawmakers. In addition, in the early 1960s several courts held that in the absence of specific legislation arthorizing collective bargaining, government officials did not have the right to engage in such activity. Subsequently, though, the dominant trend in court decisions shifted to a more permissive position allowing collective bargaining unless it was specifically outlawed. Thus for the most part, even in the

Table 10.4. State Collective Bargaining Provisions Established by Legislation or Administrative Fiat

State	Employees Covered				
	State	Local	Police	Firefighters	Teachers
Alabama	—	—	—	Y	Y
Alaska	X	X	X	X	X
Arizona	Y	Y	Y	Y	Y
Arkansas	—	—	—	—	—
California	X	X	X	X	X
Colorado	—	—	—	—	—
Connecticut	X	X	X	X	X
Delaware	X	X	X	X	X
Florida	X	X	X	X	X
Georgia	—	—	—	X	—
Hawaii	X	X	X	X	X
Idaho	—	—	—	X	X
Illinois	X	X	X	X	X
Indiana	X	X	X	X	X/Y
Iowa	X	X	X	X	X
Kansas	Y	Y	Y	Y	X
Kentucky	—	—	X	X	—
Louisiana	—	X[a]	—	—	—
Maine	X	X	X	X	X/Y
Maryland	—	X	—	—	X
Massachusetts	X	X	X	X	X
Michigan	X	X	X	X	X
Minnesota	X/Y	X/Y	X/Y	X/Y	X/Y
Mississippi	—	—	—	—	—
Missouri	Y	Y	—	Y	—
Montana	X	X	X	X	X/Y
Nebraska	X	X	X	X	Y
Nevada	—	X	X	X	X
New Hampshire	X	X	X	X	X
New Jersey	X	X	X	X	X
New Mexico	X/Y	—	—	—	—
New York	X	X	X	X	X
North Carolina	—	—	—	—	—
North Dakota	Y	Y	Y	Y	X
Ohio	X	X	X	X	X
Oklahoma	—	X	X	X	X
Oregon	X	X	X	X	X
Pennsylvania	X/Y	X/Y	X	X	X/Y

(continued)

Table 10.4. *Continued*

State	Employees Covered				
	State	Local	Police	Firefighters	Teachers
Rhode Island	X	X	X	X	X
South Carolina	—	—	—	—	—
South Dakota	X	X	X	X	X
Tennessee	—	—	—	—	X
Texas	—	—	X	X	—
Utah	—	—	—	—	—
Vermont	X	X	X	X	X
Virginia	—	—	—	—	—
Washington	X	X	X	X	X
West Virginia	Y	Y	Y	Y	Y
Wisconsin	X	X	X	X	X
Wyoming	—	—	—	X	—

X: collective bargaining provisions; Y: meet and confer provisions; X/Y collective bargining on some issues, meet and confer on others.
Note: Administrative fiat includes, for example, civil service regulation, executive order, or attorney general opinion.
[a]Public transit workers only.
Source: Adapted from Richard C. Kearney, *Labor Relations in the Public Sector* (New York: Marcel Dekker, 1984). Updated by *Labor Relations Reporter*, "State Labor Laws." (Washington, D.C.: BNA, 1989–1990).

absence of specific statutory authorization, governmental jurisdictions may establish programs for labor relations and collective bargaining.

Since 1959, when Wisconsin became the first state to enact a comprehensive law governing public sector labor relations, well over half of the states have followed suit. By 1982, 40 states had relatively well-developed public sector labor relations policies—a remarkable change had occurred during the previous two decades. Yet the specific scope and nature of the states' policies and programs continue to vary widely (Table 10.4). There has been some tendency to distinguish between state and local employees and to differentiate among occupations in the various state regulations. Thus, firefighters, police, teachers, and other employees in a given state may face disparate conditions when seeking to collectively bargain. Moreover, a teacher, firefighter, or other employee who moves from one state to another may find that the available collective bargaining process varies substantially (see Table 10.4). While there are a number of advantages in this situation, including the flexibility for each state to adopt labor relations practices that are especially tailored to its particular political, economic, and employment conditions, there has nevertheless been a demand for a federal statute to guarantee uniform collective bargaining for state and local employees. Such a law would simplify the task of organized labor and enable the judicial and administrative rulings concerning labor relations in one state to be applied in another. However, there seems to be little enthusiasm for such a statute today, given that organized labor's influence is waning, so many states are in difficult fiscal times, and the Republican presidential administration is displaying no interest in the issue.

State labor relations can still be divided into the "meet and confer" and "negotiations" approaches. The former is premised on notions of sovereignty and the inequality of the partners involved in collective bargaining. This model closely resembles the Kennedy program; management retains many rights and may retain the final authority in all matters affecting personnel administration. The negotiations approach, on the other hand, has as its model labor relations in the private sector. Here management maintains whatever authority it is able to retain in the face of collective agreements; relationships are premised on equality between the parties engaged in the bargaining process. The majority of states having comprehensive labor relations programs have opted largely for the negotiations approach, although some have pursued the other course. Yet the evidence suggests that the latter, as can be observed in federal developments, is something of an interim measure and that as employees, government officials, the public, and politicians become more accustomed to collective bargaining in the public sector, almost all programs will emphasize negotiations and a specific format for resolving impasses.

Impasse resolution remains the most difficult problem confronting labor relations in the public sector. Impasses result when the parties to a contract negotiation cannot agree on an item (or items) within the scope of *mandatory* bargaining. In the private sector, impasses are frequently resolved through the application of economic force, such as strikes and lockouts. For the most part, however, such approaches are deemed unsuitable to the public sector, so that some other ways of resolving protracted disputes over mandatory bargaining items must be developed. The states have addressed this problem in a variety of ways. The most common approach begins with mediation of one sort or another and, where this is inadequate, escalates to fact-finding with nonbinding recommendations. Many states go a step further and require binding arbitration. Techniques for mediation, fact-finding, and arbitration vary widely and are discussed in the next chapter.

For the most part, state legislation is similar to federal statutes and regulations prohibiting strikes by public employees. There is, of course, a longstanding common law prohibition against such strikes and they are therefore illegal even where no explicit statutes exist. Nevertheless, several states have addressed the issue and allow strikes for some categories of public servants. Where states have outlawed strikes, the remedies for breaches of the prohibition generally include some form of injunctive relief obtained through judicial action or the issuance of cease-and-desist orders by the administrative agency responsible for the labor relations program (often called a public employment relations board or PERB). Statutes may also provide for the discipline of violating unions and employees. Here, the New York State Taylor Act continues to stand out for its practicality. In the event of what appears to be an illegal strike, the chief legal officer of the employer involved is required to seek an injunction against the union in the state supreme court. The public employer is directed to deduct two days pay for each day an employee was out on strike in violation of the act. Such employees are also to be placed on probation for a year, thereby jeopardizing their civil service status. Other disciplinary measures and even dismissal are permitted. The act further provides for fines against unions engaging in strikes in violation of injunctions and for the suspension of certain beneficial procedures such as dues checkoffs.

Nothing stands out more in public labor relations than the fact that the outlawing of strikes does not necessarily prevent them. In consequence, some states have legalized strikes for at least some categories of public employees and have sought to regulate them in some fashion (see Chapter 11).

The federal labor relations program protects the right of employees to refuse to join or support employee organizations. In general, state regulations also protect these rights. However, under the Supreme Court's decisions in *Abood* v. *Detroit* (1977) and *Chicago Teachers Union* v. *Hudson* (1986; see Chapters 9 and 11), public employees can be constitutionally required to pay a fee (counterpart fee or "fair share") to unions representing them in collective bargaining even though they are not members of these organizations. On the other hand, the Court left no doubt that enforced membership, through a "union shop," "closed shop," or "maintenance of membership" requirement, would be an unconstitutional violation of the public employee's First Amendment rights.

Conclusion

At this point, it is appropriate to reconsider the immense change that has taken place in the development and scope of public sector collective bargaining. About five decades ago, New York State's highest court had occasion to remark that "to tolerate or to recognize any combination of civil service employees of the Government as a labor organization or union is not only incompatible with the spirit of democracy, but inconsistent with every principle upon which our government is founded." Today, at least 80 percent of the states have statutory provisions for some kind of public sector labor relations, and even in the others public employees are free to exercise their First Amendment constitutional rights by joining unions. More important, despite the fragmented nature of public sector collective bargaining, a comprehensive labor relations model is emerging. It consists of

1. Recognition of employee rights to organize and bargain collectively, or to refrain from joining labor organizations
2. Recognition of employer rights in a "management rights clause" such as is found in the federal labor relations program
3. Inclusion of an administrative agency, such as the FLRA or state public employment relations board, to oversee the labor relations process and make rulings on matters of unit determination, negotiability, and unfair labor practices
4. Standards for bargaining unit determination
5. Procedures for recognizing unions as exclusive bargaining agents
6. A delineated scope of bargaining
7. Impasse resolution procedures
8. Provisions for union security arrangements (see Chapter 11)
9. A statement of unfair labor practices, often including strikes

This model bears both similarities and dissimilarities to practices in the private sector under the National Labor Relations Act (NLRA). The similarities lie in recognition of the right to organize and to bargain collectively, in the principle of exclusive recognition, in the creation of an administrative agency to oversee the operation of the collective bargaining process and to adjudicate disputes pertaining to its operation, and in the statement of unfair labor practices. In some ways, however, the dissimilarities are more profound. First, it must be remembered that whereas in the private sector it has been the federal government that writes the rules for collective bargaining, in the public sector governments write their own rules. Second, these rules may specify a broad set of "management rights" that seriously reduce the available scope of bargaining. Third, the impasse resolution procedures legislated for the public sector diverge very substantially from private sector practices, especially when it comes to arbitration of economic interests. Fourth, the outlawing of strikes and lockouts, which are viewed as integral to the private sector model, continues to place public sector labor relations on a dramatically different footing.

Because the public sector model diverges substantially from private sector practices, it often involves different politics and tactics. Moreover, it operates in a different personnel environment and has different consequences for personnel management generally. These are the subjects of the next chapter.

Bibliography

Balfour, Alan. *Union-Management Relations in a Changing Economy.* Englewood Cliffs, N.J.: Prentice Hall, 1987.

Barrett, Jerome T. *Labor-Management Cooperation in the Public Service.* Washington, D.C.: International Personnel Management Association, 1985.

Douglas, Joel M. "Public Sector Unionism: New Approaches—New Strategies," in Carolyn Ban and Norma M. Riccucci (eds.), *Public Personnel Management—Current Concerns, Future Challenges.* White Plains, N.Y.: Longman Press, 1991.

————. "Collective Bargaining for Public Sector Supervisors: A Trend Towards Exclusion?" *Public Administration Review*, 19 (November-December 1987).

Ferman, Louis (ed.) *The Future of American Unionism.* Beverly Hills, Calif.: Sage Publications, 1984.

Hill, Herbert. *Black Labor and the American Legal System.* Madison: The University of Wisconsin Press, 1985.

Kearney, Richard C. *Labor Relations in the Public Sector.* New York: Marcel Dekker, 1984 (second edition forthcoming).

Levitan, Sar and Alexandra Noden. *Working for the Sovereign: Employee Relations in the Federal Government.* Baltimore: Johns Hopkins University Press, 1983.

Lipset, Seymour Martin (ed.). *Unions in Transition.* San Francisco: Institute for Contemporary Studies, 1986.

Mosher, Frederick. *Democracy and the Public Service,* 2nd ed. New York: Oxford University Press, 1982.

Riccucci, Norma M. *Women, Minorities and Unions in the Public Sector.* Westport, Conn: Greenwood Press, 1990.

————. and Carolyn Ban. "The Unfair Labor Practice Process as a Dispute-Resolution Technique in the Public Sector: The Case of New York State," *Review of Public Personnel Administration*, 9 (Spring 1989).

Rosenbloom, David H. "The Federal Labor Relations Authority," *Policy Studies Journal*, 17 (Winter 1988–1989).

————. and Jay M. Shafritz. *Essentials of Labor Relations.* Englewood Cliffs, N.J.: Reston/Prentice Hall, 1985.

Stieber, Jack. *Public Employee Unionism: Structure, Growth Policy.* Washington, D.C.: Brookings Institution, 1973.

Sulzner, George T. "Public Sector Labor Relations: Agent of Change in American Industrial Relations?" in James L. Perry (ed.), symposium, *Review of Public Personnel Administration*, 5 (Spring 1985).

Troy, Leo. "Public Sector Unionism: The Rising Power Center of Organized Labor," *Government Union Review*, 9 (Summer 1988).

11
Labor Relations: Process, Participants, Tactics, and Politics

Prologue: The Demise of PATCO

It isn't often that a strike results in the total destruction of a union. Of course, the Professional Air Traffic Controller Organization (PATCO) was an exceptional union in a great many respects. It was one of the very few unions that supported the Republican presidential nominee, Ronald Reagan, for the presidency in 1980. It was the first major union to make concerns such as job strss and burnout significant collective bargaining issues. And it was so sure of itself as a union that couldn't be beaten by management that it overwhelmingly rejected an average annual salary offer of $38,000 in favor of striking.

On July 29, 1981, 95 percent of PATCO's 13,000 members, the traffic "cops" at the nation's airports, voted to reject the federal government's final offer. They insisted upon getting twice-a-year cost-of-living increases that would be 1½ times greater than inflation, a 4-day, 32-hour work week without a compensating salary cut, and retirement after 20 years at 75 percent of base salary. One striking controller stated the feelings of thousands: "Where are they going to get 13,000 controllers and train them before the economy sinks? The reality is, we are it. They have to deal with us."

But the Reagan administration was equally determined in its resolve to keep the planes flying. First, it cut back on many scheduled flights and reduced the staff at some of the smallest airports. Then it put air traffic control supervisors (who were not members of the union) and some retired controllers back into service and ordered as many military controllers as could be spared to civilian duty stations. Finally, President Reagan addressed the entire nation on televison. After reminding the American public that it is illegal for federal government employees to strike against their employer and that each controller signed an oath asserting that he or she would never strike, he proclaimed: "They are in violation of the law, and if they do not report for work within 48 hours, they have forfeited their jobs and will be terminated." About 1,000 controllers took the president at his word and reported back to work. Most of the rest thought that he was just bluffing.

Then a ghoulish wait began. It would only take one serious accident and the deaths of innocent passengers for the situation to turn in the union's favor. PATCO was loudly critical of the safety of what it called the nation's "fill-in" air traffic control system. The president of PATCO said: "I hope that nothing happens!" He told the Secretary of Transportation: "If passengers are killed, it'll be your responsibility." Fortunately, while there were near misses, no one was hurt. There were no accidents.

The strike continued and the president showed that he wasn't bluffing after all. Over 11,000 controllers received formal letters of dismissal. PATCO's assets were frozen by court order, some PATCO leaders were literally taken away to jail in chains, and the Department of Transportation started formal proceedings to decertify the union.

With its members fired, with practically no public support, and with the fill-in system working better every day, PATCO—the union that had broken ranks with labor to support Republican presidential candidate Reagan—called for labor solidarity. The response was minimal. The major labor leaders verbally supported the strike and deplored the president's efforts at "union busting," but did nothing else. United Auto Workers President Douglas Fraser said that the strike "could do massive damage to the labor movement. That's why PATCO should have talked to the AFL-CIO council"—before they struck. Had any of the major airline unions joined in the strike, the system would surely have been shut down. But none of these unions felt that they had any obligation to support the controllers in any way that mattered.

In late October the Federal Labor Relations Authority formally decertified PATCO—the first time that it had ever done so to any union of federal government workers. In December, PATCO was forced to file for bankruptcy. In the end over 11,000 of the controllers who stayed on strike lost their jobs permanently.

The PATCO episode illustrates several aspects of public sector labor relations. First, it exemplified the passing of labor relations from a period in which unions were relatively secure to one in which they were increasingly vulnerable. Public opinion in favor of containing the cost of government by adopting labor-saving technologies and contracting out to private firms became a major force in many local governments. Unions found themselves doing the unthinkable: bargaining over pay freezes, reductions, givebacks, subcontracting, cutbacks,

What Is NATCA?

The National Air Traffic Controllers Association (NATCA) is the collective bargaining agent or union for air traffic controllers in this nation. It won representational rights in 1987, and as of 1990 had approximately 8,000 members (this is over 50 percent of the air traffic controller work force). NATCA, founded on the principle of "safety above all," is affiliated with District One of the Marine Engineers' Beneficial Association, AFL-CIO. It has no ties to the Professional Air Traffic Controllers Organization (PATCO), which was decertified in 1981 for striking.

and more authority for management. Second, once again the symbolic importance of federal labor relations was made clear. Just as the Kennedy executive order helped legitimize public sector collective bargaining in state and local governments, Reagan's union busting showed the public and governments throughout the nation that strikes could be broken and that a determined government could find a way to cope with work stoppages. Third, Reagan's handling of PATCO demonstrated the importance of the legal procedures that govern public sector collective bargaining. Collective bargaining can sometimes be lawless and chaotic, but it is always fundamentally rooted in a legal framework. Governmental employers, like their employees, may choose to overlook the law regulation collective bargaining when they deem it necesary or desirable, but they can also invoke it when it is to their advantage. Illegal strikes were frequently tolerated in the 1960s and early 1970s, but Reagan's message to PATCO was as clear as Coolidge's to Boston's finest—flaunt the law at your own peril. This chapter picks up on these themes in discussing the process, participants, tactics, and politics of public sector labor relations. We begin with a thorough analysis of the process, from which much of the rest follows.

The Right to Join and Form Unions

Although once widely denied, the right to join and form unions is now secure for most public employees. However, the position of supervisors remains problematic. Here is a clear case of the difficulty of trying to transfer the private sector model to the public sector. In private corporations, managers are not unionized. Whatever the legal basis of the organization, they are considered part of the employer. The Taft-Hartley act (1947) excludes private sector supervisors from membership in bargaining units. In the public sector, however, a markedly different situation prevails. The employer is the

Montplaisir, et al. v. Leighton,
875 F.2d 1 (1st Cir. 1989)

Facts—In 1981, Paul Montplaisir and three others were employed as air traffic controllers at the Nashua, New Hampshire, Federal Aviation Administration (FAA) facility. All four were members of the Professional Air Traffic Controllers Organization
(PATCO). On August 3, 1981, PATCO struck. Montplaisir and his three coworkers
were dismissed from their jobs for participating in the strike. They are now seeking
remediation under a state malpractice statute against Leighton, who served as
PATCO's general counsel during the strike. These former air traffic controllers are
claiming that the lawyer encouraged the unlawful strike and negligently advised them
and other traffic controllers that they ran no risk of losing their jobs by participating
in the strike.

Issue—Are the former air traffic controllers entitled to relief under state malpractice
legislation for losses suffered by participating in the PATCO strike?

Discussion—The U.S. Court of Appeals for the 1st Circuit ruled that Title VII of
the Civil Service Reform Act (CSRA) of 1978 provides an exclusive remedy for
such claims as those brought by Montplaisir and his co-workers. The court went
on to add that the former air traffic controllers "stand in a singularly poor position
to assert a right of recovery against lawyer-defendants for counseling the [strike]....
It was plaintiffs' union which masterminded the strike effort....It was no secret that
strikes against the federal government were illegal....The 'bad advice' which the
attorneys reportedly gave was that plaintiffs would probably incur no penalty for
violating the statute because 'there is no way that the government can...fire 15,000
air traffic controllers'....Thus assured that they could act with impunity, the [air traffic
controllers] proceeded to flout the law. Having been caught in toils of their own
construction, plaintiffs have little basis for asking us to poke a hole in CSRA's
regulatory net for their aid and succor."

public or its representative (i.e., the government). Supervisors do not make
decisions related to profits and losses and do not have an economic situation
vis-à-vis their employer that differs much, if at all, from rank-and-file
employees. They are not paid out of company profits. Moreover, public personnel law often treats supervisors no differently from other employees, as
in the case of political neutrality and residency regulations, for example. As
a result of prevailing civil service law, public sector supervisors also tend
to have a narrower scope of authority over rank-and-file personnel than do
private managers. Thus, the issue is whether or not public supervisors have
interests or positions sufficiently different from those of other public employees
to limit their right to join and form unions.

Leaving aside the very thorny question of what constitutes a bona fide
supervisor (something upon which jurisdictions tend to differ), the following

situation prevails. While constitutional law appears to guarantee the right of supervisors to join and form unions, it also appears that they may legitimately be excluded from joining unions with rank-and-file members. The rationale behind this approach is that where supervisors belong to unions with non-supervisory members, their loyalties may be divided between the union and the employer. Consequently, they might fail to enforce disciplinary measures, work rules, and even official policy. However, allowing supervisors to join unions does not guarantee them a right to bargain collectively. For example, in some jurisdictions, certain categories of supervisors are afforded full collective bargaining rights either in separate autonomous bargaining units or in "mixed" units, where supervisors belong to units with rank-and-file (i.e., nonsupervisory) employees. In those same jurisdictions, other categories of supervisors may be completely excluded from collective bargaining, or they may be afforded meet-and-confer rights (see Table 11.1).

National Labor Relations Board (NLRB) v. *Yeshiva University and Yeshiva Faculty Association,*
444 U.S. 672 (1980)

Facts—In 1974, the Yeshiva Faculty Association filed a representation petition with the National Labor Relations Board (NLRB) seeking to unionize full-time faculty members at Yeshiva, a private university. The university opposed the petition, arguing that faculty members are managerial or supervisory personnel and therefore not eligible, in accordance with the National Labor Relations Act (NLRA), to bargain collectively. The NLRB granted the union's petition. The bargaining unit consisted of assistant deans, the departmental chair, and faculty at all ranks (i.e., from instructor to full professor). The university refused to bargain with the union, based on the aforementioned ground.

Issue—Are faculty members, at least at private-sector universities, managers or supervisors within the meaning set forth by the NLRA, and hence ineligible for collective bargaining?

Discussion—The U.S. Supreme Court in *Yeshiva* held that the faculty at Yeshiva "exercise authority which in any other context unquestionably would be managerial ...They decide what courses will be offered, when they will be scheduled, and to whom they will be taught. They debate and determine teaching methods, grading policies and matriculation standards." To this extent, the Court said that "faculty [exercise] supervisory and managerial functions and [are] therefore excluded from the category of employees entitled to benefits of collective bargaining under the NLRA."

Although *Yeshiva* pertains only to private universities and colleges, some public colleges and universities have sought to apply the ruling to their own institutions in order to deny faculty collective-bargaining rights.

Table 11.1. Public Sector Supervisors' (PSS) Collective Bargaining Rights

Jurisdiction	Coverage	Complete exclusion of PSS	Separate bargaining units for PSS	Mixed units[a]
Alabama	Firefighers			X
Alaska	General Unit		X	
	Teachers	X		
	Ferry employees			X
California	State civil service		X	
	State non-civil service			X
	Local Government			X
	Public School		X	
	Higher education		X	
	Firefighters			X
Connecticut	State employees			X
	Municipal employees		X	
	Teachers	X		
Delaware	General unit			X
	Public school	X		
	Transit employees			X
	Police and fire			X
District of Columbia	All public employees		X	
Florida	All public employees			X
Georgia	Firefighters			X
Hawaii	All public employees		X	
Idaho	Firefighters	X		
	Teachers	X		
Illinois	Public employees	X		
	Educational employees	X		
Indiana	Teachers	X		
Iowa	General unit	X		
	Firefighters			X
	Judicial employees			X
Kansas	General unit	X		
	Teachers	X		
Kentucky	Firefighters			X
	Police			X

(continued)

Table 11.1. *Continued*

Jurisdiction	Coverage	Complete exclusion of PSS	Separate bargaining units for PSS	Mixed units[a]
Maine	State employees		X	
	Municipal, county, school		X	
	University employees		X	
	Judicial employees		X	
Maryland	Teachers	X		
	Noncertified public school		X	
Massachusetts	General unit			X
	Police and fire			X
Michigan	General unit		X	
	Police and fire			X
Minnesota	All public employees		X	
Missouri	General unit			X
Montana	General unit	X		
	Nurses			X
Nebraska	General unit		X	
	Teachers			X
Nevada	Local government employees		X	
New Hampshire	All public employees		X	
New Jersey	All public employees		X	
	Police and fire			X
New Mexico	State employees	X		
New York	General unit			X
North Dakota	Teacher and school administrators		X	
Ohio	General unit	X		
Oklahoma	Police and fire	X		
	Public school employees	X		
Oregon	General unit	X		

(continued)

Table 11.1. *Continued*

Jurisdiction	Coverage	Complete exclusion of PSS	Separate bargaining units for PSS	Mixed units[a]
Pennsylvania	General unit		X	
	Police and fire			X
	Transit employees			X
Rhode Island	State employees		X	
	State police	X		
	Municipal employees	X		
	Teachers	X		
	Municipal employees			X
	Firefighters			X
South Dakota	All public employees	X		
Tennessee	Teachers			X
	Transit employees			X
Texas	Police and Fire			X
Vermont	State employees		X	
	Municipal employees	X		
	Teachers		X	
Virgin Islands	General unit		X	
Washington	Municipal employees			X
	Teachers		X	
	Community college district			X
	Higher education classified			X
	Port District			X
	Ferry Employees			X
	Utility districts			X
Wisconsin	State employees		X	
	Municipal employees	X		
	Police and fire			X
Wyoming	Firefighters			X

[a]The presumption in favor of PSS inclusion was deemed to be controlling. Unless the legislation had a specific exclusion or designated unit placement, supervisory employees are presumed to have bargaining rights in mixed units with rank-and-file employees.

Source: Adapted from Joel M. Douglas, *At the Bargaining Table: The Status of Public Sector Supervisory, Managerial and Confidential Employees* (Alexandria, Va.: International Personnel Management Association, 1989).

Which arrangement is best? It all depends on the character of the collective bargaining process in the particular jurisdiction. In general, though, it appears that mixed supervisory-nonsupervisory units are most likely to militate against effective supervision and management for productivity and efficiency. At the same time, the total exclusion of supervisors from the labor relations process makes sense only insofar as employees who are defined as supervisory are distinct in their duties and relationship to the employer. Even then, the meet-and-confer approach would seem to be sensible.

A second problem under the heading of joining and forming unions is that the employer, though interested in the outcome of such efforts, must scrupulously avoid becoming involved in unionizing activities. Among other things, the employer cannot make any effort to dominate a union, show favoritism toward a particular union, or prohibit employees from soliciting membership, distributing literature, or displaying support for a union during nonwork time at the place of employment. Surveillance and interrogation of employees or threats or promises to them have also been ruled unfair labor practices.

Establishing the Collective Bargaining Relationship

Federal, state, and local regulations concerning the collective bargaining process vary widely. Where collective bargaining is sanctioned by law, practice, or judicial interpretation, several steps may be necessary before a union can collectively bargain on behalf of its employees:

1. It must be determined whether or not the employees are covered by the regulations in force. This is not always as easy as it sounds because there are seemingly innumerable quasi-public, quasi-private boards and commissions in operation in the United States. The National Labor Relations Act (NLRA), which governs collective bargaining in the private sector, excludes states and their political subdivisions from its coverage. The courts have tended to define the latter in terms of how their officials are selected, whether they have the power of eminent domain, and whether they can issue federallly tax-exempt bonds. Nevertheless, the situation can be problematic. In one set of decisions, the New York State Public Employment Relations Board (PERB) held that the Nassau County library system was not a public employer within the meaning of the governing Taylor Law whereas the National Labor Relations Board (NLRB) held that it was not a private employer! Interstate and international bridge commissions or authorities also present substantial problems of interpretation.

2. Then there is the question of whether the organization employees are joining or forming can be considered a labor union. In general, such an organization would have to involve employee participation and deal with

employers concerning wages, grievances, labor disputes, hours, and working conditions. Depending upon state law, it might have to place primary emphasis on such activities. In addition, unions must be free of corrupt practices, may be subject to elaborate financial disclosure and antidiscrimination provisions, and may be formally required to refrain from striking. Again, the issues are hardly clear-cut: it has been ruled that an organization composed solely of supervisors in the federal service could not be considered a union, but also that an organization solely of students at Wayne State University could be so defined.

3. Once it has been determined that the employees in question are "public" and that they are seeking to join or form a "union," a process for showing interest and holding elections is generally necessary. Often, a showing of interest requires that a union have the support of at least 30 percent of the employees in the proposed bargaining unit. This support can be conveyed to the employer by a submission of membership cards, authorizations to have dues checked off by the employer, or some form of petition. When such a showing is made, an election will ordinarily be held. For a union to become the exclusive representative of the employees in the unit, it must generally receive a majority vote of the ballots cast.

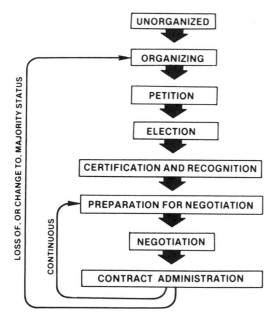

Figure 11.1. Typical sequence of organizing events. *Source*: U.S. Office of Personnel Management, *Manager's Handbook* (Washington, D.C.: U.S. Government Printing Office, 1979), p. 137.

This approach makes nonvoters irrelevant to the outcome of the election. Consequently, it probably tends to encourage employees to participate. The election will give employees the opportunity to vote for "no representative" as well as for one or more unions. If there are more than two options on the ballot and none gets a majority, either no union will be certified as the exclusive agent or a runoff election among the two options receiving the most votes will be held, depending upon prevailing regulations. If no union is elected, an "election bar" may take effect. Depending upon the jurisdiction, union electoral activity may be barred anywhere from one to two years.

What can be granted by election can also be taken away by election. Unions can be decertified or replaced by others. This process may be initiated by employees, who may have to demonstrate a 30 percent showing of interest in decertification. Provisions concerning the employer's right to begin a decertification process vary. In any event, however, such an action would have to be taken strictly in good faith and not as a means of harassing a union. Decertification procedures may be prohibited by law within a fixed period of the original granting of recognition or at times when the expiration of contracts or agreements is imminent. The purpose of this practice is to afford a degree of stability to representation. If a decertification election is held, then the union must again muster majority support or lose its status as exclusive representative.

Unit Determination

We have been discussing the process of establishing the public sector collective bargaining relationship as though the nature of bargaining "units" is self-evident. However, this is not always the case. The nature of a unit—its size, and kinds of employees in it, occupationally and sometimes socially—has a great bearing on the outcome of representational elections. Hence, unit determination is inherently political. The following are among the criteria typically considered:

1. A clear and identifiable community of interest among the employees
2. Effective dealings with the unit and efficient operations
3. A history of representation
4. The level of authority of the employees and the officials with whom they might bargain
5. Agreement between the parties
6. The convenience of the employer

Typically, professional employees will not be forced into units with nonprofessionals.

In recent years, some public employers have opted for larger units. These have the advantage of reducing fragmentation and its concomitant tendencies toward constant chaotic bargaining and competition among the units. Massachusetts presents a good example. It rejected units based on departments and placed employees into the following ten statewide units:

Professional	*Nonprofessional*
Administrative	Clerical and administrative
Health care	Service, maintenance, and institutional
Social and rehabilitative	Building trade and crafts
Engineering and science	Institutional security
Education	Law enforcement

Florida, Iowa, Hawaii, New York, New Jersey, Washington, Minnesota, Wisconsin, Pennsylvania, Kansas, and Alaska are other states having at least one statewide bargaining unit.

Although the criteria for unit determination may be spelled out in some detail, like so much of public sector labor relations, the establishment of bargaining units is inherently political. Units should be designated that facilitate the representation of employees since that is the main purpose of collective bargaining. But this might require that employees with related yet different occupations be placed in separate units. It might even require that employees having the same occupation but engaging in it in different workplaces be afforded representation through separate units. For instance, academic employees of the State University of New York are in one statewide bargaining unit even though the character of their jobs and the requirements placed upon them varies considerably from, say, the State University at Buffalo to the State College at Plattsburg. Employees therefore might prefer smaller units. However, unless the employees are essential to the public interest, small units will probably be less powerful than large ones. So employees are faced with a serious trade-off. So are unions, which may find it easier to organize smaller, less powerful units. From their perspectives, however, seeking to represent a diverse body of employees at the bargaining table may place great strains on the union's internal political processes. A union leader who fails to reconcile differences among sizable groups in a bargaining unit is not likely to win much from management or even remain a union leader for long. Nowadays the public employer tends to prefer larger units for the sake of convenience—but at a price. The public policy favoring collective bargaining will be frustrated if there is neither rhyme nor reason to the creation of units. A large number of small units also enables employers to engage in divide-and-conquer strategies and to prevent the potentially devastating effects of a statewide strike.

The Scope of Bargaining

Once a collective bargaining relationship is established, the nature of the scope of bargaining becomes of crucial importance (Figure 11.2). It is possible to classify issues concerning the scope of bargaining into three categories: (1) items upon which bargaining is mandatory, (2) items upon which it is permitted, and (3) items upon which it is prohibited. However, where specific items will fall varies widely with the regulations of various jurisdictions.

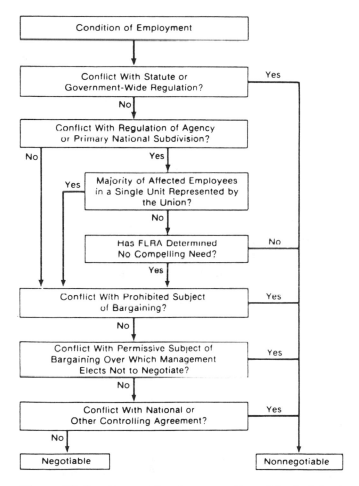

Figure 11.2. Determining the scope of bargaining in federal employment: *Source: The Federal Labor-Management Consultant* (Washington, D.C.' U.S. Office of Personnel Management, November 2, 1979).

For example, most federal employees cannot bargain over wages and hours, but this is very much what collective bargaining in municipalities is generally about. In the private sector, bargaining refers to "wages, hours, and other terms and conditions of employment." However, in the public sector it is common to exclude matters controlled by civil service legislation and to specify a set of management rights that are beyond the scope of bargaining. Matters that fall within the scope of any agency's "mission" are also commonly outside the scope of bargaining. Today the tendency is to consider other matters to be within the scope of bargaining unless specifically excluded by statute, court decision, or PERB ruling. This is especially true of matters having a primary impact on the welfare of the employee rather than upon the operating effectiveness of the government as a whole. Sometimes an even weaker test is used—the subject will be within the scope of bargaining if it bears a "significant relation" to working conditions defined within the mandatory or permitted bargaining categories.

But what is a primary impact or significant relation? Here are some puzzlers that demonstrate the politics of public sector collective bargaining. Each is an issue of public policy that some might think better resolved through the processes of representative government than by collective bargaining. However, each is undeniably a working condition of great consequence to the public employees involved:

1.   The number of police officers assigned to a squad car
2.   The conditions under which police can use deadly force
3.   The weaponry and protective gear used by police
4.   The right of firefighters to carry weapons
5.   The decentralization or consolidation of school systems
6.   School discipline
7.   School calendars
8.   The quality and technology of patient care in public mental health facilities
9.   The number of pupils per classroom in public schools
10. Observance of Martin Luther King, Jr. Day as a state or municipal holiday

The importance of the scope of bargaining exceeds mere delineation of what the parties can seek to negotiate. It places very serious constraints on management and is related to the use of impasse procedures. In general, management cannot unilaterally alter a working condition that has been defined within the scope of mandatory bargaining. This may be true even if the collective bargaining contract has expired, but labor negotiations are underway. Failure to reach agreement on a mandatory item triggers impasse resolution procedures at the appropriate time. This is an area in which bilateralism or

Fort Stewart Schools v. *Federal Labor Relations Authority (FLRA),*
110 S. Ct. 2043 (1990)

Facts—During a round of collective negotiations, Fort Stewart Schools, a federal
government employer (owned and operated by the Army at a military facility in
Georgia), refused to negotiate with the union, the Fort Stewart Association of
Educators, over wages and fringe benefits. The employer claimed that such matters
were not subject to negotiations under Title VII of the Civil Service Reform Act
(CSRA) of 1978. The union appealed to the FLRA, which ruled that the union's
proposals to bargain over a salary increase, paid leave, and milage reimbursement
were negotiable under the CSRA.

Issue—Were the union's proposals related to "conditions of employment" within
the meaning of the CSRA and therefore subject to negotiations?

Discussion—The U.S. Supreme Court first acknowledged that the "wages and fringe
benefits of the overwhelming majority of Executive Branch employees are fixed by
law, in accordance with the General Schedules of the Civil Service Act...and are
therefore eliminated from the definition of 'conditions of employment.'" Thus, for
most federal employees, unions cannot bargain over wages and fringe benefits; rather,
they are determined by Congress.

But, the question remained, could federal employees not covered by the General
Schedule (GS) or other systems that are provided for by federal statute bargain over
wages? In a unanimous decision, the Supreme Court said that employees of such
schools as Fort Stewart are "among a miniscule minority of federal employees whose
wages are exempted from operation of the General Schedules." For these and other
federal employees not covered by the GS, wages need not be set by Congress. Rather,
the Court said that unions may negotiate with their employers over such issues as
wages and fringe benefits.

codetermination by management and labor is required by the contemporary
public sector collective bargaining process. In addition, management will most
likely be required to consult with unions if it seeks to alter a working condition within the permitted bargaining category. In this case, although a sincere
effort is necessary, it is not required that the parties reach an agreement. It
is important to bear in mind that a kind of common law of the workplace
is frequently recognized that limits management's right to alter unilaterally
even working conditions that are not directly spelled out in negotiated labor
contracts.

Unfair Labor Practices and Good Faith

Unfair labor practices (ULPs) are serious breakdowns of properly functioning
labor relations. The following employer practices are typically considered
unfair:

1. Interfering in any way with the exercise of employee rights under the collective bargaining statute
2. Interfering in any way with the formation or administration of an employee organization, including trying to assist in its formation
3. Encouraging or discouraging membership in a labor organization through personnel actions directed toward specific employees or groups of employees
4. Discriminating against an employee in any way because he or she has filed charges or given testimony under the statute, or because he or she has or has not joined or been active in an employee organization
5. Denying the rights of an exclusively designated agent
6. Refusing to submit to (or avoiding) required impasse procedures
7. Instituting a lockout
8. Violating the terms of the collective bargaining agreement
9. Failure to bargain in good faith

The latter condition requires some further explanation.

The question of good faith sometimes arises in negotiations. In general, bargaining in good faith requires that the parties genuinely seek to reach a negotiated agreement. It does not require that such an agreement be reached, but rather that the parties not engage in negotiations with the intention of frustrating the process. The requirement of good faith has some important consequences for public employers. They must delegate enough authority and trust to their negotiators or any agreements reached with labor will have little chance of becoming binding. Yet it is also axiomatic that whoever negotiates for the public employer cannot compel elected legislative and executive officials to agree to the terms of the proposed contract. Consequently, a fine line often exists as to whether the public employer has truly granted its negotiators enough authority or whether it is using them to engage in "surface bargaining." The latter is generally a breach of good faith and is aimed at using the negotiator to reduce labor's demands with the intention of subsequently reducing them even further by rejecting any proposed contract agreement that is reached.

Sometimes the requirement of good faith may also require that the public employer vigorously participate and make sensible counterproposals. Remember that without the right to strike, labor may have trouble making the employer take its proposals seriously. A unilateral change in working conditions after the expiration of a contract while negotiations for a new one are going on may also be considered a show of bad faith, or even a ULP. The same may be true of an employer's ettempt to bypass union leaders and speak directly to its employees concerning working arrangements subject to collective bargaining. The employer may also be required to submit information to employee unions, even though this information may weaken the employer's position. If an employer claims "inability to pay" for labor's demands for wages, hours, and so forth, the employer will generally be required to open its books to union scrutiny.

Labor organizations are also prohibited from engaging in ULPs and breaches of good faith. Among the practices typically prohibited are the following:

1. Interfering in any way with the exercise of employee rights under the statute
2. Interfering in any way with a public employer with respect to protecting the exercise of employee rights under the statute or selecting a bargaining representative
3. Refusing to engage in mandated impasse procedures
4. Engaging in or instigating a strike or other job action where prohibited
5. Hindering or interfering with an employee's work performance or productivity
6. Refusing to meet and bargain collectively in good faith

International Association of Firefighters (IAFF) v. City of Homestead, **291 So. 2d 38 (Fla. Ct. App. 1974)**

Facts—In January of 1971, the city of Homestead, Florida, recognized the IAFF as the exclusive bargaining agent for city firefighters. The city council subsequently named the city manager as the bargaining representative for the city (i.e., management). In November of 1971, negotiations commenced with the understanding that a final agreement between labor and management would require approval by the city council. In January of 1972, the city council met to review the collective bargaining agreement entered into by the IAFF and the city manager. It proceeded to renegotiate the entire contract, changing every provision that had been agreed upon by the union and city manager.

Issue—Has the city met its obligation to negotiate in good faith with the IAFF? Did the city grant to the city manager the authority needed to enter into a contract with the union?

Discussion—The Florida appeals court said that Article I, Section 6 of the constitution of the state of Florida grants public employees the right to bargain collectively. Several courts in Florida have ruled that this section of the state constitution imposes a duty upon the public employer to negotiate in good faith with its employees' bargaining representative. The court thus found the city in violation of good faith bargaining. It said that the city's "conduct in attempting to renegotiate the entire contract after the lengthy negotiations between the Union and the City Manager, indicates that the bargaining...was only surface bargaining and not a good faith effort by the City to reach agreement with [the union]."

Unions are generally also subject to a number of structural requirements. These pertain to their internal governance, which must be democratic, and their finances, which cannot be corrupt. Unions are also prohibited from discriminating against members or would-be members on the basis of such factors as race, color, religion, national origin, and sex. They also may be required to be "loyal," not subversive, to the United States and/or the jurisdiction in question. Unions enjoying exclusive recognition are prohibited from discriminating against nonmembers in the bargaining unit, that is, they have a legal "duty of fair representation," whereby the union must represent and treat all unit members fairly and equally.

Impasse Resolution

If an agreement between a union and an employer cannot be reached on matters within the scope of mandatory bargaining, some method of impasse resolution may be used. In some cases the choice of method, if any, is left to the parties to the negotiations. In others, impasse procedures are mandated by the labor relations statute. In states having comprehensive public sector labor relations programs, the PERB or equivalent agency must generally be notified that the parties are at an impasse before impasse resolution procedures are undertaken. Typically, three kinds of procedures are used as mechanisms for resolving impasses and thereby avoiding breakdowns of the collective bargaining process to the point where illegal strikes occur or employees are forced to work without a contract. These are mediation, fact-finding, and arbitration.

Mediation involves efforts of a third-party neutral participant to persuade those involved in the dispute to reach a settlement. Mediation cannot work if all of the concerned parties do not support it. It is by nature a voluntary process. Where there is an aura of distrust between the disputants, each side may be unwilling to make compromises, lest these become the basis upon which bargaining takes place if the mediator's efforts ultimately fail. Mediation may also represent an effort by the disputants to avoid difficult and prolonged bargaining, although mediators may simply recommend further direct negotiations. Mediators can be private individuals, but in most cases they are supplied by a government agency, such as the Federal Mediation and Conciliation Service. Mosts state labor laws provide for mediation, and over half of the states offer mediation services.

Mediation is a highly informal process and much of the information about it is anecdotal. Generally, one supposes, the mediator meets jointly and individually with the disputants. He or she tries to keep them talking to each other and at the bargaining table. Part of the mediator's work is to develop a better climate for negotiations and to try to make the parties more skillful at bargaining. Another part is to try to help the parties to reach a substantive

Karahalios v. National Federation of Federal Employees (NFFE),
489 U.S. 527 (1989)

Facts—Efthimios Karahalios was employed by the Defense Language Institute as
a Greek language instructor. He was not a member of the NFFE, but belonged to
its bargaining unit. In 1976, the Language Institute reopened the heretofore defunct
position of course developer. Karahalios applied and was subsequently hired for this
position. Simon Kuntelos who had held this position before it was abolished, sought
to return to the job without going through the competitive application process. Kuntelos
filed a grievance, and the NFFE was successful in getting the position declared vacant. Kuntelos was eventually reassigned to his old position of course developer.
Karahalios then filed a grievance for which the NFFE refused to participate in because
of its previous support for Kuntelos. Karahalios filed suit in federal court against
not only the institute, but also against the union, claiming that the union breached
its duty of fair representation.

Issue—Did the NFFE breach its duty of fair representation by refusing to process
the grievance filed by Karahalios?

Discussion—The federal district court ruled that the union did violate its fair representation duty. However, the appeals court and then the U.S. Supreme Court ruled that
federal employees cannot bring duty of fair representation suits against their unions
in the federal courts; rather, they are limited to filing such suits with the Federal
Labor Relations Authority (FLRA). The Supreme Court said that the Civil Service
Reform Act of 1978 recognizes that unions have a duty to represent all of its bargaining
unit members. But the Court went on to say that "an administrative remedy for its
breach is expressly provided for before the FLRA, created by Congress" to enforce
such duties as fair representation.

agreement. This may involve determining what each side will agree to and
then formulating an acceptable package to which the two sides can subscribe.
Sometimes agreement can be facilitated merely by the choice of the right words
in proposals and counterproposals.

Mediation is prized for its flexibility. However, it also has some
drawbacks. There is no finality to it. Moreover, skillful mediators, who may
be difficult to find in any case, may forge agreements by using language that
has somewhat different meanings to management and labor. In this event,
disputes may resurface in the form of grievances after the contract has been
signed. According to Richard Kearney, mediation is *least* successful (1) in
large jurisdictions, (2) where the parties have gone to impasse frequently,
(3) where the basic dispute involves the employer's ability to pay, and (4)
where the parties face strong external pressures to avoid compromise. Conversely, successful mediation appears to depend very heavily upon timing

and trust. It must begin after an impasse has been reached but before positions have hardened so much that compromise is unlikely. If the mediator loses the trust of one side and is viewed as an ally of the other, the process is bound to fail.

Fact-finding involves a third party in more of an investigatory and judicial role. The objective is for a neutral observer to review the key aspects of a dispute and issue a report. The report may simply state the fact-finder's view of the facts or it may include recommendations for a resolution of the dispute. The report may be public or reserved to the parties and any appropriate governmental agencies. Actually, the term *fact-finding* may be something of a misnomer. According to the late Jerry Wurf, who was a powerful leader of the American Federation of State, County, and Municipal Employees (AFSCME), "the parties usually know and understand the facts. The problem is that these facts are interpreted from positions of self-interest and therefore lead rational people to conflicting conclusions." In a sense, fact-finding really amounts to a form of voluntary arbitration. There will be pressure on the parties to accept the fact-finder's report and recommendations, if any, but they are not bound by it and are free to seek a different resolution. More than thirty states provide for fact-finding in public sector disputes. It tends to work well in part because there is often considerable pressure on the parties to accept a fact-finder's "neutral" or "fair" recommendation. Like mediation, fact-finding depends heavily upon the trust of the two sides in the impartiality of the third party.

Arbitration is another kind of third-party intervention. It can take several forms, but it is always primarily judicial in character. The arbitrator or panel of arbitrators holds hearings, receives evidence, hears the perspectives of the parties to the dispute, and makes recommendations (often called "awards") as to how the impasse should be resolved. Arbitration abandons the hope that the parties to a dispute can reach an agreement themselves. Rather, its purpose is to formulate a contract per se. Since arbitration moves away from self-determination in the workplace by imposing conditions, it is seldom used to resolve impasses over economic interests (as opposed to grievances) in the private sector.

There are several forms of arbitration. It can be voluntary or compulsory, depending upon how the parties enter into it. Compulsory arbitration is frequently found in states with comprehensive labor legislation and is used where other impasse procedures have failed or are deemed inappropriate. Arbitration can also be binding or nonbinding, depending on whether the parties are required to adhere to the arbitrator's award. Nonbinding arbitration is similar to fact-finding and suffers from a lack of finality. Arbitration can also take a form called "final offer" or "last best offer." This requires the parties to the impasse to submit their final offers for resolution to the arbitrator.

Disadvantages of Fact-Finding and Arbitration

Despite the benefits of fact-finding and arbitration as means of resolving disputes, they do have their limitations.

First, although fact-finding and arbitration have been widely acclaimed as providing the final solutions to collective bargaining disputes, neither really guarantees the reestablishment of labor-management relations harmony. Since the fact finder's report is advisory it may be totally rejected by either or both parties. If this occurs the parties may well be back where they started or perhaps even worse off. If the fact finder's report is only partially rejected, an additional effort at settlement is dictated by the need for the parties to meet and negotiate some adjustment or compromise which will bring them to settlement. In this subsequent negotiation there is always a chance of stalemate recurring. In a few States the designating agencies may make arrangements for offering additional mediation services. However, the use of such steps beyond fact finding is discouraged, because it tends to invite bypassing of mediation at its proper place in the system.

There is some question as to whether even arbitration achieves the finality for which it is acclaimed. It is always possible for one of the parties to continue to press the other to adjust the arbitrator's award more to its liking. Even if there is no such restructuring by the parties themselves and the award is implemented as written, there is still the prospect that it will not be accepted. Even though the award is presumably final and binding, there is a body of experience which suggests that dissatisfaction by either party may preclude a complete compliance with its terms.

The Montreal Police strike of a few years ago occurred in defiance of a final and binding arbitration award. Although we have not yet had out-and-out strikes in the U.S. under such circumstances, there have been occasional protests through slowdowns, sick outs, and the like, demonstrating rank-and-file objections to an award. As arbitration of impasse disputes expands, so too will the likelihood of objections to imposed awards.

Second, the issuance of a fact-finding report recommending specific dispositions of disputed issues undoubtedly deadlocks the parties by creating a vested interest for the successful proponents of those issues. This problem is of course much less likely to exist in arbitration, although it might occur if one of the parties sought the agreement of the other to modify the award.

In both arbitration and fact-finding, the neutral's determination may thus become a strait jacket. This may be a more serious problem where findings are offbase, unrealistic, or impractical of attainment. It virtually precludes any flexibility for subsequent negotiations toward a more workable agreement. Thus when the document makes a finding which favors one part of the constituency, the interests represented thereby become virtually immutable, and it is difficult, at best, to then negotiate those "victories" away.

Finally, neither fact finding nor arbitration can guarantee a final document which can be hailed as the true substitute for the strike, i.e., can produce that result which

(continued)

Disadvantages of Fact-Finding and Arbitration *(continued)*

would have been reached if the parties had been in a position to negotiate their agreement to finality without the intervention of fact finding or arbitration. Fact finders, with their inability to bind the parties to their recommendations, must place extensive (if not excessive) emphasis on acceptability as distinguished from equity. Arbitrators, on the other hand, working in a more legalistic and antiseptic atmosphere, are usually deprived of any insight into the true priorities of the parties. It is difficult for them to ascertain acceptability, and hence, equity tends to be emphasized. This would be true even if the parties themselves might have preferred to have settled on a more acceptable, though less equitable, package. Finality may be stimulated or achieved, but the "best" package for both parties may not be the end result.

Arnold Zack, *Understanding Fact Finding and Arbitration in the Public Sector* (Washington, D.C.: U.S. Government Printing Office, 1980), pp. 12–13.

In "whole-package" final offer arbitration, the arbitrator is required to choose the complete final offer of one side or the other without modification as his or her award. In "issue-by-issue" final offer arbitration, the arbitrator still cannot modify the proposals of the two sides, but he or she can choose the final offer of one on an issue, such as wages, and the final offer of the other on another issue, such as fringe benefits. The efficacy of final offer arbitration is that it prods the parties to put forward reasonable demands. If the union or the employer puts forth the unreasonable proposals, the other's will almost certainly be chosen. Thus, the best way of attaining demands is to make only those that are reasonable. However, there has been enough irrationality in public sector labor relations during the past two decades to at least raise the specter of both parties putting forward unreasonable demands, in which case final offer arbitration compels the arbitrator to choose an unsatisfactory solution. This possibility highlights the danger of such arbitration and some argue that final offer arbitration should only follow fact-finding and should give the arbitrator the option of using the fact finder's recommendations as the binding award. This practice has been used in Iowa.

In theory, arbitration can take any of these forms since they speak to different aspects of the process. It can be voluntary or compulsory, binding or nonbinding, conventional or final offer. In practice, however, the public sector has tended to opt for the compulsory/binding approach, with increasing attention paid to the final offer format. But this approach to impasse resolution is not without potential difficulties. The essence of the problem was well captured by Detroit Mayor Coleman Young's complaint about compulsory/binding arbitration for police and firefighters under Michigan law: "...Arbitration has been a failure. Slowly, inexorably, compulsory arbitration destroys sensible financial management. The arbitrators seem to believe there is no limit to how much of our money they should spend." Indeed, in his view arbitration awards "have caused more damage to the public service in Detroit than the strikes they were designed to prevent." In short, the issue is one of standards.

Arbitrators must consider several standards in making awards or in choosing between final offers. *Acceptability* is crucial, especially in nonbinding arbitration. The parties must be willing to live with the award and willing to work in the public interest under it. Acceptability generally depends on getting the two parties to agree that the award reflects the balance of economic power between them. Since arbitration is viewed as a substitute for strikes and lockouts (i.e., the use of economic force), acceptability seeks to substitute the result that would have most likely occurred had the parties been free to use economic weapons.

Equity refers to the fairness of the resolution. Here economic strength is not the main concern. Rather such matters as comparability become important. But one of the problems is, comparable to whom? Should pay scales and fringe benefits for police in Detroit be compared to (1) firefighters in Detroit, (2) police in New York City, (3) police in Los Angeles, Cleveland, Buffalo, or (4) police in the suburbs of Detroit? Trying to establish comparable wages for dissimilar occupations is even more difficult than establishing true pay comparability between different public jurisdictions or between public employees and their closest private sector counterparts.

Ability to pay is another standard. It is obvious that arbitration awards must be concerned with the employer's ability to pay. However, there are some serious complications with this standard. How can one determine a public employer's ability to pay? What will happen to the tax base if taxes are raised? Is the budget "padded" enough to sustain an increase in employee compensation? These questions may have no undisputed answers. However, from an arbitrator's point of view, it may be unreasonable for the public employer to ask its employees to work for less than the going market rate. The same employer could not, for example, go to a pencil company and say, "You have very fine pencils and our bureaucrats need many of them, but we'll have to pay you less than the going price because that price is simply more than we can afford." But if it is absurd for a city to plead poverty in buying other supplies, why would it be reasonable in buying labor? Faced with this question, some arbitrators are inclined to downgrade the importance of ability to pay except in cases where the employer is obviously in very dire financial straits. Remember, unless arbitrators protect employees against unreal inability-to-pay claims, civil servants, who are constrained by residency requirements and prohibitions on political activity and strikes, may be easily victimized.

The *public interest* is another standard that arbitrators should take into account in the public sector. The public, as taxpayers, citizens, and recipients of public services and regulations, has a strong interest in the outcome of public sector labor negotiations and impasses. But how is the public interest to be ascertained in any particular dispute? This is another question without a clear answer. However, it has led many to consider whether arbitrators in the public sector should receive special training and whether public sector labor relations statutes should provide more explicit definitions of the public interest.

In passing, at least three additional approaches to impasse resolution should be mentioned. *Mediation and arbitration* (Med-Arb) combines those two functions in a single third party. The objective is to use mediation to resolve as many issues as possible and then arbitrate those that remain. It is thought that it induces the parties to take sensible positions lest the arbitrator rule against them at a later stage. This approach was used successfully by the U.S. Postal Service in 1978, but experience with it has been limited. Wisconsin began using it for municipal employees in 1978, apparently with some success. Some public employers have relied on the use of *labor-management committees* for resolving impasses. Massachusetts and Indiana have had limited experience with this approach, which requires the establishment of a committee representing labor, public employers, and the public interest. A committee of this type could intervene in disputes directly or it could specify which impasse procedures should be followed. Finally, some jurisdictions provide for *public referendums* to resolve limited collective bargaining issues. This practice is not common but has been used in some cities in Colorado.

The Trouble with Third Parties

Many labor relations participants and expert observers consider third-party intervention to be undesirable in principle. The history of the labor movement in the United States has manifested a strong commitment to voluntary "codetermination" of wages, hours, and working conditions generally. Many believe that labor peace and equity can be best achieved through collective bargaining between management and labor, absent outside intervention or settlements imposed by third parties. The two sides know their workplace best and are likely to be more committed to an agreement if it is reached voluntarily. Many believe that the tendency to rely on third-party neutrals inherently undercuts vigorous collective bargaining.

Specifically, the following effects have been identified, although their prevalence is unknown:

1. *The ritualism effect*—Since the parties are aware that a dispute may go to impasse resolution procedures, they may engage in grandstanding for

an outside audience, such as the public or the union members. Negotiators may seek to consolidate their constituencies. For instance, Kearney reports that a Long Island, New York police association once demanded "eighty-five concessions, including a gymnasium and swimming pool, seventeen paid holidays, including Valentine's Day and Halloween."

2. *The chilling effect*—The chilling effect also encourages extreme demands, but it does so on the assumption that the dispute will go to impasse resolution procedures and the third party will seek to "split the difference." In that case, making concessions early would not be sensible.

3. *The narcotic effect*—Impasse resolution procedures can become seductive and addictive. The parties may come to rely on outsiders to do their work for them. Unlike other narcotics, such an effect may actually save money by avoiding futile and long bargaining sessions. It may also ease interpersonal contact between management and labor since they do not have to engage in genuine conflict at the bargaining table.

Finally, many critics believe that there are simply not enough qualified mediators, fact finders, and arbitrators available to the public sector. In part, this is because many of the professionals, who may engage in these roles interchangeably, have most of their experience in the private sector, which, as we have noted, sometimes differs considerably from the context of public labor relations. To a large extent, third parties are chosen from lists supplied by the American Arbitration Association, the National Center for Dispute Settlement, or the Federal Mediation and Conciliation Service, none of which specializes in the resolution of public sector disputes. In some states, the PERB or equivalent administrative agency will seek to assure that third parties are sufficiently versed in their state's public sector context.

Strikes

If an impasse is not resolved, a strike may occur. This represents the ultimate breakdown of the collective negotiations process and in theory, at least, should be at last resort. Although strikes are now legal for some public employees under certain circumstances in several states (see Table 11.2), the strike question continues to loom large in public sector labor relations. Here again we see the problematic nature of trying to adapt private sector practices to the public sector. The strike is a fundamental feature of the private sector process: denying it in the public sector, while nevertheless roughly paralleling other private sector practices, tends to create an imbalance between the parties. This may dictate the use of the strike, even though illegal, for essentially political purposes. Indeed, analysts of the causes of strikes in the public sector have sometimes come to the conclusion that most public sector strikes are unpredictable, perhaps because predicting their political use remains

Table 11.2. Public Employees with the Right to Strike, as of 1990

State	Employees covered
Alaska	All public employees except for police and firefighters
California	All but police and firefighters, *providing* a court or California PERB does not rule that striking is illegal[a]
Hawaii	All public employees
Idaho	Firefighters and teachers
Illinois	All public employees except for police, firefighters, and paramedics
Minnesota	All public employees except for police and firefighters
Montana	All public employees
Ohio	All public employees except for police and firefighters
Oregon	All public employees except for police, firefighters, and correctional officers
Pennsylvania	All public employees except for police, firefighters, prison guards, guards at mental hospitals, and court employees
Rhode Island	All public employees
Vermont	All public employees except for correctional officers, court employees, and state employees
Wisconsin	All public employees except for police, firefighters, and state employees

[a]The California State Supreme Court, in *County Sanitation District* v. *L.A. County Employees Association* (699 P.2d 835, 1985), said that unless expressly prohibited by statute—or case law—striking by public employees is not illegal. Firefighters are prohibited by statutory law, police by case law.
Source: Adapted from Richard C. Kearney. *Labor Relations in the Public Sector* (New York: Marcel Dekker, 1984). Updated by "State Labor Laws," *Labor Relations Reporter*, (Washington, D.C.: BNA, 1989–1990).

elusive. Moreover, public sector strikes often seem tied as much to the personalities of union leaders and government officials as to prevailing economic conditions.

Collective bargaining in the public sector can be a highly politicized process. Agreements are not necessarily hammered out solely on the basis of rationality and compromise. They are often dictated almost entirely by political muscle. This is perhaps the main reason why labor leaders and unionists so

Mayor Jackson Breaks a Strike

On January 7, 1974, Maynard H. Jackson, Jr., became the first African American to be inaugurated as the chief executive of a major city in the South. Atlanta, the city "too busy to hate," had given some credence to its motto. As with many another African-American politician Jackson's political base had always included large elements of the poor. But during the fourth year of his mayoralty he fired almost a thousand of Atlanta's lowest-paid municipal workers. He called it "the most painful task" of his public career.

In March of 1977 Atlanta's sanitation and public works employees were earning an average of $7,500 a year. Organized by the American Federation of State, County, and Municipal Employees (AFSCME), the mostly African-American workers were negotiating for a 50-cent-an-hour increase, about $1,000 a year more for each worker. The mayor, a former labor lawyer and long-time union supporter, conceded that the workers deserved a raise, but felt that granting it would cost the city $5 million more than it could afford. Borrowing to meet the union demands would hardly help Atlanta's double-A credit rating—such tactics had contributed significantly to New York City's much publicized financial woes. The mayor mused, "Maybe the union thought that because I'm liberal, because I'm black, I would respond to any demand." But the mayor stood firm. And the union walked out.

The strike didn't last long. Just less than 1,000 of the 2,400 sanitation and public works employees actually walked off the job. Those who did were sent letters by the mayor advising that if they did not immediately return to work, they would be formally dismissed. The strike continued. The dismissals took effect. Thereupon the mayor invited the fired workers to reapply for their old jobs. About one-third of the fired strikers immediately broke ranks and accepted the mayor's offer. About two weeks into the strike the union offered to end the strike if the workers could be reinstated without penalty. Mayor Jackson said that he could not accept the union's suggestion because more than 200 new workers had already been hired to replace the strikers. A month after the strike began less than 300 of the original strikers were still out. The mayor offered them first crack at new vacancies during the next year.

The union viewed things differently. Their members hadn't had a general salary increase in three years. Their analysts asserted that Atlanta had available millions of dollars in uncollected taxes and millions more in budget surpluses. AFSCME has comparatively few members in the South. A successful strike in Atlanta would encourage recruitment throughout the region. The union spent $60,000 for advertisements in the national print media that attacked both Atlanta and its African-American mayor. But the ad campaign backfired. African Americans were offended because the ads attacked Maynard Jackson personally. Whites were offended because the ads attacked Atlanta. Jerry Wurf, the international president of AFSCME , was forced to admit, "Atlanta was a special case and we screwed it up."

No mayor, county executive, or governor wins a strike with dramatic gestures and appealing rhetoric alone. On the strike issue Maynard Jackson had the enthusiastic

(continued)

Mayor Jackson Breaks a Strike *(continued)*

support of the white middle class, the bankers, the NAACP, and the Urban League. The most surprising, and ironic, support came from Martin Luther King, Sr., whose more famous son and namesake was assassinated a decade earlier while supporting striking sanitataion workers in Memphis, Tennessee. In these times of fiscal awareness, the mayor had obviously struck a responsive chord in the citizenry when he vowed, "Before I take the city into a deficit financial position, elephants will roost in the trees." The mayor was up for reelection in November of 1977, less than six months after the strike. While there was some doubt about his prospects of being reelected before strike, there was none afterward.

strongly support the right to strike and engage in strikes even when contrary to law. The strike is the ultimate weapon in labor's arsenal. Many labor leaders and sympathizers believe that the prohibition of the right to strike is a denial of a fundamental and inherent right. Moreover, they are wont to claim that collective bargaining can never be more than a charade in the absence of the right to strike. It is felt that management will not take labor negotiations seriously unless the worker has some sanction available. In the absence of the right to strike, management may be patronizing at best, or at worst obstructionist. Yet in the view of many labor leaders, collective bargaining depends upon the rough equality of the parties; as a process it "transforms pleading to negotiation." In theoretical consequence, a strike or the threat of one is an essential part of labor-management negotiations.

But what about the society as a whole? Clearly, the state performs vital functions. While some of these are analogous or identical to those which are performed by the private sector, some are uniquely governmental. Hence the society may pay a very heavy price for strikes in the public sector, not just in terms of lost work days, but in terms of the disruption of essential functions. This is exacerbated by the fact that in many cases the state has a monopoly over services which, if disrupted, cannot be obtained in another fashion. At a given moment, the cost of a strike by strategically placed public employees is likely to appear greater than the cost of reaching a settlement. The public's inconvenience and the elected officials' quest for reelection may make it difficult for the government to take a hard-line stance even though the financial plight of cities has made officials and the public more willing to tolerate inconvenience or even chaos. Public employees are then in a strong position to make gains that they otherwise would not make. And, the gains go beyond economic matters to include the right to participate in policymaking over such issues as classroom size and the number of police officers assigned to a patrol car.

Each side in the strike controversy raises valid questions. Sam Zagoria, as director of the Labor-Management Relations Service established by the National League of Cities, the U.S. Conference of Mayors, and the National Association of Counties, distilled the arguments of both sides of the strike question.

In his view, the proponents of strikes have to deal with the following challenges:

1. There is no need to legalize strikes because most contracts are negotiated without the threat of a strike.
2. Granting the right to strike would considerably enhance the political power and lobbying abilities of unions. Given the voting power of organized public sector labor and its already formidable political strength, a grant of strike rights would place management in an unenviable position in collective bargaining. This situation might be different if unions were willing to accept restrictions on their political activities.
3. The strike, at least on a prolonged basis, is a weapon of doubtful might. The employer stands to gain financially, at least in the short run, as taxes and other revenues come in even though services are not rendered. In addition, prolonged or exceedingly disruptive strikes may cause sentiment to shift away from the unions, thereby strengthening management's position at the bargaining table.
4. When strikes are called by such vital services as police and fire, the strike may take on an overkill character. The lost services cannot be purchased from a competitor. The whole community becomes a "hostage" for the union.
5. The strike is labor's counterpart to the lockout, but since the latter is inappropriate in the public sector, the former is also unnecessary and undesirable.

On the other hand, those who support prohibitions on the right to strike must also face some serious difficulties:

1. The right of workers in the private sector to strike has long been guaranteed. Those public workers who perform similar functions, such as selling liquor, driving buses, teaching, collecting garbage, and nursing, cannot justifiably or logically be treated differently and in a discriminatory fashion.
2. Prohibitions against strikes and court orders forcing public workers to stay on the job are not effective mechanisms for dealing with labor disputes. Fines and the imprisonment of labor leaders may solidify their tenure.
3. In the absence of a strike potential, what assurances will labor have that management will bargain in good faith?

4. Strikes already occur and they do not tend to create the destruction claimed by opponents of the strike.
5. By legalizing the strike, fewer resources will be spent by management in attempting to prevent them; more time and effort will then be placed on substantive issues.
6. Many states have already legalized the strike, even for such vital service employees as police and fire.

The logical path in dealing with strikes, whether legal or illegal, is to make them the least desirable alternative and one which is undertaken only after other possible means of settling disputes have been tried and found unsatisfactory. Experience in San Francisco, Atlanta, Chicago, and with PATCO has shown that strikes are no longer inevitably successful.

Grievances

However they are derived, public sector collective bargaining agreements will tend to have a similar set of clauses. Among these are

Preamble

Recognition and union rights clause

Management rights clause

Mutual compliance clause

Grievance procedure clause

Work hours and overtime clause

Vacation and holidays clause

Leave of absence clause

Fringe benefits clause

Duration of the contract clause

"Zipper clause" (indicating that the agreement constitutes the entirety of the agreed-upon contractual arrangements and that new elements will not be added, i.e., the agreement is "zipped up")

"Savings clause" (indicating that if for any reason part of the agreement is deemed illegal, the rest will still be considered binding upon the parties)

Clauses dealing with antidiscrimination, residency requirements, and union political activities may also be found in some contracts.

Once the contract has been put into effect, the parties must learn to live with it. This may be easier said than done because contract language is often complex and ambiguous. Some contracts run as long as 100 pages or more and present an awesome barrier to being understood fully by any public manager. Inevitably, contracts will use such ambiguous terms as "reasonable notice" of overtime assignments, "just and sufficient cause" for discipline, or "equitable distribution" of overtime. And what's reasonable, just, or equitable in the eyes of the manager may appear arbitrary or unfair to the employee. Somehow disputes over the meaning of the contract must be resolved. Typically this is accomplished through the creation of a grievance procedure.

Grievances generally arise within the realm of the contingent provisions of a contract. These are personnel provisions where it is expected that change will commonly occur during the life of the contract. For example, discharges, layoffs, reductions in force, promotions, discipline, and transfers are among a contract's contingent provisions. The grievance occurs when the employee and/or the union reasonably believe that the contract is being violated in a personnel action of this type.

Most public and private sector labor contracts now provide for a mechanism to resolve such grievances. Although there is considerable variation, at least three steps are common. First, the employee and a union steward bring the complaint to the attention of the supervisor. This step is informal and oral. It is hoped that the matter will be quickly resolved. If the grievance is not resolved, a second step may be taken. A formal, written complaint is forwarded to the next highest management level. If there is still no resolution, the grievance may be advanced to the third stage, which is arbitration by a neutral third party. Since the collective bargaining contract exists between the employer and the union (not the individual employees), the union's agreement may be necessary before the employee can pursue a grievance. This is especially likely for steps 2 and 3. It should also be noted that in some cases there will be several levels of managerial review prior to permitting the grievance to go to binding arbitration.

Some grievances involve the rights of the union as an organization and the public employer. For example, these might arise in the context of granting released time to union stewards, union security arrangements, and the right of unions to disseminate information at the workplace. Such grievances are generally brought to management's attention and then, if not resolved, submitted to binding arbitration.

More than 80 percent of all public sector negotiated grievance systems end with binding arbitration. This process can cut deeply into what were once managerial prerogatives to assign work and discipline and direct employees. The *Digest of Labor Arbitration Awards in the Federal Service* provides a large sample of the kinds of matters that have been subjected to binding grievance arbitration. The following will provide a flavor of what transpires:

Did the employer violate the agreement by changing the work week and requiring grievants to work on Sunday without overtime pay? (Yes)

Did management violate the agreement when it refused to issue the grievant safety shoes? (Yes)

Was the 5-day suspension of the grievant warranted by his use of threatening and abusive language against a supervisor and a fellow employee? (No)

Did management violate the agreement by requiring male employees to wear neckties? (Yes)

Was the change of grievant's work location a violation of the agreement? (Yes)

Was the grievant forced to take substantially more night shift duty than circumstances required due to personal favoritism of the supervisor? (Yes)

Did management have just cause to issue a 10-day suspension to the grievant for leaving the job to which she was assigned during working hours? (No)

Did the activity violate the negotiated agreement by unilaterally transferring the grievant in order to remove him from the supervision of his future wife? (Yes)

Grievances can be time consuming and expensive nuisances. If they go to arbitration, the arbitrator's decision may become part of "custom and practice" in the workplace and serve as a continuing constraint on management. Grievances also emphasize the adversarial quality of labor relations and may impede cooperation. In general, both labor and management would prefer to reduce the number of grievances, especially those going beyond the first step. Sometimes a union will use the grievance system to harass a manager. However, perhaps as frequently or more so, a union will feel compelled by its obligation to represent all employees in the bargaining unit equally to persue a grievance that it would rather avoid. The U.S. Office of Personnel Management has published some tips for managers on keeping the number of grievances to a minimum:

Be alert to the usual causes of grievances. Don't knowingly violate the contract.

Keep workers informed regarding the quality of their work.

Correct minor irritations promptly.

Encourage constructive suggestions.

Keep promises.

Assign work impartially to employees with equal skill and ability.

Explain your orders unless they are obvious.

Be consistent unless there is an obvious reason for change.

Explain change, even when the change doesn't require negotiation.

Act as soon as possible on requests.

Avoid showing favoritism.

If you must take corrective action, don't make it a public display.

Of course, even in the best of circumstances grievances will occasionally arise. As a result, some labor relations programs have paid atention to reducing the time and money costs of arbitration. The hiring of permanent arbitrators to hear cases on an expedited or even instant basis is one approach being tried in the private sector. So far, however, such approaches do not seem to have made much headway in the public sector.

In passing, it should be noted that sometimes the grievance system is but one of several channels an employee can pursue in protesting a personnel action. In addition, there are typically statutorily based adverse action appeals systems and equal employment opportunity (EEO) complaint systems. Under some procedures the employee is given the choice of pursuing one of these to the exclusion of the others. In other cases, however, they may be used serially or even simultaneously. One of the reasons for this is that the same personnel action may have several components. For instance, a minority employee may be demoted in violation of a labor contract's seniority clause (a grievance), but also due to prohibited discrimination (an EEO matter) and in violation of civil service rules (an adverse action appeal).

The Union Leader

The labor relations process outlined in this chapter can be used in many different ways to different ends. The formal process is very important to the nature of collective bargaining, but the participants in that process are also crucial to public sector labor relations.

As we have noted throughout our discussion of public sector labor relations, politics is at the very heart of the process. This is a major reason why public sector labor relations patterned upon private sector practices initially turned out to be so chaotic. Public economies are not private economies. Mayors and governors are not simply managerial executives. Public workers are voters whose ballots are dearly sought by their "bosses." Government services are sometimes unique. Thus it is crucial for the student of public sector labor relations to consider the position of public sector labor leaders and public officials in the context of collective bargaining, for their needs and personalities dictate much about the patterns public sector agreements will take.

Politicians, public personnel managers, and the press often see union leaders as power hungry and even sinister forces. No doubt some of them are. Even Jerry Wurf, the late president of the powerful AFSCME, AFL-CIO, was willing to say that "the labor movement in this country has had its share of opportunists and scoundrels, its quota of individuals who abused the power conferred by their constituents, and its proportion of shortsightedness and lack of vision." Perhaps because of this image, there appears to be a tendency not to take seriously the plight of the union leader or, at least, the union leader's perception of that plight.

There are a variety of reasons for this. At the heart of all of them appears to be the notion that a union leader can easily and effectively control membership. Indeed, even when the rank and file reject a contract negotiated by the leader, many may consider their action a charade to strengthen the leader's hand. There is a considerable element of truth in this outlook. The "iron law of oligarchy" as formulated by the sociologist Roberto Michels maintains that "who says organization says oligarchy." Many organizations, including unions, do seem to fit this mold. The leadership generally exercises more control and influence over the rank and file than vice versa. While there may be some organized opposition to the leadership within the union, it is seldom successful in installing its own candidates. All unions are democratically governed in a formal sense, but few have institutionalized competition, such as a two-party system. The tendency toward oligarchy is largely a result of the advantages that accrue to the leadership. The leader generally holds his position on a full-time basis. He or she is in a position to be far more knowledgeable about the union's activities, past, and budget than anyone else. Who else can be as knowledgeable about what can be obtained from those sitting across the table during negotiations? The leader also sits atop the organization's formal communications, public relations, and propaganda channels. Yet while all of these elements are substantial, especially in the hands of one who has a proven ability to succeed in a political context, union leaders profess to be constrained by their membership. There is little reason to doubt that this is a genuine feeling.

The case of Victor Gotbaum is a good example of this. As executive director of the powerful District Council 37 (New York) of the AFSCME, he was generally considered one of the most powerful union leaders in the public sector. In Gotbaum's view, "the collective bargaining table becomes all important to the labor leader." While unsuccessful negotiations can undermine the leader's authority, "a good contract means that many of his errors of omission and commission will be forgiven by the rank and file for years to come—or at least for the length of the contract." Moreover, nonprofessional workers are most interested in bread-and-butter issues, which may be the most difficult to deal with in the view of the financial plight of many urban areas in the United States. Good wages and retirement plans are of the greatest importance to the rank-and-file union member and therefore are central to the leader's success. At the same time, the perception of what constitutes a "good" contract is often related to what other city workers are getting. Thus, where the city negotiates with each union separately, the union leaders may be in competition with each other as well as with dissident forces within their own organizations. Hence the union leader does not just want a contract to be approved, but rather wants it overwhelmingly ratified. Otherwise the charge of a "sellout" is inevitable and the leader may become "a sitting duck for the dissident sharpshooters within his own union." In addition, the government may place barriers in the way of the union's success. The strike, which remains the most potent weapon in labor's arsenal, may be prohibited. There may also be legal restrictions on a city's authority to bargain and strong management rights clauses. And the separation of powers may make agreements subject to further legislative approval. As a result, in Gotbaum's words, "union leaders wither and fall by the wayside with remarkable rapidity or become heroes in the eyes of the people they represent." The leadership either beats "the law and the system, or the law and the system beat them."

The way Gotbaum saw it, then, was that a union leader must be militant, where militancy means the public employer must either accommodate what may be rather farfetched demands, help the leader save face, or be prepared to cope with disruption. Thus, when a pension program demanded by Gotbaum ran into political trouble in the state legislature, he decided to display some muscle. Calling for "the biggest, fattest, sloppiest strike" in the history of New York City, he initiated massive disorder, which A. H. Raskin of the *New York Times* describes as "a two-day exhibition of urban guerrilla warfare." The strike caused "700 million gallons of raw sewage to be dumped into metropolitan waterways, shut down garbage incinerators, cut off school lunches,...and made a shambles of traffic by locking two dozen city [draw] bridges in uncrossable positions." Yet such an action is in reality an admission of failure. It may bring the benefits sought, but the price will be high for the union in terms of public opinion and, perhaps, further legal action.

The union leader is typically in a bind. The rank and file, as well as potential challengers to the leader, want more and more while the public employer may have less and less. Something has to give. Somehow the situation must be defused. Unfortunately, disaffection between politicians and municipal unions is common and often far reaching. While some politicians are able to deal effectively with union leaders, others see their responsibility toward the larger community as preventing this or simply inherit a budgetary situation that makes it impossible to meet even reasonable demands. When the union has supported the politician in the previous election, the situation may be exacerbated. The rank and file are wont to ask, "Why can't we get this from the mayor? After all, we elected her!"

Union leaders are very cognizant of another problem. Members who are opposed to the leader or the union itself may choose to drop out rather than to try to elect new union officials or change the union's policies. When this occurs, the union is still legally required to represent those bargaining unit employees who have abandoned it, just as it must represent all employees in the unit equally. Consequently, from the employee's perspective there may be no penalty for quitting a union—in fact, there may be a gain since the employee may no longer have to pay union dues. In essence, the nonmember may be a "free rider" in the bargaining unit who is represented by the union, but at no cost. This situation can impose a considerable financial burden on unions and make it all the more difficult for them to engage in effective collective bargaining. Consequently, unions have historically stressed the need for "security" arrangements. The most important for the public sector have been the following:

1. *The union shop*—All employees must join and maintain membership in the union. New employees are given a period in which to join, usually thirty days. A number of states including Alaska, Maine, Kentucky, Washington, and Vermont have authorized the union shop for some categories of public employees. However, under the U.S. Supreme Court's reasoning in *Abood* v. *Detroit Board of Education* (1977), the constitutionality of this arrangement is dubious since it uses governmental authority to compel individuals to join an organization and can consequently be seen as an abridgement of freedom of association.

2. *The agency shop and fair share*—These arrangements do not require employees to join unions, but they do require them to pay "counterpart" or "fair-share" fees. These fees may be equivalent to the union dues or they may be smaller and intended to cover only those union activities *directly* related to collective bargaining and representing the employee. Such arrangements are not considered to violate the constitutional right of freedom of association. The District of Columbia, Washington, Michigan, Montana, Rhode Island, Connecticut, Vermont, New York, Oregon, North Dakota, Hawaii, Massachusetts, Minnesota, and California are some of the states that use one of these arrangements for certain categories of public employees.

3. *Maintenance of membership*—All employees who are members of a union must maintain their membership in it, but others need not join. States such as Pennsylvania and California use this arrangement for some employees.

4. *The dues checkoff*—This is normally a way of facilitating any of the above arrangements. The employer is authorized to deduct union dues,

Chicago Teachers Union v. *Hudson*,
475 U.S. 292 (1986)

Facts—The Chicago Teachers Union represents educational employees of the Chicago Board of Education. About 95 percent of the employees are members of the union. The other 5 percent, although not union members, belong to the union's bargaining unit and, under an agency shop arrangement, are required to pay union dues. Nonunion employees filed suit against the union on the grounds that the union's procedures for considering nonmember's objections to the dues deduction were unfair and in violation of their due process rights under the Fourteenth Amendment and their First Amendment rights to freedom of expression and association.

Issue—Are procedural safeguards necessary under an agency shop agreement in order to "prevent compulsory subsidization of ideological activity by nonunion employees . . . while at the same time not restricting the union's ability to require any employee to contribute to the cost of collective-bargaining activities?"

Discussion—In a unanimous decision, the U.S. Supreme Court ruled that procedural safeguards are necessary. The Court said that "the constitutional requirements for the Union's collection of agency fees include an adequate explanation of the basis for the fee, a reasonably prompt opportunity to challenge the amount of the fee before an impartial decisionmaker, and an escrow for the amounts reasonably in dispute while such challenges are pending."

counterpart or fair-share fees from the employee's paycheck, and remit them to the union. Unions value the checkoff highly because it assures them a steady flow of revenue and makes it much easier to collect fees. The union may be required to pay the employer for the checkoff service, but like the checkoff itself this is generally a subject for collective bargaining. Since the checkoff is so valued by unions, some jurisdictions may seek to punish unions for illegal strikes by eliminating the service.

The Public Employer

One of the major characteristics of public sector labor relations is that the public employer may be highly fragmented. Frequently, there is no one person with whom the union can bargain over many matters, including wages and hours. This is especially true at the state and federal levels. However, at the local level, where public sector labor relations are generally most acute, there is usually more room for comprehensive collective bargaining.

Cities in the United States tend to fall into one of three structural categories. Over half of them use some form of mayor-council government. In some of these, mainly the smaller ones, the mayor is weak vis-à-vis the council. Here

Some Major Public Sector Unions

All Public

The American Federation of State, County, and Municipal Employees (AFSCME). It is affiliated with the AFL-CIO and has been outspoken on a number of public policy issues. AFSCME does not include federal employees.

The American Federation of Government Employees (AFGE). Most members are clerical and blue-collar workers. It is affiliated with the AFL-CIO.

The National Federation of Federal Employees (NFEE). It represents federal employees, most of whom are clerical workers and professionals.

Mixed Unions (representing both public and private sector workers)

The Service Employees International Union (SEIU). Most of its members work in hospitals, social service agencies, or are nonteaching personnel in schools. It is affiliated with the AFL-CIO.

The Laborer's International Union (LIU). The LIU represents mostly workers in departments for streets, public works, and sanitation, along with federal mail handlers. Most of its members are in private sector construction jobs. It is an AFL-CIO affiliate.

The International Brotherhood of Teamsters. The Teamsters' members are primarily in blue-collar jobs and in the protective services (police, fire, corrections).

Functionally Specific Unions

The National Education Association (NEA). The NEA has more or less transformed itself from a professional association to a union during the past decade.

The American Federation of Teachers (AFT). The AFT is affiliated with the AFL-CIO. Unlike the NEA, it has sought to organize teachers' aides, library workers, bus drivers, and noneducational employees in health care and a variety of civil service jobs.

The International Association of Fire Fighters (IAFF). The IAFF was founded in 1918. It has a highly decentralized structure allowing its locals a great deal of autonomy.

The Fraternal Order of Police (FOP). The FOP was founded in 1915. Most of its members are in north-central and southern states.

several major city posts may be filled by direct election rather than mayoral appointment, thereby limiting the mayor's ability to control important facets of the city's government. There may also be a large number of boards and commissions which are not subject to the mayor's control. The council in such a government has both legislative and executive functions. Generally, the mayor and the council have a mutual veto power over each other's actions. The authority of the mayor is far greater in the strong mayor-council variant. Here the mayor makes appointments and there are few independent units of government. The mayor and the council make policy and the former is responsible for its execution, hence the mayor has the power of appointment over department heads. The majority of large cities follow this approach.

A second structural category is the commission plan, which is not widespread among governments with more than 5,000 residents. Under this arrangement, a five-person commission is generally elected for a four-year term. Each of the commissioners is the head of an administrative department, and collectively they are the jurisdiction's chief policy maker.

Finally, there is the council-manager plan, found in about half of all cities with populations in the 10,000–500,000 range. Here the council is elected to perform the city's legislative functions. It appoints a city manager to handle administrative matters. The basic idea is that there is "no Democratic or Republican way to pave streets." In practice, the manager is not completely insulated from politics because she or he needs to curry favor with various groups and the council in order to enhance her or his power and effectiveness.

Each of these structures presents different questions with regard to collective bargaining. In council-manager cities it is usually the manager who represents the city in negotiations. In some cases, however, the council or a committee from it may perform this task. The duty may also fall upon a civil service commission. In mayoral systems, there is a tendency for the mayor to avoid being a formal party to negotiations, although he or she may nevertheless exert a great deal of influence over the collective bargaining process. The rationale for this is that the mayor may be too susceptible to electoral pressures either to stand up to unions and risk labor disruption, or to forego union support. City workers, it must be remembered, are often a very substantial voting bloc, all the more so where residency rules are in effect. Similarly, where councils or their committees are directly involved in negotiations, unions may seek to exert political pressure on them. Hence, cities may appoint nonelected officials to represent their interests. This can defuse the political situation somewhat, but where there is a wide gap between employer and employee, where conflict is prolonged or bitter, or where labor feels the bargaining arrangements are inappropriate, it is almost certain that political officials will be forced into the act.

In addition to these structural dimensions, the nature of politics is important. Where machine-style politics prevails, the "boss" will be in control of the labor situation no matter what the governmental formalities. However, in the wake of the U.S. Supreme Court's decision in *Rutan* v. *Republican Party of Illinois* (1990) (see Chapter 9), the traditional art of patronage will be both unconstitutional and more costly to practice. Where political officials are relatively weak and divided, on the other hand, and no political machine exists to exert a unifying force, labor may very well gain the upper hand. Strong governments may be the only match for strong municipal labor, and perhaps only manager, strong mayor, and machine-based systems are viable in terms of labor relations with militant unions.

Given the widespread variations in the structural and political nature of governments in the United States, it is to be expected that public officials will adopt differing views on labor relations in the public sector. Yet on the whole it appears that professional public managers and many elected and politically appointed executives have displayed hostility toward sharing their authority and resources with unions through the collective bargaining process. President Reagan's handling of the PATCO strike (discussed in the prologue to this chapter) is symptomatic of what seems to be the prevailing attitude of "management." In the mid-1970s, Alan Saltzstein reported on a survey of city managers in United States cities with populations larger than 10,000. He found that 45 percent of his respondents felt there was no way that unions could be an asset to local government. Over 20 percent of the managers declared that they worked actively to prevent or to control the growth of employee organizations. The culture of these city managers viewed "giving in" to strikers as "delinquent behavior." Nor does it appear that attitudes have changed much since then. Beginning in 1975, public employers have "won" some major strikes in cities such as San Francisco, Chicago, Atlanta, and New York. The tough attitude of public employers, and apparently the public as well, has been reflected in other ways too. For instance, it is now common for public employers to demand "give backs" in negotiations; that is, to seek to win back some benefits they agreed to grant to labor in the past. Productivity bargaining, which seeks to link wage increases to gains in productivity, has also become more common. Almost incredibly, postal unions have agreed to a system whereby new employees will be compensated at a lower rate than other employees doing the same jobs. In a dramatic policy shift, the former head of the U.S. Office of Personnel Management (OPM), Donald Devine, announced in early 1985 that agencies were to be encouraged to hire temporary employees to reduce compensation. This approach would also have the inevitable effect of weakening unions. Thus, signs of hostility to public employee unions currently abound.

Nevertheless, public sector collective bargaining is a serious fact of life for many jurisdictions. Unions are not easily busted in the manner of the Reagan-PATCO contest. Mayors in particular may find themselves under great pressure from the public, political opponents, unions, and fiscal constraints. Here we are confronted with a lack of systematic knowledge. Generally speaking, many mayors believe it is wise for elected officials to avoid direct involvement in collective bargaining. Many urban officials owe their electoral victories to union support, but they also face an electorate made up of taxpayers who are becoming increasingly sensitive to tax burdens and the disruption of urban services. Consequently, union leaders must frequently break with the elected officials they previously supported. While this is painful for both sides, it is the elected official who stands to lose most in the divorce and who will strive hardest to avoid it. Yet a mayor must be continually aware of the costs of government and the extent to which these are a function of wages and salaries. The payroll of some municipalities constitutes over 70 percent of the operating budget. Ultimately, then, the mayor will become concerned with holding the line on the cost of services, particularly where the city is in a deficit, as is now common in large urban areas. In fact, it is no longer unusual for urban services to be curtailed as a result of the employer's inability to meet the payroll.

Elected officials are especially weak with regard to their ability to respond to monetary demands. However, because of the fragmented nature of many urban governments, they may even be unable to get assorted independent boards and commissions to concur with the labor relations practices they would recommend. Mayors are also limited in the amount of time they can devote to labor matters. Municipal labor may be represented by a plethora of bargaining units and negotiations may be virtually a nonstop process. Yet the mayor has other responsibilities and must depend heavily upon a staff of labor relations experts. However, any professional staff, no matter how expert, must realize that collective bargaining in the public sector is a political process as much as an economic one. Elected officials are usually well aware of the necessity of leaving union leaders a respectable path of retreat from impossible demands. Anyone involved in public sector negotiations, must realize that under ordinary circumstances attempts at union busting, the destruction of leadership, or even seeking to levy unrealistic penalties on unions engaging in illegal activity is likely to be counterproductive. Ironically, strong union leaders who feel threatened neither within their own organization nor by city management may make for the most stable and productive kind of collective bargaining.

Tactics

The number of collective bargaining sessions that takes place in the public sector each year is huge. It would be virtually impossible to keep track of all negotiations and their outcomes, much less observe the tactics employed by each side. Necessarily, therefore, a discussion of collective bargaining tactics must be highly general.

Often the first matter is deciding how management will be represented: by personnelist, by private negotiator, by department head, or by a full-time or part-time managerial employee with labor relations responsibilities? To date, the main patterns seem to be as follows:

1. *The federal government*—Bargaining goes by agencies and the agency head usually appoints a team of full-time labor relations specialists.

2. *The states*—There is more variation here, but the state team will usually include a chief negotiator with direct responsibility to the governor, a budget officer, a personnelist, and a representative from the state agency involved.

3. *Local government*—Here there is great variety, but the emergent pattern seems to reflect state practices. Depending on the size of the city, a city manager is likely to participate directly in negotiations, appoint an assistant to do so, or use professional negotiators and labor relations specialists. The latter are commonly used in cities with 500,000 or more inhabitants, regardless of their form of government. Usually budget officers and personnelists are part of the team at the local level. Often relevant department heads are included. Mayors and members of the city council rarely sit directly on the bargaining team.

The composition of management's bargaining team is important to the success of negotiations. It is especially destructive if the participants represent different interests and constituencies, as could be the case with personnelists seeking to strengthen the career service and budget officers trying to reduce compensation packages. It is generally thought that bargaining teams should be relatively small and that a single spokesperson should be designated. The spokesperson should be the sole conduit to the media in jurisdictions where negotiations are not open to the public and press.

Richard Kearney has outlined some essential preparatory steps for management:

1. Establish the bargaining committee.

2. Analyze experience under the previous contract (if any). Pay special attention to grievances.

3. Analyze wage and benefit data with a view toward comparable jurisdictions.

4. Analyze the outcome of bargaining in comparable jurisdictions and assess the impact of personnel policy changes.

5. Confer with labor to establish the rules for the negotiations and establish schedules.

6. Establish a bargaining agenda.

Kearney suggests that once sessions begin, they should be held during working hours for one to three hours at a time.

Once bargaining begins, questions of strategy may arise. Assessments of the other side's intentions must be made. Is the union leader grandstanding for the benefit of a particular constituency? Have the ritualism, chilling, or narcotic effects set is? Is the other side's approach too "blue sky," that is to make absolutely absurd demands? Are distrust, deception, threats, and insults employed to wear the "opponent" down? Is body language being used to cajole, irritate, or otherwise affect the other side? Will "nickel and diming" be used to try to squeeze every last bit of concession from the other side? Perhaps more important, will one side demand concessions from the other as a demonstration of the other's good faith?

These and other questions arise. But finding the proper answers is not easy. Collective bargaining can be an adversary or cooperative process. Generally, perhaps, it is both at once. It is adversary when the issues are distributive; that is, where one side's gain is the other's loss. In the private sector, economic issues are usually distributive. In the public sector, distributive issues tend to involve management's authority. Cooperation is more prevalent where the issues are integrative. Here conflict is not viewed as inherent. An example might be better safety conditions for employees. Obviously, a great deal will depend upon the personalities involved and the ability of each side to assess the needs of the other.

Conflict resolution has become a field of serious academic study and practical application. Many approaches have been recommended. One of the most promising for public sector collective bargaining is proposed by Roger Fisher and William Ury in *Getting to Yes*. Called principled negotiations it recommends:

1. "Separate the people from the problem." Recognize that the problem is arriving at a workable and desirable agreement. Don't let personalities get in the way.

2. "Focus on interests, not positions." Each side will have different but often overlapping interests. By focusing on the areas where the interests are compatible or can be redefined to make them compatible, negotiators can avoid getting locked in.

3. "Invent options for mutual gain." Explore the possibilities for harmony and compatibility. Although labor and management are adversarial in important respects, it is also important to avoid concluding that they are adversaries in all respects.

4. "Insist on using objective criteria" as a means of determining what is acceptable. Since one cannot expect to dominate in every bargaining situation, it is important that the acceptability of an agreement turn on objective factors, fairly applied. For example, if management and labor

have agreed to cost-of-living increases in principle, it is important to adopt an objective measure of what the increase has actually been.

Regardless of the tactics employed, however, a "third party" called politics is likely to be on, near, or under the table.

Politics

Public sector labor relations are necessarily suffused with politics. Public employees are an important part of the electorate in many jurisdictions. Their unions engage in electoral activity and in lobbying. Agreements between unions and public employers affect the allocation of resources, tax rates, and the availability and quality of public services. Since the public is affected by collective bargaining agreements, the public may become mobilized and bring pressure to bear on the process. Presidents, governors, mayors, and legislators are elected and are often sensitive to a mobilized constituency. Union leaders are elected by union members and they too must try to please their constituents. Under these conditions a very large number of political scenarios are possible. Enough cases of public sector labor relations have been studied to suggest the following:

1. "The Calvin Coolidge." This approach is derived from Coolidge's handling of the Boston police strike. His laconic "there is no right to strike against the public safety by anybody, anywhere, anytime" was instrumental in his rise to national recognition. Similarly, President Reagan served notice that he was tough when he announced he would brook no breach of law and order by members of PATCO. Similarly, Mayor Jane Byrne of Chicago gained considerable support by riding out an illegal firefighter strike in Chicago. However, the tenacity award may go to Mayor Maynard Jackson of Atlanta, who in the face of a garbage strike in 1977 declared, "Before I take the city into a deficit financial position, elephants will roost in the trees."

2. "The symbiotic charade." Here the public employer, generally as represented by a mayor, and a union leader invent mutual gain for each other. Perhaps the best long-term example occurred in the 1950s in New York City between Mayor Robert Wagner and Michael Quill, leader of the Transport Workers Union. The typical scenario was as follows: The transport workers contract would require renewal on December 31. Quill would begin his display in November, making demand after demand, threat after threat, with a great flair and publicity. As the hour for the "obligatory" threatened New Year's Day subway strike drew near, Quill entered into a private session with Wagner. Ultimately they emerged, Quill smiling. Wagner, frowning, would mutter something along the lines of how costly the settlement would be to the city. New Year's Day, the trains ran.

Not bothering to announce the content of the proposed contract in detail, Quill would run for reelection as union leader in February on the basis of his success negotiating. His victories were overwhelming. In April, when the city budget became public, few took the time to see what the transit settlement actually cost. However, more often than not, the contracts were a paragon of reasonability. The Transport Workers Union, according to A.H. Raskin of the *New York Times*, "after the television cameras had been turned off, was a model of cooperation in raising standards of operating efficiency by permitting the squeeze-out of thousands of jobs in the deficit-ridden system." In fact, at times the transit system was seriously understaffed. At the same time, the mayor received the union's support at election time.

3. "The face saver." This occurs when both sides are truly antagonistic in a public dispute but neither wants to destroy the other. The union will not seriously seek to unhinge the politician's career and the politician will not try to bust the union. The postal strike of 1970, outlined in Chapter 10 presents a good example. Here the postal workers won the right to collective bargaining over wages, hours, and working conditions in a unique format. President Nixon was successful in obtaining the postal reorganization he sought. And the House Post Office Committee got out of the tricky politics surrounding the setting of postal wage rates. Were it not for the disruption caused by the strike and the deployment of the National Guard, the settlement might have looked like a model of integrative, principled negotiations.

4. "The so long, it's been good to know ya." More or less the opposite of the face saver, here one side or the other seriously wants to remove the opponent from the scene. This can be done quietly, as when a public official simply refuses to give a union leader enough to sustain him or her in the eyes of the rank-and-file members. Or it can be done loudly, as when Victor Gotbaum waged his "guerilla warfare" against New York, partly to unseat the mayor. This approach can be used in conjunction with the Calvin Coolidge, sometimes with devastating results.

One could describe many more scenarios. But these should be sufficient to convey the highly politicized quality of public sector labor relations. No comprehensive account of the politics of public sector labor relations can be presented because our creative politicians and union leaders are inventing new ones all the time. It should always be borne in mind, though, that the vast majority of public sector labor agreements are negotiated relatively smoothly. It's mostly the problems and disruptions that attract public attention.

Conclusion

Collective bargaining is fundamentally different from most aspects of public personnel administration. It creates a format for determining what much of the content of personnel policy will be. Much of that which was once established by personnel agencies, such as civil service commissions, is now subject to collective bargaining. In some jurisdictions this is true of pay, position classification, probation, aspects of discipline, and promotion. That is why collective bargaining is said to create codetermination. In some respects, it is an alternative system and forum for setting personnel policy and establishing personnel procedures. Its potential importance for the future of public personnel management is truly staggering.

Yet, oddly, its impact to date has been difficult to trace. Those who believed that collective bargaining would destroy the merit system have so far been proven wrong. Nor were those who argued that it would routinely bankrupt governments correct. In an age of give backs and concern with productivity, the public sector may not come close to suffering the financial harm once predicted. Moreover, while there have been some instances of damage to the public interest, chaos and anarchy have not reigned. When one comes right down to it, the impact of collective bargaining *generally* on recruitment, selection, promotion, training, technology, transfers, and work assignments seems to have been limited. The same seems to be true of compensation, though here the picture is considerably murkier. The greatest change has been that now management must share its authority over workers and the workplace with the union. That is the point of codetermination. Just as it offers new opportunities for conflict, it also offers better prospects for cooperation between management and labor.

Bibliography

Davis, Charles. "Equity vs. Fairness: The Impact of State Collective Bargaining Policies on the Implementation of Affirmative Action Programs," *Journal of Collective Negotiations in the Public Sector*, 13 (1984).

Douglas, Joel M. "Public Sector Unionism: New Approaches—New Strategies," in Carolyn Ban and Norma M. Riccucci (eds.), *Public Personnel Management—Current Concerns, Future Challenges*. White Plains, N.Y.: Longman Press, 1991.

————. "Collective Bargaining for Public Sector Supervisors: A Trend Towards Exclusion?" *Public Administration Review*, 19 (November-December 1987).

Figart, Deborah M. "Collective Bargaining and Career Development for Women in the Public Sector," *Journal of Collective Negotiations in the Public Sector*, 16 (1989).

Fisher, Roger and William Ury. *Getting to Yes: Negotiating Agreement Without Giving In*. New York: Penguin, 1983.

Gagala, Ken. *Union Organizing and Staying Organized*. Englewood Cliffs, N.J.: Prentice Hall/Reston, 1983.

Hill, Herbert. *Black Labor and the American Legal System: Race, Work, and the Law*. Madison: University of Wisconsin Press, 1985.

Kearney, Richard C. *Labor Relations in the Public Sector*. New York: Marcel Dekker, 1984 (second edition forthcoming).

Leigh, Duane E. and Stephen M. Hills. "Public-Sector, Private-Sector Differences in Reasons Underlying Expressed Union Preferences," *Journal of Collective Negotiations in the Public Sector*, 16 (1987).

Paterson, Lee and Reginald Murphy. *The Public Administrator's Grievance Arbitration Handbook*. New York: Longman, 1983.

Riccucci, Norma M. *Women, Minorities, and Unions in the Public Sector*. Westport, Conn: Greenwood Press, 1990.

Rosenbloom, David H. and Jay M. Shafritz. *Essentials of Labor Relations*. Reston, VA: Reston Publishing Co., 1985.

Smith, Charles G. Jr. "An Initial Evaluation of the Collective Bargaining Process in the Federal Service," *Journal of Collective Negotiations in the Public Sector*, 18 (1989).

Spero, Sterling. *The Labor Movement in a Government Industry*. New York: Macmillan, Co., 1927.

Wall, James. *Negotiation: Theory and Practice*. Glenview, Ill.: Scott, Foresman, 1985.

Part **V**
PRODUCTIVITY

12
Productivity Improvement

Prologue: The Meter Reader on Roller Skates—Productivity Innovation in One American City

Pittsburg, California is a typical small city of 40,000 located on the banks of Sacramento and San Jaoquin rivers about forty miles east of San Francisco. The city was originally named Black Diamond because of the extensive mining of coals in the nearby foothills and changed its name to follow its more famous eastern steel-city counterpart when steel fabrication plants were set up prior to World War I. The economic base diversified to reflect extensive commercial fishing, redwood lumber processing, and support operations for a major army base, but the military base was closed in 1954 and commercial fishing stopped three years later. Pittsburg went into the 1960s with an uncertain economic future as it tried to lure new economic and residential growth.

Possibly it was the environment of economic uncertainty, maybe it was innovative leadership, but by the 1980s Pittsburg had become a major example of productivity innovation in city management, symbolized by its "meter reader on roller skates." Specifically, the city's public service (or public works) department calculated that the cost of reading each of its 13,000 water meters bimonthly measured in staffing hours was 1.5 work years. The public service department reviewed its productivity and quality studies and found that accuracy declined after five or six hours of continuous work and that traditional work scheduling (standard forty-hour work week with holidays, breaks, and so on) wasn't conducive to getting the job done. The solution was a productivity performance concept. The meter reader gets paid by the unit—for every meter read, minus a $2.00 error rate per inaccurate reading (as reported by audit or customer complaint). The reading cycle must be completed in the appropriate weekly or monthly schedule to match billing cycles. The rest is up to the employee. The meter reader determines the daily work schedule and pay level for hours worked. Oh yes, it was the meter reader who came up with the idea of using roller skates. (It does help that this California city is predominantly flat and has the standard magnificent California weather). The result was a reduction in the overall cost of reading meters from $.78 to $.33, and the use of one meter reader compared to the previous 1.5 work years estimate.

Pittsburgh didn't stop there. It put in a number of productivity performance innovations, including paying for street sweeping by the mile, not the hour. Deductions are made for poor quality when complaints are received. (The unit goes back and redoes the portion involved.) To minimize equipment problems, no payments are made when the street sweeping equipment breaks down on the job. This makes the operating crew responsibile for preventative maintenance and street accidents. Everything is up to the operating crew but the overall result was a reduction in complaints and a $.10 to $.15 lowering of the costs per mile swept.

Perhaps the most interesting concept has been the shared savings program set up for the parks department. Concerned about a 40 percent increase in operating costs in the mid-1980s and a projected increase in park acreage for the latter 1980s of 55 percent, it created a special productivity incentive program for its employees. First, it reorganized the management team by selecting in effect a board of directors from about half of the park employees. The rest of the park employees work directly for the management group. Next, a shared savings pool was created. Taking out over a million dollars (about 60 percent of the total parks budget) this sum was put into four quarterly expense accounts. The management team tracks all the charges for supplies materials, equipment, tools, work hours, and other operating costs. Costs are compared to income for the quarter and if there are savings, 60 percent goes to the employees fund, and 40 percent to the city's general fund. The employees then decide how to distribute their savings. If expenses exceed income allotment, the employees must borrow against next quarter profits. Results for parks for the first year were impressive—a 6.3 percent return to the operating budget when park acreage had increased 11 percent and inflation was up 4 percent. The system worked because careful analysis was taken to set standards for productivity and quality of service ratios. The income allotments are adjusted to reflect a standard unit rate for maintenance. (Pittsburg was careful in setting up many of its productivity rates by comparing other California cites to make sure its standards were "fair." It also compares its costs to private sector contractors to make sure they're competitive.)

Are there implications for personnel management? Of course, there are many. The concern about increasing productivity, implementing measurement systems, and then using the measurements to change personnel practices are major parts of the productivity challenge for the public sector. In a rare bit of candor, the city noted in receiving a 1988 League of California Cities Award for Administrative Excellence:

> Employees are not satisfied with the traditional civil service system. This system generally provides all the tools necessary to deal with poor employees, but does very little to recognize good to excellent employees. Civil service traditionally gives us a merit system of pay advancement . . . in which, generally speaking, all employees who provide average service will reach the top. Employees with high performance standards quite often revert to the average when confronted with this system. . . . Pittsburg wants to recognize the good employee and management wants to spend time in developing our employee skills and productivity potential. Management spends far too much time and effort on the poor employee by concentrating on the negative reinforcement mechanisms of the civil service system.

Understanding the "Productivity Environment"

Recent initiatives throughout federal, state, and local government organizations make one point abundantly clear—government leaders and managers must do something about productivity improvement. While the "era of resource scarcity," "cutback management decade," the "period of retrenchment" (whatever term is vogue these days) is already old, the move to bolster confidence in public sector management by improving productivity or organizational efficiency remains very current and highly significant. Much is happening; many efforts currently being undertaken are ambitious experiments designed to establish new confidence in government's productive capacity and concurrently, competence.

Of course, many initiatives are not really serious and are designed only to promote images of action without bringing about change. This chapter attempts to sort out what today's "productivity environment" means for public sector organizations; how many of the current initiatives might be categorized so that planning objectives, design variables, implementation processes, and evaluation efforts can be better understood; and finally, what some of the implications are for public sector human resources management.

Everyone seems to understand that the nation has "productivity problems" these days, but not many know for sure what the causes are or even how serious these problems are. Most of the "numbers" involving productivity rates of growth are private sector parameters—and whether one reads the *Monthly Labor Review*, the *Wall Street Journal* or the *Harvard Business Review* there is a lot more disagreement about the causes and magnitude of the problem than seems possible, given a problem as immensely important as productivity is. Obviously the nation is not keeping its former pace and is lagging behind its major foreign competitors. But even here, economists and economic historians argue about whether or not that is bad or even meaningless.

Briefly, over the last forty years, the nation's mean annual increase rate in productivity has been slipping from +2.7% over the period from 1948 to 1966, to +1.6% from 1966 to 1973, to +0.7% from 1973 to 1977, to −0.9% in the period from 1979 to 1981. Thanks to better economic growth in the period from 1982 to 1985, the rate rebounded somewhat to above 2 percent, but gradually slipped again from 1985 to 1987 to under 2 percent and finished the decade on an even lower note (under 1.5 percent). As depressing as these rates are, the figures constitute a tenuous and arguable statistic. Many parts of American industry retain negative growth rates and our international competitive position has further deteriorated. While the U.S. still leads the world in productivity, there is substantial reason for concern as the recent MIT Commission on Industrial Productivity, as reported by Dertouzos in 1989, concluded:

> First, American productivity is not growing as fast as it used to, and productivity is not growing as fast as it is elsewhere, most notably in Japan. Second, other indicators of industrial performance that are less easily quantified than productivity but no less important tell a disquieting story. In such areas as product quality, service to customers, and speed of product development, American companies are no longer perceived as world leaders, even by American customers. There is also evidence that technological innovations are being incorporated into practice more quickly abroad, and the pace of invention and discovery in the United States may be slowing.

The American productivity slowdown that began in the 1970s is of particular interest to public administrators. Most economists concede three key problem aspects: (1) that American productivity was in a major slowdown from 1965 to 1980 that continues to haunt the economy; (2) that there has been a major rise in the service sector, which has lower productivity growth rates and thus far has not realized real benefits from fairly significant investments in technology, and (3) that the rate of growth of our major competitors (Japan and Germany) continues to outstrip American economic performance (see Table 12.1).

Some economists take a longer view of productivity which confirms current lags in American economic performance but reveals better marks for American accomplishments and identifies more clearly some of the cycles. A "longer view" shows that the picture is not as bleak as many alarmists would make it; but the need for concerted and positive action is still critical. This is especially significant for service sector growth, the impacts of

Table 12.1. Some Productivity and Labor Perspectives

Percentage of labor force in	Industry		Services		Capital-labor ratio growth (1950–1980)
	1965	1980	1965	1980	
U.S.	35%	31%	60%	66%	2.44%
Germany	48%	44%	42%	50%	5.66%
Japan	32%	34%	42%	55%	7.11%
U.K.	47%	38%	50%	59%	3.55%
Canada	33%	29%	57%	65%	2.95%

U.S. annual productivity growth rates	1980	1981	1982	1983	1984	1985	1986	1987	1988	1989
	−.4	1.0	−.9	2.8	2.1	1.4	2.1	1.1	2.1	.8

Ten-year labor productivity growth rates (1970s to 1980s)	U.S.	Germany	Japan	U.K.	France
	1.0%	3.0%	3.2%	2.4%	3.4%

Sources: U.S. Statistical Abstract, 1989, and William Baumol, et al., *Productivity and American Leadership: The Long View* (Cambridge, Mass.: MIT Press, 1989).

information and technology, and its evaluation of educational policies and investments. While some may be angered to find government and government enterprises categorized as a "stagnant sector" of the economy, there will be some consolation in terms of the company being kept in this group.

Arguments about causes of America's decline in productivity are even more confusing. Factors from the decline in S.A.T. scores tied to the number of hours of television watched to labor/capital substitution rates; the decline in the work ethic and in R & D spending; and marriage and divorce rates are variously cited, but the real point that should be made is that debates about productivity problems have generated a great deal of confusion in the minds of managers and personnel experts who ought to have the best idea about how and where such problems affect organizational performance.

The debate about the work ethic, especially in the public sector, bears this out. Nationally, there have been declines in worker attitudes in a number of key areas such as level of respect for the organization, perception of equity, belief in organizational responsiveness to employee problems, and disbelief in the effectiveness of advancement systems and performance evaluation systems. But do such "trends" constitute a sufficient case that the work ethic is sick in the public sector? Certainly not! Actually the opposite case can be made—that lower levels of productivity, declines in work quality, and reductions in overall organizational performance have a definite adverse affect on morale and motivation. If we then factor in the problems inherent in a 20 to 30 percent pay gap between public and private sector wages (see Chapter 5), it becomes impossible to attribute much to the work ethic or morale issue in the public sector.

Human resources managers don't need to be told that there's considerable controversy about productivity and quality problems. Any informal sample of managers can generally identify three prevailing themes: *inadequate resources, inappropriate organizational structures*, or *insufficient motivation* as major factors that adversely affect productivity. Even so, many feel more can be accomplished. An early 1982 survey report of federal managers and executives, *The Elusive Bottom Line*, by the Merit Systems Protection Board (MSPB), found that although most are positive about federal productivity, many see considerable potential for improvement. (This survey is instructive because it was taken at the start of the 1980s, when pay comparability was not a major factor.) Over 20 percent of federal executives and nearly 25 percent of mid-level managers replied that there was considerable potential to improve productivity in their organizations without increasing work force levels. Even higher percentages felt that quality could be improved without increasing staff.

There is one other argument that should be addressed about the current "productivity environment"—that most of the problems of the public sector are unique because of the service and information sector dimensions to public sector work. Briefly, the argument runs that productivity will always be more problematical because public sector efforts comprise mostly enterprises with low productivity growth rates, high labor intensities, and service considerations where effective performance can't be and shouldn't be measured through efficiency. Certainly this is true, but what public sector managers need to recognize is that it is private sector organizations that are recognizing their movement into the service information sector. They are changing and recognizing in the process how productivity equations and solutions change as a result of entry into this environment. Even private sector personnelists recognize this complexity. As an example, Walter Wriston, on his retirement in the mid-1980s as CitiBank's chief executive officer, made this remark about productivity problems and performance:

> Productivity, in the crudest sense, means output per work-hour. That's a useful enough concept in manufacturing, but what does it tell us in an information-intensive age when the vast majority of our workers are employed in the service sector? Take the financial-service industry. Once you get past counting the number of checks cleared per hour or the number of insurance claims paid, you move into the realm of subjectivity. How do you measure a loan officer's productivity?

By the number of loans he/she makes? By the size of the loans? By the number of his/her loans that are repaid on time? By the quantity of bad debt he/she creates?

These should be familiar words to almost any public sector manager because they mirror what's been said about productivity and performance in the public sector for the last thirty years. Maybe the point is that both public and private sector organizations, as they mount new productivity and work quality efforts, will have much more to learn from each other in the process.

Privatization and Productivity

One of the major factors that led to increased productivity efforts in the 1980s was the movement toward privatization. It may be somewhat of a misnomer to even label the above a "movement," but clearly both public administration theorists and practitioners are acutely aware of the increasing frequency and changes involved by contracting out, public-private partnerships,

---

Adam Smith on the Productivity of the Public Service

The labour of some of the most respectable orders in the society is, like that of menial servants, unproductive of any value, and does not fix or realize itself in any permanent subject, or vendible commodity, which endures after that labor is past, and for which an equal quantity of labour could afterwards be procured. The sovereign, for example, with all the officers both of justice and war who serve under him, the whole army and navy, are unproductive labourers. They are the servants of the public, and are maintained by a part of the annual produce of the industry of other people. Their service, how honourable, how useful, or how necessary soever, produces nothing for which an equal quantity can afterwards be procured. The protection, security and defence of the commonwealth, the effect of their labour this year, will not purchase its protection, security, and defence for the year to come. In the same class must be ranked, some both of the gravest and and most important, and some of the most frivolous professions: churchmen, lawyers, physicians, men of letters of all kinds; players, buffoons, musicians, opera-singers, opera-dancers, etc. The labour of the meanest of these has a certain value, regulated by the very same principles which regulate that of every other sort of labour; and that of the noblest and most useful, produces nothing which could afterwards purchase or procure an equal quantity of labour. Like the declamation of the actor, the harangue of the orator, or the tune of the musician, the work of all of them perishes in the very instant of its production.

Adam Smith, *The Wealth of Nations* (New York: Modern Library, 1937), p. 315.

coproduction, or whatever vehicle is being used to separate the production of public sector goods and services from their provision. From garbage collection and public works functions to human services, prisons, health care, education, and administrative services, new arrangements have been made for the delivery of public services to the public.

There is little doubt that the debate over public-private sector roles and comparable performance is just getting started. Divested now of some of the political ideology and rhetoric it accumulated in the 1980s, "privatization" may increasingly be viewed more simply as a policy choice or management decision in the 1990s. But it is critical to understand how and why governments seek to perform public tasks. Likewise, what citizens think about their public services matters—what John Donahue in his recent book *The Privatization Decision* calls "fidelity to the public's values. . . . If the citizenry cares about how goods and services are produced, about how equitably they are distributed, about the pay, benefits, and working conditions of those who produce them, then any legitimate measure of efficiency must incorporate these concerns."

Privatization is almost always predicated on assumptions about public sector versus private sector productivity rates. Although some researchers have gone to great lengths to explain why these comparisons can't be made, aren't made correctly, or even shouldn't be made in the first place, the simple truth remains that the burden of proof is on the public sector organization to demonstrate that it is not inferior in terms of productivity. This is doubly more difficult because productivity in the public sector involves multiple, often conflicting perspectives and comparisons of different services for different groups of recipients with different needs. By comparison, private sector counterparts like to make one-dimension comparisons, i.e., to stack.

While public sector organizations can certainly be faulted for not being more willing to measure productivity, one should be clear about both the context of and the reasons for that unwillingness. There are far too many systems "disincentives" built in toward productivity measurement, beginning with fears of having budgets cut, personnel levels trimmed, or other penalites for producing above budgeted levels to measurement problems that are adversely biased against public sector goods and products. The difference in perspective is far more complicated than analysts give credit for. To begin with there is the nature of work differences. For example, Barbara Stevens, in a recent article comparing public and private sector productivity, notes that there are critical differences involving "the concepts of clear, precise task definitions and job descriptions, coupled with easily identifiable responsibility for job requirements."

There is still another major difference to be considered: mainly, the precept that private sector organizations use productivity measurement and improvement in the same way that public sector organizations do. They don't. Most private sector organizations use productivity measurement systems to assign more work, more responsibility, more financial reward, more capital resources, and more power to the units that demonstrate the highest levels of productivity. Rather than cut the most productive units, they give them more resources or more rewards. This also affects the investment strategy that goes into a productivity improvement effort. Most public sector organizations commission productivity efforts by assignment without up front investment; that is, staff are reassigned or reprogrammed to take on productivity responsibilities. In short, they must be internally financed. Private sector organizations expect to pay up front costs to start a productivity improvement effort and then evaluate the results against total costs.

What Is Productivity?

Until a few years ago, governmental administrators rarely emphasized productivity improvement as a fundamental management theme. In fact, the word had an unfortunate reputation, being associated with sweatshops, time-and-motion studies, and demoralized assembly-line workers. However, the early 1970s brought a radical change when more and more public sector budgetary crunches were in sight. Coupled with the pressures of privatization and contracting out in the 1980s, the need for *productivity* improvement became more accepted. It is in harmony with public administration's major modern themes—parsimony and creative conservation. Still, many managers in the public sector have observed this development with skepticism. Fads, they reason, come and go. They hold the glum hope that all this talk about government productivity will eventually fade away.

There are good explanations for their cynicism. Many public sector activities are difficult to measure, or put another way, the costs of measurement may be so prohibitive as to outweigh the benefits in measuring productivity. We are reminded of the example of one field office that wished to measure the productivity of a new centralized typing pool (now referred to as *word processing*) to justify its establishment. A log was kept of every document received, typed, and returned-by time. At the end of the month, the unit was dismantled because productivity did not significantly increase. The real cause was not the typing arrangement but the inordinate amount of time spent keeping up the logs and compiling statistics for daily productivity reports. While there are relatively simple solutions to the above problem, the difficulty of measuring the productivity of engineers, scientists, diplomats, researchers, public relations specialists, and many other public workers is very real, so it is imperative to keep productivity in a proper perspective.

Simply stated, the purpose of productivity efforts is to get improved yield out of allocated resources. This is achieved by means of efficiency and effectiveness controls. A good way to understand the overall meaning of productivity is to think of any government organization as part of a production cycle in which resources are transformed by the agency into usable services. This means that simple systems terms can be used to show how the process works. Resources or inputs are transformed by a throughput phase into results, or outputs. In order to know if the process is doing what it should, outputs are matched with standards, or goals (see Figure 12.1). For example, a motor vehicle registration operation would use inputs of people, supplies, equipment, and facilities in order to go through the process of registering vehicles of various types of people in different types of circumstances and occupations. These registrations are one major output. However, they must meet certain standards of quality and timeliness. These standards are matched to the actual output. If the match is satisfactory, then the process is not interfered with. Often the match of output to standards will not be satisfactory; then there are three action alternatives. The first is to change the amount and/or mix of input; the second is to rearrange the organizational or management process (throughput); the third alternative is to change the standards.

The process of matching output to standards provides a measure of *effectiveness*, or quality. However, it is necessary to keep cost factors in mind, because attaining quality objectives might be done in wasteful ways. Therefore, the comparison of output to input, or the *efficiency ratio*, is also essential. Returning to the example of the motor vehicle registration operation, an

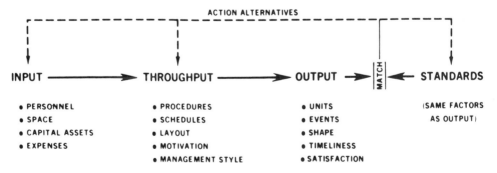

Figure 12.1. The production process and its elements. *Source*: Edward H. Downey and Walter L. Balk, *Employee Innovation and Government Productivity* (Chicago: International Personnel Management Association, 1976), p. 39. Reprinted by permission of the International Personnel Management Association, 1850 K Street, NW, Suite 870, Washington, D.C. 20006.

efficiency measure or control could be cost per license issued. This could be obtained by dividing the number of licenses issued over a given period of time (output) by the resource dollars (input) used in agency operations to produce these results. A productive process is one that optimizes both ratios of effectiveness and efficiency. This process can be summarized by the following equations:

$$\text{Productivity} = \text{effectiveness} + \text{efficiency}$$

or

$$\text{Productivity} = \frac{\text{output}}{\text{standards}} + \frac{\text{output}}{\text{input}}$$

The second equation is the same as the first, except that the terms *effectiveness* and *efficiency* are explained respectively as the ratios of output to standards and output to input. These two productivity ratios are extremely important because their analysis can lead to (1) cost reduction and service improvement, (2) more accurate planning and budget justification, and (3) better accountability to the public. Productivity improvement is most fundamentally an effort to improve work and management practices.

Measuring Productivity

All public agencies engage in activities that can be identified in terms of the direct results of the work performed. A state police department, for example, patrols lengths of highway, makes traffic arrests, investigates criminal cases, and may train local police in various police science techniques. The activities are more or less routine and the results can be described in units of output—so many arrests made, tickets issued, hours on patrol, and so on. Such units of output, while subject to statistical variation, are essentially under the control of the agency; therefore, they are amenable to some form of meaningful productivity measurement. Still, there are certain limits. If a police force sets an expected standard of two arrests per day per officer, there are certain possibilities that the resulting interpretations by police officers may bring about inappropriate results on different days. Moreover, is an arrest for rape "counted" the same as an arrest for jaywalking?

Governmental agency outputs are usually aimed at producing broad social consequences. Consider the state police department again. Its work is supposed to improve the flow of traffic, reduce accidents, and cause the crime rate to drop, yet these consequences are also affected by road maintenance, laws, and the legal system. Crime reduction is only mildly related to police actions; the efficiency of the courts and prison system as well as economic and demographic considerations may be far more important factors.

Table 12.2.   Terminology of Government Producitivity Measurement

Term	Definition
Activity	A task performed by an organization to produce a desired output. Examples include miles driven, trucks serviced, and meters read. Sometimes described as workload.
Consequence	The desired results of government programs or services such as improved citizen safety, increased longevity, and reduced infant mortality. Sometimes described as impact or outcome.
Effectiveness	The degree or extent to which program goals are met, such as percentage of population served or percentage of clients successfully treated.
Efficiency	The ratio of output to inputs such as a work performed per staff hour or downtime as a percentage of total hours. Includes productivity, unit costs, and technical efficiency.
Function	A government service such as police, fire, and education. "Function" and "service" are used synonymously.
Goal	A statement which describes what is to be accomplished by a program, service, or agency such as "insure a safe and secure environment."
Impact	The long-term effect of a program on a community or its citizens. "Impact" and "consequence" or used synonymously. See "Consequence."
Input	The resource used by an agency to produce a function or service. Examples of inputs are labor, facilities, equipment, and materials.
Outcome	Short-term impact or consequence of government action or outputs, such as increased income which might come as a result of job training.
Output	The result of work performed or produced by an agency. Outputs are what government produces. Examples of outputs are the number of individuals served, gallons of water delivered, or tons of trash collected.
Productivity	Amount of physical output per unit of input.
Productivity index	An index of the change in resources used per unit of output.
Service	A government function such as police, fire, or education. The terms "service" and "function" are used synonymously.
Social indicator	A measure of societal well-being such as longevity or happiness. These measures are of interest because they are considerations which governments wish to promote.
Workload	A measure of the amount of work performed, usually an intermediate output, such as the number of miles driven, or number of machines serviced. See "Activity."

Source: Donald M. Fisk, *Measuring Productivity in State and Local Government* (Washington, D.C.: U.S. Department of Labor, Bureau of Labor Statistics, January 1984), p. 2.

Consequently, making a case that there is a cause-and-effect connection between the direct work activities of an agency and the seeming social consequences is problematical at best. In short, while it is rational to seek to measure the activities of an agency, it is irrational to seek a measure of agency effectiveness by assessing the social impact of agency activities—the outside environment is far too complex and interrelated to allow this.

As any agency performs its assigned functions, its activities contribute to social consequences that are at the same time a product of other environmental influences. Policy makers such as executives and legislatures then have to make an informed judgment about the nature and quality of resources to be provided to individual agencies. Any state police department, returning to our example, has its yearly budget determined by the policy makers who control the budget. The decision makers must consider the social consequences of their action—obviously they will continue to fund the state police, but by how much?

Essentially all such decisions involve making a quality-of-life judgment. Should we have more police protection and spend less on education? Since an infinite number of other trade-offs are also possible, policy makers generally make decisions in small increments that deviate only slightly from the past. When policy makers decide to fund an activity, the specific amount becomes a function of the perceived social consequences of the level of funding and the ability of an agency to demonstrate that it has or can perform in an efficient and effective manner. It is only this latter part of the decisional focus that lends itself to mathematical rationality. Technical productivity measures, while primarily an internal management tool, can play a major role in making agencies more accountable to the policy makers who are accountable to the public.

What is it that can actually be measured in a governmental agency? Practically everything! However, it is crucial that the measuring instrument be appropriate to the activity being measured. Almost all governmental work lends itself to one of three measurement techniques: engineered work standards, group output trend analysis, or program output analysis (see Figure 12.2).

Highly routine and repetitive tasks easily lend themselves to *engineered work standards*—a continuation of the scientific management tradition. This approach entails dividing each job into basic work increments, assigning a time to each increment, adding these times up to get a "standard time" per unit of output, and matching the actual to the ideal time in order to measure efficiency. Engineered work standards have the advantage of providing a reasonably scientific basis to measure individual performance in many manufacturing, clerical, and maintenance jobs. A ready example of this would be data entry operations. Scientifically engineered standards can be set that define

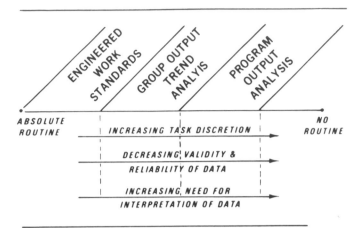

Figure 12.2. The effect of work routine upon control and measurement. *Source*: Walter L. Balk, *Improving Government Productivity: Some Policy Perspectives* (Beverly Hills, Calif.: Sage Publications, 1975), p. 333.

Productivity Measurement at the Post Office

The following is the sworn testimony of Mr. William J. Anderson, the deputy director of the General Government Division of the General Accounting Office, given on July 1, 1976, before the Subcommittee on Postal Facilities, Mail, and Labor Management of the Committee on the Post Office and Civil Service of the U.S. House of Representatives:

> Mr. Chairman and members of the committee: We appreciate the opportunity to discuss with you our work involving the Washington, D.C. City Post Office.

> As you know, our work was done in response to the June 23, 1975 request of Mr. Henderson, Chairman, Committee on Post Office and Civil Service, U.S. House of Representatives.

> Allegations of mismanagement were made by the former Capital District Manager, Mr. Carlton Beall, and were contained in a notebook of documents forwarded to us by the Committee at the time of the request.

> Specifically Mr. Henderson requested that we investigate allegations of exaggerated mail volumes and overstaffed operations at the City Post Office.

> I would like to briefly reiterate the findings in our report and describe how we arrived at our conclusions and then I will be happy to try to answer any questions you may have.

(continued)

Productivity Measurement at the Post Office (Continued)

The allegations of exaggerated mail volumes and overstaffed operations at the City Post Office were valid. However, the Postal Service was aware of the problem and had taken, and was continuing to take, actions to improve operations at that office.

As we pointed out in our report, similar problems occurred at other post offices across the country and apparently resulted from intense pressure from top management to improve productivity.

In many instances, purported productivity gains were achieved by manipulating the Postal Service's Workload Recording System which measured productivity in mail processing operations.

In November 1974, the Postmaster General sent a message to all postal managers stating that several instances of deliberate falsification of production records had been uncovered and that a grace period to correct irregularities would be given.

After the grace period, however, strict accountability for accurate and reliable data would be required and violators would be subject to dismissal.

The Workload Recording System lost its validity after Service management tried to foster competition among post offices by generating a list of top offices in productivity.

When management started the list, the Postal Service's productivity and mail volume appeared to increase nationwide. And so it did at the City Post Office.

After starting at the bottom of the list, the City Post Office reported consistently increasing mail volumes and productivity unit it ranked at or near the top.

Mr. Martin L. Simms, former Postmaster at the City Post Office, told us that when he was appointed Postmaster of the City Post Office in January 1974, he realized mail volumes being recorded were higher than those he observed and that the facility was generally overstaffed. The overstaffing resulted from inflated mail volumes.

In May 1974, Mr. Simms called a series of meetings of all tour supervisors and informed them he knew of the volume falsification and wanted it stopped immediately. He threatened to fire anyone caught falsifying volumes in the future. Mail volumes and productivity reported for June 2–28, 1974 declined 25 percent.

When the results for this period became known at the district level, Mr. Beall called Mr. Simms to his office and requested an explanation for the drop in productivity. When Mr. Simms said the prior productivity figures were false, Mr. Beall disagreed and accused him of having lost control of the City Post Office. This controversy ultimately led to an Inspection Service audit in August 1974.

The Inspection Service found that in spite of Mr. Simms' warning to cease all volume inflation, the situation had not been completely corrected. It was estimated that the total piece handlings were inflated over 60 percent.

(continued)

Productivity Measurement at the Post Office (continued)

The service now estimates it was overstated as much as 100 percent.

Their audit was supported by hours of video tape records showing individuals reweighing the mail over and over to inflate volumes and by sworn statements from supervisors and employees admitting record falsification.

The most common reasons given by employees for participating in the fabrication were the pressure from higher management to achieve production levels that were unrealistic and a belief that their career would suffer if these productivity levels were not met.

a "normal" amount of output per data entry clerk. The productivity of an individual clerk might be the number of entries made over a period of time compared to the established standards of output.

It is readily apparent that engineered work standards can only be applied to limited amounts of government work. They are not appropriate for complex, less routinized work, even if the outputs are reasonably tangible. In such cases a common approach has been to aggregate the work done by an entire group in order to develop efficiency ratios—the most common being the number of units produced per average person in the group. This kind of measure can be called *group output trend analysis*.

Consider a hypothetical automobile registration operation as an example. In this group effort, employees may switch jobs from day to day, the types of registrations may also differ in complexity as well as format, and the workload can vary according to the weather, time of day, or month. One measure of productivity would be to divide the numbers of each category of registrations completed by the work hours used each month. This can translate into so many registrations of a specific type per average workday. When this calculation is performed each month, the emerging pattern will show a trend of performance over time. A typical trend analysis would present a region of tolerance for the output of the group. Within the region of tolerance would be a historically derived standard of performance. For example, the production standard for an automobile registration operation might be 300 registrations per day, while the region of tolerance might be from 275 to 325. If performance is below 275, resources may not be used as effectively as possible; above 325 the work force may be so pressed that the quality of the work suffers. Of course, the production figures for any given day may be misleading. Decisions should only be made on data that reflect several weeks or months of output. Overall, group output trend analysis data are less

The Little Red Hen:
A Productivity Fable

Once upon a time there was a little red hen who scratched about the barnyard until she uncovered some grains of wheat. She turned to other workers on the farm and said: "If we plant this wheat, we'll have bread to eat. Who will help me plant it?"

"We never did that before," said the horse, who was the supervisor.

"I'm too busy," said the duck.

"I'd need complete training," said the pig.

"It's not in my job description," said the goose.

"Well, I'll do it myself," said the little red hen. And she did. The wheat grew tall and ripened into grain. "Who will help me reap the wheat?" asked the little red hen.

"Let's check the regulations first," said the horse.

"I'd lose my seniority," said the duck.

"I'm on my lunch break," said the goose.

"Out of my classification," said the pig.

"Then I will," said the little red hen, and she did.

At last it came time to bake the bread.

"Who will help me bake the bread?" asked the little red hen.

"That would be overtime for me," said the horse.

"I've got to run some errands," said the duck.

"I've never learned how," said the pig.

"If I'm to be the only helper, that's unfair," said the goose.

"Then I will," said the little red hen.

She baked five loaves and was ready to turn them in to the farmer when the other workers stepped up. They wanted to be sure the farmer knew it was a group project.

"It needs to be cleared by someone else," said the horse.

"I'm calling the shop steward," said the duck.

"I demand equal rights," yelled the pig.

"We'd better file a copy," said the goose.

But the little red hen turned in the loaves by herself. When it came time for the farmer to reward the effort, he gave one loaf to each worker.

"But I earned all the bread myself!" said the little red hen.

"I know," said the farmer, "but it takes too much paperwork to justify giving you all the bread. It's much easier to distribute it equally, and that way the others won't complain."

So the little red hen shared the bread, but her co-workers and the farmer wondered why she never baked any more.

Adapted from *Federal News Clip Sheet*, June 1979.

scientific than engineered work standards. While the data are less hard and reliable, they nevertheless offer considerable decision-making utility.

When it is not possible to establish engineered work standards or group output trend analysis, it is common to rely upon estimates pertaining to program schedules and completion targets. This third form of productivity measurement is called *program output analysis*. Estimates are made of the desired percentage of program completion to be achieved over the coming weeks or months. At a specific reporting date actual progress is compared to the estimates. This is essentially a way of holding managers responsible for their time; as such, it is a variant of management by objectives (MBO). Program output analysis is a very imprecise measurement device, but it is the only way to deal with those large areas of government work concerned with policy making, analysis, and evaluation: program development and implementation, and research among others.

Models of Productivity Management

Productivity management or measurement is a concept that has been a part of public administration and public personnel management since the advent of "performance budgeting" in the early 1900s in New York City. It is important to bear in mind that measurement systems seldom operate alone—they are generally found in conjunction with some type of participative management or employee involvement effort. Hybrid systems are generally the rule because measurement approaches require employee involvement and acceptance to work and participation approaches require some forms of measurement to focus problem-solving efforts and evaluate results.

Table 12.3 attempts to depict some of major models for productivity management. The word *management* is used because it more clearly communicates the objective of "improved organizational and individual performance," which goes beyond simple productivity improvement. As discussed, improvements in organizational efficiency are important, but the context is larger and the purview of any of the models reviewed here reflects this. Each model has its own specific emphasis or objective.

But, traditional approaches to productivity management need to be addressed first. Ad hoc programs, which have been used by public sector organizations for years, involve internal reforms centering on performance appraisal, compensation/incentive plans, new efforts at work redesign/job enrichment, or planning group and suborganizational productivity goals. To some degree they can be useful and effective; but it is difficult to sustain long-range progress and to institutionalize results. Actually, institutionalization of results is one of the larger problems—over time the reforms become part of the institutional framework and can actually impede further progress. This

Table 12.3. Productivity Management Models: Measurement Oriented

Model 1	Model 2	Model 3
Experimental productivity measurement	Integrated performance productivity measurement	Comprehensive productivity measurement
Emphasis on: "Knowledge" work productivity measurement	Emphasis on: Total performance management	Emphasis on: Multivariate productivity measurement systems

is not to say that job redesign (something that is an invaluable tool in productivity improvement) or any other of these ad hoc efforts should be made light of; but they are tools and can be most effectively used as part of a more comprehensive effort.

Three models are displayed in measurement-oriented appraoches. Comprehensive productivity measurement includes most of the composite work measurement techniques that have been developed by federal and state governments over the past twenty years. In terms of methods, there isn't much new; but overall application is more ambitious in terms of scope and magnitude of effort. The comprehensive approach assumes the organization's incorporation of productivity measurement into its goal-setting and budgeting processes. The second part of this model outlines some of the measurement methodologies that can be used (see Table 12.4). As such it is a lot more than the simple control/accountability systems developed in this area in the past.

Integrated performance/productivity systems (see Table 12.5), such as those developed in San Diego or Phoenix, take the measurement concept a considerable step further. Multiple measures of performance and organizational results are integrated with productivity and resource usage measures. When management involvement or participative management approaches are used to focus correctional efforts, the result is a productivity improvement effort that includes a lot more than simple or multiple productivity measurements. Perhaps the most important distinction in this recognition that "organizational" performance evaluation and productive capacity are linked. One can see the special applicability of this model to cities and local governments.

Of the measurement-oriented models, experimental productivity measurement is perhaps the most ambitious. Major experiments are underway at national and international research centers attempting to develop methods through which knowledge organizations or white-collar work can be analyzed and evaluated in terms of resource requirements, management requirements, and

Table 12.4. Comprehensive Productivity Measurement: Work Measurement Techniques

Technique	Cycle	Frequency	Complexity	Example
Supervisor's estimate	Irregular	Low	High complexity	Project work such as research and development work; laboratory experiments; planning; budget
Delphi method	Irregular	Low	High complexity	Project work such as research and development work; laboratory experiments; planning; budget; evaluation
Historical	Regular/ irregular	Low-high	Complex	Processing purchase orders; processing grant applications; processing vouchers for payment; personnel records
Modified Historical	Regular/ irregular	Mid-high	Low complexity	Processing purchase orders; processing grant applications; processing vouchers for payment; personnel records
Average case	Regular/ irregular	Low-mid	Complex	Routine inspection; processing vouchers for payment
Time Study	Regular	High	Few operations, low complexity	Factory work; support services for patient care
Predetermined time data	Regular	High	Few operations, low complexity	Support services for patient care; janitorial services; Keypunch operations

Source: Adapted from Albert Hyde, "Productivity Management for Public Sector Organizations," *Public Personnel Management*, (Winter 1985).

Table 12.5. Integrated Performance/Productivity Measurement—Total Performance Management (TPM)

Phase		Initial Steps: Organization Climate/ Communications Survey
	I	Define organizational goals and determine how TPM can help achieve those goals.
	II	Hold orientation meetings between management and employee representatives.
	III	Determine productivity indicators.
	IV	Survey employees' attitudes.
	V	Survey client/citizen satisfaction with organization's products/services.
	VI	Examine productivity indicators, employees' attitudes, and citizen satisfaction levels in organizational meetings.
	VII	Establish action plans to remedy identified problems.
	VIII	Implement action plans and evaluate results.
(Optional but suggested)	IX	Institute employee-management problem solving, communications, and team building, capacity building training effort.

Source: Adapted from City of San Diego's *Total Performance Management System Report*.

service and production capacity. Unfortunately, most of these projects are still in their initial stages of development, with early results being quite tentative. Overall, there is a great deal of promise that measurement methodologies may well advance considerably in this decade enabling public sector organizations to better understand their productive capacities.

A winter 1985 symposium in *Public Personnel Management* presented an overview of a number of cities, states, and federal agencies that have used some the models described in the figures above. Over the five-year period tracking these productivity models, there has been a fairly high mortality rate. About half of the examples cited have discontinued their programs. But this should come as no surprise, given the high failure rates of public management efforts, budgeting and personnel programs, information and computer systems, and previously announced productivity programs.

Gainsharing and Shared Savings Plans

A second series of efforts has focused on the motivation problems inherent in the work force, or more specifically, tying employee motivation directly into productivity efforts. Productivity gainsharing raises a number of significant questions about this current application of compensation and reward systems geared to organizational outcomes. The basic concept links a portion of a worker's pay to increased productivity and shares organizational savings with employees. Such arrangements were first used in the private sector (the term itself dates back to 1896 as Henry Towne's label for his firm's indirect incentive system), but now encompass many variations. Renewed interest in gainsharing in this decade parallels national concerns with declining productivity and a deteriorating international economic position. Various surveys have shown considerable usage of gainsharing plans by private sector firms, although the vast majority have been adopted only in the last ten years. Some experts see the current inspiration for gainsharing systems in the Japanese compensation method of paying out nearly 25 percent of workers' wages in two yearly bonuses that are determined by the firm's current economic performance.

Regarding public sector applications, the federal government has already accumulated considerable experience with gainsharing. The General Accounting Office (GAO) has recently evaluated eighteen Defense Department experiments with gainsharing and the Office of Management and Budget has announced its approval of "shared savings plans" in which half the budgetary savings created by productivity improvements can be returned to workers in the form of bonuses. Local government applications are just now surfacing. The GAO conducted a major survey in 1986 of Fortune 500 firms that have used gainsharing, pointing to the factors contributing to success or failure. Again, some caution is essential, as some critics have noted that private sector programs have notoriously short life spans, especially if the measurement base and participation of the work force has not been firmly established.

Summary: Will It Work? Will It Last?

Any public agency exists within an open systems environment consisting primarily of elected executives, legislators, employee unions, constituencies (e.g., clients and special-interest groups), other agencies (at the same and different levels of government), and the media. These influences are vital to the support of the agency. However, they frequently "push" at cross-purposes, making it difficult for an agency to keep its equilibrium and integrity among these pressures. One way to maintain agency balance is to develop a better language, using productivity to explain and document goals, results, and operational improvements over time. In this way agencies can become more accountable to their various publics and make more visible to those publics what they intend to do as well as their success in achieving those intentions. Public administration has already crossed into an era in which credibility will be defined by conservation of resources and the improvement of services. The continuing evolving techniques of productivity improvement naturally have great utility for internal agency control. But while these techniques can help agencies adapt to the new realities of resource scarcity, they will also force agencies to be more accountable to outside influences.

Consider the political implications of an agency's responsibility to be accountable. One could argue that since open-system influences frequently are not pushing in the same direction, it is poor strategy for an agency to make its detailed plans public. For example, suppose a community mental health operation would make its objectives visible to the point that mental retardation would seem to be taking a lower priority than alcoholism and drug rehabilitation. This would bring down the rage of those with special interests in mental retardation, thus causing hassles, external as well as internal, to the agency. These priorities become eventually visible in any event, and it is perhaps better to face angry constituents than deceive them. However, subterfuges of this kind have been used as excuses by administrators wanting to take the time to be accountable (or the risk) by stating in some detail just what their accomplishment targets and results are.

Perhaps the root of the problem is that most administrators have closed-system perspectives. They quickly sense the contrary and disorderly nature of the political environment of public programs and realize that they have very limited control over the organization's fate. Because of this they tend to fear outside disturbances and the attendant conflict and confrontation involved in becoming accountable. Why make themselves and their programs unnecessarily vulnerable? In addition, there exists a conviction that others cannot understand the complexity and professional details of many agency operations, therefore, making public plans and decisions would only confuse those on the outside and provide hostile elements with ammunition. While there is often truth to these feelings, public managers have overreacted. They all too frequently tell as little as possible, which is to say they are accountable as little as possible. In their dealings with the press and the public they engage in ham-handed or transparently slick public relations efforts in order to "sell" the public. These activities often use up considerable resources which might better be directed toward where it counts: being more productive. The net result is a lack of response to public pressures to improve management practices.

Public employees' concerns for productivity improvement efforts have hardly been enthusiastic. They are obviously fearful of management's motives and often have good reason to be. In the eyes of the rank and file, productivity rhetoric on the part of politicians and top administrators contains two equally unpleasant possibilities. Management could be intending to operate under sweatshop conditions or it could be trying to generate layoffs. These reactions are understandable when administrators have neither clear policies nor rewards that encourage employees to become part of an improvement effort. Public sector unions are not predisposed to accept productivity programs for the same reasons. Unions, based on abuses of the past as well as present, are justifiably skeptical of "productivity improvement" efforts. In addition, union leaders must be vigilant of the "trade-offs" when these efforts yield "positive " results. Suppose, for example, that employees were paid more "in line" with their output rather than in seniority. This would mean that some individuals or groups would make more money than others within the same bargaining unit. This would be further complicated by the often subjective and imprecise measurement methods that would have to be used to determine levels of output. Employee associations, especially in the public sector, then prefer to bargain for improved wages and working conditions for entire classes of employees. Differentiating wages between people or groups in the same unit based upon productivity results is just another headache to union leadership. They would much prefer to engage in efforts that have a greater and more visible payoff, such as making general unitwide improvements, expanding membership, and fighting off other unions that might want to intrude upon their turf.

Public managers are often even more opposed to productivity efforts. A major reason why public managers are not motivated to engage in strong productivity improvement efforts is that most of them simply do not understand what productivity is within a governmental context. Learning the new language and techniques of productivity is a painful process. Implementing such a program requires confronting others and taking risks. It also means change. Unfortunately, environmental constraints limit the ability of managers to take effective action. Managerial authority is eroded by executives, legislators, and constituencies. Civil service regulations often reduce the flexibility of managerial actions. Advocacy media efforts highlight the failures and tend to ignore the successes of programs. But most damaging of all is that there are generally no clear-cut rewards for public managers that encourage them to engage in productivity improvement. The atavistic outlook of many budget executives ensures that a punishment rather than a gratifying system of rewards is in operation. Typically, it is folly for an agency to announce a substantial savings brought about by a productivity improvement effort. The total amount would be promptly cut from the budget, leaving no room for improvements in the quality of services or for giving differential pay increases to those who bring about the savings.

Given these complications, it is not surprising to find that sizable numbers of public administrators prefer to keep a low profile and seek their gains through a byzantine and covert political influence process. This is not to say that no controls exist in agencies. Of course records are kept, goals established, and attempts made to record progress. After all, things do get done in public agencies and it takes a modicum of good management practices to deliver services.

What Is Productivity Bargaining?

Productivity bargaining is one of the means by which jurisdictions have sought to relate salary increases to greater productive efforts. This strategem has met with limited success. There are two basic approaches to productivity bargaining: *integrative bargaining* and *pressure bargaining*. The latter is the stuff of confrontation best illustrated by the adversary model of labor relations. Its dysfunctional consequences—strikes, hostility, and fiscal crises—are well known. The other approach—integrative bargaining—is in essence participative management. It is premised on the notion that a decrease in hostility is mutually advantageous and that management does not have a natural monopoly on brains. It is highlighted by its mutuality—a mutual definition of problems, a mutual search for alternatives, and a mutual selection of solutions. The two bargaining strategies—integrative and pressure—do not present themselves as an either/or proposition. Each side develops what it believes to be the best mix of both approaches for any given situation.

While labor-management negotiations involve an inherent degree of productivity bargaining, most deliberate efforts at it in the public sector have been at the local level.

The problem is that these controls are frequently not integrated, visible to employees, made public or used as the basis for rewarding the better managers. The Civil Service Reform Act of 1978 attempted a major step toward changing this attitude on the federal level. Provisions in the Senior Executive Service required a merit pay system that included major provisions for bonuses, promotions, and annual compensation increases that are to be linked to productivity increases. Although each agency in the federal government was to develop its own plan, it is clear to all federal government agencies that productivity improvement is to be one of the most critical factors (if not *the* most critical factor) for distributing salary increases. Unfortunately, the plans never reached the middle and bottom levels of the organization and the merit pay system failed to ignite a productivity explosion.

Finally, there has been a disturbing tendency on the part of some agencies to set up productivity systems on a zero-sum budget basis, pitting one region against another. Resources and bonuses went to the more productive regions at the expense of the less productive. Consider the case of the Social Security Administration (SSA), as reported by the GAO in a 1985 study. For years, the Atlanta region has had higher productivity rates than the San Francisco or New York regional offices. Atlanta received the benefits while New York and San Francisco, having high costs of living, complained that their federal wage dollars couldn't hire personnel of "comparable" quality to Atlanta, with its lower cost of living. Furthermore, New York and San Francisco argued that the measured system was stacked in that each SSA case represented a unit; but, higher crime, greater mobility and economic diversity, and larger language, social, and cultural differences made "cases" in New York harder than in Atlanta. Productivity measurement has to be both fair and equitable.

So, all in all, despite the promises, it is too soon to evaluate what changes will occur in the behavior of public managers and public organizations in terms of productivity improvement. Certainly there has been a pronounced shift in favorable attitudes toward productivity improvement and recognition of the problems. But to some extent, it has become just another competing management priority. This is the point raised earlier about a key difference between private sector counterparts. When they initiate a process, it requires an investment of extra resources and, at a mimimum, some type of coordination position or function to implement change. Public sector managers and personnel managers simply add to their job descriptions. Productivity remains important, but clearly, in the 1990s, the emphasis has shifted to another theme—the emergence of quality management.

Bibliography

Aft, Lawrence S. *Productivity, Measurement and Its Improvement*. Reston, Va.: Reston Publishing, 1983.

Ammons, David N. *Municipal Productivity*. New York, Praeger, 1984.

Balk, Walter L. *Improving Government Productivity: Some Policy Perspectives*. Beverly Hills, Calif.: Sage Publications, 1975.

_____ . "Symposium: Productivity in Government," *Public Administration Review* (January–February 1978).

Barbour, George P. Jr. "Measuring Local Government Productivity," *Municipal Year Book*. Washington, D.C.: International City Management Association, 1972.

Baumol, Blackman, et al. *Productivity and American Leadership: The Long View*. Cambridge, Mass.: MIT Press, 1989.

Berry, Frances S. and James E. Jarrett. *Nationwide Survey Results of State Government Productivity*. Report of State Government Productivity Research Council, April 1981.

Bendick, Marc Jr. "Privatization of Public Services: Recent Experience," in *Public-Private Partnership* edited by Harvey Brooks et al. Washington, D.C.: American Academy of Arts and Sciences, 1984.

Bish, Robert L. "Improving Productivity in the Public Sector: The Role of Contracting Out," in *Responses to Economic Change* edited by David Laidler. Toronto: University of Toronto Press, 1986.

Blinder, Alan S. (ed.). *Paying for Productivity*. Washington, D.C.: the Brookings Institution, 1990.

Brief, Arthur (ed.). *Productivity Research in the Behavioral and Social Science*. New York, Praeger, 1984.

Bullock, R. J. and E. E. Lawler. "Gainsharing: A Few Questions and Fewer Answers," *Human Resources Management* (spring 1984).

Downs, George and Patrick D. Larkey. *The Search for Government Efficiency*. New York: Random House, 1986. (See especially chapter 2, "Business versus Government: An Invidious Comparison.")

Dertouzos, Michael L., Richard K. Lester and Robert M. Solow. *Made in America*. The MIT Commission on Industrial Productivity. Cambridge, Mass , MIT Press, 1989.

Donahue, John D. *The Privatization Decision*. New York: Basic Books, 1989.

Goldoff, Anna C. with David C. Tatage. "Joint Productivity Committees: Lessons of Recent Initiatives," *Public Administration Review*, 38 (March–April, 1978).

Hatry, Harry and D. M. Fisk. *Improving Productivity and Productivity Measurement in Local Governments*. Washington, D.C.: Urban Institute, 1971.

Hayward, Nancy S. "The Productivity Challenge," *Public Administration Review* (September–October 1976).

Holzer, Marc (ed.). *Public Productivity Handbook*. New York: Marcel Dekker, 1992.

Holzer, Marc (ed.). *Productivity in Public Organizations*. New York: Dunellen, 1975.

Hyde. A. C. "Productivity Management for Public Sector Organizations," *Public Personnel Management* (winter 1985, special issue: Productivity in Government).

Kelly, Rita M. "Productivity, Societal Well-Being, and Public Policy: An Introduction and Overview," *Policy Studies Review* (February 1985).

Kettl, Donald F. "Privatization: Implications for the Public Work Force," in Carolyn Ban and Norma M. Riccucci (eds.). *Public Personnel Management: Current Concerns, Future Challenges*. White Plains, N.Y.: Longman Press, 1991.

League of California Cities Award. *1988 Annual Conference Proceedings*. Sacramento, Calif., 1988.

Lemonias, Peter J. and Brian L. Usilaner. "Productivity Measurement: A Neglected Approach for Reducing Federal Government Costs," *National Productivity Review* (spring 1984).

Mercer, James L. and Ronald J. Philips (eds.). *Public Technology: Key to Improved Government Productivity*. New York: Amacon, 1981.

Mushkin, Selma. "Productivity in the States," *State Government* (autumn 1979).

Neugarten, Dail Ann. "Themes and Issues in Public Sector Productivity," *Public Personnel Management*, 9, no. 4 (1980).

Phillips, Lou. "Productivity," in *Conference Report: Recapturing Confidence in Government—Public Personnel Management Reform*. Washington, D.C.: Office of Personnel Management, 1979.

Riggs, James L. and Glenn H. Felix. *Productivity by Objectives*. Englewood Cliffs, NJ, Prentice Hall, 1983.

Siedfried, John J. "Public Sector Productivity," *Atlanta Economic Review* 27 (September–October 1977).

Staudohar, Paul D. "An Experiment in Increasing Productivity of Police Employees," *Public Administration Review*, 35 (September–October 1975).

Stevens, Barbara. "Comparing Public- and Private-Sector Productive Efficiency: An Analysis of Eight Activities," *The National Productivity Review* (autumn 1984), pp. 395–405.

U.S. General Accounting Office. *Gainsharing: Due Efforts Highlight an Effective Tool for Enhancing Federal Productivity*. Washington, D.C.: USGAO, 1986.

U.S. General Accounting Office. *Improving Operating and Staffing Practices Can Increase Productivity and Reduce Costs in SSA Atlanta Region*. Washington, D.C.: USGAO, 1985.

U.S. Merit Systems Protection Board. *The Elusive Bottom Line: Productivity in the Federal Workforce*. Washington, D.C.: USMSPB, May 1982.

U.S. Office of Personnel Management. *Improving the Productivity of the Federal Workforce*. Report for the National Productivity Council. Washington, D.C.: USOPM (September 1979).

Washnis, George J. (ed.). *Productivity Improvement Handbook for State and Local Governments*. New York: John Wiley, 1980.

White House Conference on Productivity. *Productivity Growth: A Better Life for America*. Report to the president, 1984.

Wriston, Walter. "Obsolete Economics," *Harper's* (September 1985).

Note: The student will want to take advantage of the use of two major journals in the area of productivity management—*Public Productivity Review* and *National Productivity Review*. A comprehensive listing of the excellent work published in both of these journals would require a separate bibliography in and of itself.

13
Improving Quality

Prologue: "Getting It Right the Second Time"—Quality Improvement at NASA's Johnson Space Center

Few government agencies were more respected in the 1970s and early 1980s than the National Aeronautics and Space Administration (NASA). All of this changed with the Challenger explosion. Shortly after that terrible and traumatic event, a series of articles in the *New York Times* raised major questions about the agency's management systems, expertise, and overall competence. Making matters worse, the articles were for the most part drawn from previously reported Government Accounting Office (GAO) audits and evaluations, all of which were available to NASA's management. A crisis of confidence enveloped the agency's missions and its personnel and raised questions about the nation's space policy and future programs.

No part of the organization was more affected than the Johnson Space Center (JSC), NASA's largest and best known installation. In many respects, JSC had become synonymous with NASA and had long regarded itself as the field leader of the organization. This predominantly high technology, white-collar installation of 3,600 employes, manages a $2 billion budget, working directly with over 10,000 contract personnel in twenty-five different contract organizations in the Houston area. It also oversees another 8,000 contract personnel in California. The challenge faced by the JSC was to work with all of NASA to get the shuttle back to flight status and reinspire confidence in NASA's future missions—the space station, a lunar base, and a crew mission to Mars.

JSC chose to stay the course it had already embarked on in the early

1980s when in 1982, the NASA administrator set a goal for NASA to be nationally recognized for productivity leadership. Perhaps no organizational environment presents a more difficult climate for productivity improvement than research and development. Prior to setting this goal, JSC and NASA had relied on the "typical" cost reduction—employee suggestion programs and strategies that were pretty much meant to promote a positive image rather than require true change.

JSC decided, well before Challenger, that ad hoc productivity efforts weren't enough; that the path toward organizational improvement had to represent a mainstream effort that involved both the organization and its contractors in a new partnership. That partnership would have a goal of "team excellence," and more important, it would focus on "total quality management" (TQM) as its method of incorporating changes in organizational culture. In 1986, JSC announced its first set of three TQM initiatives:

1. *Strategic planning.* The strategic planning process involved over one-third of the civil service work force at JSC and had assessment teams identifying external and internal factors in each functional area concerning suppliers and contractors, current operational strengths and weaknesses, and performance improvement priorities. The resulting assessments were passed on to strategy development teams that identified and set goals, objectives, and organizational strategy for JSC. The last part of the planning process was reviews by implementation teams that set up action plans and schedules, milestones, and resource allocation requirements. In 1990, a review and major update of JSC's strategic plan was initiated to make revisions and develop a new set of three--to-five-year quality initiatives, goals, and plans.

2. *Employee culture study.* This process recognized the need for understanding and revitalizing the organizational culture. JSC started with standard organizational surveys and moved to its first organization-wide culture study in 1986. Twenty-five percent of its work force was asked to complete a 174-question survey that identified communications, role clarity, and career development as top concerns. Action lists were developed and sent out to supervisors, with extensive feedback going to all employees. In 1989, a second survey was sent out to test the organizational climate and identify new and reemphasize old concerns for corrective action.

3. *Team excellence improvement projects.* This implementation dimension of JSC's TQM process begins with the identification of major performance improvement areas that cut across all organizational areas (such as innovation, safety, teamwork, participation, and quality of worklife), but the impetus for change is generated by the organizational teams within the organization. They produce plans and objectives for the improvement of quality that lead to such accomplishments as redesigning the procurement process so that it cuts processing time by 25 percent, eliminating forms or reducing paper

(in one case, eliminating a form that was used over 2,000 times annually at JSC), or implementing design changes in shuttle thermal control system blankets, saving some $12 million. There is a considerable list of accomplishments.

Central to each part of JSC's TQM process is the highly participative management approach. One by-product of the process revealed in the 1986 and 1989 culture surveys was a major improvement in trust, credibility, and teamwork. JSC's team excellence approach and quality improvement process has had a positive overall effect on fostering a high-quality work environment. The other major component has been working closely with its contractors. Treating its contractors as partners, it has extended the quality process to its suppliers, vendors, and contract organizations, expecting them to work closely together in a commitment toward total quality. JSC began by sponsoring conferences to discuss quality and performance problems and now has established participative planning processes and a JSC/contractor team excellence forum.

In 1990, JSC was awarded the Quality Improvement Prototype Award by the executive office of the president. These awards go to a select few federal agencies that "serve as models to the rest of government, showing how an unswerving commitment to quality leads to better services and products, more satisfied customers, and reduced costs." JSC's response was uncharacteristically subdued, closing their award executive summary statement with the following:

> The Center is only at the beginning of its journey to Total Quality Management. A strategic approach to change has established direction and commitment. The pace of change and improvement continues to accelerate. However, much remains to be done. Plans for the Center include the establishment of more systematic tools for broadening employee involvement in continuous improvement efforts and the development of better tools and techniques for assessing progress.

One might attribute the above statement to humility and the recognition that NASA is truly getting it right the second time. But it more appropriately and realistically reflects the emerging management environment that now focuses on quality. Quality has become the management watchword for the 1990s.

The Emergence of Quality: A Public Sector Odyssey

What is TQM and what does it mean in the public sector? Organizations, both public and private, have long taken quality for granted. If there was a problem with quality or the rate of defects in organizational products or services, one simply added a quality assurance or inspection program. This function, using statistical quality assurance rates, would assure the organization that products and services were in conformance with specifications. Using the most common example, every time you purchase an item of clothing (usually, one with a pocket), you will find somewhere a tiny slip of paper with the words, "inspected by inspector 3," or whatever.

While you're still going to find those slips of paper in clothing or other products, organizations have come to regard quality assurance as the wrong approach. Modern management theory now believes that you can't build quality into products and services by inspection or administrative decree; rather, there has to be an individual commitment to build quality in by those who do the work (perhaps illustrated by the tiny slip of paper recently found in an article of clothing purchased by one of the authors, which read, "inspected by NORMA"!). This lesson has been brought home in a very dramatic way that many Americans are now quite sick at being reminded of: the private sector has had to live with the complete reversal of its reputation. Over thirty years ago, the label "made in Japan" was synonymous with cheap, inferior products. Today, it personifies high quality (backed up by various consumer reports on low defect and low repair rates). "Made in America" has unfortunately been relegated all too often to a slogan urging one to be patriotic and buy American goods to protect jobs and the economy. Least anyone in the public service think this amusing, the other classic slogan used to exemplify poor quality is that uniquely American expression, "good enough for government work." Anyway, the emphasis now is on convincing employees that product and service quality is their primary responsibility, along with forging new institutional arrangements to carry that out.

A major part of this effort is focusing on the customer or client. Governments have always had mixed feelings about the receivers of their products and services, in part because of the mixed roles they play—regulator, adjudicator, and direct and indirect service provider. Consider local governments where, from a public administration perspective, there is the most direct link between the unit providing the service and the individual receiving it. Schools, garbage collection, public works, utilities, roads, parks, and so on, are all services that the public is constantly evaluating. But based on what perspective and what range of choices? Are our local schools providing a quality product and service? Obviously, the answer greatly depends on the resource base the school district is working with, the social demographics and economics of the district, and the degree of involvement and support of the community itself. Now consider the local police force. What constitutes a quality product or service? For that matter, how should the police treat as "clients" some of their customers, ranging from those being protected, ticketed, investigated, or incarcerated?

It is more complicated in government, but it doesn't lessen the need to improve quality. A survey in the *Washington Post* (October 18, 1988) reported that the perception of the quality of services for local governments averaged 23 percent; that is, only 23 percent of those responding felt the quality of the services they received was high. This rating was even lower than the 25 percent received by used car sales personnel (the assumption implied that this is as low as one could go—no offense intended!). Still the problem here is determining how reliable the opinions of the service recipients are to begin with and how objective they are if part of the process involves evaluating whether or not they even receive the service.

In the latter part of the 1980s, some of the impetus behind productivity improvement switched over to the quality improvement movement, now known as TQM. The private sector has already been profoundly influenced by several "quality gurus," principally the works of W. E. Deming, J. Juran, and P. Crosby. Crosby and Juran (two quite separate quality consultants) advocate education and retraining workers to learn quality awareness and a zero-defects attitude that requires strict adherence to product and service specifications; that is, "conformance to requirements." On the other side is Demings's highly statistical approach to quality that requires extensive charting of reliability and defect rates as the driving force in ensuring that workers build in work quality as opposed to inspecting for it later. If these two approaches differ in method, they are in agreement on overall strategy. Most quality improvement systems stake a path keyed to policy and training dimensions, with the major emphasis on management and work force commitment.

How to make quality improvement a reality throughout the federal government is another problem. Lessons learned from the 1980s in the productivity effort convinced many that implementation could not be required or regulated from above. The means chosen for quality improvement were more oriented toward advocacy and volunteerism. To lead the effort, the Federal Quality Institute (FQI) was created in June of 1988. The FQI was charged with working with the Office of Management and Budget (OMB), the Office of Personnel Management (OPM), and the President's Council on Management Improvement to function as part clearinghouse (to disseminate information on TQM), part education center (to introduce and orient senior government officials), and part network coordinator (to distill information about TQM and agency successes to others). The FQI now oversees annual federal quality and productivity conferences, interagency quality network organizations, and the quality improvement award process.

This is a low-key approach that envisions a long-range effort with many major goals. First, employees and unions must be involved upfront followed by renewal of education and training programs. Then a concerted focus must be made on participative management and teamwork concepts that can break down the organizational barriers to quality. The technical aspects of quality improvement, assessing customer needs, assessing organizational quality and performance, and monitoring the effectiveness of TQM efforts then follow. The FQI is now working on the *Federal Total Quality Management Handbook*, which, in the introductory manual, defines quality as "meeting the customer's requirements, needs, and expectations, the first time and everytime." Since TQM is defined as a process, there is no specific set of plans and activities that must be followed to do TQM. Rather, FQI identifies several key factors that determine successful quality efforts and define the process.

1. Top management support
2. Customer/client focus
3. Long-term strategic planning
4. Employee training and recognition
5. Employee empowerment and teamwork
6. Measurement and analysis of products and processes
7. Quality assurance

For the most part, TQM efforts in the public sector have conceptually steered a course somewhere between the more strategic Crosby/Juran "conformance to requirements/behavior modification" and the more quantitative Deming "zero defects/statistical reliability measurement" approaches. Thus far, the direction of these numerous efforts has been the elevation of workers and management attitudes and levels of awareness about the significance of quality in the workplace. These efforts are loosely labeled under the most important part of the process from a TQM perspective—employee empowerment and teamwork.

Empowerment or Participative Management

Fortunately for TQM implementation, there has been considerable experience in the public sector with employee empowerment, or participative management efforts, as it is often called. (Another buzzword phrase is "quality through participation"; QTP.) In fact, the 1980s productivity programs were often based on one of the following three major participative management models:

1. *Team building*—These efforts are numerous and are best described as "prescriptive-adaptive learning." Organizations, through upper-management inspiration and approval, rebuild, retool, and restructure the ways in which organizational members operate.

2. *Quality circles*—These efforts are quite common, due in part to the extensive use of them in Japanese management, and can be identified as "voluntary-planned change." Individuals assume self-determined roles on a

voluntary basis to improve organizational outcomes and take responsibilities to plan, make, and maintain better quality.

3. *Quality of worklife* (QWL)—These programs can be thought of as "participative research-planned change." Here, individuals participate in planning, researching, implementing, and evaluating organization and individual working environment changes as part of a decision-making process based on obtaining a consensus. By definition, quality of worklife objectives are part of the goals for any organizational experimentation.

Team Building

Team building, certainly the oldest technique, involves a number of strategies designed to deal with structural rigidities, intra- and intergroup competition, and organizational unresponsiveness. Using operating teams, problem- or project-oriented teams, or management teams, organizations allow employees to address productivity and other operational problems by building flexible "semiautonomous work groups." The major emphasis is on building communication and cooperation.

Team building attempts to improve organizational quality and performance by emphasizing various techniques. Among the more prominent efforts are job enrichment (increasing the variety of tasks to be performed and the skills of the employee), encouraging greater worker cooperation, and enhancing employee autonomy. The team concept itself can be structured as one of several variations, including:

1. *Operating teams*—Groups of employees who perform their normal day-to-day tasks as a team
2. *Problem-oriented teams*—Groups of employees who are brought together to discuss or recommend solutions to specific problems
3. *Management teams*—Groups of supervisory/management personnel who work together regularly on operational problems and address problems with transcendental objectives (i.e., those that cut across organizational lines)

For a team concept to be successful, several variables must be considered. First, it is essential that teams are assigned whole tasks with identifiable, meaningful, and significant objectives. Second, members of the team must have a number of different skills required for group completion of the tasks. Third, each team must be given autonomy to make decisions about methods through which work is accomplished. Finally, and most difficult of all from a personnel perspective, evaluation of the team is based on performance of the group as a whole, rather than team contribution of the individual. Essentially, the performance appraisal concept must be group based, as opposed to individually based. There are other personnel implications that must be considered, as H. Douglas Sherwin noted in a 1976 *Harvard Business Review* article:

1. Who selects the objectives for the team?
2. Who selects the team members and based on what criteria?
3. Who is accountable for accomplishing the team's objectives?
4. How will teams be motivated and trained to order to accomplish their objectives?
5. And, as previously alluded to, how will team members be evaluated and what are the implications for the performance appraisal process?

Quality Circles

Quality circles (QCs) are a more recent technique, emerging in the early 1980s as a significant approach for dealing with barriers to organizational productivity and individual performance. The origins of QCs are generally traced to the Japanese industrial experience, where impressive productivity rates have been attributed to highly goal-oriented, solidified group activity within organizations. There is a certain irony, of course, in the fact that the Japanese attribute the original concept to American engineers who were working with developing Japanese firms in the 1950s. (Indeed, to this day, Japan's industrywide competition process for quality is named the Deming Prize after the American quality guru, W. E. Deming.)

The essential concept behind the QC is to enable a small number of key participants to do more than study or discuss problems, but to have the group plan for and implement actual solutions. In the early 1970s, the Lockheed missile division became one of the first American borrowers of the QC concept. By the early 1980s, over a dozen federal agencies and numerous state and local government agencies had instituted QC programs.

A guiding premise is that the most significant expertise of the organization is in its employees. Quality circles then, are voluntary participant work groups, functioning autonomously, that attempt to focus worker expertise on work problems, especially quality problems. To establish QCs within public sector organizations usually requires consideration of three critical factors: (1) the commitment and cooperation of management, unions and employees, and the public; (2) establishment of a measurement concept that can serve as a basis for assessment of work environment and productivity changes; and (3) identification and provision of some form of facilitative expertise to assist in organizing, focusing, and implementing QC deliberations.

Quality circles or quality improvement teams are generally defined as any group of workers from the same organizational area who meet regularly to discuss quality problems, investigate causes, recommend solutions, and implement changes when approved by management. The premise behind the

QC is that problems in quality, productivity, and motivation are widespread, that management can't solve all the problems (and, in many cases doesn't know that many of the problems exist), and that solutions are only possible when the organization relies on the "innovative power that lies within the work force." The goal then is to develop a participative management process in the organization that empowers workers to solve their own job-related problems.

The QC differs from teams or other task forces in that members select problems to work on, analyze problems and recommend solutions, have their own leadership, use trained facilitators, and generally have both leaders and members receive training. Most critical of all, the circle must be totally voluntary. In this sense, the QC is not really a program, but is a *process*. There are also key differences in the types of problems that are addressed. Quality circles focus on logistical problems and defects; administrative processes; division of functions, tasks, and staffing; reports, records, and forms; work flow; communications flow; safety; and training. They generally don't involve themselves with wages and salaries, benefits, disciplinary and grievance policies, or employment and termination policies.

Many organizations using QCs also establish some type of organizational steering committee. This committee oversees and coordinates the establishment of QCs, reviews implementation plans and makes changes as necessary, helps select circle leaders and circle facilitators. If the organization decides to establish some type of reward or recognition program, the steering committee will oversee that effort, as well as review progress of QCs to determine overall worth or success of the effort. Quality circles have had an uncertain fate thus far. Many private sector organizations have disbanded their QCs and replaced them with more informal team-building efforts. When circles fail, several factors are generally cited: (1) management ordering supervisors to volunteer as leaders or supervisors ordering employees to volunteer as members; (2) management assigning problems to QCs rather than letting them choose their own agenda, and (3) within the QCs, leadership trying to control circle activities or dominate the decision-making process.

So how then are QCs unique? First, their objectives are focused primarily on quality, not productivity, not cost reduction, not anything else. Admittedly, quality improvement ultimately leads to productivity improvement, cost reduction, and enhanced performance—but these are long-range goals that are by-products of the commitment to quality. The method of operation of the QC is also substantially different. All QC members supposedly function as equals. A consensus decision-making method is used to ensure all views have been heard and accepted. Consensus means that all members have to agree or agree not to disagree. Even the discussion method at QC meetings favors brainstorming methods designed to get the maximum number of ideas without promoting high amounts of disagreement. There is a management truism among the quality theorists that sums up this different perspective for insisting on consensus. "In America, decisions are made overnight, but take months to implement. In Japan, a decision may take months, but it is implemented overnight."

Quality of Worklife Programs

The third technique—quality of worklife (QWL) programs—involves a number of very ambitious efforts to both humanize the work environment and truly democratize the organization to develop the highest levels of employee participation possible. Few phenomena may have as much potential impact on public sector organizations as the QWL movement. Since the mid-1970s, QWL has burgeoned into an international field of research, experimentation, and development involving a significant number of business and public sector organizations. While it should be stated that QWL programs go beyond the subset of organizational development efforts initiated in the 1970s—that is, work redesign, flexible work scheduling, participative management, QCs, work humanization efforts, and so on—QWL provides a framework that integrates many of these organizational development activities.

In part, the future of the QWL movement hinges on economics. After treading water in the 1980s, the nation stands on the brink of its first major recession in the midst of a productivity slump with a number of arguments being bantered about as to the cause, extent, and significance of the "current productivity decline." As of yet, there has been little reconciliation between the needs for QWL and increased quality or productivity, except that there is general recognition that improved QWL in work environments is important to long-range productivity growth and short-range quality commitment.

The current mood is admittedly a bleak one. As public sector organizations face up to a new set of economic and political realities and confront widescale "cutback management" efforts, the expectation is that it will be hard to realize, much less remember, QWL objectives. But one should remember QWL's origins.

Efforts toward QWL were born in the early 1970s and actually accelerated following the worldwide economic slump in the mid-1970s. There were a number of reasons for this, but they all center on the increasing importance of human resources. Human resources are simply more important than ever before. Worldwide problems with increased scarcity and cost of new capital sources have resulted in organizations rethinking high-risk technology investment decisions for increasing performance, quality, and productivity. The continuing increase toward more and more service domination in our economy makes human resources even more vital.

But human resources have changed substantially over the past twenty years

What Is QWL?

It is probably best to state that an exact definition of QWL seems impossible since that would entail specifying a common work environment with a relatively homogenous set of workers and organizations. But one must conclude that QWL is more than simply increased job satisfaction or work humanization and goes beyond the number of quality and improvement, work redesign, and participative management projects currently being attempted. One of the earliest private sector experiences with QWL was at the United Auto Workers plant at Bolivar, Tennessee. From 1972 to 1979, a major joint labor-management work experimentation effort was attempted under a project concept, in which "both parties can jointly determine and implement organizational effectiveness." As Barry Macy has noted, what makes a QWL experiment work is joint agreement between labor (or unions) and management on explicit internal goals to include performance, behavioral, and affective dimensions.

What makes the Bolivar project such a significant model for QWL experimentation is that the project evaluation criteria went beyond simple short-range measure of performance (e.g., productivity, efficiency, and standards of performance) and long-range productivity measures (e.g., absenteeism, cooperation, grievances, and turnover) to focus on specific measurements of quality of work life and work environment.

Summing up, a QWL program would entail a participative management mode throughout all of its phases—research, planning, change, and evaluation. It would focus on balancing organization and individual needs in addressing productivity, performance, work environment, and quality of working life issues. It would provide for union and management representation. Above all, a QWL program should be viewed as a voluntary experiment in which the driving force should be to reengage the "expertise" of the worker to organizational and individual problems.

and organizations are having to reconfigure some of their most basic social and economic precepts about human resources utilization. Organizations are having difficulty comprehending the nature and significance of shifts in work skills, worker values, and even worker demographics. Part of this was presented in the chapter on human resources planning, but this is not new. As an early illustration, the OPM's 1981 conference report, *The Changing Character of the Public Work Force*, identified a number of the issues involved in changing work values. There was basic agreement on demographics, which were aptly summarized by Kanter and Stein in 1979:

Increase in number and proportion of women in the work force
Maintenance of job segregation and earnings gaps between females and males
Undersupply of younger, less experienced workers
Oversupply of older, more experienced workers
Increase in the amount of education (but decrease in quality) possessed by
    workers

Mixed assessment for certain protected-class groups, with varying gains and
    losses for African Americans and potentially even more serious prob-
    lems for Latinos
Decline in overall labor union membership, but growth in public sector union
    membership

But the greatest potential impact of the above trends is in the changing
nature of work values. What workers will want in the future will be determined by first identifying "who" the workers will be, what will be important to them individually and collectively, how they will work together toward
the accomplishment of both individual and organizational goals, and how such
goals will be balanced in terms of individual and organizational development
needs. This is the agenda that QWL must address.

Thus far, the concept of QWL has had considerable difficulty in generating
any real consensus about what should be done to improve work environments
and outcomes. Part of the problem is definitional in that what is supposed
to be covered by QWL is so broad and diverse that it defies analysis, much
less simple qualification. Perhaps the first comprehensive definitions of QWL
have been provided by Richard Walton, Louis Davis and James Taylor.

Walton's definition attempts to be conceptual in that it stresses criteria
for analyzing QWL change efforts. His eight categories are almost self-
explanatory so that the following listing can serve to show the range of concerns focusing on the "quality of human experience in the workplace":

Adequate and fair compensation
Safe and healthy working conditions
Immediate opportunity to use and develop human capacities
Future opportunity for continued growth and security
Social integration in the work organization
Constitutionalism in the work organization (legal rights)
Work and enhanced total life space
Social relevance of work life

Walton's early work has also attempted to stress the interrelations among
the above QWL criteria and their relationship to productivity questions. He
also adds the attitudinal variables caused by the different perspectives of various
kinds of employees who will view QWL criteria differently. What one emerges
with from Walton's work is the pessimistic realization that change will not
be easy to diagnose but that work redesign efforts will be absolutely essential.

Louis Davis's work provides a more historical attempt at definition. His
work has traced the development of the QWL concept arising principally from
a number of sources related to increasing job dissatisfaction. One major strength
of Davis's work is that it enlarges the QWL context, most notably by adding
integrated organization-plant design to the aforementioned work redesign

objective. Davis admits that there is no consensus on definition as of yet, but optimistically concludes that "more important in the long run than the development of centers or government policy is the steady growth of work reform programs and integrated organization-plant designs based on the notions of participation, cooperation, self-regulation and the complementarity of technology and people." The new designs help to demonstrate the economic effectiveness of such concepts. The firms accepting them at the same time necessarily train workers, managers and union officials who in time will transfer their skills and experience to other sites. Though secluded from public scrutiny, these developments are quietly going ahead and will presently acquire the critical momentum needed to bring awareness of the subject into the mainstream of American social thinking.

Quality of Worklife Programs: A Personnel Management Perspective

How should personnel management view QWL? Any time significant changes are made in work redesign or workers skills improvement, personnel is, by definition, involved. Obviously, QWL projects would hope to have the active participation and full support and cooperation of the personnel function (whatever that means). The reality is that the personnel function will probably be one of the most significant roadblocks to effective QWL change. Despite the fact that the 1978 Civil Service Reform Act contains provisions for demonstration projects or agency experimentation, it will be difficult to get personnel to function as a resource for change efforts as opposed to some form of arbitrator.

Why should it be this way? For one thing, QWL emphasizes a participative change process while personnel has only in the last decade come to be comfortable with its role as professional adjudicator. Second, QWL change would embrace a number of the personnel functions—classification, performance evaluation, training and development, affirmative action, employee relations—in an integrated mode. This may cause tension because personnel, especially in larger organizations, has become increasingly fragmented and specialized. Training, evaluation, and classification have all tended toward development of separate viewpoints; so instead of there being one single personnel management perspective, there may be several. While that may be of help in some QWL projects, the likelihood of personnel's contributing contradictory advice and conflicting resources to QWL seems more probable.

And yet, a strongly developed human resources management function could play a significant resource role in facilitating QWL programs and change. For one thing, a systematic evaluation of the project to include pre- and postproject measurements must be lodged in an objective location within the organization (thus precluding any consulting team doing the evaluation that assisted or facilitated the project), and personnel could effectively perform that function. But more significantly, personnel management could address in a research and analysis role a number of critical issues stemming out of QWL changes that have not been addressed.

Table 13.1 proposes such an agenda under the general concept that public personnel management should adopt a human resources management perspective. A detailed discussion of the differences between personnel management and human resources management goes beyond the scope of what's being addressed here, but it should be noted that the latter involves a much more extensive and comprehensive view of human resources utilization in both a macro and micro perspective. Perhaps one of the best illustrations is in the area of work stress. Evaluation of a major private sector QWL project showed increases in the perception of physical and psychological stress on the part of workers. Since change is considered by most psychologists and epidemiologists as an integral cause of stress, this result should be expected. But what then are the resulting outcomes over the long run in terms of: (1) positive and negative physiological stress reactions, (2) changing worker and occupational perceptions of work stresses, (3) changes in individual coping disposition and motivational strength affecting ability and desire to handle stressful work situation, (4) and long-range health effects on employees?

Table 13.1. Quality of Worklife Experimentation Evaluation Critera from a Human Resources Management Perspective

Directly related issue areas	Indirectly related issue areas
What will be the impact of increased levels of work stress on individuals?	What will be the impact of QWL on work values and workers attitudes?
How should organizations change selection/separation policies to reflect more dynamic person-work environment fit?	What types of assistance and counseling programs should organizations provide for employees as part of QWL?
How will QWL projects impact on promotion and career development for individuals?	How will QWL projects change the concepts of career management and promotion policies within organizations?
How will QWL projects change training and development programs for individuals?	How will QWL affect organizational learning?
How will performance appraisals be affected by QWL experimentation?	How will QWL projects affect general systems of performance evaluation and individual development planning?

A human resources management perspective demands systematic and longitudinal study of these issues with the hopes of developing preventative strategies to assist employees in coping and mastering more stress. A personnel management strategy, at least as it has evolved so far, either views stress as the wrong person in the wrong position *or* as an inevitable result of modern societal disruption to be handled by an employee counseling or employee assistance program (EAP). (It should be added parenthetically that transfer programs or EAPs are remedial efforts for only some personnel management functions. Many personnel managers don't view work stress as a personnel or an organizational problem.)

In sum, personnel management will undoubtedly face QWL programs in a fragmented, incremental manner. The perspectives developed and support given to QWL projects will hinge greatly on how seriously QWL is taken by organization members and how comprehensive attempts at change are.

Implications for Human Resources Management

Organizational efforts to improve quality seem certain to intensify and expand throughout the public sector. It is appropriate in this last section to address some of the implications for human resources management. There are some obvious technical problems with both measurement and participation approaches where the expertise of personnel managers is desperately needed. Fundamental issues include:

Who sets objectives and how do "program" objectives relate individual and organizational performance outcomes?

Who selects teams, QCs, or QWL project members, and according to what selection criteria, and what kind of training is provided?

How will participation and measurement efforts ensure sufficient motivation from individuals over the long run?

What are the implications for performance appraisal, individual advancement, and career development?

Quality improvement is more than a management intervention; it is an organizational effort. Deeper involvement by human resource managers in such programs is critical to their development and the integration of the ideals they convey into personnel policy. This also means that public personnel managers will have to recognize the importance of both productivity and quality improvement, both in terms of its practices and its research implications. The following suggestions might make a reasonable agenda for public management to focus on in this area.

1. *Help define quality as an organizational construct.* Organizations, in too many cases, view quality improvement as a symbolic strategy. In fact, the key factors are individuals and work groups, and the resources, management

information, technology, and organizational opportunities provided them. Public managers need to study and research organizational climate, management and individual commitment, and the impacts of organizational and work role structures on productive capacity. Special attention must be given to technology, which is now being viewed as a "cheap" way to automate work and increase work quality and reduce labor costs. Following the work of Shoshana Zuboff and her concept of "informating," true quality improvement is only possible when work is fundamentally changed and restructured, not just speeded up or redirected.

2. *Reconcile the differences between the personnel micro perspective and the organizational macro perspective.* In too many cases, employees are viewed as quality or productivity problems and measurement is oriented toward establishing control systems to account for individual performance discrepancies. In fact, the most successful programs concentrate on structural problems in organizations and emphasize the individual's role in helping to solve quality problems. Quality is an organizational management concept that must be evaluated in that context. This will also be key to resolving the dilemmas inherent in productivity gainsharing and productivity measurement. The unit of measurement just as the unit of participation must be focused on the work unit or group, not the individual.

3. *Establish an evaluation role for human resources management.* Many of the organizational efforts in quality do not have rigorous evaluation built in. A major role needs to be played in evaluating what and how quality problems or customer satisfaction are being defined, what measurements and information are being generated about organizational performance and development, and what results—in terms of levels of productivity and quality improvement, innovation, organizational performance, and organizational and individual impacts—are being achieved and sustained. Very significantly, public sector personnel management needs to play a key role in facilitating and guiding this evaluation role. Public sector budgeting and financial management must also ensure that evaluations are budgetarily objective and produce appropriate reprogramming of funding levels. Experience shows that when funding is "redistributed" from productivity managed programs to "politically" needy programs, the disincentive created is the surest known method of killing productivity management. The same will be true for quality improvement efforts.

This should come as no surprise, given the high failure rates of many public management efforts, budgeting and personnel programs, information and computer systems, and especially productivity programs. It adds special impetus to the need to establish both the above-mentioned evaluation capacity and to change expectations somewhat. The public sector experience confirms a well-known private sector adage—it's easy to establish a quality or productivity program; the hard part is sustaining it. Skeptisim runs deep, especially when participative management is the principal vehicle for change. A recent survey of private sector firms by the American Society for Quality Control, as reported by Swoboda in 1990, showed that the majority of employees surveyed said that their companies talked a lot about quality improvement, but only a third felt their employer was really committed to doing anything. The biggest reason cited was empowerment—over two-thirds responding said they had been asked to be involved in workplace decision making, but fewer than 15 percent indicated that they had been given any power to make and implement such decisions. In the final analysis, this may be the most important lesson public managers will have to learn about quality improvement in the 1990s.

Bibliography

Aft, Lawrence S. *Productivity, Measurement, and Its Improvement*. Reston: Reston Publishing, 1983.

Balk, Walter L. *Improving Government Productivity: Some Policy Perspectives*. Beverly Hills, Calif.: Sage Publications, 1975.

————. "Symposium, Productivity in Government," *Public Administration Review* (January–February 1978).

Barbour, George P. Jr. "Measuring Local Government Productivity," *Municipal Year Book* (Washington, D.C.: International City Management Association, 1972).

Berry, Frances S. and James E. Jarrett. "Nationwide Survey Results of State Government Productivity," *Report on State Government Productivity Research Council* (April 1981).

Burkhead, Jesse and Patrick Hennigan. "Productivity Analysis: A Search for Definition and Order," *Public Administration Review* (January–February 1978).

Butler, M. A. "Quality Leadership Equals Quality Service," *The Bureaucrat* (Summer 1990).

Capozzola, John M. "Productivity Bargaining: Problems and Prospects," *National Civic Review*, 65 (April 1976).

Cohen S. and R. Brand. "Total Quality Management in the U.S. Environmental Protection Agency," in both *Public Productivity and Management Review* (Fall 1990).

Committee for Economic Development. *Improving Productivity in State and Local Government*. New York: Committee for Economic Development, 1976.

Crosby, P. *Quality is Free*. New York: McGraw-Hill, 1979.

Davis, Louis E. and James C. Taylor. *Design of Jobs*. Middlesex, U.K.: Penguin Books, 1962.

Deming, W. E. *Out of the Crises*. Cambridge, Mass.: MIT Center for Advanced Engineering Study, 1986.

Federal Quality Institute. *Introduction: Total Quality Management Handbook*. Washington, D.C., 1990.

Federal Quality Institute. *Introduction: Prototype Award Report: Total Quality Management at NASA's Johnson Space Center*. Washington, D.C., 1990.

Fremont, E.G. "Productivity Bargaining That Really Is," *Personnel*, 49 (January–February 1972).

Ginzberg, Eli. *Good Jobs, Bad Jobs, and No Jobs*. Cambridge, Mass.: Harvard University Press, 1979.

Goldoff, Anna C. with David C. Tatage. "Joint Productivity Committees: Lessons of Recent Initiatives," *Public Administration Review*, 38 (March–April, 1978).

Greiner, John M. "Motivating Improved Productivity: Three Promising Approaches," *Public Management*, 61 (October 1979).

Hatry, Harry and D. M. Fisk. *Improving Productivity and Productivity Measurement in Local Governments*. Washington, D.C.: Urban Institute, 1971.

Hayward, Nancy S. "The Productivity Challenge," *Public Administration Review* (September–October 1976).

Hinrichs, John R. *Practical Management for Productivity*. New York: Van Nostrand Reinhold, 1978.

Holzer, Marc (ed.). *Productivity in Public Organizations*. New York: Dunellen, 1975.

Horton, Raymond D. "Productivity and Productivity Bargaining in Government: A Critical Analysis," *Public Administration Review*, 36 (July–August 1976).

Improving Productivity in State and Local Government. New York: Committee for Economic Development, 1976.

Juran, J. *Juran on Leadership for Quality*. New York: McGraw-Hill, 1988.

Kanter, Rosabeth Moss and Barry A. Stein. *Life in Organizations*. New York: Basic Books, 1979.

Lemonias, Peter J. and Brian J. Usilaner, "Productivity Measurement: A Neglected Approach for Reducing Federal Government Costs," *National Productivity Review* (spring 1984).

Levitt, Theodore. "Management and the 'Post-Industrial' Society," *Public Interest* (summer 1976).

McKersie, R. B. and L. C. Hunter. *Pay Productivity and Collective Bargaining*. London: Macmillan, 1973.

Mercer, James L. and Ronald J. Philips (eds.). *Public Technology: Key to Improved Government Productivity*. New York: Amacon, 1981.

Milakovich, M. M. "Total Quality Management for Public Sector Productivity Improvement," *Public Productivity & Management Review* (fall 1990).

Mushkin, Selma. "Productivity in the States," *State Government* (autumn 1979).

Neugarten, Dail Ann. "Themes and Issues in Public Sector Productivity," *Public Personnel Management*, 9, no. 4 (1980).

Perrine, J. L. "Federal Quality Institute: Quest for Quality," *The Bureaucrat*; Summer 1990.

Phillips, Lou. "Productivity," in *Conference Report: Recapturing Confidence in Government—Public Management Reform*. Washington, D.C.: Office of Personnel Management, 1979.

Rees, Albert. "Improving the Concepts and Techniques of Productivity Measurement," *Monthly Labor Review*, 102 (September 1979).

Rosow, Jerome M. (ed.). *Productivity: Prospects for Growth*. New York: Van Nostrand Reinhold 1981.

Ross, John P. and Jesse Burkhead. *Productivity in the Local Government Sector*. Lexington, Mass.: Lexington Books, 1974.

Sherwin, H. Douglas. "Management of Objectives," *Harvard Business Review*, 3 (May–June, 1976).

Siedfried, John J. "Public Sector Productivity," *Atlanta Economic Review* 27 (September–October 1977).

Staudohar, Paul D. "An Experiment in Increasing Productivity of Police Employees," *Public Administration Review*, 35 (September–October 1975).

Swoboda, Frank. "Empowering the Rank and File," *Washington Post* (September 30, 1990).

U.S. Merit Sysems Protection Board. *The Elusive Bottom Line: Productivity in the Federal Workforce*. Washington, D.C.: May 1982.

U.S. Office of Personnel Management. *Improving the Productivity of the Federal Workforce*. Report for the National Productivity Council, September 1979.

Walton, Mary. *The Deming Management Method*. New York: Perigee Press, 1986.

Walton, Richard E. "Quality of Worklife Activities: A Research Agenda," *Professional Psychology* (June 1980).

Washnis, George J. (ed.). *Productivity Improvement Handbook for State and Local Governments*. New York: John Wiley, 1980.

White House Conference on Productivity. *Productivity Growth: A Better Life for America*. Reports to the president, 1984.

Wise, Charles R. and Eugene B. McGregor Jr. "Government Productivity and Program Evaluation Issues," *Public Productivity Review*, 1 (March 1976).

Zuboff, Shoshana. *In the Age of the Smart Machine*. New York, NY: Basic Books, 1988.

Part **VI**
HUMAN RESOURCES
DEVELOPMENT

14

Training and Development

Prologue: Teaching Employees a "New Way to Think"—A Case Study on the Limits to Training and Development

Pacific Bell is not a public sector organization, but its experience with a major leadership development program it conducted for some 15,000 of its employees in the mid-1980s provides a spectacular case study of training and development. Pacific Bell is, of course, the phone company, or rather a "baby Bell" branch, as they have been called since the breakup or divestiture of AT&T in early 1984. Concerned about the impacts of divestiture and the need for a new business ethic in its newly acquired, deregulated, and more competitive environment, top management committed the entire organization to a major leadership development initiative called "Krone." The plan was to give each of its 60,000 plus employees training through ten two-day sessions held once a quarter; the program started in earnest in early 1986. A year and a half later, the Krone program was making headlines in the San Francisco papers and even ended up as a story in *Newsweek*.

Because Pacific Bell is, after all, a private sector organization, its training and development decisions are confidential. But given that it also has a monopoly on local phone service and its rates are regulated, the media was quick to pick up the scent for what was reported as a program costing "ratepayers more than $30 million a year or $2.30 per customer." This prologue attempts no value judgements; it simply reviews reporter Kathleen Pender's account in the *San Francisco Chronicle* of March 23, 1987, which generated tremendous controversy over the value and appropriateness of such a training effort.

457

What was Krone all about? The name itself refers to a California consultant, Charles Krone, a major pioneer and innovator in organization development. Pacific Bell employed a team of consultants associated with Krone to develop its program. In terms of approach, Krone's concept is, as the *San Francisco Chronicle* article reports, "that people are not taught how to think. Krone attempts to improve thinking by making people conscious of their thought processes. He also tries to get all employees involved in management by giving them a common language and framework for solving business problems." The media also questioned some of the philosophical foundations to the Krone approach, which the press claimed were developed out of the work of an early twentieth century Russian philosopher and spiritualist, G. I. Gurdjieff.

Pacific Bell defended its Krone training program by noting that Krone had been used with considerable success at a number of major corporations, which found that people completing the program (i.e., the "Kronies") were more productive, energetic, and creative. Pacific Bell argued that the program was designed to encourage both teamwork and creativity, and that the small groups of employees who had been "Kroned" in the early 1980s were the ones who "were making the greatest improvement toward the bottom line." It was only logical to want to expand the program to everyone, especially since "departments that had gone through the program were having trouble communicating with those who had not."

Communication itself became another part of the controversy. The common language and framework that the Krone program called for resulted in a special vocabulary or nomenclature. Goals became "end-state visions"; agreements were "alignments"; a plan was a "path foward." Concepts such as "levels of energy," "purposefulness," and "intentionality" are important to decision making and teamwork. The special vocabulary invited criticism and even ridicule. Some Pacific Bell employees who were interviewed about the program criticized it as a culture imposed by top management that, in the words of one employee quoted in the newspaper article, "teaches people to put peer pressure on anyone who strays from the party line." Another employee was quoted as saying: "It's like a dress code for your mind." Responding to these criticisms were other managers and employees who felt that the Krone training was useful, more common sense than anything else, and helpful in alerting everyone to the new challenges facing the organization.

From a training and development perspective, it is instructive to wonder how any major organization would react to seeing its primary leadership development program being spread out across the pages of the local newspaper as a source of controversy at best, and ridicule at worst. In Pacific Bell's case, it was announced that the Krone program would be reviewed and modified, and individual rights would be carefully protected. The program, however, never fully recovered from the *San Francisco Chronicle*'s lead story that started out, "A new corporate philosophy based in part on an Eastern mystic's teachings is sweeping through Pacific Bell, and although some employees have embraced its unusual language and rituals, others feel they are being coerced into adopting a new way of thinking."

This is certainly an interesting case study for public sector organizations to ponder and it is one that points out a very significant change that has occurred over the last two decades—the emergence of training and development as a major organizational function that actually rivals personnel management itself.

Training and Development in "Hard Times"

Traditionally, of all the major functions of personnel, training and development has been the most neglected. Any organization is necessarily concerned with maintaining its operational status and accordingly will identify its staffing requirements, make decisions about where its employees will work in fulfilling those requirements, evaluate and advance its employees, and recruit and hire new employees to replace those who leave. Only after all of these priorities are attended to will an organization provide for some form of training and development in an effort to improve the capabilities of its employees. Given the scarce resources environment that many public organizations inhabit, there is generally little doubt as to which will be the first area to be sacrificed in a budget crunch. The 1980s is a textbook example of this resources challenge.

But there is more to this problem than simple neglect or fiscal scarcity. Employee training and development efforts place the public organization in somewhat of a dilemma since such efforts entail the expenditure of public

---

How Much Does the Federal Government Spend on Training?

The most recent published estimates report that total expenditures on federal training are about $550 million for 2.2 million federal civilian workers (excluding the U.S. Postal Service). This sum amounts to approximately 0.8 percent of the amount spent on federal payroll. In contrast, one estimate for all Fortune 500 firms places training expenditures at 3.3 percent of payroll, and many progressive and successful firms spend 5 to 10 percent of payroll on employee training and development.

Leadership for America: Rebuilding the Public Service. The National Commission on the Public Service (Volcker Commission), (Washington, D.C., 1989), p. 141.

Table 14.1. Employer-Paid Training Courses (1984)

Industry	Percentage of total courses	Percentage of training done inside
Total number of courses	14,800	—
Government	9.7	78
Agriculture	.7	62
Mining	1.6	77
Construction	2.2	59
Manufacturing	18.5	66
Transportation, communications, utilities	7.9	75
Trade	8.6	74
Finance, insurance, real estate	9.4	63
Services	41.4	69

Source: Adapted from Anthony P. Carnevale and Harold Goldstein, "Schooling and Training for America: An Overview,"in Louis A. Ferman et al. (eds.), *New Developments in Worker Training: A Legacy for the 1990s* (Madison, Wis.: Industrial Relations Research Association, 1990).

funds to develop human resources over which the organization has no real control. Although some organizations, like the military, have linked many of their training programs to contractual arrangements, whereby individuals promise to stay in the organization for certain periods of time (or provide reimbursement for the training received), most public organizations view training expenditures as a less-than-certain investment.

There are other conceptual problems inherent in training. Just as employees as individuals differ, they naturally have differing training needs. Should training programs be shaped to fit the individual needs of the employee or the overall needs of the organization? An agency may develop one set of training assumptions tailored to meet what it considers to be its short- and long-range needs (in that order). At the same time, an individual employee will have, depending upon his or her previous background and aptitudes, an independent set of training assumptions oriented toward different long- and short-range needs (in this order). There is a continuous degree of conflict between the assumed training needs of the organization and the assumed training needs of the individual. The task of any manager—indeed, an essential function—is to ensure equity for both sides, to the organization as well as to the individual. This question of equity is further complicated by the fact that more and more public employees (and their unions) take the view that training opportunities are basically another fringe benefit and should be part of the employee's compensation package.

Training has always been viewed as a stepchild in the personnel and human resource management family. Consequently, it has usually been one of the first areas to be sacrificed. Training has had an especially tough time in terms of budgets. Since so many jurisdictions meet budget shortages via meat-axe approaches (for example, invariably they will cut certain categories of line-item expenditures which are reputed to be "luxuries," such as outside area travel, consultants' fees, and training program costs), training has found itself hard-pressed to maintain any continuity, much less identity. Under these circumstances, trainers have had to abandon programs and jobs only to be replaced by new trainers who have subsequently become equally frustrated; and so the cycle continues.

Despite these obstacles, public sector organizations have placed an increased emphasis on training and development. While there has always been surface acceptance, the increasing commitment to training and development programs by many private and public sector organizations comes as somewhat of a surprise to many observers, especially in the public sector. Proof that there is such a trend can be seen in the establishment of larger and more sophisticated training programs, greater numbers of staff being hired as training specialists, and increasing support for external educational and tuition assistance programs. There is also a somewhat more tenuous factor—the coming of age of a distinct literature in training and development, marked by a number of major books, symposia, journals, technical reports, and newsletters that cover training.

In spite of sporadic program development and intermittent resource availability, training as an organizational function has survived and even begun to prosper. Why this is happening now is less certain, but very significant pressures are coming from individual employees, both directly and indirectly. Direct pressure is represented by employee interests and demands for obtaining training for both maintaining current work skills and developing new ones. Indirect pressure comes from supervisors and managers, many of whom have been troubled by their perceptions of an increasing gap between work requirements and what individuals are capable of doing.

This indirect source of pressure is a complex factor. In a sense, it is a lament along the lines of the "our children can't read" syndrome associated with our educational system. Many supervisors feel that employees don't know or meet their basic skill requirements; for example, how to type, compute,

Training in the Federal Civil Service

Training in the federal Civil Service runs the gamut from remedial development of basic clerical and office skills to advanced programs for senior executives. Most federal agencies have written training policies, and all operate or support some training activities for their employees. Although OPM sets overall policy and provides general guidance, agencies are free to develop their own plans, design their own programs, and allocate resources as necessary to meet their perceived needs. There are only a few common points in the careers of government employees where most agencies provide for regular training:

- The OPM requires that all agencies "consider" the training needs of employees newly assigned to supervisory roles. Most agencies follow OPM guidelines and provide newly appointed supervisors with 80 hours of supervisory training. In some instances the supervisory training is provided through OPM programs; in other instances agencies conduct their own in-house programs using agency employees or contracted instructors.

- The OPM requires that virtually all candidates for senior executive service positions complete a two-week OPM executive development course, or an acceptable substitute. These mandated programs have become a staple offering of OPM's three executive seminar centers. In addition, candidates for and incumbent members of the Senior Executive Service may participate in one of the residential programs of the Federal Executive Institute (FEI), located in Charlottesville, Virginia. The FEI program is perhaps the only experience that bonds senior members of the civil service, providing them with some measure of unity and common experience.

Leadership for America: Rebuilding the Public Service. The National Commission on the Public Service (Volcker Commission),(Washington, D.C., 1989), p. 141.

weld, write, or analyze. Part of this is certainly a problem stemming from our educational system and its difficulties. But another part surely involves our obsession with credentials and certification, which is often totally unrelated to entry-level jobs and the specific skills required to perform adequately. A further source of indirect pressure is that work responsibilities are changing more rapidly in the current dynamic social technological environment. Work skills are subject to considerable obsolescence, a factor only barely discussed by most of the literature.

The consequences of the above pressures are more readily identifiable. Supervisors are more supportive of training programs (within reason, of course) and expect to receive a fair share of training opportunities to develop and reward their employees. Employees want their "share" as well, and they expect to have both formal training during work time and informal training on the job. Perhaps James O'Toole has said it best: "Most workers have an

---

Leadership

The only real training for leadership is leadership: You do not learn it by being an assistant or a deputy, only by being a boss. The advice Peter O'Toole gave to Michael Caine was that if he wanted to be a leading actor he must only play leading parts: much better to play Hamlet in Denver than Laertes on Broadway. In the same way, the best way to learn how to lead a big organization is by leading smaller ones.

Antony Jay, *Management and Machiavelli: An Inquiry into the Politics of Corporate Life* (New York: Holt, Rinehart and Winston, 1967), p. 177.

---

innate desire to grow ... Apparently being able to satisfy the desire to grow and to learn on the job enhances worker self-esteem, satisfaction, loyalty, motivation, and *occasionally*, productivity."

Training has arrived and now constitutes one of the most significant personnel management functions. It's so significant, in fact, that many training offices are being established outside the usual personnel organization, frequently under the separate title of human resources development. A set of questions to personnel managers is emerging: Where does the training and development function belong? What should it consist of? How shall it be controlled?

Training and Personnel Relationships

If there is such a thing as a traditional approach to personnel management, it clearly includes training. Training is part of the process of development that advances and maintains individuals within an organization. While the words *training* and *development* have often been used interchangeably, there is a highly significant line of demarcation between the two. Training is a tool; it is instruction in a myriad of forms and settings, where both technical and conceptual knowledge and skills are imparted to employees, both nonmanagers and managers. Development is a process of advancing or progressing within an organization while aquiring skills and experience. Development incorporated all training and previous job assignments and organizational experiences into a total capability package. Viewed in this light, training is a primary tool or method of facilitating development. It will necessarily vary depending upon the stage of development and the aspect of work involved. What kinds of training programs will be offered and what emphasis will be placed on employee development are usually based on several key criteria: (1) that training be job- or career-related; (2) that it be relevant to enhancing advancement potential; (3) that it be useful in improving organizational effectiveness, and (4) that it be of sufficient relevance and interest to employees. In the public sector, decisions about training programs are more often focused on the first criterion mentioned—job- or career-relatedness. In fact, this criterion is generally used as a guideline by most personnel units to approve or deny requests by employees for training.

But how do the objectives of training and development fit into the objectives of personnel management? This can only be answered in organizational terms. First, what are the functions of personnel? What is personnel designed to do? As already mentioned, the most realistic answer is to ensure organization continuity or organizational survival. What personnel is most concerned with is making sure that organizations, through the people in the organization who make it up, have "human continuity."

Unfortunately, personnel all too often uses its responsibility in this area much too narrowly. Personnel generally sees its function as making sure that the organization can at any point bring to bear on any type of problem the right kinds of people to provide the right kinds of solutions. Personnel purports to develop those people, place them in the organization in the right positions, and ensure that for those people who are leaving the organization, there are adequate replacements. Training, then, has its place in this organizational human resources cycle—staffing, placement, advancement, training and development, replacement, and informational support.

However, what seems conceptually logical falls far short in practice. Personnel management has often so specialized its functions that its focus has become concerned largely with the impacts of its own services. Personnel often doesn't compare in any systematic fashion *how* or even *if* it should face an organizational resource problem—for example, by new hiring, reassignment or transfer, training, *or* job redesign or some combination of these options. Rather, it prefers to solve recruitment, assignment, training, and work organizational problems as they are handed down to personnel management specialists and different personnel management divisions. Personnel all too often and by its own choice prefers to facilitate the implementation of organizational solutions rather than actively help shape the decision in the problem-solving phase.

Trainers, as a result, have become increasingly concerned about what they view as personnel's self-prescribed isolationism. In many cases, this has moved training toward secession. Trainers seek autonomy in part to establish the creditability of their trade and in part to avoid the regulatory image that personnel so often conjures up. In a sense, trainers want to disassociate themselves from "those people who are always saying no because of this regulation or that"; they want to establish their own image. Further impacting this movement toward autonomy has been the drive to contract out training, or what is commonly referred to as "outsourcing." Much of the movement toward outsourcing has been caused by public sector organizations requiring that training pay for its own costs by charging organizational unit fees for each employee who attends a training course. From a management perspective, this has a number of implications. First, it forces training programs to adopt a value-added mentality. Since the organization is paying fees to cover training costs, then the organization will want to ensure that it is getting its money's worth. Second, the fees charged invite a comparison to the competition (in short, other training sources). This is particularly the case with technology or computer training or other highly specialized training courses. Organizations can "shop around" and compare what it would cost to send their employees to a computer software supplier, a university, or other training supplier that offers its own training courses taught by its experts.

But increasingly in the 1980s, contracting out training was applied to more and different types of programs. Montgomery County, Maryland (a suburban county on the north border of Washington D.C.) contracted out its basic management development program. Dennis Misler, the county's training director, explains in a 1986 *Public Personnel Management* article that the county's six-person training staff was only able to offer four sections each year to approximately 100 of the 1,300 supervisors in the county. Simple math dictated that at that rate, the county would have needed over thirteen years to reach existing supervisors, not to mention any new supervisors hired or promoted. The county was facing a severe budget crisis and opted to reduce its training staff by two-thirds. Half the savings were returned to fund outside contracts for contracted training courses. Eight contractors were selected after a carefully developed request for proposal (RFP) was submitted and responded to with 159 different new course proposals in a highly competitive local area. The county was able to revamp its management program and offer at least some courses in the program to over 1,200 supervisors the first year. By the mid 1980s, four of the original contractors remained with the city and supervisory participation remained quite high. From Misler's standpoint, this was a major success. In his words,

> It has been a happy marriage. Ironically, as the training unit got smaller, it became able to do more.... Contracting out and the circumstances that brought it about in Montgomery County at first seemed like the death knell for training. It has in fact turned out to be an injection of invigorating new life.

The above case well illustrates some of the advantages from a resources perspective for outsourcing. But there are major implications. Training staffs still require the expertise to plan and prioritize training needs and then evaluate and assess outcomes. Freedom from the direct instructional responsibility does not mean that training staffs are nothing more than contract management specialists. Training must continue the major effort it embarked upon in the late 1970s to professionalize itself. This process begins with training staff

Training for Results

Training is inevitable. Like old age, it attacks each of us whether we like it or not. At birth, or before, we begin training to operate within our environments. When the training is satisfactory, we speak of adjustment or adaptation to life. When the training is unsatisfactory, the result is failure, neurosis, or perhaps psychosis. This generalization provides a fairly valid basis for further discussion of training or development, since any action taken to train an individual must be considered in the light of his or her prior experience and the behavior which must be developed in the current environment.

But if training is inevitable, why all the fuss about training program development, development planning, need identification, etc., in an organization? It would seem that since "Experience is the best teacher," training in an organization is also inevitable. All that is really needed is a hire and a job; in time the hire will be trained.

An intelligent management looks at this inevitable process and asks some questions. Is experience actually the best teacher? What is the cost of training a qualified person? How do we know when the person has been trained? How long do we mean when we say, "In time, the hire will be trained?" Most important, management asks, "How do we know that the person has been trained to meet the goals we have set?"

These questions and the implications they raise require that training or personnel development be clearly defined in terms of management's goals, the fulfillment of which is the organization's first concern. From this viewpoint, training must be evaluated in terms of its contribution to these goals. The first question is not how, or even who but rather why. If experience is the "trainer" who can best help the organization meet its goals, then experience will be chosen to run the training function.

Malcolm W. Warren, *Training for Results* (Reading, Mass.: Addison-Wesley, 1979), p.1. © 1979 Addison-Wesley Publishing Company, Inc. Reprinted with permission.

who are being urged to move through their own professional development process. The American Society for Training and Development (ASTD), which has long played a key role in developing the training and development profession and professionalizing training, has issued numerous statements on what this must include. The ASTD's required activity categories include:

1. Analyzing needs and evaluating results
2. Designing and developing training programs and materials
3. Delivering training and development programs and services
4. Advising and counseling
5. Managing training activities
6. Maintaining organization relationships

7. Doing research to advance the training field
8. Developing professional skills and expertise
9. Developing basic skills and knowledge

The impact of "professionalization" on training's separate identity remains to be seen. Certainly such an effort takes training far beyond presenting orientation programs, explaining affirmative action policies, and providing forty hours of supervisory management training for new supervisors. And it means more than simply negotiating contractors' proposals and doing contract oversight. Above all, trainers must be concerned about human development objectives and then focus on upgrading the activities and techniques to be used. These objectives can be condensed into three critical functions:

- To plan what people need to know, both now and in the future
- To stress the ability to communicate and apply—to ensure that what needs to be known is actually learned and used
- To be *seriously* involved with the whole process of human development in helping people learn more about themselves

To do the above requires accomplished expertise in the methods of training, planning training, and training evaluation.

Methods of Training

The primary variables that organizations consider when implementing their training objectives are format (i.e., in what way and by whom should training be presented) and time (i.e., how often and how long should training sessions last). It is generally assumed that training programs with longer time intervals between the program segments will have more impact than those with segments that are bunched together. This is especially true for supervisory training, where some form of behavior modification is the ultimate objective. While there is a great variety of training formats, almost all would fall into one of the following general categories:

1. *Skills training or demonstration*—Training to teach specific craft or equipment skills, either in-house or through an outside contractor where the employee receives initial or refresher instruction about specific processes or skills.
2. *Coaching or on-the-job training*—Direct personal instruction, usually in the work setting where an "expert" oversees initial work efforts by a learner and provides corrective advice and continued monitoring of work output.
3. *Formal-informal lecture or classroom instruction*—A variety of classroom methods are available to organizations whereby they can assemble and

What are the Implications of the Demographic Changes in the Work Force for Training and Development?

First, government agencies will need to begin to conduct more extensive needs assessments to determine the types of training and development experiences that are needed to meet both organizational and individual needs. Specifically, government agencies will need to conduct organizational analyses to determine the existing levels of support, both financial and philosophical, available to training and development efforts, and work to increase those levels of support, as necessary. Further, government agencies will need to conduct demographic analyses focusing on protected class people, including older workers, examine current training and development practices, determine the extent to which these practices meet the needs of these demographic groups, and develop new training and development programs, as appropriate.

Second, since the available pool of entry level workers will include increasing numbers of individuals who have had inadequate education and training opportunities, government agencies must be willing to provide more training in basic remedial skills.... Given the decreased number of entry-level employees, government agencies must be more willing to establish integrated recruitment and training programs that are based on potential and aptitude for necessary knowledge, skills and abilities (KSAs) rather than current possession. For example, . . .New York State has adopted a grow-your-own approach to meeting work force needs that includes pre-employment training and job preparation for underskilled applicants, school-to-work bridge programs for non-college bound students, and traineeship, internship, apprenticeship and transition programs.

Third, government agencies need to examine their current organizational climates and provide necessary training to the people already in the organization in order to make the organizational culture more receptive to people from all cultures, to women and to older workers....Affirmative actions programs have been designed to recruit underrepresented people to the workplace. They have not, however, focused on creating supportive work environments. As the demographic changes bring new people into the workplace, it is the responsibility of the organization to provide work environments that are free from discrimination and that value diversity.

Carolyn Ban, Sue Faerman, and Norma M. Riccucci, "Productivity and the Personnel Process," in Marc Holzer (ed.), *Public Productivity Handbook* (New York: Marcel Dekker, 1992).

instruct groups of employees or assist employees in obtaining instruction on their own at nearby academic institutions. Organizations can and often do provide tuition reimbursement for outside course work that can be shown to be job related.

4. *Sensitivity or "T-group" training*—A group of techniques have evolved from this concept of assembling small groups of employees to directly and openly approach problems of human behavior and interpersonal

New York State conducts training programs in a variety of areas. *Source*: New York Civil Service, Albany, New York.

relationships. Used as a major tool to developing more "sensitive" and aware managers, sensitivity training usually requires the services of a professional "facilitator" and relies heavily on the willingness of individuals to confront emotional and subjective aspects of their behavior openly.

5. *Job rotation programs*—This technique can be established on a number of levels and is designed to provide employees with varying work tasks and assignments in order to increase employee experience. Some offices have developed limited versions of this concept (usually called cross-functional training), in which each job and thus the entire work of the office is learned by each employee. More formal systems also exist in which new employees are rotated through different offices to facilitate organizational familiarity or develop more general work skills.

6. *Special conferences and seminars*—These are special meetings of employees to discuss and exchange ideas about process, problems, and techniques. The great advantage of this conference or "retreat" concept

lies in assembling employees away from day-to-day operations to focus on a specific agenda that is usually change-oriented.

7. *Modeling, simulation, and self-paced learning training*—A plethora of simulated real-life situations have been developed to provide individuals with various contrived experiences. Many "games" involve extensive applications of role-playing, which affords participants the opportunity to view, analyze, and practice behavior patterns and related outcomes. Some of the major advances in this area involve the use of computers and videos that rely on self-paced learning methods, whereby the individual reads, responds, and is evaluated at the end of each session. Technology and computer training is especially well-suited for this type of training method.

8. *Exchange and sabbatical programs*—The concept of getting the individual out of the organizational environment and into a totally different one for a substantial period of time—up to two years—represents the most advanced training concept. Exchange programs are worked out between different organizations to send their professionals to work in new positions, while sabbaticals involve sending an individual off to an academic or research program.

The Intergovernmental Personnel Act of 1970, by authorizing the temporary assignment of personnel between the various jurisdictional levels and educational institutions, initially did much to advance the exchange concept and is a good example of such talent-sharing experiences. The determinator of which training methods should be employed will depend on the subject matter, the instructional preferences of the employees involved, and the appropriateness of the method to the organizational environment. Unfortunately, little systematic work has been done in the training field to keep track of what kinds of methods work better with what kinds of subjects and what types of employees.

Career Development and the Employee

Training and development are also vital to the employee's perspective of what is termed career development. A career can be defined as the sequence of positions within job fields that an individual holds over time. Career planning and development is the ongoing process of evaluating an individual's strengths and weaknesses in order to determine a personal strategy by which to pursue individual growth. Unfortunately many individuals don't know what they want in the way of a "career" path, and their organizations frequently don't have any better idea about what their employees should be doing in this regard. But generally speaking, there are four basic phases of career development:

Entry phase—A break-in time period in which the new employee will achieve a journeyworker's level (i.e., adequate working level of operational competence)

Specialist phase—A period in which the employee concentrates on performing a set of specific work assignments involving technical and work skills

Generalist phase—A period in which specific technical skills are less important and more supervisory responsibilities are involved

Management phase—A period in which the employee assumes responsibilities for administering and directing work operations, for managing the execution of programs, and for the formulation of plans for future organizational action

Essentials of an Effective Executive Developmental System

The following elements or characteristics can be found in the most successful programs now in operation.

1. *Top Management Support*—The head of the organization is personally committed to the program, provides personal direction and support, and communicates his or her interest and support to the management team and to the employees.

2. *An Active Executive Resources Board (ERB)*—The Executive Resources Board made up of senior officials actively oversees and evaluates the XD program. This is the same board which oversees other SES activities, including merit staffing for career appointments to the SES.

3. *An Executive Development Policy*—Such a policy is formally developed and broadly communicated throughout the organization. It defines the purpose and objectives of the XD program for incumbents and candidates and delineates the roles and responsibilities of the head of the organization, the Executive Resources Board or Boards, other agency executives, support staff and program participants. There are clear statements that participants for the agency SES candidate development program will be selected on a merit basis and that participants who successfully complete the program will be prime candidates for future appointment to the SES. The fact that the program will contribute affirmative action goals is stated.

4. *An Executive Personnel Planning System*—Such a planning system projects executive needs based on such considerations as program and organizational changes, retirements, fallback as a result of performance deficiencies, and planned reassignments of SES members. It includes plans for executive development programs to meet anticipated needs.

5. *Merit Selection of Participants in SES Candidate Development Programs*—The merit selection system identifies the eligible population from which participants

(continued)

Essentials of an Effective Executive Developmental System *(continued)*

will be selected. This includes qualified individuals from other Federal agencies, and may include individuals from other levels of government, universities and the private sector. It reflects a positive effort to include women and minority citizens and the handicapped in the competition and is consistent with the Uniform Guidelines on Employee Selection Procedures (1978). It limits the number selected to no more than twice the number of persons needed to fill SES vacancies projected for the upcoming two-year period.

6. *Planned Developmental Activities*—Developmental activities are planned to match organizational and individual needs. Organizational needs are determined through a systematic analysis of the competencies required in the organization's executive positions. These needs are related to the developmental needs of prospective or incumbent executives through the Individual Development Plan (IDP).

   (a) Developments of SES candidates. The SES candidate development program gives an opportunity for participants to assess personal strengths and needs prior to planning developmental activities. The IDP is used in selecting development assignments and other program activities. Line and staff assignments in field and headquarters organizations are made available as necessary. The IDP places significant obligations upon the agency and the participants. However, it may be modified if conditions change.

   In addition to formal training in managerial theory and practice as may be needed, the program provides an orientation to executive management in the agency involving contact with the key executives who manage major agency functions. The program also focuses on the clients of the organization in order to give insight regarding the organization's impact upon them.

   Regular assessments of participants' progress are made during the course of the program and periodic coaching and counseling sessions are held with senior executives and staff specialists. Participants who do not make satisfactory progress are released from the program.

   (b) Development of SES members. The SES member program provides for individual development plans which are tied to the performance evaluation cycle. These IDP's focus on building upon individual strengths, identifying individual needs, expanding general executive competencies, and preparing members for future assignments. Short term or more extended developmental experiences are designed to:

   (i) Meet organizational needs for managerial improvement and increased productivity.

   (ii) Help SES members to keep abreast of professional, technical, managerial, social and political areas.

   (iii) Meet individual SES members' needs for intellectual and personal growth and development

   Beginning in July 1981, SES member programs will include executive sabbaticals for carefully selected members.

(continued)

Essentials of an Effective Executive Developmental System *(continued)*

7. *Use of Program Graduates*—Executive development program graduates are placed in positions where their increased competencies are used. The Executive Resources Board assigns substantial weight for completion of the XD program when selecting persons for SES positions. Graduates are also assigned to responsible GS-15 positions in their own organizations, given inter- and intraagency assignments or placed on special task force projects.
8. *Staff and Budget Support*
   (a) Staffing. The agency provides a staff large enough to operate and maintain the XD program and develops them to the level of competency required to support the program.
   (b) Budgeting. The agency identifies and earmarks full costs of executive development in advance, budgeting funds as needed.
9. *Evaluation*—The agency periodically evaluates its program against established objectives and makes needed revisions.

Executive Development: An Overview for Agency Officials (Washington, D.C.: U.S. Office of Personnel Management, September 1979).

While employees may pursue a career path in any of the latter three phases, many employees are expected to and do chart their career path through each of the four phases culminating in a top managerial position. Training priorities obviously vary for each of the career path phases. Presumably new employees are hired with a modicum of skills so that they are capable of immediately performing work related to their assignment. The primary development need here is to acquaint new employees with the organizational structure in which they have been placed. Some form of orientation can generally accomplish this. As employees become full-fledged specialists, their development needs will require even more knowledge of organizational structure and increased technological skills. They must stay abreast of changes in the state of the art concerning their specialties. Generalists will be concerned both with technical advances and the direct oversight of the specialists. Development here will necessarily involve interpersonal social skills.

Managers must be fully adept with those interpersonal skills relating to the communication, motivation, and leadership aspects of employee interactions. How many individuals must develop along these last lines will depend upon the organization's hierarchical structure. Training and development programs can and should be tailored to individuals at each level of development. This in itself is one definition of the objectives for a training and development program.

One of the first examples of a career development guide or model, which presents training objectives for the organization to provide and the employee to achieve, is one that was developed by the U.S. Department of Labor in the late 1970s and that is still used in different formats. The department created model career patterns for its various occupational fields. It has literally charted out the various phases of myriad careers by grade level, indicating the objectives for each phase, desirable assignments, and appropriate education and training activities. Employees wishing to advance themselves would now know what is specifically expected of them in one career period if they are to be advanced to the next. Of course, as with any such program, there is always the possibility that luck or politics will intervene in the normal process; but at the very least, the rules of the game—the way to the top—have been laid out for all to see.

For the most part, public organizations have been hard pressed to provide such career planning models for their employees. As early as the 1970s, the former U.S. Civil Service Commission conducted a nationwide study of training and employee development and found that the major problems with training were not so much the result of budgetary vendettas, but rather of the creation of an integrated cause-and-effect cycle—the "disincentives process." Of course, budgetary shortfalls in the 1980s complicated training and development opportunities; but the disincentives process still remains a compelling argument for why individuals question the value of training and development, regardless of the method used.

The process has been described as follows:

1. The benefits of training and development are not clear to top management.
2. Top management rarely evaluates and rewards managers and supervisors for carrying out effective training and development.
3. Top management rarely plans and budgets systematically for training and development.
4. Managers usually do not account for training and development in production planning.
5. Supervisors have difficulty meeting production norms with employees in training and development.
6. *Therefore*, supervisors and managers train and develop employees unsystematically and mostly for short-term objectives.

There are two problems immediately apparent with the disincentives process. First, adequate methods do not exist to demonstrate the potential benefits of training to managers, and consequently, top management is inclined to focus its attention on and allocate its resources to areas where returns are more evident. This is especially true in the public sector where political executives only have a comparatively brief time in which to make a "record" to run on in the next election. There is simply no short-term payoff on long-term training and development programs. The second general problem is the perennial difficulty of sparing individuals to take training when they are severely needed for day-to-day operations. Actually, it is not uncommon for some employees to be more excusable than others; an employee may have good reason for pause if and when he or she is selected for a training "opportunity." The conventional wisdom was always that, out of any group of managers or employees attending a training program, about a third assigned to have training regard it as a reward; a third felt they were sent there as a subtle punishment (to get them out of the organizational way for a while); and a third had no clear idea of why they were there, except that there was a quota to fill and money budgeted for the program (in other words, someone had to go).

Yet the real point is that training, to be most effective in development, must be planned in advance so that employees see how the training fits into their career paths. To integrate training effectively into career development requires two levels of planning. The first occurs on an individual level where employees schedule and evaluate what kinds of training they will need and when. The second level involves planning the total training program for the organization, or what is termed *training needs assessment*.

On Planning Training

"Failing to plan is planning to fail," or so the management adage goes. Few would argue that some form of planning effort for training is a vital first stage in developing training programs (see Figure 14.1). Planning is so significant in the training and development area that it falls under its own title: training needs assessment. If training is to be effective, it is argued, a careful diagnosis of what training is needed is essential. As a diagnostic tool, needs assessment will ensure that training is relevant to both the short-run performance deficiencies and long-run career development needs of employees by identifying training priorities. In the current environment of resource scarcity, the necessity of making such determinations seems almost absolute.

Of course, the planning of training goes beyond identifying what subject areas training should be conducted in. Needs assessment rightfully must consider the level of training needed for different kinds of employees, the best learning sequence for conducting the training, and the most effective methods and techniques of presenting the training. While more attention is being paid to these latter problems of level, sequence, and methods, the major difficulty facing most trainers is to ascertain what training employees need.

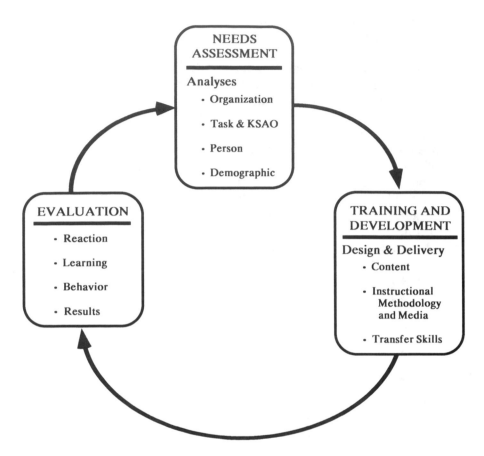

Figure 14.1. A systems approach to training and development. *Source*: Carolyn Ban, Sue Faerman, and Norma M. Riccucci, "Productivity and the Personnel Process," in Mark Holzer (ed.)., *Public Productivity Handbook* (New York: Marcel Dekker, forthcoming).

A variety of techniques of needs assessment has been established; most training handbooks and numerous how-to-do-it training publications review some of the possible methods, such as interviews, discussion meetings, questionnaires, review of career plans, critical incident analysis, task or job analysis, and review of performance appraisal data. These techniques fall into six generally accepted categories:

1. Survey of employees
2. Interviews of employees, supervisors, or work experts
3. Review of performance evaluation and assessment center data
4. Model career planning
5. Human resources information systems approaches
6. Job analysis

The first, employee surveys, involves written individual opinion questionnaires (in which individuals are asked to estimate their skill levels, corresponding training needs, and interests). A second approach involves extensive interviewing of a sample of individuals, supervisors, or work experts in specific occupational or job categories. The oral interview may be both direct (e.g., what kinds of training do you need?) or indirect (e.g., How would you go about doing this kind of task or handling this type of situation?). This format requires that the interviewer identify a training or skill need level that is related to job performance and level. A third approach involves a review of performance evaluation reports or assessment center data results whereby supervisors or some designated group review individual performance records, tests, inspection reports, career plans, and/or other data in order to assess what the most relevant training programs to offer various employees would be.

Model career planning, a concept used and documented quite extensively by the U.S. Department of Labor, constitutes a fourth approach, whereby each functional or occupational work category is planned out against time and career grade objectives with approximate work assignment and training program objectives. Such model career paths are usually planned and modified by work groups of highly superior professionals in the various categories. The model career path functions quite similarly to a college bulletin, which lists courses and degree requirements. Both the individual and the supervisor retain the option to make choices and select only those developmental experiences that they deem appropriate.

The fifth approach, commonly referred to as HRIS, after the U.S. State Department's Human Resources Information Systems (HRIS) Project (pioneered in the 1970s), involves the development of an extensive computerized position-person inventory data system. HRIS can compare all position requirements against the current skill levels of employees and project training priorities. HRIS, as a highly sophisticated computer and data concept, conceptualizes training as one of several planning alternatives for professional development, and compares training to position redesign, employment, and placement options.

The sixth and last approach is that of functional job analysis, where managerial positions are analyzed for functions, activities, and tasks performed. This level of detail affords a further basis for the determination of the corresponding knowledge, skills, and aptitudes needed to perform each task successfully. Functional job analysis involves extensive survey work and position analysis on a continuing basis.

Training is still in development in terms of validating the most appropriate methods for assessing the need for training. There are still problems inherent in the definition of need. Most troublesome is time. What is the need for training for work being performed now and what will it be for work that is to be done three to five years from now? What if present work skills and most probable future work skills are in conflict? What then should be the training program? A good example can be seen in dictation skills. Should secretaries and clerks be given training in a skill fast reaching obsolescence? The problem of time is further complicated by opinion, specifically different people's opinions about individual training needs. Conversely, what does an organization do about all the employees it has now given personal computers to who have never learned to type?

When it comes to "training needs," we have to consider the opinions of superiors, subordinates, peers, and professional training specialists. All can be involved in the process of identifying training needs, and all are likely to have different opinions.

Still, what individuals want to do is as important as any other factor in the needs assessment process. Training needs assessment strives to be what Roger Kaufman and Fenwick English have defined as "a humanizing process to help make sure that we are using our time and the learner's time in the most effective and efficient manner possible." After all, learners count, too.

On Evaluating Training

Last but not least, the problem of evaluation stands at the core of the entire training and development knot. While many an annual report will boast of the employees who have been trained during the past year, such statistics must be viewed with great suspicion. It is a common mistake to assume that the number of individuals who have been subjected to a training experience is equal to the number of individuals who have acquired a new skill or expertise. The only way of even knowing what has been gained through training is to have developed evaluation criteria prior to all training experience. Without base points of performance, subsequent attempts to measure results will be futile. A further distinction must be made between measurement, which quantifies the results of training, and evaluation, which seeks to ascertain whether a training effort is worth its cost. A principal factor in the disincentive cycle of training is that public managers generally have neither measures of training effectiveness nor evaluations of training program utility.

Evaluations of training and development efforts are necessarily multifaceted. Do you measure the individual's subjective reaction to a training experience or do you seek an objective measure of what was learned? Another approach is to measure the change in job behavior—perhaps an increase in productivity—that might have occurred as a result of training. But if large elements of the organization have been recently taught new techniques, a more rational method of assessing utility would be to seek a measure of overall organizational effectiveness. Did it increase, decrease, or stay the same?

If a training effort seeks to prepare employees for positions that lend themselves to engineered work standards, then corresponding evaluations will be relatively simple mathematical efforts. However, as work moves up the scale of task ambiguity, corresponding training efforts and their evaluations become more difficult to design, conduct, and measure. Training can be said to be validated if quantifiable measures of its effectiveness can be produced. But while many of the individual training elements of a management development program may be amenable to validation, management development itself in almost all jurisdictions is undertaken as an "act of faith."

The act may be covered in social science rhetoric, but it is faith—not science—that causes public organizations to put resources into management development, because these programs have simply not been validated. There are two basic reasons for this—time and numbers. Remember, the federal government was not even authorized to spend any significant sums on training until passage of the Government Employees Training Act of 1958. Even today, while most state and local jurisdictions have training efforts, most do not have extensive training staffs. The movement toward outsourcing, especially as a result of budgetary shortfalls, generally reduces the number of training staff who are available to plan and evaluate training programs. Of course, a public sector agency can contract out the evaluation of the training to an outside consultant. But that means contracting out the evaluation of contractors doing the training!

As the number of public managers who have had the opportunity to participate in a comprehensive management development program increases, there should be growing confidence in training evaluation. Even if there aren't large-scale studies that empirically demonstrate the utility of the components of such programs, further funding of them will continue to be matters of faith. Part of it is an act of faith—and it is a faith that most managers and personnelists subscribe to. But part of it is also a recognition that training and development are critical dimensions of human resources managment; that the technical, technological, and managerial requirements of most public sector jobs are

What Is Evaluation?

...evaluation is an information gathering process that should not be expected to reach decisions that declare a program totally good or poor. Instructional programs are never complete but instead are designed to be revised on the basis of information obtained from evaluations that examine relevant multiple criteria that are both free from contamination and reliable. One role of the previously described need assessment process is to suggest relevant criteria which can be utilized to measure the achievement of the multiple objectives of the training program. Evaluation must be treated as one part of a long term systematic approach to the *development* of effective programs. Unless such a systematic approach is developed, the feedback process that could result from effectively designed evaluations built around relevant multiple criteria has been more likely to conclude in emotional reactions rather than decisions to use the information to improve programs.

The better experimental procedures control more variables permitting a greater degree of confidence in specifying program effects. While the constraints of the training environment may make laboratory type evaluation impossible to achieve, an awareness of the important factors in experimental design makes it possible to conduct a useful evaluation. Certainly, the real world has many constraints and these affect the designs employed. Thus, a pure do-nothing control group is sometimes not useful in the examination of instructional programs. At least, this author would not be interested in being flown across the Atlantic Ocean in a 747 jet plane by a pilot who was randomly placed in the uninstructed control group. However, there are many instances where controls consisting of the old technique as compared to the institution of a new type of program are appropriate. It is time to begin comparing methodologies to the constraints of the environment. This process should be characterized by careful consideration of threats to validity, and the creative application of design methodology to the questions being investigated.

Irwin L. Goldstein, "The Pursuit of Internal and External Validity in the Evaluation of Training Programs," *Public Personnel Management*, 8 (November-December, 1979), p. 419. Reprinted by permission of the International Personnel Management Association, 1850 K Street, N.W., Suite 870, Washington, D.C. 20006.

not static. In fact, the reverse is the case; job dimensions are so dynamic that ongoing evaluation of training to ensure that "learners" are satisfactorily mastering new skills and competencies and applying them effectively in their positions is critical.

Of course, that still leaves the difficulty of deciding upon what evaluation approach to use. It is much easier to determine whether employees found a specific training program interesting, well organized, and relevant than to survey individuals and units several months later to see if productive job behavior changes have occurred that can be attributed to a specific training program. Furthermore, most jurisdictions that are beginning the task of assembling or reassembling a major training effort see the thorny problems of evaluation as a second priority. Their rationale, which is basically "let's build a good program first, and then we'll worry about evaluation," seems quite logical.

But the fact is that training evaluation has now been upgraded from simply a cost-benefit resource question to a new series of questions about validation. Reflecting a more scientific perspective, training programs in public organizations must stand on the same grounds as examinations and promotion decisions. This will mean at a minimum, the development of performance-relevant training programs that must be capable of demonstrating improvement in appropriate skills.

As such, the training evaluation question, which essentially focuses on the more intangible aspects of improving employee morale and perceptions, must yield to more rigorous evaluation questions. Consequently, validity in the context of the evaluation of training can be conceptualized, as Irwin Goldstein has hypothesized, in a hierarchy of four stages:

1. The validity of the training itself based upon demonstrated performance in the training environment
2. Performance validity based upon demonstrated performance on the job
3. Intraorganizational validity, which considers the question of the training program's generalizability to new groups of trainees in the same organization
4. Interorganizational validity, which considers the training program's generalizability to trainees in different organizations

These stages of training validity necessarily incorporate increasingly difficult levels of measurement. Most public sector organizations have been hard-pressed to reach much beyond the first stage. Most simply choose to administer various forms of subjective questionnaires to trainees about their reactions. Some, like the military, use extensive pre- and posttesting procedures to determine what was learned.

But how much of this newly learned knowledge is imparted on the job (performance validity) is only indirectly addressed. Postcourse questionnaires to supervisors and employees asking numerous subjective questions about job improvement are very general and of little utility in producing any real measurement. As for inter- and intraorganizational validity, a great deal must still be done before these dimensions are successfully integrated into training evaluation. Perhaps it is in this sense that the experience of many public sector organizations with outsourcing or contracting out of training programs provides a silver lining. Much more emphasis has been placed on evaluation and developing more comprehensive and

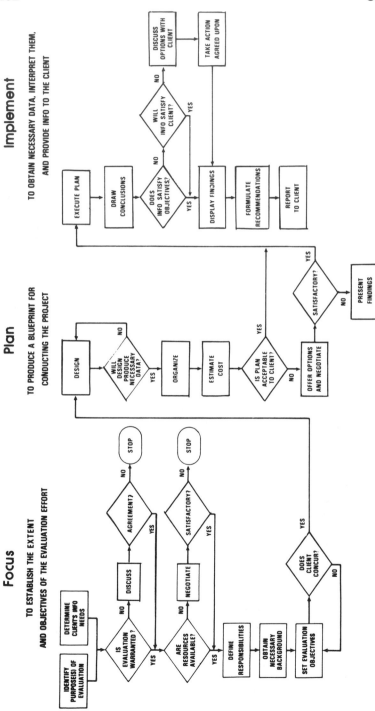

Source: U.S. Civil Service Commission, *A Process for the Evaluation of Training* (Washington, D.C.: U.S. Government Printing Office, 1978), p. viii.

sophisticated evaluation methods to demonstrate that the training contractor is in compliance and that the programs contracted for are effective in meeting the organization's needs.

Without evaluation processes being established, there is literally no way that anyone will ever be able to assess what has been accomplished or answer such questions as: More or less training? Better or worse management development? Provided in house or contracted out? But evaluation, as critical as it is, must be kept in context. The problems here must be addressed in tandem with the changes facing training in the coming decade.

Training and Development in the 1990s

The 1980s was a tenuous decade for the public sector for a variety of reasons, including diminishing economics and finances, tight budgets, political pressures to privatize, vanishing credibility of the value of the public service, bureaucrat bashing, and greater cynicism among public employees. Governments at all levels were pressed to be more efficient, more effective, and more accountable, all the while having to do more with less. On top of these requirements, governments have had to spend more time on public relations, building a better image, and proving that they are worth the resources allotted them. Learning to do more with less about bigger problems for an increasingly disbelieving and unforgiving public constituted a severe test.

Training and development played a crucial role in helping governments face the challenges of the 1980s. Its importance was greatly magnified by the "pay gap" issue in which wages fell considerably behind the private sector (see Chapter 5). Organizations used their training and development funding as "investment budgets" both to develop younger and newly hired employees at a faster pace, and to "reward" employees with training programs that they were interested in. Major investments were made in computer and technology training as public sector organizations moved dramatically to use more computers to automate work requirements and enhance productivity.

While training staffs were often reduced and training budgets cut back, there was access to more organizational resources for training in many cases. In the 1960s and 1970s, training was more centralized, with personnel being sent to courses provided by training departments. By the 1980s, there were more choices, and departments within various jurisdictions would often contract out for their own training programs. In this decentralized environment of the 1980s and now the 1990s, training is more competitive with a lot more choices. Universities. professional organizations, and consultants provide inexpensive training programs (both general and tailored) at the organization's facility. Increasingly, there are more computer-based and video training

packages that can be purchased externally or even developed internally to
enhance training opportunities. This explosion in training sources and delivery
methods reflects a very different future of human resources development.
Robert L. Craig (the editor of the ASTD's *Training and Development Handbook*) made a series of observations about the trends that will dominate training until the year 2000. He wrote, in an article appearing in the winter 1986
issue of *Public Personnel Management*:

> A good, close look at the current trends in employer-provided education and
> training may be a bit unsettling for trainers, but the picture is pretty clear—the
> job is going to be tougher.... Some of the major and more obvious trends are:
> (1) human resource development [HRD] in the world of work is massive and
> growing (it's already bigger than many realize); (2) it is getting too big and im-
> portant to be ignored by mainstream interests—senior management at the
> organization levels and policy makers at the national affairs level; (3) HRD is
> going to be counted and measured increasingly with much the same intensity
> as other vital organizational functions; (4) HRD professionals can expect greater
> exposure and accountability; and (5) a larger share of employee training will
> be provided by external suppliers and line functions.

These trends simply confirm that tight budgets or not, training and development has created its identity with a corresponding set of major roles and responsibilities. Training and development will be driven by two major forces: (1)
the quality of the work force and the need for new work force knowledge
and skills to combat obsolescence and keep pace with dynamic job and
technology demands, and (2) the increasing expectations of workers who will
view training and development as a major factor in their selection and retention
decisions. In effect, it will be increasingly challenged by an expanding, highly
results-oriented, more decentralized environment. Interestingly, its success
in this environment will greatly determine whether training and development
will truly become a human resources development endeavor, or simply a
catalog of training options, contracts, and development programs.

Bibliography

Baird, L. S. et al. (eds.). *The Training and Development Sourcebook*. Amherst,
    Mass.: Human Resources Development Press, 1983.

Baird, L. S. and Kram, Kathy L. *Career Dynamics: Matching the Super-
    visor/Subordinate Relationship Organizational Dynamics*, vol 11, no. 4,
    spring 1983.

Bellman, Geoffrey. "Doing More with Less," *Public Personnel Management*,
    vol. 15, no. 4 (winter 1986).

Benford, Robert J., William E. Brooks, Stephen X. Doyle, and Michael T. Tedd. "Training for Results," *Personnel* (May-June 1979).

Brown, F. Gerald and Kenneth R. Wedel. *Assessing Training Needs*. Washington, D.C.: National Training Development Service Press, 1974.

Byers, Kenneth T. (ed.). *Employee Training and Development in the Public Service*. Chicago: International Personnel Management Association, 1970.

Clement, Ronald W. "Testing the Heirarchy Theory of Training Evaluation," *Public Personnel Management*, vol. 11, no. 2, (summer 1982).

Cooke, Kathleen. "A Model for the Identification of Training Needs," *Public Personnel Management* (July-August 1979).

Craig, Robert L. "The Future of HRD: It's Going to Get Tougher," *Public Personnel Management*, vol. 15, no. 4 (winter 1986).

Craig, Robert (ed.). *Training and Development Handbook*. New York: McGraw-Hill, 1987.

Cross, L. "Career Management Development: A System That Gets Results," *Training and Development Journal*, vol. 37, no. 2 (February 1983).

Ferman, Louis A., et al. (eds), *New Developments in Worker Training: A Legacy for the 1990s*. Madison, Wis.: Industrial Relations Research Association, 1990.

Frank, William W. and Robert Hayes. *Training Needs Survey*. Ithaca, N.Y.: Cornell University, 1973.

Fraser, Richard F., John W. Gore, and Chester C. Cotton. "A System for Determining Training Needs," *Personnel Journal* (December 1978).

Gardner, James E. *Helping Employees Develop Job Skills: A Casebook of Training Approaches*. Washington, D.C.: Bureau of National Affairs, 1976.

Garson, G. David. "Personnel Training and Development," in Jack Rabin et al. (eds.), *Handbook on Public Personnel Administration and Labor Relations*. New York: Marcel Dekker, 1983.

Goldstein, I. L. *Training: Program Development and Evaluation*, 2nd ed. Monterey, Calif.: Brooks/Cole, 1986.

————. "Training: Methodological Considerations and Empirical Approaches," symposium for *Journal of Human Factors*, 20, no. 2 (April 1978).

Gordon, Michael E. "Planning Training Activity," *Training and Development Journal*, 27 (January 1973).

Hamblin, A. C. *Evaluation and Control of Training*. New York: McGraw-Hill, 1974.

Hinch, Gerald K. and Clement D. Pangallo. "Federal Training in Tight Budget Years," *Public Personnel Management*, vol. 15, no. 4 (winter 1986).

Hyde, Albert C. and Jay M. Shafritz. "Training and Development: Problems and Prospects," symposium in *Public Personnel Management* (November-December 1979).

Jones, Andrew N. *Combatting Managerial Obsolescence*. Oxford: Philip Allan, 1980.

Kaufman, Roger and Fenwick W. English. *Needs Assessment: Concept and Application*. Englewood Cliffs, N.J.: Educational Technology Publishers, 1979.

Kirkpatrick, Donald L. "Evaluating In-house Training Programs," *Training and Development Journal* (September 1978).

_____. "Effective Supervisory Training and Development," *Personnel*, part 1 (November-December 1984), part 2 (January-February 1985).

Knowles, Malcolm S. *The Adult Learner: A Neglected Species*. Houston: Gulf Publishing, 1973.

_____. "Gearing Up for the Eighties," *Training and Development Journal* (July 1978).

Laird, Dugan. *Approaches to Training and Development*, 2nd ed. Reading, Mass.: Addison-Wesley, 1985.

Mager, Robert F. *Developing Attitudes toward Learning*. Palo Alto, Calif.: Fearon Publishing, 1968.

_____. *Preparing Instructional Objectives*. Palo Alto, Calif.: Fearon Publishing, 1962.

McCullough, Richard C. (ed.) "Training in Tough Times," *Public Personnel Management*, vol. 15, no. 4 (Winter 1986 special issue).

Michalak, Donald F. and Edwin G. Yager. *Making the Training Process Work*. New York: Harper & Row, 1979.

Misler, Dennis I. "Management Development and More: Contracting Out Makes It Possible," *Public Personnel Management*, vol. 15, no. 4 (winter 1986).

Nadler, Leornard. *Developing Human Resources*, 2nd ed. Austin, Tex.: Learning Concepts, 1979.

Odiorne, George S. *Training by Objectives: An Economic Approach to Management Training*. New York: Macmillan, 1970.

O'Toole, James. "Integrating Work and Learning," *Training and Development Journal* (June 1977).

Otto, Calvin P. and Rollen O. Glaser. *The Management of Training: A Handbook for Training and Development People*. Reading, Mass.: Addison-Wesley, 1970.

Passett, Barry A. *Leadership Development for Public Service*. Houston, Tex.: Gulf Publishing, 1971.

Patton, Arch. "The Coming Flood of Young Executives," *Harvard Business Review*, 54 (September-October 1976).

Pender, Kathleen. "Pac Bell's New Way to Think," *San Francisco Chronicle* (March, 23, 1987).

Pomerleau, Raymond. "The State of Management Development in the Federal Service," *Public Personnel Management*, 3 (January-February 1974).

Rich, Wilbur C. "Career Paths for Public Managers: Upward but Narrow," *Personnel*, (July-August 1984).

Saint, Alice M. *Learning at Work: Human Resources and Organizational Development*. Chicago: Nelson-Hall, 1974.

Salinger, Ruth D. *Disincentives to Effective Employee Training and Development*. Washington, D.C.: U.S. Civil Service Commission, 1973.

————. and Ruth Kletnick *Determining the Need for Training*. Washington, D.C.: U.S. Office of Personnel Management, 1984.

Sims, Ronald R., John G. Veres, and Susan Heninger. "Training for Competence," *Public Personnel Management*, 18 (spring 1989).

Sylvia, Ronald D. and C. Kenneth Meyer. "An Organizational Perspective on Training and Development in the Public Sector," in Stephen Hays and Richard Kearney (eds.), *Public Personnel Administration*. Englewood Cliffs, N.J.: Prentice-Hall, 1990.

Training Needs Assessment: A Study of Methods, Approaches, and Procedures Used by Government Agencies. Philadelphia: Regional Training Center, 1978.

Ulshcack, Francis L. *Human Resource Development: The Theory and Practice of Needs Assessment*. Reston, Va.: Reston, 1983.

U.S. General Accounting Office. *Training Budgets: Agency Budget Reductions in Response to the Balanced Budget Act*. July 1986.

Warren, M.W. *Training for Results*, 2nd ed. Reading, Mass.: Addison-Wesley, 1969.

Watson, Charles E. *Management Development through Training*, Reading, Mass.: Addison-Wesley, 1979.

Wexley, Kenneth N. and Gary P. Latham. *Developing and Training Human Resources in Organizations*. Glenview, Ill.: Scott, Foresman, 1981.

Zeira, Yoram. "Is External Management Training Effective for Organizational Change?" *Public Personnel Management* (November-December 1978).

15
Performance Appraisal

Prologue: The Debate Over Merit Pay

Few things seem more basic to a personnel system than the requirement to appraise individual performance regularly and ensure that the organization uses this information in making training, compensation, and advancement decisions. The federal government initially addressed the appraisal process with the enactment of the Performance Rating Act of 1950. The act provided guidelines for appraisal goals and processes and included rules for removing those individuals with unsatisfactory performance ratings. But dissatisfaction with performance appraisal (for reasons soon to be explained) ran rampant over the 1960s and 1970s, and, when the Civil Service Reform Act (CSRA) was passed in 1978, a major target for change was the performance appraisal process. The CSRA established a merit pay system to cover supervisors and managers from GS-13 to GS-15 and also required that compensation decisions be linked with employee appraisals. In essence, performance appraisals were to serve as the primary basis for annual salary changes.

But, the merit pay rapidly drew fire from all sides. Hampered severely by limited funding levels (it was tied to General Schedule funding), the initial procedures were extremely cumbersome and ineffective. As the Merit Systems Protection Board (MSBP) concluded its 1988 study, *Toward Effective Performance in the Federal Government*:

> There were many complaints that the procedures were so complex that employees could not understand how their increases were derived. Employees also were concerned about the fairness of the Performance Appraisal System which was the basis for the merit pay and cash award determinations.

In 1984, merit pay was replaced with a new pay-for-performance system called PMRS, or the Performance Management and Recognition System. Interestingly, Congress "sunseted" PMRS with a five-year lifeline, requiring legislation to revive it after September 1989. The details were as follows. Performance appraisals were to have five rating levels ranging from 1 (unacceptable) to 3 (fully successful) to 5 (two levels above fully successful). Employees rated 3 or above would get the full general annual pay increase with some kind of merit increase based on their overall rating and where they stood in terms of pay. Level 5 awards range from a minimum of 2 percent to a maximum award of 10 percent of their pay. Provisions existed to give exceptions up to 20 percent. Level 4 employees were intended to obtain some kind of award and level 3 employees were also eligible for a similar type of award. Those below level 3 were penalized. Level 2 employees were to get only 50 percent of the general pay raise and level 1 employees received no increase at all. All the funding for these performance awards was to come from a performance award budget of 1.5 percent of the total salary budget for all PMRS employees. Again, the system was to apply to all supervisors and managers from GS- 13 to GS-15.

But even the revised PMRS, which most federal personnel offices felt was an improvement over the original merit pay plan, ran into trouble. To begin with, there simply wasn't enough money in the budget to reward all the high performers. Consider MSPB's findings in it 1987 report, *Performance Management and Recognition System*, that over two-thirds of all employees covered under PMRS had bonus-eligible ratings of 4 or 5 in the first year of the new plan! Agencies varied considerably in their ratings, which further discredited the system. Managers at the Departments of Justice and State were rated the highest (48 percent and 59 percent, respectively had ratings of 5), while managers at the Departments of Labor and Treasury had tougher ratings (8 percent and 7 percent, respectively, had ratings of 5). Could this mean that one set of agencies had much better managers than another or, is it that one set of performance raters took the rating process more seriously? Even the Office of Personnel Management (OPM) was not immune from rate inflation. Of its eligible managers, 10 percent had ratings of 5 but 40 percent had ratings of 4.

Faced with inflated ratings, agencies either enforced informal quotas (limiting the number of high ratings) or developed subtle rotation polices, whereby one group of managers would get the high ratings one year and a second set would get the high ratings the next. The system's credibility was ripped apart by the resulting chaos. In MSPB's merit systems principles survey, as reported in *Performance Management and Recognition System*, nearly 70 percent of all top supervisors and managers responding agreed that there was an arbitrary limit on the number of high performance ratings. An even more

Obstacles to Taking Formal Actions Against Poor Performers

Federal government supervisors,* when asked, "To what extent, if any, are each of the following an obstacle in taking formal action against employees?" responded:

Factors	Great or considerable extent	Some extent	Little or no extent
Lack of support from higher management	25%	25%	47%
Possibility of lowering office morale	7%	23%	67%
Results do not justify the effort	31%	24%	40%
Too many reviews/appeals	41%	19%	35%
Possibility of a labor relations complaint	22%	17%	56%
Possibility of a discrimination complaint	22%	16%	56%
Possibility of a whistleblower complaint	6%	9%	78%
Lack of technical assistance	18%	21%	55%

*Based on a sample of 21,620 employees.

U.S. Merit Systems Protection Board, *Federal Personnel Policies and Practices* (Washington, D.C.: USMSPB, 1987), p. 11.

critical question drew this mixed response. Forty-five percent agreed with the statement that if they performed better on the job, they would likely be paid more while nearly 39 percent disagreed.

But despite problems with employee perceptions and inflated ratings, concern about PMRS was overshadowed by the increasing pay gap (for a further discussion, see Chapter 5 on classification and compensation). As the sunset date approached, Congress moved to extend PMRS for an additional two years, or until March 1991. In the interim, OPM commissioned a major study by the National Academy of Sciences for completion in early 1991 and established a Pay for Performance Management Committee to make recommendations for action by November 1991. The latter committee is charged with reviewing pay raises in general and to evaluate all the studies to date on pay-for-performance problems experienced by the federal government. Another wrinkle in the equation was the enactment of the 1990 Pay Reform Act, which authorizes agencies to award time off as a performance incentive. Where will it all go? The debate on pay-for-performance will be decided in 1991, since Congress is unlikely to set up another extension. OPM will then be forced to act. Performance ratings remain a major obstacle, and, through it all, public personnel administration will continually be asked to explain why it has been unable to reform the basic performance appraisal process after nearly three decades of concentrated, but largely failed effort.

The Problem of Performance Appraisal

Few problems have been as vexing to personnel administrators as that of performance appraisal. Certainly it is the most maligned area of personnel and in many cases seems to be tolerated only because no one can think of any realistic better alternatives. At stake is a process that should control the development and growth of the organization itself. Performance appraisal can be restated as a series of questions: What qualities are we now recognizing, rewarding, and developing in employees? What messages are we conveying to individuals about their behavior, skills, and attitude? What ideal qualities do we wish to see developed and enhanced in our employees for the accomplishment of our objectives in the future? (See Figure 15.1.)

The development process, however, is rarely considered in a long-range perspective. The functions that performance appraisal seeks to support are much more short-range, relating to positions being held now or, at best, the next promotion. Even career systems, with their "tenure" reviews, generally have very static views of the qualities built into their minimal standards for career status. This static focus of performance appraisal is well reflected in the major functions it is designed to serve, such as:

1. To change or modify dysfunctional work behavior
2. To communite to employes managerial perceptions of the quality of their work
3. To assess skill deficiencies in employees and to recommend appropriate compensation levels
4. To assess whether or not the present duties of an employee's position have an appropriate compensation level
5. To provide a documented record for disciplinary and separation actions

In theory, performance appraisal is well suited to supporting these functions. But in reality, most performance evaluation systems have not been very successful. Why? The main reason may be because supervisors have a great deal of difficulty writing useful and objective performance reports. They submit appraisals that tend to be very subjective, impressionistic, and noncomparable to the reports of other raters. Strong-minded supervisors with very high standards will do their better employees an injustice when compared with raters

Human Resources Management Factors (Individual)	Traditional Personnel Management Factors (Organization)
1. *Equity*—Does appraisal measure accurately, without bias, skills/potential of employees.	1. *Linkage to Compensation/Productivity*—documents productivity objectives to lead to some form of reward.
2. *Development*—Does appraisal help individuals grow: vertically; (i.e. role/responsibility/horizontally (i.e. master various skills, work content).	2. *Career Selection*—Organization identifies best, selects out worst.
3. *Individuation/Security*—Does appraisal help to maintain individuals in their jobs and their careers.	3. *Training Needs Assessment*—Identify performance gaps.
4. *Participation*—How do individuals participate in the appraisal process.	4. *Improving Supervisory-Subordinate Communication.*
5. *Integration/Support of other HRM* functions.	5. *Documentation of Work Agreements*—Used to provide form of accountability for areas of high task ambiguity and employee independence.

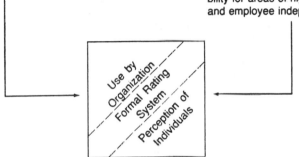

Figure 15.1. The objectives of performance appraisal viewed from two perspectives. *Source*: Albert C. Hyde, "Performance Appraisal in the Post Reform Era," *Public Personnel Management*, vol. 11, no. 4 (Winter 1982), p. 297.

who have low standards or are less professional. The result is a vast quantity of inflated reports filled with superlatives; in effect, any review of performance appraisals boils down to a consideration of who wrote the report, what other reports have they prepared, and what didn't they say that they should have said. More often than not, reports submitted on employees will reflect primarily the strengths and weaknesses of the rater (the impact of this factor substantially limits the validity and use of any individual performance appraisal). To complicate matters even further, supervisors are often not sure "what" is really being rated—their subordinates' work performance, or their own writing ability.

Another difficulty with the concept of performance appraisal is that some

Fundamental Flaws in Employee Performance Appraisal

Consider the pyramiding required for performance appraisal to be objective. Most contemporary organizations are not assembly lines with clear inputs and material outputs. The majority of occupations are office based and deal with intangible information exchanges. Especially in the public sector we serve diverse clientele, respond to requests, and communicate. Our days are varied; they vary by season, budget cycle, and externally generated deadlines. All these activities are somewhat artificially gathered under the umbrella and named such and such unit, agency, or department. Such organizations are vastly complex macroorganizations made up of already extremely complex subgroups in turn made up of multifaceted individuals. Out of this "primordial stew" we first evaluate jobs by breaking them down to minute components, attempting thereby to distill the essential tasks by removing their human incumbents from consideration. We then articulate a position classification system that arrays clusters of tasks according to various criteria by which their comparative worth can be assessed . . . We must then take *each* task or cluster of tasks and figure out precisely what level of performance, or which performance targets, may be termed "unsatisfactory," "needs improvement," "satisfactory," "fully satisfactory," and "outstanding." Once all this has been done we then ask a supervisor semiannually or annually to take the results of this fantastic series of abstract calculations, now reduced to a form, and use it to gauge the complex, interdependent, variegated activities of individual job incumbents. The end result of this process is to be objective data of sufficient validity to compare and reward or punish employees from across the entire organization.

If, for public relations purposes, or to save face, the political powers that be feel the need to maintain some sort of performance appraisal system, let them have the shadow of one. They will, over time, probably become that anyway as organizations adjust to the human reality that full-blown, objective, performance audits simply cannot be done . . . that seems to be the direction that the federal government was heading as it switched from the extremely punitive Merit Pay System . . . to the more lenient and flexible Performance Management and Recognition System in 1984. . . . A less complicated approach that I recommend in order to establish a defensible legal base for the occasionally needed adverse personnel action—firing or demoting, for example—is a simple form outlining position duties with only two rating categories: "unsatisfactory" and "fully satisfactory." . . . "Courts do not reject the subjective approach." You just have to be consistent in your subjectivity.

Whatever the strategy, we should work to abolish or mitigate formal performance appraisal as we know it.

Charles J. Fox. "Employee Performance Appraisal: The Keystone Made of Clay," in Carolyn, Ban and Norma M. Riccucci (eds.). *Public Personnel Management: Current Concerns, Future Challenges* (White Plains, N.Y.: Longman Press, 1991), pp. 63 and 68.

of the functions it is designed to serve conflict with each other. For example, appraisal of performance (what has been done on the job) and potential (the capacity to do other jobs) may be in contrast to one another in that the qualities desirable for performance in one job aren't necessarily those needed in a higher-level job. The individual who works well independently in one particular job may be a total loss in another job that requires considerable social interaction.

Perhaps the best assessment of the general utility of performance appraisal systems has been provided by Harry Levinson, who wrote in a *Harvard Business Review* article that despite its significance for effective management and the great deal of effort expended in developing such systems, the results have been fairly dismal. Levinson asserts that "there are few effective established mechanisms to cope with either the sense of inadequacy managers have about appraising subordinates, or the paralysis and procrastination that result from guilt about playing God." To those who might argue that these problems are deficiencies of individual managers and not of the managerial system, Levinson holds that "even if that were altogether true, managers are part of the system. Performance appraisal needs to be viewed not as a technique but as a process involving both people and data, and as such the whole process is inadequate."

Probably one of the most damning indictments of performance appraisal systems can be found in comparing the viewpoints of employees themselves over time. In OPM's 1979 *Federal Employee Attitudes* survey, only about half of the 14,000 employees who participated in the survey felt their performance appraisals were accurate and fair; over half thought their superiors gave the same rating regardless of performance. The 1979 report summary, in a model of understatement, observed that "the current usefulness of performance feedback is questionable at best." The report found that "almost half of the employees said their performance ratings are not useful in assessing their strengths and weaknesses, improving their performance or determining their contribution to the organization. Even more say that feedback is not helpful either in planning for or receiving needed training."

A decade later, the MSPB stated in its 1989 report, *Working for America* (involving over 16,000 federal-worker respondents), that two-thirds of all employees feel their ratings are accurate but that over 60 percent now receive ratings of above fully satisfactory. So, even when rating inflation largely dominates, there still remains a significant portion of employees who disagree with their ratings. Furthermore, over 60 percent of the survey respondents reported that they had little or no involvement in the determination of their performance standards. The survey ratings don't differ much from OPM's central personnel data files on the distribution of performance ratings. The MSPB concluded:

> What is to be made of a performance rating system in which two-thirds of all employees are rated "above the norm" on their performance? What, indeed, when most of the remaining one-third are rated as meeting the "fully successful" norm

and many of them disagree with the accuracy of their ratings? What do these employee responses say about the system? Or about the perception of a "fully successful" rating?

Can the same discouraging note be sounded for state and local government efforts? The credibility of performance appraisal programs at the state and local level is probably even lower because many jurisdictions don't have ongoing systems or they use only the most cursory types of evaluation reporting formats. While there are many exceptions, the overall record here is certainly no better than that of the federal government or of private industry. Of course, private industry has found traditionally that unless the evaluations are kept confidential, they too end up overinflated and of little use.

The Traditional Approach to Performance Appraisal

The standard method of performance appraisal is a written performance evaluation report prepared by the supervisor for a specific time period of an employee's performance. Many jurisdictions require annual evaluations and tie time-in-grade salary increases to satisfactory performance. Written evaluations generally include one or more of the following:

1. A delineation of specific duties and responsibilities
2. Specification of objectives or results to be produced for the time period (as previously agreed upon)
3. Rating scales to evaluate specific performance factors
4. A narrative about specific work accomplishments
5. A rating and/or narrative about the employee's potential for advancement
6. An overall scoring of the employee's performance

Most written evaluations begin with some form of descriptive listing of the work being accomplished. This provides a frame of reference for reviewing the report and can often be used for classification purposes. A more elaborate aspect of this type of work specification is to spell out performance objectives or indicate work products that will be produced over a certain period. In addition, this type of performance-by-objectives narrative normally includes a section to indicate any special circumstances or environmental constraints that may arise during the rating period. While this approach seems well designed to clarify working objectives, the written objectives tend to be either too vague or simply unmeasurable. There is no way to evaluate the apparent difficulty or the qualitative aspect of meeting the objective, much less to make valid comparisons against other reports. Too many unanswered questions remain: Were they appropriate for the individual? Were they actually under the individual's control? What do the objectives indicate about the "how" of performance as opposed to the "what"?

Rating scales represent a "multichoice" dimension of the performance report. The degree to which closed-ended scales or forced choices are used will increase the degree of capability to compare reports. Scales can be of several varieties, the most common being continuous (or integer) scales and discontinuous (discrete-unit) scales. The latter, a discrete-unit scale, forces the rater to choose one out of the four or five responses that is most descriptive, as seen in the following example:

Written
communication _____ Does not get ideas across clearly on paper.

_____ Can do simple drafting. Writing often lacks clarity, brevity, or effectiveness. Composition usually requires extensive editorial revision.

_____ Writing is understandable, to the point, and acceptably organized. Composition usually requires little editing.

_____ Writes clearly and effectively. Composition and style are admirably suited to the objective. Product rarely requires editing.

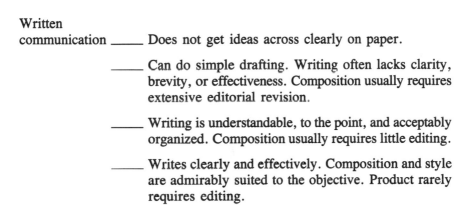

Do Federal Government Employees See a Link Between Pay and Performance?

Here is how federal government employees* responded to the following question: "If you perform better in your present job, how likely is it that you will receive more pay?"

Pay category of respondent	Percentage responding very likely or somewhat likely
Prevailing rate	33
General Schedule (GS)	30
Performance Management and Recognition System (GM)	45
Senior Executive Service	39

*Based on a sample of 21,620 employees.

U.S. Merit Systems Protection Board, *Federal Personnel Policies and Practices* (Washington, D.C.: USMSPB, 1987), p. 7.

_____ Composition has all qualities of excellence: clarity, precision, conciseness, good organization, persuasiveness, and style. Only occasional minor editing is ever required.

A continuous scale provides more latitude for choice, in that the rater scores the quality on a scale of 1 to 10 (or whatever) and is provided with descriptions of certain interval points on the scale, as the following example shows:

Dependability __0__ Fails to follow instructions, unable to meet commitments or complete work on time.

__1__

__2__

__3__ Needs undue amount of supervision to comply with instructions or to meet deadlines and commitments.

__4__

__5__ Conscientious and steady worker. Fulfills commitments, meets deadlines, and produces useful work with normal supervision.

__6__

__7__ Conscientious and reliable worker. Completes each task, meets deadlines and commitments with a minimum of supervision.

__8__

__9__

__10__ Invariably meets the most difficult deadlines and commitments. Follows through even without special supervision.

The narrative portions of a written evaluation report can be undirected and designed to allow the rater maximum discretion, or they can be directed so that the rater must describe preselected qualities, providing examples and a general assessment of the quality involved. Narrative exercises can also be designed to address areas for improvement or weaknesses, in an effort to combat inflated performance reports. Unfortunately, this tends to encourage supervisors to search for and relate weaknesses that are not really weaknesses or are so general as to be applicable to everyone.

Since written evaluations can be constructed in various ways, there is a tendency to constantly experiment and change the format of the performance evaluation report. In actuality, this represents an attempt by personnel managers to continually change the evaluation "system" so as to beat down "inflated reports." Making constant revisions in the reporting format may achieve the objective of keeping the system one step ahead, but at the cost of making historical comparisons of performance reports virtually impossible and creating uncertainty among supervisors as to what the "current" instructions are for completing the reports.

The inadequacies of written evaluation reports have led to the use of other methods of performance appraisal that essentially reflect different modes of the standard written evaluation technique. Many of these new methods have focused on changing who actually writes the performance report. Four such methods are:

1. *Self-appraisals*—Where individuals write some form of narrative or submit some work product to document their work performance.
2. *Peer ratings*—Where each individual rates every other employee in the division or office at a parallel level in the organization.
3. *Subordinate ratings*—Where the subordinates rate the performance of a supervisor.
4. *Group or external ratings*—Where an independent rater, usually a counselor or other qualified expert, will rate performance based on selected interviews or on-the-job visits. Assessment centers would be an example.

By changing the rater, an entirely different perspective can be obtained. However, the use of new performance appraisal methods seems to primarily represent a general dissatisfaction with traditional written reports. Most studies have found no significant relationships between size or type of organization and the type of performance appraisal system in existence. If there is no trend toward one particular system, it is also difficult to say whether these new modes of evaluation represent advances in evaluation methodologies. They do indicate, however, a trend toward more collaborative systems. The 1989 MSPB study *Working for America* addressed some possible changes. It asked about the possibility of converting performance ratings to a pass-fail approach—60 percent disagreed. The idea of limiting the number of high performance ratings was suggested—50 percent disagreed. Figure 15.2 shows the responses to the survey question regarding other involvement in the rating process. Fifty-six percent reject the idea of involving co-workers or peers, 27 percent reject second level supervisors and 7 percent even reject individual

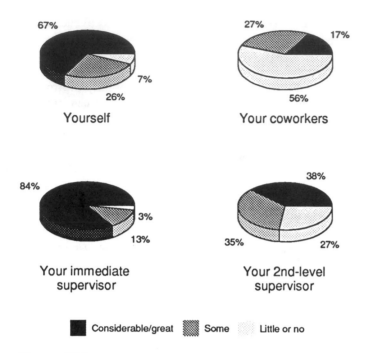

67%

7%

26%

Yourself

27%

17%

56%

Your coworkers

84%

3%

13%

Your immediate
supervisor

38%

35%   27%

Your 2nd-level
supervisor

■ Considerable/great ▨ Some ▨ Little or no

Figure 15.2.   Who should be allowed to provide input into performance ratings? Note: "No basis to judge" responses omitted. *Source*: U.S. Merit Systems Protection Board, *Working for America* (Washington, D.C. USMSPB, 1990), p. 17.

involvement. To this end, performance appraisal seems destined to be subject to both universal complaint and universal rejection of ideas for change. This is not to imply that appraisal hasn't changed at all; indeed, it has gone through a profound metamorphosis over the past two decades.

Changing the System: The Behavioral Focus

Beginning in the 1970s, a new focus emerged from the failures of the past. While it would be unfair to attribute it to any one specific source, the works of John Campbell, Larry Cummings and Donald Schwab have been particularly significant in signaling this change. In brief, the argument has been to shift performance measurement to observable work *behaviors* as opposed to measures of organization effectiveness. The point is that effectiveness generally

involves additional factors that are beyond the control of the individual. The
emphasis, it was argued, should be to construct behaviorally based rating scales
or behaviorally anchored rating scales (BARS). Statistical results showed considerably less distortion, bias, and variance when this technique was used.

The new thrust in performance appraisal was to write performance standards that were behaviorally based. What was added to the methodology is
the job analysis technique that is used to determine which job behaviors are
most important and thus should be measured. Job analysis would involve an
extensive review of positions to determine what the job elements were. A
job element is defined as a distinguishable, goal-oriented unit of work required by the position. Once the job elements are listed, some form of ranking process would be used to identify which elements were critical (i.e., defined
in performance terms as an area in which below-minimum performance would
be a basis for removal or demotion). Finally, performance standards would
be established for those critical job elements and incorporated into a performance evaluation reporting format.

Degrees → Factors	Far exceeds job requirements	Exceeds job requirements	Meets job requirements	Needs some improvement	Does not meet minimum requirements
Quality	Leaps tall buildings in a single bound.	Must take running start to leap over tall buildings.	Can leap over short buildings only.	Crashes into buildings when attempting to jump over them.	Cannot recognize building at a glance.
Timeliness	Is faster than a speeding bullet.	Is as fast as a speeding bullet.	Not quite as fast as a speeding bullet.	Would you believe a slow bullet?	Wounds self with bullet when attempting to shoot.
Initiative	Is stronger than a locomotive.	Is stronger than a bull elephant.	Is stronger than a bull.	Shoots the bull.	Believes cock and bull stories.
Adaptability	Walks on water consistently.	Walks on water in emergencies.	Washes with water.	Drinks water.	Sleeps on a water bed.
Communication	Talks with God.	Talks with the angels.	Talks to himself.	Argues with himself.	Loses those arguments.

Figure 15.3. Performance guide for evaluating employees. *Source: Civil Service Journal*, 19 (April–June 1979), p. 53.

Priscilla Levinson writes in *A Guide for Improving Performance Appraisal*:

> Since job duties and performance standards are interrelated, it is common practice to develop them at the same time. Any standard needs to be consistent with the grade level of the position and reflect duties and responsibilities contained in the position description. There are several methods for analyzing jobs to develop job duties and performance standards. Whichever method is used should take into account both the quantitative and qualitative aspects of performance as well as timing and level of achievement. Quantitative measures include such things as number of forms processed, amount of time used, number of errors, number of pages typed, etc. Qualitative measures include accuracy, quality of work, ability to coordinate, analyze, evaluate, etc. Almost all jobs involve both aspects of performance, but in varying proportions depending on the nature of the job. A production job on an assembly line may depend as much on quantity as on quality of production whereas a research job may emphasize the quality of results with quantity being a minor consideration. Most work situations vary between these examples. It is easier, of course, to measure performance against standards which can be stated and measured in quantitative terms. However, a complete set of performance standards for a job probably will contain some objectives which cannot be quantitatively measured. Supervisory and managerial positions have an added component because of the nature of the positions. Some duties and responsibilities reflect individual performance. Examples are fulfilling equal employment opportunity responsibilities, recommending or making personnel decisions in accordance with merit principles, appraising subordinates fairly and accurately in accordance with previously established standards, and developing subordinates. Other duties and responsibilities of supervisors and managers reflect the performance of the organization for which the individual is responsible—i.e., the degree to which the organizational objectives are met.

This new focus places special emphasis on performance standards and how they should be developed. Levinson provides a detailed discussion of these approaches and the advantages and limitations of each:

1. Position description method
    a. *Description and uses*—The position description, in addition to containing the classification series and grade, should also serve as a written record of what the employee is expected to do. It includes information such as job duties, responsibilities, work products, and level of supervision received. It is typical for the position description to be written by a manager or supervisor and revised as needed when the duties of the job change. Refinements in the process are made by classification specialists and others who base their results on observation of employees and analysis of the job. The resulting position description is more objective and accurate than the one developed by the supervisor alone.
    b. *Advantages and limitations*—The economy, speed, convenience,

and job knowledge of a single person who knows the job thoroughly (i.e., the supervisor) are advantages of using the position description method. Shortcomings include the single point of view on which the standard is based and the supervisor's frequent lack of training in carrying out job analysis and preparing position descriptions. One of the major problems in writing job descriptions and performance standards is in incorporating the qualitative aspects of the job because they are so difficult to assess objectively.

2. Expert individual or group approach to job analysis

a. *Description and uses*—Many organizations use either a job analysis expert or a team composed of specialists in fields such as position classification, job analysis, and personnel management to improve the process of collecting data and making judgments about all of the pertinent information relating to the nature of a specific job.

As a first step, the individual specialist or the team collects such background information as organization charts, classification specifications, training manuals, and pertinent regulations. Second, a sample is selected of positions that are representative of the job, keeping in mind such factors as location, size of the organization, and amount of public contact. The next step involves gathering job data. This may be done by using one or more of the following methods: interviews, questionnaires, work plans, and job diaries or time sheets (records of job duties over a period of time). Information that is collected from different sources and obtained by more than one method of collection is more reliable than data collected from one source. At the same time that data on job duties are being obtained, information can be collected to use in developing standards to measure performance of those job duties. The final steps involve analyzing the information, knowledge, skills, abilities, and other characteristics needed for the job.

Another type of expert group approach to job analysis is called the *job element method*. It is based on quantifying the opinions of job experts who, as supervisors or as expert workers, know the requirements of the job. They work under the direction of a person who is familiar with the job element method of analysis. An interesting sidelight of this technique is a self-report checklist by which employees may describe their own qualifications in terms of the pertinent job elements. The checklist may be useful in making selections and in identifying possible causes of poor performance.

b. *Advantages and limitations*—The various methods that make use of one or more job analysis experts may be expected to yield more complete, accurate, and precise job information, which in turn leads to clearer, more useful performance standards. The job element method has the advantage of yielding job-related data that are useful for several purposes, such as developing rating checklists and constructing examinations. There is also an optional procedure for selecting job elements that are important in developing training programs. Although the job element method has been used primarily for examining blue-collar occupations, it is now being expanded to include a variety of white-collar occupations, particularly by the OPM.

3. Participative methods

a. *Description and uses*—Although the above-mentioned methods provide for obtaining job information from employees, none of them involves employees to the extent that the participative method does. Active participation is an important characteristic of techniques such as management by objectives (MBO) and the related but more limited work planning and review (WPR) systems. These systems are not, however, job analysis methods for developing performance standards for most jobs. For those higher-level jobs characterized by few measurable work products and great involvement in planning and decision making, performance standards and goals may be determined not by job analysis but by agreement between employee and supervisor using MBO and WPR methods. For most jobs, however, it is a good idea to have initial performance standards determined by job analysis, even if some of the standards may be later modified by agreement between supervisor and employee. In the participative methods, employees and their supervisors are involved in planning work, setting goals and objectives to be met, and periodically reviewing and revising work plans. Goals and objectives that meet at least minimum standards are documented in quantitative terms if possible (i.e., a specified kind and amount of work will be done within a certain time limit). Thus, employees can readily assess their progress before any formal appraisal takes place. Some participative plans have provisions for employees to actively contribute to the appraisal process by carrying out self-ratings.

Management by objectives uses a participative approach as part of a broad plan to integrate organizational and personal goals at all organizational levels. Usually, this approach calls for all employees to participate in varying degrees in setting organizational objectives as well as planning their work, appraising their performance, and planning their career development. Target dates are set, and at predetermined times, the results are measured against the projected goals. To be successful, MBO programs require of management: careful planning, active participation, follow-up, and a regular review procedure.

The WPR method, which is narrower in scope than MBO, emphasizes the periodic review of work plans by employee and supervisor to acknowledge goals reached, identify problems and hindrances, exchange ideas and information about solutions, determine areas of specific need such as training, and review and update the goals and objectives in the work plan.

b. *Advantages and limitations*—The participative approach, by being oriented to the amount and quality of work accomplished, makes it possible to appraise performance more in terms of specific work goals rather than of ambiguous personal qualities. Thus, an advantage of this method is that its emphasis is on evaluating the characteristics of the work being done, not the characteristics of the employee doing the work. Employee involvement in work planning, performance standards, and appraisals promotes fairer, more objective performance appraisal and results in improved work performance and motivation. The MBO approach appears to be more successful when applied to managerial, executive, and professional jobs than to other kinds of positions. There are some organizations, however, using variations of the participative approach in work planning and review with employees in other occupational fields at several organizational levels.

Assessment Centers

Some have advocated abandoning the idea of individual performance appraisal altogether. Their alternative is to develop an external methodology for discovering what qualities were essential for successful performance in the organization. This concept involves establishing an assessment center for identifying individuals with future executive potential.

Actually, the term assessment center never implies a particular place; rather, it is a method—a comprehensive standardized measurement process that requires the employees being evaluated to participate in simulated real-life situations. Multiple evaluation techniques are used that include a range of approaches to simulating work situations: group discussions, in-basket exercises, simulation of interviews with subordinates, oral presentations, and written communication exercises. The assessment center is designed to evaluate candidates in a number of stressful situations over a period of several days for behaviors and abilities that are crucial for successful performance. How does an organization know which behaviors and abilities to test for? This information is provided by a job analysis of potential future positions. If first-line supervisors are being evaluated for middle-management potential, then the assessment center's exercise should test for the traits via a job analysis so that assessment center exercises could be selected or invented to test for those qualities.

The assessment center concept is far from new. Assessment center techniques were used by the German Army for selecting officers in World War I. The American Office of Strategic Services (OSS) used them for selecting secret agents in World War II. However, the assessment center concept did not reach American industry until the mid-1950s when AT&T pioneered a program. The practice spread during the 1960s, but it wasn't until 1969 that a government agency, the Internal Revenue Service, used assessment center methodology on a large scale. Today, such techniques have been used by government agencies at all jurisdictional levels, including the state of Illinois, the city of Philadelphia, and a host of federal agencies.

Typical Assessment Center Exercises

Assigned Role Group Discussion.   In this leaderless group discussion, participants, acting as a city council of a hypothetical city, must allocate a one-million dollar federal grant in the time allotted or make other judgments on the varying proposals offered. Each participant is assigned a point of view to sell to the other team members and is provided with a choice of projects to back and the opportunity to bargain and trade off projects for support.

Nonassigned Role Group Discussion.   This exercise is a cooperative, leaderless group discussion in which four short case studies dealing with problems faced by executives working in state government agencies are presented to a group of six participants. The participants act as consultants who must make group recommendations on each of the problems. Assessors observe the participant's role in the group and the handling of the content of the discussion.

In-basket Exercise.   Problems that challenge middle- and upper-level executives in state governments are simulated in the in-basket exercise. These include relationships with departmental superiors, subordinates and peers, representatives of other departments, representatives of executive and legislative branches, the public, and the news media. Taking over a new job, the participant must deal with memos, letters, policies, bills, etc., found in the in-basket. After the in-basket has been completed, the participants is interviewed by an assessor concerning his/or handling of the various in-basket items.

Speech and Writing Exercises.   Each participant is given a written, narrative description of a policy, event, situation, etc. and three specific situational problems related to the narrative, each requiring a written response. The participant is also required to make a formal oral presentation, based upon the background narrative description, before a simulated news conference attended by the Capitol Press Corps and interested government officials and citizens (assessors).

Analysis Problem.   The analysis problem is an individual exercise. The participant is given a considerable amount of data regarding a state agency's field operations, which he/she must analyze and about which he/she must make a number of management recommendations. The exercise is designed to elicit behaviors related to various dimensions of managerial effectiveness. The primary area of behavior evaluated in this exercise is the ability to sift through data and find pertinent information to reach a logical and practical conclusion.

Paper and Pencil Tests.   Three different commercially available objectively scoreable tests are included in the assessment: a reading test used for self-development purposes, a reasoning-ability test, and a personality test. The latter two are being used experimentally at present, and as with the reading test, are not made available during assessor discussions.

William C. Byham and Carl Wettengal, "Assessment Centers for Supervisors and Managers," *Public Personnel Management*, 3 (September–October 1974), p. 241. Reprinted by permission of the International Personnel Management Association, 1850 K Street, N.W., Suite 870, Washington, D.C. 20006.

The assessors used in an assessment center are usually employees in the organization who are several levels higher than the candidates and have been specially trained in assessment center evaluation methods. The assessors function as a team—usually one assessor for each of two candidates—and they rotate so they can observe different candidates in each exercise. After the candidates have completed their exercises, the team of assessors confers and produces a report or assessment for each candidate.

Assessments are frequently used as justifications for both advancement and career development opportunities. It is not uncommon for an employee's assessment to recommend a particular course of training that could compensate for a noticed deficiency. To assure the validity of an assessment process and to meet equity requirements, assessment center exercises must demonstrably test for qualities that can be shown to be necessary to the job level in question. Position requirements, which must be determined through a prior job analysis, are reviewed and those that can be assessed adequately by the employee's current job performance should be deleted since the appropriate evaluation mechanism for "current" performance is the regular performance appraisal.

While the assessment center methodologies are still so new as to be aptly termed experimental, they have proven to be substantially more reliable predictors of future performance than traditional written examinations or panel interviews. But while assessment centers may have resolved one set of problems, they also generate their own unique problems. At present, most organizations base their decisions on who will be assessed on some form of supervisor's recommendation or individual voluntary basis. As the assessment center concept is more widely adopted, one question will become more and more commonplace: If the door to management development and advancement goes through the assessment center, who will be the gatekeeper? Unless the organization can afford to process its entire management cadre through assessment centers, those individuals not selected for attendance might justifiably conclude they have been negatively evaluated because the organization did not judge them to be worthy of formal evaluation. The decision (or nondecision) not to send an individual to an assessment center while peers are being sent could even have considerable legal ramifications. Since management development funds will continue to be a scarce resource, any jurisdiction implementing an assessment center program must also be concerned with designing an equitable nomination process.

Another potential problem with assessment centers is that they may be too efficient in replicating existing management values. A possible danger in any assessment center program is that the assessors will seek to reproduce themselves by scoring high those individuals who tend to reflect their personalities, leadership styles, and lengths of hair; or that the exercises used will self-select the past. The last thing any management development program should do is produce a management corps with the same values and attitudes as the previous managerial generation. The best way of guarding against this potential nightmare is to use the organization's best and most active line managers as assessors. It should go without saying that any manager the organization would wish to use as a "full-time assessor" should not be allowed to assess anyone. This especially includes the personnel operatives. Personnel's job is to facilitate a decisional task that belongs to line management. Another possibly dysfunctional aspect of an assessment center program is the "crown prince" phenomenon. Some individuals who do exceedingly well at the assessment center may feel that their future is so assured that their on-the-job performance slackens. No organization should rely entirely on assessment center reports. Such scores comprise only one of a variety of factors that should be considered when it is time to make decisions on management development and advancement. The above-mentioned caveats notwithstanding, assessment centers have already proven to be of such value that personnelists should not only be aware of their procedures, but they should also be prepared to install centers in their own organizations.

Bibliography

Adelsberg, Henri van. "Relating Performance Evaluation to Compensation of Public Employees," *Public Personnel Management*, 7 (March–April 1978).

Bann, Charles and Jerald Johnson. "Federal Employee Attitudes Toward Reform: Performance Evaluation and Merit Pay," in Patricia W. Ingraham and Carolyn Ban (eds.). *Legislating Bureaucratic Change: The Civil Service Reform Act of 1978*. Albany, N.Y.: SUNY-Albany Press, 1984.

Basnight, Thomas and Benjamin W. Wolkinson. "Evaluating Managerial Performance: Is Your Appraisal System Legal?" *Employee Relations Law Journal* (autumn 1977).

Beer, Michael and Robert Rich. "Employee Growth through Performance Management," *Harvard Business Review* (July–August 1976).

Borman, W. D. and Marvin Dunnette. "Behavior-based versus Trait-Oriented Performance Ratings: An Empirical Study," *Journal of Psychology*, vol. 60 (1975).

Brinkerhof, Derek W. and Rosabeth Moss Kanter. "Appraising the Performance of Performance Appraisal," *Sloan Management Review* (Spring 1980).

Bray, Douglas W. "The Assessment Center Method," in *Training and Development Handbook*, 2nd ed., edited by Robert L. Craig. New York: McGraw-Hill, 1976.

Brumback, Gary B. "Toward a New Theory and System of Performance Evaluation: A Standardized, MBO-oriented Approach," *Public Personnel Management*, 7 (July–August 1978).

Burke, Ronald J. "Why Performance Appraisal Systems Fail," *Personnel Administration* (May–June 1972).

Byham, William C. and Carl Wettengel. "Assessment Centers for Supervisors and Managers," *Public Personnel Management*, 3 (September–October 1974).

Campbell, John P. et al. "The Development and Evaluation of Behaviorally Based Rating Scales," *Journal of Applied Psychology*, vol. 57 (1973).

Cascio, Wayne F. "Scientific, Legal and Operational Imperatives of Workable Performance Appraisal Systems," *Public Personnel Management*, 11 (1982), pp. 367–375.

Cascio, Wayne F. and H. John Bernardin. "Implications of Performance Appraisal Litigation for Personnel Decisions," *Personnel Psychology*, vol. 34, 1981.

Clark, Cynthia et al. "Job Elements and Performance Appraisal," *Management* (September 1979).

Clement, Ronald W. and Eileen K. Aranda. "Performance Appraisal in the Public Sector: Truth or Consequences," *Review of Public Personnel Administration* (fall 1984).

Cummings, Larry L. and D. P. Schwab. *Performance in Organizations: Determinants and Appraisal*. Glenview, Ill.: Scott, Foresman, 1973.

Daley, Dennis M. "Monitoring the Use of Appraisal-By-Objectives in Iowa: Research Note," *Review of Public Personnel Administration*, vol. 3, no. 3 (1983), pp. 33–44.

———. "An Examination of the MBO/Performance Standard Approach to Employee Evaluation: Attitudes toward Performance Appraisal in Iowa," *Review of Public Personnel Administration*, vol. 6, no. 1 (1985), pp. 11–28.

Davies, C. and A. Francis. "The Many Dimensions of Performance Measurement," *Organizational Dynamics*, 3 (winter 1975).

Enell, John W. and George H. Haas. *Setting Standards for Executive Performance*. New York: American Management Association, 1960.

Feild, Hubert S. and William H. Holley. "Performance Appraisal: An Analysis of State-wide Practices," *Public Personnel Management*, 4 (May–June 1975).

————. "The Relationship of Performance Appraisal System Characteristics to Verdicts in Selected Employment Discrimination Cases," *Academy of Management Journal*, vol. 25 (1982).

Finn, R. H. and P. A. Fontaine. "Performance Appraisal: Some Dynamics and Dilemmas," *Public Personnel Management* (fall 1984).

Fox, Charles J. "Employee Performance Appraisal: The Keystone Made of Clay," in Carolyn Ban and Norma M. Riccucci (eds.). *Public Personnel Management: Current Concerns, Future Challenges*. White Plains, N.Y.: Longman Press, 1991.

Fox, William M. "Consentient Merit Rating: A Critical Incident Approach," *Personnel*, vol. 58, no. 3 (1981), pp. 72–78.

Gabris, Gerald T. "Can Merit Pay Systems Avoid Creating Discord Between Supervisors and Subordinates?: Another Uneasy Look at Performance Appraisal," *Review of Public Personnel Administration*, vol. 7, no. 1 (1986), pp. 70–89.

Gabris, Gerald T. and Kenneth Mitchell. "Merit Based on Performance Appraisal and Productivity: Do Employees Perceive the Connection?" *Public Productivity Review*, vol. 9 (1985), pp. 311–327.

Gaertner, Karen N. and Gregory H. Gaertner. "Performance Evaluation and Merit Pay: Results in the Environmental Protection Agency and the Mine Safety and Health Administration," in Patricia W. Ingraham and Carolyn Ban (eds.). *Legislating Bureaucratic Change: The Civil Service Reform Act of 1978*. Albany, N.Y.: SUNY Press, 1984.

————. "Performance-Contingent Pay for Federal Managers," *Administration and Society*, vol. 17 (1985), pp. 7–20.

Geis, A. Arthur. "Making Merit Pay Work," *Personnel*, vol. 64, no. 1 (1987), pp. 32–60.

Halachmi, Arie and Marc Holzer. "Merit Pay, Performance Targeting, and Productivity," *Review of Public Personnel Administration*, vol. 7, no. 2 (1987), pp. 80–91.

Heyel, Carl. *Appraising Executive Performance*. New York: American Management Association, 1958.

Holley, William H. and Hubert S. Field. "Will Your Performance Appraisal Hold Up in Court? *Personnel*, vol. 59 (1982).

Hughs, Garry L. and Erich P. Prien. "An Evaluation of Alternate Scoring Methods for the Mixed Standard Scale," *Personnel Psychology*, vol. 39 (1986), pp. 839–848.

Huse, Edgar. "Performance Appraisal: A New Look," *Personnel Administration*, 30 (March–April 1967).

Hyde, Albert C. and Wayne Cascio. "Performance Appraisal in the Post Reform Era," a symposium in *Public Personnel Management* (winter 1982).

Kane, Jeffrey S. and Kimberly A. Freeman. "MBO and Performance Appraisal: A Mixture That's Not a Solution, Part 1," *Personnel*, vol. 63, no. 12 (1986), pp. 26–36.

————. "MBO and Performance Appraisal: A Mixture That's Not a Solution, Part 2," *Personnel*, vol. 64, no. 2 (1987) pp. 26–33.

Kearney, William J. "The Value of Behaviorally Based Performance Appraisals," *Business Horizon*, 19 (June 1976).

Kleiman, Lawrence S. and Richard L. Durham. "Performance Appraisal, Promotion and the Courts: A Critical Review," *Personnel Psychology*, vol. 34 (1981).

Koontz, Harold. *Appraising Managers as Managers*. New York: McGraw-Hill, 1971.

Kopelman, Richard E. "Linking Pay to Performance Is a Proven Management Tool," *Personnel Administrator*, vol. 28, no. 10 (1983), pp. 60–68.

Koss, Margo et al. *Do Employee Performance Appraisal Systems in State and Local Governments Contribute to Productivity Improvements? Can They?* Washington, D.C.: the Urban Institute, 1978.

Landy, Frank J. et al. "Behaviorally Anchored Scales for Rating the Performance of Police Officers," *Journal of Applied Psychology* (December 1976).

————. and James L. Farr. "Performance Rating" *Psychologic Bulletin*, vol. 87 (1980).

Latham, Gary P. and K. N. Wexley. "Behavioral Observation Scales for Performance Appraisal Purposes," *Personnel Psychology*, vol. 30 (1977).

Latham, Gary P., Lise M. Saari, and Charles H. Fay. "BOS, BES, and Baloney: Raising Kane with Bernardin." *Personnel Psychology*, vol. 33 (1980), pp. 815–821.

Lazer, Robert I. and Walter S. Wikstrom. *Appraising Managerial Performance: Current Practices and Future Directions*. New York: the Conference Board, 1977.

Levinson, H. "Appraisal of What Performance?" *Harvard Business Review*, 54 (July–August 1976).

Levinson, Priscilla. *A Guide for Improving Performance Appraisal: A Handbook*. Washington, D.C.: U.S. Office of Personnel Management, 1979.

_____. and Mary Sugar. "Performance Evaluation and Rating," *Civil Service Journal*, 18 (July–September 1977).

Linenburger, Patricia and Timothy J. Kearney. "Performance Appraisal Standards Used by the Courts," *Personnel Administrator* (May 1981).

Lovrich, Nicholas P. Jr., Paul L. Shaffer, Ronald H. Hopkins, and Donald A. Yale. "Do Public Servants Welcome or Fear Merit Evaluation of Their Performance?" *Public Administration Review*, vol. 44 (1980), pp. 214–222.

MacLane, Charles N. "The Design and Development of an Inter-Organizational Performance Evaluation and Referral System," U.S. Office of Personnel Management technical memorandum 79-19. Washington, D.C., 1978.

McConkie, Mark L. "A Clarification of the Goal Setting and Appraisal Processes in MBO," *Academy of Management Review*, vol. 4 (1979), pp. 29–40.

McCrensky, Edward. "Increasing the Effectiveness of Staff Performance Appraisal Systems," *Public Personnel Management*, 7 (July–August 1978).

McEvoy, Glenn M. "Predicting Managerial Performance: A Seven Year Assessment Center Validation Study," *Proceedings of the Academy of Management*, vol. 48 (1988), pp. 277–281.

McGregor, Douglas. "An Uneasy Look at Performance Appraisal," *Harvard Business Review* (May–June 1957; reprinted May–June 1975).

McNish, Linda C. "A Critical Review of Performance Appraisal at the Federal Level: The Experience of the PHS," *Review of Public Personnel Administration*, vol. 7, no. 1 (1986), pp. 42–56.

Marcoulides, George A. and R. Bryant Mills. "Employee Performance Appraisal: A New Technique," *Review of Public Personnel Administration*, vol. 8, no. 3 (1988), pp. 105–115.

Meyer, H. H. "The Pay-for-Performance Dilemma." *Organizational Dynamics* (Winter 1975).

————. E. Kay, and J. R. French Jr. "Split Roles in Performance Appraisal," *Harvard Business Review*, 43 (January–February 1965).

Millard, C. W., F. Luthans, and R. L. Otteman. "A New Breakthrough for Performance Appraisal," *Business Horizons*, 19 (August 1976).

Morrisey, George L. *Appraisal and Development through Objectives and Results*. Reading, Mass.: Addison-Wesley, 1972.

Murphy, Kevin P. and Joseph I. Constons. "Behavioral Anchors as a Source of Bias of Rating," *Journal of Applied Psychology*, vol. 72 (1987), pp. 573–577.

Nachmias, David and Paul J. Moderacki. "Patterns of Support for Merit Pay and EEO Performance: The Inherent Difficulties of Implementing Innovation," *Policy Studies Journal*, vol. 11 (1982), pp. 318–327.

Nalbandian, John. "Performance Appraisal: If Only People Weren't Involved," *Public Administration Review* (May–June 1981).

Nigro, Lloyd G. "Attitudes of Federal Employees Toward Performance Appraisal and Merit Pay: Implications for CSRA Implementation," *Public Administration Review*, vol. 41 (1981), pp. 84–86.

————. "CSRA Performance Appraisals and Merit Pay: Growing Uncertainty in the Federal Work Force," *Public Administration Review*, vol. 42 (1982), pp. 371–375.

Oberg, Winston. "Make Performance Appraisal Relevant," *Harvard Business Review*, 50 (January–February 1972).

O'Toole, Daniel E. and John R. Churchill. "Implementing Pay-for-Performance: Initial Experiences," *Review of Public Personnel Administration*, vol. 2, no. 3 (1982), pp. 13–28.

Pearce, Jone L. and James L. Perry. "Federal Merit Pay: A Longitudinal Analysis," *Public Administration Review*, vol. 43 (1983), pp. 315–325.

Pearce, Jone L., William B. Stevenson, and James L. Perry. "Managerial Compensation Based on Organizational Performance: A Time Series Analysis of the Effects of Merit Pay," *Academy of Managerial Journal*, vol. 28 (1985), pp. 261–278.

Perry, James L. "Merit Pay in the Public Sector: The Case for a Failure of Theory," *Review of Public Personnel Administration*, vol. 7, no. 1 (1986), pp. 57–69.

————. "Linking Pay to Performance: The Controversy Continues," in Carolyn Ban and Norma M. Riccucci (eds.). *Public Personnel Management: Current Concerns, Future Challenges*. White Plains, N.Y.: Longman Press, 1991.

Pierson, Ralph M. "Performance Evaluation: One More Try," *Public Personnel Management*, vol. 3, 1980.

Platz, Alan L. "Performance Appraisal: Useful but Still Resisted," *Harvard Business Review*, 53 (May–June 1975).

Rollins, Thomas. "Pay for Performance: The Pros and Cons," *Personnel Journal*, vol. 66, no. 6 (1987), pp. 104–111.

Schay, Brigitte W. "Effects of Performance-Contingent Pay on Employee Attitudes," *Public Personnel Management*, vol. 17 (1988), pp. 237–250.

Schinagl, Mary S. *History of Efficiency Ratings in the Federal Government*. New York: Bookman Associates, 1966.

Schneier, Dena B. "The Impact of EEO Legislation on Performance Appraisals," *Personnel* (July–August 1978).

Schwab, D. P., H. G. Heneman III, and T. A. Decotis. "Behaviorally Anchored Rating Scales: A Review of the Literature," *Personnel Psychology*, 28 (1975).

Schwab, Donald P. and Craig A. Olson. "Pay-Performance Relationships as a Function of Pay for Performance Policies and Practices," *Proceedings of the Academy of Management*, vol. 48 (1988), pp. 287–291.

Sherwood, Frank and Barton Wechsler. "The 'Hadacol' of the Eighties: Paying Senior Public Managers for Performance," *Review of Public Personnel Administration*, vol. 7, no. 1 (1986), pp. 27–41.

Shigher, E. A. "A Systems Look at Performance Appraisal," *Personnel Journal*, 54 (February 1975).

Stimson, Richard A. "Performance Pay: Will It Work?" *The Bureaucrat* (Summer 1980).

Swezey, Robert W. "Aspects of Criterion-Referenced Measurement in Performance Evaluation," *Human Factors* (1978).

Taylor, Robert L. and William D. Wilsted. "Capturing Judgment Policies in Performance Rating," *Industrial Relations*, 15 (May 1976).

_____ and Robert A. Zawacki. "Collaborative Goal Setting in Performance Appraisal: A Field Experiment," *Public Management*, 7 (May–June 1978).

Teel, Kenneth S. "Performance Appraisal: A Survey of Current Practices," *Personnel Journal* (May 1977).

Thayer, Fred C. "Performance Appraisal and Merit Pay System: The Disasters Multiply," *Review of Public Personnel Administration*, vol. 7, no. 2 (1987), pp. 36–53.

U.S. General Accounting Office. *Performance Management: How Well Is the Government Dealing with Poor Performance?* Washington, D.C.: USGAO, 1990.

U.S. Merit Systems Protection Board. *Federal Personnel Policies and Practices—Perspectives from the Workplace.* Washington, D.C.: USMSPB, 1987.

_____. *Performance Management and Recognition System: Linking Pay to Performance.* Washington, D.C.: USMSPB, 1987.

_____. *Working for America: A Federal Employee Survey.* Washington, D.C.: USMSPB, 1990.

U.S. Office of Personnel Management. *Federal Employee Attitudes.* Washington, D.C.: USOPM, 1979.

Wagel, William H. "A Software Link Between Performance Appraisals and Merit Increases," *Personnel*, vol. 65, no. 3 (1988), pp. 10–16.

Walker, James W. and Daniel E. Lupton. "Performance Appraisal Programs and Age Discrimination Law," *Aging and Work* (Spring 1978).

Zawacki, Robert A. and Robert L. Taylor. "A View of Performance Appraisal from Organizations Using It," *Personnel Journal*, 55 (June 1976).

Part **VII**
FUTURE CHALLENGES TO PUBLIC PERSONNEL MANAGEMENT

16

Work, Family, and the Future

Prologue: Family Leave Policies and Benefits

Kathy Consullo gave birth to a second child in November of 1989. Jim, her husband, was working as a manager for a large organization in New Hampshire at the time. Two days after their son was born, the baby underwent life-saving, emergency heart surgery. Bob kept his office apprised of the baby's condition, but eight days after the surgery, Bob's supervisor called him at the hospital, demanding to know when Bob would be returning to work. Because of his son's life-threatening condition, Bob told his supervisor he did not know exactly when he could return to work. Later that day, Bob received a mailgram informing him that he was fired. Only after the story appeared in New England newspapers was Bob invited back to work. Bob instead opted to work for another firm, where he took a pay cut of $11,000 a year. Kathy and Bob's son Anthony needs further surgery and the medical bills are mounting.

In 1990, President George Bush vetoed the Family and Medical Leave Act, which would have provided up to three months of unpaid leave for workers like Bob, with newborn babies (or other family members) needing health care or assistance. Bush justified his veto on the grounds that the law would constitute an unwarranted intrusion of government into the affairs of business. Interestingly enough, this veto came at a time when many organizations are developing policies to accommodate the needs of the growing number of working women and men with children. Various calculations and forecasts have been made about what the work force will look like in the year 2000; they all point to the significance of the substantial increase of working women

517

in particular for family leave policies and benefits to accommodate such activities as childbearing, childrearing, and care of newborn babies as well as elderly family members. As a 1988 report issued by the U.S. Department of Labor has said, "unless employers and employees can find some middle ground between the competing worlds of work and family, someone is bound to pay the price: either the women [or man] in terms of stress, or the employer, in terms of productivity. Either way, both parties lose."

Changing Demographics of the Workplace

Chapter 7 ("Equal Employment Opportunity and Affirmative Action") briefly alluded to some of the changes that are likely to occur in the workplace by the twenty-first century. The developments around women in the work force are especially relevant to work and family concerns. Granted, these concerns are certainly pertinent for men as well. But as *Opportunity 2000* has succinctly stated, it is "women, even when employed full time, [that] spend more time than men caring for dependents, whether children or elderly family members." The growing number of women in the labor force, then, has become an important concern to public as well as private sector employers. Consider the following changes, shifts, and projections reported by the U.S. Department of Labor in various reports between 1988 and 1990:

1. Women will account for 64 percent of U.S. labor force growth by the year 2000, a substantial change from a few decades ago.
2. In 1968, 42 percent of all women were in the labor force, as were 47 percent between the ages of 16 and 44. By 1989, 57 percent of all women over 16 were in the labor force.
3. In 1987, in almost 60 percent of "married-couple" families, both spouses were working. (One of the biases of these forecasts is that they ignore the existence of unmarried persons—heterosexuals, gays, and lesbians—raising families, which masks the true magnitude of "work and family" concerns.)
4. In 1960, 19 percent of mothers with young children worked outside the home; by 1988, 54 percent did. (As *Opportunity 2000* points out, white women account for most of this change, since women of color with children have almost always worked outside the home.)
5. In 1984, almost half of the mothers with a child age 1 or younger were in the labor force; by the time the youngest child reached the age of 3, the labor force participation rates of mothers was about 60 percent.
6. In 1984, about 44 percent of all African-American families were headed by women, compared to 23.2 percent of Latino families and 13 percent of white families.

7. African-American and Latino women maintaining families had lower median earnings than white women heading families and they were less likely than similar white families to have more than one wage earner.

These statistics point to the growing need and demand for benefits and policies to be shaped around workers and their families. This seems prudent, especially for public sector employers as they seek to recruit and retain the "best and brightest" employees. Notwithstanding, there is an intriguing irony surrounding the most pivotal, not to mention primal, family-related issue—pregnancy!

The Pregnancy Paradox: Benefits or Bias?

As noted above, as we move into the 1990s and beyond, employers are being encouraged to develop and implement benefit programs and policies that will make it easier for working women and men to have children without the threat of losing their jobs. In particular, a number of public sector employers, as seen in Table 16.1, are developing benefits that provide for pregnancy or childbearing leave. (The term "family" leave seems to be replacing "pregnancy," "maternity," or "paternity" leave, to reflect the desire of both working women and men to participate in childbirth and childrearing. Also, it is a more neutral term, conveying a sense of equity to those who might feel slighted by such gender-bound terms as "pregnancy" leave.)

Interestingly enough, despite the movement in this direction by some public and private sector employers, there is a lasting legacy of discrimination against women for what has been called the "womb factor" (i.e., their reproductive capabilities). Nowhere has this been more evident than in so-called protective laws, which were designed to protect pregnant women and women of "childbearing" age (whatever that means) from certain "hazards" in the workplace. Such laws, of course, did little more than frustrate women's efforts to make progress in the labor force, since the "protection" had the effect of restricting when women could work, for how long, what types of jobs they could and could not perform, and how much pay they could receive. Just as in the other facets of their lives, government and industry were able to regulate the employment of women, especially pregnant women or women in their "childbearing" years.

Well, "you've come a long way, baby," so we are told. It is the 1990s, the prelude to the twenty-first century, in which, according to a variety of economic forecasts, all of this momentous employment progress will be made by women. Yet, the legacy of "protective legislation" resounds in "fetal protection" policies. That is to say, the debate has shifted from the protection of women to the protection of fetuses that female workers are carrying or

Table 16.1. Percentage of Full-time Employees Covered by Parental Leave Policies, State and Local Governments (1987)

Employer leave policy	All employees	Regular employees	Teachers	Police and firefighters
"Maternity" leave				
Total	100	100	100	100
Eligible for paid leave	1	1	1	—
Eligible for unpaid leave	57	55	65	51
Fixed number of days available	49	47	55	41
Provided as needed[a]	5	4	6	5
Information not available on duration	4	3	4	5
Not eligible for maternity leave	43	45	35	49
"Paternity" leave				
Total	100	100	100	100
Eligible for paid leave	([b])	([b])	([b])	—
Eligible for unpaid leave	30	29	32	30
Fixed number of days available	26	26	28	26
Provided as needed[a]	2	2	2	2
Information not available on duration	2	2	3	2
Not eligible for paternity leave	70	71	68	70

Note: Includes paid or unpaid leave provided to new mothers or fathers for the specific purpose of caring for their child during the early days of its infancy. This plan is separate from any sick leave, annual leave, vacation, personal leave, or short-term disability plan that the employee may take.
[a]Plan does not specify maximum number of days.
[b]Less than 0.5 percent.

Source: Bureau of Labor Statistics, *Employee Benefits in State and Local Governments* (Washington, D.C.: U.S. Department of Labor, May 1988), p. 12.

may be carrying at some point in the future. (Do employers and law and policy makers actually believe that women as well as men will continue to believe that the safety and health of fetuses is the primary goal of such "protection" policies? There is reason to believe that these policies primarily seek not to protect fetuses but rather employers from the liability that may arise around miscarriages or related complications.)

But notwithstanding their purpose, the policies, just as in the past, adversely affect women by excluding them from more desirable high-paying jobs. Moreover, such policies infringe upon women's reproductive rights; women are once again being victimized for being pregnant and for raising a family. A perfect illustration can clearly be seen in one of the most recent judicial developments as of this writing—*International Union, UAW* v. *Johnson Controls* (1989, 1991). This case begins with the U.S. Court of Appeals for the Seventh Circuit upholding the "fetal protection" policies of Johnson

---

Views from the U.S. Supreme Court in Its 1908 Decision,
***Muller* v. *State of Oregon* (208 U.S. 412)**

In upholding the constitutionality of Oregon's "protective" statute, Supreme Court Justice Brewer, writing for the majority, had this to say:

> That woman's physical structure and the performance of maternal functions place her at a disadvantage in the struggle for subsistence is obvious. This is especially true when the burdens of motherhood are upon her. Even when they are not, by abundant testimony of the medical fraternity continuance for a long time on her feet at work, repeating this from day to day, tends to injurious effects upon the body, and, as healthy mothers are essential to vigorous offspring, the physical well-being of women becomes an object of public interest and care in order to preserve the strength and vigor of the race.

> Still again, history discloses the fact that woman has always been dependent upon man. He established his control at the outset by superior physical strength, and this control in various forms . . . has continued to the present. . . . Though limitations upon personal and contractual rights may be removed by legislation, there is that in her disposition and habits of life which will operate against a full assertion of those rights. *She will still be where some legislation to protect her seems necessary to secure a real equality of right.* . . . Differentiated by these matters from the other sex, she is properly placed in a class by herself, and legislation designed for her protection may be sustained, even when like legislation is not necessary for men, and could not be sustained. It is impossible to close one's eye to the fact that she still looks to her brother and depends upon him . . . she is so constituted that she will rest upon and look to him for protection; *that her physical structure and a proper discharge of her maternal functions . . . justifies legislation to protect her from the greed as well as the passion of man* [emphasis added].

Controls, a manufacturer of automobile batteries in Milwaukee. The policy barred women under the age of 70 (oh, that's what they mean by "of childbearing age") from certain high-paying factory jobs unless they provide medical proof that they are sterile.

The case was initially brought by a number of union workers, including a 50-year-old divorcee who was coerced into sterilization in order to keep her job. The union, UAW, challenged the policy on the grounds that it discriminated against women in violation of Title VII of the Civil Rights Act. The court ruled that the policy was a legitimate business necessity because of risks posed by exposure to high levels of lead used in battery production. It concluded that the policy was "proper and reasonably necessary to further . . . industrial safety."

If the job is so hazardous, why does the policy apply only to women? Are men immune to the absorption of lead, and wouldn't this affect their role in procreation? Indeed, the UAW provided evidence in *Johnson Controls* that fathers exposed to the levels of lead present in battery production pose the same risk to the fetus as mothers exposed to lead. As a spokesperson for the National Organization for Women (NOW) has said, the "issue is an environmental problem," and there is "a lot of strong evidence that lead affects the safety of the *whole* work force" (emphasis added). Perhaps it is not the fetus that industry seeks to protect; rather, as noted earlier, industry seeks to avoid the creation of circumstances that could lead to liability.

The U.S. Supreme Court in 1991 overturned the appellate court ruling in *Johnson Controls*. Notwithstanding, some Supreme Court justices said that a more narrowly tailored version of the Johnson Controls fetal proection

---

What Is the "Mommy Track?"

Felice N. Schwartz, founder and president of the not-for-profit research and consulting organization, Catalyst, is urging employers to "identify and nurture two separate groups [of female employees]. Treat high-potential 'career-primary' women, most of whom will be childless, just as if they were talented men. Then help 'career-and-family' women be productive—but probably not upwardly mobile . . . The notion [is to have] two classes of corporate women, only one of which makes it to the top."

Critics are arguing that this mommy track is "separate and unequal" and "will permanently derail women's careers, making them second-class citizens at work and confirming the prejudices of male executives." In essence, the "mommy tracker puts up a sign: Don't consider me for promotions now."

Adapted from *Business Week* (March 20, 1989).

policy could be legally justified. The Court's decision in *Johnson Controls*, then, is not the final word on the future of fetal protection policies. As the case law continues to unfold in this area, millions of jobs in both public and private sectors may be at stake because of the fetal risks posed by a variety of "hazardous" substances.

In addition to being denied or excluded from jobs on the basis of pregnancy or fertility, women have also been denied employee benefits for such reasons. Indeed, the Pregnancy Discrimination Act of 1978 (see box) grew out of U.S. Supreme Court decisions that restricted employee benefits available to pregnant women. In *General Electric Co.* v. *Gilbert* (1976), for example, the U.S. Supreme Court ruled that employers are *not* in violation of Title VII for gender discrimination if they deny pregnant women the "disability" benefits that all other workers are entitled to receive.

Ten years after the *Gilbert* decision, the U.S. Supreme Court issued two rulings that have further shaped the parameters of pregnancy policies in this

---

What Is the Pregnancy Discrimination Act of 1978?

An amendment to Title VII of the Civil Rights Act of 1964, which holds that discrimination on the basis of pregnancy, childbirth or related medical conditions constitutes unlawful sex discrimination. The amendment was enacted in response to the Supreme Court's ruling in *General Electric Co.* v. *Gilbert*, 429 U.S. 125 (1976) that an employer's exclusion of pregnancy related disabilities from its comprehensive disability plan did not violate Title VII. The amendment asserts that:

1. A written or unwritten employment policy or practice which excludes from employment opportunities applicants or employees because of pregnancy, childbirth or related medical conditions is in prima facie violation of Title VII.

2. Disabilities caused or contributed to by pregnancy, childbirth, or related medical conditions, for all job-related purposes, shall be treated the same as disabilities caused or contributed to by other medical conditions, under any health or disability insurance or sick leave plan available in connection with employment. Written or unwritten employment policies and practices involving matters such as the commencement and duration of leave, the availability of extensions, the accrual of seniority and other benefits and privileges, reinstatement, and payment under any health or disability insurance or sick leave plan, formal or informal, shall be applied to disability due to pregnancy, childbirth, or related medical conditions on the same terms and conditions as they are applied to other disabilities. Health insurance benefits for abortion, except where the life of the mother would be endangered if the fetus were carried to term or where medical complications have arisen from an abortion, are not required to be paid by an employer; nothing herein, however, precludes an employer from providing abortion benefits or otherwise affects bargaining agreements in regard to abortion.

(continued)

**What Is the Pregnancy Discrimination
Act of 1978? (continued)**

3. Where the termination of an employee who is temporarily disabled is caused
   by an employment policy under which insufficient or no leave is available, such
   a termination violates the Act if it has a disparate impact on employees of one
   sex and not justified by business necessity.

Jay M. Shafritz, *Dictionary of Personnel Management and Labor Relations*, 2nd edition (New
York: Facts on File, Inc., 1985).

---

country. In *California Federal Savings and Loan* v. *Guerra, Director of
Department of Fair Employment and Housing* (1987), the Court was called
upon to rule whether the Pregnancy Discrimination Act (PDA) of 1978 prohibits employment practices that "favor" pregnant women, and whether the
PDA preempts state laws on pregnancy. The case involved Lillian Garland,
who was employed by the California Federal Savings and Loan Association
(Cal Fed) as a receptionist for several years. In January of 1982, she took
a pregnancy disability leave. When she attempted to return to work in April
of that year, Garland was informed that her job had been filled and that there
were no receptionist or similar positions available.

Garland filed a complaint with the Department of Fair Employment and
Housing (hereafter, Department), which then charged Cal Fed with violating
California's Fair Employment and Housing Act (FEHA). The FEHA prohibits various forms of discrimination in employment and housing; it explicitly
prohibits discrimination on the basis of pregnancy. In addition, it requires
employers covered by Title VII of the Civil Rights Act to provide female
employees with an unpaid pregnancy disability leave of up to four months.
The Department interprets the law to require California employers to reinstate
an employee returning from a pregnancy leave to the job previously held.
The act does not compel employers to provide *paid* pregnancy leaves. Cal
Fed argued that the FEHA is inconsistent with and preempted by Title VII,
as amended by the PDA. This line of reasoning was pursued in light of Cal
Fed's interpretation that the FEHA "favors" pregnant women, but that the
PDA does not.

The U.S. Supreme Court held that the PDA does not prohibit employment practices that favor pregnant women. It further ruled that the FEHA
is not inconsistent with and thus is not preempted by Title VII, as amended
by the PDA. The Court stated that "the district court's conclusion that [Califor-
nia's FEHA] discriminates against men on the basis of pregnancy defies common sense, misinterprets case law, and flouts Title VII and the PDA."

The EEOC Guidelines on Pregnancy Discrimination

(a) A written or unwritten employment policy or practice which excludes from employment applicants or employees because of pregnancy, childbirth and related medical conditions is in prima facie violation of Title VII.

(b) Disabilities caused or contributed to by pregnancy, childbirth, or related medical conditions, for all job-related purposes, shall be treated the same as disabilities caused or contributed to by other medical conditions, under any health or disability insurance or sick leave plan available in connection with employment. Written or unwritten employment policies and practices involving matters such as the commencement and duration of leave, the availability of extensions, the accrual of seniority and other benefits and privileges, reinstatement, and payment under any health or disability insurance or sick leave plan, formal or informal, shall be applied to disability due to pregnancy, childbirth, or related medical conditions on the same terms and conditions as they are applied to other disabilities. Health insurance benefits for abortion, except where the life of the mother would be endangered if the fetus were carried to term or where medical complications have arisen from an abortion, are not required to be paid by an employee; nothing herein, however, precludes an employer from providing abortion benefits or otherwise affects bargaining agreements in regard to abortion.

(c) Where the termination of an employee who is temporarily disabled is caused by an employment policy under which insufficient or no leave is available, such a termination violates the Act if it has a disparate impact on employees of one sex and is not justified by business necessity.

(d)(1) Any fringe benefit program, or fund, or insurance program which is in effect on October 31, 1978, which does not treat women affected by pregnancy, childbirth, or related medical conditions the same as other persons not so affected but similar in their ability to work, must be in compliance with the provisions of § 1604.10(b) by April 29, 1979. In order to come into compliance with the provisions of § 1604.10(b), there can be no reduction of benefits or compensation which were in effect on October 31, 1978, before October 31, 1979 or the expiration of a collective bargaining agreement in effect on October 31, 1978, which ever is later.

(2) Any fringe benefits program implemented after October 31, 1978, must comply with the provisions of § 1604.10(b) upon implementation.

29 CFR Section 1604.10 (1980).

A week after the Supreme Court issued its ruling in *California Federal Savings and Loan*, it decided *Wimberly* v. *Labor and Industrial Relations Commission of Missouri* (1987). Linda Wimberly, in August of 1980, requested a leave for pregnancy from her employer, J.C. Penney Company. Wimberly was granted a leave, pursuant to the company's policy that any employee may take a leave of absence "without guarantee of reinstatement." Employees would be rehired only if a position was available when the employee was ready to return to work. When Wimberly returned to work after her baby was born, there were no positions available, and so she filed a claim for unemployment benefits. Wimberly was denied benefits by the state's Labor and Industrial Relations Commission (hereafter, Commission) on the grounds that a Missouri unemployment compensation law disqualifies claimants "who have left work voluntarily without good cause attributable to their work or their employer."

Wimberly filed suit against the Commission on the grounds that the Missouri statute was inconsistent with a provision of the Federal Unemployment Tax Act of 1976, which prohibits states from denying persons unemployment compensation on the basis of pregnancy. The U.S. Supreme Court ruled against Wimberly saying that the Missouri law was not inconsistent with the Tax Act, because it is a "neutral" law that denies benefits to any employees who leave their jobs voluntarily for reasons unrelated to their jobs or employers. (Incidently, most states allow women who are not reinstated after leaves of absence for pregnancy to collect unemployment compensation. Only Vermont, Minnesota, North Dakota, and Washington, D.C. have unemployment compensation laws similar to Missouri's.)

Taking the two 1987 decisions together, the Supreme Court has thus said that states are not required to develop nor are they prohibited from developing policies that favor pregnant employees. Obviously, there is a good deal of ambiguity here, thus leaving room for sharper boundaries to be drawn around employment policies that affect the "womb factor." In particular, the fate of "fetal protection" measures appears unclear at this point. It would seem, based on the Supreme Court's 1987 decisions presented above, that states could not enact (develop) restrictive "fetal protection" laws (policies). However, as *Johnson Controls* suggests, it may be the case that private sector employers may do so in the future if the policies are "narrowly tailored." For public sector employers, there is greater uncertainty, particularly in light of two 1974 U.S. Supreme Court decisions, *Cleveland Board of Education* v. *LaFleur* and *Cohen* v. *Chesterfield County School Board*. In these cases, the U.S. Supreme Court found the overly restrictive policies of school districts that forced women to leave their jobs very early during their pregnancy to be unconstitutional (see also Chapter 9). Of course, the composition of the U.S. Supreme Court is very different today as compared to 1974, and so the Court, if faced with similar circumstances, may uphold such restrictive pregnancy policies.

At least one thing is certain, however—the pregnancy paradox continues. Some public and private sector employers, sensitive to the realities of what the labor force will look like in the twenty-first century, will develop benefit packages to accommodate work and family issues in such areas as pregnancy. Other employers will end up in court seeking to justify the denial of benefits to pregnant workers or restrictive pregnancy policies under the guise that they seek to protect women or their fetuses. The economic forecasts of the labor force suggest that this latter group of employers will be at a competitive *disadvantage* "in the scramble for high-quality, productive and dedicated workers." As *Opportunity 2000* has stated, the organizations that will be "most successful in the 1990s and beyond will be those that take steps to provide equal opportunity for all workers, regardless of gender or family responsibilities."

The History of Family-Related Benefits

Employee benefits are extremely important to both public and private sector employees. And, for workers with dependents, benefit packages may be vital. Health care plans, retirement plans, and disability benefits are among those that have provided some sense of "security" to workers and their families. Today, employee benefits account for almost 30 percent of the total cost of employee compensation; with the growing complexity of family concerns and needs, this is expected to increase by the next century.

The growing emphasis on benefits, in particular family-oriented ones, represents a notable shift in values from the beginning of the twentieth century, when employers did not seek to accommodate any of their employees' nonwork needs. Extended families were the norm during this period of the nation's history; they relied on self-support and self-sufficiency, and not what were perceived at the time to be "handouts." As William J. Wiatrowski, a noted expert puts it, "Loss of income or unusual expenses were generally borne by the pooled resources of the family. The pioneer and agricultural traditions of this country had left a strong legacy of independence, and employers did not interfere."

Interestingly enough, nor did labor unions. Samuel Gompers, the first president of the American Federation of Labor (AFL) vociferously opposed compulsory employee benefits, arguing that such "interference" in affairs traditionally handled by individuals "weakens independence of spirit, delegates to outside authorities some of the powers and opportunities that rightfully

---

The "Sex Plus" Theory

"Sex plus" refers to employers classifying employees on the basis of sex *plus* another characteristic. In such cases, the employer treats a subclass of women or men disparately. For example, such a case arises when an employer hires men regardless of their parental status, but refuses to hire women with preschool-age children. In other words, an employer refuses to hire on the basis of being female *plus* having preschool age children. This type of disparate treatment is illegal under Title VII of the Civil Rights Act. (See *Phillips* v. *Martin Marietta Corp.*, 400 U.S. 542, 1971.)

belong to wage earners, and breaks down industrial freedom by exercising control over workers through a central bureaucracy." (Lane Kirkland, president of the AFL-CIO today, does not take the same position on employee benefits. Indeed, in May of 1988, the AFL-CIO celebrated and sponsored "Family Day" on the Washington Mall, demonstrating for such family services as parental leave and child care.)

By the 1920s, some employers began to offer fringe benefits as a way to hold good employees. However, because employers (like society in general) saw women as "marginal" workers whose primary responsibilities were as wives and mothers, restrictions were placed on benefits available to female workers (if, indeed, employers even hired them). While some employers provided fewer benefits to female employees than to male employees, others completely denied women any benefits.

It wasn't until the era marking America's involvement in World War II that we saw a systematic increase in employer–provided benefit programs. When this nation entered the war in 1941, employment grew at a rapid rate, and women entered the labor force in large numbers. The War Labor Board restricted wage increases during this time in order to "stabilize" wages. But to compensate for the wage restrictions, it permitted improvements to employee benefits. Employers, as such, began to offer time off with pay and limited medical care for workers and their families. Such benefits enabled women and men to spend more time with their families. In addition, the federal government established a temporary child care program with the enactment of the Lanham Act in 1941 to make it easier for mothers to work.

Following the war, men displaced women by returning to their jobs, and pre-war discrimination patterns in women's employment began to reemerge. There was a notable change in family structure in this nation resulting from the boom in marriages and children. Women, again, were expected to "keep" house. Employers, prodded in part by labor unions, responded to these developments by maintaining such benefit programs as time off with pay and medical care. Indeed, between 1945 and 1959 there was widespread adoption of such benefits into employee compensation packages. Benefit packages continued during this time and well into the early 1970s.

As we have seen, employee benefits of this general nature have not diminished in importance, yet they are somewhat anachronistic in the sense that they were and are geared toward a family structure that is no longer typical—one with a working husband, nonworking wife and school-age children. The challenge to public personnel administration and managers is to develop programs that will appropriately respond to the nature and character of American families, which are often headed by single women or have two wage earners. (This latter group has received attention by personnelists in the past under the rubric "dual-career couples.") In addition to financial reasons, women (like men) often do not desire to stay home and take care of the children. In effect, this creates a serious tension for workers with family or other nonwork responsibilities. On the one hand, they seek to nurture their careers; on the other, they want to be certain that their children (or other family members) are getting the proper care and attention. Just how well are public sector employers responding to these types of needs and desires of their employees?

Policies and Programs Aimed at Accommodating Family Responsibilities

It is amazing that in a society such as ours, which places so much value on the family and work, there is no coherent federal policy or law that enables workers to balance their career and family interests. Other than the PDA discussed above and a few government programs that provide tax deductions for employment-related child care expenses (e.g., Dependent Care Tax Credit of 1976), there is a hodgepodge approach, where family-oriented policies

Family Leave Policies in Industrialized Nations

The U.S., unlike other industrialized nations, lacks a coherent policy aimed at balancing work and family needs. In many countries, parental leave policies are government-mandated.

• *Sweden* has one of the most comprehensive parental leave policies in the world. The Child Care Leave Act of 1978 provides Swedish employees with up to 12 months leave to care for children. The leave can be split between the parents and can be taken in full or partial days until the child reaches the age of 8. Employees are paid 90 percent of their pay for 9 months and a flat rate for 3.

• *Canada* has a parental leave policy for federal public service employees. Time off is granted to both female and male employees. It is usually unpaid, but unemployment payments may be received during the leave. Other parental leave policies exist, but only in certain provinces or territories. For example, all but one of the provincial governments mandate unpaid pregnancy leave for public and private sector employees.

• The *United Kingdom* mandates parental leave for female employees under the Employment Protection Act of 1975. Six weeks of pregnancy leave can be taken at 90 percent pay. Women can also receive up to 29 weeks of unpaid leave for newborn child care.

Joseph R. Meisenheimer, "Employer Provisions for Parental Leave," *Monthly Labor Review* (October 1989).

vary by employer (see Table 16.1). The same can be said for state laws and regulations (see Table 16.2).

But, if public and private sector employers seek to attract and retain quality workers in the coming decade and beyond, they will need to develop programs that enable their employers to balance work and family obligations.

Table 16.2. States with Family and Medical Leave Laws and Regulations (as of January 1990)

State	Family leave	Medical/ pregnancy leave	Employers covered	
			State	Private
California		X	X	X
Connecticut	X	X	X	X
Florida	X		X	
Hawaii		X	X	X
Iowa		X	X	X
Kansas		X	X	X
Kentucky	X		X	X
Louisiana		X	X	X
Maine	X	X	X	X
Massachusetts	X		X	X
Minnesota	X		X	X
Montana		X	X	X
New Hampshire		X	X	X
New Jersey	X		X	X
North Carolina		X	X	
North Dakota	X		X	
Oklahoma	X		X	
Oregon	X	X	X	X
Pennsylvania	X	X	X	
Puerto Rico		X	X	X
Rhode Island	X		X[a]	X
Tennessee		X	X	X
Vermont	X	X	X	X
Washington	X	X	X	X
West Virginia	X		X	
Wisconsin	X	X	X	X

[a]Includes local governments as well.

Source: Adapted from *State Laws and Regulations Guaranteeing Employees Their Jobs after Family and Medical Leaves* (Washington, D.C.: Women's Legal Defense Fund, 1990).

Even if organizations believe that family responsibilities should be left in the hands of families, prudent employers will recognize that the work performance of its employees is affected by how well work-family obligations can be met. Indeed, a number of studies have shown that family-supportive benefit programs lead to increased worker performance and productivity.

There are a number of family-supportive policies and programs that are able to meet the needs of working parents. First and foremost, however, the organization culture and climate must be family-supportive. As Stanley Nollen has pointed out, a supportive culture is

> one in which diversity is tolerated—that is, in which there is no stifling conformity requiring everyone to dress alike, talk alike, and act alike. Instead, this type of workplace is oriented toward change and informality and stimulates rather than thwarts self-reliance. Another aspect of a supportive corporate culture is a knowledge among managers that work and family impinge on each other and that workplace events affect families just as family health affects the workplace.

In addition, personnel and human resources management must be geared toward the empowerment of employees so that they possess the resources needed to balance their work and family commitments. Empowerment in part involves employees having some control over their own jobs—what they do, how they do it, and when. Some of the benefit programs that employers establish can have such an effect. The following represents just a few of such policies and programs.

1. *Parental leave*—time off for childbirth and caring for newborn or newly adopted children.
2. *Family and medical leave*—time off so that workers can care for ill family members, whether a child, spouse/partner, or parent.
3. *Flexible work schedules*—including the following: (a) *flextime*—where employees may be required to work a certain number of hours per day (e.g., eight), but can set their own schedules (e.g., from 7 A.M. to 3 P.M. or from 10 A.M. to 6 P.M.). Employees may also be allowed to compress their work week into four days by extending the hours they work per day. (b) *flexsite*—where employees are allowed to take work home or, through "telecommuting," are allowed to work at home and communicate with their offices via computers. (c) *job sharing*—allows at least two employees to share the same job, working different hours. For example, one employee may work the "morning shift," and another the "afternoon shift." (d) *voluntary reduced work time ("V-Time")*—employees take a temporary 5 to 50 percent reduction in work time and salary for six months to a year.
4. *Employee Assistance Programs (EAPs)*—counseling programs to address

Striking a Balance Between Work and Nonwork Obligations

Employers seeking to compete for high-quality workers will need to create opportunities that not only enable employees to balance work and family obligations, but
more broadly, work and nonwork obligations. Barbara Romzek has said that
"[e]mployees have multiple commitments, many tied to roles outside of work, that
they expect to sustain. These nonwork commitments, and employees' efforts to balance
them with their work commitment, are factors which managers cannot control.
Nonetheless, personnel managers need to be aware of their impact on employee recruitment, performance, and retention. Employers need to change the way they think
about employee recruitment and retention. In particular, organizations need to change
their expectations and work policies to better allow employees the opportunity to
balance their work and personal lives. Another way to increase the retention of
employees is to provide them with experiences at work that elicit organizational commitment. Facilitating employees' ability to accommodate work and nonwork lives
is one important aspect of that work experience."

Barbara Romzek, "Balancing Work and Nonwork Obligations," in Carolyn Ban and Norma
M. Riccucci (eds.), *Public Personnel Management: Current Concerns, Future Challenges* (White
Plains, N.Y.: Longman Press, 1991).

and respond to work-family problems such as alcoholism, drug depen-
dency, financial planning, and day/child care planning.
5. *Educational and support programs*—programs enabling working parents
   to help themselves through networking, information gathering and sharing, support building, and problem solving.
6. *Elderly care*—including benefit programs that cover long-term nursing
   care.
7. *Day/child care*—including the following (see Table 16.3): (a) *on- or near-
   site child care*—sponsored by the employer (or consortium of employers),
   this enables parents to maintain contact with their children during the
   day. (b) *resource and referral services*—computer data bases, maintained
   by the employer or independent, nonprofit agencies (e.g., the Northwest
   Family Network, servicing states in the northwestern part of the country), which store information on child care providers and enable working parents to locate services compatible with their needs and preferences.
   (c) *employer subsidies*—direct reimbursement for child care expenses (or
   a portion of them). This could be part of a cafeteria-style benefit plan.
   Voucher systems are another type of employer subsidy whereby employees
   can redeem vouchers for child care at centers/homes of their choice or
   designated by the employer.

Table 16.3. The Utilization of Child Care Services by Working Women

Place of care	Percentage
Child care facility	3
Place of mother's work	8
Own home by someone else	31
Nonrelative's home	22
Grandparents' home	10
Other relatives' home	5
Kindergarten/school	1

Note: For children under five years of age.
Source: Adapted from Edward L. Suntrup, "Child-Care Delivery Systems in the Government Sector," *Review of Public Personnel Administration* (Fall 1989), p. 50.

One of the most critical problems that working parents face today is quality care for their children. This problem will only magnify in the coming years with the changing makeup of the work force, as discussed earlier in this chapter. Responding to this concern is one of the biggest challenges public and private sector employers will face. Currently, only a small percentage of employers provide on-site child care services (less than 2 percent of private employers and just over 9 percent of government employers); other types of child care services, as discussed above, may be more popular among employers, but efforts will need to be stepped up in this very critical area of personnel management.

Compared to the private sector, the federal government, according to the Office of Personnel Management (OPM), is a leader in providing child care benefits to its employees. And, there is certainly an incentive to provide such benefits, since there are between 200,000 and 300,000 parents with children under the age of five in the federal work force. Here are some federal agencies, as summarized by OPM in *Civil Service 2000*, that have developed child care programs and policies to accommodate the specific needs of their own workers.

Social Security Administration (SSA)—About 65 percent of the SSA work force is female, with about 58 percent of the women between the ages of 30 and 44. To assist its employees seeking child care, the SSA has established a telephone referral service, which matches employees with "caregivers."
National Security Agency (NSA)—About 37 percent of the NSA work force is female, and the median age of these women is 27. The NSA also employs a significant number of single male parents. Similar to the SSA, the NSA provides a child care referral service. However, according to the agency's

What Are Cafeteria-Style Benefit Programs?

Cafeteria-style benefits allow employees to select benefits from a menu of choices to best meet their needs and the changing needs of their families. For example, as Barbara Romzek states, "a divorced mother may not need family health insurance if her children are covered under their father's health insurance program. Instead, she may choose to take the benefit in the form of increased personal leave days as a way to facilitate management of her nonwork obligations. Similarly, in a two paycheck family, the family does not usually need health insurance from both employers. If the family could choose to have health insurance through one parent's employer and have dental insurance through the other parent's employer, then the family would be better able to use these benefits."

Barbara Romzek, "Balancing Work and Nonwork Obligations," in Carolyn Ban and Norma M. Riccucci (eds.), *Public Personnel Management: Current Concerns, Future Challenges* (White Plains, N.Y.: Longman Press, 1991).

personnel officials, there is a need for on-site or nearby child care facilities. Unfortunately, by the agency's own admission, the child care needs of NSA staff are not currently being met, and the problem is expected to intensify as the year 2000 approaches.

National Institutes of Health (NIH)—Over 58 percent of NIH employees are women. The NIH currently has two on-site child care centers, one that can house 65 children and the other 33. One of these centers was established in 1973 by NIH staff and parents; it represents the longest on-site child care facility in the federal government. It receives some private foundation funding and it charges fees on a sliding scale. It is anticipated that child care services will grow in demand in the coming decade.

Veterans Administration (VA)—About 65 percent of all VA employees, such as health care staff, under the age of 35 are women. As of 1987, the VA had eighteen child care facilities, accommodating over 700 children; nine additional centers are scheduled to open in the near future. It was grass-roots efforts, similar to those at NIH, that started the child care facilities, since Congress has not funded child care services at VA medical centers.

The Naval Academy—The academy has a broad mix of employees; its 2,000 or so employees range from college professors to maintenance workers. Although the Naval Academy has an on-site child care facility, it does not meet the needs of staff, who are estimated to have 381 preschool-age children and 370 school-age children.

Obviously, the federal government could not afford to provide on-site child care facilities for all of its employees. Nonetheless, as we move into the twenty-first century, the need for such family-related benefits as child care will continue to grow. The federal government, as OPM recommends, should look more closely at the alternatives to on-site facilities, including such options as referral services (for elderly care facilities as well); after-school programs; voucher systems, and cafeteria benefit programs, which distribute the benefits more equitably.

The Future

A new role set for public personnel departments appears to be gradually evolving in response to the changing needs and demands of today's and future workers. In recognition of the fact that the problems of managing the human resources of an organization must be approached comprehensively, an increasing number of public personnel departments have begun to take an expansive view of their mandate. Instead of viewing the personnel function as simply that collection of disparate duties necessary to recruit, pay, and discharge employees, they assume their appropriate mission to be the maximum utilization of their organization's human resources. There has been some success in realizing this new function for two basic reasons: (1) the maximum utilization of an organization's human resources, like economy and efficiency, is a goal that, while unattainable, can hardly be denied by top administrators, and (2) while other organizational units have operating responsibilities, there seldom exists in a public sector organization a unit specifically accountable for the maximum development of the jurisdiction's human capital. The personnel department can fill this void if it has the will. In doing so, it can not only revitalize many segments of its host organization, but can expand its responsibilities to include those of an in-house group of behavioral consultants. This expansive role will not only reduce the cost of the parent organization's operations, but will have a revolutionary effect on the content, processes, and people involved in and committed to the public personnel profession.

One aim of this book has been to foster this new public personnel role set. Many of the preceding chapters have dealt with practices to which public personnel agencies, departments, and units must continue to devote attention. But, given the evolving nature of work, how work is and will be performed and by whom, public personnel management will be challenged, as this book suggests, to expand its boundaries and horizons.

In the old days—back before the mid-1960s—no special preparation was really needed for a career in personnel. The procedural aspects of certification, classification, and examinations were learned on the job. Many a music, history, and/or English major were composing civil service examinations a few months after graduation. Validation was not a heavy concern. But, by a decade later, validation was of paramount importance. Personnel agencies now need psychologists and statisticians to write and validate examinations of all kinds. They also need specialists (if not the psychologists!) to ensure that the exams are not culturally biased. A similar story can be seen in labor relations. As the public employee union movement exploded in the late 1960s, personnel agencies were advertising for organization development and job design specialists. The 1980s saw similar searches for human resources information system specialists and productivity measurement experts. The 1990s will require a new breed of personnelists; those who possess the skills necessary to manage a very culturally diverse work force, and who are able to meet the needs and demands of these new workers.

Such issues as equal employment opportunity, affirmative action, training, adequate/equitable pay, labor-management relations, and employees' family obligations will continue to be placed high on the public personnel agenda. How well public personnel and human resources managers of today and tomorrow can address these concerns will help determine the quality of public sector work forces at all levels of government.

Bibliography

Civil Service 2000. Washington, D.C.: U.S. Office of Personnel Management, June 1988.

Cook, Alice H. "Public Policies to Help Dual-Earner Families Meet the Demands of the Work World," *Industrial and Labor Relations Review*, 42 (January 1989).

Gelb, Joyce and Marian Lief Palley. *Women and Public Policies*. Princeton, N.J.: Princeton University Press, 1982.

Halachmi, Ari. "Information Technology, Human Resources Management and Productivity," in Carolyn Ban and Norma M. Riccucci (eds.). *Public Personnel Management: Current Concerns, Future Challenges*. White Plains, N.Y.: Longman Press, 1991.

Greenhouse, Linda. "Court Backs Right of Women to Jobs with Health Risks." *New York Times*, March 21, 1991, A1/B12.

Hayden, Delores. *Redesigning the American Dream: The Future of Housing, Work and the Family*. New York: W.W. Norton, 1984.

Huckle, Patricia. "The Womb Factor: Policy on Pregnancy and the Employment of Women," in Ellen Boneparth and Emily Stoper (eds.). *Women, Power and Policy*, 2nd ed. New York: Pergamon Press, 1988.

International Union, UAW v. *Johnson Controls* 886 F.2d 871 (7th Cir. 1989), overturned, 59 *Law Week* 4209 (March 20, 1991).

Lenhoff, Donna R. and Sylvia M. Becker. "Family and Medical Leave Legislation in the States: Toward a Comprehensive Approach," *Harvard Journal on Legislation*, 26 (1989).

Lewin, Tamar. "Battle for Family Leave Will be Fought in States," *New York Times* (July 27, 1990), p. A8.

————. "View on Career Women Sets Off a Furor," *New York Times* (March 8, 1989), p. A18.

Magid, Renee Y. "When Mothers and Fathers Work: How Employers Can Help," *Personnel* (December 1986).

Meisenheimer, Joseph R. "Employer Provisions for Parental Leave," *Monthly Labor Review*, U.S. Department of Labor (October 1989).

Monthly Labor Review, special issue on family, U.S. Department of Labor (March 1990).

Nollen, Stanley, D. "The Work-Family Dilemma: How HR Managers Can Help," *Personnel* (May 1989).

Opportunity 2000. Washington, D.C.: U.S. Department of Labor (September 1988).

Romzek, Barbara S. "Balancing Work and Nonwork Obligations," in Carolyn Ban and Norma M. Riccucci (eds.). *Public Personnel Management: Current Concerns, Future Challenges*. White Plains, N.Y.: Longmand Press, 1991.

Shinn, Marybeth, Nora W. Wong, Patricia A. Simko, and Blanca Ortiz-Torres. "Promoting the Well-Being of Work Parents: Coping, Social Support, and Flexible Job Schedules," *American Journal of Community Psychology*, 17 (1989).

Suntrup, Edward L. "Child-Care Delivery Systems in the Government Sector," *Review of Public Personnel Administration*, 10 (fall 1989).

Taylor, Stuart. "Jobless Pay After Pregnancy Limited," *New York Times* (January 22, 1987), p. B17.

————. "Job Rights Backed in Pregnancy Case," *New York Times* January 14, 1987), p. A1.

Wiatrowski, William J. "Family-related Benefits in the Workplace," *Monthly Labor Review*, U.S. Department of Labor (March 1990).

Work and Family Responsibilities: Achieving a Balance. New York: the Ford Foundation, March 1989.

Workforce 2000. Indianapolis, Ind.: Hudson Institute, June 1987.

Index

Aaron, Henry J., 246

Abood v. Detroit Board of Education (1977), 297, 317, 355, 394

Aft, Lawrence S., 432, 453

AIDS (AIDS testing), 244, 245, 308, 310, 311, 313, 314

Adams, John, 5, 239

Adelsberg, Henri van, 508

Administrative Careers with America (ACWA), 196, 197

Adverse effect, 224

Adverse impact (*also see* "4/5ths" rule), 175, 176, 224

Adverse-inference rule, 224

Advisory Committee on Federal Pay, 150, 152

AFSCME (see American Federation of State, County and Municipal Employees)

Age Discrimination in Employment Act of 1967, 236

Agency shop (fair share), 297, 323, 394, 395

Air traffic controllers, 47, 359–361

Albemarle Paper Company v. Moody (1975), 171, 197

Albrecht, Maryann H., 247

American Arbitration Association, 383

American Federation of Government Employees (AFGE), 396

American Federation of Labor (AFL), 319, 320, 334

American Federation of Labor–Congress of Industrial Organizations (AFL–CIO), 323, 345

American Federation of State, County and Municipal Employees (AFSCME), 396

American Federation of State, County and Municipal Employees (AFSCME) v. Washington State and *Washington State v. AFSCME* (1983, 1985), 249, 259–261, 269, 275

American Federation of Teachers (AFT), 396

American Society for Public Administration (ASPA), 76

American Society for Quality Control, 453

American Society for Training and Development (ASTD), 466
Americans with Disabilities Act (ADA) of 1990, 244, 245
Ammons, David N., 432
Angelo v. Bacharach Instrument Co. (1977), 274
Aranda, Eileen K., 509
Arbitration, 330, 345, 354, 378–382
Argyris, Chris, 143, 162
Armstrong, Daniel L., 128
Aron, Cindy Sondik, 212, 246, 272
Aronson, Albert H., 62
Aronson, Sidney, H., 23
Arthur, Chester A., 3, 4, 15–17, 31
Arvey, Richard D., 188, 198
Ash, Ronald A., 198
Ashe, R. Lawrence, 198
Asher, Janet, 247
Asher, Jules, 247
Assembled examinations, 185, 186
Auster, Ellen, 272
Authorization card, 323

Baird, Lloyd, 128
Balfour, Alan, 357
Balk, Walter L., 416, 420, 432, 453
Balkan, David B., 162
Ban, Carolyn, 62, 63, 70, 93, 162, 164, 195, 198, 316, 357, 468, 476
Banfield, Edward C., 23
Bann, Charles, 508
Barbour, George P. Jr., 432, 453
Bargaining agent, 323
Bargaining unit, 323
Barnard, Chester I., 74, 75, 93
Barrett, Jerome T., 357
Bartholomew, D. J., 128
Bayes, Jane, 248, 273
Beatty, James R., 162
Beatty, Richard W., 111, 118, 162
Becker, Sylvia M., 537
Behaviorally anchored rating scales (BARS), 501
Bell, D. J., 128

Bellman, Geoffrey, 484
Bellone, Carl J., 63
Bendick, Marc Jr., 432
Benford, Robert J., 485
Benge, Eugene J., 145
Berger, Philip K., 94
Bergmann, Barbara R., 272
Bernstein, Marver, 39, 63
Berry, Francis S., 432, 453
Berry, Mary Francis, 268
Berwitz, Clement, 198
Bill of Rights, 279, 280
Bish, Robert L., 432
Bishop v. Wood (1976), 306, 317
Bittker, Boris, 247
Blakely, Robert T., 128
Blank, Rebecca M., 162
Blinder, Alan S., 433
Blue-collar work, 132, 137
Board of Regents v. Roth (1972), 287, 305, 317
Bolt, Robert, 80
Bona fide occupational qualification (BFOQ), 217, 225
Bona fide seniority system, 234
Bond v. Madison County Mutual Insurance Co. (1981), 274
Borman, W. D., 508
Bottom-line concept, 225, 236
Bowey, Angela, 162
Brand, R., 453
Branti v. Finkel (1980), 281, 282, 296, 317
Brennan v. Prince William Hospital Corp. (1974), 274
Brief, Arthur, 433
Briggs v. City of Madison (1982), 274
Brinkerhof, Derek W., 508
Brown, F., 485
Brownlow Committee (*also see* President's Committee on Administrative Management), 37, 38, 40
Brownlow, Louis, 37
Brumback, Gary B., 509
Buchanan, James, 9
Bullock, R. J., 433

Burack, Elmer H., 128
Burke, Ronald J., 509
Burkhead, Jesse, 453
Bush, George, 30, 153, 156, 171, 208, 296, 517
Business necessity, 225
Bussey, Ellen M., 63
Butler, M. A., 453
Byham, W. C., 198

Cafeteria-style benefit programs, 534
California Federal Savings and Loan v. Guerra (1987), 524, 525
California State Employees Assoc. v. State of Connecticut (1983), 274
Campbell, Alan K., 22, 55, 63
Campbell, Joel T., 198
Campbell, John, 500
Campion, Michael A., 198
Capozzola, John M., 453
Career service, 9, 10
Carnevale, Anthony P., 460
Carpenter, William Seal, 23
Carroll, James D., 284, 316
Carter, Jimmy, 5, 21, 40, 41, 45, 150, 218, 267
Cascio, Wayne, 102, 103, 128, 184, 198, 509
Cathcart, David A., 198
Cayer, N. Joseph, 63
Chalk v. U.S. District Court (1988), 245, 249
Challenger (explosion), 437, 438
Chi, Keon, S., 273
Chicago Teachers Union v. Hudson (1986), 297, 315, 317, 355, 395
Child Care (*see* Day care)
Chilling effect, 225
China Lake (Naval Weapons Center) demonstration, 55, 131–133, 152
Christensen v. Iowa (1977), 275
Churchill, Winston S., 186
Civil Rights Act of 1964, 168, 169, 171, 204, 205, 215, 238, 242, 257
  Title VII of, 169, 171, 204, 205, 257

Civil Rights Act of 1990, 171, 208
Civil Rights Act of 1991, 171
Civil Service Commission, U.S., 4, 5, 14–16, 21, 22, 25, 29, 30, 33, 37, 39–41, 47, 58, 60, 65, 222
Civil Service Reform Act of 1978, 5, 21, 22, 40, 44, 45, 52, 55, 62, 335, 337, 345
  Title VI of, 55, 131, 133, 152
  Title VII of, 337, 345, 350
Civil Service 2000, 99, 114, 245
Clark, Cynthia, 509
Clark, Harry L., 119, 128
Clark, Timothy B., 152, 162
Classification Act of 1923, 36, 137, 212
Classification Act of 1949, 38, 137, 138
Clay, Henry, 7, 9
Clement, Ronald W., 485, 509
Cleveland Board of Education v. LaFleur (1974), 298, 299, 317, 526
Cleveland Board of Education v. Louderville (1985), 306, 317
Cleveland, Grover, 16
Closed shop, 355
Clowes, Kenneth W., 128
Codd v. Velger (1977), 306, 317
Cohen v. Chesterfield County School Board (1974), 298, 317, 526
Cohen, Michael, 63, 150
Cohen, S., 453
Coil, Ann, 128
Commission on Civil Rights, U.S., 268
Commission on the Status of Women, 215
Committee on Administrative Management (Brownlow Committee), 37, 38, 40, 64
Committee on Equal Employment Opportunity, 215
Committee on Government Employment Policy, 214
Concurrent validity (*also see* Validity), 190
Congressional Joint Commission on Reclassification of Salaries, 136
Connecticut v. Teal (1982), 236, 249
Consent decree, 225

Construct validity (*also see* Validity), 191
Content validity (*also see* Validity), 189
Contract bar, 323
Cook, Alice, 273, 536
Cook, Charles, 23
Cooke, Kathleen, 485
Coolidge, Calvin, 320, 402, 403
Coproduction, 414
Council of State Governments, 269
County of Washington, Oregon v. Gunther
    (1981), 258, 259, 262, 267, 272,
    275
County Sanitation District v. L.A. County
    Employees Association (1985), 384
Couturier, Jean J., 20, 23, 63
Craft, Protective and Custodial (CPC) pay
    plan, 137
Craig, Robert L., 484, 485
Cranston, Alan, 264, 267
Crenson, Matthew A., 23
Criterion-related validity (*also see* Valid-
    ity), 189
Cronback, Lee J., 198
Cronin, Thomas I., 63
Crosby, P., 441, 442, 454
Cross, L., 485
Crouch, Winston W., 63
Cultural biases, 187, 188, 231
Cummings, Larry, 500, 509
Cummings, Thomas G., 157, 158, 163
Curtis, George William, 83, 293
Cutback management, 104, 409, 446

Dalby Michael T., 23
Daley, Dennis M., 509
Daley, Richard J., 278
Davey, Bruce W., 128
Davis v. California (1979), 275
Davis, Charles, 404
Davis, Louis E., 160, 163
Day (child) care, 245, 532
DeGive, G., 128
Delphi technique, 112, 113, 119, 120, 121
Deming, W. E., 441, 444, 454
Demonstration projects, 45, 55, 62,
    131-133, 152

[Demonstration projects]
China Lake (Naval Weapons Center)
    demonstration project, 131, 132,
    133, 152
Pacer Share (McClellan Air Force Base)
    demonstration project, 131-133,
    152
Department of Treasury, IRS v. Federal
    Labor Relations Authority (1990),
    329
Dertouzos, Michael L., 433
DeSanto, John F., 128, 162
Devine, Donald, 47, 55, 398
Discriminatory impact, 169, 170
Disparate effect, 226
Doctrine of privilege, 283, 288, 290, 294
Doctrine of substantial interest, 287, 288
Doherty, Mary H., 163
Donahue, John, 414, 433
Donovan, J. J., 198
Doss, Marion, 300, 316
Dothard v. Rawlinson (1977), 217
Douglas, Joel M., 357, 366, 404
Downey, Edward H., 416
Downs, George, 433
Downsizing, 104, 112
Drazin, Robert, 272
Dresang, Dennis L., 23, 63, 247
Drucker, Peter, 140, 141, 163
Drug testing, 308-313
Dues checkoff, 304, 323, 349, 355, 394,
    395
Duggan, Martin L., 163
Duty of fair representation, 376, 377

Eisenhower, Dwight D., 30
Eisinger, Peter K., 247
Elazar, Daniel J., 80-82, 93
Elderly care, 532
Elliot, Robert H., 198, 247
Elrod v. Burns (1976), 277, 281, 282,
    296, 297, 301, 315, 317
Employee assistance program (EAP), 451,
    531, 532
English, Fenwick, 478, 486

Equal Employment Opportunity Act of 1972, 169, 204, 216, 242
Equal Employment Opportunity Commission (EEOC), 21, 44, 46, 51, 215, 216, 218, 219, 223, 247, 267, 348
Equal Employment Opportunity program (federal), 21, 41, 44, 51, 52, 215, 216, 218, 220, 221
Equal Pay Act of 1963, 252, 257, 258
Equal pay for equal work, 136, 212, 252, 267
Eriksson, Erik M., 23
Ethics in Government Act of 1978, 79
Evans, Sara M., 271, 273
Executive leadership, 32, 41, 45
Executive Order 8802, 213
Executive Order 10988, 336, 342, 344
Executive Order 11491, 336, 337
Executive Order 12564, 309

Face validity (also see Validity), 191
Fact-finding, 324, 330, 345, 354, 378, 379, 380
Faerman, Sue, 468, 476
Fair Employment Practice Committee, 213
Fair Employment Practices Board, 213
Fair share (see Agency shop)
Faley, Robert H., 188
Family and Medical Leave Act of 1990, 517
Family leave (see Maternity leave)
Featherbedding, 324
Federal Employees Pay Council, 150
Federal Employees Pay Equity Act of 1984, 267
Federal Executive Institute, 75
Federal Labor Relations Authority (FLRA), 23, 44, 51, 346, 347–351, 360
Federal Labor Relations Council (FLRC), 44
Federal Mediation and Conciliation Service, 376, 383
Federal Pay Comparability Act of 1970, 149, 150

Federal Pay Reform Act of 1990, 154, 491
Federal Personnel Management Project, 21
Federal Quality Institute (FQI), 441, 442
Federal Salary Act of 1967, 149
Federal Salary Reform Act of 1962, 149
Federal Service Entrance Exam (FSEE), 193
Federal Service Impasses Panel (FSIP), 347, 349
Federal Service Labor–Management Relations Statute (also see Title VII of the Civil Rights Act of 1978), 345, 350
Federal wage system (FWS), 132
Federal Women's Program, 210, 211, 215, 218, 223
Ferman, Louis, 357, 485
Fetal protection policies (laws), 521, 522, 526
Figart, Deborah, 404
Fillmore, Millard, 9
Finn, R. H., 510
Fish, Carl Russell, 23, 94
Fisher, Roger, 401, 404
Fisk, Donald M., 418
Flexsite, 531
Flextime, 531
Foley v. Connelie (1978), 305
Ford, Gerald, 288, 296, 349
Foreign Service, 30
Foreign Service Officers exam, 191
Forrer, J., 163
Fort Steward Schools v. Federal Labor Relations Authority (1990), 373
"4/5ths" rule (also see Adverse impact), 175, 176
Fowler v. New York City Department of Sanitation (1989), 314, 317
Fox, Charles J., 494, 510
Fox, William M., 510
Francoeur v. Corroon & Black Corp. (1982), 275
Frank, William W., 485
Fraser, Richard F., 485
Fraternal Order of Police, 396

Fraternal Order of Police v. City of Philadelphia (1987), 300, 317
Fredlund, Robert F., 163
Free rider, 324, 394
Freedman, Anne, 63
Freedom of Information Act, 44, 51
Freeman, Kimberly A., 511
Full Employment Act of 1946, 107
Fullilove v. Klutznick (1980), 249

Gabris, Gerald T., 510
Gaertner, Gregory H., 510
Gaertner, Karen N., 510
Gagala, Ken, 405
Gainsharing, 161, 162, 427, 428
Gandy, Jay A., 198
Ganschinietz, Bill, 163
Gardner, James E., 485
Garfield, James A., 3-6, 16
Garson, G. David, 485
Gawthrop, Louis, 39, 63
Gelb, Joyce, 536
General Electric Co. v. Gilbert (1976), 523
Geis, A. Arthur, 510
Gerson, S. R., 163
Ghiselli, Edwin E., 199
Gilbert, G. Ronald, 163
Gillespie, Jackson E., 128
Gilmour, Robert, 64
Ginsburg, Eli, 177
Ginsburg, Sigmund S., 94
Glover v. Eastern Nebraska Community Office of Retardation (1989), 310, 311, 313, 314, 317
Gobal, Pati C., 248
Goldberg, Alan, 247
Goldman, Deborah D., 316
Goldman, Eric F., 12
Goldoff, Anna C., 433, 454
Goldstein, Harold, 460
Goldstein, Irwin L., 480, 485
Golembiewski, Robert T., 63, 150
Gomez-Mejia, Juis R., 162
Gompers, Samuel, 320, 527

Good faith bargaining, 373-375, 387
Goodnow, Frank, 141
Gordon, Michael E., 485
Gotbaum, Victor, 392, 393
Gouldner, Alvin W., 76, 94
Governing, 151
Government Employees Training Act of 1958, 479
Government Executive, 152
Graham, Michael, 251
Granger, Gideon, 209
Grant, Ulysses S., 10, 13-16, 29
Greenhouse, Linda, 171, 199, 247, 536
Greenough, William C., 163
Greer, Charles R., 128
Grievances (grievance arbitration), 388-391
Griggs v. Duke Power Company (1971), 167, 169-171, 175, 183, 184, 188, 199, 249
Grimes, Andrew J., 94
Grossman, Paul, 200, 243
Guiteau, Charles, 3, 4, 6
Gurdjieff, G. I., 458

Hackman, Richard, 160, 163
Halachmi, Arie, 164, 510, 536
Hall, Chester, 63
Hall, Francine, 247
Halloran, Daniel F., 182
Hampton, Robert, 63
Harding, Warren, 320
Harley v. Schuylkill County (1979), 314, 317
Harriman, Ann, 163
Hartman, H. J., 274
Harvey, Donald R., 63
Hatch Acts (1949, 1950), 50, 293, 294-296, 347
Hatry, Harry, 433
Hawkins, Jacquelyn J., 247
Hayden, Delores, 536
Hayes, Rutherford B., 3, 15, 16
Hays, Steven, 200
Hayward, Nancy S., 433, 454

Heclo, Hugh, 63
Heisal, W. Donald, 200
Heneman, Herbert G., 128
Heninger, Susan, 487
Hill, Herbert, 357, 405
Hinch, Gerald K., 486
Hispanic Employment Program, 215–216
    218, 223
Hofstadter, Richard, 10, 23
Holley, Meridew, 149, 164
Holley, William H., 511
Holmen, Milton G., 199
Holmes, Steven A., 208
Holzer, Marc, 433, 454, 468, 476
Hood, David, 248
Hoogenboom, Ari, 14, 18, 24
Hoover Commissions (First and Second),
    38
Horn, Jack C., 247
Horn, Patrice D., 247
Horner, Constance, 47, 219
Horrigan, Michael, 273
Horton, Raymond D., 454
Howard, Lawrence C., 180
Howell, William C., 199
Huckle, Patricia, 536
Hudson Institute, 97
Hughs, Garry L., 511
Human Resources Information Systems
    (HRIS) Project, 477
Hunter, J. E., 199
Hunter, R. F., 199
Hyde, Albert C., 129, 164, 201, 426, 433,
    486, 493, 511

Impasse (impasse resolution), 328, 330,
    331, 344, 345, 350, 356, 376–378,
    380, 382, 383
Ingraham, Patricia W., 63, 94, 195, 198
Injunction, 324
Intergovernmental Personnel Act of 1970
    (IPA), 58, 60, 61, 470
International Association of Firefighters
    (IAFF), 396

International Association of Firefighters
    (IAFF) v. City of Homstead (1974),
    375
International Personnel Management
    Association (IPMA), 76, 177, 194
International Union, UAW v. Johnson
    Controls (1989, 1991), 521, 522,
    523, 526, 537
Ippolito, Richard A., 164
Iran-Contra Affair, 75
Iron law of oligarchy, 392
Isaac, Stephen, 199

Jackson, Andrew, 7, 8, 10, 17, 229, 277
Jackson, Daine P., 247
Jackson, Maynard H. Jr., 385, 386
Jacobson, Larry S., 128
Jakus, Larry, 64
Jay, Anthony, 463
Jefferson, Thomas, 7, 32, 78, 229, 293
Jenckes, Thomas A., 12, 13
Jensen, Ollie A., 164
Job enlargement, 158–160
Job Evaluation and Pay Review Task
    Force, 144
Job Evaluation Policy Act of 1970, 144
Job enrichment, 158–160
Job rotation programs, 469
Job sharing, 531
Johansen, Elaine, 247, 273
Johnson v. Transportation Agency of Santa
    Clara County (1987), 170,
    203–206, 231, 232, 249
Johnson, Andrew, 12, 19
Johnson, Jerald, 508
Johnson, Lyndon B., 19, 86, 215
Johnson, Paul, 203–205
Johnston, William B., 129
Josephson, Matthew, 24
Joyce, Diane, 203–205
Juran, J., 441, 442, 455

Kahalas, Harvey, 128
Kane, Jeffrey S., 511

Kanter, Rosabeth Moss, 455, 508
Karahalios v. National Federation of
    Federal Employees (NFFE) (1989),
    377
Kaufman, Herbert, 63, 73, 83, 94
Kaufman, Roger, 478, 486
Kearney, Richard C., 200, 353, 357, 377,
    383, 384, 400, 405
Kearney, William J., 511
Kellam, S., 31
Kelley v. Johnson (1976), 298, 317
Kelly, Rita Mae, 248, 273, 433
Kettl, Donald F., 433
Kennedy, John F., 3, 86, 214, 215, 342,
    344, 345, 354
King, Francis P., 163
Kingsley, J. Donald, 19, 24, 86, 94
Kirkland, Lane, 528
Kirkpatrick, Donald L., 486
Knights of Labor, 333
Knowles, Malcolm S., 486
Knudsen, Steven, 63
Kopelman, Richard E., 511
Kramer, Kenneth W., 64
Kranz, Harry, 248
Krislov, Samuel, 178, 199, 229, 248
Krone, 457
Krone, Charles, 458

Labor Agreement Information Retrieval
    System (LAIRS), 349
Labor-management cooperation (commit-
    tees), 332, 382
Labor-Management Relations Service, 387
Laborers International Union (LIU), 396
Laird, Dugan, 486
Landy, Frank J., 511
Larkey, Patrick D., 433
Last-in, first-out (LIFO) seniority system,
    234
Latham, Gary P., 488, 511, 512
Laurent, Anne, 310
Lawsche, C. H., 199
Lazear, Edward, 273

Leckelt v. Board of Commissioners (1990),
    249
Ledvinka, James, 199
Lee, Robert D. Jr., 64, 113, 129
Leigh, David R., 129
Leight, Duane E., 405
Leininger, Wayne, E., 128
Lemonias, Peter J., 434, 455
Lemons v. Denver (1980), 275
Lenoff, Donna R., 537
Levine, Charles, 104, 105, 129
Levinson, Harry, 495, 512
Levinson, Priscilla, 502, 512
Levitan, Sar, 357
Levitt, Theodore, 455
Lewin, Tamar, 537
Lewis, William G., 248
Lincoln, Abraham, 9, 11, 32
Lipset, Seymour Martin, 357
Lloyd-LaFollette Act of 1912, 84, 335,
    336
Locality pay, 154
Lockout, 324, 331
Lorance v. AT&T (1989), 207, 249
Lougy, Cameran M., 246
Lovrich, Nicholas P., 248, 512
Loyalty-security regulations, 284
Lucianouic, William M., 113, 129
Luevano v. Campbell, 194
Luevano v. Devine, 194
Lust, John, 164
Luton, Larry S., 273

Maccoby, Michael, 164
Machiavelli, Niccolo, 67, 69
MacKinnon, Catharine A., 248
MacLane, Charles N., 512
Macy, John W. Jr., 86, 94
Magid, Renee Y., 537
Maintenance of membership, 355, 394
Mainzer, Lewis C., 24
Malek, Fred, 67
Malek Manual, 67, 95
Management by objectives (MBO), 424,
    504, 505

Marcy, William L., 7, 9
Markey, James P., 273
Markov chains, 113
Martin v. Wilks (1989), 207, 249, 304, 317
Martin, Andrew Ayers, 248
Massachusetts Board of Retirement v. Murgia (1976), 300
Matarazzo, J. D., 199
Maternity (pregnancy or family) leave, 230, 288, 298, 517, 519, 520, 524, 526, 529–531
McBain, Howard Lee, 24
McCarthy v. Philadelphia Civil Service Commission (1976), 298, 317
McCarthy, Eugene M., 164
McClellan Air Force Base (*also see* Pacer Share demonstration project), 131–133, 152
McClung, Glenn, 199
McCullough, Richard C., 486
McEvoy, Glenn M., 512
McGregor, Eugene B. Jr., 456
McKersie, R. B., 455
McKinley, William, 30, 84
McKinney, Jerome B., 180
McLaughlin v. Tilendis (1968), 351
McNish, Linda C., 512
Med-arb (mediation-arbitration), 382
Mediation (mediating), 324, 330, 354, 376, 377, 382
Meet and confer, 327, 363, 367
Meisenheimer, Joseph R., 529, 537
Memphis v. Stotts (1984), 234, 249
Mercer, James L., 434, 455
Meriam, Lewis, 24, 94
Merit pay, 45, 46, 54, 431, 489
Merit System Standards of 1979, 38
Merit Systems Protection Board (MSPB), 23, 43, 44, 46, 47, 49, 52, 349
Meritor Savings Bank v. Vinson (1986), 242, 249
Meshoulam, I., 128
Metro Broadcasting v. F.C.C. (1990), 207, 250
Metz, Maida, 64

Meyer, C. Kenneth, 487
Michael, William B., 199
Michels, Roberto, 392
Milakovich, M. M., 455
Milkovich, George, 164
Miller, James R., 129
Miller, Theodore K., 64
Mills, D. Quinn, 129
Mills, Stephen M., 405
Misler, Dennis, 465, 486
Mitchell, Kenneth, 510
Mommy track, 522
Monroe, Michael L., 140
Montplaisir, et al. v. Leighton (1989), 362
Morgan, H. Wayne, 14
Morris, Edmund, 33
Morrison, Malcolm H., 129
Mosher, Frederick C., 64, 94, 357
Mosher, William E., 19, 24, 86, 94
Mt. Healthy City School District Board of Education v. Doyle (1977), 307, 317
Moynihan, Daniel P., 68
Muller v. State of Oregon (1908), 521
Multiemployer bargaining, 325
Murphy, Kevin P., 513
Murphy, Lionel V., 24
Murphy, Reginald, 405
Mushkin, Selma, 434, 455

Nachmias, David, 513
Nader, Ralph, 39
Nadler, Leonard, 486
Naff, Katherine C., 129, 164
Nalbandian, John, 513
Narrowly tailored (narrow tailoring), 206, 207, 219, 303
National Academy of Public Administration, 164
National Air Traffic Controllers Association (NATCA), 361
National Association of Letter Carriers (NALC), 334
National Association of Letter Carriers (NALC) v. CSC (1972), 294, 295, 317

National Center for Dispute Settlement, 383
National Civil Service League, 20, 21, 85
National Civil Service Reform League, 16, 83
National Commission on the Public Service (*also see* Volcker Commission), 90–94, 151, 152, 164, 459, 462
National Committee on Pay Equity, 262, 264
National Education Association (NEA), 396
National Federation of Government Employees (NFFE), 396
National Federation of Postal Clerks, 334
National Labor Relations Act (NLRA), 356, 367
National Labor Relations Board (NLRB), 322, 345, 367
National Labor Relations Board v. Yeshiva University (1980), 363
National Municipal League, 85
National Treasury Employees Union v. Von Raab (1989), 308, 310, 317
Naval Ocean Systems Center (*also see* Demonstration projects), 131
Nelson, Ardel, 163
Nelson, Barbara J., 271, 273
Neuberger, Thomas Stephen, 248
Neugarten, Dail Ann, 248, 434, 455
Neutral competence, 32, 41
New York Civil Service Reform Association, 16
New York State Center for Women in Government, 144
New York State Civil Service Department, 142, 213, 469
New York State Taylor Act, 355
Newman, Constance, 47, 156
Neihaus, Richard J., 129
Nigro, Lloyd G., 513
Nixon, Richard, 20, 27, 39, 67, 215, 288, 345, 403
Nkomo, Stella M., 129
Noden, Alexandra, 357

Nollen, Stanley D., 531, 537
Norton, Eleanor Holmes, 237, 267

Oakar, Mary, 264
Obuchowski, C., 200
O'Connor v. Ortega (1987), 307, 308, 318
Office of Affirmative Employment Programs, 218
Office of Federal Equal Employment Opportunity, 223
Office of Personnel Management (OPM), 21, 22, 41, 42, 47, 55, 58, 60
Office of Special Counsel (OSC), 43, 44, 47, 49, 52
Office of Systems Innovation and Simplification (OSIS), 133
Oldham, Greg R., 160, 163
Oliver, Philip M., 144, 164
Oliver Report, 144
Open shop, 325
Ortiz-Torres, Blanca, 537
O'Toole, James, 462, 487

PACE (*see* Professional and Administrative Careers Exam)
Pacer Share (McClellan Air Force Base) demonstration project, 131, 132, 133, 152
Palley, Marian Lief, 536
Participative management, 442, 445
Participatory bureaucracy, 290
PATCO (*see* Professional Air Traffic Controller Organization)
Paternity leave, 520
Paterson, Lee, 405
Patronage, 10, 12, 14, 33, 278, 281, 282, 289
Patten, Thomas H. Jr., 64
Patterson v. McLean Credit Union (1989), 207, 250
Patton, Arch, 487
Pay banding, 132–134
Pay Equity Act of 1983, 264
Pay for Performance Management Committee, 491

Pearce, Jone L., 64, 513
Pender, Kathleen, 457, 487
Pendleton Act of 1883, 3, 4, 11, 13, 16, 18, 21, 29, 30, 40, 56, 83, 183, 293
Pendleton, Clarence, 268
Pendleton, George H., 16
Penner, Maurice, 165
Performance Management Recognition System (PMRS), 55, 490, 491
Perlman, Kenneth, 165, 199
Perrine, J. L., 455
Perry, James L., 64, 513, 514
Perry, Lee T., 129
Personnel Administrator v. Feeny (1979), 301, 302, 318
Personnel Classification Board, 137
Petrakis, Beth Ann, 64
Phillips, Lou, 434
Pickering v. Board of Education (1968), 291, 318
Pierce, Franklin, 7, 9
Polygraph tests, 286
Pomerleu, Raymond, 164
Postal Alliance, 334
Postal Reorganization Act of 1970, 337, 345
Postal Service, U.S., 28, 382
Postal strike, 345–347
Powell, Norman J., 24
Power v. Barry County (1982), 275
Predictive validity (*also see* Validity), 190
Pregnancy Discrimination Act of 1978, 523–525, 529
Pregnancy leave (*see* Maternity leave)
President's Committee on Administrative Management (*also see* Brownlow Committee), 37, 64
President's Council on Management Improvement, 441
Price Waterhouse v. Hopkins (1989), 207, 250
Privatization, 413–415
Productivity bargaining, 398, 431
Professional Air Traffic Controller Organization (PATCO), 359–361, 388, 398, 402

Professional Airways Systems Specialists v. FLRA (1987), 350
Professional and Administrative Careers Exam (PACE), 51, 191, 193–195, 197, 218–219
Protected class, 227
Public employment relations board (PERB), 355, 367, 372, 376, 383
Public trust, 332

Quality circles (QC), 442, 444, 445, 451
Quality of worklife (QWL), 443, 446–451
Quill, Michael, 402
Quinn, Robert E., 248

Rabin, Jack, 248
Ramirez, Blandina Cardenas, 268
Ramspeck Act of 1940, 84
Rank-in-person, 181
Rank-in-position, 181
Rankin v. McPherson (1987), 291, 292, 315, 318
Raskin, A. H., 393, 403
Raytheon Co. v. Fair Employment & Housing (1989), 250
Reagan, Ronald, 30, 46, 47, 55, 60, 167, 267, 291, 359–361, 398, 402
Reasonable accommodation, 227
Rees, Albert, 455
Regents v. Bakke (1978), 206, 250
Rehabilitation Act of 1973, 243–245
Reichenberg, Neil E., 248
Reliability, 185, 191
Remick, Helen, 249, 273
Remsay, Arch S., 165
Representative bureaucracy, 228–230
Restrictive credentialism, 227
Retroactive seniority, 228
Riccucci, Norma M., 62, 70, 93, 162, 164, 200, 255, 266, 273, 316, 357, 476
Rich, Wilbur C., 130, 487
Richmond v. Croson (1989), 207, 250
Riggs, James L., 434

Rightful place, 228
Riordon, William L., 20
Ritzer, George, 94
Roberts, Robert, 300, 316
Robertson, David E., 200
Rollins, Thomas, 514
Romzek, Barbara, 532, 534, 537
Roosevelt, Franklin D., 37, 213
Roosevelt, Theodore, 12, 33, 84, 134,
    178, 209, 293
Rosen, Bernard, 64
Rosenbloom, David H., 24, 63, 94, 199,
    200, 216, 249, 284, 316, 357, 405
Rosenthal, Harvey, 64
Rosow, Jerome M., 455
Rouleau, Eugene, 200
Rowland, Kenndrith M., 130
Rule of three, 15
Rutan v. Republican Party of Illinois
    (1990), 30, 64, 282, 397

Saint, Alice M., 487
Salinger, Ruth D., 487
Saltzein, Alan, 398
Sandver, Marcus, 128
Savas, D. E., 94
Sayre, Wallace, 24, 139, 165
Scab, 325
Scales, R. Jr., 200
Scarpello, Vida G., 199
Schay, Brigitte W., 514
Schedule B appointment, 195, 196
Scheibal, William, 273
Schein, Edgar H., 130, 200
Schlei, Barbara, 200, 243
Schneier, Craig, 118
School Board of Nassau County v. Arline
    (1987), 245, 250
Schultz v. Wheaton Glass Co. (1970), 252
Schwab, Donald, 500, 509, 514
Scientific management, 35, 419
Scope of bargaining, 325, 344, 347, 371,
    372, 376
Seidman, Harold, 64
Senior Executive Service (SES), 45, 46,
    52, 54, 431

Seniority systems, 234
Sensitivity (T-group) training, 468, 469
Service Employees International Union
    (SEIU), 342, 396
Sexual harassment, 238–242
Shafritz, Jay M., 22, 24, 30, 60, 61, 64,
    69, 71, 74, 77, 84, 94, 95, 129,
    165, 168, 216, 228, 248, 357
Shared savings plan, 427, 428
Sharkansky, Ira, 95
Sharon, Milton I., 25
Sharon Report, 25
Shelton v. Tucker (1960), 296, 318
Sherwin, H. Douglas, 444, 455
Sherwood, Frank, 514
Shinn, Marybeth, 537
Shop steward, 325
Siedfried, John J., 434, 455
Siegel, Gilbert B., 165
Simko, Patricia A., 537
Sims, Ronald R., 487
Skinner v. Railway Labor Executives
    (1989), 310, 318
Smith, A. R., 128
Smith, Charles, 405
Smith, Darrell Hevenor, 24
Smith, Robert D., 182
Smith, Russ, 165
Snell v. Suffolk County (1985), 220
Snepp v. U.S. (1980), 318
Sorauf, Frank J., 64
Sorenson, Elaine, 274
Sovereignty, 328, 335, 338
Spanish-Speaking Program (federal), 215,
    223
Spann, Jeri, 249
Spaulding v. University of Washington
    (1984), 275
Spero, Sterling, 405
Spoils system, 5, 7–9, 11, 58, 83, 139,
    283, 293
Stanley, David T., 36
Staudohar, Paul D., 434, 456
Steel, Brent S., 248
Steele, Christine E., 193
Steelworkers v. Weber (1979), 205, 206,
    250

Steiber, Jack, 358
Stein, Barry A., 455
Stenberg, Carl, 342
Stevenson, William B., 513
Stewart, Frank Mann, 24
Storing, Herbert, 289
Strategic planning, 438
Strike (striking), 325, 328, 331, 333, 343, 344, 359–361, 383–388, 402
Strivastva, S., 157, 158, 163
Sugarman v. Dougall (1973), 287, 318
Sulzner, George T., 358
Summers, Scott L., 130
Suntrup, Edward L., 533, 537
Superconciliation, 330
Supervisors bargaining rights, 364–366, 369, 370
Suskin, Harold, 165
Swoboda, Frank, 456
Sylvia, Ronald D., 200, 487

T-group training (*see* Sensitivity training)
Taft-Hartley Act of 1947, 336, 361
Taft, William Howard, 32, 134
Tatage, David C., 433, 454
Taylor, Frederick, 35
Taylor, James C., 160, 163
Taylor Law, New York State, 367
Taylor, Stuart, 537
Taylor, Vernon T., 200
Team building, 442–445
Teamsters Union, International Brotherhood of, 342, 396
Tennessee Valley Authority, 30
Tenopyr, Mary L., 200
Tenure of Office Act of 1867, 12
Texas Department of Community Affairs v. Burdine (1981), 275
Thayer, Fred C., 515
Thomas, Clarence, 249, 267
Thomas, John C., 200
Thompson, Duane E., 200
Thompson, Frank J., 67, 95, 150, 165, 316
Thompson, Suzanne, 273

Thompson, Toni A., 200
Thorne v. City of El Segundo (1983), 300, 318
Thorpe, Richard, 162
Thurston, Dona, 119, 128
Time-and-motion study, 141
Title VI of the Civil Service Reform Act of 1978 (*also see* Demonstration projects), 55, 131, 133, 152
Title VII of the Civil Rights Act of 1964, 169, 171, 204, 205, 257
Title VII of the Civil Service Reform Act of 1978 (*also see* Federal Service Labor-Management Relations Statute), 337, 345, 350
Tolchin, Martin, 24, 88
Tolchin, Susan, 24, 88
Total quality management (TQM), 438–442
Towne, Henry, 161, 428
Townsend, Robert, 190
Training needs assessment, 475
Transport Workers Union (TWU), 402, 403
Trattner, M. H., 200
Treiman, D. J., 274
Trice, Harrison, M., 94
Troy, Leo, 358
Truman, Harry S., 37, 214
Trumbull, Lyman, 13

Ulschack, Francis, 130, 487
Unassembled exams, 185
Unfair labor practice (ULP), 326, 345, 346, 350, 356, 373, 374
Uniform Guidelines on Employee Selection Procedures, 172, 173, 175–177
Uniformed services, 255
Union security arrangements, 394, 395
Union shop, 297, 326, 329, 355, 394
Unit determination, 329, 340, 356, 369, 370
United Auto Workers (UAW), 360
United Public Workers v. Mitchell (1947), 294, 295, 318

U.S. v. Georgia Power Company (1973), 171
U.S. v. Paradise (1987), 250, 302, 304, 318
U.S. v. South Carolina (1978), 177, 201
Ury, William, 401, 404
Uyar, Kivilcim M., 130

Validity, 182, 184, 185, 189–191
Van Maanen, John, 201
Van Riper, Paul P., 24
Vaughn, Robert G., 95, 249, 317
Veres, John G., 487
Veteran's preference, 21, 45, 237, 238, 301
Veteran's Preference Act of 1944, 84
Vietnam, 75
Vin Rijn, Paul, 129
Volcker Commission (*also see* National Commission on the Public Service), 90–94, 151, 152, 164, 459, 462
Volcker, Paul A., 92, 151
Voluntary reduced work time (V-Time), 531

Wachtel, Marjorie, 152, 162
Wagel, William H., 515
Wagner, Robert, 402
Walker, Alfred, 130
Walker, James W., 107, 109, 123, 130, 515
Wall, James, 405
Walton, Mary, 456
Walton, Richard, 448, 456
War on poverty, 19
Wards Cove v. Atonio (1989), 167, 169, 170, 171, 175, 176, 177, 183, 184, 201, 207, 250
Warren, M. W., 488
Washington v. Davis (1976), 176, 201, 250, 301, 302, 318
Washington, George, 7, 208
Washington, Harold, 57
Washnis, George J., 434, 456

Watson, Charles E., 488
Watson, Thomas, 158
Watergate, 40, 75
Weber, Max, 5, 65
Werthman, Michael S., 23
Wexley, Kenneth N., 488
Whistleblower Protection Act (WPA) of 1989, 49, 52
Whistleblowing, 44, 45, 47, 49, 50, 52, 289
White, Leonard D., 10, 24
White, Robert D., 166
Whitman, Torry S., 129, 201
Wiatrowski, William J., 527, 537
Wiens, A. M., 199
Wilkins v. University of Houston (1981), 275
Williams, R. L., 201
Wilson, James Q., 23, 78, 95
Wilson, T., 247
Wilson, Woodrow, 31, 35, 65, 82, 83, 95, 141, 211
Wimberly v. Labor and Industrial Relations Commission of Missouri (1987), 525, 526
Winn, Russ, 166
Wirtz v. Wheaton Glass Co. (1970), 275
Wise, Charles R., 456
Wisniewski, Stanley C., 249
Witt, Elder, 151, 166
Wolohojian, George, 105, 129
Women in the federal service (*also see* Federal Women's Program), 210
Women's Legal Defense Fund, 530
Wong, Nora W., 537
Woodland v. City of Houston (1990), 286
Work force planning, 107, 110, 112–114, 121
Work force 2000, 97–99, 107, 245, 246
Work planning and review (WPR) system, 504
Work to rule, 326
Workforce 2000, 97–99, 113, 129
Wriston, Walter, 412, 435
Wurf, Jerry, 378, 392

Wygant v. Jackson Board of Education
    (1986), 303, 318

Yeshiva University (see *National Labor
    Relations Board v. Yeshiva Uni-
    versity*)
Young, Coleman, 380
Young, Lisa, 253

Zack, Arnold, 380
Zagoria, Sam, 387
Zawacki, Robert A., 515
Zeidner, Rita L., 201
Zeira, Yoram, 488
Zipper clause, 326, 388
Zone of indifference, 74, 75
Zuboff, Shoshana, 452, 456